MW00583305

Philostratus's *Heroikos*

Society of Biblical Literature

Writings from the Greco-Roman World

John T. Fitzgerald, General Editor

Editorial Board

David Armstrong
Elizabeth Asmis
Brian E. Daley, S.J.
David G. Hunter
David Konstan
Michael J. Roberts
Johan C. Thom
Yun Lee Too
James C. VanderKam

Number 6

Philostratus's *Heroikos*:
Religion and Cultural Identity
in the Third Century C.E.

Philostratus's *Heroikos*

Religion and Cultural Identity in the Third Century C.E.

Edited by

Ellen Bradshaw Aitken
Jennifer K. Berenson Maclean

Society of Biblical Literature
Atlanta

PHILOSTRATUS'S *HEROIKOS*:
Religion and Cultural Identity
in the Third Century C.E.

Library of Congress Cataloging-in-Publication Data

Philostratus's Heroikos : religion and cultural identity in the third century C.E. / edited by Jennifer K. Berenson Maclean and Ellen Bradshaw Aitken.

p. cm. — (Writings from the Greco-Roman world ; v. 6)
Most of the essays in this volume were first presented at a conference held in May 2001 at Harvard Divinity School, "Philostratus's Heroikos, Religion and Cultural Identity."
Includes bibliographical references and indexes.
ISBN 1-58983-091-1 (pbk. : alk. paper)

1. Philostratus, the Athenian, 2nd/3rd cent. Heroicus. 2. Dialogues, Greek—History and criticism. 3. Civilization, Greco-Roman, in literature. 4. Trojan War—Literature and the war. 5. Christianity and literature—Rome. 6. Religion and literature—Rome. 7. Protesilaus (Greek mythology) 8. Religion in literature. 9. Heroes in literature. I. Maclean, Jennifer K. Berenson, 1963– II. Aitken, Ellen Bradshaw, 1961– III. Series.

PA4272.A45P5 2005b
183.1—dc22 2004016062

04 05 06 07 08 09 10 11 5 4 3 2 1

The book is printed in the United States of America
on recycled, acid-free paper.

Table of Contents

Acknowledgments

The community of scholarship that this volume represents was made possible by funding from a number of sources. Roanoke College, Harvard Divinity School, and the Department of the Classics, Harvard University, provided funding for the conference, "Philostratus's *Heroikos,* Religion, and Cultural Identity," held at Harvard Divinity School, Cambridge, Massachusetts, 4–6 May 2001, at which many of the essays were first presented. In addition, this conference was supported by a 2001 Research and Technology Grant from the Society of Biblical Literature. Roanoke College also provided generous funding for research and the preparation of this volume through multiple grants extending from spring 2000 through fall 2003. For all of these grants we wish to record our thanks.

We are also deeply grateful to those whose practical contributions and wise counsel made this volume possible: Elizabeth Busky, Judith A. Chien, Gary G. Gibbs, Katherine Burton Jones, Whitney A. M. Leeson, Sarah Lefebvre, James Long, Anna Miller, James M. Ogier, Catherine Playoust, and Emily Ann Schmidt. The interlibrary loan and public service personnel, particularly Pat Scott at Roanoke College's Fintel Library and Renate Kalnins and Michelle Gauthier at the Andover-Harvard Theological Library, provided invaluable assistance. We also wish to thank the editorial staff of the Society of Biblical Literature, particularly Rex Matthews and Bob Buller, for their unflagging enthusiasm for this project. The editor of this series, John Fitzgerald, and an anonymous reviewer furnished discerning comments; for their contributions we are most appreciative. We are also grateful to Gregory Nagy for his manifold encouragement of this endeavor and support of our involvement with the undying glory of the hero Protesilaos.

Our families—William Porter and Iain, Rachel, and Duncan Maclean—have also been unstinting in their devotion and patience during the preparation of this volume. To them we offer special thanks for their plentiful good humor and loving support.

Ellen Bradshaw Aitken
Montreal, Quebec

Jennifer K. Berenson Maclean
Salem, Virginia

Abbreviations

AB	Anchor Bible
Acc. trag.	Ribbeck, Otto. *Tragicorum Romanorum fragmenta*
ABD	*Anchor Bible Dictionary*
AcOr	Acta orientalia
ACW	Ancient Christian Writers
AJA	*American Journal of Archaeology*
AJP	*American Journal of Philology*
AnBib	Analecta biblica
AncSoc	*Ancient Society*
ANRW	*Aufstieg und Niedergang der römischen Welt: Geschichte und Kultur Roms im Spiegel der neueren Forschung*
AR	*Archiv für Religionswissenschaft*
ASAA	*Annuario della Scuola Archeologica di Atene*
Ath. Mitt.	*Mitteilungen des deutschen archäologischen Instituts (Athenische Abteilung)*
AThR	*Anglican Theological Review*
BCH	*Bulletin de correspondance hellénique*
BDAG	Bauer, W., F. W. Danker, W. F. Arndt, and F. W. Gingrich. *Greek-English Lexicon of the New Testament and Other Early Christian Literature*
BJRL	*Bulletin of the John Rylands University Library of Manchester*
ByzZ	*Byzantinische Zeitschrift*
CAH	Cambridge Ancient History
CBQ	*Catholic Biblical Quarterly*
CIL	*Corpus inscriptionum latinarum*
CIS	*Corpus inscriptionum semiticarum*
CJ	*Classical Journal*
CP	*Classical Philology*
CQ	*Classical Quarterly*
CRAI	Comptes rendus de l'Académie des inscriptions et belles-lettres
CSCO	Corpus scriptorum christianorum orientalium
DK	Diels, H., and W. Kranz. *Die Fragmente der Vorsokratiker*
FGrH	Jacoby, F. *Die Fragmente der griechischen Historiker*

GCS	Die griechische christliche Schriftsteller der ersten [drei] Jahrhunderte
GRBS	*Greek, Roman, and Byzantine Studies*
Hell	*Hellenica: Recueil d'épigraphie, de numismatique et d'antiquités grecques*
Her.	Philostratus *Heroikos*
Hist.	Herodotus *Histories*
HSCP	*Harvard Studies in Classical Philology*
HTR	*Harvard Theological Review*
HTS	Harvard Theological Studies
IG	*Inscriptiones graecae*
IGR	*Inscriptiones graecae ad res romanas pertinentes*
Il.	Homer *Iliad*
ILS	*Inscriptiones latinae selectae*
Ist. Mitt.	*Mitteilungen des deutschen archäologischen Instituts (Abteilung Istanbul)*
JAC	Jahrbuch für Antike und Christentum
JBL	*Journal of Biblical Literature*
JDAI	*Jahrbuch des (kaiserlichen) deutschen archäologischen Instituts*
JEH	*Journal of Ecclesiastical History*
JHS	*Journal of Hellenic Studies*
JR	*Journal of Religion*
JRA	*Journal of Roman Archaeology*
JRS	*Journal of Roman Studies*
JSNT	*Journal for the Study of the New Testament*
JTS	*Journal of Theological Studies*
KlPauly	*Der kleine Pauly*
LCL	Loeb Classical Library
LIMC	Ackerman, H. C., and J.-R. Gisler. *Lexicon iconographicum mythologiae classicae*
LSJ	Liddell, H. G., R. Scott, and H. S. Jones. *A Greek-English Lexicon*
LXX	Septuagint
NRSV	New Revised Standard Version
NTS	*New Testament Studies*
Od.	Homer *Odyssey*
OLA	Orientalia lovaniensia analecta
OrChr	*Oriens christianus*
OrChrAn	Orientalia christiana analecta
PCG	Kassel, R., and C. Austin. *Poetae Comici Graeci*

PG	Patrologia graeca
PMG	Page, D. L. *Poetae Melici Graeci*
PP	*La Parola del passato*
PW	Pauly, A. F. *Paulys Realencyclopädie der classischen Altertumswissenschaft*
RAC	Kluser, T., et al. *Reallexikon für Antike und Christentum*
RAr	*Revue archéologique*
REA	*Revue des études anciennes*
REG	*Revue des études grecques*
RevPhil	*Revue de philologie*
SBLDS	Society of Biblical Literature Dissertation Series
SBLMS	Society of Biblical Literature Monograph Series
SBLTT	Society of Biblical Literature Texts and Translations
SBLWGRW	Society of Biblical Literature Writings from the Greco-Roman World
SecCent	*Second Century*
SHA	Scriptores Historiae Augustae
SNTSMS	Society for New Testament Studies Monograph Series
SÖAW	Sitzungen der österreichischen Akademie der Wissenschaften in Wien
SSN	Studia semitica neerlandica
ST	*Studia theologica*
Sylloge[3]	Dittenberger, W. *Sylloge Inscriptionum Graecarum*, 3d ed.
TAPA	*Transactions of the American Philological Association*
TDNT	Kittel, G., and G. Friedrich. *Theological Dictionary of the New Testament*
TLG	*Thesaurus linguae graecae*
TU	Texte und Untersuchungen
VC	*Vigiliae christianae*
WUANT	Wissenschaftliche Untersuchungen zum Alten und Neuen Testament
WUNT	Wissenschaftliche Untersuchungen zum Neuen Testament
ZNW	*Zeitschrift für die neutestamentliche Wissenschaft und die Kunde der älteren Kirche*
ZPE	*Zeitschrift für Papyrologie und Epigraphik*

Concerning Transliteration

In this translation, we have adopted the following system for spelling the Greek names and the few other Greek words that appear. Names that have passed in common English usage appear in their generally familiar forms: for example, Corinth, Euripides, Helen, Cassandra, and Achilles. Names that are much less familiar are transliterated according to the guidelines in the *Chicago Manual of Style*, 15th edition, with the exception that the circumflex (ˆ) is used to mark long vowels: for example, Protesilaos, Akhelôos, Idomeneus, and Borysthênes.

Contributors

Ellen Bradshaw Aitken
Associate Professor of Early Christian History and Literature
McGill University

Susan E. Alcock
John H. D'Arms Collegiate Professor of Classical Archaeology and Classics
University of Michigan

Hans Dieter Betz
Shailer Mathews Professor Emeritus of New Testament
University of Chicago Divinity School

Alain Blomart
Visiting Professor of Greek Philology
University of Barcelona

Walter Burkert
Emeritus Professor of Classical Philology
University of Zurich

Casey Dué
Assistant Professor of Classics
University of Houston

Simone Follet
Professor Emerita of Ancient Greek
University of Paris Sorbonne

Sidney H. Griffith
Professor of Semitic Languages and Literatures
Catholic University of America

Jackson P. Hershbell
Emeritus Professor of Classics
University of Minnesota

Christopher Jones
George Martin Lane Professor of the Classics and History
Harvard University

Jennifer K. Berenson Maclean
Associate Professor of Religion
Roanoke College

Francesca Mestre
Professor of Greek Philology
University of Barcelona

Gregory Nagy
Francis Jones Professor of Classical Greek Literature and
Professor of Comparative Literature, Harvard University
Director of the Center for Hellenic Studies

Corinne Ondine Pache
Assistant Professor of Classics
Yale University

Jeffrey Rusten
Professor of Classics
Cornell University

M. Rahim Shayegan
Musa Sabi Assistant Professor of Iranian
University of California, Los Angeles

James C. Skedros
Associate Professor of Early Christianity and Byzantine History
Holy Cross Greek Orthodox School of Theology

Tim Whitmarsh
Reader in Greek Literature
University of Exeter

Introduction

Ellen Bradshaw Aitken and
Jennifer K. Berenson Maclean

"Religion was, and remained, good to think with," concludes Mary Beard in her discussion of the religions of late Republican Rome.[1] In other words, discussions about cultic practice in antiquity provided a rhetorical site for the construction, negotiation, and display of the central values of human and political life. Philostratus's *Heroikos* demonstrates a similar point, namely, that hero cult "was . . . good to think with." Stories about the heroes, descriptions of cultic practice at the tombs of heroes, accounts of interactions between heroes and other humans all proved good material for thinking about cultural identity, the maintenance of empire, and questions of lifestyle and ethics. This is the central proposal that guides the collection of essays in this volume.

This volume centers on the relationship between religion and the construction of cultural identity in the *Heroikos*. "Religion" is understood here broadly, encompassing cultic practice, community formation and character, ethical values, and beliefs. We might approach the *Heroikos* with a number of questions in mind. For example, how does this text demonstrate contemporary practices of Homeric criticism? How does it draw upon and extend established literary conventions of its day? What are its sources? Can the dialogue reveal specific rituals of hero cult as practiced in Philostratus's day? The answers to these questions come to play in any attempt to understand the religious ethos of the *Heroikos* and its use for a larger cultural agenda. It is our contention, however, that the religious interests of the dialogue are intimately related to Philostratus's interests in the literary act of re-creating a coherent Greek identity for the Greek elites of the Roman Empire in the early third century C.E. Samson Eitrem and Teresa Mantero depict Philostratus's purpose as primarily religious, albeit with a larger cultural agenda;[2] Graham Anderson understands the dialogue as an intellectual exer-

[1] Mary Beard, John North, and Simon Price, *Religions of Rome*, Vol. 1: *A History* (Cambridge: Cambridge University Press, 1998), 166.

[2] Eitrem regarded the *Heroikos* as a serious effort to promote hero worship. However, he also claimed that the *Heroikos* had a "national purpose": by present-

cise bordering on the frivolous.[3] The contributions in this volume instead highlight in various ways the literary, religious, political, and topographical strategies deployed in the *Heroikos* for the fashioning of a cultural identity. Philostratus's text thus serves as an instance of the construction and promotion of cultural meaning for his time. The reader will have to judge if the essays brought together here successfully work toward a comprehensive and compelling argument for the specific agenda that we propose.

Most of the essays in this volume were first presented at a conference held in May 2001 at Harvard Divinity School, "Philostratus's *Heroikos*, Religion, and Cultural Identity." This conference, cosponsored by the Divinity School and the Department of the Classics at Harvard University, as well as by Roanoke College and the Society of Biblical Literature, brought together scholars across disciplinary boundaries around a common text. The conversation that Philostratus's *Heroikos* sparked among classicists, archaeologists, biblical scholars, historians, and theologians of early Christianity, as well as scholars of Persian and Syrian studies, demonstrates that heroes and hero cult remain "good to think with." In particular, along with the host of other topics raised by this single text, heroes and hero cult shed light upon questions, concepts, and interests shared by those devoted to the study of antiquity. Such a discussion sharpens the categories of analysis, uncovers our assumptions (as, for example, about "belief" or "coming back to life," which are both key to the *Heroikos*), and juxtaposes texts often kept in separate disciplinary boxes (what, for example, does Pausanias have to do with Tertullian?). We present these essays here in order to continue this conversation among scholars and students. In addition to the essays from the conference, we have included two previously published articles. Walter Burkert's classic "Jason, Hypsipyle, and New Fire

ing ideal men of the past, Philostratus indirectly combated anything anti-Hellenic and thus promoted Hellenic culture. Samson Eitrem, "Zu Philostrats *Heroikos*," *Symbolae Osloenses* 8 (1929): 1–56, especially 5–6. Mantero argues that Philostratus hoped to achieve a revitalization of hero cults. Mantero also discusses the pro-Hellenic tendencies in the *Heroikos*, suggesting that Philostratus was promoting a Greek identity in the face of the syncretistic tendencies of the Severan dynasty. Teresa Mantero, *Ricerche sull'* Heroikos *di Filostrato* (Genoa: University of Genoa, Istituto di Filologia Classica e Medioevale, 1966), 227–28.

[3] Anderson sees little "pious purpose" in Philostratus's reworking of myth. He argues that Philostratus's interest in hero cult and Protesilaos is only "a preliminary excursus before the main subject—the correction of Homer." Graham Anderson, *Philostratus: Biography and* Belles Lettres *in the Third Century A.D.* (London: Croom Helm, 1986), 253.

at Lemnos: A Study of Myth and Ritual" is one of the few studies of the cultic material in the *Heroikos*. Hans Dieter Betz's "Hero Worship and Christian Beliefs: Observations from the History of Religion on Philostratus's *Heroikos*" appears here in English translation for the first time. Betz's article is the first exploration of the relationship of the *Heroikos* to early Christianity since the work of Samson Eitrem more than seventy years earlier.

A brief introduction to the *Heroikos* itself is in order, especially for those unfamiliar with this work.[4] The *Heroikos* is a dialogue between a Phoenician merchant and the man who tends the vineyard and gardens around the tomb of a hero. Through the voice of the vinedresser, a third character "appears": the hero Protesilaos, the first Greek warrior to die in the Trojan War (Homer *Il.* 2.695–710). Protesilaos not only aids the vinedresser in gardening, but also discusses the Trojan War and Homer's poems, while inculcating in him a philosophic approach to life (*Her.* 2.6–5.5). In addition to its obvious composition as a dialogue,[5] the *Heroikos* also draws upon various aspects of both popular and more sophisticated literature. In particular, the influence of Plato's *Phaedrus*, sophistic rhetorical exercises, as well as novelistic techniques and thematic interests are abundantly evident in the text. In 2001 we published an English translation of the *Heroikos* in this series. A summary of the text can be found in the introduction to that volume as well as in the article by Hans Dieter Betz in this volume.[6] Because the articles published here stand as independent works of scholarship, authors to varying

[4] References to the *Heroikos* follow the chapter and paragraph divisions assigned to the text on the basis of content by Ludo de Lannoy in his critical edition, *Flavii Philostrati Heroicus* (Berlin: Teubner, 1977). Earlier scholarship on the *Heroikos* frequently employs the page numbers of vol. 2 of Carl Ludwig Kayser's *editio minor* of the works of Philostratus (Leipzig: Teubner, 1870; repr. Hildesheim: Olms, 1964). It may be useful to reader to note, moreover, that citations of the *Heroikos* in Henry George Liddell and Robert Scott, comp. *A Greek-English Lexicon* (rev. ed. Henry Stuart Jones; Oxford: Clarendon, 1989) also refer to Kayser's *editio minor* of 1870, but employ Kayser's chapter and paragraph numbers rather than the page numbers.

[5] The *Heroikos* is indebted to Plato and the development of the genre of the dialogue by other writers of the Second Sophistic, especially Lucian's *Charon* and Dio Chrysostom's *Euboikos*.

[6] Jennifer K. Berenson Maclean and Ellen Bradshaw Aitken, trans. *Flavius Philostratus: Heroikos* (SBLWGRW 1; Atlanta: Society of Biblical Literature, 2001), xxxvii–xl. A summary also appears in the student edition of the *Heroikos*: Jennifer K. Berenson Maclean and Ellen Bradshaw Aitken, trans., *Flavius Philostratus: On Heroes* (SBLWGRW 3; Atlanta: Society of Biblical Literature, 2003),

degrees retell the story of the *Heroikos* as an integral part of their arguments.

Flavius Philostratus composed the *Heroikos* no earlier than 222–235 C.E. and no later than 244–249 C.E., although the immediacy of the reference to the athlete Helix (*Her.* 15.8–10) suggests the early years of Alexander Severus's reign (222–235 C.E.).[7] Philostratus was part of a cultural phenomenon he termed the "Second Sophistic."[8] In addition to delivering extemporaneous public speeches and educating the young, sophists participated prominently in religious festivals and acted as advisors to cities.[9] Moreover, like Philostratus, most sophists came from wealthy families, and their reputations were enhanced by holding public offices and acting as benefactors of their cities. Thus the sophist's social role was considerably more than teacher of elite youth or public entertainer. For Philostratus, his connections with the imperial court and its politics seem to have guided at least some of his literary productions. He was introduced to the Severan court during the reign of Septimius Severus, whose wife, Julia Domna, had already gathered around her intellectuals of varying interests (*Life of Apollonius* 1.3). Julia Domna's interest in Apollonius of Tyana led to her commissioning Philostratus to write his biography, which at least in part must have been seen as a justification for the imperial family's devotion to Apollonius.[10] Philostratus's composition of the *Heroikos* was no doubt equally influenced by Caracalla's imitation of Alexander the Great's sacrifices at Achilles' tomb in 214 C.E. (Dio Cassius *Roman History* 78.16.7).[11]

Sophists thus had considerable opportunity and power to influ-

---

xliii–xlv. In the present volume, authors at times rely upon this translation, but at other times provide their own. The divergent renderings point to different ways of understanding this fascinating text. Translations of the *Heroikos* into other modern languages are listed in the bibliography of this volume. Many of the issues touched upon in this brief introduction have been addressed in the introduction to *Flavius Philostratus: Heroikos*. Interested readers may wish to consult that introduction for more detailed argumentation.

[7] The essays in this volume represent a diversity of opinion on the dating of the *Heroikos*. As editors we have not imposed our own conclusions on the contributors' work.

[8] For a discussion of Philostratus's construction of the Second Sophistic and its descent from Gorgias, see Anderson, *Philostratus*, 11–12.

[9] Glen W. Bowersock, *Greek Sophists in the Roman Empire* (Oxford: Clarendon, 1969), ch. 2. On Philostratus's offices in Athens, see among others, Simone Follet, *Athènes au IIe et au IIIe siècle: Études chronographiques et prosopographiques* (Paris: Les Belles Lettres, 1976), 101–103 and her essay in this volume.

[10] On the difficulties of distinguishing heroes from holy men, see the essay by Christopher Jones in this volume.

ence the cultural productions and values of their day. They moved among the cultural and political elites of their cities, were sought-after teachers for their children, and had as a primary goal the welfare of their cities. Many like Philostratus were also influenced by imperial politics and concerns. The specific goals of the Second Sophistic centered on the celebration and preservation of Greek culture in the context of a multicultural empire. In all aspects of their rhetorical creations, the Second Sophistic looked to the past to justify the prominence of the Greek-educated elite in the Roman world and to maintain Greek identity through the promotion of *paideia*, which Jaap-Jan Flinterman defined as the "absolute familiarity with literary culture."[12] The *Heroikos* is clearly the product of this literary and cultural movement. The setting, the detailed descriptions of the heroes' physical appearance and their characters, "the pictorial creation of vivid and memorable scenes,"[13] the correction of Homer,[14] and elaborately composed speeches and chreia all reveal Philostratus's sophistic education and literary panache.[15] Our suggestion then that, through the *Heroikos,* Philostratus sought to promote not only a cultural agenda, but also one with close connections to imperial concerns is fully within the goals of the Second Sophistic and the particular experience of Philostratus.

The *Heroikos* must also be set in the context of the ongoing veneration of Protesilaos. Only two sanctuaries dedicated to Protesilaos are attested: the sanctuary in Phulakê, where athletic contests were held in his honor (*Her.* 16.5; Pindar *Isthmian* 1.30, 58 and scholia), and the sanctuary at Elaious on the Chersonesus, which provides

[11] Philostratus probably traveled with the empress's entourage until at least 217, the year of Caracalla's murder and his mother's suicide. The details of Philostratus's career after 217 are unfortunately few.

[12] Jaap-Jan Flinterman, *Power,* Paideia, *and Pythagoreanism: Greek Identity, Conceptions of the Relationship between Philosophers and Monarchs and Political Ideas in Philostratus'* Life of Apollonius (Dutch Monographs on Ancient History and Archaeology 13; Amsterdam: Gieben, 1995), 233. On the sophists' nostalgia for the Greek past, see E. L. Bowie, "Greeks and their Past in the Second Sophistic," *Past and Present* 46 (1970): 3–41; revised in *Studies in Ancient Society* (ed. M. I. Finley; London: Routledge, 1974); Graham Anderson, *The Second Sophistic: A Cultural Phenomenon in the Roman Empire* (London and New York: Routledge, 1993), esp. chs. 1–5.

[13] Anderson, *Philostratus*, 241, 243.

[14] On the correction of Homer in the *Heroikos* and vitality of the tradition, see the essay by Francesca Mestre in this volume.

[15] Jeffrey Rusten examines literary allusions in the *Heroikos* in his essay, "Living in the Past: Allusive Narratives and Elusive Authorities in the World of the *Heroikos,*" in this volume.

the setting for the *Heroikos* (Herodotus *Hist.* 7.33.1; 9.116–120; Thucydides *Peloponnesian War* 8.102.3; Strabo *Geography* 13.1.31; 7.frg. 51). The latter site has been discovered, but excavation has not yielded any artifacts helpful for reconstructing the cult in the Greek or Roman periods.[16] According to Pausanias, the whole of Elaious was dedicated to Protesilaos, and there he received divine honors.[17] Pausanias's description of the wealth of the sanctuary's treasury, presupposed by the story of its plundering by Artayktes (Herodotus *Hist.* 7.33.1; 9.116–120), stands in marked contrast to the description of the sanctuary in the dialogue, where the foundations are the only remaining indications of its former greatness and the cult statue is badly worn and stands apart from its original base (*Her.* 9.5–6).[18]

The few images of Protesilaos that are extant attest to his symbolic, if not cultic, role in the cities of Macedonia and Thrace.[19] Based in part on the description of the cult statue in *Her.* 9.6 and 10.3–5, Gisela Richter identified a marble Roman copy of a Greek bronze as Protesilaos.[20] Protesilaos appears on coins from Skionê (fifth and fourth centuries B.C.E.), Thessaly (early third century B.C.E.), and Elaious (late second century C.E.); these coins depict him in the act of disembarking or standing on the prow of a ship.[21] Similar poses appear on a late geometric vase and an early classical intaglio.[22] A late-fourth-century B.C.E. relief, found in Sigeion and

[16] R. Demangel, *Le tumulus dit de Protésilaos* (Fouilles du corps d'occupation français de Constantinople 1; Paris: De Boccard, 1926).

[17] Pausanias *Description of Greece* 1.34.2. Herodotus (*Histories* 9.120.3) employs the terminology of hero cult, whereby a hero becomes θεός when immortalized after death. The description of Protesilaos's cult in the *Heroikos* also suggests that he received divine honors; see Mantero, *Ricerche*, 104–6, 115.

[18] Susan E. Alcock ("Material Witness: An Archaeological Context for the *Heroikos*," in this volume) documents archaeological evidence for patterns of construction, concentration, and convergence of memorial sanctuaries in this period.

[19] On the *Heroikos*'s connections to the northern Aegean, see the essay by Simone Follet in this volume.

[20] Gisela Richter, "A Statue of Protesilaos in the Metropolitan Museum," *Metropolitan Museum Studies* 1 (1928–1929): 187–200; see also José Dörig, "Deinoménès," *Antike Kunst* 37 (1994): 67–80. This statue appears as the frontispiece of our *Flavius Philostratus: Heroikos* (p. vii) and *Flavius Philostratus: On Heroes* (p. v). For alternative identifications, see Hans Christoph Ackermann and Jean-Robert Gisler, eds., *Lexicon Iconographicum Mythologiae Classicae (LIMC)* (8 vols.; Zurich: Artemis, 1981–1997), s.v. Protesilaos, no. 14.

[21] *LIMC*, s.v. Protesilaos, nos. 10–11; Jean Babelon, "Protésilas à Scioné," *Revue Numismatique*, 5th ser., 3 (1951): 1–11; Louis Robert, *Études de numisma-*

belonging to an Attic treaty inscription, possibly depicts Protesilaos in the company of Athena and another heroic figure.[23]

Following the suggestion of Hans Dieter Betz that the *Heroikos* should be read in a religious-political framework, we now turn to the political context of the *Heroikos*'s composition.[24] Protesilaos's role as defender of Greek territory against the outrages of a foreigner was well known (Herodotus *Hist.* 9.116–120). In the *Heroikos,* Protesilaos and Achilles play the roles of avenging *revenants* against characters foreign or "other" from the Hellenic perspective (see, e.g., *Her.* 4.2; 19.5–9; 56.6–10, 11–17). The composition of the *Heroikos* in the early third century C.E., during the later Severan period, situates it in a time when the government of the Roman empire faced threats of "foreignness" on two fronts. First, the imperial family itself was often perceived as not authentically Greek. Many of the Severan emperors and their powerful wives were Syrian[25] and to the consternation of some did not hesitate to introduce their ancestral religious practices into the established cults of Rome.[26] Second, in the early 230s Alexander Severus launched a campaign against the Sasanids in response to

---

tique Grecque (Paris: Collège de France, 1951). The coin from Elaious appears as the frontispiece of *Flavius Philostratus: Heroikos* (p. viii) and *Flavius Philostratus: On Heroes* (p. vi). Vermeule identifies the hero depicted on the reverse of an early-third-century C.E. bronze coin from Philippopolis in Thrace as Protesilaos, but we find this identification questionable; see Cornelius C. Vermeule, "Protesilaos: First to Fall at Troy and Hero in Northern Greece and Beyond," in *Florilegium Numismaticum: Studia in Honorem U. Westermark* (Numismatiska Meddelanden 38; Stockholm: Svenska Numismatiska Föreningen, 1992), 341–42, figs. 1 and 2.

[22] *LIMC*, s.v. Protesilaos, no. 12. Vermeule, "Protesilaos," 342–44, fig. 4.

[23] See L. Budde and R. V. Nicholls, *A Catalogue of the Greek and Roman Sculpture in the Fitzwilliam Museum Cambridge* (Cambridge: Cambridge University Press, 1964), 11–12, no. 27, plate 5; Vermeule, "Protesilaos," 344. Budde and Nicholls's cautious identification of the figure as Protesilaos rests upon a badly damaged inscription, which they reconstruct in light of the provenance of the find at Sigeion.

[24] See the article by Betz, pp. 25–47 in this volume. On the importance of political context, see also Mantero, *Ricerche*, 227–28; Georges Radet, "Notes sur l'histoire d'Alexandre: II. Les théores Thessaliens au tombeau d'Achille," *REA* 27 (1925): 81–96.

[25] Phoenicia was part of the Roman province of Syria, which in 194 C.E. Septimius Severus divided into Syria Phoenice (governed from Tyre) and Syria Coele (governed from Antioch). The city of Emesa, the home of Julia Domna, Julia Mamaea, and Julia Soemias, was located in eastern Syria Phoenice. On the Phoenician and Syrian identification of the Severan emperors and their wives, and the relation to the Phoenician merchant in the *Heroikos*, see the article by Ellen Aitken in this volume.

their invasion of Roman Mesopotamia.[27] With accusation of foreignness within the leadership of the empire and actual foreigners making incursions into Roman territory, the Severans needed to defend Severan cultural solidarity with the Greek world.

We suggest that the *Heroikos*, through the figure of the Phoenician merchant, may well have been intended to present the Severan dynasty (in particular its women) as authentically Greek. In addition, the *Heroikos* may have been written in order to promote Greek (and hence Roman) identity, fortitude, and piety, by re-creating in a way worthy of imitation the memory of the preeminent heroes of the Trojan War.[28] The Amazons,[29] whose unsuccessful attack on the abode of Achilles serves as the final narrative within the *Heroikos*, may thus represent the contemporary foreign threat to Greek identity, and Achilles' destruction of the Amazons, the certainty of Roman success against the Sasanids—so long as the heroes receive due honor.

The dialogue's three characters—Protesilaos, the vinedresser, and the Phoenician—serve as a useful way of organizing the contributions to this volume.[30] The hero *Protesilaos* is not only the object of cult, but also the avenue through which the reader learns the pat-

[26] E.g., the introduction into Rome of the Syrian sun god and Elagabalus's installation of the Black Rock of Emesa on the Palatine (Herodian *History* 5.5.8; SHA *Elagabalus* 3.4).

[27] In the 220s, the Sasanid ruler Ardašīr I declared his intent to reclaim the full extent of the Persian empire. Fergus Millar, *The Roman Near East: 31 B.C.–A.D. 337* (Cambridge, Mass.: Harvard University Press, 1993), 146–47; Glen W. Bowersock, *Roman Arabia* (Cambridge, Mass.: Harvard University Press, 1983), 126–28. Anthony Birley (*Septimius Severus: The African Emperor* [London: Eyre and Spottiswoode, 1971], 278) dates the accession of Ardašīr to 226 C.E., his invasion of Roman Mesopotamia to 230, and Alexander Severus's campaign to 231–232. For a thorough examination of the political positioning of Rome, see the essay by Rahim Shayegan in this volume.

[28] On the re-presentation of the heroes in accord with the virtues of the Hellenistic and Roman worlds, see the essay by Francesca Mestre in this volume.

[29] On the literary topos of the Amazons, see Josine H. Blok, *The Early Amazons: Modern and Ancient Perspectives on a Persistent Myth* (Religions in the Greco-Roman World 120; Leiden: Brill, 1995), especially 182, 441; John Boardman, "Herakles, Theseus, and the Amazons," in *The Eye of Greece: Studies in the Art of Athens* (ed. D. C. Kurtz and B. Sparkes; Cambridge: Cambridge University Press, 1982), 1–28. According to Herodotus (*Hist.* 9.27), before the Battle of Plataea the Athenians referred to the Amazons' invasion. The story also appears in Aeschylus's *Eumenides* (657–666), first performed during the Persian Wars; see Blok, *The Early Amazons*, 182.

[30] Needless to say, the connections among essays in this volume transcend this classification schema. We have tried to alert readers in the footnotes in this introduction to connections among essays in different sections.

terns of proper cultic veneration of heroes as well as the dire price paid for failing to give heroes their due. The first section of this volume contains essays that center on the hero, the rituals of hero cult, and the religious experiences of the hero's devotee. The *vine-dresser*, presented more as a sophist than a cultic functionary (*Her.* 4.4–10), oversees and mediates the hero's bounty, which occurs in the form of both an abundant garden and sage advice. The essays in this part of the volume revolve around the strategies by which the text cultivates—or, to use the postmodern building metaphor, constructs—cultural values in relation to preexisting values, texts, and trends. The *Phoenician*, by no means the least important member of the dialogue, gradually moves from being a stranger to the world of the heroes to a devotee. This character is an excellent symbol for the interest of this text in a specific area of cultural construction: redefining Greek culture in contrast to its binary other—the foreigner. The essays in this last section of the volume address the ways in which this text formulates the opposition between Hellene and foreigner and attempts to persuade the reader to identify herself as Hellene rather than foreigner.

PROTESILAOS: THE WITNESS OF THE HEROES

As the title clearly indicates, Philostratus's *Heroikos* is a dialogue about heroes, cataloging and describing the heroes on both the Hellenic and Trojan sides of the Trojan War. Protesilaos, the first to die in the war, and Achilles, the central figure of the *Iliad*, are preeminent in Philostratus's treatment. Significant attention is also given to Palamedes, who is said to be neglected by Homer, and Odysseus, whose Homeric protrait is significantly revised through this text. Yet the *Heroikos* is a "heroic" dialogue not only because it is *about* heroes, but also in the sense that the information it conveys about the heroes is presented as stemming directly from the authority of the hero Protesilaos. This is the literary fiction of the dialogue, namely, that all the vinedresser tells the Phoenician is what he has received from his own encounters and conversations with Protesilaos, who though dead appears regularly in his sanctuary. In this respect, Protesilaos is the not-so-silent partner in the dialogue, never appearing or speaking in person, but serving as the source of all the "true" knowledge that the vinedresser now communicates. The extended use of indirect discourse in the vinedresser's speeches, all premised on an implicit "Protesilaos says," demonstrates this chain of communication. It is the direct experience and observation of the hero (whose soul is "now free from the body and its diseases"; *Her.* 7.3) that is the source of what really happened at Troy and afterward. The word of the hero who has returned to life and speaks to his worshipers thus has ultimate truth value in the dialogue. This revealed knowledge functions as the final authority in the *Heroikos*.

In the *Heroikos*, moreover, Protesilaos is not simply a source of knowledge; he is also the object of cultic devotion. Set within the bucolic grove of the hero's sanctuary, the conversation between the vinedresser and the Phoenician includes details about the cult statue and its surroundings, the votive offerings the hero prefers, the oracles sought and given at the hero's tomb, and the avenging appearances of the hero as *revenant*. Similarly, Achilles appears in the dialogue not only as a hero of long ago, but as the inhabitant of a sanctuary in the Black Sea and as the sometime recipient of honors at his tomb in the Hellespont. The dialogue, moreover, evinces concern with the tombs and honors for numerous other heroes; heroes are clearly the subjects not only of stories but also of cultic practice.

The *Heroikos* does more than describe the cults of heroes. As Casey Dué and Gregory Nagy demonstrate, the *Heroikos* stands in a more complex relationship to hero cult. They argue that the *Heroikos*'s interest in both narrative and cult, within the ideals of the Second Sophistic, manifests the overall concept of the ancient Greek hero in both its literary and religious dimensions. They show, moreover, how the dialogue utilizes the language of initiation into hero cult in order speak of the special knowledge and experience available to the Phoenician through belief in and devotion to Protesilaos. In other words, the dialogue begins to enact the initiation of the Phoenician and thus itself participates in the practices of hero cult.

In "Singing Heroes—The Poetics of Hero Cult in the *Heroikos*," Corinne Pache examines the dimension of intimacy and emotion in hero cult as they are represented in the dialogue. What does it mean to "love" the hero or to "enjoy" the hero's company? Connecting such desire to the practices of singing and lamentation in hero cult, Pache locates the *Heroikos* in the context of earlier Greek ritual practices, but indicates the new concern with doubt, persuasion, and conversion as aspects of initiation. Hans Dieter Betz also explores the worship of heroes in the *Heroikos*, but focuses on the relationship between hero cult and Christian beliefs about the death and resurrection of Jesus. In what ways did early Christians respond to the prevalence of hero cult in the first through third centuries C.E.? Betz's examination of the *Heroikos*, complemented by the other discussions of hero cult in Philostratus, provides useful categories with which to answer this question.

Other contributions set the treatment of heroes and hero cult in the *Heroikos* within a larger cultural, political, and religious context. Christopher Jones considers the difficulties in the Roman imperial period of categorizing heroes, holy men, and other "divine" figures, with particular reference to Apollonius of Tyana, the subject of Philostratus's other major work. His article thus extends the discussion of hero cult beyond the cults of the legendary heroes of Trojan times to the veneration of more recent figures. Alain Blomart looks more broadly at the phenomenon of the transfer of hero cults in ancient Greece, inquiring into the multiple political motivations for this religious action. Blomart's work draws our attention to the *localization* of hero cult and its consequences for granting status and power to a city or region. Given the *Heroikos*'s particular concern with the cults of the northern Aegean (see Follet's article in part three), this argument helps to elucidate the possible political dimensions of Philostratus's work.

The local Lemnian traditions of cult attested in the *Heroikos* are the subject of Walter Burkert's article, "Jason, Hypsipyle, and New Fire at Lemnos: A Study in Myth and Ritual," reprinted here. This detailed analysis of rites that Philostratus cites as analogous to the cultic practices for Achilles illumines the relationship between narrative and ritual in Greek religion and argues that the consideration of ritual is indispensable to the study of myth, as myth is also indispensable for the interpretation of ritual. Burkert's methodological considerations require us to ask also about the nature of the evidence about cult provided in the *Heroikos*. Without question, when the *Heroikos* includes "description" of ritual, what we have instead is the literary inscription of religious practice, shaped through the rhetoric and broader interests of the dialogue. Rather than mining the dialogue for information about the ritual practices of hero cult,

[31] Albert Henrichs ("Keeping Dead Heroes Alive: The Revival of Hero Cult in the *Heroikos*" [paper presented at "Philostratus's *Heroikos*, Religion, and Cultural Identity," Harvard Divinity School, Cambridge, Mass., 4 May 2001]) has shown, moreover, that when Philostratus utilizes the practices of hero cult in the dialogue, he does so with considerable acumen for technical terminology and specificity.

we may look rather at how and to what ends Philostratus uses hero cult in all its splendor, together with stories about the heroes, as material for a rich literary composition.[31]

THE VINEDRESSER: STRATEGIES FOR THE CONSTRUCTION OF CULTURE

When he is not entertaining visiting merchants, the main speaker of Philostratus's dialogue, the vinedresser (ὁ ἀμπελουργός), is occupied with viticulture and the cultivation of fruit, nuts, and grain. He is, moreover, the caretaker of Protesilaos's sanctuary, devoting himself to the upkeep of the walkways and leaving suitable gifts for the hero. Protesilaos, for his part, instructs the vinedresser not only in the ways of heroes but with more practical skills as well, including the proper way to protect vines, water flowers, and plant trees. For the vinedresser, the art of cultivation derives from the hero. In contrast to those who defiled the sanctuary by their actions, the vinedresser cultivates the sanctuary as a place for the philosophical way of life (*Her.* 2.6) and the acquisition of wisdom (*Her.* 4.10). The vinedresser thus serves as an apt metaphor for the multiple ways in which the dialogue itself "cultivates" a way of life, in keeping with the philosophical and cultural values of the Second Sophistic.

The essays in part two of this volume attend variously to the cultivation or construction of culture in and through the *Heroikos*. One important area of investigation is the authoritative sources that Philostratus employed in the dialogue and his handling of them. Francesca Mestre considers Philostratus's treatment of Homer and his attempts to bring Homer up-to-date for a Greek readership under the Roman Empire. Demonstrating the degree to which the dialogue remains anchored in Homer, even while refuting and correcting the poems, Mestre indicates the importance of Homer as a sign of identity. Jeffrey Rusten also discusses the sources for Philostratus's "evidence" about heroes and prodigious sights, such as the bones of giants. He argues for the highly allusive texture of the dialogue and notes the diverse yet elusive character of many of the references Philostratus makes. His discussion of Philostratus's sources for the reports of bone finds around the Mediterranean complements Simone Follet's essay on Philostratus's knowledge of the northern Aegean; both consider the role of Philostratus's personal observation in the composition of the *Heroikos*. In "Material

Witness: An Archaeological Context for the *Heroikos*," Susan E. Alcock correlates Philostratus's literary cultivation of a memory of the heroic past to the patterns of the material construction of the past by Greek elites in the Roman Empire. The correlation helps us to appreciate anew the tension between panhellenic tendencies and local traditions both in the literature of the Second Sophistic and also in the treatment of sanctuaries, tombs, and other cult sites. Taken together these essays indicate the range of practices—literary, material, and cultic—available for the cultivation of a distinct cultural identity.

Early Christian communities contemporary with Philostratus were likewise engaged in the cultivation of identity, both communal and personal. Jackson P. Hershbell examines the practices of veneration of heroes, saints, and martyrs as evidence for common cultural patterns of worship. Wrestling with the category of "hero" for Jesus and Christian martyrs, Hershbell looks at the formative influence of a "hero cult paradigm" on the practices and beliefs of early churches. James Skedros also explores the nexus of ritual actions evident in the *Heroikos* with the practices of third-century Christians, especially the interest in dreams and visions, the materiality of cult, the negotiation of daimonic powers, and the bones of the special dead. Hero cult is sometimes assumed to have operated within a religious milieu distinct from that of early Christianity. It is over against this unwarranted assumption that Skedros argues that hero cult and Christianity shared a common milieu, and thus that neither can be rightly understood without taking the other into consideration. Jennifer Berenson Maclean brings the *Heroikos* and the Gospel of John into conversation with each other and argues that the pattern of hero cult found in the *Heroikos*, in which the hero becomes intimate with worshipers through his epiphany, communicates wisdom, and inculcates a particular ethical stance, is the precise way in which the Johannine community understood its relationship to Jesus.[32]

[32] The range of practices available for the cultivation of a distinct cultural identity has been illumined further by Froma Zeitlin in "Viewing the Heroes: Philostratus's *Heroikos* and the Culture of Visuality in the Second Sophistic" (paper presented at "Philostratus's *Heroikos*, Religion, and Cultural Identity," Harvard Divinity School, Cambridge, Mass., 4–6 May 2001).

THE PHOENICIAN: HELLENES AND FOREIGNERS

The arrival of a merchant at the sanctuary of Protesilaos provides the opportunity for this extended conversation among Phoenician, vinedresser, and hero. Although the Phoenician clearly speaks Greek and has the benefit of a Greek education, he is immediately cast as a foreigner, although not so much a "barbarian" as one foreign to the realities of the heroes—both past and present. His reticence to believe in the continued power of the heroes is eventually overcome, and a new relationship with Protesilaos is forged: the merchant sheds his allegiance to money and luxury and becomes obedient and devoted to the hero, and even an initiate into his cult. This movement from cultural outsider to intimate insider is perhaps the transformation Philostratus hoped his readers would achieve: to understand properly what constitutes a Greek cultural identity, to fulfill the ethical ideals inherent in that worldview, and vigorously to defend it.

The essays in part three of this volume all contribute to understanding Philostratus's project of cultural definition and identification. Simone Follet, in her essay "Philostratus's *Heroikos* and the Regions of the Northern Aegean," by paying attention to the geographical references in the text, begins the project of elucidating Philostratus's understanding of Greek identity. After examining the inscriptional evidence for the Philostrati's connection to various geographical locations, Follet identifies the northern Aegean as a particular area with which Philostratus demonstrates himself quite familiar; his descriptions of both its landscapes and modes of life are realistic and trustworthy. This essay urges us to consider Philostratus's trustworthiness in another area: his descriptions of cult activities, an issue of great importance if Philostratus is indeed urging his readers to adopt a particular kind of religious observance.[33]

Drawing on the literature of travel writing, Tim Whitmarsh's "The Harvest of Wisdom: Landscape, Description, and Identity in the *Heroikos*" likewise addresses cultural identity. The sanctuary of Protesilaos is cast as both Hellenic space par excellence and as a liminal space where what is foreign is both near and far and where the crucial distinctions are either maintained or lost. The reader,

[33] This essay, with its emphasis on inscriptional evidence, may be read fruitfully in conjunction with the essay in this volume by Susan E. Alcock, who explores broad trends in the changing religious landscape of the Greek world.

Whitmarsh argues, must enter the *Heroikos* as an outsider like the Phoenician, whose foreignness is constructed in the traditional opposition between rural and urban, especially in its economic aspects. The Phoenician's encounter with the metaphysically dynamic gardens of Protesilaos provides an extreme—and perhaps overly idealistic—model the reader might use to reconfigure his or her cultural identity.

As is clear from Whitmarsh's essay, the Phoenician is central to the *Heroikos*'s construction of both Greek identity and foreignness. The essay by Jennifer Berenson Maclean offers a detailed exploration of the Phoenician's characterization within the dialogue. Paying attention to both the character's self-presentation and his construction by the vinedresser, Maclean argues that his intitial position as unabashed sybarite is gradually overcome as he moves from skepticism concerning the heroes, to belief in their present power, and finally to devotion and perhaps even initiation into the hero's mysteries. The Phoenician's sybaritic outlook is forsaken through a reorientation of his priorities: the hero's wisdom—true knowledge of the Greek tradition—is of greater value than his ship's cargo. His former life is recognized as not simply barbaric, but subhuman, and through his transformation he achieves his true homecoming.

The essay by Ellen Aitken offers a reading of the *Heroikos* in the context of Severan politics. The Phoenician, whose dialogic purpose Aitken analyzes through the traditional charcterization of Phoenicians in Greek literature, also plays a large role in her essay. The ultimately pious Phoenician, she suggests, is used by Philostratus to defend the piety of the most prominent Phoenician (i.e., Syrian) family in the empire: the Severan royal family. Aitken is also attuned to the gendered discourse of foreignness; in particular, the dialogue's emphasis on victory over true foreigners—the Amazons—is intended to signal Roman victory over the Sasanians, who had recently breached the eastern borders of the empire.

The political interests of Aitken's contribution dovetail with the essay by Rahim Shayegan, who brings to the study of the *Heroikos* the perspective of Persian sources, too often ignored by or inaccessible to classicists. Shayegan explores how both Romans and the inheritors of the Persian domains created specific political identities vis-à-vis one another through their creative (i.e., manipulative) revival of their respective pasts, especially as regards the heroes and the need for imitation of them. In particular, Shayegan analyzes the tension in Alexander Severus's political positioning between a defensive military posture and the expectation that he imitate Alexander in his relationship with the East.

Sidney Griffith's essay on third-century Syriac Christianity highlights the fact that early Christian communities were also found beyond the eastern borders of the Roman Empire. It thus serves as a counterpart to Rahim Shayegan's essay on the Roman relations with Parthia in the Severan period. Even as we locate early Christianity as one of the cults of the Roman Empire, it is also important to recall the uneasy relationship that at least some early Christian groups had with imperial rule.[34] Griffith's essay also opens the door to further research on the geographical and theological particularity of a set of early Christian communities in Syria and the East. This particularity is critical to any understanding of the relationship of hero cult and the stories about heroes to the development of early Christianity. Rather than proceeding by painting a picture of influence in broad strokes, it is more productive to inquire into the tendencies in a given locale with a distinctive heritage to incorporate an available repertoire of practices and stories about the heroes into shaping a Christian way of life. In particular, attention to hero cult may shed light on how the cultural and political borders between Romans and Syrians were negotiated by early Christians. The *Heroikos*'s interest in Hellenes and foreigners is thus of importance for understanding early Christians who may have straddled these borders both geographically and conceptually.

THE *HEROIKOS* AND EARLY CHRISTIANITY

Philostratus's *Life of Apollonius of Tyana* is far better known to students of New Testament and early Christianity than is his *Heroikos*. In small part this is because the *Life* has long been available in English translation, but largely it is due to the text's emphasis on the portrait of the "holy man," which rendered it useful for comparison with the depictions of Jesus in the canonical Gospels. The *Heroikos* raises somewhat different questions for the study of early Christianity, questions that center less on the genre of the Gospels or the question of the uniqueness of the person or work of the historical Jesus, and more on the practices for a continuing relationship with

[34] See, for example, the articles collected in Richard A. Horsley, ed., *Paul and Empire: Religion and Power in Roman Imperial Society* (Harrisburg, Penn.: Trinity Press International, 1997).

the divine and the holy. The religious interests of the *Heroikos* speak to concerns of early Christian communities and thinkers such as the ways of understanding the body and its continued existence after death, the authority of ancient traditions, the methods for gaining knowledge of and ξυνουσία ("communion") with the divine. That is, early Christian communities were reckoning with many of the issues also addressed by Philostratus, among which were the relation of an emerging canon of texts to local traditions, the proper cultic worship of Christ (including both ritual and formal doctrinal statements), the proper veneration of martyrs, and the definition of community in contrast to what was considered "foreign" or "decadent."

Some of the essays in this volume (Betz, Hershbell, Skedros, Maclean, and Griffith) explicitly address the relationship between the *Heroikos* and early Christianity. We have chosen not to separate these pieces into their own section. Rather we incorporate them into the organizing categories of how the *Heroikos* thinks with heroes, worshipers, and foreigners. In doing so, we recognize that what we call "Christianity" in the second and third centuries was a fluid religious phenomenon, or set of phenomena, very much in the formative phase. Simon R. F. Price has argued that the landscape of religious groups in this period is best envisaged in terms of overlapping circles ("Venn diagrams," to borrow a metaphor from set theory).[35] In general we may say that formative Christianity thus shares with the other religions of the Roman Empire a wide range of strategies for community formation, initiation, cultic practice, ethics, and the acquisition of knowledge and power. In this volume the essays that engage early Christianity indicate that many of the modes of religious and cultural meaning-making and practice that we find in the *Heroikos* were also deployed by early Christian writers and communities.

Our goals for this collection of essays are not only that it will engender further scholarly discussion about the *Heroikos*, but also that it will inspire the use of Philostratus's dialogue in the classroom. The essay by Casey Dué and Gregory Nagy describes their experience using the text in a course on Homer, heroes, and Hel-

[35] Simon R. F. Price, "Religious Pluralism in the Roman World: Pagans, Jews, and Christians" (paper presented at the Annual Meeting of the Society of Biblical Literature, Nashville, Tenn., November 2000). Price argues for the importance of recognizing clusters of religious markers in any given case, rather than placing the evidence in impermeable categories of religious identity, e.g., Jewish *or* Christian; Isis *or* Mithras.

lenic civilization. Our own experiences with using the *Heroikos* in teaching about first- through third-century Christianity in its historical context similarly indicate the numerous opportunities the text offers for understanding, for example, what it entails to be a religious person in antiquity. The essays in this volume may thus be useful as guides to students with regard to particular aspects of this rich text.

Part I

Protesilaos: The Witness of the Heroes

Singing Heroes—The Poetics of Hero Cult in the *Heroikos*

Corinne Ondine Pache

> *"With regard to giants," replied Don Quixote, "there are different opinions as to whether they ever existed or not . . . on the island of Sicily, shoulder-bones, arm-bones and leg-bones have been found, the size of which shows that they belonged to giants as tall as towers: geometry puts this truth beyond all doubt."*
>
> —Cervantes, *Don Quixote*[1]

In this essay, I explore the poetic, emotional, and ritual dimensions of hero cult as presented in Philostratus's *Heroikos*.[2] After a short digression on hero cult in the Greek period, I focus on the emphasis placed on the emotional bond between worshiper and hero, as well as the important role played by hymns and laments in the narrative. I propose to investigate these twin themes in depth by focusing on examples provided by Philostratus himself, and particularly the cult of Melikertês. Because Philostratus associates hymns and laments with initiation or mystery cults, I also consider the link between hero and mystery cult in the *Heroikos*, as well as in earlier Greek texts. The link between these two forms of ritual, I argue, is already present in the classical sources, yet while the connection between mystery and hero cult is not unique to the Roman period, the function of initiation in Philostratus's narrative is different; it

[1] Miguel de Cervantes Saavedra, *The Ingenious Hidalgo Don Quixote de la Mancha* (trans. John Rutherford; New York: Penguin, 2001), 495. On ancient fossils' influence on beliefs, see Adrienne Mayor, *The First Fossil Hunters: Paleontology in Greek and Roman Times* (Princeton: Princeton University Press, 2000).

[2] I would like to thank Ellen Aitken and Jennifer Maclean for inviting me to the conference "Philostratus's *Heroikos*, Religion, and Cultural Identity." I also gave a version of this paper at "A Symposium on Hero Cults in the Greek East During the Empire" at the University of Chicago. My warmest thanks to Sulo Asirvatham, Judy Barringer, Claude Calame, Betsy Gebhard, Albert Henrichs, and Gregory Nagy for their help and advice.

expands in order to accommodate skepticism and include conversion. Whereas the reality of heroes is implicitly accepted as fact in archaic and classical sources, in the *Heroikos* their existence needs to be established through a series of proofs; the reader, along with the Phoenician merchant of the dialogue, undergoes an initiation of sorts. The central role of initiation into the mystery of the hero in the narrative reflects historical changes in the perception of cult heroes in the imperial period. Just as we see a gradual movement from unquestioning belief in heroes to skepticism, and from hearing about heroes to reading about them, we also see a shift from mourning to communion with the hero come back to life.

Before examining hero cult in the *Heroikos*, I would like to backtrack and turn for a moment to Greek hero cult in general. By "hero cult," I mean the combination of myths and rituals associated with the worship of heroes. Starting in the archaic period, some human beings are assigned the status of hero after their death and become objects of worship and recipients of animal sacrifice.[3] Because of the local nature of most hero cults, allusions to ritual practice (as Gregory Nagy and Albert Henrichs have argued) tend to be implicit rather than explicit in archaic and classical literature. Although allusions to hero cult per se are scarce in Greek poetry, allusions to heroes themselves, their deeds, lives, and deaths, are plentiful.[4] Myths and rituals in honor of heroes not only fulfill important religious functions, but the narrative of the hero's death and heroization must also have been a source of aesthetic pleasure that finds its way both in literary and visual representations.

Traditionally, the connection between worshiper and hero is established through ritual, and the relationship between hero and worshiper is conceived in terms of reciprocity through cult and not in terms of a close personal bond: the hero is conceptualized as a "deceased person," in Burkert's formulation, "who exerts from his grave a power for good or evil and who demands appropriate

[3] Walter Burkert, *Greek Religion* (Cambridge, Mass.: Harvard University Press, 1985), 203–13.

[4] On the implicitness of hero cults in epic, see Gregory Nagy, *The Best of the Achaeans: Concepts of the Hero in Archaic Greek Poetry* (2d ed. rev.; Baltimore: Johns Hopkins University Press, 1999), 9–11, and Gregory Nagy, "The Sign of the Hero: A Prologue," in *Flavius Philostratus: Heroikos* (trans. Jennifer K. Berenson Maclean and Ellen Bradshaw Aitken; SBLWGRW 1; Atlanta: Society of Biblical Literature, 2001), xv–xxxv; in drama, see Albert Henrichs, "The Tomb of Aias and the Prospect of Hero Cult in Sophokles," *Classical Antiquity* 12 (1993): 165–80.

honour."[5] There are, however, two important exceptions to this general rule. Two texts in extant Greek literature depict a hero simultaneously as the recipient of cult and as alive: the *Heroikos*, and some six hundred years earlier, Sophocles' *Oedipus at Colonus*. Sophocles' play depicts Oedipus as if he were already a cult hero *before* his death, while Philostratus depicts heroes *after* their deaths as very much alive to their worshipers. I will come back to other affinities between these two texts, but for now what I wish to emphasize is their extraordinary status. Oedipus notwithstanding, hero cult in the archaic and classical period is a highly ritualized form of worshiping the dead.

Hero cult continues to thrive in the Greek world beyond the classical era, and by the Hellenistic period, this answer to death becomes so popular that private citizens routinely heroize dead members of their own families. By the time of Philostratus's *Heroikos*, we also see a renewal of interest in the earlier Greek heroes in the Roman East.[6] Dennis Hughes recently suggested that among the attractions of the traditional heroes was the link they can provide with the past, both mythical and historical. He argues, "Hero cult—with its political and historical as well as religious dimensions—played a particularly important role in the 'Greek Renaissance', the revival of civic and national pride and identity in Greece under Roman rule." He also notes that, at a time when the distance between worshipers and gods increases, worshipers grow closer to their heroes and worship them not only as a way of identifying themselves with the Greek past, but also because they hope to join the old heroes in the life to come.[7]

When we turn to the *Heroikos*, we find that the promise of hero cult lies not only in the hope of joining ancient heroes in the afterlife, but very much in the possibility of enjoying their company in the here and now. The *Heroikos* records the conversation between a vinegrower and a traveling Phoenician merchant that takes place at Elaious on the north shore of the Hellespont. At the beginning of the dialogue, the merchant makes clear that he does not believe in

[5] Burkert, *Greek Religion*, 203.

[6] For the controversy about dating the *Heroikos*, see Maclean and Aitken, *Philostratus: Heroikos*, xlii–xlv.

[7] Dennis D. Hughes, "Hero Cult, Heroic Honors, Heroic Dead: Some Developments in the Hellenistic and Roman Periods," in *Ancient Greek Hero Cult: Proceedings of the Fifth International Seminar on Ancient Greek Cult, Organized by the Department of Classical Archaeology and Ancient History, Göteborg University, 21–23 April 1995* (ed. Robin Hägg; Stockholm: Åströms, 1999), 173–74.

heroes, and the vinegrower proceeds to persuade him of their existence.

Some scholars have dismissed the third-century C.E. work as a sophistic exercise with no religious import.[8] Others take the *Heroikos* at its word and argue that the concern with hero cult is indeed serious and central to the dialogue.[9] Without denying the obvious literary aspects of Philostratus's text, I agree with the latter group of scholars that the discourse about heroes must be understood within the framework of a society in which hero cult was a common practice, and a society in which Philostratus's readers would have had no problems recognizing the ritual vocabulary associated with hero cults.

Hans Dieter Betz argues that the movement from skepticism to belief is one of the major themes of the *Heroikos*, and indeed the whole dialogue revolves around the Phoenician's change of attitude toward the worship of heroes.[10] There is a progression in the types of evidence the vinegrower uses to convince his interlocutor of the existence of heroes: he starts with his encounter with the hero Protesilaos, which represents a turning point in his own life, then goes on to the scientific proof afforded by the existence of large bones and to what he learned about other heroes directly from Protesilaos. After a section devoted to the correction of Homer's account of epic heroes, the vinegrower goes on to describe the proper performance of heroic rituals.

The vinegrower never has any doubts about the reality of heroes, and his life changes for the better when he decides to follow the hero Protesilaos's advice and moves to the country. He considers the hero to be both an adviser and a companion. The friendship the vinegrower enjoys with the risen Protesilaos, however, is not unique, and he gives other examples of heroes who have come back to life.

Even when one encounters heroes, it is not always easy to recognize them. When ghosts (εἴδωλα) first appear, the vinegrower explains to the Phoenician, the identity of each is not immediately

[8] Graham Anderson, *Philostratus: Biography and* Belles Lettres *in the Third Century A.D.* (London: Croom Helm, 1986), 247–48.

[9] Teresa Mantero, *Ricerche sull'* Heroikos *di Filostrato* (Genoa: University of Genoa, Istituto di Filologia Classica e Medioevale, 1966), 1–18; Hans Dieter Betz, "Hero Worship and Christian Beliefs: Observations from the History of Religion on Philostratus's *Heroikos*," 25–47 in this volume. See also Maclean and Aitken, *Philostratus: Heroikos*, xlii–xlv.

[10] Betz, "Hero Worship and Christian Beliefs."

obvious. Heroes may appear in many different guises—they can change their appearance, their age, or their armor—and it can be a tricky task to recognize a hero from one time to the next (*Her.* 21.1–8).

To illustrate the difficulty in identifying heroes, the vinegrower tells the story of a Trojan farmer who particularly favors the hero Palamedes. The farmer is described as having deep sympathy for Palamedes' suffering and his horrific death at the hands of his comrades. The farmer often goes to the shore where Palamedes was stoned to death; he brings offerings to the hero's grave and sings dirges for him. After the farmer displays his admiration for Palamedes in these and other ways, the hero decides to visit and reward his admirer, whom he describes as his ἐραστής ("lover"). Palamedes appears to the farmer as he tends his vine:

> «σὺ γινώσκεις με» ἔφη «γεωργέ;»—«καὶ πῶς» εἶπεν, «ὃν οὔπω εἶδον;»—«τί οὖν» ἔφη, «ἀγαπᾷς ὃν μὴ γινώσκεις;» ξυνῆκεν ὁ γεωργὸς ὅτι Παλαμήδης εἴη· καὶ τὸ εἶδος ἐς ἥρω ἔφερε μέγαν τε καὶ καλὸν καὶ ἀνδρεῖον, οὔπω τριάκοντα ἔτη γεγονότα· καὶ περιβαλὼν αὐτὸν μειδιῶν «φιλῶ σε, ὦ Παλάμηδες» εἶπεν, «ὅτι μοι δοκεῖς φρονιμώτατος ἀνθρώπων γεγονέναι καὶ δικαιότατος ἀθλητὴς τῶν κατὰ σοφίαν πραγμάτων.»
>
> "Do you recognize me, farmer?" He answered, "How would I recognize you whom I have never seen?" "Then *do you love him* [ἀγαπᾷς] whom you do not recognize?" said the other. The farmer realized that it was Palamedes, and he reported that the hero's image was tall, beautiful, and brave, although he was not thirty years old. The farmer embraced him and said with a smile, "*I love you* [φιλῶ σε], Palamedes, because you seem to me to be the most sensible of all and the most fair champion in deeds of skill." (*Her.* 21.5–6)

As soon as Palamedes mentions love (ἀγαπᾷς), the farmer recognizes the hero. In this passage, there is an intimate emotional bond between worshiper and hero, and loving the hero comes to the same thing as physically seeing him.

Just before this epiphany, one of the ways in which the farmer shows his devotion to Palamedes is by experiencing the sufferings (πάθος) of the hero as well as singing laments (ἐθρήνει) for him. Mourning, paradoxically, revives the hero for the worshiper. Love and lament are keys to the hero's coming back to life.

Later in the dialogue, another passage demonstrates a similar conflation of loving and seeing, or loving and recognizing. The vinegrower tells the Phoenician what Protesilaos told him about Achilles' physical appearance. He starts with Achilles' hair, "lovelier than gold," and then goes on to his nose, brow, and eyes:

> ὁρμήσαντος δὲ συνεκπηδᾶν τῇ γνώμῃ, τοῖς τε ἐρῶσιν ἡδίω αὐτὸν φαίνεσθαι.
>
> "When he is rushing on," [he adds,] "[his eyes] spring out along with his purpose, and he seems more lovely than ever *to those who love* [τοῖς ἐρῶσιν] *him*." (*Her*. 48.2)

In the case of the farmer and Palamedes, loving precedes, and perhaps causes, the hero's epiphany. In the second instance, loving and seeing are synchronous. Clearly, then, seeing, loving, and knowing the hero are all intertwined.

The same language of love and desire is used in the dialogue both of longing for the hero and also of longing for knowledge about the hero. Desire to learn is often described in terms of πόθος and ἔρως. The Phoenician, in particular, emphasizes his thirst for knowledge:

> ἃ ποθῶ μαθεῖν, ξυνίης δή γε· αὐτὴν γὰρ τὴν ξυνουσίαν, ἥτις ἐστί σοι πρὸς τὸν Πρωτεσίλεων.
>
> You know at any rate what *I long to learn* [ποθῶ μαθεῖν], and especially about this association you have with Protesilaos. (*Her*. 7.1)

And again a little later:

> ποθοῦντι ἀποδίδως, ἀμπελουργέ, τὸν περὶ αὐτῆς λόγον· σπάνιον δὲ οἶμαι ἀκούσεσθαι.
>
> You tell the story to one *who longs* for it [ποθοῦντι], vinegrower. And I believe I will seldom hear it. (*Her*. 23.2)

Similarly, the hero Palamedes himself is described as a lover of wisdom (σοφίας ἐρῶν, *Her*. 23.24).[11]

Nagy argues that epic heroes are eroticized already in Homer's *Iliad* where yearning for the hero is conventionally described in the language of desire (πόθος). This happens when the warriors of Phthia "long" for their leader, Protesilaos, in Book 2 (*Il*. 2.703, 709) and again in Book 23, when the Achaeans "long" for Patroklos (*Il*.

[11] Other example of ἔρως for knowledge or wisdom: *Her*. 23.1; 23.36.

23.16).[12] The same verb, ποθεῖν, is used in both instances. Yet, the discourse of love is nowhere as strikingly explicit as it is, almost a thousand years later, in the *Heroikos*, with the hero Palamedes' description of his follower as an ἐραστής ("lover"), and his tacit self-definition as his worshiper's ἐρώμενος ("beloved"). It is not only the intimate emotional bond between hero and worshiper that is surprising, but the physical reality of the hero's presence and the individual nature of his relationship with worshipers.

While the emotional intensity of the bond between hero and worshiper in the *Heroikos* is unique, Philostratus also focuses on more conventional forms of worship. We saw how the Phoenician is both skeptical about heroes, yet eager to learn more about them at the beginning of his conversation with the vinegrower. Later in the dialogue, once it becomes clear that the Phoenician is no longer hostile to the idea of the reality of heroes in general, the vinegrower starts to discuss *ritual* in more details.

I would like to focus on a passage that describes the cult of Achilles and compares it with the cults of Melikertês and the children of Medea. This passage comes close to the end of the dialogue, as the vinegrower and his interlocutor start to discuss the cult of Achilles. The vinegrower tells the Phoenician about the strange mixture of rites performed by the Thessalians in honor of Achilles:

> καὶ μὴν καὶ ὕμνων ἐκ Θετταλίας ὁ Ἀχιλλεὺς ἔτυχεν, οὓς ἀνὰ πᾶν ἔτος ἐπὶ τὸ σῆμα φοιτῶντες ᾖδον ἐν νυκτί, τελετῆς τι ἐγκαταμιγνύντες τοῖς ἐναγίσμασιν, ὡς Λήμνιοί τε νομίζουσιν καὶ Πελοποννησίων οἱ ἀπὸ Σισύφου.
>
> From Thessaly, of course, Achilles also received *hymns*, which they sang at night when they visited his tomb every year, *mixing something of an initiatory rite* with their *heroic offerings*, just as both the Lemnians and the Peloponnesians descended from Sisyphus practice. (*Her.* 52.3)

While the Greek word τελετή can be an unmarked term for ritual in general, it also has a more specific meaning of "initiation" and in some cases "initiation into mysteries." As Arthur Darby Nock has shown, the terminology of initiation and mystery acquired a generic quality as mysteries became increasingly popular in the Hellenistic period and later.[13] Yet, because the narrative here

[12] Nagy, "The Sign of the Hero," xxvii n. 20.

[13] On τελετή as an initiation term, see Walter Burkert, *Ancient Mystery Cults* (Cambridge, Mass.: Harvard University Press, 1987), 9. Arthur Darby Nock,

emphasizes that the ritual in honor of Achilles is a *mixture* of different rituals, and since τελετή is contrasted with ἐναγίσματα, a technical term for the type of bloody animal sacrifices preferred by the dead and heroes, I take τελετή in this passage in its specialized sense as initiatory rites.

When he learns of the rites in honor of Achilles, the Phoenician confesses that this is a subject of great interest to him. The vinegrower cautions him that a digression into these practices might be time-consuming, but encouraged by the Phoenician's enthusiasm ("the soul's cargo," as he puts it, "is sweeter to me and more profitable"; *Her.* 53.3), he agrees that digressions make for worthwhile conversation, and he elaborates the comparison by specifying that he was comparing the ritual for Achilles with two Peloponnesian rites in particular:

> τὰ μὲν γὰρ Κορινθίων ἐπὶ Μελικέρτῃ (τούτους γὰρ δὴ τοὺς ἀπὸ Σισύφου εἶπον), καὶ ὁπόσα οἱ αὐτοὶ δρῶσιν ἐπὶ τοῖς τῆς Μηδείας παισίν, οὓς ὑπὲρ τῆς Γλαύκης ἀπέκτειναν, θρήνῳ εἴκασται τελεστικῷ τε καὶ ἐνθέῳ· τοὺς μὲν γὰρ μειλίσσονται, τὸν δὲ ὑμνοῦσιν.
>
> The rites of the Corinthians for Melikertês (for these people are those whom I called the descendants of Sisyphus) and what the same people do for Medea's children, whom they killed for the sake of Glaukê, resemble a *lament* that is both *initiatory* and *inspired*, for they *propitiate* the children and *sing hymns* to Melikertês. (*Her.* 53.4)

The rituals mentioned in this passage are comparable because they all consist of a *mixture*. Let us look carefully at the terminology used by the vinegrower: he specifies that the rites for Melikertês and those for the children of Medea are similar in that they resemble a lament (θρῆνος), which is of an initiatory nature (τελεστικός), as well as divinely inspired (ἔνθεος). He does mention that "they," the Corinthians, killed the children of Medea, but he does not refer to the circumstances of the death of Melikertês. While worshipers propitiate (μειλίσσονται) the children of Medea, they perform hymns for Melikertês. Μειλίσσειν is a verb typically used to describe offerings to the dead or to heroes.[14] Both these

"Hellenistic Mysteries and Christian Sacraments," in *Essays on Religion and the Ancient World* (ed. Zeph Stewart; 2 vols.; Oxford: Clarendon, 1972), 2:798.

[14] Burkert, *Greek Religion*, 195.

cults, then, like the one in honor of Achilles, consist of a blend of initiation rituals and heroic offerings.

In all three cases—Achilles, Melikertês, children of Medea—Philostratus also describes the rites in terms of singing. The performance of mourning songs in the context of hero worship is nothing unusual, but the emphasis in these two passages is on the link between singing and initiation: the performance of hymns and laments is, in fact, what defines these rites as τελεταί, as rituals of an initiatory nature.[15]

Why are laments so important in the cults of Melikertês, the children of Medea, and Achilles? We have seen, in the case of Palamedes, how a lament can be a prelude to the hero's epiphany, and singing a θρῆνος is clearly an effective means of communication with the hero as we see in these three cases. Yet what are we to make of Philostratus's insistence on describing these cults as similar to initiation rituals? Moreover, is this link between hero cults and initiation typical of the Roman period?

While the connection between initiation and hero cult is made explicit in the *Heroikos*, can the same be said about earlier Greek sources? Angelo Brelich already suggested in his 1958 book on hero cult that there is a type of hero who is closely connected to mysteries.[16] Not surprisingly, he refers to Philostratus's description of the cults of Melikertês and the children of Medea. Yet he also points out that Euripides already had his Medea describe the ritual in honor of her children in terms of initiatory rite:

> οὐ δῆτ᾽, ἐπεί σφας τῇδ᾽ ἐγὼ θάψω χερί,
> φέρουσ᾽ ἐς Ἥρας τέμενος Ἀκραίας θεοῦ,
> ὡς μή τις αὐτοὺς πολεμίων καθυβρίσῃ
> τύμβους ἀνασπῶν· γῇ δὲ τῇδε Σισύφου

[15] See Margaret Alexiou, *The Ritual Lament in Greek Tradition* (Cambridge: Cambridge University Press, 1974), 61–62 and nn., for laments in honor of cult heroes (lament for Leukothea in Thebes, Achilles at Elis, and the Bakchiadai at Corinth) and lamentation in the Dionysiac and Orphic tradition. For more on the cult of Achilles on Leukê, see Guy Hedreen, "The Cult of Achilles in the Euxine," *Hesperia* 60 (1991): 313–30. For the cult of Achilles in the *Heroikos*, see Ellen Bradshaw Aitken, "The Cult of Achilles in Philostratus' *Heroikos*: A Study in the Relation of Canon and Ritual," in *Between Magic and Religion: Interdisciplinary Studies in Ancient Mediterranean Religion and Society* (ed. Sulochana R. Asirvatham, Corinne Ondine Pache, and John Watrous; Lanham, Md.; Rowman & Littlefield, 2001), 127–35. On τελετή as a term used to describe mysteries, see Burkert, *Ancient Mystery Cults*, 9–11.

[16] Angelo Brelich, *Gli eroi greci: Un problema storico-religioso* (Rome: Edizioni dell'Ateneo, 1958), 118–23. See also Nagy, "The Sign of the Hero."

σεμνὴν ἑορτὴν καὶ τέλη προσάψομεν
τὸ λοιπὸν ἀντὶ τοῦδε δυσσεβοῦς φόνου.

Indeed no, *I shall bury them* with my own hand,
Taking them to the *sanctuary* of Hera the goddess of
Akraia,
So that none of my enemies may outrage them,
Tearing up their graves. And on this land of Sisyphus
I shall enjoin a *solemn festival and initiation rituals*
For the rest of time *as a compensation* for this impious
murder. (Euripides *Medea* 1377–1383)

The sources describing the cult in honor of the children of Medea are few and not always in agreement. Parmeniskos, an Alexandrian grammarian of the second and first centuries B.C.E., reports that the cult in honor of the children was instituted by the Corinthians after some sort of a plague (λοιμός) struck the city. The Corinthians consulted the oracle, which told them to establish a cult in honor of the children in order to expiate their guilt and appease the wrath of Hera. And from that time on, seven boys and seven girls were chosen every year from the Corinthian aristocracy to serve in the temple of Hera for one year.[17] Pausanias, who is the other main source for the ritual, is silent about this yearly rite of segregation in his second-century C.E. guidebook to Greece. According to him, his contemporaries have abandoned the rituals (θυσίαι) in honor of the children of Medea. He mentions that Corinthian children used to cut their hair and wear dark clothes in honor of the dead heroes, but that the custom ended with the sack of Corinth by the Romans in 146 B.C.E. (*Description of Greece* 2.3.7). Aelian, on the other hand, writing after Pausanias, disagrees and claims that the Corinthians still perform sacrifices for the children in his own time, but he speaks in terms of heroic sacrifices (ἐναγίζουσι, *Varia historia* 5.21). Although Pausanias's and Aelian's versions are difficult to reconcile, and regardless of whether the rituals were still performed in the Roman period, we should nonetheless note that Euripides, the scholia to the *Medea*, and Pausanias all describe the ritual in terms of initiation.

When we turn to Melikertês, we find that the Isthmian myth is well documented in earlier sources, and although they disagree on details, the same basic elements are found in most versions of the story: baby Melikertês dies when his mother Ino tries to escape the murderous fury of her husband, Athamas, by jumping into the sea

[17] Scholia to Euripides *Medea* 264 = *FGrH* 417 F 3.

from the White Rock, holding her son in her arms. The Nereids welcome her, and she is deified as Leukothea, while the body of her son, Melikertês, is brought ashore at the Isthmus by a dolphin. There Sisyphus finds the body, gives him a funeral, and establishes the Isthmian Games in honor of the boy, renamed Palaimôn. Pindar is the earliest source to mention the ritual established by Sisyphus in honor of the dead child:

> Αἰολίδαν δὲ Σίσυφον κέλοντο
> ᾧ παιδὶ τηλέφαντον ὄρσαι
> γέρας φθιμένῳ Μελικέρτᾳ.
>
> They ordered Sisyphus, the son of Aiolos,
> to establish an *honor that can be seen from afar*
> for the dead child Melikertês. (Pindar *Isthmian* frg. 6.5 Maehler)

Pindar's "honor that can be seen from afar" clearly refers to the cult in honor of Melikertês. The Greek word γέρας can be understood both literally and metaphorically, as both a physical monument and the institution of a festival in honor of the dead hero.[18] The myth of Melikertês appears not only in lyric poetry, but also in tragedy as well as in Hellenistic poetry.[19] Yet, as Helmut Koester argues in a

[18] For τηλέφαντος γέρας as a panhellenic festival in honor of Melikertês, see Elizabeth R. Gebhard and Matthew W. Dickie, "Melikertes-Palaimon, Hero of the Isthmian Games," in Hägg, *Ancient Greek Hero Cult*, 161. I argue elsewhere (*Baby and Child Heroes in Ancient Greece* [Urbana: University of Illinois Press, 2004]) that the adjective τηλέφαντος refers both to time and space; the word has the connotation both of "appearing" and "speaking." In the case of Pindar's *Isthmian* fragment, the τηλέφαντον γέρας belongs to the rhetoric of cult: I suggest that it refers both to a concrete visible heroic shrine built in honor of Melikertês, as well as to the poetic narrative of the hero's death.

[19] We know that Aeschylus and Sophocles each composed an *Athamas* (actually, Sophocles is the author of two plays of the same name); there is also a *Phrixos* by Sophocles, as well as two *Phrixos* plays by Euripides; see Timothy Gantz, *Early Greek Myth: A Guide to Literary and Artistic Sources* (Baltimore: Johns Hopkins University Press, 1993), 179. Euripides' lost *Ino* can be reconstructed via Hyginus's *Fabula* 4. Euripides (*Medea* 1282–1291) mentions the story of Ino and Melikertês and describes Palaimôn, the son of Leukothea, as the guardian of ships (*Iphigenia in Tauris* 270–271). The scholia to Pindar's *Isthmian Odes* also gives many details about the myth and ritual in honor of Melikertês (Anders Björn Drachmann, *Scholia vetera in Pindari Carmina* [3 vols.; Teubner; Amsterdam: Hakkert, 1966–67], 3:192–95). In Hellenistic poetry, Melikertês becomes an angry baby requiring human sacrifice: see Callimachus *Causes* 4; *Diegesis* frg. 91 Pfeiffer, where Lesbians sacrifice babies on the altar of Melikertês at Tenedos; Lycophron *Alexandra* 229 mentions Melikertês as a baby slayer (βρεφοκτόνος) and the scholia add that the son of Ino is especially honored in Tenedos, where he receives sacri-

1990 article, the cult in honor of Melikertês begins to be described as a mystery cult in our literary sources only in the Roman period.[20]

Pausanias describes the temple of Melikertês-Palaimôn, which he places "to the left" within the sanctuary of Apollo at Isthmia. The ἄδυτον, an underground chamber, is where Palaimôn is supposed to be hidden—and anyone, either Corinthian or foreign, who falsely swears an oath there has no way to escape his oath (Pausanias *Description of Greece* 2.2.1). It is unclear from Pausanias's description whether the ἄδυτον was part of the temple or a different structure altogether.

Near where the temple of Palaimôn should have been according to Pausanias, excavators found the foundations of an earlier stadium, as well as the concrete foundation of a Roman building. An earlier cult place for Melikertês was probably located somewhere in this area, but all remains were obliterated during the destruction of Corinth by Mummius (146 B.C.E.). The earliest remains, however, that can be directly linked with Melikertês are from two sacrificial pits from the first century C.E. filled with animal bones, pottery, and lamps of a unique shape unknown anywhere else in Greece. The Palaimônion was rebuilt in the Roman period, and the temple as it stood in the second century C.E. has been reconstructed from representations on coins from the Isthmus and Corinth.[21]

What about the cult, then, and the lament that is both "initia-

---

fices of babies (schol. *Alexandra* 229 Scheer). The emphasis on human sacrifice in the Hellenistic sources is inconsistent with what we know about heroic rituals: while it is frequent for the spirits of young victims to take revenge on their living counterparts—as is the case with the children of Medea, for example, who cause all Corinthian infants to die—there is no evidence of any hero cults requiring human victims. The function of such myths may be apotropaic. For a different interpretation, cf. Elizabeth Gebhard, who argues that the story of the death of Melikertês fits a pattern of myths dealing with child sacrifices performed in times of crisis to save a city. "Child in the Fire, Child in the Pot: The Making of a Hero" (paper presented at the Seventh International Seminar on Ancient Greek Cult, Göteborg University, Sweden, 16–18 April 1999), to be published in the proceedings of this conference. We find another such myth, of course, in the *Heroikos*, in the story of Achilles requesting that a young Trojan girl be left on the beach for him, only to be torn apart limb from limb (*Her.* 56.10), but here the murder of the young woman is the result of Achilles' anger against the Trojans rather than a sacrifice per se.

[20] See Helmut Koester, "Melikertes at Isthmia: A Roman Mystery Cult," in *Greeks, Romans, and Christians: Essays in Honor of Abraham J. Malherbe* (ed. David Balch, Everett Ferguson, and Wayne A. Meeks; Minneapolis: Fortress, 1990), 355–66.

[21] For lamps, see Oscar Broneer, *Isthmia III: Terracotta Lamps* (Princeton: American School of Classical Studies at Athens, 1977) and Koester, "Melikertes at

tory and inspired"? Philostratus is, in fact, not our only source for this aspect of the ritual. Plutarch also mentions the cult in his life of Theseus:

> ὁ γὰρ ἐπὶ Μελικέρτῃ τεθεὶς αὐτόθι νυκτὸς ἐδρᾶτο, τελετῆς ἔχων μᾶλλον ἢ θέας καὶ πανηγυρισμοῦ τάξιν.
>
> For the contest established *in honor of Melikertês* was taking place there at night, organized like an *initiatory ritual* [τελετή] rather than like a spectacle or public festival. (Plutarch *Theseus* 25.5)

In this passage, Plutarch is distinguishing between the panhellenic athletic games, which he claims were founded by Theseus, and the ἀγών in honor of Melikertês, which he describes as already in place by the time Theseus came to the Isthmus. Plutarch uses the traditional ritual syntax ἐπί plus the dative to indicate that the ἀγών is offered to Melikertês as a compensation for his death. This ἀγών, however, is not a simple public athletic festival, but rather it is organized like an initiatory ritual (τελετή), which takes place at night.

Another important source for the cult of Melikertês-Palaimôn is Philostratus's *Imagines*. I want to focus more particularly on a few sentences referring to the ritual:

> ὁ θύων ἐν Ἰσθμῷ δῆμος—εἴη δ᾽ ἂν ὁ ἐκ τῆς Κορίνθου—καὶ βασιλεὺς οὑτοσὶ τοῦ δήμου—Σίσυφον αὐτὸν ἡγώμεθα—τέμενος δὲ τουτὶ Ποσειδῶνος ἠρέμα τι προσηχοῦν θαλάττῃ—αἱ γὰρ τῶν πιτύων κόμαι τοῦτο ᾄδουσι—τοιάδε, ὦ παῖ, σημαίνει· ἡ Ἰνὼ τῆς γῆς ἐκπεσοῦσα τὸ μὲν ἑαυτῆς Λευκοθέα τε καὶ τοῦ τῶν Νηρηίδων κύκλου, τὸ δὲ τοῦ παιδὸς ἡ γῆ Παλαίμονι τῷ βρέφει χρήσεται. καταίρει δὲ ἤδη ἐς αὐτὴν ἐπὶ δελφῖνος εὐηνίου, καὶ ὁ δελφὶς τὰ νῶτα ὑποστρωννὺς φέρει καθεύδοντα διολισθάνων ἀψοφητὶ τῆς γαλήνης, ὡς μὴ ἐκπέσοι τοῦ ὕπνου· προσιόντι δὲ αὐτῷ ῥήγνυταί τι κατὰ τὸν Ἰσθμὸν ἄδυτον διασχούσης τῆς γῆς ἐκ Ποσειδῶνος, ὅν μοι δοκεῖ καὶ Σισύφῳ τούτῳ προειπεῖν τὸν τοῦ παιδὸς εἴσπλουν καὶ ὅτι θύειν αὐτῷ δέοι. θύει δὲ ταῦρον τουτονὶ μέλανα ἀποσπάσας οἶμαι αὐτὸν ἐκ τῆς τοῦ Ποσειδῶνος ἀγέλης. ὁ μὲν οὖν τῆς θυσίας λόγος καὶ ἡ τῶν θυσάντων ἐσθὴς καὶ τὰ ἐναγίσματα, ὦ παῖ, καὶ τὸ σφάττειν ἐς τὰ τοῦ Παλαίμονος

Isthmia," 359–60; for the temple, see Oscar Broneer, *Isthmia I: Temple of Poseidon* (Princeton: American School of Classical Studes at Athens, 1977). For a recent discussion, see Elizabeth Gebhard, "The Beginnings of Panhellenic Games at the Isthmus," in *Akten des Internationalen Symposions Olympia 1875–2000* (ed. Helmut Kyrieleis; Mainz am Rhein: Zabern, 2002), 221–37.

ἀποκείσθω ὄργια—σεμνὸς γὰρ ὁ λόγος καὶ κομιδῇ ἀπόθετος ἅτ' ἀποθειώσαντος αὐτὸν Σισύφου τοῦ σοφοῦ· σοφὸν γὰρ ἤδη που δηλοῖ αὐτὸν ἡ ἐπιστροφὴ τοῦ εἴδους—τὸ δὲ τοῦ Ποσειδῶνος εἶδος, εἰ μὲν τὰς Γυρὰς πέτρας ἢ τὰ Θετταλικὰ ὄρη ῥήξειν ἔμελλε, δεινὸς ἄν που ἐγράφετο καὶ οἷον πλήττων, ξένον δὲ τὸν Μελικέρτην ποιούμενος ὡς ἐν τῇ γῇ ἔχοι, μειδιᾷ καθορμιζομένου καὶ κελεύει τὸν Ἰσθμὸν ἀναπετάσαι τὰ στέρνα καὶ γενέσθαι τῷ Μελικέρτῃ οἶκον. ὁ δὲ Ἰσθμός, ὦ παῖ, γέγραπται μὲν ἐν εἴδει δαίμονος ἐνυπτιάζων ἑαυτὸν τῇ γῇ, τέτακται δὲ ὑπὸ τῆς φύσεως Αἰγαίου καὶ Ἀδρίου μέσος κεῖσθαι καθάπερ ἐπεζευγμένος τοῖς πελάγεσιν. ἔστι δὲ αὐτῷ μειράκιον μὲν ἐν δεξιᾷ, Λέχαιόν τοι, κόραι δὲ ἐν ἀριστερᾷ· θάλατται δὲ αὗται καλαὶ καὶ ἱκανῶς εὔδιοι τῇ τὸν Ἰσθμὸν ἀποφαινούσῃ γῇ παρακάθηνται.

This people sacrificing at the Isthmus, that would be the people of Corinth, and the king of the people here is, I think, Sisyphus himself; this is the sacred precinct of Poseidon, which resounds gently with the sea, for the leaves of the pine trees sing in this way, and this, my boy, is what it means: Ino, after she threw herself into the sea, became Leukothea and one of the circle of the Nereids; as for her son, the earth will benefit from the baby Palaimôn. Already he puts into port on the well-disposed dolphin, and the dolphin carrying the sleeping child spreads his back, slipping through the calm sea noiselessly, so that the child may not be waken from his sleep. And with him approaching, an ἄδυτον breaks forth out of the earth split apart by Poseidon, who, it seems to me, is announcing the child's sailing-in to Sisyphus here, and also that he should sacrifice to the child. And Sisyphus sacrifices this black bull here, having dragged him away from the herd of Poseidon. The *λόγος of the sacrifice* and the *attire* worn by those sacrificing as well as *the offerings*, my boy, and *the slaying* must be kept *for the secret rites of Palaimôn.* For *the λόγος is holy*[22] and altogether *secret*, since Sisyphus the wise himself deified it. That Sisyphus is wise is indeed shown by the thoughtfulness of his appearance. As for the face of Poseidon, if he were about to break the Gyrean rocks or the Thessalian mountains, he would certainly have been depicted as terrible and such as someone striking a blow, but since he is receiving him as a guest so that he might keep him in his land, he smiles

[22] Euripides uses same word when he describes Medea establishing a σεμνὴν καὶ τέλη ritual. For ἱερὸς λόγος in the context of mysteries, see Burkert, *Ancient Mystery Cults*, 69–70.

> at the child coming into harbor, and orders the Isthmus to unfold its breast and become a home for Melikertês. The Isthmus, my boy, is painted in the form of a δαίμων sprawling himself on the land, and he has been appointed by nature to lie between the Aegean and the Adriatic as if he were yoking the two seas together. There is a young man on the right, Lechaios probably, and girls on the right, who are the two seas, beautiful and suitably calm, lying beside the land representing the Isthmus. (Philostratus *Imagines* 2.16)

Neither the "λόγος of the sacrifice," the attire worn by the people performing the sacrifice, the offerings, nor the way of killing the animal, are to be disclosed. "For the λόγος is holy [σεμνός] and altogether secret [ἀπόθετος]." Never mind that this prohibition is transgressed in this image, which shows precisely what must be kept secret.

The "λόγος of the sacrifice" (ὁ τῆς θυσίας λόγος) is in itself a mysterious phrase: is it referring to the language used during the sacrifice, the order in which it is performed, the beliefs of the participants, or the story behind it?[23] I suggest it refers to the narrative dealing with the death and coming back to life of the hero Melikertês. We see a similar preoccupation in the *Heroikos*, with the vinegrower carefully distinguishing between which part of the λόγος of Protesilaos can be told and which parts must be kept secret.

Aelius Aristides also mentions the cult of Melikertês at the end of his hymn to Poseidon. He wonders whether the story of Melikertês and Ino should be described as a story (λόγος) or a myth (μῦθος), and is distressed at the idea that the goddess Leukothea might have undergone the sufferings ascribed to the mortal Ino (*Sacred Discourses* 46.32–34). Thus, for him, Leukothea must have been a goddess from the beginning, and since there can be no evil among the gods (*Sacred Discourses* 46.36), he rejects the violent details of the narrative: Leukothea actually never threw herself into the sea, and neither was the child Melikertês snatched away—according to Aristides, he was actually entrusted to Poseidon as a source of delight and a gift (ἄθυρμα καὶ δῶρον).[24]

[23] On cult of Melikertês being secret (ἀπόρρητα), cf. Libanius *Or.* 14.65 Foerster.

[24] There is an intriguing precedent for this story, of course, in the myth of Poseidon falling in love with another beautiful young boy, Pelops (see Pache, *Baby and Child Heroes in Ancient Greece*).

When it comes to the cult of Melikertês, Aristides describes it in much the same terms as Philostratus:

> Παλαίμονα δὲ καὶ εἰπεῖν καλὸν καὶ τοὔνομα αὐτοῦ ὀνομάσαι καὶ ὅρκον ποιήσασθαι καὶ τῆς τελετῆς τῆς ἐπ' αὐτῷ καὶ τοῦ ὀργιασμοῦ μετασχεῖν—τοσοῦτος τις ἵμερος πρόσεστι τῷ παιδί—καὶ ἰδεῖν γε καὶ ἐν γράμματι, . . . ὅπου δὲ καὶ ἐπ' αὐτῶν τῶν νώτων τῆς θαλάττης, ὅπου δὲ καὶ ἐν ταῖς χερσὶν τῆς μητρὸς τὸ θάλος τοῦ παιδὸς καὶ τὴν ὥραν καὶ τὸ ἄνθος. ταῦτα γὰρ θεάματα θεαμάτων ἥδιστα καὶ ἰδεῖν γε καὶ ἀκοῦσαι.
>
> It is good to talk about Palaimôn and say his name and swear his oath, as well as to take part in the initiation ritual [τελετή] and the celebration of secret rites [ὀργιασμός] in his honor, and also—so great is the desire [ἵμερος] attached to the boy—to see in the picture the bloom and freshness and flower of the boy when he is on the back of the sea, and when he is in his mother's arms. For these are the sweetest of sights to see and to hear. (Aelius Aristides *Sacred Discourses* 46.40 Keil)

Aristides specifically describes the rites in honor of the hero as initiatory. Not only does he use the nouns τελετή and ὀργιασμός, which are associated with initiation rituals, but like Plutarch he also uses the traditional ritual syntax ἐπ' αὐτῷ, which in combination with the noun τελετή means "to be initiated into the mysteries of the hero." Although Aristides just dismissed the story of Ino and Melikertês throwing themselves into the sea, the picture he describes seems to show precisely this scene: the mother holding her child in the sea, and the child being carried forth by the sea. Two aspects of Aristides' description are particularly intriguing: Aristides insists on both the importance of *speaking* about Palaimôn (both talking about him and saying his name), as well as the pleasure inherent in *seeing* the boy.

The mention of swearing an oath in the name of Palaimôn recalls Pausanias's description of the ἄδυτον at Isthmia where worshipers actually swear oaths. Pausanias's claim that Palaimôn is hidden (κεκρύφθαι) begs the question: does Melikertês ever appear to his worshipers? Pausanias describes another ἄδυτον in the context of a hero cult, that of the oracle of the hero Trophônios at Lebadeia, where in order to consult the oracle, the worshiper descends into an underground χάσμα. Once they reach the inner sanctum (ἄδυτον), worshipers learn the future. According to Pausanias, there is no single way of doing this, but some learn through seeing, others through hearing (*Description of Greece* 9.39.11).

Aristides uses a series of adjectives associated with youth to describe Palaimôn in his mother's arms: θάλος, ὥρα, ἄνθος. All belong to the metaphorical world of flowers and spring, and all draw attention to Palaimôn's youth and beauty. What about the ἵμερος evoked by Aristides? The word can express longing or yearning, but also love and desire. This is the word used by Philostratus, for example, when he describes how desire is awakened in Achilles and Helen after they hear descriptions of each other. Yet, in the case of Melikertês, Aristides is not talking about romance, but about a dead, heroized child. At first glance, it may seem that the ἵμερος described by Aristides is caused by the vision of the boy's image, but on closer examination it becomes clear that this ἵμερος is very closely related to what precedes as well; it is the participation in the rites (τελετή, ὀργιασμός) and oath, as well as the description of the picture that follows, that awakens the ἵμερος for the hero in the worshiper. Moreover, Aristides emphasizes at the end of the passage that these sights are the sweetest to *see* and to *hear* (καὶ ἰδεῖν γε καὶ ἀκοῦσαι), making it very clear that both components are essential. In some way, then, ἵμερος is closely linked with initiation into the mystery of the hero Melikertês. Something similar seems to be at work in the *Heroikos*, where we see worshipers falling in love with heroes. Indeed, in some cases, loving a hero seems to be a form of initiation.

How early, then, can we trace back a link between a hero cult and a mystery cult? I have mentioned Sophocles' *Oedipus at Colonus* as an important exception in the way in which it conceptualizes a living being as a hero. Sophocles' last tragedy also provides an intriguing perspective on the link between initiation and hero cult. The play describes the death and heroization of Oedipus in the grove of the Eumenides at Kolônos. Although Oedipus is still alive, other characters are aware of his status as cult hero and of the powers he can exercise as such. As Claude Calame has shown, Sophocles superimposes a pattern of initiation into the Eleusinian mysteries onto the narrative of the death of Oedipus.[25] While this

[25] See Jacques Jouanna, "Espaces sacrés, rites et oracles dans *l'Oedipe à Colone* de Sophocle," *REG* 108 (1995): 38–58; Lowell Edmunds, "The Cults and the Legend of Oedipus," *HSCP* 85 (1981): 221–38; Lowell Edmunds, *Theatrical Space and Historical Place in Sophocles'* Oedipus at Colonus (Lanham, Md.:

does not necessarily mean that the ritual in honor of Oedipus was in fact a mystery cult, the very fact that Sophocles can make such an analogy is intriguing.

If a link, however tenuous, between hero cult and mystery rites can already be attested for the fifth century B.C.E., then the initiatory nature of the cults of Melikertês, of the children of Medea, as well as of Achilles described in the *Heroikos* is perhaps not an exception or a late (Roman) development, but rather represents a particular strand of hero cult that was there all along.[26]

What about the role of initiation and mysteries in the *Heroikos* in general? While the existence of heroes is a given in the classical period, in Philostratus's narrative, initiation becomes a prerequisite to perception. I return to an episode at the very beginning of the dialogue:

> καὶ οὔπω, ξένε, τῶν ἀηδόνων ἤκουσας, οἷον τῷ χωρίῳ ἐναττικίζουσιν, ἐπειδὰν δείλη τε ἥκῃ καὶ ἡμέρα ἄρχηται.
>
> "Stranger," says the vinegrower, "*you have not yet heard the nightingales that sing here in the Attic manner* both when evening comes and when day begins." (*Her.* 5.4)

Here again, let me turn to Sophocles: the allusion to nightingales recalls Antigone's description of Kolônos at the beginning of the play, where nightingales are a defining feature:

> χῶρος δ' ὅδ' ἱερός, ὡς σάφ' εἰκάσαι, βρύων
> δάφνης, ἐλαίας, ἀμπέλου· πυκνόπτεροι δ'
> εἴσω κατ' αὐτὸν εὐστομοῦσ' ἀηδόνες·
>
> But this place is *sacred*, one may clearly surmise,
> luxuriant
> with laurel, olive and vine. A throng of feathered
> *nightingales* sing their blessed song within it. (*Oedipus at Colonus* 16–18 Blundell)

And later in the play, the chorus echoes Antigone's words in their description of the sacred grove:

Rowman & Littlefield, 1996); Claude Calame, "Mort héroïque et culte à mystère dans l'*Oedipe à Colone* de Sophocle: Aspects rituels au service de la création mythique," in *Ansichten griechischer Rituale: Geburtstags-Symposium für Walter Burkert, Castelen bei Basel, 15. bis 18. Marz 1996* (ed. Fritz Graf; Stuttgart: Teubner, 1998), 326–56.

[26] For heroic cults "di carattere misterico," see Brelich, *Gli eroi greci*, 121.

εὐίππου, ξένε, τᾶσδε χώ—
ρας ἵκου τὰ κράτιστα γᾶς ἔπαυλα,
τὸν ἀργῆτα Κολωνόν, ἔνθ'
ἁ λίγεια μινύρεται
θαμίζουσα μάλιστ' ἀη—
δὼν χλωραῖς ὑπὸ βάσσαις,
τὸν οἰνωπὸν ἔχουσα κισ—
σὸν καὶ τὰν ἄβατον θεοῦ
φυλλάδα μυριόκαρπον ἀνήλιον
ἀνήνεμόν τε πάντων
χειμώνων·

In this country of fine horses, stranger,
You have reached the mightiest shelter upon earth,
White Kolônos.
The clear-toned nightingale,
Frequenting it most,
Pipes plaintively within green glades,
Occupying the wine-dark ivy
And the foliage of the god
Where none may step, with untold berries, out of the
sun
Out of the wind of all storms. (*Oedipus at Colonus* 669–678 Blundell)

Two keywords in these two passages, Kolônos and nightingale, evoke concerns closely linked to mourning and hero cults. The noun κολωνός here refers to the sacred grove near Athens where the heroization of Oedipus takes place. Nagy argues that the word is consistently associated with hero cult and is often used as a marker of the hero's grave. Indeed it appears in the *Heroikos*, where it is used to describe the mound that extends over the grave of the hero Protesilaos (*Her.* 9.1). The same term later on describes the grave of Achilles and Patroklos (*Her.* 51.12).[27] Moreover, like the White Rock that marks the entrance to the underworld in archaic Greek poetry, it can also be perceived, metonymically, as the boundary as it were between life and death.[28]

Just as important as the word κολωνός is the presence of nightingales singing in these two passages. The presence of nightingales at Kolônos is no coincidence. Nightingales are often connected with

[27] See Nagy, "The Sign of the Hero," xxxiii n. 34.

[28] On the associations between Kolônos and the White Rock, see Gregory Nagy, "Phaethon, Sappho's Phaon, and the White Rock of Leukas: 'Reading' the Symbols of Greek Lyric," in *Greek Mythology and Poetics* (Ithaca, N.Y.: Cornell University Press, 1990), 223–62.

mourning in the context of hero cults, and more particularly they mourn the death of the poet par excellence, Orpheus:

> ὁ δὲ Μυρσίλος ὁ τὰ Λεσβιακὰ συγγεγραφώς φησιν, τῆς Ἀντισσαίας ἐν ᾧ τόπῳ μυθολογεῖται καὶ δείκνυται δὲ ὁ τάφος ὑπὸ τῶν ἐγχωρίων τῆς τοῦ Ὀρφέως κεφαλῆς, τὰς ἀηδόνας εἶναι εὐφωνοτέρας τῶν ἄλλων.
>
> And Myrsilos, who wrote the *Lesbiaka*, says that in Antissaia, in the place where the tomb for the head of Orpheus is reported to be and shown by the inhabitants, *the nightingales are more melodious than others.* (*FGrH* 477 F 2)

Here Myrsilos describes how the inhabitants of Lesbos describe the place where the grave for the head of Orpheus is in terms of the nightingales who sing there more melodiously than others. Similarly, according to Pausanias, the Thracians say that the nightingales that nest on Orpheus's grave, which they claim is in Thrace, sing more loudly and in a sweeter manner than other nightingales (*Description of Greece* 9.30.6). The Greeks traditionally understood the song of the nightingale as a song of lament,[29] and clearly this is how the vinegrower understands it when he tells the Phoenician that he has not yet heard the nightingales singing. But what interests me even more is the Phoenician's answer, in which he makes a distinction between lamenting and singing:

> δοκῶ μοι ἀκηκοέναι ξυντίθεσθαί τε μηδὲ θρηνεῖν αὐτάς, ἀλλὰ ᾄδειν μόνον.
>
> "I think that I have heard them and I agree that they *do not lament*, but *only sing*." (*Her.* 5.5)

Is this an indication of the Phoenician's utter failure to understand what is really at stake? Remember what the vinegrower said: "You have not *yet* heard the nightingales that sing here in the Attic manner both when evening comes and when day begins." By link-

[29] Calame, "Mort héroïque et culte à mystère," 238 n. 16, with references. For nightingales in Sophocles, see Charles Segal, *Tragedy and Civilization: An Interpretation of Sophocles* (Cambridge, Mass.: Harvard University Press, 1981; repr., Norman: University of Oklahoma Press, 1999), 373–75, with n. 34; see also Aara Suksi, "The Poet at Colonus: Nightingales in Sophocles," *Mnemosyne* 54 (2001): 646–58. For the nightingale as metaphor for poetic authority, see Gregory Nagy, *Poetry as Performance, Homer and Beyond* (Cambridge: Cambridge University Press, 1996), passim, especially 7–9, 57–66, 207–13; for the nightingale in the context of mourning, see Nicole Loraux, *Mothers in Mourning* (Ithaca, N.Y.: Cornell University Press, 1998), 57–65, 105.

ing the nightingales to Attica, the vinegrower makes clear both the literary and ritual connection to the classical past. The Phoenician merchant perhaps catches the literary allusion, but not the ritual one. He cannot hear the nightingales' lament *yet* because he is not yet initiated into the mysteries of hero cult. By the end of the dialogue, however, the Phoenician has been persuaded and is ready to understand, and perhaps experience, the bond between worshiper and hero.

Laments and hymns clearly are at the center of hero worship in the *Heroikos*, but this is also something we see at work in other sources: telling the story of the hero, singing of him, and lamenting him are constantly described as the focus of the cult of Melikertês and of Achilles, for example. Lamenting the hero is a form of community for the worshipers, and perhaps the beginning of an initiation into the mysteries.

Before I turn to my conclusion, I would like to go back once more to initiation as it is described in the *Heroikos*. As many have noticed before, the Phoenician undergoes an initiation of sorts himself in the course of the narrative:[30] at the beginning of the dialogue, he makes it clear he does not believe in heroes; by the end, he is so entranced by the vinegrower's narrative that he asks to come back the next day to hear more about yet another subject. Through hearing the vinegrower's stories, the Phoenician merchant begins to see a truth he had not suspected even existed before, and by the end of the dialogue he claims that his soul's cargo is more valuable than that of his ship, and that he would rather delay his business than miss the opportunity to hear more from the vinegrower and Protesilaos himself.

The Phoenician merchant realizes that he cannot ask about certain subjects, such as Protesilaos coming back to life, but there is one topic he is particularly interested in: he wants to hear about the place where the rivers Kôkytos, Pyriphlegethôn, and Akherousias flow, or the place—as we know it from the *Odyssey*—which is just beyond the White Rock, beyond the world of the living, beyond everyday consciousness:[31]

> τοὺς δὲ Κωκυτούς τε καὶ Πυριφλεγέθοντας καὶ τὴν Ἀχερουσιάδα καὶ τὰ τοιαῦτα τῶν ποταμῶν τε καὶ τῶν λιμνῶν ὀνόματα καὶ νὴ

[30] See Mantero, *Ricerche sull'* Heroikos, 61–64, and Betz, "Hero Worship and Christian Beliefs," 25–47.

[31] See Nagy, *Greek Mythology and Poetics*, 236.

Δία τοὺς Αἰακοὺς καὶ τὰ τούτων δικαστήριά τε καὶ δικαιωτήρια αὐτός τε ἴσως ἀπαγγελεῖς καὶ ξυγχωρεῖ διηγεῖσθαι.

On the *Kôkytoi* and the *Pyriphlegethontes* and the *Akherousiada*, and such names of rivers and seas, and, by Zeus, the Aiakidai and their courts of justice and places of punishments, you yourself will perhaps report and he [Protesilaos] will agree to set forth the details. (*Her*. 58.3)

The vinegrower advises him to set sail or, if the winds should be bad, to come back the next day. The Phoenician merchant does not hesitate and reiterates that he wants to hear more:

πείθομαί σοι, ἀμπελουργέ, καὶ οὕτως ἔσται· πλεύσαιμι δὲ μήπω, Πόσειδον, πρὶν ἢ καὶ τοῦδε ἀκροάσασθαι τοῦ λόγου.

I believe in you, vinedresser, and so shall it be. May I not sail, by Poseidon, before I listen to this *story* as well. (*Her*. 58.6)

Kôkytos, Pyriphlegethôn, and Akherousias: Wailing, Blazing Fire, and Woe, these are the topics the Phoenician wants to learn more about, and this, it seems to me, is the perfect way to conclude an initiation into the mysteries of the hero: in the *Heroikos*, the λόγος of death and mourning literally gets the last word of the dialogue.

In conclusion, the *Heroikos* uses the same ritual vocabulary and concept of the hero used by the poets of the classical period. The roles played by mourning, love, and πόθος reflect earlier Greek practices, yet the dialogue also fundamentally differs from the earlier tradition. The need for persuasion and the "scientific," or to echo Don Quixote, the "geometric," nature of the evidence represent new developments. The vinegrower's belief in heroes, just like Don Quixote's belief in giants, is being challenged by his interlocutor and the burden of proof is on the believer. The *Heroikos* depicts worshipers who still empathize with, mourn, and love the hero, but belief in the existence of heroes is no longer a given. While earlier hero cults already exhibit aspects that we associate with mystery cult, something new is at work in the *Heroikos*, where the mystery is closely connected with doubt and the need for persuasion and conversion. And, through conversion and initiation, the hero becomes alive to the worshiper.

Hero Worship and Christian Beliefs: Observations from the History of Religion on Philostratus's *Heroikos**

Hans Dieter Betz

The growth of ancient hero worship at the time of Christianity's origin poses all kinds of questions for the historian of religion and exegete of the New Testament. It is, however, surprising that even relevant works seldom explore these questions.[1] The term ἥρως is not found in the New Testament and early Christian literature, a fact which is in striking contrast to the great popularity of hero worship in the environment of early Christianity. One must draw from Celsus's polemics in order to understand that the silence of early Christian literature cannot be accidental. In a long quotation in Origen's *Against Celsus* 2.55,[2] Celsus raises the question of why Christians are not content to understand Jesus' resurrection appearances as analogous to appearances of comparable figures such as, for example, Zamolxis among the Scythians, Pythagoras in

* [*Ed.:* This article originally appeared as "Heroenverehrung und Christusglaube: Religionsgeschichtliche Beobachtungen zu Philostrats *Heroicus*," in *Griechische und Römische Religion* (ed. Hubert Cancik; vol. 2 of *Geschichte—Tradition—Reflexion: Festschrift für Martin Hengel zum 70. Geburtstag*; ed. Hubert Cancik, Hermann Lichtenberger, and Peter Schäfer; Tübingen: Mohr Siebeck, 1996), 119–39. It has been translated by Jackson P. Hershbell. We thank Hans Dieter Betz and Mohr Siebeck Verlag for permission to translate and reproduce this essay here. Translations of the Greek have been added when necessary. Translations of the *Heroikos* are our own; translations of biblical passages follow the New Revised Standard Version.]

[1] See Samson Eitrem, "Heros," PW 8.1 (1913): 1111–45; Arthur Darby Nock, "The Cult of Heroes," *HTR* 37 (1944): 141–74, repr. in *Essays on Religion in the Ancient World* (ed. Zeph Stewart; 2 vols.; Oxford: Oxford University Press, 1972), 2:575–602; Walter Burkert, *Greek Religion* (Cambridge, Mass.: Harvard University Press, 1985), 190–208; trans. of *Griechische Religion der archaischen und klassischen Epoche* (Stuttgart: Kohlhammer, 1977); Wolfgang Speyer, "Heros," *RAC* 14 (1988): 861–77, esp. 871–72; Abraham J. Malherbe, "Herakles," *RAC* 14 (1988): 559–83; Scott Scullion, "Olympian and Chthonian," *Classical Antiquity* 13 (1994): 75–119.

[2] Henry Chadwick, trans. and ed., *Origen: Contra Celsum* (Cambridge and New York: Cambridge University Press, 1953), 109. For Origen's dispute with Celsus, see especially the following passages: 3.34–37, 80–81; 7.68–70.

Italy, Rhampsinitus in Egypt, Orpheus, Protesilaos, Herakles, and Theseus. If Celsus's arguments are allowed to stand, the question arises why very early Christian belief in Jesus Christ did not in fact lead to a hero cult.[3] If one views the phenomena with Celsus's eyes in the context of the history of comparative religion, one also sees that the miraculous deeds of Jesus, his violent death on the cross, and his appearances after death could easily have led to the development of a Christian hero cult.[4] On this point, Celsus definitely had correct insight; he would have even declared himself in agreement with veneration of Jesus as a hero (*Against Celsus* 7.68–70).[5] To be sure, Origen raises his strongest objection primarily at this point, since for him worship of the supreme God and his Logos, the first-born of creation (*Against Celsus* 2.31; 7.70 and passim), is involved. On the other side stands the orator and philosopher of religion, Philostratus, who dedicated himself to the programmatic upgrading of Greek culture, including its religion. In contrast to Celsus, Philostratus endeavored to make a positive use of θεῖος ἀνήρ figures such as Apollonius of Tyana (*Life of Apollonius*),[6] heroes of the Homeric world worshiped by the populace (*Heroikos*), and the great Sophists (*Lives of the Sophists*). The fact is that Philostratus, in contrast to Celsus and Lucian,[7] never mentioned Christianity, although one must probably assume that he had knowledge of it.[8]

In what follows, the thesis will be put forth that early Christology consciously avoided developing veneration of Jesus Christ as a hero. Given that hero worship enjoyed increasing popularity in the

[3] See also my comments in "Das Problem der Auferstehung Jesu im Lichte der griechischen magischen Papyri," in *Hellenismus und Urchristentum* (vol. 1 of *Gesammelte Aufsätze;* Tübingen: Mohr Siebeck, 1990), 234–36, as well as Glen W. Bowersock, "Resurrection," in *Fiction as History: Nero to Julian* (Berkeley: University of California Press, 1994), 99–119.

[4] Veneration of heroes including Jesus existed among the Gnostics. For the texts, see Speyer, "*Heros*," 875–76.

[5] As is known, the emperor Alexander Severus is said to have kept in his *lararium* an image of Apollonius of Tyana next to those of Christ, Abraham, Orpheus, and others (SHA *Alexander Severus* 29.2).

[6] On this matter, see Wolfgang Speyer, "Zum Bild des Apollonius von Tyana bei Heiden und Christen," in *Frühes Christentum im antiken Strahlungsfeld: Augewählte Aufsätze* (WUNT 50; Tübingen: Mohr Siebeck, 1989), 176–92, esp. 179–82.

[7] See my essay, "Lukian von Samosata und das Christentum," in *Hellenismus und Urchristentum*, 10–21.

[8] The relationship of Philostratus to Christianity involves a difficult question that cannot be discussed here.

ancient world, this refusal cannot be based on lack of awareness. Is there indication of a conflict concerning this matter in very early Christian literature? To these problems the following discussion is directed. In part I, Philostratus's *Heroikos*, one of the most important writings for the topic of the hero cult, will be examined. In the course of this discussion, concepts and facts from the history of religion will be emphasized in comments and footnotes, thereby illuminating the parallels in very early Christian literature. A second part (II) evaluates the results further and thus has connection to a thesis of Samson Eitrem, unjustly overlooked at present. According to this thesis, the theme of a hero Christology is already addressed in the New Testament.

I. PHILOSTRATUS'S *HEROIKOS*

Flavius Philostratus's dialogue *Heroikos*[9] is worth serious consideration as evidence for non-Christian religion in the second and third centuries C.E. In view of Ulrich von Wilamowitz-Moellendorff's disparaging judgments[10] and those of Martin Nilsson,[11] it is no surprise that Philostratus's *Heroikos*,[12] unlike his *Life of Apollonius* composed a short time earlier, has for many years received little attention.[13]

[9] In what follows the work will be cited by chapter and paragraph, according to the edition of Ludo de Lannoy, *Flavii Philostrati Heroicus* (Bibliotheca Teubneriana; Leipzig: Teubner, 1977). Specific references are from the index to that volume.

[10] Ulrich von Wilamowitz-Moellendorff, *Der Glaube der Hellenen* (3d ed.; 2 vols.; Darmstadt: Wissenschaftliche Buchgesellschaft, 1959), 2:513–14.

[11] Martin P. Nilsson, *Geschichte der griechischen Religion* (2d ed.; 2 vols.; Munich: Beck, 1961), 2:564–65.

[12] The dialogue is dated 214/215 C.E. and is connected with Caracalla's crossing the Hellespont. On this point, see Karl Münscher, "Die Philostrate," *Philologus* suppl. 10/4 (1907): 469–558, esp. 504ff.; Wilhelm Schmid and Otto Stählin, *Geschichte der griechischen Literatur* (2 vols.; Handbuch der Altertumswissenschaft; Munich: Beck, 1924), 2.2:778; Friedrich Solmsen, "Philostratus," PW 20.1 (1941): 124–77, for the *Heroikos* see esp. cols. 154–59.

[13] Confinement to the *Life of Apollonius* has led to a one-sided and insufficient assessment, especially in New Testament research. To this assessment belong the recent studies of Erkki Koskenniemi, *Apollonios von Tyana in der neutestamentlichen Exegese: Forschungsbericht und Weiterführung der Diskussion* (WUNT 2/61; Tübingen: Mohr Siebeck, 1994). The study, composed as a Christian apologetic, treats neither the *Heroikos* nor the total work of Philostratus in the context of his time (see especially the remarks on pp. 184–87: "Die Intentionen des Philostratos").

Eitrem's learned study of 1929[14] is an exception, to which the following interpretation is substantially indebted.[15]

Wilamowitz-Moellendorff has described quite well how the Severan emperor's last attempts to renew belief in the ancestral Hellenic gods failed.[16] But as Eitrem correctly saw, hero worship remained as strong as ever among the populace. He cited many reasons for this phenomenon.[17] If the imperial reformation was ready to surrender the Olympian gods, then it quite logically focused on the still vibrant spheres of religious life in which hero worship had an ever increasing popularity. In contrast to the ancient gods, heroes are accessible to and can be experienced by all human beings. Eyewitnesses report bodily appearances (ἐπιφάνειαι): one can see them with one's own eyes and even touch them. Thus, the entire program of Philostratus must also be especially viewed as having religio-political, and not only literary-aesthetic, dimensions.[18] If the empress Julia Domna introduced Philostratus to the scholarly circle gathered about her in Rome[19] and commissioned him to write a work such as *Life of Apollonius*,[20] then the *Heroikos* was composed

[14] Samson Eitrem, "Zu Philostrats *Heroikos*," *Symbolae Osloenses* 8 (1929): 1–56. Concerning Eitrem (1872–1966), see Fritz Graf's introduction to Samson Eitrem's "Dreams and Divination in Magical Ritual," in *Magika Hiera: Ancient Greek Magic and Religion* (ed. Christopher A. Faraone and Dirk Obbink; Oxford and New York: Oxford University Press, 1991), 175–76.

[15] See also the appropriate appreciation of Albrecht Dihle, *Greek and Latin Literature of the Roman Empire: From Augustus to Justinian* (London and New York: Routledge, 1994), 343; trans. of *Die griechische und lateinische Literatur der Kaiserzeit* (Munich: Beck, 1989): "Thus this writing [the *Heroikos*] by Philostratus is a valuable piece of evidence for the growing influence of folk belief on the religious notions of educated people. This influence was strongest in the late classical age, whereas the ideas of the post-Hellenistic educated classes were largely influenced by the rationalistic legacy of that period." [*Ed.:* This quotation has been altered to match the published English translation.]

[16] Wilamowitz-Moellendorff, *Der Glaube der Hellenen*, 2:511–13.

[17] Eitrem, "Zu Philostrats *Heroikos*," 1–7.

[18] Schmid and Stählin (*Geschichte*, 2.2:778) have correctly emphasized that "the dialogue strives to be a Platonic dialogue, although it soon becomes a lecture. It is especially interesting for us as an attempt to win new powers from Greek religion by descending into the depths of common belief still insolently derided by Lucian (*The Lover of Lies, or the Doubter*), and to promote anew the most popular form of religious veneration, that is, the cult of heroes."

[19] See on this point Glen W. Bowersock, *Greek Sophists in the Roman Empire* (Oxford: Clarendon, 1969), 101–9; Francesca Ghedini, *Giulia Domna tra Oriente e Occidente: Le fonti archaeologiche* (Rome: "L'Erma" di Bretschneider, 1984), 10–11.

[20] Philostratus expresses himself about the work's origin in *The Life of Apollonius* 1.3; cf. also *Lives of the Sophists*, p. 622–23 Kayser.

with a similar purpose and spirit. This dialogue is thus concerned with more than warmed-over "ghost stories" or "rehashing the ancient belief in heroes" by "this shabby sophist."[21] Certainly the *Heroikos* is a "sophistic showpiece,"[22] propaganda for the glorification of an idyllic and naive piety, as hardly experienced by the learned Philostratus himself. Yet he must have had great hopes for its dissemination:[23] "the graves of the dead had more carrying capacity than the columns of the temple."[24]

1. SKEPTICISM AND CREDIBILITY

An introductory story which frames the *Heroikos* (1.1–5) introduces the main persons of the dialogue, who, as contemporary types, remain nameless. Their chance meeting brings two men into conversation who seem at first wholly different, but who prove to be similar on a very deep level. One is a Phoenician businessman from the region of Sidon and Tyre, a proud, strutting, self-confident figure, dressed in a fashion characterized as Ionic and decadent, now spreading over Syria. During his sea journey a diminishing wind forced him to land on the Thracian Chersonesus to wait for better weather. Here he encounters a thoroughly hospitable and pious vinedresser who leads a retired life on his small country estate and enjoys the abundant gifts of his fruitful garden. He is also, as soon becomes apparent, a "modern" human being, trained in philosophy (*Her.* 2.6), who has turned his back on the life and activities of the city. The difference between both men is that the Phoenician is an unbelieving skeptic[25] and thus a contrast to the vinedresser's profound piety.[26] But no matter how much of a skeptic the Phoenician presents himself as being, the vinedresser irresistibly captivates him. He is the kind of skeptic who is filled "with quiet longing for

[21] Wilamowitz-Moellendorf, *Der Glaube der Hellenen*, 2:514.

[22] Nilsson, *Geschichte*, 2:563–64.

[23] See also *Life of Apollonius* 4.11–16.

[24] Eitrem, "Zu Philostrats *Heroikos*," 2.

[25] ἀπιστεῖν serves throughout as a term of religious skepticism: *Her.* 3.1; 7.11; 7.12; 8.1; 8.2; 8.4; 8.12; 8.17; 8.18; 17.1; 18.1; 23.22; 33.8; 43.1; 51.12; ἀπιστῶς 7.9; cf. ἀγνοεῖν 23.5. This linguistic usage is close to that of the New Testament; see Mark 6:6; 9:24; 16:11, 16; Matt 13:58; Luke 24:11, 41; John 20:27; Acts 26:8.

[26] The faith of the vinedresser in his hero is comparable to Christian linguistic usage, described generally as πιστεύειν (*Her.* 3.1; 7.10; 23.5; 44.5; 50.3; 51.5; πιστός 8.14); lack of faith he condemns as ἀδικία (cf. ἀδικεῖν) 4.11; 7.8; 17.1; 17.2; 33.6; 33.32; 43.15; ἀδικία 48.5; ἄδικος 12.1; 20.2; 31.6; 33.6; 35.11; 46.3).

faith."[27] This inner desire moves him continually to ask the vinedresser for new and, so to speak, scientifically verifiable evidence. To counter the Phoenician's objections, the vinedresser, whose belief is removed from all doubts, has available a virtually inexhaustible supply of proofs. The skeptic inquires; the pious provides particulars (*Her.* 6.1; 7.1).

2. COMMUNITY OF LIFE WITH THE HERO

A long conversation begins about the vinedresser's communion (ξυνουσία)[28] with the hero Protesilaos.[29] The hero, a Thessalian, is already mentioned by Homer (*Il.* 2.695–710; 13.681; 15.705; 16.286), who refers to him as the first Achaean killed while landing on the coast of Trojan territory. But as the astonished Phoenician learns, Protesilaos lives again after his death, and together with the vinedresser, he pursues agriculture (ζῇ καὶ γεωργοῦμεν, *Her.* 2.8). Protesilaos appears with regularity, gives the vinedresser professional advice, and protects his property from intruders and dangers.[30] We learn that the hero has indeed been restored to life on two occasions. In Troy he died because of Helen, but because of his love for Laodameia, in Phthia he was restored to life (ἀναβιοῦν).[31] Thereafter he died again and even convinced Laodameia to follow him into Hades.[32] But now he is again returned from Hades and is alive, as is clear from his regular appearances. More detailed circumstances are a secret of the mysteries (Μοιρῶν τι ἀπόρρητον, ὥς

[27] Like many skeptics the Phoenician is at the same time superstitious, as Eitrem ("Zu Philostrats *Heroikos*," 8; in reference to his attention to omens, see below) rightly observed. Fervent prayers also do no harm to his skepticism (*Her.* 2.3; 6.2; 7.8; 16.6; 20.3; 43.2; 43.3; 53.1; 58.3; 58.6).

[28] For this important word, see *Her.* 4.11; 7.1; 7.3; 43.16; 48.5; cf. ξύνειμι 5.1; 9.7; 11.8; 45.2. σύνειμι 4.10; 31.3.

[29] Concerning this hero, see G. Radke, Protesilaos, PW 43.half vol. (1957): 932–39; Walter Burkert, *Homo Necans: The Anthropology of Ancient Greek Sacrifical Ritual and Myth* (Berkeley: University of California Press, 1983), 243–47; trans. of *Homo Necans: Interpretationen griechischen Opferriten und Mythen* (Religionsgeschichtliche Versuche und Vorarbeiten 32; Berlin: de Gruyter, 1972); *LIMC*, s.v. "Protesilaos."

[30] He is for the vinedresser almost a πάρεδρος δαίμων, as the Greek magical papyri know such a one; the difference is, of course, that Protesilaos does not allow himself to be forcibly summoned by magical formulae.

[31] The word ἀναβιοῦν is in Philostratus's vocabulary downright technical (see *Her.* 2.9; 2.10; 5.2; 9.5; 58.2). In early Christian literature it is found only in *2 Clement* 19.4. For its usage in the Greek novels, see Bowersock, *Fiction*, 111–13.

[32] For the details, see Radke, "Protesilaos," cols. 933–36.

φασι, κρύπτων, *Her.* 2.11; cf. *Her.* 58.2). But the vinedresser gives assurance that not only Protesilaos, but other Trojan heroes still appear on the Trojan plain, clad in their martial attire, shaking their plumed helmets, and making a din with their weapons (*Her.* 2.11).

The Phoenician can scarcely believe what he hears, but he would like to learn more. The two men decide to sit down in the vineyard, which is described in its full magnificence, including the sacred paths (ἱεροὶ δρόμοι) on which the hero exercises (*Her.* 3.1–6).

The vinedresser reveals that his country estate is the remainder of his former holding, saved by Protesilaos's intervention. At one time, the vinedresser lived in the city, had teachers and studied philosophy, but allowed his landed property to deteriorate. Then he experienced a lack of money, had to get credit, and finally even suffered hunger after being deprived of his landed property by a swindler.

In his need, he turned to Protesilaos, asking him for advice and help. The hero did not respond at first, and because of neglect and the ensuing forwardness on the vinedresser's part he was even annoyed. But Protesilaos finally heard him, and furnished him with an oracular command: "Change your attire!" (μεταμφίασαι, *Her.* 4.9). He interpreted this command to mean that he had to change his whole way of life (μεταβαλεῖν κελεύει με τὸ τοῦ βίου σχῆμα, *Her.* 4.10). In accord with this interpretation of the oracle, he turned his back on urban life and withdrew to what remained of his estate, thanks to Protesilaos's help.[33] There he dedicated himself wholly to a life in accord with nature and hero worship, and was provided amply with fruits of the earth, medical advice, and wise instruction.

Thus it is a personal conversion experience with the hero that forms the beginning of his veneration of Protesilaos. The vinedresser's effort is therefore directed to overcoming the Phoenician's skepticism and to converting him to belief in heroes. An additional intention may, of course, be the conversion of the reader (*Her.* 3.1).

3. AN ARETALOGY OF HERO BELIEF

In the dialogue itself Philostratus lets the vinedresser present a detailed aretalogy of belief in heroes,[34] which in its several attempts

[33] The swindler, a certain Xeinis from the Chersonesus, was eliminated through an epiphany and by the miraculous punishment of blinding (*Her.* 4.2).

[34] Eitrem correctly speaks of an aretalogy, for it involves a collection of reports about the powerful deeds of the heroes ("Zu Philostrats *Heroikos*," 10), "They are pagan aretalogies, which truly, in several respects, exceed the Christian."

summarizes those elements that are best suited to the task of breaking through the very thin surface of the imperial age's skepticism.

Before the main dialogue can begin, however, a transition intervenes (*Her.* 6.1–7.12) in which the Phoenician discloses that his meeting with the vinedresser is not accidental, but can only have occurred as a result of divine providence (κατὰ θεόν, *Her.* 6.2; 6.7). A vision in a dream about the Homeric catalog of ships, which he first interpreted falsely, has now revealed through its fulfillment its true meaning.

As the goal of his inquiries the Phoenician would like to come to understand what is involved in the ξυνουσία of Protesilaos, what it means to the vinedresser, and whether his report of Trojan events agrees with the poets, or whether they did not know some things and falsely presented others.

Since the Phoenician doubts that Protesilaos could know something about the Trojan War because he was, after all, slain before the war actually began, he must allow himself to be corrected by the vinedresser from a philosophical perspective. After his purification from the body (τὸ καθαρεῦσαι τοῦ σώματος, *Her.* 7.3), Protesilaos had direct contact with the gods and thus knew the true events at Troy even before Homer knew them, a knowledge in which the vinedresser now shares and with which he can critically correct Homer. The vinedresser promises to show honor to the hero, a φιλόσοφός τε καὶ φιλαλήθης ("both learned and truth-loving"; *Her.* 7.8), by proclaiming to the Phoenician the whole truth, this mother of virtue (μήτηρ ἀρετῆς, *Her.* 7.8).

In opposition, the Phoenician professes his faith in a quite commonplace form of enlightenment. While growing up, he threw off his childhood belief and recognized that it was based on nothing more than the lies of poets (μυθολογία); as an example he refers to the heroes' legendary size. Against such supernatural humbug, he claims, only the doctrine that the human being is the measure of all things has worth (*Her.* 7.9–11).

At the start of the main section of his speech (ἀρχὴ τοῦ λόγου, *Her.* 7.12), the vinedresser refutes in his first argument the Phoenician's objection to the stories of the superhuman size of the heroes. If the Phoenician is still able to dismiss the story of the miraculous discovery of Ajax's grave as an old wives' tale for which there are no eyewitnesses (*Her.* 8.1–2), the vinedresser proceeds to present him with archaeological evidence in the form of a whole catalog of discovered bones which can only be those of heroes, and which were partly examined by himself.[35] The catalog begins with the discovery of Orestes' bones by the Lacedaemonians in Nemea, and its culmination is reached with Herakles' bones, which lay dedicated in Olympia. This chain of archaeological evidence smoothly sweeps away the Phoenician's unbelief. He is ashamed that his unbelief has rested merely on a lack of information, and he praises the vinedresser because of his profound knowledge (*Her.* 8.3–18).

The second argument is focused on Protesilaos himself and is thus intended to show that the stories concerning him are by no means untrustworthy (*Her.* 9.1–18.1). The vinedresser begins with a description of Protesilaos's grave, which is located on the southern point of the Chersonesus peninsula near the town of Elaious, opposite Troy on the western side of the Hellespont. The huge elms which stand on the grave mound were planted by the nymphs as a "sign" (σῆμα) and represent, in accord with a special law, the deadly fate (πάθος)[36] of Protesilaos. On Ilion, that is, on the side turned toward Troy, the trees thrive and lose their leaves prematurely, as was also the fate of the hero; the trees on the western side, turned away from Troy, are strong and healthy (*Her.* 9.1–4). The shrine itself is still extant, but it is in ruins since its destruction by the Medes. Protesilaos's statue still stands and depicts him as a commander on a ship's prow. The likeness is, of course, weathered by time and by the many anointings and the attaching of prayers; to the vinedresser it means nothing; indeed, he knows the hero incomparably better from his own perception (*Her.* 9.5–7).

What follows is of paramount importance as evidence, namely, the vinedresser's detailed description of Protesilaos's physical appearance, which he may enjoy four to five times a month (*Her.* 10.1–11.6). The hero appears as a young man, not quite twenty, a

[35] The theme of the giants, much discussed in antiquity, is hereby mentioned. See Friedrich Pfister, *Der Reliquienkult im Altertum* (2 vols.; Religionsgeschichtliche Versuche und Vorarbeiten 5; Giessen: Töpelmann, 1909–1912), 2:425–28; Wolfgang Speyer, "Gigant," *RAC* 10 (1978): 1247–76, esp. 1251.

[36] The term πάθος designates the "sufferings" of the hero (*Her.* 2.9; 7.9; 8.6; 9.2; 12.1; 18.5; 20.3; 21.2; 25.15; 31.7; 33.6; 53.20). In regard to Christ's sufferings, this term is found in Christian literature for the first time in the writings of Ignatius; see Walter Bauer, Frederick W. Danker, W. F. Arndt, and F. W. Gingerich, eds., *A Greek-English Lexicon of the New Testament and Other Early Christian Literature* (3d ed.; Chicago: Chicago University Press, 2000), s.v. πάθος, 1. Insofar as the heroes' sufferings are a focus of tales, a question arises regarding the possible reference to Jesus' Passion Narrative in the Gospels, which could be examined further. See also Adela Yarbro Collins, "The Genre of the Passion Narrative," *ST* 47 (1993): 3–28.

figure of great beauty reminiscent of the athletes' statues in the gymnasia. He even permits himself to be embraced and kissed[37] and enjoys flowers and wreaths, quite like a cheerful bridegroom. He is full of humor, but for all that he is also judicious and even applies his hand to agriculture, as he has, in general, proven himself an expert gardener.[38]

Where does the hero live when he is not with the vinedresser? The Phoenician wants to know. The vinedresser also has information on this point: sometimes he lives in Hades, sometimes in Phthia or the Troad, where he hunts boar and deer with his friends, after which he takes an afternoon siesta in the vinedresser's garden. In Hades he is also with Laodameia, who moves among a great company of heroines such as Alcestis, Euadnê, and others (*Her.* 11.7–8).

After that the Phoenician asks about the hero's food and drink.[39]

[37] The theme of the embrace and kiss is a topos in this literature: see *Her.* 11.2, Χαίρει περιβάλλοντι καὶ ξυγχωρεῖ φιλεῖν τε αὐτὸν καὶ τῆς δέρης ἐμφορεῖσθαί γε ("He enjoys my embrace and allows me to kiss him and cling to his neck"; see further *Her.* 21.6; 51.13). It is precisely this expression of love that the resurrected Jesus withholds from Mary Magdalene at the grave in the garden (John 20:17: μή μου ἅπτου, οὔπω γὰρ ἀναβέβηκα πρὸς τὸν πατέρα, "Don't touch me, for I have not yet ascended to my Father"). In Gnostic writings, however, the topos in the sense of a mystical love-relationship between Jesus and Mary Magdalene is worked out. For the texts and prevailing discussion, see Walter Bauer, *Das Leben Jesu im Zeitalter der neutestamentlichen Apokryphen* (Tübingen: Mohr Siebeck, 1909), 258–79; Gerd Lüdemann, *Die Auferstehung Jesu: Historie, Erfahrung, Theologie* (Göttingen: Vandenhoeck & Ruprecht, 1994), 194–96.

[38] For Protesilaos as γεωργός and κηπουρός ("farmer" and "gardener"), see *Her.* 4.12; 4.1; 11.4–6. Cf. Mary Magdalene, who confuses Jesus with a gardener (John 20:14–17). For a comparison of God with a gardener, see also Origen *Against Celsus* 4.69, in the edition of Chadwick, *Contra Celsum*, 139, with further citation of passages.

[39] The question of the common meal (*theoxenia*) with the hero is a further topos. See Nock, "The Cult of Heroes," 585–86; Scullion, "Olympian and Chthonian," 114–15; M. H. Jameson, "Theoxenia," in *Ancient Greek Cult Practice from the Epigraphic Evidence: Proceedings of the Second International Seminar on Ancient Greek Cult, Organized by the Swedish Institute at Athens, 22–24 November 1991* (ed. Robin Hägg; Svenska Institutet i Athen 8/13; Stockholm: Åströms, 1994), 35–57. The problem is tricky because conclusions can be drawn from it regarding bodily existence: ξυσσιτοῦνται δὲ ἀλλήλοις ἢ οὐ θέμις; ("Do they eat together, or is that not their custom?"; *Her.* 11.9) New Testament reports of the Lord's Supper also reveal a definite caution. Only Luke speaks of the risen Jesus' taking a meal (Luke 24:41–43; Acts 1:4; 10:41; cf. the interpretation in Ignatius *To the Smyrnaeans* 3.3). It is notable that in the Emmaus story (Luke 24:30, 35) and in the institution narratives of the Lord's Supper there is only mention of Jesus breaking and distributing bread, but not of Jesus eating it. The matter of Christ's presence in the Lord's Supper also has many layers. On the one hand, he is con-

The vinedresser replies that he has never come upon Protesilaos unawares while he was eating or drinking, but in the evening the vinedresser always offers him some Thasian wine, which the hero himself has cultivated, just as in summer and fall he offers ripe fruit at midday, and in the spring a cup of milk, on which occasions he expressly invites Protesilaos to partake.[40] He withdraws, and the offerings disappear in a very short time (*Her.* 11.9).

What information does Protesilaos give about his premature death? The vinedresser can report that the hero deplores his death as an unjust fate and attributes everything to a spiteful daimon.[41] The scar of his wound can still be seen on his hip, but the wound itself he threw off with his body (σῶμα, *Her.* 12.4).[42]

Unusual is the description of Protesilaos's athletic activity: he does martial exercises except for archery, and he does gymnastic exercises except for wrestling: archery reveals the coward, wrestling, the clumsy. Boxing he practices as shadow boxing; he tosses the discus over the clouds, and in the footrace he is so fast that he

---

sidered absent until his *parousia* (1 Cor 11:23–26; Mark 14:22–25; see also John 21:1–14); on the other hand, concepts such as κοινωνία τοῦ σώματος τοῦ Χριστοῦ ("a sharing in the body of Christ"; 1 Cor 10:16), κυριακὸν δεῖπνον ("the Lord's supper"; 1 Cor 11:20) and τράπεζα κυρίου ("table of the Lord"; 1 Cor 10:21) presuppose a presence of the Christ. This is, of course, different from that of a hero. See also Bauer, *Das Leben Jesu*, 259–61 (see also 316–18); Betz, "Das Problem der Auferstehung Jesu," 249–50; Lüdemann, *Die Auferstehung*, 182–83.

[40] The invitation formula presupposes that it involves an offering for the hero: ἰδού σοι, λέγω, τὸ τῆς ὥρας νᾶμα, σὺ δὲ πῖνε ("'Behold,' I say, 'here is the flowing essence of the season for you. Drink'"; *Her.* 11.9). For similar formulae in Achilles Tatius, see Bowersock, *Fiction*, 125–28. Contast the Lord's Supper, which is not an offering meal for a hero. Rather, the offering is now the exalted one in whom these now celebrating the Lord's Supper share (1 Cor 10:16, 18). Also, the invitation formula is spoken directly by Jesus only in Matthew's version: πίετε ἐξ αὐτοῦ πάντες ("'Drink from it, all of you'"; Matt 26:27). In the other versions the formulae are only given by description.

[41] ἐλεεῖ, ξένε, τὸ ἑαυτοῦ πάθος καὶ τὸν δαίμονα, ἐφ᾽ ᾧ τότε ἦν, ἄδικόν γε ἡγεῖται καὶ βάσκανον μὴ συγχωρήσαντα οἷ τὸν γοῦν πόδα ἐς τὴν Τροίαν ἐρεῖται ("My guest, he regrets his suffering, and the daimon who was against him at that time he considers unjust and malicious since, although his foot was compliant, it was not fixed firmly in Troy"; *Her.* 12.1).

[42] Philostratus apparently presupposes here a difference between a corporeal and incorporeal body; on the latter a scar is still visible. Compare the stigmata of the risen Jesus (Luke 24:39–40; John 20:20, 25–27), which can be both seen and touched; in the New Testament there are only reports of the disciples seeing Jesus, but not touching him (but compare 1 John 1:1). Later interpretations also speak of the disciples touching him (Ignatius *To the Smyrnaeans* 3.2). For the texts see Bauer, *Das Leben Jesu*, 259–61; Betz, "Das Problem der Auferstehung Jesu," 244, 248–50; Lüdemann, *Die Auferstehung*, 166, 182–84, 190, 200–202.

leaves no tracks behind.[43] The ten-yard-long foot tracks on the paths result, however, not from the footrace, but from walking and from sport; when running he moves above the ground as if he ran over the water's waves (*Her.* 13. 1–3).[44]

In general, Homer underestimated Protesilaos in this regard. By contrast the poet intentionally overrated Achilles and underrated Odysseus, while Protesilaos exceeded Achilles even in much, above all in shield-to-shield fighting. At this point, the vinedresser begins to report his thoroughgoing criticism of the heroes in Homer's account: Homer omitted important episodes, and his description of many episodes was distorted (*Her.* 13.3–15.10).

The Phoenician's next question concerns the healing of diseases. What does Protesilaos have to show? The vinedresser gives assurance that the hero heals all illnesses, and therefore many pray to him: consumption, dropsy, eye diseases, malaria are named. He also knows magical incantations and techniques (ἐπῳδαὶ καὶ τέχναι) for amorous affairs, but he wants nothing to do with adultery and has even frustrated adultery by means of miraculous punishment (*Her.* 16.1–3).[45]

The section ends with a summary of the hero-theology (*Her.* 16.4–17.6): the heroes stand between the gods and human beings. They know less that the gods, but more than human beings. To this category belong figures like the Boeotians Amphiaraos and his son Amphilokhos (Homer *Od.* 15.244–248, 253) as well as the Thracian Marôn (Homer *Od.* 9.197–215) and Rhêsos (Homer *Il.* 10.435–445, 474–484). Toward human beings these heroes appear helpful and

[43] See *Epistle to the Apostles* 11.22 according to C. D. G. Müller's translation in Wilhelm Schneemelcher, ed., *Neutestamentliche Apokryphen* (5th ed.; Tübingen: Mohr Siebeck, 1987) 1:211: ". . . see if my foot steps on the ground and leaves a trace. For it is written in the prophets: 'a ghost, a daimon, leaves no trace on the ground.'"

[44] Probably an allusion to the miracle topos of walking on the water is present here: μετέωρος γάρ τις καὶ οἷον ἐπικυματίζων αἴρεται ("because he is raised off the ground and like someone floating on the waves"; *Her.* 13.3). Cf. the references in Gerd Petzke, *Die Traditionen über Apollonios von Tyana und das Neue Testament* (Studia ad corpus hellenisticum Novi Testamenti 1; Leiden: Brill, 1970), 176–78; Hans Dieter Betz, *Lukian von Samosata und das Neue Testament: Religionsgeschichtliche und paränetische Parallelen* (TU 76; Berlin: Akademie-Verlag, 1961), 166–67; Adela Yarbro Collins, "Rulers, Divine Men, and Walking on the Water (Mark 6:45–52)," in *Religious Propaganda and Missionary Competition in the New Testament World: Essays Honoring Dieter Georgi* (ed. Lucas Bormann, Kelly Del Tredici, and Angela Standhartinger; Leiden: Brill, 1994), 207–27.

[45] Philostratus here emphasizes an ethical point of view which no doubt criticizes pertinent deficiencies in current erotic conjurations.

kind, but if they are insulted and neglected by a lack of faith, their anger must be reckoned with.

4. THE PRESENT ACTIVITY OF THE TROJAN HEROES

Impressed by these proofs, the Phoenician shows himself ready to give up his unbelief, but this only serves to increase his interest in Trojan events. He wants to learn more about the manner in which the Trojan heroes still appear and act in the present.

The vinedresser can report that cowherds and shepherds on the Trojan plain have numerous stories to report about such appearances, from which, on the basis of specific indications, they are able to read portending fortune or misfortune. They thus consider it advisable to placate the heroes by appropriate offerings. Downright dangerous in this respect is Ajax's grave: Ajax, because of insult and neglect by shepherds, took terrible vengeance on their herds. The Phoenician is above all interested in Hektor, however, especially in his statue in Ilion, which is so filled (ἔμπνους) with magnificent loveliness and spirit that it draws the observer to touch it. Much good emanates from this statue, and for this reason many also pray to it; contests (ἀγῶνες) were also organized in his honor. Such veneration excites Hektor so that the statue begins to sweat (*Her.* 19.3–4). By contrast, the hero appeared to an arrogant young man of Assyrian descent who slandered him. Hektor appeared to him on his way home in order to destroy him with a horrible punishment (*Her.* 19.5–7).

A special section is devoted to Palamedes (*Her.* 20.3–21.9), a wise hero whose similar fate binds him with the vinedresser. Both were ruined by an enemy who obtained an unjust ruling against them (*Her.* 20.2). The Phoenician, whom this theme moves to tears, ascertains that their association in suffering is so close that it must arouse sympathy. For just as a common interest in good things may cause envy, so shared suffering may lead to mutual love, because each person responds to sympathy by showing sympathy for the other (*Her.* 20.3).[46]

[46] This community of suffering which binds the heroes with one another and with the vinedresser seems based on the Golden Rule (cf. Matt 5:7): ἀγαθῶν μὲν γὰρ κοινωνία τίκτει ποτὲ καὶ φθόνον, ὅσοι δ' ἂν κοινωνήσωσι συμφορῶν, ἀγαπῶσιν ἀλλήλους τὸν ἔλεον τοῦ ἐλέου ἀντιδιδόντες ("Sharing good things sometimes brings forth envy, but those who share misfortunes are fond of each other and return compassion for compassion"; *Her.* 20.3). For the concept of κοινωνία, see Nock, "The Cult of

The vinedresser can report that appearances of Palamedes' εἴδωλον are seen in Troy. To be sure, there are such frequent appearances of Trojan heroes there that their identification is often difficult. Nevertheless, they are distinguishable by their form (ἰδέα), age, and weapons. Concerning Palamedes, the vinedresser has a story to relate about a farmer from Ilion who shared in Palamedes' woeful fate by performing proper mourning rites on that spot on the shore where the hero was stoned to death by the Achaeans. He chose the sweetest grapes, gathered them in a mixing bowl, and celebrated a drinking bout with Palamedes. The farmer also had a dog named "Odysseus" because the dog, like Odysseus, was a perfidious flatterer; as Odysseus would have deserved, the dog was thus beaten and scolded. Palamedes wanted to show kindness to this farmer and appeared to him embodied, as he was just about to tie up a grapevine. A dialogue ensued during which the farmer did not recognize Palamedes as he spoke to him: "Do you recognize me, farmer?" But he replied: "How could I since I have never seen you?"[47] Palamedes' following question, "You love one whom you do not know?" then enables the farmer to recognize the one who stands before him.[48] He describes the hero as tall, handsome, and manly in form, about thirty years old. The farmer embraces him while smiling and makes a declaration of love: "I love you, Palamedes, for you seem to me to be the smartest of human beings, and the most just athlete in matters of wisdom who, however, has suffered deplorably from the Achaeans because of Odysseus's machinations. Were Odysseus's grave close by, I would long ago have dug it up and destroyed it, for he is repugnant to me and worse than the dog I keep in his place." But Palamedes asked forbearance for Odysseus, since he already had taken legal proceedings against him in Hades. As a reward, Palamedes gave the farmer an amulet to protect his vines against the dreaded hail.

5. A CORRECTION OF HOMER

The following part of the *Heroikos* contains an extensive emendation or correction (ἐπανόρθωσις) of Homer combined with a catalog

---

Heroes," 583–89, 597–98; compare the New Testament teaching of the κοινωνία τῶν παθημάτων ("participation in sufferings," Phil 3:10; 1 Cor 10:16; 2 Cor 1:5–6; 1 Thess 2:14; Col 1:24; 1 Pet 4:13).

47 Cf. the dialogue between the risen Jesus and Peter (John 21:15–17).

48 For ἀναγνώρισις ("recognition"), cf. Luke 24:16–31; John 20:14–16, 24–29; 21:15–17.

of Trojan heroes (*Her.* 22.1–57.16). It is again the vinedresser who gives a detailed report about what Protesilaos related to him on this topic: he begins with Achilles' deeds, to which he returns several times (*Her.* 22.1–23.25; 25.16–17; 42.4–57.17). Here Protesilaos offers a wealth of important material for the history of religion, drawing partly from literary sources and partly from local legends;[49] a thorough discussion of these would, however, exceed the scope of this essay.

After a brief description of the battles during the Achaeans' landing (*Her.* 23.2–30) and an observation on Homer's portrayal of them (*Her.* 24.1–25.18), there begins a series of panegyrics on the heroes of Troy, first on the Achaeans, starting with Nestor (*Her.* 26.1–36.1), and then on the Trojan side, starting with Hektor (*Her.* 36.2–42.4). That Protesilaos knows both the Achaean heroes and the opposing Trojans is not astonishing for a δαίμων, but where did Homer learn about events on the opposing Trojan side? For an answer the vinedresser develops a theory which does not simply fall back on the poet's divine inspiration (*Her.* 43.6–44.4). According to this theory, Homer was a human being, and his songs are a human creation for which he collected material from local traditions about the heroes. In addition to this, he traveled to Ithaca because Odysseus's ghost was still active there. In an interview with the dead (ψυχαγωγία) Homer reached an agreement with Odysseus: he would report to Homer the true course of events at Ilion, and Homer would confer fame on him while being silent about Odysseus's crimes against Palamedes, who was truly superior to him. One can rely on this bargain, for "the souls of the dead are least likely to speak falsely in the presence of blood and offering pits" (*Her.* 43.14; cf. Homer *Od.* 10.517ff.; 11.23ff.).

Before Homer's departure, Odysseus makes a kind of confession because of his complicity in Palamedes' murder (cf. also *Her.* 33.31). Odysseus reports that Palamedes' sense of justice (δίκαι) demanded that he, Odysseus, know about his crimes (ἀδικία) and that the judges and avengers in the underworld keep ready fearsome punishments. But the less that is known and believed about his crimes against Palamedes in the upper world, so much less will he, Odysseus, have to suffer in the underworld. If Homer thus does not allow Palamedes to reach Ilion and is silent about his cleverness, there is a chance—because Homer is such an authority on the sub-

[49] See Heinrich Grentrup, "De *Heroici* Philostratei fabularum fontibus" (diss.; University of Münster, Westphalia, 1914).

ject—that even that story handed down by other poets would be rejected as unworthy of belief. Thus, the wily Odysseus saw to it that Homer doubtless knew the unadorned truth, but at the same time tendentiously tailored his report in favor of Odysseus (*Her.* 43.15–16).

After further observations about Homer's native land (*Her.* 44.1–5), the vinedresser proceeds to an introduction of Achilles, which, because of its wealth of detail, is to be viewed as the culmination of the catalog of heroes (*Her.* 45.1–57.17). It is, of course, assumed that the vinedresser got the whole report from Protesilaos (*Her.* 45.2).

First of all, Achilles' childhood is described, his mysterious birth from Thetis, a sea goddess, who appeared to his father Peleus as a φάσμα ("apparition"). She loved him and announced, "I will give to you, Peleus, a son, one who is superior to any mere mortal" (ἐγὼ δέ σοι καὶ παῖδα, εἶπεν, ὦ Πηλεῦ, δώσω κρείττω ἀνθρώπου, *Her.* 45.3). The centaur Kheirôn is appointed as tutor to the young Achilles. He now nourishes him with honeycomb and deer marrow. From Kheirôn, Achilles also learned various sports and skills in warfare. As a young man Achilles therefore appeared with radiant handsomeness and an unusual physique. But since he showed uncontrolled anger, Kheirôn instructed him in music and song. At his request Calliope, the Muse, appeared to Achilles in sleep, and revealed that his future would not be that of a poet, but of a warrior, and thus he would be granted only as much skill in the arts as he needed. A poet would later come to celebrate his deeds appropriately (*Her.* 45.4–7).

Of further importance is the vinedresser's information about the connection between the legends of Achilles and Theseus (*Her.* 45.8–46.7; cf. Plutarch *Theseus* 35)[50] and about the miraculous weapons of Achilles: the mysterious spear fashioned from ash wood (*Her.* 46.7; cf. *Her.* 45.4), which Homer also describes (*Il.* 16.140–144; 19.387–391), and the famous shield, which differs from Homer's description (*Her.* 47.1–5).

After this, there is a thorough description of the form (εἶδος) of Achilles: his head of hair, his nose, his eyebrows, and above all, his very expressive eyes. His character was manifested by the way he held his head high. Among the heroes he was one of the most just (δικαιότατος), partly because of his nature, partly because of the

[50] For the myth and cult of Theseus, see Henry J. Walker, *Theseus and Athens* (Oxford and New York: Oxford, 1995).

education he received from Kheirôn. He had little regard for wealth and possessions, which caused him to quarrel with Agamemnon, Odysseus, and other Achaeans. The account of these events again gives the vinedresser, who has Protesilaos as his source, ample opportunity to set Homer straight (*Her.* 48.1–18). The barbaric and cruel manner in which Achilles dragged Hektor's corpse shows his daimonic nature, at which the Trojans were also shocked.[51] As his anger because of Palamedes and his revenge on Hektor for Patroklos and Antilokhos prove, Achilles' most daring deeds are the ones undertaken for the sake of his friends; he confirms this himself in conversation with Ajax (*Her.* 48.18–21). In general, Achilles had a close relationship with his friends, especially Ajax, whom he considered his head, and Patroklos, whom he considered his hands (*Her.* 48.22).

The physical description of Patroklos (*Her.* 49.1–3), and the depiction of Achilles' horses (*Her.* 50.1–3), which Homer falsely considered immortal (*Il.* 16.154; cf. 19.405–424; 23.276–277), is followed by an account of Achilles' death. Homer reported this correctly (*Her.* 51.1). As the horse Xanthos (*Il.* 19.417), his mother, Thetis (*Il.* 21.277–278), and the dying Hektor (*Il.* 22.359–360) predicted, he was killed by Apollo's arrow and by Paris, a victim of murderous cunning (δολοφονηθείς, *Her.* 51.1). On the third day after his death, Polyxena, Priam's daughter betrothed to Achilles, sacrificed herself on Achilles' grave (*Her.* 51.2–6). The dirge for Achilles was enormous; even the Black Sea participated in it, agitated by the Nereids, and the hair-raising lamentations of Achilles' mother were heard by the whole army throughout the night (*Her.* 51.7–11).

Greatest attention is given to Achilles' grave cult. The vinedresser points to the grave mound, which is within sight on the other side of the Hellespont on the promontory of Sigeion. The Achaeans built the tumulus, working together after they buried Achilles beside Patroklos. About the burial rites it is reported that Hellas collected the most precious gifts as an offering to the dead, that hardly anyone neglected the ritual cutting of hair, and that much of the booty of war was piled on the funeral pyre. Then Achilles' son Neoptolemos surprisingly came to Troy to contribute his offerings. Many had thrown themselves down on the grave before the return from Troy, as if the Achaeans wanted to embrace Achilles at their departure (*Her.* 51.13).

[51] Achilles is regarded as a δαίμων and δαιμόνιος (*Her.* 48.15; 48.19).

To the grave cult that arose from Thessaly belonged hymns which were sung at a night vigil during a yearly visit to the grave. An initiation into the mysteries was also added to the offerings for the dead, apparently by transferal of the cults from Lemnos and Corinth: . . . ἀνὰ πᾶν ἔτος ἐπὶ τὸ σῆμα φοιτῶντες ᾖδον ἐν νυκτί, τελετῆς τι ἐγκαταμιγνύντες τοῖς ἐναγίσμασιν, ὡς Λήμνιοις τε νομίζουσι καὶ Πελοποννησίων οἱ ἀπὸ Σισύφου ("[hymns which] they sang at night when they visited his tomb every year, mixing something of an initiatory rite with their offerings to the dead, as both the Lemnians and the Peloponnesians descended from Sisyphus practice"; *Her.* 52.3).

At the mention of Sisyphus, the Phoenician interrupts the vinedresser in order to urge him to a digression (ἐκβολή) concerning the Corinthian celebration of the hero Melikertês. After initial resistance, the vinedresser is ready to enlighten his visitor about this theme, of which he has apparently heard some things already (*Her.* 53.1–3). The mourning rites going back to Sisyphus (θρήνῳ εἴκασται τελεστικῷ τε καὶ ἐνθέῳ, "[they] resemble a lament that is both initiatory and inspired"; *Her.* 53.4) are conceived, on the one hand, to placate Medea because of her murdered children and, on the other hand, to praise Melikertês. The vinedresser does not disclose more at this point, but explains the relevant rites of the Lemnians (*Her.* 53.5–7). After this, the sacrificial cult of the Thessalians, which the oracle of Dodona imposed on them, is described in detail. A procession of ships organized yearly sails from Thessaly to Troy in order to bring offerings to Achilles, partly as to a god (σφάττειν τὰ μὲν ὡς θεῷ) and partly as to one of the dead buried there.

First, the offering to the dead is described. A ship with black sails was sent from Thessaly, on which fourteen sacred ambassadors, two bulls—one white, the other black—as well as all other necessities, including wood, fire, and water, were available. Before the landing at night a hymn was offered to Thetis, which the vinedresser quotes. After the landing, the noise of war was created with beating on shields and a kind of running dance with invocation of Achilles. Then the grave mound was splendidly garlanded, the sacrificial pits (βόθροι) dug, and the black bull slaughtered (ὡς τεθνεῶτι ἔσφαττον, "they slaughtered [the black bull] as to one who is dead"; *Her.* 53.11). To the sacrificial meal for the dead not only Achilles, but also Patroklos, was invited.

After the offering (ἐντεμόντες δὲ καὶ ἐναγίσαντες, "after they slit the victim's throat and made this sacrifice"; *Her.* 53.13) one returned again to the shore, where the white bull was slain for

Achilles as if to honor a god (ὡς θεῷ, *Her.* 53.13). First, the sacred barley came out of the basket, and then with the burning of the entrails the ceremony on the mainland was concluded; the Thessalians took the sacrificial animal itself on board the ship the following morning in order to avoid having the feast in enemy territory (*Her.* 53.9–14).

Unfortunately, these time-honored rites later fell into disuse,[52] and renewal of Achilles' cult first took place through the efforts of Alexander the Macedonian, son of Philip. Alexander consciously associated himself with Achilles and chose him as his ξύμμαχος for his campaign against Darius. Alexander's cavalry gathered at that time for prayer, sacrifice, and martial exercises at Achilles' grave and summoned him along with his steeds, Balios and Xanthos, to battle. After Alexander's victory, these cultic tributes were again neglected, and as a result a fundamental turning point was reached, because Achilles was thereafter hostile to the Thessalians and punished them with continued harm (*Her.* 53.14–17).

Protesilaos reported further details about Achilles' transformation into a dangerous daimon. Four years ago, as he was in the habit of doing on occasion, he took a boat trip to Achilles. At that time, however, he fell out with Achilles when he wanted to dissuade him from his harsh, harmful punishments of the Thessalians. But Achilles was not willing to agree to anything, but threatened instead a yet more frightening catastrophe from the sea. It happened, however, that this catastrophe involved neither crop damages nor flood tides, but a legal charge made by Achilles and Thetis together against the Thessalians because of their misuse of shellfish from which purple is extracted. The production of this valuable dye was a forbidden business, severely punished. Fear of a general penalty then caused many Thessalians to sell their belongings and leave their land, in order to avoid punishment (*Her.* 53.14–23).

The stories which Protesilaos can report about the famous Black Sea island of Leukê are also uncanny. Poseidon had allowed the island of Leukê to arise from the sea at Thetis's request, in order to serve as a meeting point and home for Achilles and Helen. On this uninhabited and desolate island stands only a temple with statues of Achilles and Helen. Visitors may not remain overnight on the island because Achilles and Helen continue to hold drinking parties there, during which Achilles recites his own and Homeric

[52] See also the parallel passages in *Life of Apollonius* 4.16.

poems. Protesilaos has shared with the vinedresser several of Achilles' poems from the previous year, and the vinedresser gives the Phoenician a sample (*Her.* 54.1–55.21).

Further stories about Achilles' influence on the island conclude the report. These are genuine horror stories, like the one about the dismemberment of a Trojan maiden from Priam's family at the hands of Achilles (*Her.* 56.1–11) and the one about his brutal destruction of the Amazons (*Her.* 57.1–17). These stories emphasize the contrast between Achilles, an unpredictable and dangerous daimon, and Protesilaos, the good and gentle helper of the vinedresser.

Through all these stories and also in the epilogue, the Phoenician's thirst for knowledge becomes unquenchable. Questions such as exactly how Protesilaos returned to life await information from the vinedresser (τὸ μὲν ὅπως αὐτὸς ἀναβεβίωκεν οὐκέτ' ἂν ἐροίμην, "I would no longer ask how he himself returned to life"; *Her.* 58.2). But unfortunately no answer to the question is allowed; it must remain a secret of the mysteries (ἐπειδὴ ἀβεβήλῳ τε καὶ ἀπορρήτῳ φῄς αὐτὸν χρῆσθαι τούτῳ τῷ λόγῳ, "since you say that he treats that story as inviolable and secret"; *Her.* 58.2).[53] Then there are questions about the Underworld, Kôkytos and Pyriphlegethôn, the Akherousian lake, and still other matters.

But evening has come and the vinedresser is tired. So the Phoenician must wait for another occasion; he concludes with a prayer to Poseidon: May this god not allow him to sail away before he has heard these other stories as well (*Her.* 58.1–6).

II. CHRIST'S APPEARANCES AND THE EMPTY GRAVE

Eitrem concludes his previously mentioned essay, "Zu Philostrats *Heroikos*," with two excurses, the first of which treats the theme of "the σύστασις and light conjuring in magic" (pp. 49–53). At the end of this excursus, there are but a few brief "observations on the appearances of Christ" which provide an interesting thesis for us. According to this thesis, the reports about the post-Easter appearances of Christ and his συνουσίαι with his disciples represent a kind of "interim 'hero stage' of Christ." This thesis is merely mentioned

[53] Compare the question of the Corinthians which Paul reports in 1 Cor 15:35, πῶς ἐγείρονται οἱ νεκροί; ποίῳ δὲ σώματι ἔρχονται; ("How are the dead raised? With what sort of body do they come?") The apostle answers the question in what follows, but he also points out that it concerns a μυστήριον ("mystery"; 1 Cor 15:51).

by Eitrem and is illustrated by several references to parallels to the hero cult in the Gospels and in the *Acts of the Apostles*.[54]

What Eitrem has in mind is plausible. The gospel texts allow the conclusion that their authors knew about the possibility of a resurrected Jesus as a hero. Moreover, the legends circulating in Christian communities suggest that perception of the post-Easter appearances of Jesus was already headed in this direction. As shown above, such a development can hardly be a surprise, for the violent, premature death of Jesus brought about by an unjust legal verdict, as well as the appearances after his death, correspond to the basic pattern of a hero cult. The stories of his childhood, taken from the tradition by Matthew and Luke into their gospels, treat the well-known motifs of a divine descent and a genealogical affiliation with the ancestors Abraham and David. The miracle stories portray Jesus' helpful deeds to humans. His wise teachings and scriptural interpretation have a revelatory character. His death, although a result of human arbitrariness, is in accord with God's will. God has thus transformed his shameful death on the cross by his resurrection into the salvation event on which the Christian community bases its existence. The epiphanies in which the resurrected one "appears" (John 20:14; 21:1; Acts 1:3) and again "disappears" (Luke 24:31; Acts 1:2, 10–11) lead to cultic veneration by his disciples. The apostate disciples who have all left him (Mark 14:50, 52) are won back by these appearances. Their ἀπιστία (Mark 16:11, 14, 16; Luke 24:11, 41; John 20:27) is redeemed by their πίστις (Mark 16:13, 17; John 20:8, 25, 29, 31). The denier Peter, the unbelieving James, brother of the Lord, the persecutor Paul, all became apostles and leaders of Christian communities (1 Cor 15:5–10). The stories of the risen Christ's appearances always have, in their own way, these transformations in view, in that in the course of which problematic themes such as fear, recognition and identification of the resurrected one, seeing and touching as well as the communal meal, are also treated.

In the final analysis, however, it cannot be overlooked that the gospel writers are opposed to a heroic kind of Christology.[55]

[54] To this and other parallels references have already been made in part I. In evaluating these parallels, consideration must be given to the fact that hero worship had been widespread in the whole Hellenic world for a long time. The stories collected by Philostratus are based mostly on older traditions, for which a dependency on early Christian literature cannot be shown.

[55] With a view to the gospel of Mark, Adela Yarbro Collins also makes this claim; see her "The Empty Tomb and Resurrection According to Mark," in *The*

In general, as has been well known for a long time, the evangelists' endeavor was to limit the time period of Jesus' post-Easter appearances between the resurrection and ascension. Christ's elevation[56] assigns to him the highest place at God's right hand, and this excludes a hero-Christology as unsuitable for Christian belief. The very admission of a temporally limited hero's existence can be considered an allusion to the fact that the way to a Christology in the manner of Hellenistic heroes had already been tried in the tradition, but that its further propagation should be checked by this temporal limitation.

In the expression of this theological decision, which indeed set the course for christological development, the tradition of an empty grave also appears to have played a special role.[57] As shown before, the most important component of a hero cult is probably the hero's grave, because it is on his grave that cultic tributes and sacrifices are made. Hero cults are all grave cults, and where there is no grave, a hero cult is hardly conceivable. Normally the heroes' bones are believed to be present in the grave, but empty graves are also respected if these bear witness to the hero's presence by other signs and wonders.[58] Some heroes even had several graves because cultic veneration at several places made this necessary. The angel's announcement at Jesus' grave, "he has risen, and is not here" (ἠγέρθη, οὐκ ἔστιν ὧδε, Mark 16:6) makes a hero cult impossible at the decisive point. That Jesus' grave is declared "empty" apparently excludes an interpretation of his manner of existence as a chthonic hero, whose presence is bound up with the grave. Jesus' resurrection was instead interpreted by a Christology of elevation according to which he took his place at God's right hand as ruler of the

Beginning of the Gospel: Probings of Mark in Context (Minneapolis: Fortress, 1992), 119–48; the chapter appeared in a revised form with the title "Apotheosis and Resurrection" in *The New Testament and Hellenistic Judaism* (ed. Peder Borgen and Søren Giversen; Århus: Århus University Press, 1995), 88–100. But if Collins means that Jesus was directly transported from the grave to heaven (see p. 147, repr. p. 100), do not the foretold appearances in Galilee (Mark 16:7; cf. 14:27) contradict this view? Cf. also Adela Yarbro Collins, "From Noble Death to Crucified Messiah," *NTS* 40 (1994): 481–503.

[56] For pertinent ideas see Georg Bertram, "Erhöhung," *RAC* 6 (1966): 22–43.

[57] The extensive literature about this theme cannot be discussed here. For the current state of the discussion, see Betz, "Das Problem der Auferstehung Jesu," 245–47; Collins, *The Beginning of the Gospel*, 119–48; Collins, "Apotheosis and Resurrection," 88–100; Lüdemann, *Die Auferstehung*, 32–33, 43, 67–69, 141–53, 156–57, 216–22.

[58] See Georg Strecker, "Entrückung," *RAC* 5 (1962): 461–76, esp. 468–70.

cosmos.[59] The result of such a Christology was that his universal presence was bound together with the Holy Spirit and with the word of proclamation.[60]

[59] See, in addition, the essays in the volume edited by Martin Hengel and Anna Maria Schwemer, *Königsherrschaft Gottes und himmlischer Kult im Judentum, Urchristentum und in der hellenistischen Welt* (WUANT 55; Tübingen: Mohr Siebeck, 1991).

[60] The difference becomes clear, for example, with the comparison of the presence of the risen Jesus in the pre-Lukan Emmaus story (Luke 24:15–31), which comes close to that of the heroes, and the rather different presence of the cosmocrator in the gospel of Matthew (Matt 18:20; 25:40, 45; 28:18–20).

Illuminating the Classics with the Heroes of Philostratus

Casey Dué and Gregory Nagy

In this essay we make a case for adopting Philostratus's *Heroikos* as an introductory-course text in conjunction with older masterpieces of Greek poetry and prose.* The *Heroikos* has not traditionally been used in introductory literature and civilization classes, in part because there has not been an English translation available for use as a textbook. Now that a student edition of the *Heroikos* exists, we are confident that the reading of this classic of the Second Sophistic can enhance any undergraduate or graduate course centering on Greek civilization, literature, myth, or religion.

The two of us have personal experience in team-teaching an undergraduate course that featured the *Heroikos* in English (thanks to Jennifer Berenson Maclean and Ellen Bradshaw Aitken, who kindly gave us permission to use a preliminary version of their translation). We adopted the *Heroikos* as a primary text to be read in a class that we taught in the fall of 1999, "The Concept of the Hero in Greek Civilization." Other primary texts included the Homeric *Iliad* and *Odyssey*, Herodotus, and nine tragedies selected from the works of Aeschylus, Sophocles, and Euripides.

This class is a large core-curriculum lecture course that has been offered yearly for more than two decades to an average of around three hundred and fifty students, none of whom is assumed to have any prior background in classics, let alone ancient Greek. In the 1999 version of the course, we required the *Heroikos* to be read in its entirety. The students were assigned Philostratus's *Heroikos* immediately after they had completed the *Iliad* and *Odyssey*, in the same week that they read selections from Herodotus and Pausanias concerning hero cult. For our discussions with the students, we emphasized the sections on Protesilaos (*Her.* 9.1–23.30) and Achilles (*Her.* 44.5–57.17).

* All translations of the *Heroikos* are by Jennifer K. Berenson Maclean and Ellen Bradshaw Aitken [*Flavius Philostratus: Heroikos* (SBLWGRW 1; Atlanta: Society of Biblical Literature, 2001)]. All other translations are our own, except where indicated.

By including the *Heroikos* in the assigned reading for the course, we were able to address directly both of the historical dimensions of ancient Greek heroic traditions, cult as well as literature. When readers are exposed to the *Iliad* and *Odyssey* for the first time, references to the immortalization of heroes after death and their status as religious beings are most difficult to grasp, since such references are almost never explicit. With Philostratus's *Heroikos* as a background, the reader begins to appreciate how much of epic and dramatic language resonates with religious undertones. The surface meaning of key heroic terms can be juxtaposed with a deeper, sacred meaning intended for those "in the know," the initiated worshipers. In the lectures on the *Iliad* and *Odyssey* as well as tragedy, the religious significance of such terms as τιμή and σῆμα were emphasized, and these key Greek terms were included in a glossary as part of the course sourcebook.[1] Reading the *Heroikos* was the context for confronting these terms for the first time in their explicitly cultic contexts. Building on the background provided by Philostratus's *Heroikos*, students had the opportunity to juxtapose the implicit references to hero cult in the *Iliad*, *Odyssey*, and Greek tragedy with the explicit worship of heroes in cult. Moreover, by combining the *Heroikos* with selections from Herodotus and Pausanias, we were able to give students a sense of the continuity of heroic traditions over the course of more than a thousand years.

Finally, the learning experience to be gained from reading the *Heroikos* is practically unique in conveying the realities of how it must have felt for a worshiper to participate in hero cult. The *Heroikos* conveys more than any other work of literature the emotional ties that bind hero and worshiper together. This deeply personal aspect of hero cult is perhaps the most difficult thing to learn about ancient Greek heroes if the reader relies on archaic and classical Greek literary sources alone. The relationship portrayed in Philostratus's *Heroikos* between the pious vinedresser and the charismatic cult hero Protesilaos illustrates most vividly the practice of hero cult as a personal experience, thereby offering students and experts alike an unparalleled insight into what was for the ancient Greeks the everyday life-sustaining practice of worshiping heroes.

[1] For τιμή see Gregory Nagy, *The Best of the Achaeans: Concepts of the Hero in Archaic Greek Poetry* (Baltimore: Johns Hopkins University Press, 1979; 2d ed., with new introduction, 1999), 72–83 and 118. For σῆμα see Gregory Nagy, "The Sign of Protesilaos," *ΜΗΤΙΣ: Revue d'anthropologie du monde grec ancien* 2/2 (1987): 207–13.

The new student edition of the *Heroikos* by Ellen Aitken and Jennifer Maclean now makes possible for the first time the inclusion of the *Heroikos* in courses taught in translation.[2] In our introductory essay to that volume, entitled "Preliminaries to Philostratus's *On Heroes*," we discuss several examples of the continuity between classical literature and the literary world of the Second Sophistic in the conceptualization of the cult hero. In doing so we show that there is a great deal to be gained by reading and teaching these works together. The text that follows is a slightly modified version of that same essay.

THE HEROES OF PHILOSTRATUS'S *HEROIKOS*: FICTION, EPIC, AND HERO CULT

In the literature of the so-called Second Sophistic era (around 60 to 230 C.E.), as best exemplified by Philostratus's *Heroikos* (written toward the end of this era), ancient readers were treated to claims of a truer and more accurate account of the Trojan War—truer even than the version they were used to reading in the epic poetry of the Homeric *Iliad* and *Odyssey*. In the polished prose of the *Heroikos*, such a claim was made not by the author himself, Philostratus, but by a creation of the author. This creation is a fictional character known simply as ἀμπελουργός, "vinedresser," who is telling another character—a mysterious Phoenician—all about an ancient hero who fought and died at Troy. This hero, Protesilaos by name, now communicates mysteriously from beyond the grave his eyewitness accounts about what really happened in the Trojan War and beyond. Similar claims were made by shady "authors" like Dictys of Crete and Dares the Phrygian, offering what were described as eyewitness accounts.

What was the cause for such intense interest in trying to validate the stories of the Trojan War? For an answer, it is essential to understand the agenda underlying the stories themselves. The Trojan War was viewed by the ancients as the primary testing ground for the ancient concept of the hero. The heroes who populated the stories about the Trojan War were the primary focus of interest. These heroes were the real agenda.

In ancient Greek myth, heroes were humans, male or female, of

[2] Jennifer K. Berenson Maclean and Ellen Bradshaw Aitken, trans., *Flavius Philostratus: On Heroes* (SBLWGRW 3; Atlanta: Society of Biblical Literature, 2003).

the remote past, endowed with superhuman abilities and descended from the immortal gods themselves. The prime example is Akhilleus, more commonly known as Achilles in the English tradition. This, the greatest hero of the Homeric *Iliad*, was the son of Thetis, a sea-goddess known for her far-reaching cosmic powers.

There was a major problem, however, with the actual stories that were told about such heroes. The classical versions of these stories had been crystallized in the epic poetry of Homer and, later on, in the dramas of Aeschylus, Sophocles, and Euripides. As literature, the media of epic and drama could be seen as perfect expressions of classical ideals. By the time of the Second Sophistic, however, these same media were far less than perfect in expressing the essence of the ancient heroes. What seemed to be missing in the classical media? It was the older concept of the *cult* hero, which continued to be a vital part of the overall concept of the hero in the era of the Second Sophistic. In this era, even new fiction seemed superior to classical epic and drama in giving full expression to that older concept.

The cult hero, the object of hero cult, was a basic historical fact of Greek civilization. Hero cult was the traditional practice of worshiping heroes, and the evidence for it goes back at least as far as the "Geometric" period of the first millennium B.C.E.[3] There is broad cultural evidence indicating that hero cult in ancient Greece was not created out of epic stories like those of the *Iliad* and *Odyssey* but was in fact independent of them. The epic stories, on the other hand, were actually based on the religious practices, though not always directly.

Paradoxically, references to the practice of worshiping heroes are not obvious—at first sight—in the prime media of archaic and classical Greek literature that deal most directly with heroes. Current research on the traditions underlying the Homeric *Iliad* and *Odyssey* as well as the dramas of Aeschylus, Sophocles, and Euripides has demonstrated the pervasive influence of hero cults in shaping the media of epic and drama, but the fact remains that most

[3] On the history and archaeology of hero cults, see Anthony M. Snodgrass, *An Archaeology of Greece: The Present State and Future Scope of a Discipline* (Berkeley: University of California Press, 1987), 159–65. Two pathfinding general works on hero cults are Angelo Brelich, *Gli eroi greci: Un problema storico-religioso* (Rome: Edizioni dell'Ateneo, 1958), and Friedrich Pfister, *Der Reliquienkult im Altertum* (2 vols.; Giessen, Germany: Töpelmann, 1909–1912). Specialized works include Corinne Pache, *Baby and Child Heroes in Ancient Greece* (Urbana: University of Illinois Press, 2004).

references to the actual cults of heroes are only implicit in these forms of archaic and classical Greek literature.[4] It is the historians of the classical period who give us the earliest explicit references to hero cults, and the most prominent example is the narrative of Herodotus about the cult of Protesilaos at Elaious (*Hist.* 7.33; 9.116–120).[5] Yet, even in the medium of classical Greek historiography, the actual meaning of such a hero cult remains something of a mystery. That mystery, as we shall see later, is intentional.

As Ellen Aitken and Jennifer Maclean show clearly in their detailed introduction to Philostratus's *Heroikos*, the numerous references in this work to the hero cults of Protesilaos, Achilles, Ajax, and other heroes of the epic tradition reflect accurately the historical realities of hero cults as they persisted into the third century C.E. They show further that the traditionalism of Philostratus's *Heroikos* in its treatment of hero cults is not necessarily at odds with the literary and philosophical modernities that pervade this masterpiece of the Second Sophistic era of Hellenic civilization.

A key aspect of these modernities is the use of fiction.[6] The framing devices used by authors of the Second Sophistic to claim authenticity are patently fictional. Yet, at the same time, the authors of works like the *Heroikos* of Philostratus and the *Journal of the*

[4] For epic, see Nagy, *Best of the Achaeans*, 9–11 (also p. vii in the new introduction). For drama, see Albert Henrichs, "The Tomb of Aias and the Prospect of Hero Cult in Sophokles," *Classical Antiquity* 12 (1993): 165–80. In Homeric usage, a key word for implicitly referring to the cult of a hero is σῆμα, meaning "sign, signal" *and* "tomb [of a hero]": see Nagy, *Best of the Achaeans*, 340–43; cf. Henrichs, "The Tomb of Aias," 171–72.

[5] See Nagy, "The Sign of Protesilaos," and Gregory Nagy, *Pindar's Homer: The Lyric Possession of an Epic Past* (Baltimore: Johns Hopkins University Press, 1990), 268–73, as well as Deborah Boedeker, "Protesilaos and the End of Herodotus' *Histories*," *Classical Antiquity* 7/1 (1988): 30–48.

[6] See, for example, Ewen L. Bowie, "Philostratus: Writer of Fiction," in *Greek Fiction: The Greek Novel in Context* (ed. J. R. Morgan and Richard Stoneman; New York: Routledge, 1994). Bowie notes that "the fictional dialogue had a long and respectable ancestry in Greek prose" (p. 184) and goes on to highlight a "second level of fiction," that is, the content of the given dialogues. This content includes narratives about the Trojan War not found in Homer, information about the afterlife and cult of Achilles, as well as an account of the powers and habits of the hero Protesilaos. Very many of these framing narratives involve discovery of ancient writing in tombs. For examples of other truth-claiming framing devices see Nathaniel Edward Griffin, *Dares and Dictys: An Introduction to the Study of Medieval Versions of the Story of Troy* (Baltimore: J. H. Furst, 1907), 14 n. 1; Stefan Merkle, "Telling the Truth of the Trojan War: The Eyewitness Account of Dictys of Crete," in *The Search for the Ancient Novel* (ed. Joseph Tatum; Baltimore: Johns Hopkins University Press, 1994), 195 n. 8, and discussion below.

Trojan War attributed to Dictys of Crete strive to emphasize the truth and credibility of their accounts. As Stefan Merkle points out, Dictys of Crete presents himself as a reliable historian. Dictys is represented as referring to his own credibility as an eyewitness and claims to have questioned other eyewitnesses. He uses the rhetoric and methods of historiography to distinguish between versions and to provide the most reliable account.[7] Merkle also notes that, unlike the literary game of Lucian's *The Dream, or The Cock*, there are no parodic features in Dictys. The unadorned style of the military diary is adopted in order to give the account the greatest weight.[8]

Philostratus's *Heroikos* is similar in that there are no parodic features that undermine the authority of the framing narrative. The vinedresser who tends the sacred grove of the cult hero Protesilaos engages in a dialogue with a Phoenician who seems to know nothing about Greek hero cult.[9] The vinedresser communes frequently with the hero and has heard from him a more accurate account of the Trojan War.[10] This account (as mediated through the vinedresser) not only directly contradicts Homer in many places, but it also includes narratives that are not featured in the Homeric tradition:

> *Phoenician:* And, vinedresser, what would be the contest over the shield?[11] No poet has mentioned it, nor does it appear in any story of the Trojan War.
>
> *Vinedresser:* That, my guest, you will say about many matters, because the hero tells many things about warriors as well as deeds of battles that are not yet known to most people. This is the reason. He says that, in their passion for the poems of Homer, most people, looking only at Achilles and Odysseus, neglect good and brave men, so that some are not remembered at all, and for others Homer dedicates a trireme of four verses. (*Her.* 14.1–2)

Philostratus, through the experiences of a worshiper of Protesilaos,

[7] Merkle, "Telling the Truth," 185.

[8] Merkle, "Telling the Truth,"193.

[9] Note the Phoenician's questions in *Her.* 2.7–11.

[10] In *Her.* 23.1 the vinedresser says that Protesilaos has told him a story that is unknown to Homer and all other poets. In *Her.* 25.1–18 the vinedresser relates the faults that Protesilaos finds in Homer's account (as well as the things for which he praises Homer).

[11] That is, the contest that takes place in the course of the war against the Mysians in *Her.* 23.2–30.

claims to bring to light narratives about heroes that are not featured prominently in the panhellenic *Iliad* and *Odyssey*.

Philostratus uses the authority of a warrior hero who was reportedly present at Troy, seeking thus to authenticate narratives about the various other heroes who fought there. According to epic, Protesilaos was the first warrior to die at Troy (*Il.* 2.701–702). He was thus an eyewitness—as a warrior—only to the beginning of the war. Nevertheless, according to the vinedresser, once freed from the body after death, Protesilaos could "observe the affairs of mortals" (*Her.* 7.3). Thus both the Dictys narrative and the *Heroikos* make use of an authoritative heroic source who, in communication with the participants in the Trojan War, corrects and supplements the Homer-centric understanding that most people of the day would have had about the Trojan War, particularly with respect to the heroes who fought there.

The vinedresser particularly calls attention to heroes who are not mentioned in the *Iliad* or *Odyssey* or who have only a few verses devoted to them in these epics. Protesilaos himself belongs to the latter group. The cult of this particular hero in the Chersonesus is featured prominently at the end of Herodotus's *Histories*, and it stems from an old tradition.[12] Narratives about Protesilaos associated with that cult must have existed in classical times and possibly even earlier. It could be argued that the *Heroikos*, far from being a playful fiction or a literary game, is a revival of those narratives, an assertion of the "truth" about that hero. It is possible that the other heroes and narratives that are featured prominently in the *Heroikos*, such as those about Achilles on the so-called White Island, are also connected with a renewed interest in the cult of various heroes.[13]

The question must then be asked: To what extent did such writers of the Second Sophistic as Philostratus and the author behind Dictys of Crete conceive of their works as fictional? As Ewen Bowie has pointed out, a fictional frame does not suffice to make the overall work a fiction: the fictional dialogue, after all, is a common feature of Greek philosophical writings.[14] In the case of the *Heroikos*, the presence of polemic should perhaps be our first indication

[12] Herodotus *Hist.* 9.116. See Nagy, "The Sign of Protesilaos."

[13] For the White Island and the cult of Achilles in the area of the Black Sea, see Guy Hedreen, "The Cult of Achilles in the Euxine," *Hesperia* 60/3 (1991): 313–30. For the renewed interest in hero cults in the Second Sophistic, with particular reference to the *Heroikos* and the cult of Protesilaos, see Christopher P. Jones, "Time and Place in Philostratus' *Heroikos*," *JHS* 121 (2001): 141–48.

[14] Bowie, "Philostratus," 184.

that something important is at stake when Philostratus the author asserts his version of the Trojan War. In the *Heroikos*, Philostratus indirectly attacks the credibility of Dictys's account of the Trojan War in at least two places.[15] The *Journal of the Trojan War*, attributed to Dictys of Crete, purports to be a journal kept by a companion of the Cretan hero Idomeneus during the Trojan War. This work is contradicted in Philostratus's *Heroikos* when Protesilaos is cited as saying that Idomeneus never participated in the Trojan War, thereby implicitly denying the authenticity of Dictys's eyewitness report (*Her*. 30.1). It is also asserted in the *Heroikos* that the use of writing was first invented by Palamedes, a prominent figure associated with the Trojan War (*Her*. 33.1). This assertion, implying that writing was not yet in use at the time of the Trojan War, seems once again to challenge the framing narrative of Dictys. The narrative of Philostratus undermines the narrative of Dictys in the process of asserting the accuracy of Philostratus's own account.

Framing narratives of authentication can be found in the literature of many cultures. A less extraordinary but nevertheless comparable attempt to authenticate a new narrative of the past may be found in the Roman historian Sallust's *Jugurtha* (17):

> But what people first inhabited Africa and what people came later or in what way they became mixed together, although my account is different from the report that most people have heard, nevertheless how I have interpreted it using Punic books which are attributed to King Hiempsal, and how the cultivators of the land themselves think that it happened, I will relate as briefly as possible.

Sallust here claims to provide a more accurate history of Africa on the basis of his access to a special source: books, written in another language, attributed to an important historical figure from Numidia.

Another notable example comes from the early medieval Irish evidence. It is an anecdote, dated to the ninth century C.E.,[16] concerning the rediscovery of a supposedly lost book, the *Táin Bó Cuailnge* ("The Cattle Raid of Cooley"), which is a collection of

[15] See Merkle, "Telling the Truth," 193–94.

[16] The anecdote is entitled *Dofallsigud Tána Bó Cuailnge* and was published at pp. 433–34 of Heinrich Zimmer, "Keltische Studien," *Zeitschrift für vergleichende Sprachforschung* 28 (1887): 417–689. It is taken from the *Book of Leinster* (twelfth century C.E.), on which see the next note.

"epic" narratives about Ireland's greatest heroes.[17] This anecdote is in effect a "charter myth,"[18] explaining the essence of the *Táin*.[19] In terms of the myth, this book of narratives, the *Táin*, is equivalent to an integral epic performance. The myth narrates how this book had once been lost and how the assembled poets of Ireland "could not recall it in its entirety," since they knew only "fragments" (*bloga*).[20] In a quest to find the lost integral book, the poet Muirgen happens to travel past the tomb of Fergus mac Roich, one of the chief heroes featured in the narrative of the *Táin*. It is nighttime. Muirgen sits down at the gravestone of the tomb, and he sings an incantation to this gravestone "as though it were Fergus himself."[21] Responding to the incantation, Fergus himself appears in all his heroic glory, and he "recited to him [= to Muirgen] the whole *Táin*, how everything had happened, from start to finish."[22] As in Philostratus's *Heroikos*, we see that the superhuman consciousness of the hero can take over or even possess the narration of epic.

Confronted with the idea that an oracular cult hero possesses total mastery of epic narrative, our first impression is that this idea cannot be reconciled with what we find in Homeric poetry. According to the poetics of the Homeric *Iliad* and *Odyssey*, it is of course the Muses who "inspire" epic narrative. At first glance then these

[17] There are two main surviving recensions of the *Táin*, as attested in two manuscript families: (1) the *Book of the Dun Cow* (*Lebor na hUidre*, twelfth century C.E.) and the *Yellow Book of Lecan* (fourteenth century C.E.) and (2) the *Book of Leinster* (twelfth century C.E.). For a translation, see Thomas Kinsella, *The Táin: From the Irish Epic Táin Bó Cuailnge* (Oxford: Oxford University Press, 1969).

[18] On the concept of "charter myth," see especially p. 5 of Edmund R. Leach, "Critical Introduction" to Mikhail I. Steblin-Kamenskij, *Myth* (trans. Mary P. Coote; Ann Arbor, Mich.: Karoma, 1982), 1–20.

[19] There is a translation provided by Kinsella, *The Táin*, 1–2.

[20] Kinsella, *The Táin*, 1. The concept of a *blog* ("fragment") of a corpus that has disintegrated is a traditional theme found in the charter myths of many cultures; for a brief survey, see Gregory Nagy, *Homeric Questions* (Austin: University of Texas Press, 1996), 70–74.

[21] Kinsella, *The Táin*, 1.

[22] Kinsella, *The Táin*, 1–2. The point of this charter myth, then, is that the corpus of the *Táin* is reintegrated in performance, and thus the "lost book" is finally recovered, even resurrected. See Nagy, *Homeric Questions*, 70, following especially pp. 284 and 289 of the discussion in Joseph F. Nagy, "Orality in Medieval Irish Narrative," *Oral Tradition* 1 (1986): 272–301. On traditional metaphors about a book (or a library of books) as a corpus destined for resurrection, see pp. 196–98 of Gregory Nagy, "The Library of Pergamon as a Classical Model," in *Pergamon: Citadel of the Gods* (ed. Helmut Koester; HTS 46; Harrisburg, Penn.: Trinity Press International, 1998), 185–232.

goddesses of memory seem to be the sole source for the superhuman consciousness that informs the content of Homeric poetry and gives it the authority to tell about the gods and heroes of heroic times. This authority, however, is actually shared with the heroes who are "quoted" by Homeric performance, as a closer look at the *Iliad* and *Odyssey* reveals clearly.

In his book about the "quotations" of heroes in Homeric poetry, Richard Martin has demonstrated that the "voice" of the poet becomes traditionally identified with the "voices" of the heroes quoted by the poetic performance:

> My central conclusion is that the *Iliad* takes shape as a poetic composition in precisely the same "speaking culture" that we see foregrounded in the stylized words of the poem's heroic speakers, especially those speeches designated as *muthos*, a word I redefine as "authoritative speech-act." The poet and the hero are both "performers" in a traditional medium. The genre of muthos composing requires that its practitioners improve on previous performances and surpass them, by artfully manipulating traditional material in new combinations. In other words, within the speeches of the poem, we see that it is traditional to be spontaneous: no hero ever merely repeats; each recomposes the traditional text he performs, be it a boast, threat, command, or story, in order to project his individual personality in the most convincing manner. I suggest that the "voice" of the poet is the product of the same traditional performance technique.[23]

Recent ethnographic work on oral poetic performance traditions has provided typological parallels in support of Martin's demonstration. In the *Sîrat Banî Hilâl* epic singing tradition of the poets of al-Bakâtûsh in contemporary Egypt, for example, Dwight Reynolds has sought—and found—an analogy for Martin's model of the interchangeable "voice" of poet and hero in epic performance:

> [T]he social reality of the al-Bakâtûsh poets involves a distinctly negative position for the epic singer within the greater social hierarchy; in marked contrast to the poet's marginalized status in village society, however, are the

[23] Richard P. Martin, *The Language of Heroes: Speech and Performance in the Iliad* (Myth and Poetics; Ithaca, N.Y.: Cornell University Press, 1989), xiv.

> moments of centrality, power, and "voice" he achieves in epic performance. This disjunctive persona has produced not only a fascinating process of deep self-identification with the epic tradition on the part of the poets, but has clearly, over generations, shaped and indeed constituted many aspects of the content of the epic itself—an epic tradition, as I have termed it, of heroic poets and poetic heroes.[24]

There is also a plethora of ethnographic work that documents the widespread mentality of heroic "possession," in which the consciousness of the poet is "possessed" by the consciousness of the hero as soon as the poet, in performance, starts "quoting" the hero.[25] As one ethnographer puts it, there can be "a transition from a story *about* a spirit, to one told *to* a spirit, to one told *by* a spirit."[26]

We may infer, then, that Philostratus's *Heroikos* has preserved for us the memory of oral epic traditions in which heroes are being "quoted" through the supernatural consciousness of the heroes themselves. This is not to say, however, that the *Heroikos* itself represents a direct continuation of such oral traditions. We have little doubt that the oral traditions of composition-in-performance, as still reflected in the hexameter poetry of the *Iliad* and *Odyssey* and

[24] Dwight Fletcher Reynolds, *Heroic Poets, Poetic Heroes: The Ethnography of Performance in an Arabic Oral Tradition* (Ithaca, N.Y.: Cornell University Press, 1995), 208; at p. 207, Reynolds quotes the formulation of Martin (*The Language of Heroes*, xiv) as a heuristic paradigm for his own ethnographic fieldwork.

[25] For a particularly valuable collection of examples, see Stuart H. Blackburn, Peter J. Claus, Joyce B. Flueckiger, and Susan S. Wadley, eds., *Oral Epics in India* (Berkeley: University of California Press, 1989), especially Peter J. Claus, "Behind the Text: Performance and Ideology in a Tulu Oral Tradition," 55–74. At p. 60, Claus notes, "In his performance the possessed priest must not only recite Kordabbu's story, but also assume his character and dramatically portray his exploits for several hours on end."

[26] See Claus, "Behind the Text," 74, who adds, "Accompanying these transitions are shifts in verbal style: from the third person pronominal referent, to the second, to the first. There are also changes in the behavior of the performers and the audience." In this comparative context, it is relevant to reconsider Philostratus *Her.* 12.3, where Protesilaos ἐπαινεῖ ("confirms") the words spoken by Homer "to" (ἐς) himself, not "about" himself. The implication of ἐπαινεῖ is that Protesilaos "confirms" (*Il.* 2.695–709) the short narrative about his epic deeds at Troy, by way of *reperforming* these Homeric verses. On the poetics of authentication-by-reperformance, as implied by the verb ἐπαινέω, see the comments on the use of this word by Lycurgus *Against Leocrates* 102, at p. 129 n. 16 of Gregory Nagy, "Homer and Plato at the Panathenaia: Synchronic and Diachronic Perspectives," in *Contextualizing Classics: Ideology, Performance, Dialogue. Essays in Honor of John J. Peradotto* (ed. Thomas M. Falkner, Nancy Felson, and David Konstan; Lanham, Md.: Rowman & Littlefield, 1999), 123–50.

of the Epic Cycle in general, had been dead for well over half a millennium by the time Philostratus composed the *Heroikos*. Still, it is essential to stress that the traditions of hero cults were evidently still alive in the era of Philostratus. Moreover, the archaic mentality of seeking communion with the consciousness of cult heroes was likewise still alive. Even though the Homeric poems and the Epic Cycle were now literary rather than oral traditions, they still preserved, as traditions per se, a vital link with the rituals of hero cult. The *Heroikos* bridges the chasm between the mythical world of epic heroes and the ritual world of cult heroes. In this masterpiece of the Second Sophistic, a continuum is still felt to exist between these two diverging worlds. The spirit of this age is captured by the following formulation of the would-be initiate Phoenician in *Her*. 6.3: "I dreamed I was reading aloud (ἀναγινώσκειν) the epic verses (ἔπος plural) of Homer."

INITIATION INTO THE MYSTERIES OF HEROES: ANCIENT GREEK HERO CULT AND THE *HEROIKOS*

A telling feature of Philostratus's traditionalism is his consistent use of mystical language in referring to the cult hero Protesilaos. Throughout Philostratus's *Heroikos*, there is a sharp contrast being made between the special understanding of the initiated—in this case, he happens to be a local Greek "vinedresser" in the hero's sacred space—and the everyday understanding of the uninitiated—in this case, he happens to be a nonlocal non-Greek, from Phoenicia. This special understanding is conveyed by words that have a special meaning for the initiated but an everyday meaning for the uninitiated. The process of initiation allows the new initiate—hereafter we will refer to him as the "initiand"—to transcend the everyday meaning of words and to achieve a special understanding of their sacral meaning.

At the beginning of the *Heroikos*, the reader learns that Protesilaos experienced not one but two resurrections in the heroic past. The first time, the hero came back to life at Phthia in Thessaly after his death at Troy, all because of his love for his bride Laodameia (ἀναβιῴη, *Her*. 2.9). Then he died a second time—and again it was because he loved his bride—only to come back to life a second time thereafter (ἀναβιῶναι, *Her*. 2.10). Just exactly how he came back for the second time, however, is not revealed even to the initiate, the vinedresser, who says to the initiand, the Phoenician, that Protesilaos chooses not to tell that particular "sacred secret," that particular ἀπόρρητον (*Her.* 2.11).[27]

That was then, in the heroic past. Now, however, in the everyday present, the living hero continues to come back again and again, as a sacred epiphany or apparition, much like other heroes of the heroic past who likewise "appear in epiphanies" or "show up" (φαίνονται, *Her.* 2.11). So speaks the initiated vinedresser, and the Phoenician admits that he has a hard time believing all this: "I do not believe," he says (ἀπιστῶ, *Her.* 3.1). In other words, the initiand is not yet an initiate. Still, he wants to be a "believer" (πιστεύων, *Her.* 3.1). The initiate responds by proceeding to tell the initiand all about the epiphanies of Protesilaos, describing the cult hero's interventions into the world of the everyday. Where is Protesilaos most likely to be sighted? The initiate reveals an array of places where the hero may "show up," as it were: sometimes he is in the Chersonesus, sometimes in Phthia, sometimes in Troy—a most notable of locations for frequent sightings of heroes who died in the Trojan War—and sometimes he is back in Hades (*Her.* 11.7). It is in Hades that he continues to have sex with his beloved bride Laodameia (*Her.* 11.8).

As the narrative of the hero's epiphanies proceeds, a gentle breeze carries the sweet aroma of flowers in bloom, and the initiand is feeling refreshed (*Her.* 3.2–5). He remarks that the plant life literally "breathes out" (ἀναπνεῖ) a sweetness of its own (*Her.* 3.3). It is the right season, the exact time, the perfect moment: it is the ὥρα (*Her.* 3.2, 5). One can begin to sense the hero's sacred presence. Through a sort of metonymy, the breath of the hero himself ani-

[27] It is relevant to note the suggestive use of the word πάθος ("experience") in an earlier context, "He himself [Protesilaos] does not speak about his own experiences [πάθη]" (*Her.* 2.9). The speaker goes on to say that the ἀπόρρητον ("sacred secret") belongs to the Moirai ("Fates"; *Her.* 2.11). In the formulaic language of epic diction, the name *Prôtesi-lâos* seems to be associated with the word πρῶτος ("first"), in the sense that this hero was the first Achaean to die at Troy (*Il.* 2.702: πρώτιστος). But the name seems also to be associated with the root of πε-πρω-ται ("it is fated"; as in *Il.* 18.329), in that Protesilaos is linked with traditional epic narratives about the fate of the Achaean λαός or "people" (Nagy, *Best of the Achaeans*, 70). A turning point in the plot of the *Iliad* is the moment when the fire of Hektor reaches the ships of the Achaeans, and here the narrative focus centers on the ship of Protesilaos himself (*Il.*15.704–705, 716–718; see also 16.286). This same precise moment is figured as a turning point for the very destiny of all Hellenes as descendants of the epic Achaeans, in that the *Iliad* equates the threat of destruction for the Achaeans' ships with the threat of extinction for the Hellenes that are yet to be (Nagy, *Best of the Achaeans*, 335–37).

mates the atmosphere, and Protesilaos is now revealing (ἀποφαίνω) the scent of the blossoms at their sweetest (*Her.* 11.3).[28] The hero's presence smells sweeter than myrtles in autumn (*Her.* 10.2).[29] The perfect moment or ὥρα, in all its natural beauty, becomes the ultimate epiphany of the cult hero.[30]

[28] Such a traditional metonymy depends on a preexisting traditional metaphor that pictures an interchangeability between breath and wind, on which see Gregory Nagy, "As the World Runs Out of Breath: Metaphorical Perspectives on the Heavens and the Atmosphere in the Ancient World," in *Earth, Air, Fire, Water: Humanistic Studies of the Environment* (ed. Jill K. Conway, Kenneth Keniston, and Leo Marx; Amherst: University of Massachusetts Press, 1999), 37–50.

[29] In contexts of beautiful natural settings, the cult hero is conventionally eroticized, as here in *Her.* 10.2–4 and elsewhere; see especially *Her.* 11.2, describing the urge of the worshiper to embrace and kiss the hero. A sense of personal intimacy is conveyed by the worshiper of the hero when he says about Protesilaos (*Her.* 9.7): "I spend time with him [αὐτῷ γὰρ ξύνειμι], and no cult statue [ἄγαλμα] can be sweeter [ἥδιον] than he, that one [ἐκεῖνος]." The worshiper's experience of the hero as a real person, not as a cult statue (ἄγαλμα), is here conveyed by the deictic pronoun ἐκεῖνος ("that one"), which is conventionally used to refer to a hero who appears in an epiphany (see Nagy, *Pindar's Homer*, 200–201, with special reference to Mimnermus and Sappho). The deixis of ἐκεῖνος conveys the remoteness ("that" not "this") of the hero, even in the immediacy of his epiphany. The gap between the superhuman and the human is so great that it sets the superhuman apart from the human even in the process of attempting to bridge that gap in an epiphany. The human response is a sense of longing and yearning as experienced even during the immediacy of an epiphany. We refer again to *Her.* 11.2, describing the urge of the worshiper to embrace and kiss the cult hero. The convention of eroticizing this sense of longing and yearning is implicit, we further suggest, in the epic usage of ποθέω ("long for, yearn for"), as at *Il.* 2.703, 709. On one level of meaning, the warriors native to Phthia long for the epic hero Protesilaos as their leader. On a deeper level, however, the reference implies the emotional response of native worshipers who are "yearning" for their local cult hero in all his immanent beauty; we may compare the application of ποθέω to Patroklos at his funeral, *Il.* 23.16. For other Homeric examples of similar two-level references to heroes of epic/cult, see Gregory Nagy, *Greek Mythology and Poetics* (Ithaca, N.Y.: Cornell University Press, 1990), 132–34, on the usage of the word δῆμος (in the sense of "local district") as an index of localized cult practices.

[30] On the religious mentality of equating ritual perfection with beauty itself, see in general the work of Pache, *Baby and Child Heroes*. The concept of ὥρα as the "right season" conveys the context of ritual perfection and correctness; in that sense, ὥρα is conceived as the perfect moment of beauty, as in Philostratus *Her.* 3.2, 5. The Modern Greek adjective *oréos* (ὡραῖος), derived from ὥρα, means "beautiful." On the formal and semantic connections of ὥρα and Hêra and ἥρως ("hero"), see Nagy, *Homeric Questions*, 48 n. 79: heroes become "seasonal" after they die and achieve mystical immortalization, but they are "unseasonal" during their own lifetime in the heroic age (thus, for example, Achilles while he is alive in his own epic narrative is described as παν-α-ώριος, "the most unseasonal of them all," in *Il.* 24.540). The formal connections between ὥρα and hero cult are evident in *Her.* 18.2–3, a passage that describes in explicit terms the ritually correct times (ὧραι) for

The secrets of the cult hero Protesilaos are clearly visible to the initiate: since these are things that are θεῖα ("divine") and μεγάλα ("larger than life"), they will not escape the notice of those who are "cultivated" (χαρίεντας; *Her.* 3.2). For the uninitiated, however, these same secrets are veiled in language that expresses what seems quite ordinary and everyday on the surface. About the cult hero Protesilaos, the initiate starts by saying to the uninitiated: "He lives [ζῇ] here, and we work the land [γεωργοῦμεν] together" (*Her.* 2.8). What image in life could be more straightforward, more everyday, than life itself? When the initiand follows up by asking whether Protesilaos "lives" in the sense that he is "resurrected" (ἀναβεβιωκώς), the initiate replies: "He himself does not speak about his own experiences [πάθος plural]" (*Her.* 2.9). This absolutizing declaration is then followed by a series of qualifications: contradicting what he has just said, the initiate now goes on to say that the hero Protesilaos does indeed speak about his own death at Troy, about his first resurrection, and about his second death—though he does not speak about his second resurrection (*Her.* 2.9–11).

A vital question remains: How can a cult hero like Protesilaos actually communicate with those who are initiated into his mysteries? According to the traditional mentality of hero cults, the answer is simple: whenever they come back to life, cult heroes are endowed with a superhuman consciousness. This consciousness of the hero, activated by hero cult, performs the basic function of ensuring the seasonality of nature, and it manifests itself in such specific functions as the healing of humans or animals or plants: in *Her.* 4.10, for example, Protesilaos is described as the ἰατρός ("healer") of sheep, beehives, trees.[31]

For this superhuman consciousness to be activated, the cult hero must be *consulted*. In the case of Philostratus's *Heroikos*, we see that a cult hero like Protesilaos has to be actively consulted by his worshipers: from the very beginning, in fact, the intent of the

---

slaughtering herd animals as sacrifices to cult heroes; in this particular context, diseases afflicting herd animals are said to be caused by an angry Ajax, *in his capacity as a cult hero*. In this context, such a belief is linked to the myth about the ritually incorrect slaughter of herd animals by Ajax (as dramatized, for example, in Sophocles' *Ajax*).

[31] On the "iatric" function of cult heroes, see in general Brelich, *Gli eroi greci*, 113–18. Cult heroes, when they feel benign, will cure illnesses afflicting humans, animals, and plants—just as they will inflict these same illnesses when they feel malign (see the previous note). On the φρίκη or sacred "frisson" induced by a cult hero's presence, see *Her.* 6.4; 8.11; 18.4; etc.

chief character, the worker in the vineyard of Protesilaos, is to make this cult hero his own personal "advisor" (ξύμβουλος, *Her.* 4.7).[32] Whenever the ritual of consultation would fail, the worshiper says that he could know for sure, since the cult hero would be silent (ἐσιώπα, *Her.* 4.7). By contrast, the success of the consultation is manifested whenever the cult hero speaks.

Such consulting of oracular cult heroes concerns not only the fundamentals of nature. It concerns also the fundamental nature of the heroes themselves. Their heroic essence has two aspects, one of which is defined by epic narrative traditions like the *Iliad* and *Odyssey*, while the other is defined by hero cult. In Philostratus's *Heroikos*, these two aspects of the hero are treated holistically as integral parts of a single concept. Thus the process of consulting oracular heroes leads to the initiate's knowledge about their epic aspects, as well as their ritual aspects. As the initiate declares, cult heroes have their own knowledge of epic narrative because they are endowed with μαντικὴ σοφία ("the skill of a seer [μάντις]"), and there is an "oracular" principle (χρησμῶδες) operating within them (*Her.* 7.3). That is why a hero like Protesilaos "sees all the way through" (δι-ορᾷ) the poems of Homer (*Her.* 7.4), knowing things that go beyond his own experiences when he, Protesilaos, had lived in the past of heroes (*Her.* 7.5–6); the hero even knows things about which Homer himself did not sing (*Her.* 7.5).

In sum, the *Heroikos* provides a model of poetic inspiration that centers on the superhuman consciousness of the oracular hero, which has a totalizing control of epic narrative. As we have seen, this model is not an innovation but an archaism, stemming from oral poetic traditions that predate even the Homeric traditions of the *Iliad* and *Odyssey*. Philostratus's *Heroikos* makes it clear that heroes cannot be defined exclusively in terms of their epic dimensions, though this aspect becomes vitally important in the history of ideas about heroism, especially in view of the ultimate cultural prestige surrounding the prime medium that conveys these ideas, Homeric poetry. For Philostratus, the prestige of Homer and the Homeric hero is a given. In the *Heroikos*, however, he goes further,

[32] See also *Her.* 14.4: Protesilaos is an "advisor" to athletes who cultivate him (cf. *Her.* 15.5, where Protesilaos is said to give oracular advice, χρῆσαι, to an athlete who consults him on how to win). Already in Homeric poetry, we see implicit references to consultations of cult heroes: in *Il.* 10.415, for example, Hektor βούλας βουλεύει ("plans his plans") at the σῆμα ("tomb") of Ilos, a stylized cult hero of Ilion.

far further, by reconnecting that epic prestige with the sacred charisma possessed by the hero in cult.

CONTINUITY AND TRADITION IN PHILOSTRATUS'S *HEROIKOS*

As noted above, references to the immortalization of heroes after death and their status as cult figures are almost never explicit in the *Iliad* and *Odyssey*.[33] Implicit references to hero cult, however, are pervasive. Indeed, much of epic diction resonates with religious undertones, resulting in a superficial meaning for certain key terms, as well as a deeper, sacred meaning for those "in the know"—the initiated worshipers. Philostratus's *Heroikos*, although composed many centuries after our *Iliad* and *Odyssey*, helps us to connect with the mentality of hero cults that lies beneath the surface of Homeric poetry. A closer examination of a few selected passages will illustrate the continuity of hero-cult narratives about the immortality of heroes that can be traced in the *Heroikos*. These same passages can in turn enhance our understanding of archaic and classical Greek poetry.

In *Iliad* 23, the ψυχή of Patroklos visits Achilles in a dream and entreats Achilles to bury him in a golden amphora that Thetis gave to Achilles in anticipation of his death:

> Do not bury my bones apart from yours, Achilles,
> but together, as we were raised in your house . . .
> so may the same vessel contain both our bones,
> the golden amphora, which your lady mother gave you.[34]
> (*Il.* 23.83–84, 91–92)

This golden amphora is one of the only concrete symbols of Achilles' immortality after death in the *Iliad*.[35] The golden amphora

[33] For an exception to this formulation see Casey Dué, "Achilles' Golden Amphora and the Afterlife of Oral Tradition in Aeschines' *Against Timarchus*," *CP* 96 (2001): 33–47.

[34] See *Od.* 24.73–77, "Your mother gave you a golden amphora and said that it was the gift of Dionysos, the work of most famous Hephaistos. In this amphora lie your white bones, radiant Achilles, and mixed with them are the bones of the dead Patroklos, son of Menoitios." In *Her.* 56.5 the vinedresser mentions a story about a golden pitcher (κάλπις) that appeared, apparently mysteriously, on Chios, but declines to tell the tale because, he says, it is so well known. It is likely that this golden pitcher is also to be connected with the immortality of the cult hero.

[35] For the golden amphora as a symbol of immortality see Nagy, *Best of the Achaeans*, chs. 9–10. See also Andrew Stewart, "Stesichoros and the François Vase," in *Ancient Greek Art and Iconography* (ed. Warren G. Moon; Madison: University of Wisconsin Press, 1983), 53–74, who argues for a compositional unity to

signals the reassembly of Achilles' bones and his transformation into an immortalized hero after death. Elsewhere in the poem, however, only his short life and his grief while alive are emphasized. The anticipation of the finality of Achilles' death is so great that the mourning for Achilles begins while he is still alive. Similarly, Odysseus and Telemachus are lamented by Penelope repeatedly throughout the *Odyssey*.[36]

The religious dimension of Homeric poetry aids our interpretation of these lament-filled passages. As Nagy has argued, the funeral rituals and lamentation of the *Iliad* and *Odyssey* are a reflection of actual cult practice in the worship of heroes like Achilles and Odysseus as religious figures.[37] The songs of lament for Achilles and Odysseus within the epic are an important part of ritual lamentation for the hero on the part of the communities for whom the epics are performed.[38]

---

the so-called François Vase centered on the golden amphora depicted on it. The wedding of Peleus and Thetis is set amid narratives that explore the tensions between mortality and immortality, peerless heroism and savage wrath, and mighty prowess and terrible hubris in the figure of Achilles. Stewart notes (p. 66), "Appropriately, all these themes intersect in the motif of Dionysos's amphora and its twin promises of death and immortality."

[36] *Od.* 1.363–364; 4.716–741, 800–801, 810–823; 18.202–205, 603–605; 20.57–90; 21.54–57, 356–358.

[37] See Nagy, *Best of the Achaeans*, 94–117, especially 116–17, "As Rohde [1898] himself had noticed, the Funeral of Patroklos at *Iliad* XXIII has several features that connote the rituals of hero cults. For example, the wine libation (XXIII 218–221) and the offering of honey with oil (XXIII 170; cf. xxiv 67–68) 'can hardly be regarded as anything but sacrificial.' Such marginal details of cult, as also the integral element of singing lamentations at XXIII 12 and 17, give ritual *form* to the **ákhos** of Achilles for Patroklos at XXIII 47. Even the central epic action of Book XXIII, the Funeral Games of Patroklos, has ritual form. In Homeric narrative, the funeral of a hero is the primary occasion for athletic contests (XXIII 630–631: Amarynkeus; xxiv 85–86: Achilles himself). In classical times, local athletic contests were still motivated as funeral games for the epichoric hero (cf., e.g., Pausanias 8.4.5). As a general principle, the **ágôn** was connected with the cult of heroes, and even the Great Panhellenic Games were originally conceived as funeral games for heroes. The custom of mourning for Achilles at the beginning of the Olympics (Pausanias 6.23.3) is a striking instance of this heritage. As a parallel, epic offers a corresponding single event in the mourning for Patroklos that inaugurates the Funeral Games in Book XXIII. Even though there are hints within the *Iliad* that the Funeral of Patroklos is presented as a grand beginning of cult (XXIV 592–595), the overt singularity of the event forced Rohde to rule it out as a parallel to the cult of heroes, which is recurrent. And yet, the *Iliad* itself is a singularity. What is recurrent in ritual is timeless in the epic tradition, just like the **kléos áphthiton** of Achilles."

[38] On Greek laments in general see the seminal work of Margaret Alexiou, *Ritual Lament in the Greek Tradition* (2d ed.; Lanham, Md.: Rowman & Littlefield, 2002).

Similarly, Briseis's lament for Patroklos in *Iliad* 19 expresses private grief that becomes transformed into a collective sorrow for her audience both within the epic and beyond it:

> So she spoke lamenting, and the women wailed in
> response,
> with Patroklos as their pretext, but each woman for her
> own cares. (*Il.* 19.301–302)

Briseis's song extends not only to the collective experience of the women around her who lament their fallen husbands, but to the audience of the epic as well.[39] Dué has argued that Briseis's lamentation for Patroklos is also a lament for Achilles.[40] Her lament becomes on the level of cult a communal expression of lamentation for Achilles as hero. It is not insignificant then that the final lament of the *Iliad*, sung by Helen (who is the cause of the war), ends not with the antiphonal wailing of the women (as at 6.499; 19.30; 22.515; and 24.746), but of the Trojan people: "So she spoke lamenting, and the people [δῆμος] wailed in response" (*Il.* 24.776).

We may compare the lamentation for Achilles before his death in the *Iliad* to the very full description of his funeral in the *Odyssey*:

> "Happy [ὄλβιος] son of Peleus, Achilles like the gods," answered the ghost [ψυχή] of Agamemnon, "for having died at Troy far from Argos, while the best of the Trojans and the Achaeans fell around you fighting for your body. There you lay in the whirling clouds of dust, all huge and hugely, heedless now of your horsemanship. We fought the whole of the livelong day, nor should we ever have left off if Zeus had not sent a storm to stay us. Then, when we had borne you to the ships out of the fray, we laid you on your bed and cleansed your fair skin with warm water

[39] For a similar transformation of the laments of women into a collective, civic sorrow, see Charles P. Segal's discussion of Euripides' *Hippolytus* 1462–1466 in *Euripides and the Poetics of Sorrow* (Durham, N.C.: Duke University Press, 1993), 121; and Laura McClure, *Spoken Like a Woman: Speech and Gender in Athenian Drama* (Princeton: Princeton University Press, 1999), 41 and 156. Thomas M. Greene has noted that lamentation in epic collapses the boundaries between the audience and the heroic past, producing "a hallowed communion between the two" ("The Natural Tears of Epic," in *Epic Traditions in the Contemporary World: The Poetics of Community* [ed. Margaret Beissinger, Jane Tylus, and Susanne Wofford; Berkeley: University of California Press, 1999], 195). He argues that the *telos* of most of the European poetry known as epic is tears, and that through tears the communion between past and present is most accessible.

[40] See Casey Dué, *Homeric Variations on a Lament by Briseis* (Lanham, Md.: Rowman & Littlefield, 2002).

and with ointments. The Danaans tore their hair and wept bitterly round about you. Your mother, when she heard, came with her immortal nymphs from out of the sea, and the sound of heavenly wailing went forth over the waters so that the Achaeans quaked for fear. They would have fled panic-stricken to their ships had not wise old Nestor whose counsel was ever truest checked them saying, 'Hold, Argives, flee not, sons of the Achaeans, this is his mother coming from the sea with her immortal nymphs to view the body of her son.'

Thus he spoke, and the Achaeans feared no more. The daughters of the old man of the sea stood round you weeping bitterly, and clothed you in immortal raiment. The nine muses also came and lifted up their sweet voices in lament—calling and answering one another; there was not an Argive but wept for pity of the dirge they chanted. Days and nights seven and ten we mourned you, mortals and immortals, but on the eighteenth day we gave you to the flames, and many a fat sheep with many an ox did we slay in sacrifice around you. You were burnt in raiment of the gods, with rich resins and with honey, while Achaean heroes, horse and foot, clashed their armor round the pile as you were burning, with the tramp as of a great multitude. But when the flames of heaven had done their work, we gathered your white bones at daybreak and laid them in ointments and in pure wine. Your mother brought us a golden amphora to hold them—gift of Dionysos, and work of Hephaistos himself; in this we mingled your bleached bones with those of Patroklos who had gone before you, and separate we enclosed also those of Antilokhos, who had been closer to you than any other of your comrades now that Patroklos was no more.

Over their bodies we the sacred army of Argive spearmen piled up a huge and perfect tomb, on a jutting headland, by the wide Hellespont, so that it may be bright from afar for men coming from the sea, both those who are now and those who will be in the future. Your mother begged prizes from the gods, and offered them to be contended for [ἀγών] by the noblest of the Achaeans. You must have been present at the funeral of many a hero, when the young men gird themselves and make ready to contend for prizes on the death of some great chieftain, but you never saw such prizes as silver-footed Thetis offered in your honor; for the gods loved you well. Thus even in death your κλέος, Achilles, has not been lost, and your name lives evermore among all humankind. (*Od.* 24.35–95)[41]

In the *Odyssey* tradition, the spectacular funeral, prominent tomb, and the lamentation of not only the Nereids but also the Muses themselves are a prelude to Achilles' immortality in song, his κλέος.[42]

The lamentation for heroes within epic is a reflection of ritual lamentation on the part of the community outside of epic. There are clear traces we can find in the hero cults of Achilles in the classical and even postclassical periods. To cite just one example, let us consider a custom in Elis that Pausanias mentions in connection with various local athletic traditions. On an appointed day at the beginning of the Olympic Games, as the sun is sinking in the west, the women of Elis perform various rituals to worship Achilles (τοῦ Ἀχιλλέως δρῶσιν ἐς τιμήν), and the ritual that is singled out specifically is that of mourning (κόπτεσθαι, Pausanias *Description of Greece* 6.23.3).[43]

But whereas the mortality of the hero is emphasized in Homeric epic and in many rituals concerning heroes, it is likely that the immortalization of the hero after death played a role in the epic traditions that have come down to us as the Epic Cycle. These poems, attributed to various authors such as Arctinus of Miletus or Lesches of Mytilene, announce themselves as being more locally oriented than the *Iliad* or *Odyssey*.[44] Because they are more local in orientation, the poems of the Epic Cycle include relatively more

[41] Translation after Samuel Butler, trans. *The Odyssey* (London: Longmans, Green & Co., 1900).

[42] κλέος is fame or glory, especially the fame or glory that comes from being glorified by poetry or song; see Nagy, *Best of the Achaeans*, 16–18.

[43] For this and other examples of cult practices in honor of Achilles, see Martin P. Nilsson, *Griechische Feste* (Leipzig: Teubner, 1906), 457, as well as Hedreen, "Cult of Achilles."

[44] The *Iliad* and the *Odyssey*, by contrast with the Epic Cycle, were never explicitly said to belong to any one city. Many cities laid claim to being the birthplace of "Homer." See Thomas W. Allen, *Homer: The Origins and the Transmission* (Oxford: Clarendon, 1924), 11–41. On the local, that is, relatively less panhellenic nature of the poems of the Cycle, see Nagy, *Pindar's Homer*, 70–79, as well as Jonathan S. Burgess, "The Non-Homeric *Cypria*," *TAPA* 126 (1996): 77–99. For more on the Epic Cycle in general, see Malcolm Davies, *The Epic Cycle* (Bristol: Bristol Classical Press, 1989), and Jonathan S. Burgess, *The Tradition of the Trojan War in Homer and the Epic Cycle* (Baltimore: Johns Hopkins University Press, 2001).

romance, fantasy, folktale, and local color.[45] The poems of the Cycle survive only in fragments and in the summaries written by an ancient scholar named Proclus; our knowledge of their contents is therefore limited.[46] The summaries of Proclus, moreover, are not an entirely accurate reflection of the poems in their earliest stages.[47] Nevertheless, the surviving summaries and fragments give us an indication of the traditional content of epic poetry that was composed and performed within the same tradition as the *Iliad* and *Odyssey*.

In the *Aithiopis*, as it is summarized by Proclus, Thetis snatches the corpse of Achilles from his funeral pyre and transports him to the island of Leukê:

> Then they hold funeral rites for Antilokhos and lay out Achilles' corpse; Thetis comes with the Muses and her sisters and makes a lament [θρῆνος] for her son. After that, Thetis snatches him off the pyre and carries him over to the island Leukê. But the Achaeans heap up his burial mound and hold funeral games.

Nagy has shown that the verb *ἀναρπάζω* ("snatch") used here has a special meaning in connection with the death of heroes. *ἀναρπάζω* is the verb most commonly used in narratives of the abduction by divinities of mortals who subsequently become immortalized.[48] Such mortals include Phaethôn and Ganymede. In the *Aithiopis* tradition, Achilles died and was buried, but was subsequently imagined to come back to life as an immortalized hero on the so-called White Island, the island of Leukê.

Philostratus's *Heroikos* represents a continuation of archaic beliefs about the death (accompanied by intense lamentation and elaborate funerals) and the subsequent immortalization of heroes. The following is the vinedresser's account of the burial and tomb of Achilles at Troy:

[45] See J. Griffin, "The Epic Cycle and the Uniqueness of Homer," *JHS* 97 (1977): 39–53, and Davies, *The Epic Cycle*, 9–10, who view these elements as signs of inferior poetry; contrast Nagy, *Pindar's Homer*, 60–61 and 70–71.

[46] It is not known whether this Proclus is the Neoplatonist of the fifth century C.E. or another man from the second century C.E. See Burgess, *The Tradition of the Trojan War*, 12.

[47] On the earliest recoverable scope and content of the poems of the Epic Cycle, see especially Davies, *The Epic Cycle;* Ross Scaife, "The *Kypria* and Its Early Reception," *Classical Antiquity* 14 (1995): 164–92; Burgess, "The Non-Homeric *Cypria*"; and Burgess, *The Tradition of the Trojan War*, 143–48.

[48] Nagy, *Best of the Achaeans*, 192–98.

> This hill, my guest, which you see standing in line with the headland, the Achaeans erected when they came together at the time when Achilles was mingled with Patroklos in the tomb and bequeathed to himself and that man the loveliest shroud. For this reason they who praise the marks of friendship sing of him. He was buried most spectacularly of mortals with all that Hellas offered to him. The Hellenes no longer considered it proper after Achilles' death to wear their hair long, and they piled up in mass on a funeral pyre their gold and whatever each of them had, whether he had brought it to Troy or had taken it as booty, both right then and when Neoptolemos came to Troy. For Achilles obtained glorious gifts again from both his child and the Achaeans, who were trying to show in return their gratitude to him. (*Her.* 51.12–13)

The vinedresser believes that the Greeks of Achilles' day began to confer a hero's honors upon Achilles immediately after his death. These honors included a spectacular burial, precious gifts, and perpetual mourning as expressed in the form of shorn hair.

The vinedresser goes on to describe in the course of the dialogue many rituals performed at the tomb of Achilles by worshipers of the vinedresser's own day, a direct continuation of those ancient rites. According to the vinedresser, moreover, Achilles continues to have an existence beyond death, much like the primary hero of the dialogue, Protesilaos. As in the *Aithiopis* tradition, Achilles lives on the island known as Leukê, the White Island. His companion on this island is none other than Helen of Troy. She is immortal, and so too has Achilles become immortal after death. Passing sailors can hear him singing songs, and visitors to the island can sometimes experiences frightening epiphanies by this hero.

In the preceding discussion we have already noted that Protesilaos is a cult hero who, according to the vinedresser, has died and been resurrected not once, but twice. Thus Achilles and Protesilaos are both heroes who die an unseasonably early death in epic, but live on as immortalized heroes in cult. The description of Protesilaos's tomb captures perfectly these two aspects of the hero:

> Listen to such stories now, my guest. Protesilaos does not lie buried at Troy but here on the Chersonesus. This large κολωνός here on the left no doubt contains him. The nymphs created these elms around the κολωνός, and they made, I suppose, the following decree concerning these trees: "Those branches turned toward Ilion will blossom

> early and will then immediately shed their leaves and perish before their season (this was indeed the misfortune of Protesilaos), but a tree on the other side will live and prosper." All the trees that were not set round the grave, such as these in the grove, have strength in all their branches and flourish according to their particular nature. (*Her.* 9.1–3)

Most noteworthy is the use here of the word κολωνός, which we propose to translate as "landmark" in this context. It marks the mound, surrounded by elm trees, that "extends over" (ἐπέχει) the body of the cult hero Protesilaos at Elaious in the Chersonesus. At *Her.* 51.12, this same word κολωνός designates the mound that the Achaeans built (the verb here, ἀγείρω, suggests a piling of stones) over the bodies of Achilles and Patroklos, situated on a headland overlooking the Hellespont, thus facing the mound of Protesilaos on the other side of the strait.

At *Her.* 53.10–11, κολωνός refers again to the tomb of Achilles, and here the word is used synonymously with σῆμα (the "tomb" or "sign" of the hero; *Her.* 53.11). In Sophocles' *Oedipus at Colonus*, the place-name Κολωνός refers to a sacred grove (690, 889) where Oedipus's body is destined to receive an οἶκος, that is, an "abode" befitting a cult hero (627).[49] There is a metonymy implicit in the name: κολωνός as a landmark becomes, by extension, the name of the whole sacred grove—and, by further extension, the name of the whole deme of Attica in which the grove is situated. Moreover, the landmark is associated with a stone called the Θορίκιος πέτρος (1595), sacred to Poseidon, which marks the last place where Oedipus is to be seen before he is mystically engulfed into the earth. As Nagy argues elsewhere, the metonymy extends even further: the inherited imagery of the Θορίκιος πέτρος as a mystical "white rock" becomes coextensive with the description of Kolônos itself as a white rock shining from afar (690; ἀργής).[50]

Such connections between classical literature and the literary world of the Second Sophistic reveal strong undercurrents of continuity in conceptualizing the cult hero. Still, the traditions of hero cult were never fully spelled out in the classical period of Greek civilization. Only in the era of the Second Sophistic do these traditions—and the charismatic heroes who populate them—become manifest. Philostratus's *Heroikos*, this masterpiece of

[49] On this context of οἶκος, see Nagy, *Pindar's Homer*, 269.
[50] See Nagy, *Greek Mythology and Poetics*, 231.

Second Sophistic, is not only the best literary source for understanding the ancient concept of the cult hero in Greek civilization. It is the only work of literature where the overall concept of the ancient Greek hero—in its religious as well as literary dimensions—is given a chance to reveal itself in all its wondrous splendor. Philostratus's *Heroikos* is the perfect literary initiation into a full understanding of what it really is to be a hero in the ancient Greek world.

Apollonius of Tyana, Hero and Holy Man*

Christopher Jones

The Greek world under Roman rule teemed with strange people, both living and dead. Thus a certain Epicrates of Nakrason in Mysia, probably in the first century of our era, set aside lands in order to build and maintain the monument (μνημεῖον) of his deceased son, the "hero Daiphantos." He was motivated "not only by my affectionate feeling towards my child, but by the fact that the hero often visited me in dreams, signs and visions."[1] In the next century, Alexandra, a priestess of Demeter at Miletos, consulted Apollo of Didyma about mysterious occurrences during her tenure: "The gods have never been so visible by means of apparitions (ἐπιστάσεις), sometimes by means of virgins and women, sometimes through men and boys: why is this, and is it a good sign?"[2] In the same century, the same god received an enquiry from the citizens of Pergamum: "Where was it permitted (ὅσιον) to bury the heroes Marcellus and Rufinus, because of the virtue they had shown in their past life?" (Rufinus was a Roman consular and a benefactor of the city, the builder of the well-known temple of Zeus Asclepius in the Asclepieion).[3]

* I presented a preliminary version of this essay at the conference "Philostratus's *Heroikos*, Religion, and Cultural Identity"; I am grateful to the organizers of the conference for inviting me, and to all attending the conference who improved this paper by their comments. References to Philostratus's *Life of Apollonius* are made by book and chapter of the *editio minor* of C. L. Kayser (*Flavii Philostrati Opera* [2 vols.; Leipzig: Teubner, 1870–1871]), followed by Kayser's page and line numbers (K). Research on this paper has been greatly facilitated by use of the *TLG*, CD-ROM #E (1999).

[1] Peter Herrmann and Kemal Ziya Polatkan, *Das Testament des Epikrates und andere neue Inschriften aus dem Museum von Manisa* (SÖAW 265.1; Vienna: Böhlau, 1969), 7–36. Jeanne Robert and Louis Robert, "Bulletin épigraphique," *REG* 83 (1970): 438–41 no. 512.

[2] Albert Rehm, *Die Inschriften* (vol. 2 of *Didyma*; ed. Theodor Wiegand; Berlin: Mann, 1958), no. 496. Louis Robert, "Addenda aux Tomes I–X," *Hell* 11/12 (1960): 543–46. Robin Lane Fox, *Pagans and Christians* (New York: Knopf, 1987), 102–3.

[3] Christian Habicht, *Die Inschriften des Asklepieions* (Altertümer von Pergamon 8.3; Berlin: de Gruyter, 1969), no. 2.

There was therefore a wide range of possible relationships between ordinary mortals and extraordinary beings such as holy men, heroes, δαίμονες, not to mention lesser and greater gods. Correspondingly, there were many ways of negotiating these relationships. There were of course always oracles—more and more in fact, as the traditional sites such as Delphi received increasing competition from others such as Lebadeia, Didyma, Claros, Mallos, Abônuteichos. Rather than going to the trouble and expense of consulting one of these traditional sites, you could turn to some local source. This might be a legendary hero such as Protesilaos at Elaious, or a recently deceased member of your own community, such as the respectable citizen Neryllinus of Alexandria in the Troad.[4] For retail services, especially ones involving not merely prediction but power over the future, there was always the ready recourse of magic, though that carried manifold risks, not merely from failure of the experiment (as for Apuleius's Lucius), but also from the law.[5]

It is hardly surprising, then, that it was often a pressing question how to categorize those persons, living or dead, who somehow stood outside the mortal sphere. Was someone who could foretell the future an impostor (γόης) or a man in touch with the divine (θεῖος ἀνήρ)? Is my deceased son actually a hero, and should I follow his orders issued from the other world, or is this merely the delusion of a grieving parent? And what about figures of the past? Is it true that a statue of the Corinthian general Pellichos can step down from its pedestal and walk around my neighbor's house at night (Lucian *The Lover of Lies, or The Doubter* 18–20)? Is it true that Plato was mysteriously fathered by Apollo, or is that just a fantasy of the Platonists (Plutarch *Table-Talk* 717d–718b)?

Philosophers in fact caused particular difficulties of classification, since their mode of life and their devotion to knowledge seemed often to place them above the normal level and in close contact with the divine. As we have seen, the Platonists nourished legends of the master's divine birth, and observed his birthday with especial reverence. But, surprising as it at first seems, Epicurus too received very similar cult from his followers, as Lucretius attests:

[4] Christopher P. Jones, "Neryllinus," *CP* 80 (1985): 40–45. Marijana Ricl, *The Inscriptions of Alexandreia Troas* (Inschriften griechischer Städte aus Kleinasien 53; Bonn: Habelt, 1997), no. 22 and T 144.

[5] Note Philostratus's hostile remarks about contemporary magic, *Life of Apollonius* 7.39 (292.23–293.26 K).

deus ille fuit, deus, inclute Memmi ("a god he was, a god, illustrious Memmius"; *On the Nature of Things* 5.8).[6] Pythagoreans were famous for their reverence towards "the master," and even Lucian, when called upon to say something unkind about him, still feels it wise to ask his forgiveness and to describe him as "a wise man of divine intellect" (σοφὸς ἀνὴρ καὶ τὴν γνώμην θεσπέσιος, *Alexander the False Prophet* 4).

One Pythagorean of the first century of our era, perhaps the most important after the founder, was to cause great problems of classification. This is Apollonius from the considerable city of Tyana in southern Cappadocia, whose works included a *Life of Pythagoras*.[7] For Apollonius's own reputation we do not have much to go on before the second quarter of the third century, when Philostratus of Athens produced his massive biography. Enough survives from before Philostratus, however, to show that the question of classifying Apollonius was already under intense debate. It is not clear whether the Moiragenês whose work Philostratus so contemptuously dismisses was favorable to his subject, though it seems likely that he was.[8] The Maximus who wrote about the young Apollonius's stay in Cilician Aigeae was certainly favorable, and as master of the emperor's correspondence he must have been a person of high standing (Philostratus *Life of Apollonius* 1.3; 1.12 [4.7–9; 11.28–30 K]; *FGrH* 1066).

The turning point for Apollonius's reputation appears to have come through someone even more highly placed in imperial society, that is, Julia Domna, the widow of Septimius Severus and the mother of his successor, Caracalla. Philostratus claims to have been on close terms with Domna and a member of what he calls her "circle." She urged him to write the *Life of Apollonius* and supplied him with hitherto unknown materials in the form of the notebooks of Damis, a kind of Sancho Panza to Apollonius.[9] (This is not the place to enter into the debate over the authenticity of these materi-

[6] Diskin Clay, "The Cults of Epicurus," *Cronache Ercolanesi* 16 (1986): 11–28.

[7] *Suda* A 3420 = *FGrH* 1064 T 9, F 1, 2. All *FGrH* references are to *Biography: Imperial and Undated Authors* (ed. J. Radicke; *FGrH* Part 4 A, fasc. 7; Leiden: Brill, 1999). I am not persuaded by P. Gorman, "The 'Apollonius' of the Neoplatonic Biographies of Pythagoras," *Mnemosyne* 38 (1985): 130–44.

[8] D. H. Raynor, "Moeragenes and Philostratus: Two Views of Apollonius of Tyana," *CQ* 34 (1984): 222–26. *FGrH* 1067.

[9] Circle of Domna and materials of Damis: *Life of Apollonius* 1.2 (3.27–4.7 K) = *FGrH* 1065 T 1. On Damis see *FGrH* pages 162–63.

als, though I incline to believe that they existed only in Philostratus's vivid imagination.)

The influence of Domna seems to have induced Caracalla to become a devotee of Apollonius, or at least to show him extraordinary honor. He built a sanctuary (ἡρῷον) in his honor in Tyana, situating it near the meadow in which Apollonius had been born.[10] Caracalla and his mother passed jointly through Tyana on their way to the East in 215 C.E., and this may be when the emperor determined to honor the city's most famous son.[11]

Though Philostratus received his materials from Julia Domna, and so before 217 C.E., he published the *Life of Apollonius* after her death, probably during the reign of Alexander Severus, who came to the throne in 222 C.E. Why Philostratus persisted with the project after the death of his patroness it is impossible to say: perhaps he continued to receive imperial support since, if we can believe the *Augustan History* (SHA), Alexander Severus kept a statue of Apollonius in his private chapel, together with those of Christ, Abraham, and Orpheus (SHA *Alexander Severus* 29.2; *FGrH* 1064 T 10).

Whatever his motives, Philostratus consistently represents Apollonius as "divine" (θεῖος), though he does so with caution, usually making characters in the work use the adjective rather than expressing his own opinion.[12] Thus when he first introduces Apollonius in the *Life* he says that "he approached wisdom more divinely [θειότερον] than Pythagoras" (*Life of Apollonius* 1.2 [2.17–18 K]). Soon after, he states his intention of describing "the ways of his wisdom, through which [ways] he came close to being considered divine and supernatural" (τοῖς τε τῆς σοφίας τρόποις, ὑφ' ὧν ἔψαυσε τοῦ δαιμόνιός τε καὶ θεῖος νομισθῆναι). The more enlightened characters in the work address or speak of Apollonius as divine: thus the "Median" king Vardanês, the Indian king Phraôtês, the chief gymnosophist Iarchas (*Life of Apollonius* 1.21; 2.40; 3.28 [22.24–25; 82.29–30; 106.3 K]). The Roman emperor Vespasian

[10] Dio Cassius *Roman History* 78.18.4 (*FGrH* 1064 T 5), presumably the same as the ἱερόν mentioned by Philostratus in *Life of Apollonius* 1.5 (5.3–5 K), and see further below.

[11] Helmut Halfmann, *Itinera principum: Geschichte und Typologie der Kaiserreisen im Römischen Reich* (Stuttgart: Steiner, 1986), 224, 227–29.

[12] For a recent discussion of Apollonius as θεῖος ἀνήρ, reaching some of the same conclusions, see David S. du Toit, *Theios Anthropos: Zur Verwendung von "theios anthrôpos" und sinnverwandten Ausdrücken in der Literatur der Kaiserzeit* (Tübingen: Mohr Siebeck, 1997), 276–320.

also tells Apollonius that he will think everything that issues from him divine (*Life of Apollonius* 5.36 [196.10–11 K]). For his part, Apollonius refers to others as divine: Pythagoras, Socrates, Iarchas, and the gymnosophists in general, and even (when speaking before Domitian) Vespasian (*Life of Apollonius* 8.7.4; 6.19; 6.3; 7.14; 8.7.3 [307.21; 232.12; 207.2; 267.60; 306.16 K]).

Lesser beings, however, have to be persuaded of Apollonius's "divinity" by miracles. An unsympathetic centurion promises to consider him divine if he deters the man from cutting off the sage's head (*Life of Apollonius* 7.21 [275.28–32 K]); Damis only realizes his divinity when he miraculously removes his chains (*Life of Apollonius* 7.38 [292.18–20 K]), and the Greeks in general think him divine after his acquittal by Domitian (*Life of Apollonius* 8.15 [332.26–28 K]).

In several places, Philostratus links "divinity" with "wisdom" (σοφία), and especially prophetic wisdom, which he sees as a gift granted only to those who practice the greatest purity of body and soul, and this is perhaps the most persistent thread in his presentation of Apollonius as "divine" (*Life of Apollonius* 2.29; 2.37; 3.42 [71.3; 79.1–4; 117.1–18 K]). At the same time, there are hints of an even higher exaltation. The gymnosophists predict that Apollonius will "seem a god not only after death, but in his lifetime too" (*Life of Apollonius* 3.50 [121.13–14 K]). In his trial before Domitian he is accused of receiving obeisance like a god (*Life of Apollonius* 7.20; 7.21 [274.6; 275.21–23 K]); the emperor further accuses him of considering certain of his own enemies gods, but Apollonius replies that he considers only the Indians Iarchas and Phraôtês "worthy of the title" (*Life of Apollonius* 7.33 [287.7–11 K]). But the boundary between "seeming divine" and "seeming a god" is perilously narrow, and these last passages probably should not be taken to imply that Apollonius was worshiped as a god in his own lifetime, at least in public cult: of course private individuals had great freedom to declare other humans their personal gods.[13] In sum, Philostratus's Apollonius is regarded as "divine" (θεῖος) by others, and to some extent by the author himself, because of his love of wisdom and the ascetic lifestyle which made his senses especially susceptible to the future: he is not however presented as more than

[13] Arthur Darby Nock, "Notes on Ruler-Cult," in *Essays on Religion and the Ancient World* (ed. Zeph Stewart; 2 vols.; Oxford: Clarendon, 1972), 1:144–45; repr. from *JHS* 48 (1928).

fully human, as a demigod (ἡμίθεος), a hero (ἥρως), or a god in human disguise.

On the subject of Apollonius's final disappearance, the author is especially cautious. He reports several versions about Apollonius's end, "if he had an end" (εἴγε ἐτελεύτα, *Life of Apollonius* 8.29 [341.13 K]), a phrase which evoked a memorable poem of Cavafy. One of these versions involves his "end" in Ephesus, while two others involve disappearances inside temples; Philostratus clearly favors the second of these, in which Apollonius vanishes into the temple of Diktynna in Crete (*Life of Apollonius* 8.30 [341.25–342.24 K]). Such disappearances of course have a long history in many cultures: Plutarch has an interesting meditation on the subject in connection with the disappearance of Romulus, citing two famous earlier examples, Aristeas of Prokonnêsos and Kleomêdês of Astypalaia (*Romulus* 28).

While Philostratus does not fully endorse any of these versions, he insists that he had never come across either a real tomb of Apollonius or a cenotaph (ψευδοτάφιον), though he had traveled through most of the known world. There was however a sanctuary in his honor at Tyana (ἱερόν) erected at imperial expense, "since kings have thought him worthy of the honors granted to themselves" (*Life of Apollonius* 8.31 [344.1–6 K]). In addition, Philostratus expresses no doubt about a story, which in fact he may have invented, that the late Apollonius appeared to a young student at Tyana in his sleep. The student had been praying in vain to Apollonius to reassure him about the immortality of the soul, and the philosophic *revenant* duly gave him a disquisition couched in eight hexameter lines, a virtual oracle (*Life of Apollonius* 8.31 [342.30–343.29 K]). Just as this dream recalls the dream of Apollonius's mother at the beginning of the work, so Philostratus finally leaves it open exactly how he classifies his subject—never saying in his own person that Apollonius was "divine," nor affirming positively that he disappeared in the fashion of an Aristeas or a Kleomêdês, though strongly suggesting that he did.

Whatever the views about Apollonius's true nature that had prevailed before Philostratus, we can be certain that an exact contemporary held one diametrically opposite to his. The historian Cassius Dio, who as a senator and consular was more highly placed in Severan society than Philostratus, mentions Apollonius twice in his *Roman History*. Once he does so merely as "a certain Apollonius of Tyana," who witnessed the assassination of Domitian by a sort of second sight, a story also told by Philostratus (*Roman History* 67.18.1). In the other, Dio criticizes Caracalla for his devotion to "magicians and impostors" (μάγοι καὶ γόητες), including Apollonius of Tyana, for whom he built what Dio calls a ἡρῷον (*Roman History* 78.18.4; *FGrH* 1064 T 2, 5). Exactly what does Dio mean by ἡρῷον? Did Caracalla in fact revere Apollonius as a hero? What would follow if he did? Why does Philostratus never apply the term to Apollonius, though heroes form the entire subject of another of his works?

To answer these questions fully would require a long excursion into the implications of the word "hero" in the Roman Empire. In brief, there are now several kinds of heroes. There are what we can call "legendary" or "mythical" heroes of the type of Protesilaos or Hektor, though their worshipers would not have considered them mythical. These had sanctuaries (ἱερά) and issued oracles (χρησμοί), much as Philostratus describes Apollonius doing.[14] But there are also what we may call "social" heroes, that is, persons who lived in historical time, and received honors after their deaths from their families or fellow-citizens. These are found already in the classical period; Thucydides has given a fine description of the heroization of Brasidas at Amphipolis in Thrace (*Peloponnesian War* 5.11.1). However, such social heroes are especially frequent in the Greek portion of the Roman Empire. They may be buried in a public space, such as an agora or a gymnasium, though also in a private tomb, and such burial places are regularly called ἡρῷα. After the Hellenistic period, there seems no evidence for such social heroes receiving priests or other manifestations of public cult, or for their resting places to be called sanctuaries (ἱερά). Nor do they usually issue oracles or predictions, though they may appear to the living in dreams and visions. Above all, such heroes are typically local: only occasionally do we hear of a single person recognized as a hero in several communities, and this is when his family is allied to families elsewhere.[15] Such social heroes in fact retain a feature in common with local heroes of an older type: to cite Arthur Darby Nock, "Per-

[14] Protesilaos's sanctuary: *Her.* 9.5. Sanctuary of Hektor: *Her.* 19.3–4. Oracles of both heroes: Lucian *Parliament of the Gods* 12, cf. *Her.* 15.3; 15.6.

[15] Hero in several communities: thus Titus Statilius Lamprias of Epidaurus: F. Hiller von Gaertringen, *Inscriptiones Epidauri* (*IG* 4.1; Berlin: de Gruyter, 1929), nos. 82–86; for a revised text of no. 86, see SEG 35, no. 305; on the chronology, see A. S. Spawforth, "Families at Roman Sparta and Epidauros: Some Prosopographical Notes," *Annual of the British School at Athens* 80 (1985): 251–54.

haps the one constant element in the use of the term 'hero' is that the figures so designated are not of national or universal significance."[16]

By contrast, "divine men" or occasionally "divine women" also have their antecedents in the classical period—Pythagoras or Empedocles for example—but they too continue to flourish under the Roman Empire, though as a much rarer type than heroes and heroines. Several of the men about whom Lucian writes, Peregrinus Prôteus, Alexander of Abônuteichos, even the Cynic Dêmônax, belong in this category. Sometimes we learn about them from inscriptions. Thus the children of a priestess called Ammias at Thyatira in Lydia join with "the initiates of the gods" (οἱ μύσται τῶν θεῶν) to set up an altar beside her tomb. The altar is inscribed with a declaration of Ammias herself: "If anyone wishes to hear the truth, let them make any prayer they wish at the altar, and it will be granted through a vision, by day or night."[17]

The question therefore arises: which of the two was Apollonius, a "hero" as Cassius Dio implies, or a "holy man" as Philostratus does? The testimony of Dio might not seem to weigh much in such a question, since he uses "hero" and ἡρῷον for the deified emperors, when we know that in fact they were never so called. During their lifetimes, they may be called "most divine" (θειότατος): in their lifetimes they may also be called "gods" (θεοί), and are always gods after their death and consecration. Dio's departure from normal usage in this case may reflect his discomfort about the divinization of rulers, a feeling he shares with other imperial writers such as Plutarch.[18]

In the case of Apollonius, I incline to believe that both Dio and

[16] Arthur Darby Nock, "The Cult of Heroes," in *Essays on Religion and the Ancient World* (ed. Zeph Stewart; 2 vols.; Oxford: Clarendon, 1972), 2:593–94; repr. from *HTR* 37 (1944).

[17] Louis Robert, *Études anatoliennes: Recherches sur les inscriptions grecques de l'Asie Mineure* (Paris: De Boccard, 1937), 129–33, no. 6; P. Herrmann, *Tituli Lydiae: Regio septentrionalis ad Orientem vergens* (vol. 5.2 of *Tituli Asiae Minoris*; Vienna: Verlag der Österreichischen Akademie der Wissenschaften, 1989), no. 1055, with bibliography.

[18] ἡρῷον of Caesar: Cassius Dio *Roman History* 47.18.4, 19.2; cf. the ἡρῷον of Augustus, Cassius Dio *Roman History* 56.46.3. For Dio's use of ἥρως as an equivalent of the Latin *diuus*, see e.g. *Roman History* 51.20.6 (Julius Caesar), 56.41.9 (Augustus). θειότατος and θεῖος applied to emperors: J. Rougé, "Ὁ ΘΕΙΟΤΑΤΟΣ ΑΥΓΟΥΣΤΟΣ," *RevPhil* 43 (1969): 83–92. Attitudes of Dio and others to divinization: Glen W. Bowersock; "Greek Intellectuals and the Imperial Cult in the Second Century A.D.," in *Studies on the Eastern Roman Empire: Social, Economic and Administrative History, Religion, Historiography* (Goldbach, Germany: Keip,

Philostratus are correct, and that their different choice of words results from their different perspectives. Dio may well be right that Apollonius was worshiped as a hero at Tyana, as for example the great benefactor Rufinus was at Pergamum, and that his cult-place in his native city was a ἡρῷον. Philostratus, however, thinks of Apollonius not from the local point of view, as when Caracalla honored him at Tyana, but in terms of the reverence paid to him more generally as a "divine man." The picture which Maximus gave of the young Apollonius at Aigeae seems already to have reflected this point of view, and by the later third century (again, if we can believe the *Augustan History*) the sage's portrait was set up in many temples. Several such portraits are known or can be inferred. An inscribed block, which was published only in the 1970s, comes from Mopsuestia in Cilicia, and probably dates to the third or fourth century. It served as a lintel over some kind of shrine of Apollonius, and the epigram carved on it was meant to accompany a portrait, which may have been a statue, a bust, or a tondo. The stone is broken at the left-hand end, so that the beginnings of all four lines are lost. Still, enough survives to show that here too Apollonius was not explicitly called either a hero or a god. Rather, he was someone "named after Apollo" who "extinguished the wanderings of men" (ἀνθρώπων ἔσβεσεν ἀμπλακίας) and was sent by heaven (or taken up into heaven) "to drive out the sorrows of mortals" (θνητῶν ἐξελάσειε πόνους). Such a description fits very well a person close to the gods, a θεῖος ἀνήρ. A more recent discovery at Aphrodisias in Caria shows that a tondo portrait of him formed part of a series which also contained portraits of other exceptional humans such as Pythagoras, Pindar, Socrates, Aristotle, and Alexander of Macedon; here the architectural context may have been a Neoplatonic schoolhouse.[19]

Thus Philostratus seems to have ignored the heroic aspect of Apollonius, perhaps considering it too local and confined, and has deliberately emphasized the philosopher's career as one of incessant wandering and spiritual benefaction, much as the epigram from

1994), 293–326; repr. from *Le culte des souverains* (ed. Willem den Boer; Entretiens sur l'Antiquité Classique 19; Geneva: Hardt, 1973).

[19] Portraits at Tyana: *Life of Apollonius* 8.29 (341.22–23 K). In many temples: SHA *Aurelian* 24.5 (*FGrH* 1064 T 11). Inscription of Mopsuestia: SEG 28, no. 1251; *FGrH* 1064 T 6; Dietrich Berger and Johannes Nollé, *Tyana: Archäologisch-historische Untersuchungen zum südwestlichen Kappadokien* (Inschriften griechischer Städte aus Kleinasien 57; Bonn: Habelt, 2000), 420–22, no. 112. Portrait at Aphrodisias: R. R. R. Smith, "Late Roman Philosopher Portraits from Aphrodisias," *JRS* 80 (1990): 141–44.

Mopsuestia does. In the end, certainly, it was Philostratus's view that prevailed, not the hostile one of Apollonius's critics such as Cassius Dio. As several studies have shown, despite the attempt of certain pagans to set him up as a rival to Jesus of Nazareth, and even with the triumph of Christianity, Apollonius's reputation as a beneficent wonder-worker survived remarkably intact.[20] In no small way, it was Philostratus who prepared the way for his passage into the new worlds of Byzantium and Islam; and Byzantium returned the favor by transmitting the *Life of Apollonius* to us.

[20] W. L. Dulière, "Protection permanente contre des animaux nuisibles assurée par Apollonius de Tyane dans Byzance et Antioche: Evolution de son mythe," *ByzZ* 63 (1970): 247–77. W. Speyer, "Zum Bild des Apollonios von Tyana bei Heiden und Christen," *JAC* 17 (1974): 47–63. Maria Dzielska, *Apollonius of Tyana in Legend and History* (Rome: Bretschneider, 1986).

Transferring the Cults of Heroes in Ancient Greece: A Political and Religious Act

Alain Blomart

This essay concerns the introduction of the cults of new or foreign divinities and heroes in the Greco-Roman world.[1] Were some heroes and gods considered "new," not in fact ancient religious figures, rediscovered and revitalized in particular circumstances? It is important to establish the political and cultural context into which a foreign cult and its statue were imported, for instance, Athens, Sparta, or Rome. What were the authorities' reasons for importing new heroic cults or for turning ancestors or forgotten figures into heroes? And why did they transfer their body or relics at the time of an important public ceremony, before establishing a cult to them?

Contemporary and historical examples indicate the political importance of the cult of heroes and of the transfer of heroic (or religious) relics in any period and in any place. In May 2000 American newspapers reported the return of the coffin of the Armenian general Drastamat ("Dro" Kanayan), who had fought for the independence of Armenia, defeating the Turks and saving his nation in 1918. When Armenia was overrun by the Soviets in 1920, Dro sought refuge in Cambridge, Massachusetts, where he died and was buried. Since the breakup of the Soviet Union in 1991, "the Armenian government has embarked on a project to restore the nation's lost heritage and heroes, by repatriating the remains of Dro and others with full honor."[2]

Another recent example comes from France. On 23 November 1996, during the presidency of Jacques Chirac, the writer André

[1] A preliminary version of this research was published in French under the title: "Les manières grecques de déplacer les héros: Modalités religieuses et motivations politiques," in *Héros et héroïnes dans les mythes et les cultes grecs: Actes du colloque organisé à l'Université de Valladolid, 26–29 May 1999* (ed. Vinciane Pirenne-Delforge and Emilio Suárez de la Torre; Kernos suppl. 10; Liège, Belgium: Centre international d'étude de la religion grecque antique, 2000), 351–64.

[2] J. Crittenden, "Armenian Hero Laid to Rest after Journey from Watertown," *Boston Herald,* 29 May 2000. I would like to thank Jennifer K. Berenson Maclean for this reference.

Malraux, who had died twenty years previously, was consecrated as a national hero, and his ashes were transferred to the Pantheon in Paris. Malraux had participated in the government of Charles de Gaulle and was an ideal symbol for Chirac, anxious to improve his image during a time of internal political conflict.

Many other examples can be mentioned. On 15 December 1840, the ashes of the Emperor Napoleon were brought back from the island of Saint Helena to the Invalides in Paris on the orders of King Louis-Philippe, who like Chirac was keen to increase his popularity at a time of political unrest.[3]

Additional examples date from the Middle Ages. La Sainte Chapelle was built in Paris by King Louis IX in 1246 to house the relics of the Passion of Christ inside the city's Royal Palace. This was a political act aimed at affirming the primacy of the French nation.

In 1035 a church in Waltham in Great Britain was built by Tovi the Proud as a result of the transfer of a religious relic. Tovi was a Danish nobleman dependent on King Cnut the Great, whose empire included all the southern part of England. Tovi transferred a crucifix from the hill Montacute (in Somerset, in the southwest of Great Britain)—where it was found—to Waltham, thirty miles away from London, in the center of the British part of Cnut's empire. This transfer of relics was a clear transfer of power.[4]

My aim is to show that the creation and the transfer of the cults of heroes in antiquity worked in the same way. The body or the relics of heroes were considered to have a special power to protect the place or the city that hosted them. This is why many Greek cities claimed the possession of one and the same hero: as we know, it is common to find various tombs of the same hero in many different places in Greece. There were many cults of heroes in Greece and many different contexts for their creation or their introduction. To date, no systematic study has classified these different contexts, particularly the context of war. My essay will try to fill this gap and thus has three goals:

[3] A. Moreau, "Le retour des cendres: Oreste et Thésée, deux cadavres au service de la propagande politique," in *Mythe et politique: Acts du colloque de Liège, 14–16 septembre 1989* (ed. François Jouan and André Motte; Paris: Société d'édition "Les Belles Lettres," 1990), 209–18.

[4] J.-Cl. Schmitt, "Translation d'image et transfert de pouvoir. Le crucifix de pierre de Waltham (Angleterre, XIe–XIIIe siècle)," *Bulletin de l'institut historique belge de Rome* 69 (1999): 245–64.

1. To review several examples of transferring heroic cults. My examples will not be exhaustive, but will focus only on the archaic and classical periods. I aim to emphasize the mechanisms and the reasons for the transfers of these heroic cults.
2. To summarize, compare, and classify the different contexts.
3. To emphasize the features that defined and characterized the creation and transfer of cults among the Greeks. To this end, I will compare the Greek ways of transferring heroic cults with those of the Roman world and the ritual of the *evocatio*, which I have studied in depth in other articles.[5]

I. THE TRANSFER OF HEROIC CULTS IN ARCHAIC AND CLASSICAL GREECE

First I shall briefly analyze some well-known examples from the archaic period. Let us begin with Solon. The Athenians had tried in vain to take the island of Salamis in the years 636–632 B.C.E. About thirty years later, Solon also attempted to seize the island, which was under the domination of the Megarians. Following the advice of the oracle of Delphi, Solon went to the island at night and made a secret sacrifice to the heroes who protected the island, that is, to Periphêmos and Kykhreus (Plutarch *Solon* 9).[6] The main elements of this episode can be summarized as follows: Solon went to the place to be conquered and summoned the heroes that protected it, but he did not transfer the relics or the statues to Athens, as became common practice later on.

The second example concerns the island of Aegina, which also interested the Athenians. From the end of the sixth century B.C.E.

[5] Alain Blomart, "Die *evocatio* und der Transfer 'fremder' Götter von der Peripherie nach Rom," in *Römische Reichsreligion und Provinzialreligion* (ed. Hubert Cancik and Jörg Rüpke; Tübingen: Mohr Siebeck 1997), 99–111; "Evocatio," *RGG* 2:1750; "Devotio," *RGG* 2:775.

[6] See Mario Manfredini and Luigi Piccirilli, *La vita di Solone* (Milan: Mondadori, 1977), 134 (on Periphêmos and Kykhreus); Luigi Piccirilli, "Solone e la guerra per Salamina," *Annali della Scuola Normale Superiore di Pisa, Cl. di Lettere e Filosofia* 8.1 (1978): 11 (on the chronology of the conquest of Salamis); E. Kearns, *Heroes of Attica* (London: University of London, 1989), 46–47; on the political context, see Louise-Marie L'Homme-Wéry, *La perspective éleusinienne dans la politique de Solon* (Geneva: Droz, 1996), and Louise-Marie L'Homme-Wéry, "Les héros de Salamine en Attique: Cultes, mythes et intégration politique," in Pirenne-Delforge and Suárez de la Torre, *Héros et héroïnes*, 333–49 (esp. 338–39).

onward, there were several disputes and clashes between Aegina and Athens. The history of this rivalry is well known. I would simply emphasize the fact that by the beginning of the fifth century the Athenians had been unable to subdue the island by military means; as a result they offered religious honors to the protecting hero of the island, giving the hero Aiakos a new shrine on the agora.[7] In this case a hero who was the protector of an island that the Athenians coveted was honored by the construction of a sanctuary in Athens itself.[8]

A third example is the transfer of a hero's relics from the conquered land to Athens. The bones of Theseus were allegedly transferred to Athens in 476/5 B.C.E. after being discovered on the island of Skyros, a strategic outpost between Athens and her colonies of Thrace.[9] It was Cimon who decided to transfer these relics to the agora of Athens, with processions and sacrifices. The political reasons for this are well known: Cimon wanted to justify the colonization of Skyros and to reinforce Athenian imperialism in the Aegean Sea; it was also an important political coup in the fight for supremacy with his rival Themistocles.[10] Pausanias accounted for this transfer as follows: possessing the relics of Theseus was the only way to take Skyros, which was protected by their sacred power (*Description of Greece* 1.17.6 and 3.3.7).[11]

[7] It was the oracle of Delphi that advised the Athenians not to attack Aegina for thirty years and to build a shrine to Aiakos (Αἰακῷ τέμενος ἀποδέξαντας); the Athenians did not make any truce and the war went on until the submission of Aegina in 457 B.C.E., but the shrine (τέμενος) was built. On the oracle and the transfer of Aiakos and the Aiakidai, see Herodotus *Hist.* 5.89; 8.64; see also Friedrich Pfister, *Der Reliquienkult im Altertum* (2 vols.; Giessen: Töpelmann, 1909–1912), 2:462; N. G. L. Hammond, "The War between Athens and Aegina circa 505–481," *Historia* 4 (1955): 406–9; W. G. Forrest, "Oracles in Herodotus," *Classical Review* NS 8 (1958): 123, on the date of the oracle; Kearns (*Heroes of Attica*, 47) compares this event with a Roman *evocatio*. On the war between Aegina and Athens, see Thucydides *Peloponnesian War* 1.108.4; Diodorus Siculus *Library* 11.78.3–4; see also Thomas J. Figueira, "The Chronology of the Conflict between Athens and Aegina in Herodotus Bk. 6," *Quaderni urbinati di cultura classica* 28 (1988): 49–89, and his *Athens and Aigina in the Age of Imperial Colonization* (Baltimore: Johns Hopkins University Press, 1991), 104–14.

[8] Moreover, the kind of monument dedicated to Aiakos (a tomb, which was also an altar) is kept secret by the Aeginetans, just like the name of the protecting divinity in the Roman world (Pausanias *Description of Greece* 2.29.8).

[9] Edouard Will, *Le monde grec et l'Orient* (vol. 1 of *Le Vè siècle [510–403]*; Paris: Presses universitaires de France, 1972), 136; Moreau, "Le retour des cendres," 217.

[10] A. J. Podlecki, "Cimon, Skyros, and 'Theseus' Bones,'" *JHS* 91 (1971): 141–43.

[11] For other explanations, see Thucydides *Peloponnesian War* 1.98.2 (conquest of Skyros); Nepos *Cimon* 2.5; Diodorus Siculus *Library* 4.62.4; 11.60.2 (regret of

Let us turn now to another context: the transfer of the relics of the enemy's hero to the place to be conquered. This was the case of Rhêsos in 437 B.C.E. After several failed attempts to colonize Thrace at the beginning of the fifth century,[12] the oracle advised the Athenians to go to Troy to fetch the bones of Rhêsos, the mythical king of the Thracians, who had fought there (Homer *Il.* 10.465–502; Euripides *Rhesus* 665–680).[13] The Athenian general Hagnôn founded Amphipolis allegedly thanks to the power of the hero's relics. He then built a monument to Rhêsos[14] as well as a temple to his mother Clio, one of the Muses.[15]

Another example of an enemy hero whose relics were used to protect the Athenians is found in the myth of Eurystheus. The Herakleidai, in the tragedy of the same name—written by Euripides in 430 B.C.E.—are pursued by Eurystheus, king of Argos, and seek refuge in Attica. The Athenian king Dêmophôn takes them under his protection, leads the struggle against Eurystheus, and defeats him. At the end of the tragedy, Eurystheus asks the Athe-

---

the Athenians who had banned their national hero); Plutarch *Cimon* 8; *Theseus* 35.8–36.3 (ghost of Theseus appearing to the Athenian soldiers at Marathon); Aelius Aristides *In Defense of the Four* 561 and 688 Dindorf (famine). See Pfister, *Der Reliquienkult im Altertum*, 1:198–204 and 440; A. Mastrocinque, "Gli dei protettori della città," in *Religione e politica nel mondo antico* (ed. Marta Sordi; Milan: Vita e pensiero, 1981), 10–11; J. Von Ungern-Sternberg, "Das Grab des Theseus und andere Gräber," in *Antike in der Moderne* (ed. Wolfgang Schuller; Xenia 15; Konstanz: Universitätsverlag Konstanz, 1986), 321–29; Claude Calame, *Thésée et l'imaginaire athénien: Légende et culte en Grèce antique* (Lausanne: Editions Payot, 1990), 265–66 and 430–31; Robert Parker, *Athenian Religion: A History* (Oxford: Clarendon, 1996), 168–70.

[12] Catharine C. Lorber, *Amphipolis: The Civic Coinage in Silver and Gold* (Los Angeles: Numismatic Fine Arts International, 1990), 1–14; C. Pelekidis, "Les Grecs en Thrace: Les premiers rapports entre les Grecs et les Thraces," in *La Thrace* (ed. V. Papoulia et al.; Athens: n.p., 1994), 98–114.

[13] See Mastrocinque, "Gli dei prottetori della città," 12.

[14] Schol. Aeschines 34 Dindorf; Euripides *Rhesus* 279–280; Schol. Euripides *Rhesus* 347; Thucydides *Peloponnesian War* 4.102; Diodorus Siculus *Library* 12.68.2; Polyaenus *Strategica* 6.53. See D. Asheri, "Studio sulla storia della colonizzazione di Anfipoli sino alla conquista macedone," *Rivista di filologia e d'istruzione classica* 95 (1967): 5–30 (history); Wolfgang Leschhorn, *Gründer der Stadt: Studien zu einem politisch-religiösen Phänomen der griechischen Geschichte* (Stuttgart: Steiner, 1984), 148–56; Irad Malkin, *Religion and Colonization in Ancient Greece* (Leiden: Brill, 1987), 81–84.

[15] The myth and the cult of Rhêsos were invented by analogy with Orpheus and Protesilaos: Philippe Borgeaud, "Rhésos et Arganthoné," in *Orphisme et Orphée: En l'honneur de Jean Rudhardt* (ed. Philippe Borgeaud; Geneva: Droz, 1991), 51–59.

nians to bury him in Attica,[16] in order to protect Athens against the Spartan attacks.[17]

The example of Oedipus is similar. In Sophocles' *Oedipus at Colonus*, performed for the first time in 401 B.C.E, the hero asks to be buried in Athens, where he is a foreigner, rather than in Thebes, whence he had been banished. As in the example of Eurystheus, Oedipus announces that his relic will be beneficial to Athens.[18]

Thus far, all the examples have referred to Athens. Let us look now at two examples from Sparta. The first is very well known: the transfer of the relics of Orestes, exemplifying the return of an indigenous hero from abroad to his original city. Around 550 B.C.E., on the advice of the Delphic oracle, the Spartans went to Tegea in Arcadia and took the bones of Orestes, which were preserved in that city: this was a famous topic in antiquity, still mentioned in Philostratus's *Heroikos*.[19] According to the ancient authors, the transfer of Orestes' bones was the only way to defeat the Tegeans.[20] This act corresponded with a change in Spartan foreign politics and with the beginning of the Peloponnesian League. Rather than seeking total conquest of the Peloponnesus, from then on Sparta formed alliances with the other cities on the basis of a common hero. There were also domestic reasons for the return of Orestes' relics to Sparta. First, the absence of his cult was felt as a lack, given that the

[16] In Pallênê or Trikorythos or also in Megaris according to different versions mentioned by Kearns, *Heroes of Attica*, 49.

[17] The different locations suggested for the tomb of Eurystheus are all located at places of strategic importance in case of invasion: Euripides *Children of Herakles* 1026–1044. See Marie Delcourt, *Légendes et cultes de héros en Grèce* (Paris: Presses universitaires de France 1942), 50; A.-J. Festugière, "Tragédie et tombes sacrées," in *Études d'histoire et de philologie* (Paris: Vrin, 1975), 22–23.

[18] Oedipus has two sanctuaries in Athens: a tomb on the Areopagus and a *hêrôon* in the north of the city, in Kolônos Hippios: Sophocles *Oedipus at Colonus* 72, 92–93, 287–288, 389–390, 459–460, 576–578. See Festugière, "Tragédie et tombes sacrées," 15–20; Eugene Taylor Thompson, "The Relics of the Heroes in Ancient Greece" (Ph.D. diss., University of Washington, 1985), 266 (references on the tomb of Oedipus); Pierre Vidal-Naquet, "Oedipe entre deux cités: Essai sur Oedipe à Colone," in *Mythe et tragédie en Grèce ancienne* (ed. Jean-Pierre Vernant and Pierre Vidal-Naquet; 2 vols.; Paris: Éditions la découverte, 1986), 2:175–211; Kearns, *Heroes of Attica*, 50–51.

[19] For the list of bone finds mentioned by Philostratus (*Heroikos* 8, esp. 8.3 on Orestes) and by other authors, see Jeffrey Rusten, "Living in the Past: Allusive Narratives and Elusive Authorities in the World of *Heroikos*," 143–58, in this volume.

[20] Herodotus *Hist.* 1.67–68; Diodorus Siculus *Library* 9.36.2–3; Pausanias *Description of Greece* 3.3.6; Aelius Aristides *In Defense of the Four* 561–562 Dindorf; Solinus *Collection of Memorable Things* 1.90.

other Pelopides had a cult in Sparta: for instance Menelaos and Helen (in the village of Therapnê) as well as Agamemnon and Cassandra (in Amyklai) from the beginning of the seventh century onward.[21] For the Spartans, Orestes was not a foreign hero, but a local king (Pausanias *Description of Greece* 2.18.6), and we know how important it was for the Spartan kings, alive or dead, to remain in Sparta or to return there: the transfer of the bodies of the kings Leonidas, Agêsilaos, and Agêsipolis bears witness to this. Finally, we know from Herodotus that there were tensions between the aristocracy and the kings Anaximandras and Aristôn about their succession (Herodotus *Hist.* 5.39–41; 6.61);[22] there were also rivalries between the aristocrats themselves in the seventh century. Against this background, Orestes, who did not belong to any aristocratic family in particular, was common to all the Spartans and helped to unify them and resolve the political and social conflicts.[23]

A second Spartan example refers to Teisamenos, the son of Orestes and the king of the Achaeans. The bones of Teisamenos were transferred from Helikê (in Achaea) to Sparta, probably after the return of the relics of Orestes, around 560 B.C.E. This move permitted the Spartans to ally with Helikê, the most important city in Achaea at that time, the city that hosted the pan-Achaean cults of Zeus Homarios and Poseidon Helikonios, and probably also the center of the Achaean federation. So Helikê was strategically important to the Spartans; politically speaking, the transfer of a cult from this city to Sparta was a powerful symbol (Pausanias *Description of Greece* 7.1.8).[24]

[21] According to the most widespread tradition, from the end of the eighth century to the beginning of the fifth century, the dynasty of Agamemnon reigned in Laconia, either in Sparta or Amyklai, and not in the Argolid. See Moreau, "Le retour des cendres," 211. On the different shrines found near Sparta, see Isabelle Ratinaud-Lachkar, "Héros homériques et sanctuaires d'époque géométrique," in Pirenne-Delforge and Suárez de la Torre, *Héros et héroïnes*, 250–53.

[22] As François de Polignac has indicated to me, the account of Herodotus in *Hist.* 6.61, which presents the third spouse of Aristôn as predestined to become the queen, was possibly elaborated during the reign of Aristôn to justify his marriage.

[23] See Moreau, "Le retour des cendres," 209–14; A. Pariente, "Le monument argien des 'Sept contre Thèbes,'" in *Polydipsion Argos: Argos de la fin des palais mycéniens à la constitution de l'Etat classique. Freibourg, Suisse, 7–9 May 1987* (ed. Marcel Piérart; BCH suppl. 22; Paris: De Boccard, 1992), 221 (about the Peloponnesian League); D. Boedeker, "Hero Cult and Politics in Herodotus: The Bones of Orestes," in *Cultural Poetics in Archaic Greece* (ed. Carol Dougherty and Leslie Kurke; Cambridge: Cambridge University Press, 1993), 164–77.

[24] See particularly D. M. Leahy, "The Bones of Tisamenus," *Historia* 4 (1955): 26–38.

II. CLASSIFICATION OF THE TRANSFER OF HEROIC CULTS

These different examples may be classified into three main categories, according to the circumstances and reasons for the transfer of the cult. The first category is the *return of a local hero* to his original city. For ideological reasons, a city's authorities may decide at a specific moment to bring back the body or the relics of a national hero:[25] this transfer is a symbolic indication of political change. This is the case for Theseus, Orestes, and Teisamenos. Two other examples, unrelated to Athens and Sparta, reflect the same kind of motivation. The hero Arkas, whose relics were transferred within Arcadia, from Mainalos to Mantinea, in 422 B.C.E.: this transfer symbolized the political reinforcement and expansion of the city of Mantinea, which sought to establish an Arcadian league independent of Sparta (Pausanias *Description of Greece* 8.9.3–4; 8.36.8).[26] Another example is the case of Aristomenês, whose relics were transferred from Rhodes to Messene in the fourth century. Aristomenês was a "national" hero of Messenia who resisted against the Spartans in the sixth century B.C.E., but two centuries later, more exactly in 371 B.C.E., his relics were transferred to commemorate the Theban victory over the Spartans. This transfer corresponded to the liberation of Messenia from Spartan domination and the foundation of Messene (Pausanias *Description of Greece* 4.14.7; 4.24.3; 4.27.6; 4.32.3–6).[27] The first category of transfers of heroic cults confirms the political and strategic role that was given to the shrines of heroes, as Susan Alcock also notes.[28]

The second category is the *acceptance of a foreign hero* by a city in order to take advantage of his protective power. For instance, the Theban Oedipus and the Argian Eurystheus were foreigners who took refuge in Athens. If the Athenians agreed to bury them within their walls, the foreign heroes agreed in exchange to protect them with their talismanic power.[29] Another example, unrelated to

[25] Besides, the returns of these heroes are important only for the city to which the relics returned—i.e. for Athens, Sparta, Mantinea, and Messene—not for the city to which the hero was exiled and from where his relics came.

[26] See Madeleine Jost, *Sanctuaires et cultes d'Arcadie* (Paris: Vrin, 1985), 549; Boedeker, "Hero Cult and Politics in Herodotus," 171.

[27] See Mastrocinque, "Gli dei prottetori della città," 12–13; L. Lacroix, "Quelques aspects du 'culte des reliques' dans les traditions de la Grèce ancienne," *Bulletin de la classe des Lettres de l'Académie Royale de Belgique* 75 (1989): 80.

[28] Susan E. Alcock, "Material Witness: An Archaeological Context for the *Heroikos*," 159–68 in this volume.

[29] On the hero as a talisman for the city, see especially Angelo Brelich, *Gli eroi greci: Un problema storico-religioso* (Rome: Edizioni dell'Ateneo, 1958); Casey Dué

Athens or to Sparta, is the case of Hektor, whose relics were transferred from the Troad to Thebes, where they helped to rid the city of the plague and to restore prosperity (Pausanias *Description of Greece* 9.18.5; Lycophron *Alexandra* 1204–1205).[30]

The third category is linked to "mythological wars."[31] This kind of transfer consisted in the *appropriation of the power of an enemy's hero* with or without the transfer of relics. The purpose was to deprive the enemy city of the protective power of its hero and thus to conquer it.[32] This was the case of the heroes of Salamis, Periphêmos and Kykhreus. Their sacred power was taken over by Solon the Athenian, who placated them by making a sacrifice and thus conquered the island. In the same way, the Athenians feared that their protecting heroes could be captured by their enemies, who might come and sacrifice to them: note, for instance, the inviolable tombs of Praxithea's daughters that protected Athens (Euripides *Erechtheus* frg. 65A, lines 87–89 Pintaudi).[33] In the case of Aegina, its inhabitants sent the statues of the Aiakidai to help the Thebans in war against the Athenians around 506 B.C.E. A little later, the Athenians failed to recapture the statues of Damia and Auxesia from the inhabitants of Aegina. According to the ancient authors, this is why the Athenians could not take hold of Aegina. Finally, the Athenians built a temple to Aiakos—the hero of Aegina—in Athens in order to gain his protective power. A last example, mentioned above (p. 89), concerned the bones of the Thracian hero Rhêsos that were also transferred in a context of war by the Athenians from Troy to Amphipolis.

The Athenians, however, were not the only ones to use mytho-

---

and Gregory Nagy, "Illuminating the Classics with the Heroes of Philostratus," 49–73 in this volume.

[30] See Ernst A. Schmidt, *Kultübertragungen* (Giessen, Germany: Töpelmann, 1909), 110; Pfister, *Der Reliquienkult im Altertum*, 441. On the talismanic power of relics or images, see Christopher A. Faraone, *Talismans and Trojan Horses: Guardian Statues in Ancient Greek Myth and Ritual* (New York: Oxford University Press, 1992).

[31] This expression is used by Pariente, "Le monument argien," 219.

[32] Giulia Sissa and Marcel Detienne, *La vie quotidienne des dieux grecs* (Paris: Hachette, 1989), 216: "qu'un ennemi en découvre le chemin et y sacrifie le premier, et aussitôt la puissance des protecteurs se voit menacée de détournement" ("If an enemy discovers the way to a city and is the first to sacrifice on this place, there is an immediate threat that the power of its protectors will be appropriated by the enemy").

[33] See Sissa and Detienne, *La vie quotidienne des dieux grecs*, 285–86; Kearns, *Heroes of Attica*, 48. On the heroes Erechtheus and Praxithea, see Jon D. Mikal-

logical wars of this kind. For instance, at the time of the return of the bones of Orestes and Teisamenos, there was fierce rivalry between Sikyôn and Argos. Kleisthenês of Sikyôn deprived the Argian hero Adrastos of his cult in Sikyôn. He also transferred to Sikyôn the relics of the Theban Melanippos, the mythical enemy of Argos who was one of the opponents of the Seven against Thebes. It was probably at the same period that the Argians built a *hêrôon* to the chiefs of the war against Thebes in their agora as a symbol of the military power of Argos.[34] Similar mythological wars are also attested in the Spartan world. For instance, between 555 and 540 B.C.E., at the battle on the river Sagra (in the south of Italy), the Spartans agreed to help the Locrians against Croton and to send them the statues that usually accompanied the Spartan armies (Herodotus *Hist.* 5.75): the statues were transferred by boat to Locri (Diodorus Siculus *Library* 8.32; Justin *Epitome* 20.2.12–14).[35] Another example refers to Alkmênê, the Mycenaean heroine who had fled to Boeotia: her relics were brought back to Sparta at the beginning of the fourth century by the Spartan king Agêsilaos, as the final attempt to reaffirm Spartan domination several years before the beginning of the Theban hegemony (Plutarch *On the Spirit of Socrates* 5).[36]

III. COMPARISON OF GREEK AND ROMAN PRACTICES

A comparison of the main contexts in which cults were transferred in Greece with the practices of Rome will allow us to reach a better definition of Greek practices.

The first defining characteristic of the Greek customs is the transfer of cults of *heroes*, much more than cults of *gods*, as was the case in the Roman world. Generally the Greeks did not take over the statues and the gods of enemy cities as the Romans did. The only exception is Alexander the Great, who often worshiped the gods of enemy cities during his conquests. For instance, before besieging the city of Tyre, he sacrificed to Melqart (under the name of Herakles) as well as to Apollo. Alexander announced that Herakles had appeared to him in a dream and stretched his hand out to

son, *Honor Thy Gods: Popular Religion in Greek Tragedy* (Chapel Hill: University of North Carolina Press, 1991), 32–34.

[34] Pariente, "Le monument argien," 219–21.

[35] See Pritchett, *The Greek State at War*, 16, 21.

[36] See Mastrocinque, "Gli dei prottetori della città," 12.

him from the walls of the city; after his victory, Alexander paid tribute to Herakles with sacrifices, processions, athletic and naval competitions, and other votive offerings. As far as Apollo is concerned, some inhabitants of the city said that the god had appeared to them to announce that he did not agree with what happened in the city and that he preferred to be on the side of Alexander: the inhabitants responded by attaching golden chains to the big statue of Apollo so that the god could not flee. Alexander nevertheless took hold of the city, and the inhabitants thought that the gods had abandoned them and had been taken over by Alexander (Diodorus Siculus *Library* 17.40.2; 17.41.7–8; Curtius *History of Alexander* 4.2.2–3, 17; 4.3.21–22; Plutarch *Alexander* 24.5–7; Arrian *Anabasis* 2.15.7; 2.18.1; 2.24.6). I cannot here study in depth the religious customs of Alexander. In brief, except in the case of this conqueror, generally it was not the gods but the *heroes* who could be taken over by Greek cities. It has already been shown that the hero had a close tie to a territory or a colony of which he was often the protector or the founder.[37] The cult of a hero preserved the prosperity of the city and guaranteed its future, as was the case of the mythical heroes of Troy, Troilos and Laomedôn,[38] and of many other examples, including the cults of Achilles and Protesilaos who protected the region of Troy and the Hellespont, as Philostratus described in the *Heroikos*.[39]

The second characteristic of the Greek practice of transferring

[37] A. Snodgrass, "Les origines du culte des héros dans la Grèce antique," in *La mort: Les morts dans les sociétés anciennes* (ed. Gherardo Gnoli and Jean-Pierre Vernant; Cambridge: Cambridge University Press, 1982), 107–19; A. Schachter, "Policy, Cult, and the Placing of Greek Sanctuaries," in *Le sanctuaire grec* (ed. O. Reverdin and B. Grange; Geneva: Fondation Hardt, 1992), 52–53; Irad Malkin, "Land Ownership, Territorial Possession, Hero Cults, and Scholarly Theory," in *Nomodeiktes: Greek Studies in Honor of Martin Ostwald* (ed. Ralph Mark Rosen and Joseph Farrell; Ann Arbor, Mich.: University of Michigan Press, 1993), 227–31; François Jouan, "Héros d'Euripide et dieux des cités," *Kernos* 11 (1998): 65.

[38] On the death of Troilos, killed by Achilles, see Homer *Il.* 24.257; Schol. Apollodorus 3.151; Apollodorus *Epitome* 3.32. On the entry of the wooden horse and the damage of Laomedôn's tomb, see Proclus *Chrestomathia* 107.8. See Albert Severyns, *Le cycle épique dans l'école d'Aristarque* (Liège, Belgium: Champion, 1928), 305–7, 352–56; C. Bérard, "Récupérer la mort du prince: Héroïsation et formation de la cité," in Gnoli and Vernant, *La mort,* 94.

[39] Philostratus *Her.* 44.5–57.17 (on Achilles) and 1.1–6.6; 9.1–7; 14.4; 16.1, etc. (on Protesilaos). On their cults in the *Heroikos,* see for instance Teresa Mantero, *Ricerche sull'* Heroikos *di Filostrato* (Genoa: University of Genoa, Istituto di Filologia Classica e Medioevale, 1966), 100–119 (Protesilaos) and 126–28 (Achilles); Guy Hedreen, "The Cult of Achilles in the Euxine," *Hesperia* 60/3 (1991): 313–30.

cults is the lack of ritual and juridical elements in comparison with the Roman world. The most revealing Roman custom is the *evocatio*, which included prayers and sacrifices carried out before transferring a god from one place to another. I have shown elsewhere that the *evocatio* was not limited to the cities near Rome[40] nor to foreign gods in a context of war, as was thought at the beginning of the twentieth century.[41] Some literary texts, rarely mentioned, indicate that the *evocatio* was also used in a context of peace and was also applied to Roman gods.[42] It seems to me that it was the *evocatio* that marked the difference between a ritual transfer of statues and a simple capture. According to the Romans, a ritual was necessary to transfer the gods, to ask them for their agreement, and to enter into a contract with them in order to avoid their anger.[43] Moreover, the reasons that cults of conquered cities were only sometimes transferred to Rome were political and legal: if a city was deprived of its status after conquest by the Romans (in accordance with the legal principle of *capitis deminutio*),[44] the gods could not

[40] An inscription found in Turkey suggests that the *evocatio* could be also used far away from Rome and was in fact much more frequent than was thought: see also Macrobius *Saturnalia* 3.9.9–13, who mentions several cities (Fregellae, Gabii, Veii, Fidenae, Carthage, Corinth, etc.) where a *devotio* and consequently also an *evocatio* were used. See A. Blomart, "Die *evocatio* und der Transfer 'fremder' Götter," 99–111; "Evocatio," *RGG* 2:1750; "Devotio," *RGG* 2:775. On the Turkish inscription, see *AE* (1977): no. 816; A. Hall, "New Light on the Capture of Isaura Vetus by P. Servilius Vatia," *Akten des VI internationalen Kongresses für griechische und lateinische Epigraphik, München 1972* (Munich: Beck, 1973), 568–71; J. Le Gall, "Evocatio," in *L'Italie préromaine et la Rome républicaine* (ed. Jacques Heurgon; 2 vols.; Rome: École française de Rome, 1976), 1:519–24.

[41] Georg Wissowa, "Evocatio," PW 6.1 (1907): 1152–53, and Georg Wissowa, *Religion und Kultus der Römer* (2d ed.; Munich: Beck, 1912), 374; Vsevolod Basanoff, *Evocatio: Étude d'un rituel militaire romain* (Paris: Presses universitaires de France, 1947), 196.

[42] *Terminus*: Livy *History of Rome* 1.55 and Servius *Commentary on Virgil's Aeneid* 9.446. *Curiae*: Festus *Glossaria Latina*, s.v. *novae curiae*, 180 L. *Vulcanus*: Vitruvius *On Architecture* 1.7.1. *Dei inferi*: Festus *Glossaria Latina*, s.v. *tauri ludi*, 478 L.

[43] Servius *Commentary on Virgil's Aeneid* 2.351; Macrobius *Saturnalia* 3.9.2. A ritual was also necessary to enter enemy territory (cf. the fetial priests) and to modify the status of a place (cf. rites at the foundation of a colony).

[44] The Roman jurists themselves compared the changed status of a territory with the modified status of a man: Pomponius in *Digesta* 11.7.36, Mommsen: Cum *loca* capta sunt ab hostibus, omnia desinunt religiosa vel sacra esse, *sicut homines* liberi in servitutem perveniunt: quod si ab hac calamitate fuerint liberata, quasi quodam postliminio reversa pristino statui restituuntur ("When places have been conquered by enemies, everything there stops being religious or sacred, just as the free men become slaves: when they are liberated from this calamity, they return to their previous state in accordance with a sort of postliminium").

stay in a territory without juridical status and had to be transferred to Rome.[45]

In contrast, the transfer of a religious power in the Greek world was much less legalistic and ritualized, although there were, of course, Greek prayers in the context of war. For instance, we know the prayer of the Spartan king Archidamos before he took the city of Plataea in 429 B.C.E. It is true that this prayer aims to avoid the anger of the gods and the heroes and to gain their consent, but its purpose was not to ritualize the territory, to make a contract with the gods, or to ask them to change sides. The purpose was to call the gods and the heroes of the land to witness (ἐς ἐπιμαρτυρίαν καὶ θεῶν καὶ ἡρώων τῶν ἐγχωρίων) and to apologize to them:

> Ye gods and heroes who protect the land of Plataea, be our witnesses that we did no wrong in the beginning, but only after the Plataeans first abandoned the oath we all swore did we come against this land, where our fathers, invoking you in their prayers, conquered the Persians, and which you made auspicious for the Hellenes to fight in, and that now also, if we take any measures, we shall be guilty of no wrong; for though we have made them many reasonable proposals we have failed. Grant therefore your consent, that those be punished for the wrong who first began it, and that those obtain their revenge who are seeking to exact it lawfully. (Thucydides *Peloponnesian War* 2.74.2–3 Smith)

Another interesting example is provided by the prayers that the Athenians said to all the gods (εὔχεσθαι τοῖσι θεοῖσι) before the battle of Salamis in 480 B.C.E. They also called to the heroes of Salamis, Ajax and Telamôn, for help (ἐπικαλεῖσθαι).[46] Moreover, the Athe-

[45] We can make a comparison between the Roman public and private law about the notion of transfer of power and assets. The father had the *patria potestas* on his descendants, and if the son disappeared or lost his status (for instance by being under enemies' power), his assets returned (that is to say, were transferred) to the father; he could now make a new testament and ignore his son (Julius Paulus *Ad Sabinum* D 28.2.31). These relationships based on power and transfer of assets can, in my view, be compared with the relationships of domination Rome exerted over the provincial cities.

[46] There is no Greek word equivalent to the Roman *evocare,* except ἐκκαλεῖν used by Plutarch (*Roman Questions* 61), to translate this Roman concept. The other words that mean "praying" (εὔχεσθαι, ἀρᾶσθαι) and "calling up the gods" (ἐπικαλεῖν, παρακαλεῖν, and ἀνακαλεῖν) do not indicate the idea of moving and leaving a place, as is the case for *e-vocare*. παρακαλεῖν and ἐπικαλεῖν are the most frequent words: the first has a general meaning and the second is often used in a context of sacrifice or oath. ἀνακαλεῖν is used especially to mean a magic prayer. On εὔχεσθαι: see, among

nians sent a boat to Aegina to summon Aiakos, the father of Telamôn, and the other sons of Aiakos (Peleus and Phôkos) and to ask for their help (παρακαλεῖσθαι).[47]

In these two examples, the prayer was used to ask for the help of gods in order to achieve victory.[48] It was a deed of humility and not a contract as in the Roman world.

In conclusion, I hope to have shown the differences between the Greek customs and the Roman ones, especially the importance of heroes in Greece for the protection of a territory and the lack of ritual and juridical elements in the Greek way of transferring cults. Another specifically Greek feature was the variety of transfers of heroic cults, which I have classified into three main categories: the return of local heroes, the acceptance of a foreign hero, and the appropriation of the power of an enemy's hero. The only real similarity between the Greek and Roman customs was their political motivation. The Athenians, the Spartans, and the Romans generally transferred gods or heroes as a symbol of their domination of the cult's city of origin. Moreover, the transfer of a cult could have internal motivations. Fetching or bringing back a heroic cult to Athens or Sparta was a way of reaffirming the greatness of the city and of reinforcing its cultural identity.[49]

---

others, Homer *Il.* 3.296; Herodotus *Hist.* 8.64; Thucydides *Peloponnesian War* 3.58. See Leonard Muellner, *The Meaning of Homeric εὔχομαι through Its Formulas* (Innsbrucker Beiträge zur Sprachwissenschaft 13; Innsbruck: Institut für Sprachwissenschaft der Universität Innsbruck, 1976). D. Aubriot-Sévin, *Prière et conceptions religieuses en Grèce ancienne jusqu'à la fin du Ve siècle av. J.-C.* (Lyon: Maison de l'Orient méditerranéen, 1992), 199–253. On ἀρᾶσθαι, see Homer *Il.* 1.35 (Apollo) and 6.115 (the gods); *Od.* 2.135 (Erinys); Sappho frg. 22 Lobel-Page (Aphrodite); see Aubriot-Sévin, *Prière et conceptions religieuses en Grèce ancienne*, 295–401. On ἐπικαλεῖν, see Herodotus *Hist.* 1.199 (Mylitta); 2.39; 3.8 (Dionysos and Aphrodite during an oath); 8.64 (Ajax and Telamôn); Aristophanes *Lysistrata* 1280 (Artemis, Apollo, Dionysos, and Zeus as testimonies); Diodorus Siculus *Library* 5.79.4 (Idomeneus and Meriones). On παρακαλεῖν, see Plato *Laws* 666b (Dionysos); Xenophon *Hellenica* 2.4.17 (Enyalios); Plutarch *Themistocles* 15.2 (Aiakidai); Arrian *Discourses of Epictetus* 3.21.12 (gods). On ἀνακαλεῖν, see, among others, Herodotus *Hist.* 9.90 (gods); Plato *Republic* 394a (Apollo); Sophocles *Women of Trachis* 910 (demon) and *Oedipus at Colonus* 1376 (vengeful divinities).

[47] Herodotus *Hist.* 8.64.83 and 121; Plutarch *Themistocles* 15. See W. Kendrick Pritchett, *The Greek State at War* (5 vols.; Berkeley: University of California Press, 1979), 3:15; Mikalson, *Honor Thy Gods*, 30.

[48] Aubriot-Sévin, *Prière et conceptions religieuses en Grèce ancienne*, 117–18. On the divinities called up before the battle (especially Artemis Agrotera and Ares), see Raoul Lonis, *Guerre et religion en Grèce à l'époque classique: Recherches sur les rites, les dieux, l'idéologie de la victoire* (Paris: Belles Lettres, 1979), 109, 118–20.

[49] I thank François de Polignac for his comments and Mike Maudsley for improving my English text, as well as the Spanish Ministry of Education, which awarded me a research grant at the University of Barcelona.

Jason, Hypsipyle, and New Fire at Lemnos: A Study in Myth and Ritual*

Walter Burkert

History of religion, in its beginnings, had to struggle to emancipate itself from classical mythology as well as from theology and philosophy; when ritual was finally found to be the basic fact in religious tradition, the result was a divorce between classicists, treating mythology as a literary device, on the one hand, and specialists in festivals and rituals and their obscure affiliations and origins on the other.[1] The function of myth in society was studied by anthropolo-

* [*Ed.:* This article was originally published in *Classical Quarterly* NS 20 (1970): 1–16. We thank Oxford University Press for permission to reprint it here. It was also reprinted, with some corrections and additions by the author, in Richard Buxton, ed., *Oxford Readings in Greek Religion* (Oxford and New York: Oxford University Press, 2000), 227–49. To faciliate appreciation of the article, we have added translations where necessary; unless otherwise noted, the translations are our own.]

[1] This paper was read at the Joint Triennial Classical Conference in Oxford, September 1968. The notes cannot aim at completeness of bibliography. The preponderance of ritual as against myth was vigorously stated by W. Robertson Smith (*Lectures on the Religion of the Semites* [Edinburgh: Black, 1889; 3d ed.; London: Black, 1927], ch. 1), pressed further by Jane Harrison: myth "nothing but ritual misunderstood" (*Mythology and Monuments of Ancient Athens* [London: Macmillan, 1890], xxxiii). In Germany, it was the school of Albrecht Dieterich who concentrated on the study of ritual. Thus mythology is conspicuously absent from the indispensable handbooks of Martin P. Nilsson (*Griechische Feste von religioser Bedeutung* [Leipzig: Teubner, 1906] and *Geschichte der griechischen Religion* [2 vols.; Munich: Beck, 1941–1950; 3d ed.; Munich: Beck, 1967–1974], vol. 1) and Ludwig Deubner (*Attische Feste* [Berlin: Keller, 1932]), whereas Ulrich von Wilamowitz-Moellendorff stated that mythology was the creation of poets: "Der Mythos . . . entsteht in der Phantasie des Dichters" (*Der Glaube der Hellenen* [2 vols.; Berlin: Weidemann, 1931–1932], 1:42). Mythology tried to reestablish itself in the trend of phenomenology and C. G. Jung's psychology, largely ignoring ritual: cf. the surveys of Jan de Vries, *Forschungsgeschichte der Mythologie* (Freiburg: Alber, 1961); Karl Kerényi, *Die Eröffnung des Zugangs zum Mythos* (Darmstadt, Germany: Wissenschaftliche Buchgesellschaft, 1967); "die Religionswissenschaft ist vornehmlich Wissenschaft der Mythen" (Karl Kerényi, *Umgang mit Göttlichem* [Göttingen: Vandenhoeck & Ruprecht, 1955], 25).

gists,[2] the interrelation of myth and ritual was stressed by orientalists,[3] but the classicists' response has been mainly negative.[4] It cannot be denied that Greeks often spoke of correspondence of λεγόμενα and δρώμενα ("what is said" and "what is done"),[5] that rituals are usually said to have been instituted "on account of" some mythical event; but it is held that these myths are either "aetiological" inventions and therefore of little interest, or that "well-known types of story" have been superimposed on "simple magical rites and spells" as Joseph Fontenrose concluded from his study of

[2] Bronislaw Malinowski, *Myth in Primitive Psychology* (London: Paul, Trench, Trubner & Co., 1926); Clyde Kluckhohn, "Myths and Rituals: A General Theory," *HTR* 35 (1942): 45–79.

[3] Samuel H. Hooke (editor of *Myth and Ritual* [London: Oxford University Press, 1933]), defining myth as "the spoken part of the ritual," "the story which the ritual enacts" (p. 3); Samuel H. Hooke, *Myth, Ritual, and Kingship* (Oxford: Clarendon, 1958). Theodor H. Gaster, *Thespis: Ritual, Myth, and Drama in the Ancient Near East* (2d ed.; Garden City, N.Y.: Doubleday, 1961). Independently, W. F. Otto, in his *Dionysos: Mythos und Kultus* (Frankfurt am Main: Klostermann, 1934), spoke of "Zusammenfall von Kultus und Mythos" (p. 43 and passim). In fact connections of myth and ritual had been recognized by F. G. Welcker and, in an intuitive and unsystematic manner, by Ulrich von Wilamowitz-Moellendorff ("Der mythische Thiasos aber ist ein Abbild des im festen Kultus gegebenen," in *Euripides Herakles* [3 vols.; Berlin: Weidmann, 1889], 1:85; cf. Ulrich von Wilamowitz-Moellendorff, "Hephaistos," *Nachrichten von der Königliche Gesellschaft der Wissenschaften zu Göttingen. Historisch-philologische Klasse* 3 (1895): 217–45, 234f., on the binding of Hera; repr. in *Kleine Schriften* (5 vols.; Berlin: Academie, 1962–1971), 2:5–35. In the interpretation of Greek tragedy, due attention has been paid to ritual, cf., e.g., E. R. Dodds, *Euripides: Bacchae* (2d ed.; Oxford: Clarendon, 1960), xxv–xxviii.

[4] Nilsson, *Geschichte der griechischen Religion*, 1:14 n. with reference to Malinowski: "für die griechischen Mythen trifft diese Lehre nicht zu"; cf. Bronislaw Malinowski, *Cults, Myths, Oracles, and Politics in Ancient Greece* (Lund: Gleerup, 1951), 10; H. J. Rose, "Myth and Ritual in Classical Civilization," *Mnemosyne* 4th ser. 3 (1950): 281–87; A. N. Marlow, "Myth and Ritual in Early Greece," *BJRL* 43 (1960–1961): 373–402; Joseph Fontenrose, *The Ritual Theory of Myth* (Berkeley: University of California Press, 1966). As a consequence, historians of religion turn away from the Greek, cf. Mircea Eliade, "Schöpfungsmythos und Heilsgeschichte," *Antaios* 9 (1968): 329, stating "daß wir nicht einen einzigen griechischen Mythos in seinem rituellen Zusammenhang kennen."

[5] With regard to mysteries, as Nilsson (cf. n. 4 above) remarks (Galen *On the Use of Parts* 6.14 [3:576 Kühn]); Pausanias *Description of Greece* 1.43.2; 2.37.2; 2.38.2; 9.30.12; cf. Herodotus *Hist.* 2.81; 2.47; 2.51; M. N. H. van den Burg, "ΑΠΟΡΡΗΤΑ ΔΡΩΜΕΝΑ ΟΡΓΙΑ" (diss., Amsterdam, 1939), not because there was nothing similar in non-secret cults, but because only the secrecy required the use of general passive expressions such as λεγόμενα, δρώμενα. Ritual as μίμησις of myth, e.g., Diodorus Siculus *Library* 4.3.3; Stephanus of Byzantium, s.v. Ἄγρα. Cf. Achilles Tatius *The Adventures of Leucippe and Cleitophon* 2.2: τῆς ἑορτῆς πατέρα διηγοῦνται μῦθον.

Python: "The rituals did not enact the myth; the myth did not receive its plot from the rituals."[6]

Still, a formula such as "simple magical rites" should give rise to further thinking. Life is complex beyond imagination, and so is living ritual. Our information about ancient ritual is, for the most part, desperately scanty, but to call it simple may bar understanding from the start; the simplicity may be just due to our perception and description. It is true that we do not usually find Greek myths as a liturgically fixed part of ritual; but this does not preclude the possibility of a ritual origin of myth; and if, in certain cases, there is secondary superimposition of myth on ritual, even the adopted child may have a real father—some distant rite of somehow similar pattern. Only detailed interpretation may turn such possibilities into probability or even certainty. But it is advisable to remember that those combinations and superimpositions and aetiological explanations were made by people with first-hand experience of ancient religion; before discarding them, one should try to understand them.

One of the best-known Greek myths, from Homer's time (*Od.* 12.70) throughout antiquity, is the story of the Argonauts; one incident, the "Lemnian crime" followed by the romance of Jason and Hypsipyle, enjoyed proverbial fame. That it has anything to do with ritual, we learn only through sheer coincidence: the family of the Philostrati were natives of Lemnos, and one of them included details of Lemnian tradition in his dialogue *Heroikos*, written about 215 C.E.[7] The Trojan[8] vinedresser of Elaious who is conversant with the ghost of Protesilaos describes the semi-divine honors allegedly paid to Achilles by the Thessalians long before the Persian war, and he illustrates them by reference to certain Corinthian rites and to a festival of Lemnos; the common characteristic is the combination of propitiation of the dead, ἐναγίσματα, with mystery-rites, τελεστικόν:

[6] Joseph Fontenrose, *Python* (Berkeley: University of California Press, 1959), 461–62, against Hooke (above, n. 3) and Jane E. Harrison who wrote "the myth is the plot of the δρώμενον" (*Themis: A Study of the Social Origins of Greek Religion* [2d ed.; Cambridge: Cambridge University Press, 1927], 331).

[7] On the problem of the Philostrati and the author of the *Heroikos*, Karl Münscher, "Die Philostrate," *Philologus* suppl. 10/4 (1907): 469ff.; Friedrich Solmsen, "Philostratus," PW 20 (1941): 154–59; on the date of the *Heroikos*, Münscher, "Die Philostrate," 474, 497–98, 505; Solmsen, "Philostratus," 154.

[8] [*Ed.:* Burkert rightly omitted "Trojan" in the reprinting of this article in Buxton, *Greek Religion*.]

> ἐπὶ δὲ τῷ ἔργῳ τῷ περὶ τοὺς ἄνδρας ὑπὸ τῶν ἐν Λήμνῳ γυναικῶν ἐξ Ἀφροδίτης ποτὲ πραχθέντι καθαίρεται μὲν ἡ Λῆμνος †καὶ καθ' ἕνα τοῦ ἔτους† καὶ σβέννυται τὸ ἐν αὐτῇ πῦρ ἐς ἡμέρας ἐννέα· θεωρὶς δὲ ναῦς ἐκ Δήλου πυρφορεῖ, κἂν ἀφίκηται πρὸ τῶν ἐναγισμάτων, οὐδαμοῦ τῆς Λήμνου καθορμίζεται, μετέωρος δὲ ἐπισαλεύει τοῖς ἀκρωτηρίοις, ἔς τε ὅσιον τὸ ἐσπλεῦσαι γένηται. θεοὺς γὰρ χθονίους καὶ ἀπορρήτους καλοῦντες τότε καθαρόν, οἶμαι, τὸ πῦρ τὸ ἐν τῇ θαλάττῃ φυλάττουσιν. ἐπειδὰν δὲ ἡ θεωρὶς ἐσπλεύσῃ καὶ νείμωνται τὸ πῦρ ἔς τε τὴν ἄλλην δίαιταν ἔς τε τὰς ἐμπύρους τῶν τεχνῶν, καινοῦ τὸ ἐντεῦθεν βίου φασὶν ἄρχεσθαι.
>
> And the island of Lemnos is purified every year for the deed once done to the men on Lemnos by their wives at Aphrodite's instigation. The fire on Lemnos is extinguished for nine days. A sacred ship from Delos, however, carries the fire, and if it arrives before the offerings for the dead, it puts in nowhere on Lemnos, but rides at anchor off the headlands out at sea until sailing into the harbor is permitted by divine law. For then, while invoking chthonian and ineffable gods, they keep pure, I think, the fire that is out on the sea. Whenever the sacred ship sails in and they distribute the fire both to its new abode and to the forges of the artisans, from that source is the beginning of new life. [*Ed.: Her.* 53.5–7 de Lannoy][9]

It is frustrating that one important detail, the time of the festival, is obscured by corruption. The reading of the majority of the manuscripts, καθ' ἕκαστον ἔτος, is too obvious a correction to be plausible. But the ingenious suggestion of Adolf Wilhelm[10] to read καθ' ἐνάτου ἔτους has to be rejected, too: it introduces an erroneous orthography

[9] Ch. 19 § 20 in the edition of Gottfried Olearius (Leipzig: Thomas Fritsch, 1709; followed by Kayser) = ch. 20 § 24 in the edition of Anton Westermann (Paris: Didot, 1849; followed by Nilsson, *Griechische Feste,* 470) = 2.207 of the Teubner edition (Carl Ludwig Kayser [Leipzig: Teubner, 1870–1871]); critical editions: Jean François Boissonade (Paris: n.p., 1806), 232; Carl Ludwig Kayser (Zürich: Meyer & Zeller, 1844; 2d ed. 1853), 325. καὶ καθ' ἕνα τοῦ ἔτους is found in three codices (γ, φ, ψ) and apparently in a fourth (p) before correction; the printed editions, from the Aldina (1503), dropped the καί at the beginning; Boissonade and Westermann adopted καθ' ἕκαστον ἔτος found in the other manuscripts. Kayser lists 32 codices altogether.

[10] Adolf Wilhelm, "Die Pyrphorie der Lemnier," *Anzeiger der Akademie der Wissenschaften in Wien. Philosophisch-historische Klasse* 76 (1939): 41–46, followed by Marie Delcourt, *Héphaistos ou la légende du magicien* (Paris: Société d'édition "Les Belles Lettres," 1957), 172–73; Nilsson, *Geschichte der griechischen Religion,* 1:97 n. 6. Samson Eitrem ("Philostratea: Ad textum dialogi Heroici adnotationes," *Symbolae Osloenses* 9 [1930]: 60) tried καθαίρονται ἡ Λῆμνος καὶ <οἱ Λήμνιοι> καθ' ἕνα κατ' ἔτος.

of old inscriptions into a literary text of the imperial age, it gives an unattested meaning to κατά with genitive,[11] and it fails to account for the καί; it is as difficult to assume two unrelated corruptions in the same passage as to imagine how the misreading of ἐνάτου should have brought forth the superfluous καί. Looking for other remedies, one could surmise that a masculine substantive, required by καθ' ἕνα, is missing, hiding in that very καί: καιρὸν καθ' ἕνα τοῦ ἔτους—an unusual word-order, modeled on Herodotus's frequent χρόνον ἔπι πολλόν and similar expressions and thus combining archaism with peculiarities of later Greek.[12] Of course it is possible that more serious corruption has occurred; still the traditional emendation καθ' ἕκαστον ἔτος may not be far off the mark as to the content: Achilles received his honors which the Lemnian custom is meant to illustrate, ἀνὰ πᾶν ἔτος too (*Her.* 207.2 Kayser [*ed.: Her.* 52.3 de Lannoy]).

Nilsson, in *Griechische Feste* (p. 470), has Philostratus's account under the heading "festivals of unknown divinities." This is an excess of self-restraint. There is one obvious guess as to which god must have played a prominent role in the fire festival: Lemnos is the island of Hephaistos,[13] the main city is called Hephaistia throughout antiquity, it has the head of Hephaistos on its coins. Incidentally, one Lucius Flavius Philostratus was ἱερεὺς τοῦ ἐπωνύμου τῆς πόλεως Ἡφαίστου ("priest of Hephaistos, the eponymous [god] of the city") in the third century C.E. (*IG* XII 8.27). But Hephaistos is the

[11] κατά c. gen. "down to a certain deadline" in the instances adduced by Wilhelm: a contract κατ' εἴκοσι ἐτῶν, κατὰ βίου, κατὰ τοῦ παντὸς χρόνου. Cf. Wilhelm Schmid, *Der Attizismus in seinem Hauptvertretern von Dionysius von Halikarnass bis auf den zweiten Philostratus* (5 vols.; Stuttgart: Kohlhammer, 1887–1897), 4:456.

[12] Moeris *Atticist*: ὥρα ἔτους Ἀττικοί, καιρὸς ἔτους Ἕλληνες; cf. Schmid, *Der Attizismus*, 4:361. For inversion of word-order, cf. *Her.* 12.2 [*ed.: Her.* 35.9 de Lannoy]: κρατῆρας τοὺς ἐκεῖθεν.

[13] Homer *Il.* 1.593; *Od.* 8.283–284 with schol. and Eustathius 157.28; Apollonius of Rhodes *Argonautica* 1.851–852 with schol.; Nicander *Theriaca* 458 with schol., etc.; cf. Wilamowitz-Moellendorff, "Hephaistos"; C. Fredrich, "Lemnos," *Ath. Mitt.* 31 (1906): 60–86, 241–56; L. Malten, "Hephaistos," *JDAI* 27 (1912): 232–64 and Malten, "Hephaistos," PW 8 (1913): 315–16. Combination with the fire-festival: Friedrich G. Welcker, *Die aeschylische Trilogie: Prometheus und die Kabirenweihe zu Lemnos* (Darmstadt: Leske, 1824), 155–304, esp. 247ff.; Johann J. Bachofen, *Das Mutterrecht* (Stuttgart: Krais & Hoffman, 1861), 90; repr. in *Gesammelte Werke* (7 vols.; Basel: Schwabe, 1943), 2:276; Fredrich, "Lemnos," 74–75; Delcourt, *Héphaistos*, 171–90, whereas Lewis R. Farnell, *Cults of the Greek States* (5 vols.; Oxford: Clarendon, 1896–1909), 5:394, concluded from the silence of Philostratus that the festival was not connected with Hephaistos. The importance of the craftsmen was stressed by Welcker, *Die aeschylische Trilogie*, 248; Delcourt, *Héphaistos*, 177. That the festival belongs to Hephaistia, not Myrina, is shown by the coins already used by Welcker, *Die aeschylische Trilogie*; cf. n. 36 below.

god of fire, even fire himself (*Il.* 2.426): the purification of the island of Hephaistos, brought about by new fire, was a festival of Hephaistos. Philostratus indeed alludes to this: the new fire, he says, is distributed especially "to the craftsmen who have to do with fire," i.e., to potters and blacksmiths. The island must have been famous for its craftsmen at an early date: the Sinties of Lemnos, Hellanikos said (*FGrH* 4 F 71), invented fire and the forging of weapons. The "invention," the advent of fire, is repeated in the festival. It is true that Philostratus mentions Aphrodite as the agent behind the original crime: she ought to have a place in the atonement, too.[14] But the question: to which god does the festival "belong," seems to be rather a misunderstanding of polytheism: as the ritual mirrors the complexity of life, various aspects of reality, i.e., different deities, are concerned.[15] The "beginning of a new life" at Lemnos would affect all the gods who played their part in the life of the community, above all the Great Goddess who was called Lemnos herself.[16]

To get farther, it is tempting to embark on ethnological comparison. Festivals of new fire are among the most common folk customs all over the world; striking parallels have been adduced from the Red Indians as well as from East Indian Burma;[17] and one could refer to the Incas as well as to the Japanese. Nilsson, wisely, confines himself to Greek parallels, not without adding the remark (*Griechische Feste*, 173): "Daß das Feuer durch den täglichen Gebrauch . . . seine Reinheit verliert, ist ein überall verbreiteter Glauben" ("That fire loses its purity through daily use is a ubiqui-

[14] Cf. Apollonius of Rhodes *Argonautica* 1.850–852, 858–860; a dedication Ἀ]φροδίτει Θρα[ικίαι from the Kabeirion of Lemnos, see Silvio Accame, "Iscrizioni del Cabirio di Lemno," *ASAA* NS 3–5 (1941–1943): 91 no. 12; a temple of Aphrodite at Lemnos, schol. Statius *Thebaid* 5.59; the κρατίστη δαίμων in Aristophanes' *Lemniai* (frg. 365) may be the same "Thracian Aphrodite."

[15] The sacrificial calendars regularly combine different deities in the same ceremonies; cf. as the most extensive example the calendar of Erchiai, Georges Daux, "La grande démarchie: Un nouveau calendrier sacrificiel d'Attique (Erchia)," *BCH* 87 (1963): 603–34. Sterling Dow, "The Greater Demarkhia of Erchia," *BCH* 89 (1965): 180–213.

[16] Photius, Hesychius, s.v. μεγάλη θεός = Aristophanes frg. 368; Stephanus of Byzantium, s.v. Λῆμνος. Pre-Greek representations: Fredrich, "Lemnos," 60–86 with pl. VIII and IX; A. Della Seta, "Arte Tirrenica di Lemno," *Archaeologike Ephemeris* (1937): 644, pl. 2 and 3; Greek coins in Barclay V. Head, *Historia Numorum* (2d ed.; Oxford: Clarendon, 1911), 263.

[17] Fredrich, "Lemnos," 75; J. G. Frazer, *The Golden Bough* (12 vols.; 3d ed.; London: Macmillan, 1911), 8:72–75; 10:136; generally on fire-festivals: 2:195–265; 10:106–11:44.

tous belief"). "Ubiquitous belief" is meant to explain the ritual. Where, however, one ought to ask, do such ubiquitous beliefs come from? The obvious answer is: from the rituals.[18] People, living with their festivals from childhood, are taught their beliefs by these very rituals, which remain constant as against the unlimited possibilities of primitive associations. Thus the comparative method does not, by itself, lead to an explanation, to an understanding of what is going on—if one does not take it for granted that whatever Greeks or Romans told about their religion is wrong, but what any savage told a merchant or missionary is a revelation. At the same time, by mere accumulation of comparative material, the outlines of the picture become more and more blurred, until nothing is left but vague generalities.

In sharp contrast to the method of accumulation, there is the method of historical criticism; instead of expanding the evidence, it tries to cut it down, to isolate elements and to distribute them neatly to different times and places. The πυρφορία described by Philostratus connects Delos and Lemnos. This, we are told, is an innovation which betrays Attic influence. The suggestion cannot be disproved, though it is remarkable that Philostratus wrote at a time when Lemnos had just become independent from Athens, that the Athenians got their new fire not from Delos, but from Delphi (Plutarch *Aristides* 20), and that the role of Delos as a religious center of the islands antedates not only Attic, but plainly Greek influence.[19] Still, the critical separation of Lemnian and Delian worship has its consequences: if the Lemnians originally did not sail to Delos, where did their new fire come from? Obviously from an indigenous source: the miraculous fire of Mount Mosykhlos.[20] This fire has a

[18] Usually "beliefs" are traced back to emotional experience; but cf. Claude Lévi-Strauss, *Le totémisme aujourd'hui* (Paris: Presses universitaires de France, 1962), 102f.: "Ce ne sont pas des émotions actuelles, ressenties à l'occasion des réunions et des cérémonies qui engendrent ou perpétuent les rites, mais l'activité rituelle qui suscite les émotions" ("[I]t is not present emotions, felt at gatherings and ceremonies, which engender or perpetuate the rites, but ritual activity which arouses the emotions"). [*Ed.:* The English translation is that of Rodney Needham, *Totemism* (Boston: Beacon, 1963).]

[19] F. Cassola, "La leggenda di Anio e la preistoria Delia," *PP* 60 (1954): 345–67; there is an old sanctuary of the Kabeiroi on Delos, Bengt Hemberg, *Die Kabiren* (Uppsala: Almqvist & Wilksells, 1950), 140–53; the Orion myth combines Delos and Lemnos, below, n. 25.

[20] Fredrich, "Lemnos," 75; with reference to a custom in Burma, Frazer, *Golden Bough*, 10:136; Malten, "Hephaistos," *JDAI* 27 (1912): 248f.; Fredrich, however, thinks that the earth fire came to be extinguished at an early date.

curious history. The commentators on Homer and Sophocles and the Roman poets clearly speak of a volcano on Lemnos;[21] this volcano was active in literature down to the end of the nineteenth century, with some scattered eruptions even in later commentaries on Sophocles' *Philoctetes*,[22] though geographical survey had revealed that there never was a volcano on Lemnos at any time since this planet has been inhabited by *homo sapiens*.[23] Thus the volcano disappeared, but its fire remained: scholars confidently speak of an "earth fire," a perpetual flame nourished by earth gas on Mount Mosykhlos. As earth gas may be found nearly everywhere and fires of this kind do not leave permanent traces, this hypothesis cannot be disproved. Nothing has been adduced to prove it either. The analogy with the fires of Baku ought not to be pressed; no reservoir of oil has been found at Lemnos.

There is no denying that "Lemnian fire" was something famous and uncanny. Philoktêtês, in his distress, invokes it:

> ὦ Λημνία χθὼν καὶ τὸ παγκρατὲς σέλας ἡφαιστότευκτον.
>
> Land of Lemnos and almighty fire made by Hephaistos.
> (Sophocles *Philoctetes* 986–987 Lloyd-Jones)

[21] κρατῆρες: Eustathius 158.3; 1598.44; schol. Sophocles *Philoctetes* 800, 986; Valerius Flaccus *Argonautica* 2.332–339; Statius *Thebaid* 5.50, 87; Statius *Silvae* 3.1.131–133. Less explicit: Heraclitus *Allegoriae* 26.15 (echoed by Eustathius 157.37, schol. *Od.* 8.284) ἀνίενται γηγενοῦς πυρὸς αὐτόματοι φλόγες (Félix Buffière [*Allégories d'Homère* (Paris: Société d'édition "Les Belles Lettres," 1962)] keeps the manuscript reading ἐγγυγηγενοῦς, "un feu qu'on croirait presque sorti de terre," but this is hardly Greek); *Acc. trag.* frg. 532 Ribbeck "nemus exspirante vapore vides . . . ." is incompatible with the volcano-, though not with the earth-fire-hypothesis.

[22] Ludwig Preller and Carl Robert, *Griechische Mythologie* (4th ed.; 2 vols.; Berlin: Weidmann, 1894–1926), 1:175, 178; Richard C. Jebb, *Sophocles: The Philoctetes* (vol. 4 of *Sophocles: Works*; 7 vols.; Cambridge: Cambridge University Press, 1890–1924), 243–45; Paul Mazon, *Philoctète; Oedipe à Colone* (vol. 3 of *Sophocle*; ed. Alphonse Dain and Paul Mazon; Paris: Société d'édition "Les Belles Lettres," 1955–1960), note on verse 800.

[23] Karl Neumann and Josef Partsch, *Physikalische Geographie von Griechenland* (Breslau: Koebner, 1885), 314–18, who immediately thought of the earth fire; cf. Fredrich, "Lemnos," 253–54; Malten, "Hephaistos," *JDAI* 27 (1912): 233; Malten, "Hephaistos," PW 8 (1913): 316; Nilsson, *Geschichte der griechischen Religion*, 1:528–29; R. Hennig, "Altgriechische Sagengestalten als Personifikation von Erdfeuern," *JDAI* 54 (1939): 230–46. Earth fires are well attested at Olympos in Lycia (Malten, "Hephaistos," PW 8 [1913]: 317–19), where the Hephaistos-cult was prominent, and at Trapezus in Arcadia (Aristotle *On Marvelous Things Heard* 127; Pausanias *Description of Greece* 8.29.1) and at Apollonia in Epirus (Theopompus, *FGrH* 115 F 316) without the Hephaistos-cult.

Antimachus mentions it in comparison (frg. 46 Wyss):

> Ἡφαίστου φλογὶ εἴκελον, ἥν ῥα τιτύσκει
> δαίμων ἀκροτάτης ὄρεος κορυφαῖσι Μοσύχλου.
>
> like the flame of Hephaistos which a daimon prepares
> at the peaks of lofty Mount Mosykhlos.

This fire on the summit of the mountain is in some way miraculous, δαιμόνιον—but τιτύσκει (after *Il.* 21.342) is hardly suggestive of a perpetual flame. There is, however, another invocation of Lemnian fire in the *Philoctetes:* τῷ Λημνίῳ τῷδ' ἀνακαλουμένῳ πυρὶ ἔμπρησον ("burn me with this fire that is invoked as Lemnian"; Sophocles *Philoctetes* 800–801 Lloyd-Jones), the hero cries. ἀνακαλουμένῳ has proved to be a stumbling-block for believers either in the volcano or the earth fire.[24] ἀνακαλεῖν, ἀνακαλεῖσθαι is a verb of ritual, used especially for "imploring" chthonic deities: Deianeira implores her δαίμων (Sophocles *Women of Trachis* 910), Oedipus at Kolônos his ἀραί (Sophocles *Oedipus at Colonus* 1376). Thus ἀνακαλουμένῳ seems to imply a certain ceremony to produce this demoniac fire; it is not always there. Understood in this way, the verse turns out to be the earliest testimony to the fire-festival of Lemnos; it confirms the guess that the fire was not brought from Delos at that time. How the fire was kindled in the ritual may have been a secret. Considering the importance of Lemnian craftsmen, the most miraculous method for χαλκεῖς would be to use a χαλκεῖον, a bronze burning-mirror to light a new fire from the sun.[25] Hephaistos fell on Lemnos

[24] Meineke and Pearson changed the text to ἀνακαλούμενον, Mazon translates "que tu évoqueras pour cela," though keeping ἀνακαλουμένῳ; Jebb translates "famed as," with reference to *Electra* 693, where, however, ἀνακαλούμενος is "being solemnly proclaimed" as victor.

[25] Ancient burning-mirrors were always made of bronze; the testimonies in J. Morgan, "De ignis eliciendi modis," *HSCP* 1 (1890): 50–64; earliest mention: Theophrastus *On Fire* 73; Euclid *Optics* 30 (burning-glass: Aristophanes *Clouds* 767); used in rituals of new fire: Plutarch *Numa* 9 (Delphi and Athens, first century B.C.E.); Heraclitus *Allegoriae* 26.13: κατ' ἀρχὰς οὐδέπω τῆς τοῦ πυρὸς χρήσεως ἐπιπολαζούσης ἄνθρωποι χρονικῶς χαλκοῖς τισιν ὀργάνοις ἐφειλκύσαντο τοὺς ἀπὸ τῶν μετεώρων φερομένους σπινθῆρας, κατὰ τὰς μεσημβρίας ἐναντία τῷ ἡλίῳ τὰ ὄργανα τιθέντες.

Parallels from the Incas, Siam, China: Frazer, *Golden Bough*, 2:243, 245; 10:132, 137. Fredrich, "Lemnos," 75 n. 3, thought of the burning-mirror in connection with the myth of Orion, who recovers his eyesight from the sun with the help of the Lemnian Kedaliôn (Hesiod frg. 148 Merkelbach and West). "Fire from the sky" lit the altar at Rhodes, the famous center of metallurgy (Pindar *Olympian* 7.48). The practice may have influenced the myth of Helios's cup as well as the theories of Xenophanes and Heraclitus about the sun (21 A 32, 40; 22 A 12, B 6 DK).

from heaven, the *Iliad* says (*Il.* 1.593), on Mount Mosykhlos, native tradition held;[26] he was very feeble, but the Sinties at once took care of him. In the tiny flame rising from the tinder in the focus, the god has arrived—alas, this is just a guess. But it seems advisable to send the earth-fire of Mosykhlos together with the volcano after the volcanic vapors of Delphi, which, too, vanished completely under the spade of the excavators; the miracles of ritual do not need the miracles of nature; the miracles of nature do not necessarily produce mythology.

To get beyond guesses, there is one clue left in the text of Philostratus: the purification is performed "on account of the deed wrought by the Lemnian women against their husbands." It is by myth that ancient tradition explains the ritual. Modern scholarship has revolted against this. As early as 1824, Friedrich Gottlob Welcker found a "glaring contrast" between the "deeper" meaning of the festival and the "extrinsic occasion" said to be its cause.[27] Georges Dumézil,[28] however, was able to show that the connection of myth and ritual, in this case, is by no means "extrinsic": there is almost complete correspondence in outline and in detail.

The myth is well known:[29] the wrath of Aphrodite had smitten the women of Lemnos; they developed a "foul smell" (δυσωδία) so awful that their husbands, understandably, sought refuge in the arms of Thracian slave-girls. This, in turn, enraged the women so much that, in one terrible night, they slew their husbands and, for the sake of completeness, all the male population of the island. Thereafter Lemnos was a community of women without men, ruled by the virgin queen Hypsipyle, until the day when the ship arrived, the Argo with Jason. This was the end of Lemnian celibacy. With a rather licentious festival the island returned to bisexual [*ed.:* i.e., heterosexual] life. The story, in some form, is already known to the *Iliad:* the son of Jason and Hypsipyle is dwelling on Lemnos, Eunêos, the man of the fine ship.

[26] Galen *Opera Omnia* 12:173 Kühn; cf. *Acc. trag.* 529–31 Ribbeck.

[27] Welcker, *Die aeschylische Trilogie*, 249–50.

[28] Georges Dumézil, *Le crime des Lemniennes* (Paris: Geuthner, 1924).

[29] Survey of sources: Wilhelm H. Roscher, *Ausführliches Lexikon der griechischen und römischen Mythologie* 1:2853–56 (Klügmann); 2:73–74 (Seeliger); 5:808–14 (Immisch); Preller and Robert, *Griechische Mythologie*, 2:849–59; cf. Ulrich von Wilamowitz-Moellendorff, *Hellenistische Dichtung in der Zeit des Kallimachos* (2 vols.; Berlin: Weidmann, 1924), 2:232–48. Jason, Hypsipyle, Thoas, Euneos in Homer: *Il.* 7.468–469; 14.230; 15.40; 21.41; 23.747; cf. Hesiod frg. 157, 253–256 Merkelbach and West.

With this myth, the fire ritual is connected not in a casual or arbitrary manner, but by an identity of rhythm, marked by two περιπέτειαι ("reversals"): first, there begins a period of abnormal, barren, uncanny life, until, secondly, the advent of the ship brings about a new, joyous life—which is in fact the return to normal life.

Correspondences go even farther. The mythological *aition* compels us to combine with the text of Philostratus another testimony about Lemnian ritual, which, too, is said to be a remnant of the Argonauts' visit. Myrsilos of Lesbos is quoted for a different explanation of the infamous δυσωδία: not Aphrodite, but Medea caused it; in accordance with the older version ousted by Apollonius,[30] Myrsilos made the Argonauts come to Lemnos on their return from Kolchis, though the presence of Medea brought some complications for Jason and Hypsipyle. The jealous sorceress took her revenge: καὶ δυσοσμίαν γενέσθαι ταῖς γυναιξίν· εἶναί τε μέχρι τοῦ νῦν κατ' ἐνιαυτὸν ἡμέραν τινά, ἐν ᾗ διὰ τὴν δυσωδίαν ἀπέχειν τὰς γυναῖκας ἄνδρα τε καὶ υἱεῖς ("and [they say] that foul smell comes upon the women, and until now there is a certain day each year when the women because of the foul smell keep away from both their husband and their sons").[31]

Thus one of the most curious features of the myth reappears in ritual, at least down to Hellenistic times: the foul smell of the women, which isolates them from men. Evidently this fits very well into that abnormal period of the purification ceremony. Extinguishing all fires on the island—this in itself means a dissolution of all normal life. There is no cult of the gods, which requires incense and fire on the altars, there is no regular meal in the houses of men during this period, no meat, no bread, no porridge; some special vegetarian diet must have been provided. The ἑστία, the center of the community, the center of every house is dead. What is even more, the families themselves are broken apart, as it were by a curse: men cannot meet their wives, sons cannot see their mothers. The active part in this separation of sexes is, according to the text

[30] Pindar *Pythian* 4.252–257.

[31] *FGrH* 477 F 1a = schol. Apollonius of Rhodes *Argonautica* 1.609/19e; F 1b = Antigonus Carystus *Collection of Paradoxical Stories* 118 is less detailed and therefore likely to be less accurate: κατὰ δή τινα χρόνον καὶ μάλιστα ἐν ταύταις ταῖς ἡμέραις, ἐν αἷς ἱστοροῦσιν τὴν Μήδειαν παραγενέσθαι, δυσώδεις αὐτὰς οὕτως γίνεσθαι ὥστε μηδένα προσιέναι. Delcourt (*Héphaistos*, 173 n. 2) holds that only the information about Medea goes back to Myrsilos; but the scholiast had no reason to add a reference to "contemporary" events, whereas Myrsilos was interested in contemporary *mirabilia* (F 2; 4–6). Welcker (*Die aeschylische Trilogie*, 250) already combined Myrsilos's with Philostratus's account.

of Myrsilos, played by the women; they are the subject of ἀπέχειν. They act together, by some sort of organization; probably they meet in the streets or the sanctuaries, whereas the male population is scared away. Thus the situation in the city closely reflects the situation described in the myth: disagreeable women rule the town, the men have disappeared.

Dumézil already went one step farther and used the myth to supplement our information about the ritual. There is the famous fate of King Thoas, son of Dionysos, father of Hypsipyle: he is not killed like the other men; Hypsipyle hides him in a coffin, and he is tossed into the sea.[32] Valerius Flaccus (*Argonautica* 2.242ff.) gives curious details: Thoas is led to the temple of Dionysos on the night of the murder; on the next day, he is dressed up as Dionysos, with wig, wreath, garments of the god, and Hypsipyle, acting as Bacchant, escorts the god through the town down to the seashore to see him disappear. It is difficult to tell how much of this Valerius Flaccus took from older tradition;[33] the general pattern, the ἀποπομπή ("sending away") of the semi-divine king, the way to the sea, the tossing of the λάρναξ ("chest") into the water surely goes back to very old strata.[34] It is fitting that the new life, too, should arrive from the sea—ἀποπομπή and *adventus* correspond.

One step further, beyond Dumézil's observations, is to realize that the bloodshed wrought by the women, the killing of the men,

[32] Apollonius of Rhodes *Argonautica* 1.620–626; Theolytos, *FGrH* 478 F 3; Xenagoras, *FGrH* 240 F 31; and Kleon of Kurion in schol. Apollonius of Rhodes *Argonautica* 1.623/6a; cf. Euripides *Hypsipyle* frg. 64.74ff.; 105ff. Bond; Hypoth. Pi. *N.* b, iii. 2, 8–13 Drachmann; Kylix Berlin 2300 = John D. Beazley, *Attic Red-figure Vase-painters* (2d ed.; Oxford: Clarendon, 1963), 409, no. 43 = Gisela M. A. Richter, *The Furniture of the Greeks, Etruscans, and Romans* (London: Phaidon, 1966), pl. 385.

[33] Cf. Roscher, *Lexikon* 5:806 (Immisch). Domitian had made a very similar escape from the troops of Vitellius in 68 C.E.: *Isiaco celatus habitu interque sacrificulos* (Suetonius *Domitian* 1.2; cf. Tacitus *Histories* 3.74; Josephus *Jewish War* 4.11.4; another similar case in the civil war, Appian *Civil Wars* 4.47; Valerius Maximus 7.3.8).

[34] This is the manner of death of Osiris, Plutarch *Isis and Osiris* 13.356c. Parallels from folk-custom: Wilhelm Mannhardt, *Wald- und Feldkulte* (2 vols.; Berlin: Gebrüder Borntraeger, 1875–1877), 1:311ff.; Frazer, *Golden Bough*, 2:75; 4:206–12; Dumézil, *Le crime*, 42ff. Hypsipyle is a telling name; "vermutlich war Hypsipyle einst eine Parallelfigur zu Medea: die 'hohe Pforte' in ihrem Namen war die Pforte der Hölle" (Ulrich von Wilamowitz-Moellendorff, *Griechische Tragoedien* [7th ed.; Berlin, 1926], 3:169 n. 1)—or rather, more generally, the "high gate" of the Great Goddess. The same name may have been given independently to the nurse of the dying child—another aspect of the Great Goddess (*Homeric Hymn to Demeter* 184ff.)—at Nemea.

must have had its counterpart in ritual, too: in sacrifices, involving rather cruel spectacles of bloodshed.[35] It would be impossible to "call secret gods from under the earth" (*Her.* 53.6 de Lannoy) without the blood of victims, flowing into a pit, possibly at night; the absence of fire would make these acts all the more dreary. Women may have played an active part in these affairs; at Hermionê, in a festival called Chthonia, four old women had to cut the throats of the sacrificial cows with sickle swords (Pausanias *Description of Greece* 2.35). In Lemnos, a ram-sacrifice must have been prominent; a ram is often represented on the coins of Hephaistia.[36] The fleece of a ram, Διὸς κῴδιον, was needed in many purification ceremonies;[37] incidentally, the Argonauts' voyage had the purpose of providing a ram's fleece.

Most clearly the concluding traits of the myth reflect ritual: the arrival of the Argonauts is celebrated with an *agôn;* the prize is a garment.[38] This is as characteristic a prize as the Athenian oil at the Panathenaia, the Olympian olive-wreath in Olympia; the Lemnian festival must have ended with an *agôn*, though it never attained panhellenic importance. The garment, made by women, ἀγλαὰ ἔργα ἰδυῖαι, is a quite fitting gift to end the war of the sexes; if Jason receives the garment of Thoas (Apollonius of Rhodes *Argonautica* 4.423–434), continuity bridges the gap of the catastrophe. There is one more curious detail in Pindar's account of the Lemnian *agôn:* the victor was not Jason, but a certain Erginos, who was conspicuous by his untimely gray hair; the others had laughed at him.[39]

[35] Cf. Walter Burkert, "Greek Tragedy and Sacrificial Ritual," *GRBS* 7 (1966): 102–21.

[36] Cf. Alfred von Sallet and Julius Friedlaender, *Beschreibung der antiken Münzen* (Königliche Museen zu Berlin; Berlin: Spemann, 1888–1894), 1:279–83; Head, *Historia Numorum*, 262–63; Arthur B. Cook, *Zeus: A Study in Ancient Religion* (3 vols.; Cambridge: Cambridge University Press, 1914–1940), 3:233–34; Hemberg, *Kabiren*, 161. A similar ram-sacrifice has been inferred for Samothrace, Hemberg, *Kabiren*, 102, 284. Instead of the ram, the coins of Hephaistia sometimes have torches, πῖλοι (of Kabeiroi–Dioskouroi), and *kerykeion*, also vines and grapes; all these symbols have some connection with the context of the festival treated here.

[37] Nilsson, *Geschichte der griechischen Religion*, 1:110–13; Pausanius *Attic Lexica* δ 18 Erbse.

[38] Simonides 547 Page, *PMG;* Pindar *Pythian* 4.253 with schol.; cf. Apollonius of Rhodes *Argonautica* 2.30–32; 3.1204–1206; 4.423–434.

[39] Pindar *Olympian* 4.23–31; cf. schol. 32c; Callimachus frg. 668. Here Erginos is son of Klymenos of Orchomenos, father of Trophônios and Agamêdês (another pair of divine craftsmen, with a fratricide-myth, as the Kabeiroi), whereas Apollonius of Rhodes *Argonautica* 1.185, after Herodorus, *FGrH* 31 F 45/55, makes

Erginos "the workman," gray-haired and surrounded by laughter, but victorious at Lemnos after the ship had arrived—this seems to be just a transformation, a translation of Hephaistos the gray-haired workman, who constantly arouses Homeric laughter.[40] Thus the myth itself takes us back to the fire-festival: this is the triumph of Hephaistos, the reappearing fire which brings new life, especially to the workmen in the service of their god. It is possible that laughter was required in the ritual as an expression of the new life—as in Easter ceremonies, both the new fire and laughter, even in churches, are attested in the Middle Ages.[41] Another peculiarity seems to have been more decidedly "pagan": surely neither Aeschylus nor Pindar invented the unabashed sexual coloring of the meeting of Lemniads and Argonauts; in Aeschylus, the Lemniads force the Argonauts by oath to make love to them.[42] Behind this, there must be ritual *αἰσχρολογία* ("foul language") or even *αἰσχροποιία* ("physical degradation") at the festival of license which forms the concluding act of the abnormal period.

Many details are bound to escape us. Hephaistos, at Lemnos, was connected with the Kabeiroi. The Kabeirion, not far from Hephaistia, has been excavated; it offers a neat example of continu-

---

him son of Poseidon, from Miletus, cf. Wilamowitz-Moellendorff, *Hellenistische Dichtung*, 2:238.

[40] The constellation Erginos–Jason–Hypsipyle is akin to the constellation Hephaistos–Ares–Aphrodite in the famous Dêmodokos hymn (Homer *Od.* 8.266–366): another triumph of Hephaistos amidst unextinguishable laughter. A special relation to Lemnos is suggested by a pre-Greek vase fragment, found in a sanctuary in Hephaistia (A. Della Seta, *Archaeologike Ephemeris* [1937]: 650; Ch. Picard, "Une peinture de vase lemnienne, archaïque, d'après l'Hymne de Démodocos: Odyss., VIII, 256 sqq.," *Revue Archéologique* ser. 6, 20 [1942–1943]: 97–124; to be dated about 550 B.C.E., as B. B. Shefton kindly informs me; cf. Delcourt, *Héphaistos*, 80–82): a naked goddess vis-à-vis an armed warrior, both apparently fettered. This is strikingly reminiscent of Dêmodokos's song, as Picard and Delcourt saw, though hardly a direct illustration of Homer's text, rather of "local legend" (cf. Knud Friis Johansen, *The Iliad in Early Greek Art* [Copenhagen: Munksgaard, 1967], 38, 59), i.e., a native Lemnian version. The crouching position of the couple reminded Picard of Bronze Age burial customs; anthropology provides examples of human sacrifice in the production of new fire: a couple forced to mate and killed on the spot (cf. Eduard Pechuel-Loesche, *Volkskunde von Loango* [vol. 3.2 of *Die Loango-Expedition ausgesandt von der deutschen Gesellschaft zur Erforschung Aequatorial-Africas. 1873–1876*; Stuttgart: Strecker & Schröder, 1907], 171ff.). Surely Homer's song is more enjoyable without thinking of such a gloomy background.

[41] Mannhardt, *Wald- und Feldkulte*, 502–8; Frazer, *Golden Bough*, 10:121ff.; on "risus Paschalis," Paul Sartori, *Sitte und Brauch* (3 vols.; Leipzig: Heims, 1910–1914), 3:167.

[42] Frg. 40 Mette; cf. Pindar *Pythian* 4.254; Herodorus, *FGrH* 31 F 6.

ity of cult from pre-Greek to Greek population, but it did not yield much information about the mysteries, except that wine-drinking played an important role.[43] Myth connects the Kabeiroi of Lemnos with the Lemnian crime: they left the accursed island.[44] Since their cult continued at Lemnos, they evidently came back, when the curse had come to an end. In Aeschylus's *Kabeiroi*, they somehow somewhere meet the Argonauts; they invade the houses and mockingly threaten to drink everything down to the last drop of vinegar.[45] Such impudent begging is characteristic of mummery;[46] these Kabeiroi, grandchildren of Hephaistos, reflect some masked club, originally a guild of smiths, probably, who play a leading role at the purification ceremony anyhow. It is tempting to suppose that the ship of the Argonauts arriving at Lemnos really means the ship of the Kabeiroi; being associated with seafaring everywhere, it fits them to arrive by ship. The herald of the Argonauts who rises to prominence only in the negotiations of Argonauts and Lemniads is called Aithalidês, "man of soot";[47] this binds him to the blacksmiths of Lemnos; the island itself was called Aithalia.[48] These Kabeiroi—blacksmiths would, after a night of revel, ascend Mount Mosykhlos with their magic cauldron and light the fire, which was then, by a torch-race, brought to the city and distributed to sanctuaries, houses, and workshops—seductive possibilities.

Equally uncertain is the connection of the purification cere-

---

[43] Preliminary report, "Lavori della Scuola Italiana a Lemnos nel 1939," *ASAA* NS 1–2 (1939–1940): 223–24; inscriptions: Silvio Accame, "Iscrizioni del Cabirio di Lemno," *ASAA* NS 3–5 (1941–1943): 75–105; Giancarlo Susini, "Note di epigrafia lemnia," *ASAA* NS 14–16 (1952–1954): 317–40; D. Levi, "Il Cabirio di Lemno," in *Charisterion Anastasion K. Orlandos* (4 vols.; Athens: n.p., 1966), 3:110–32; Hemberg, *Kabiren*, 160–70. Wine-vessels bore the inscription Καβείρων. Kabeiroi and Hephaistos: Akousilaos, *FGrH* 2 F 20; Pherekydes, *FGrH* 3 F 48 with Jacoby ad loc.; O. Kern, "Kabeiros und Kabeiroi: Samothrake," PW 10 (1913): 1423–50; this is not the tradition of Samothrace nor of Thebes (where there is one old Κάβιρος, Nilsson, *Geschichte der griechischen Religion*, vol. 1, pl. 48, fig. 1), and thus points towards Lemnos. In the puzzling lyric fragment (adesp. 985 Page, *PMG*), Kabeiros son of Lemnos is the first man.

[44] Photios, s.v. Κάβειροι· δαίμονες ἐκ Λήμνου διὰ τὸ τόλμημα τῶν γυναικῶν μετενεχθέντες· εἰσὶ δὲ ἤτοι Ἥφαιστοι ἢ Τιτᾶνες.

[45] Frg. 45 Mette; that the Kabeiroi are speaking is clear from Plutarch's quotation (*Table-Talk* 633a): αὐτοὶ παίζοντες ἠπείλησαν.

[46] K. Meuli, "Bettelumzüge im Totenkult, Opferritual und Volksbrauch," *Schweizer Archiv für Volkskunde* 28 (1927–1928): 1–38.

[47] Apollonius of Rhodes *Argonautica* 1.641–651; cf. Pherekydes *FGrH* 3 F 109.

[48] Polybius *Histories* 34.11.4; Stephanus of Byzantium, s.v. Αἰθάλη.

monies with the digging of "Lemnian earth." Λημνία γῆ, red-colored clay, described by Dioscorides and Galen, formed an ingredient of every oriental drugstore down to this century;[49] superstition can even outlive religion. Travelers observed how the clay was dug under the supervision of the priest at the hill, which, by this, is identified as Mount Mosykhlos; in the time of Galen, it was the priestess of Artemis[50] who collected it, throwing wheat and barley on the ground, formed it into small disks, sealed it with the seal of a goat, and sold it for medical purposes. The priestess of the goddess operating at the mount of Hephaistos—it is possible to connect this with the fire festival. Indeed it is all the more tempting because, owing to the continuity of ritual, this would give a clue as to the date of the festival: Lemnian earth was collected on 6 August; this corresponds with the time of Galen's visit.[51] Late summer is a common time for new-year festivals in the ancient world; incidentally, the μύσται ("initiates") of the Kabeiroi at Lemnos held conventions in Skirophoriôn,[52] that is, roughly in August. Still, these combinations do not amount to proof.

One question has been left unsolved: what about the recurrent δυσωδία ("foul smell")? Can this be more than legend or slander?[53] The simple and drastic answer is given by a parallel from Athens: the authority of Philochoros[54] (*FGrH* 328 F 89) is quoted for the

[49] Fredrich, "Lemnos," 72–74; F. W. Hasluck, "Terra Lemnia," *Annual of the British School at Athens* 16 (1909–1910): 220–30; F. L. W. Sealey, "Lemnos," *Annual of the British School at Athens* 22 (1918–1919): 164–65; Cook, *Zeus*, 3:228ff.; Dioscorides *Materials of Medicine* 5.113; Galen *Opera Omnia* 12:164–75 Kühn (on the date of his visit to Lemnos, Fredrich, "Lemnos," 73 n. 1, 76 n. 1: late summer 166 C.E.). According to Dioscorides, the blood of a goat was mixed with the earth, but Galen's informants scornfully denied this. The "priests of Hephaistos" used the earth to heal Philoktêtês: schol. AB B 722; Philostratus *Her.* 6.2 [*ed.: Her.* 28.6 de Lannoy]; Pliny *Natural History* 35.33. Philoktêtês' sanctuary, however, was in Myrina (Galen *Opera Omnia* 12:171 Kühn).

[50] Possibly the "great Goddess," cf. above, n. 16.

[51] Cf. n. 49 above.

[52] Accame, "Iscrizioni del Cabirio di Lemno," *ASAA* NS 3–5 (1941–1943): 75ff. no. 2, no. 6, but no. 4 Hekatombaiôn.

[53] General remarks in Dumézil, *Le crime*, 35–39. Welcker (*Die aeschylische Trilogie*, 249) thought of some kind of fumigation. Cf. Frazer, *Golden Bough*, 8:73 for the use of purgatives in a New Fire festival. A marginal gloss in Antigonus Carystus *Collection of Paradoxical Stories* 118 (cf. n. 31 above) mentions πήγανον, cf. Jacoby, *FGrH* 3 comm. 437 n. 223.

[54] E. Gjerstad ("Das Attische Fest der Skira," *AR* 27 [1929–1930]: 201–3) thinks Philochoros misunderstood the sense of the ritual, which was rather "aphrodisiac"; though he recognizes himself that short abstinence enhances fertility.

fact that the women ἐν (δὲ) τοῖς Σκίροις τῇ ἑορτῇ ἤσθιον σκόροδα ἕνεκα τοῦ ἀπεχέσθαι ἀφροδισίων, ὡς ἂν μὴ μύρων ἀποπνέοιεν ("at the festival of the Skira [the women] usually ate garlic because of abstaining from sex, so that they would not smell of perfumes"). Thus we have an unmistakable smell going together with disruption of marital order, separation of the sexes, at the Skira. The women flock together at this festival according to ancient custom,[55] and Aristophanes' fancy has them plan their *coup d'état* on this occasion (*Women of the Assembly* 59). But there is even more similarity: the main event of the Skira is a procession which starts from the old temple of the Acropolis and leads towards Eleusis to the old border-line of Attica, to a place called Skirôn. The priest of Poseidon–Erechtheus, the priestess of Athena, and the priest of Helios are led together under a sunshade by the Eteobutadai:[56] Erechtheus is the primordial king of Athens; he left his residence, the myth tells us, to fight the Eleusinians ἐπὶ Σκίρῳ ("at Skirôn") and disappeared mysteriously in the battle; his widow became the first priestess of Athena.[57] Thus we find in Athens, on unimpeachable evidence, the ritual ἀποπομπή ("sending away") of the king, which was inferred from myth for the corresponding Lemnian festival. At Athens, the concluding *agôn* has been moved farther away: the "beginning of new life" is the Panathenaia in the following month, Hekatombaiôn, the first of the year. If the perennial fire in the sanctuary of Athena and Erechtheus, the lamp of Athena, is refilled and rekindled only once a year,[58] this will have happened at the Panathenaia when the new oil was available and used as a prize for the victors. The month Skirophoriôn coincides approximately with August, the time of the digging of Lemnian earth. The name Σκίρα is enigmatic, but most of the ancient explanations concentrate on some stem σκιρ- (σκυρ-) meaning "white earth," "white clay," "white rock." The place Skirôn is a place where there was some kind of white earth, and Theseus is said to have made an image of Athena out of white earth and to have carried it in procession when he was about to leave

[55] *IG* II/III^2 1177.8–12: ὅταν ἡ ἑορτὴ τῶν Θεσμοφορίων καὶ Πληροσίαι καὶ Καλαμαίοις καὶ τὰ Σκίρα καὶ εἴ τινα ἄλλην ἡμέραν συνέρχονται αἱ γυναῖκες κατὰ τὰ πάτρια.

[56] Lysimachides, *FGrH* 366 F 3; schol. Aristophanes *Women of the Assembly* 18; fullest account: Gjerstad, "Attische Fest," 189–240. Deubner's treatment (*Attische Feste*, 40–50) is led astray by schol. Lucian p. 275.23ff. Rabe; cf. Walter Burkert, "Kekropidensage und Arrhephoria," *Hermes* 94 (1966): 23–24, 7–8.

[57] Euripides *Erechtheus* frg. 65 Austin; death and tomb of Skiros: Pausanias *Description of Greece* 1.36.4.

[58] Pausanias *Description of Greece* 1.26.6–7.

Athens.[59] Were the *σκίρα* some kind of amulets "carried" at the *σκιροφόρια*, though less successful in superstitious medicine than their Lemnian counterparts?

There was another festival at Athens where the women ate garlic in considerable quantities:[60] the Thesmophoria. This festival was among the most widespread all over Greece, and there must have been many local variants; but there are features strikingly reminiscent of the pattern treated so far: there is the disruption of normal life, the separation of sexes; the women gather (cf. n. 60) for three or four days, they live at the Thesmophoriôn in huts or tents; in Eretria they did not even use fire (Plutarch *Greek Questions* 31). They performed uncanny sacrifices to chthonian deities; subterranean caves, *μέγαρα*, were opened, pigs thrown down into the depths; probably there was a bigger, secret sacrifice towards the end of the festival. In mythological fantasy, the separation of the sexes was escalated into outright war. The lamentable situation of the κηδεστής ("kinsman by marriage") in Aristophanes' *Thesmophoriazusae* is not the only example. The Laconian women are said to have overpowered the famous Aristomenês of Messene, when he dared to approach them at the time of the Thesmophoria; they fought, by divine instigation, with sacrificial knives and spits and torches—the scenery implies a nocturnal ἀπόρρητος θυσία ("secret sacrifice"; Pau-

[59] *Anecdota Graeca* (ed. Immanuel Bekker; 3 vols.; Berlin: Nauckium, 1814–1821), 304.8: Σκειρὰς Ἀθηνᾶ· εἶδος ἀγάλματος Ἀθηνᾶς ὀνομασθέντος οὕτως ἤτοι ἀπὸ τόπου τινὸς οὕτως ὠνομασμένου, ἐν ᾧ γῆ ὑπάρχει λευκὴ . . . (shorter *Etymologicum Magnum* 720.24); schol. Pausanias p. 218 Spiro: σκιροφόρια παρὰ τὸ φέρειν σκίρα ἐν αὐτῇ τὸν Θησέα ἢ γύψον· ὁ γὰρ Θησεὺς ἀπερχόμενος κατὰ τοῦ Μινωταύρου τὴν Ἀθηνᾶν ποιήσας ἀπὸ γύψου ἐβάστασεν (cf. Ulrich von Wilamowitz-Moellendorff, "Pausanias-Scholien," *Hermes* 29 [1894]: 243; slightly corrupt *Etymologicum Genuinum* p. 267 Miller = *Etymologicum Magnum* p. 718.16, more corrupt Photius, *Suda*, s.v. Σκίρα, who speak of Theseus's return); schol. Aristophanes *Wasps* 926: Ἀθηνᾶ Σκιρράς, ὅτι γῇ (τῇ codd.) λευκῇ χρίεται. A. Rutgers van der Loeff, "De Athena Scirade," *Mnemosyne* NS 44 (1916): 102–3; Gjerstad, "Attische Fest," 222–26; Deubner, *Attische Feste*, 46–47, tried to distinguish Σκίρα and Ἀθηνᾶ Σκιράς; Deubner, *Attische Feste*, 46 n. 11, even Σκίρα and the place Σκῖρον (Σκίρον? Herodian *History* 3.1.385.1–4; 3.2.581.22–31 Lentz [cf. Stephanus of Byzantium, s.v. Σκίρος] seems to prescribe Σκῖρον; Σκίρα Aristophanes *Thesmophoriazusae* 834; *Women of the Assembly* 18); *contra* Jacoby, *FGrH* 3B suppl., nn. 117–18. The changing quantity (cf. σῖρός) is less strange than the connection σκιρ-, σκυρ- (cf. LSJ, s.v. σκῖρον, σκῖρος, σκίρρος, σκῦρος), which points to a non-Greek word. On Σκῦρος (cf. Orus *Etymologicum Magnum* 720.24) Theseus was thrown down the white rock (Plutarch *Theseus* 35).

[60] *IG* II/III^2 1184: διδόναι . . . εἰς τὴν ἑορτὴν . . . καὶ σκόρδων δύο στατῆρας. On Thesmophoria, Nilsson, *Griechische Feste*, 313–25; *Geschichte der griechischen Religion*, 1:461–66; Deubner, *Attische Feste*, 50–60.

sanias *Description of Greece* 4.17.1). The women of Kyrênê, at their Thesmophoria, smeared their hands and faces with the blood of the victims and emasculated King Battos, who had tried to spy out their secrets.[61] The most famous myth in this connection concerns those women whom Euripides already compared with the Lemniads (*Hecuba* 887): the Danaids. They slew their husbands all together at night, too, with one notable exception, as at Lemnos: Lynkeus was led to a secret escape by Hypermestra the virgin. As the Argives kept the rule of extinguishing the fire in a house where somebody had died,[62] the night of murder must have entailed much extinguishing of fires. Lynkeus, however, when he was in safety, lit a torch in Lyrkeia, Hypermestra answered by lighting a torch at the Larisa, ἐπὶ τούτῳ δὲ Ἀργεῖοι κατὰ ἔτος ἕκαστον πυρσῶν ἑορτὴν ἄγουσι ("for this reason the Argives hold every year a beacon festival"; Pausanias *Description of Greece* 2.25.4 Jones). It is questionable whether this ritual originally belongs to the Danaid myth;[63] the word-play Lyrkeia–Lynkeus does not inspire confidence. The myth at any rate has much to tell about the concluding *agôn*, in which the Danaids were finally given to husbands.[64] After the outrage against nature, a new life must begin, which happens to be just ordinary life. But it is Herodotus who tells us that it was the Danaids who brought to Greece the τελετή ("rites") of Demeter Thesmophoros, i.e., introduced the festival Thesmophoria.[65] Thus the similarity of the myths

[61] Aelian frg. 44 = *Suda*, s.v. σφάκτριαι and θεσμοφόρος. Nilsson, *Griechische Feste*, 324–25.

[62] Plutarch *Greek Questions* 24.296F.

[63] Cf. Nilsson, *Griechische Feste*, 470 n. 5; Apollodorus *Library* 2.22; Zenobius 4.86, etc. point to a connection of Danaid myth and Lerna (new fire for Lerna: Pausanias *Description of Greece* 8.15.9).

[64] Pindar *Pythian* 9.111ff.; Pausanias *Description of Greece* 3.12.3; Apollodorus *Library* 2.22. Dumézil, *Le crime*, 48ff., discussed the similarities of the Argive and the Lemnian myth, without taking notice of the Thesmophoria.

[65] Herodotus *Hist.* 2.171: τῆς Δήμητρος τελετῆς πέρι, τὴν οἱ Ἕλληνες θεσμοφόρια καλέουσι . . . αἱ Δαναοῦ θυγατέρες ἦσαν αἱ τὴν τελετὴν ταύτην ἐξ Αἰγύπτου ἐξαγαγοῦσαι καὶ διδάξασαι τὰς Πελασγιώτιδας γυναῖκας. The connection of Danaoi and Egypt is taken seriously by modern historians (George L. Huxley, *Crete and the Luwians* [Oxford: n.p., 1961], 36–37; Frank H. Stubbings, CAH 18:11ff. [*ed.:* CAH 2.1: 635–38]; Peter Walcot, *Hesiod and the Near East* [Cardiff: Wales University Press, 1966], 71); Epaphos may be a Hyksos name. Now Mycenean representations mainly from the Argolid show "Demons" (cf. Nilsson, *Geschichte der griechischen Religion*, 1:296–97) in ritual functions—procession, sacrifice—whose type goes back to the Egyptian hippopotamus-goddess Taurt, "the Great One" (cf. Roscher, *Lexikon* 5:878–908 [Roeder]). S. Marinatos (*Proceedings of the Cambridge Colloquium on Mycenaean Studies* [ed. L. R. Palmer and John Chadwick; Cambridge: Cambridge University Press, 1966], 265–74) suggests identifying them with the Δίψιοι of

of the Danaids and Lemniads and the similarity of the rituals of Thesmophoria and the Lemnian fire-festival is finally confirmed by Herodotus, who connects myth and ritual.

One glance at the Romans: their μέγιστος τῶν καθαρμῶν ("the greatest of purification rituals"; Plutarch *Roman Questions* 86) concerns the *virgines Vestales* and the fire of Vesta, and it covers a whole month. It begins with a strange ἀποπομπή ("sending away"): twenty-seven puppets are collected in sanctuaries all over the town, brought to the *pons sublicius*, and, under the leadership of the *virgo*, thrown into the Tiber. They are called Argei, which possibly just means "gray men."[66] There follows a period of Lent and abstinences: no marriage is performed in this period,[67] the *flaminica*, wife of the *flamen Dialis*, is not allowed to have intercourse with her husband. From 7 to 15 June, the temple of Vesta is opened for nine days; the *matronae* gather, barefoot, to bring offerings and prayers. Especially strange is the rule of the Matralia on 11 June: the *matronae*, worshiping Mater Matuta, are not allowed to mention their sons; so they pray for their nephews. Finally on 15 June the temple of Vesta is cleaned; *quando stercus delatum fas* ("when the refuse has been removed"), ordinary life may start again. The correspondence with the Lemnian πυρφορία is striking: the ἀποπομπή and tossing into the water, the separation of the sexes, of man and wife, even of mother and son, while the fire is "purified" on which the *salus publica* is thought to depend.

Linear B texts. If these "Demons" were represented by masks in ritual (Emil Herkenrath, "Mykenische Kultszenen," *AJA* 41 [1937]: 420–21), it is tempting to see in this ritual of the "Great Goddess," influenced from Egypt, the Thesmophoria of the Danaids. Cf. also n. 34 above.

[66] Cf. Georg Wissowa, *Religion und Kultus der Römer* (2d ed.; Munich: Beck, 1912), 420; Kurt Latte, *Römische Religionsgeschichte* (Munich: Beck, 1960), 412–14; on Vestalia: Wissowa, *Religion und Kultus der Römer*, 159–60; Latte, *Römische Religionsgeschichte*, 109–10; on Matralia: Wissowa, *Religion und Kultus der Römer*, 111; Latte, *Römische Religionsgeschichte*, 97–98; Gerhard Radke, *Die Götter Altitaliens* (Munich: Aschendorff, 1965), 206–9; Jean Gagé, *Matronalia* (Brussels: Latomus, 1963), 228–35. The flogging of a slave-girl at the Matralia has its analogy in the role of the Thracian concubines at Lemnos and the hair-sacrifice of the Thracian slave-girls in Erythrai (below, n. 68). With the "tutulum" (= *pilleum lanatum*, Suetonius *apud* Servius *Commentary on Virgil's Aeneid* 2.683) of the Argei, cf. the πῖλοι of Hephaistos and Kabeiroi (above, n. 34).

[67] Plutarch *Roman Questions* 86.284F: no marriage in May; Ovid *Fasti* 6.219–234: no marriage until 15 June, the *flaminica* abstains from combing, nail-cutting, and intercourse.

Enough of comparisons;[68] the danger that the outlines of the picture become blurred as the material accumulates can scarcely be evaded. Whether it will be possible to account for the similarity of pattern which emerged, by some historical hypothesis, is a formidable problem. There seems to be a common Near Eastern background; the pattern of the Near Eastern new-year festival has been summed up in the steps of mortification, purgation, invigoration, and jubilation,[69] closely corresponding, in our case, to ἀποπομπή ("sending away"), ἀπόρρητος θυσία ("secret sacrifice"), abstinences on the one hand, *agôn* and marriage on the other. There appear to be Egyptian influences; more specifically, there are the traditions about the pre-Greek "Pelasgians" in Argos, Athens, Lemnos (according to Athenian tradition), and even in Italy.[70] But there is not much hope of disentangling the complex interrelations of Bronze Age tribes, as tradition has been furthermore complicated by contamination of legends. It may only be stated that similarities of ritual ought to be taken into account in such questions as much as certain names of tribes or of gods or certain species of pottery.

Still there are some definite conclusions, concerning the problem of myth and ritual: there is correspondence which goes beyond casual touches or secondary superimposition. But for the isolated testimonies of Myrsilos and Philostratus, we would have no clue at all to trace the myth back to Lemnian ritual, as we know nothing about the Thesmophoria of Argos. But the more we learn about the ritual, the closer the correspondence with myth turns out to be. The uprising of the women, the disappearance of the men, the unnatu-

[68] There is connection between the Lemnian festival and the Chian myth of Orion (above, n. 25); a cult legend of Erythrai implies another comparable ritual: "Herakles" arrived on a raft, and Thracian slave-girls sacrificed their hair to pull him ashore (Pausanias *Description of Greece* 7.8.5–8).

[69] Gaster, *Thespis;* for necessary qualification of the pattern, Claas J. Bleeker, *Egyptian Festivals: Enactment of Religious Renewal* (Leiden: Brill, 1967), 37–38.

[70] The evidence is collected by Fritz Lochner von Hüttenbach, *Die Pelasger* (Vienna: Gerold, 1960). The Athenians used the legends about the Pelasgians, whom they identified with the Τυρρηνοί (Thucydides *Peloponnesian War* 4.109.4), to justify their conquest of Lemnos under Miltiades (Herodotus *Hist.* 6.137ff.). There was a family of Εὐνεῖδαι at Athens, acting as heralds and worshiping Dionysos Melpomenos, Johannes Toepffer, *Attische Genealogie* (Berlin: Weidmann, 1889), 181–206; Preller and Robert, *Griechische Mythologie*, 2:852–53. On Pelasgians in Italy, Hellanikos, *FGrH* 4 F 4; Myrsilos, *FGrH* 477 F 8 *apud* Dionysius of Halicarnassus *Roman Antiquities* 1.17ff.; Varro *apud* Macrobius *Saturnalia* 1.7.28f.; on Camillus–Καδμῖλος, Alfred Ernout and A. Meillet, *Dictionnaire étymologique de la langue latine* (4th ed.; Paris: Klincksieck, 1959), s.v. Camillus.

ral life without love, the blood flowing—all this people will experience in the festival, as well as the advent of the ship which brings the joyous start of a new life. So far Jane Harrison's formula proves to be correct: "the myth is the plot of the δρώμενον";[71] its περιπέτειαι ("reversals") reflect ritual actions. The much-vexed question, whether, in this interdependence, myth or ritual is primary, transcends philology,[72] since both myth and ritual were established well before the invention of writing. Myths are more familiar to the classicist; but it is important to realize that ritual, in its function and transmission, is not dependent on words. Even today children will get their decisive impressions of religion not so much from words and surely not from dogmatic teaching, but through the behavior of their elders: that special facial expression, that special tone of voice, that poise and gesture mark the sphere of the sacred; the seriousness and confidence displayed invite imitation, while at the same time relentless sanctions are added against any violation: thus religious ritual has been transmitted in the unbroken sequence of human society. By its prominence in social life, it not only provided stimulation for story-telling, but at the same time some kind of "mental container"[73] which accounts for the stability, the unchanging patterns of mythical tradition. Thus for understanding myth, ritual is not a negligible factor.

Still one can look at flowers without caring much for roots: myth can become independent from ritual; ritual origin does not imply ritual function—nor does the absence of ritual function exclude ritual origin. Ritual, if we happen to know about it, will be illustrative especially of strange features in a myth; but as these tend to be eliminated, myth can live on by its own charm. Apollonius did not bother about Lemnian festivals, and he dropped the δυσωδία ("foul smell"). The first and decisive step in this direction was, of course, Homer; or to be more exact, Greek myth found its final form in the oral tradition of skilled singers which is behind the *Iliad*, the *Odyssey*, and the other early epics. As a consequence of

[71] Harrison, *Themis*, 331.

[72] Cf. above, n. 3. In Egypt, there were clearly rituals without myths, Bleeker, *Egyptian Festivals*, 19; Eberhard Otto, *Das Verhältnis von Rite und Mythus im Ägyptischen* (Heidelberg: Winter, 1958), 1. Biologists have recognized rituals in animal behavior; cf. Konrad Lorenz, *On Aggression* (London: Methuen, 1966), 54–80.

[73] An expression coined by William F. Jackson Knight (*Cumaean Gates* [Oxford: Blackwell, 1936], 91) for the function of the mythical pattern as to historical facts.

this successful activity of ἀοιδοί ("singers") and ῥαψῳδοί ("rhapsodes") there took place, of course, all kinds of conflation, exchange, and superimposition of myths, as local traditions were adapted to "Homeric" tales. Thus myths are often attached to rituals by secondary construction; in this case, the details rarely fit. Poets and antiquarians are free to choose between various traditions, even to develop new and striking combinations. One myth may illustrate or even replace another, the motifs overlap, as the underlying patterns are similar or nearly identical.

Still more clear than the importance of ritual for the understanding of myth is the importance of myth for the history of religion, for the reconstruction and interpretation of ritual. Myth, being the "plot," may indicate connections between rites which are isolated in our tradition; it may provide supplements for the desperate lacunae in our knowledge; it may give decisive hints for chronology. In our case, Philostratus's testimony comes from the third century C.E., Myrsilos's from the third century B.C.E., Sophocles' allusion takes us back to the fifth; but as the Hypsipyle story is known to the *Iliad*, both myth and ritual must antedate 700 B.C.E. This means that not even Greeks are concerned, but the pre-Greek inhabitants of Lemnos, whom Homer calls Σίντιες, the later Greeks Τυρρηνοί.[74] Excavations have given some picture of this pre-Greek civilization and its continuity into the Greek settlement; in spite of continuous fighting and bloodshed, there seems to have been a surprising permeability in religion, in ritual, and even in myths, between different languages and civilizations, and an equally surprising stability of traditions bound to a certain place.

If myth reflects ritual, it is impossible to draw inferences from the plot of the myth as to historical facts, or even to reduce myth to historical events. From Wilamowitz down to the *Lexikon der Alten Welt*,[75]

[74] Identification of Sinties and Tyrrhenians: Philochoros, *FGrH* 328 F 100/1 with Jacoby ad loc. Main report on the excavations (interrupted before completion by the war): Domenico Mustilli, "La necropoli tirrenica di Efestia," *ASAA* 15–16 (1932–1933): 1–278; cf. Domenico Mustilli, "Efestia," *Enciclopedia dell'arte antica, classica e orientale* (7 vols.; Rome: Istituto della Enciclopedia italiana, 1958–1966), 3:230–31; L. Bernabò-Brea, "Lemno," *Enciclopedia dell'arte antica, classica e orientale* 4:542–45. It is remarkable that there are only cremation burials in the pre-Greek necropolis (Mustilli, "La necropoli tirrenica," 267–72). Wilamowitz-Moellendorff, "Hephaistos," 231, had wrongly assumed that the pre-Greek "barbarians" would have neither city nor Hephaistos-cult.

[75] Wilamowitz-Moellendorff, "Hephaistos," 231; Carl Anderson, Klaus Bartels, and Ludwig Huber, eds., *Lexikon der Alten Welt* (Zurich: Artemis, 1965), s.v. Lemnos.

we read that the Lemnian crime reflects certain adventures of the colonization period, neatly registered in *IG* XII 8, p. 2: "Graeci ± 800–post 700" inhabiting Lemnos—as if the Lemniads had been slain by the Argonauts or the Argonauts by the Lemniads. To be cautious: it is possible that the crisis of society enacted in a festival breaks out into actual murder or revolution, which is henceforward remembered in the same festival;[76] but actual atrocities by themselves produce neither myth nor ritual—or else our century would be full of both. Another historical interpretation of the myth, given by Bachofen but envisaged already by Welcker, has, through Engels, endeared itself to Marxist historians:[77] the Lemnian crime as memory of prehistoric matriarchal society. The progress of research in prehistory, however, has left less and less space for matriarchal society in any pre-Greek Mediterranean or Near Eastern civilization. Indeed Hypsipyle did not reign over men—which *would* be matriarchy—the men have simply disappeared; and this is not a matriarchal organization of society, but a disorganization of patriarchal society, a transitional stage, a sort of carnival—this is the reason why the Lemniads were an appropriate subject for comedy.[78] Social order is turned upside down just to provoke a new reversal, which means the reestablishment of normal life.

If ritual is not dependent on myth, it cannot be explained by "beliefs" or "concepts"—which would be to substitute another

[76] In several towns of Switzerland there are traditions about a "night of murder" allegedly commemorated in carnival-like customs; a few of them are based on historical facts; cf. Ludwig Tobler, "Die Mordnächte und ihre Gedenktage," in *Kleine Schriften zur Volks- und Sprachkunde* (Frauenfeld, Switzerland: Huber, 1897), 79–105.

[77] Welcker, *Die aeschylische Trilogie*, 585ff.; Bachofen, *Das Mutterrecht*, 90; cf. above, n. 13; Friedrich Engels, *Der Ursprung der Familie, des Privateigentums und des Staats* (Hottingen-Zürich: Schweizerische Genossenschaftsbuchdruckerei, 1884); Karl Marx and Friedrich Engels, *Werke* (39 vols.; Berlin: Dietz, 1961–1974), 21:47ff.; George D. Thomson, *Studies in Ancient Greek Society* (London: Lawrence & Wishart, 1949), 175 (more circumspect: George D. Thomson, *Aeschylus and Athens: A Study in the Social Origins of Drama* [London: Lawrence & Wishart, 1941; 2d ed. 1966], 287). For a cautious reevaluation of the theory of matriarchy, cf. K. Meuli in Bachofen, *Gesammelte Werke*, 3:1107–15; on the Lycians, S. Pembroke, "Last of the Matriarchs," *Journal of the Economic and Social History of the Orient* 8 (1965): 217–47.

[78] *Λήμνιαι* were written by Aristophanes (frgs. 372–91 Kassel-Austin, *PCG*), Nikochares (frgs. 14–17 Kassel-Austin, *PCG*), and Antiphanes (frgs. 142–43 Kassel-Austin, *PCG*); cf. Alexis (frg. 139 Kassel-Austin, *PCG*), Diphilos (frg. 53), and Turpilius (90–99 Ribbeck) [*ed.*: these references reflect the corrections made in the reprinting of the original article in Buxton, *Greek Religion*].

myth for the original one. Ritual seems rather to be a necessary means of communication and solidarization in human communities, necessary for mutual understanding and cooperation, necessary to deal with the intra-human problems of attraction and, above all, aggression. There are the never-dying tensions between young and old, and also between the sexes; they necessitate periodically some sort of "cathartic" discharge; it may be possible to play off one conflict to minimize the other. This is what the myth is about: love, hatred, and their conflict, murderous instincts and piety, solidarity of women and family bonds, hateful separation and lustful reunion—this is the story of Hypsipyle, this is the essence of the ritual, too; only the myth carries, in fantasy, to the extreme what, by ritual, is conducted into more innocent channels: animals are slain instead of men, and the date is fixed when the revolution has to come to an end. Thus it is ritual which avoids the catastrophe of society. In fact only the last decades have abolished nearly all comparable rites in our world; so it is left to our generation to experience the truth that men cannot stand the uninterrupted steadiness even of the most prosperous life; it is an open question whether the resulting convulsions will lead to κάθαρσις or catastrophe.

Part II

The Vinedresser: Strategies for the Construction of Culture

Refuting Homer in the *Heroikos* of Philostratus*

Francesca Mestre

ἐξ ἀρχῆς καθ' Ὅμηρον ἐπεὶ μεμαθήκασι πάντες . . .
"Since all at first have learnt according to Homer . . ."

—Xenophanes frg. 10, DK[6] (trans. Burnet)

I have chosen to start with this fragment from Xenophanes because, with the eloquence of all fragmentary texts, it bears witness to the longstanding dependence of the Greeks on Homer. This dependence is at two levels, which are often complementary. The first is the level of exemplarity: the Homeric poems present models of all behavior and knowledge ("all . . . have learnt"). The second is the level of historical authenticity: the poems' "historical" account of the events of the past, that is, the "reality" acknowledged by all the Greeks ("at first"). It goes without saying that the Homeric poems were a common point of reference throughout the history of Greek culture. At times it was the historical value of the poems that was foregrounded; at other times it was their exemplary value. In either case, they enjoyed absolute prestige in both areas, even though, also practically from the beginning, the literal authenticity of the account is often brought into question.

Homer is the first historian: he recounts the distant past of the Greeks, their common past. Once his poems were established, the history they narrate became the official history, transmitted from city to city: the epic poet tells the story of who the Greeks are—all the Greeks—who their forefathers were—all their forefathers. The epic poet also tells of where they originated as well, obviously, who they were *not*. Homer establishes for the first time the first signs of Greek identity, in opposition to the *other*. As the different types of discourse of the Greek world—historical, political, and scientific

* I would like to thank my colleague Pilar Gómez for her invaluable comments on an earlier draft of the essay and Michael Maudsley for help with the English version.

discourses—began to acquire a specificity of their own, Homer was always the first point of reference.

As for the exemplarity of what the poems narrate, a very different picture emerges. From the times of Xenophanes onward, through the pre-Socratics such as Pythagoras or Heraclitus, criticism of Homer was as constant a feature of Greek culture as was its fidelity to him. In the sixth century B.C.E. the discussion of the reliability of Homer's accounts began; the question was whether the poems should be taken literally or understood as allegories requiring correct interpretation (as Theagenês of Rhegium proposed).[1] Later, concerned with the education of the citizen in his ideal city, Plato paid less attention to the historical value of the Homeric poems than to their potentially harmful educational influence. Indeed, in the fourth century, the problem of the exemplary nature of the Homeric texts was discussed: if Homer is the source of all knowledge and all culture, and if what he describes is exemplary and serves as the basis for an educational program, how do we account for the truculent desire for vengeance, the cruelty of fathers to sons, the harsh conduct of the gods, and the atrocities that the poems describe? How could this be explained to an increasingly sophisticated society which would no longer accept visceral reactions and was acquiring moral and ethical norms of conduct according to which the primitive actions of the remote past were incomprehensible or unjustifiable? The implausibility of some of the historical events recounted could be attributed to the fact they were just that—history—and that so long had passed, but the fact that many of the actions were far from exemplary could not be explained away so easily.

Under the empire, however, the situation was very different. Greek society or, more precisely, the culturally dominant Greek elites seeking to affirm their identity by demonstrating the traits that almost exclusively defined them, were in urgent need of Homer's support. Homer now represented the glorious past, the past that united and defined Greek identity. The Greeks under the empire needed common models that would admit those qualified to form part of the elite, models common enough to hide their internal divisions and distinctive enough to protect them from outside influences that might represent a threat or an interference—the new Roman customs, for example, or the emergence of the Christians, treated with contempt at that time. However, rather than being

[1] Theagenês of Rhegium frg. 2, DK^6.

political or religious opposition it was fundamentally cultural, with a very important meaning. Inside the idea of culture, or even language,[2] there were many other questions of a moral, ethical, and political nature. The Greek elites, who wrote in Attic Greek, were the direct heirs of the Greek past, of the grandeur of the heroes and their feats. They wished to be acknowledged as the guardians of those heroic values, which many knew and practiced, but only *belonged* to those who formed part of the group—without this opposition ever amounting to any form of resistance.[3] In this regard as well, Homer was the ideal source of moral and political authority.

But for this very reason Homer had to be corrected. If Homer described the past, the past must be as historically authentic as possible. There was no place for symbols or allegory; the account must appear plausible to the contemporary reader. It must be revised, especially its paradigmatic aspects. The question was not merely one of hermeneutics.[4]

Corrections of Homer in the works of the writers of the imperial era are commonplace.[5] Some authors refuted Homer's work in its entirety: in his famous *Troikos* (*Or.* 11), Dio Chrysostom stated that Paris was one of Helen's suitors, along with Menelaus, and since Paris was chosen, the marriage was legitimate. On this account, the Trojan War was not waged to avenge a deceived husband. For the Achaeans, and in particular for Agamemnon, the significance of the marriage was that Paris was claiming something that belonged to Greece; this was the reason for the campaign against Paris and against Troy (*Troikos* 61–64). So, according to Dio, Homer is lying. Indeed, for the mentality of the beginning of the second century C.E. it would have been far easier to accept that the Achaeans went to Troy to protect their interests and to conquer

[2] Cf. Simon Swain, *Hellenism and Empire: Language, Classicism, and Power in the Greek World A.D. 50–250* (Oxford: Clarendon, 1996), 46–51.

[3] Swain, *Hellenism and Empire*, 112: ". . . the past setting of the ancient Greek novel appealed to the Greek elite because of the role of the past in their ideology of power. They enjoyed the past in the novel for exactly the same reason they enjoyed it in the world of declamation oratory and civic life."

[4] Nor is the Alexandrian editors' elimination of verses that were incompatible with the Homeric "temperament": The case of Menelaus is a clear example; cf. Bryan Hainsworth, *The Iliad: A Commentary. Books 9–12* (vol. 3 of *The Iliad: A Commentary*, ed. G. S. Kirk; Cambridge and New York: Cambridge University Press, 1993), 175–76.

[5] According to Glen W. Bowersock (*Fiction as History: Nero to Julian* [Berkeley: University of California Press, 1994], 21), Homeric revisionism is one of the subjects of the production of fiction.

new wealth rather than merely to save someone's honor; equally, it was perfectly plausible that Homer was obliged to write the story he did to content his public, since this was how he made his living (*Troikos* 15). And above all, it was plausible in the context of this speech, because Dio was doing exactly the same thing: the *Troikos* was in all likelihood composed to be delivered in Troy. This was the time of the empire, and according to the official Roman tradition, Troy was the ancestor of Rome, just as the Achaeans were the ancestors of the Greeks. So one could hypothesize that the Trojans were in fact the victors.

There are other refutations of points of detail, both in the poems and as regards the figure of Homer himself. Most of them, in my view, refer to the ἦθος of the characters, including Homer; although they are points of detail, they are highly significant in each case.[6]

The works of Philostratus, in particular the *Heroikos*, are among the most valuable examples of these revisionist practices during the imperial era. For some scholars, in fact, this revisionism is the work's sole objective; that is, the rest of the themes in the *Heroikos*, its narrative structure and the contents, are only there to authorize this correction of Homer, to stress the veracity of a series of events via the presentation of a "correct" version.[7]

The Greek elites of the imperial era coexisted with the Romans. The Greeks were not alone in seeking to preserve their cultural manifestations; the imperial court was also keen that Greek culture should survive, in order to appropriate a certain amount of history and civilization for themselves. The source of authority that the past represented for the Greeks was also of great interest to the Romans, and so cultural manifestations were resurrected. These manifestations all had a certain religious element; though their recovery was artificial from a religious perspective, there is no denying their cultural vitality. This resurrection was extremely

[6] Cf., for example, the treatment of Penelope in the *Euboikos* (*Or.* 7) by Dio Chrysostom, or the great rejection of the heroic condition that Lucian's *Dialogues of the Dead* represents; on this, see Francesca Mestre, "Por qué miente Homero (Una visión histórica sobre los poemas homéricos en época imperial)," in *Actas del X congreso español de estudios clásicos: 21–25 de septiembre de 1999* (ed. Emilio Crespo and Maria José Barrios Castro; 3 vols.; Madrid: Ediciones Clásicas, 2000), 1:533–40.

[7] Cf. Graham Anderson, *Philostratus: Biography and* Belles Lettres *in the Third Century A.D.* (London: Croom Helm, 1986), 253: "[It] becomes too clear that the cult and powers of Protesilaos offer only a preliminary excursus before the main subject—the correction of Homer."

important because it was supported by the emperors themselves: just as Nero traveled to Greece and visited Olympia in an attempt to revive the Games,[8] in the time of Philostratus (in 214–215 C.E) Caracalla traveled to Asia Minor, visiting the Trojan Plain and paying homage to the tombs of the heroes buried there (cf. Dio Cassius *Roman History* 78.16.8; Herodian *History* 4.8.3). There are two possible interpretations of this gesture: either it was in support of a sentiment that was already alive among the Greeks under the empire, or it gave impetus to a way of recovering the past, which was to be capitalized on immediately by the cultural leaders of the moment.[9] The first explanation would represent an attempt to create a type of pagan aretalogy to challenge the Christian aretalogies, such as the lives of saints, that had already gained a certain importance in the second and third centuries C.E. The second would suggest a desire to use the heroes of the tradition to heighten the sentiment of identification: after appropriate processing by the sophists, they were to become a fundamental reference point for the definition of Greek existence.

It goes without saying that Philostratus's *Heroikos* ties in neatly with this idea of the revival of the cult of the heroes.[10] What is more, even conceding that this cult had or may have had a substantial religious component (indeed, Philostratus's re-creation clearly evokes a religious scenario in which the hero Protesilaos arises from his tomb to succor his human friends and to teach them in all senses of the term), the reference to the epic heroes is a form of metahistory. Again, the ἔπος, Homer, is the historical reference point used to speak of the past, the past re-created by those Greeks of the empire. To an extent this past was re-created to suit their own ends, but it supported Homer nonetheless.

Philostratus is a man of his times, more exactly, a member of the Greek elites under the Roman Empire. For him, the past—the past that emanates above all from Homer, but from other sources in the tradition as well—was a question of identity, in the sense that it

[8] Dio Chrysostom's *Olympic Discourse* (*Or.* 12) is an echo of this visit.

[9] Opinion is divided as to the interpretation of this imperial gesture: cf. Teresa Mantero, *Ricerche sull'* Heroikos *di Filostrato* (Genoa: University of Genoa, Istituto di Filologia Classica e Medioevale, 1966), 21–47, and Anderson, *Philostratus*, 241–57, above all.

[10] On the religious value of certain features under the Severans ("un engouement croissant pour les formes les plus irrationnelles de la ferveur religieuse") and the place of Philostratus's *Heroikos* among them, cf. Alain Billault, *L'univers de Philostrate* (Collection Latomus 252; Brussels: Latomus, 2000), 38–40.

also preserved his *status*.[11] His works, in my view, form a consistent corpus in this regard.[12] For instance, the *Life of Apollonius* is a clear example of this new pagan aretalogy. However, the characterization of the protagonist, Apollonius, is a heroic characterization. Apollonius is a new hero; he even has a ἡρῷον raised by Caracalla (as we know from Dio Cassius *Roman History* 77.18.4). This would be of little relevance to our theme if it were not because Philostratus's characterization of this new hero—a relatively recent hero, since only a century separates the Apollonius from his biographer—must bear connection to the heroes of the past: Book 4 of the *Life of Apollonius* takes Apollonius from far-off lands back to Ionia, where he is first received by the Greek oracles and, after a series of prodigious feats, predictions, and wise teachings, he goes to Ilion, where he decides to visit Achilles' ghost. The interview takes place, and the exchange coincides at many points with the section devoted to the son of Peleus and Thetis in the *Heroikos* (*Life of Apollonius* 4.11 and 16; cf. *Her.* 44.5–57.17), not only as regards Achilles himself, but also as regards Homer's descriptions of the Trojan War and the heroes. In that case, the refutation or the corrections follow the same lines, especially with reference to Palamedes. Indeed, in the *Life of Apollonius* Achilles plays the same role of legitimizing the non-Homeric versions that Protesilaos plays in the *Heroikos*.

Apollonius, this new "modern" hero, embodies the features that made the Greeks distinctive in the new world, in their new surroundings. These features create what Flinterman[13] calls "the Greek sense of superiority," which is also evident in the *Lives of the Sophists*, with the difference that in the latter work what is evoked and defined in terms of *Greekness* is the real human world, far removed from the divine world, whereas in the *Life of Apollonius*, as in the *Heroikos*, there are also elements of a religious nature. Not all these elements are active, but they evoke a certain religiosity nonetheless. As for the relation of these works to Homer, Philostra-

[11] Cf. Swain, *Hellenism and Empire*, 380–400.

[12] My starting point—perhaps taking a slight risk—is that the *Heroikos*, the *Life of Apollonius*, the *Lives of the Sophists*, and the two first books of the *Imagines*, are by the same Philostratus. On the attribution of the preserved works and the identity of the various Philostrati, see above all Jaap-Jan Flinterman, *Power, Paideia, and Pythagoreanism: Greek Identity, Conceptions of the Relationship between Philosophers and Monarchs, and Political Ideas in Philostratus'* Life of Apollonius (Amsterdam: Gieben, 1995), 5–28, which has a full bibliography on the subject.

[13] Flinterman, *Power*, 89.

tus does not in fact openly challenge the poet's account, as Dio Chrysostom does in *Troikos*. Nor does he challenge the entire system, as Lucian does in *Dialogues of the Dead*. Far from it: he means only to provide a more rational version, adapted slightly to his times.

I turn now to the *Heroikos*. The first point to make (however obvious it may sound) is that the work could not have been written without Homer, without the *Iliad* or without the *Odyssey*. From what we could call a "historical" perspective, the Achaeans' expedition to Troy provides Philostratus's work with its central theme, but in addition every episode, every anecdote, every character (on both sides), the relations between the characters—that is, the backdrop of the story—are indebted to Homer at all levels, both in terms of its structure and in terms of its content.

If this is the case, why refute Homer? And what exactly is there to refute?

The *Heroikos* neither is nor claims to be simply a commentary on the great works of the tradition or an exercise in sophistry like the μελέται.[14] It is a new model of reference for the Greek elite, the cradle of its existence and its identity. So the Homeric framework is vital, but in urgent need of a revision, a modern adaptation, a reformulation: new elements to make it accessible to the interests and concerns of Philostratus's readership—Greeks, but citizens of the Roman Empire, living at the end of the second century C.E.

Apart from the corrections of points of detail—some of which are significant, but others less so—the reformulation or renewal of the tradition that derives from Homer has three key elements. The first is the treatment of the mythical characters, the second the treatment and characterization of contemporary characters (the vinedresser and the Phoenician), and finally, the incorporation of other more modern accounts characteristic of contemporary literary genres. These three elements are the basis for the formulation that Philostratus presents, and all three, in their ways, refer to Homer either to contradict him, to add to him, or also to follow him faithfully.

The mythical characters are presented as individuals, in a more humanized form than in the Homeric model: the hero is not now the representative of a collective endeavor. He is a man—a great man, but

[14] It is probably this as well; cf. Bowersock, *Fiction as History*, 111–12; Anderson, *Philostratus*, 241–43; Billault, *L'univers de Philostrate*, 139–40.

a man nonetheless[15]—although the juxtaposition of acts of extreme cruelty and vengeance alongside acts underpinned by a profound sense of justice is hard to explain.[16] Even the theme of death and immortality, key to the ancient religiosity of the hero, has been particularized. The heroes are dead, but their ghosts are still useful to humans; they have a certain transcendence over them but above all a utility for them; they advise people how to manage their fields and teach them how to pay homage, even if it is to themselves. It is true that the description of the heroes harks back to ancient times—their superhuman stature, their physical beauty, and their courage (*Her.* 7.9–12; 8.14–17; 10.1–4; 22.1–4)—but their ἦθος and their conduct no longer prize honor above all else. Other values, we might say more conventional ones, now take priority: honesty, sincerity—this is why Odysseus comes off so badly—goodness, and the sense of justice, the family, marriage, and so on (*Her.* 11.4–6; 21.1–9). Protesilaos himself is described as a model husband, concerned with his wife's well-being (*Her.* 2.7; 11.1). In the characterization of Achilles, personal aspects of the life of the hero of heroes are stressed for the first time—they had never been considered important before. His marital commitments, to Polyxena during his lifetime and to Helen after death, account for a large part of what we learn of the son of Peleus and Thetis, along with his childhood and some details of his family life (*Her.* 46.1–7; 51.1–13).

In the characterization of the two contemporary characters who act out the dialogue, the vinedresser and the Phoenician, there are also elements that shed light on the reliability of Homer. The first point is that the foreigner, the Phoenician, is Homer's principal spokesman; that is to say, he upholds the immutable version of the myth. At the beginning the Phoenician is unwilling to believe anything that strays from the original version, even though he accepts that Homer's story contains a substantial amount of fiction (*Her.* 7.1–2; 7.9–10). He prefers to believe this fiction rather than a variant of it, even when this variant is presented to him as the reality.

[15] Cf. Pilar Gómez and Francesca Mestre, "Lo religioso y lo político: Personajes del mito y hombres de la historia," in *Estudios sobre Plutarco: Misticismo y religiones mistéricas en la obra de Plutarco* (ed. A. Pérez Jiménez and F. Casadesús Bordoy; Actas del VII Simposio Español sobre Plutarco, Palma de Mallorca, 2–4 noviembre 2000; Madrid-Málaga: Ediciones Clásicas & Charta Antiqua, 2001), 365–78.

[16] The example of Achilles is particularly significant; he exacts vengeance by quartering a Trojan girl whom he orders to be taken to the island of Leukê (*Her.* 56.10); cf. also Hektor, who murders a young Assyrian for confusing his statue with one of Achilles and then disposes of the body (*Her.* 19.3–7).

The vinedresser, for his part, skillfully persuades the Phoenician of this, thanks to the prodigious fact that he is the spokesman of Protesilaos (*Her.* 8.18). From this point on, the Phoenician's keenness to hear more stories becomes insatiable, until he understands what he hears as something different, not as a correction of the same account but a new one, referring more or less to the same story but a new version, without interferences. So the Phoenician can continue to paraphrase Homer in the conversation, but what the vinedresser–Protesilaos says is taken as new, as another piece in the collection. So the fact that the Phoenician is a foreigner does not stop him from having the same points of reference as regards the Greeks, even though he does not share this identity,[17] or at least does not share it in the same way.

The debt to Homer is visible even in the construction of the dialogue. The vinedresser and the Phoenician converse, and the one seeks to persuade the other in the fashion of Odysseus and Eumaios in Book 14 of the *Odyssey*. As Anderson rightly observes,[18] there are many coincidences: there is a discussion on what is true and what is false (*Od.* 14.321–334); a dream concerning what is happening and what is about to happen is recounted (*Od.* 14.495–499); there is a test of the truth (*Od.* 14.363–400); they speak of the hero's wife—Penelope, Laodameia—(*Od.* 14.244); and in both cases even the dog is mentioned (*Od.* 14.29–38).

Also, as we said above, in some cases the refutation consists in introducing more modern aspects into the characterization of the personae and the heroes. These features, related for the most part to the everyday lives of individuals, are now attributed to the heroes, something that the ideology of the epic did not contemplate. They are far removed from the ἔπος, but not from the new type of hero that the sophists propagate: the protagonists of the love and adventure romances, so human and often so banal, but representative of the ideal model of the man in the street. Philostratus adds a number of novelesque touches to the lives and feats of the heroes in an attempt to bring the protagonists of the myths closer to the present.[19] Of the mythical character only a certain authority is preserved,

[17] Cf. Marcello Massenzio, "Prefazione," in *Filostrato: Eroico* (ed. and trans. Valeria Rossi; Venice: Marsilio, 1997), 13; on the universality of Greek culture on the one hand and the exclusive nature of the "inheritance" on the other, cf. Swain, *Hellenism and Empire*, 9–13.

[18] Cf. Anderson, *Philostratus*, 249–50.

[19] This procedure is found also in most of the other writers of the era, including Dio Chrysostom, Lucian, and even Plutarch, each after their own fashion.

and, above all, Philostratus strives to attribute divine wisdom to the heroes.

It is clear that the *Heroikos*, as a whole, takes Homer as a reference. When it suits the author to do so, the content of the poems is amended, contradicted, or added to. Nonetheless, as we have seen, it is not a mere exercise in refutation. Philostratus, anchored in the tradition, also has recourse to other cultural aspects of the ancient Greek world to construct his work.

The framework in which, or the backdrop against which, the initiation of the non-Greek into the new Greek *imaginaire* takes place—where the Phoenician will learn, as he learned in Homer, what is Greek in the eyes of the Greeks—is not Homeric. The recreation of a *locus amoenus* in which to situate the focal conversation is closer to the tradition of the Platonic dialogue (cf. especially *Phaedrus* 230b–c), inherited in turn from Hesiod's *Theogony*. It goes without saying that the magic of the setting, the country landscape and the time of day—noon or nighttime—also has its own tradition inside the Hellenistic pastoral,[20] which was followed by the novel[21] and other writings by authors of the Roman era.[22] All these backdrops become the ideal framework for bringing out ancient polarities: the *country* and the *city*—the vinedresser has left the city because only the country lifestyle permits contact with supernatural beings[23]—the *Greek* and the *non-Greek*—we have already spoken of the Phoenician as a foreigner, though familiar with Greek culture, as are all people—and finally, the *initiated* and the *uninitiated*, another way of denoting those who belong to the group and those who do not.

Strictly speaking, however, the most striking refutation of Homer in the *Heroikos* concerns an absence. Palamedes is not even mentioned in Homer, which suggests that he did not participate in the Trojan War. But in Philostratus's account, Palamedes is the

[20] I refer above all to Theocritus.

[21] I refer now to the novel by Longus (*Daphnis and Chloe* 2.4.1) in which Eros appears to reveal amorous sentiments to the young adolescents.

[22] Cf., merely as an example, Lucian *Anacharsis* 16: before embarking on his account of initiation into the Greek way of life, Solon invites Anacharsis to find a suitable place; the fact that it is noon, when the heat is at its most intense, means that they have to find a place in the shade and with some breeze.

[23] See here the parallel with the life of the hunter in the mountains of Euboea in Dio Chrysostom *Euboikos;* on the interpretation of life in nature, see Francesca Mestre, "Urbanidad y autosuficiencia: La moneda no es *physis*," in *Actas del XIII simposio nacional de estudios clásicos* (La Plata, Argentina: Universidad Nacional de La Plata, 1997), 239–45.

greatest hero of all times, unaccountably ignored by Homer.[24] What is more, to counterbalance the exaltation of the figure of Palamedes, Philostratus censures the figure of Odysseus, so much so that it becomes the explanation of Homer's inexplicable oversight (*Her.* 43.10–16).

Yet did Homer omit all mention of Palamedes for a particular reason, or should we assume that if Palamedes does not appear in the poems it is because there is no tradition that links him to them, that is, his traditions are all more modern or unconnected to the epic? What I have said about this thus far provides a possible answer: Philostratus, being who he is and living in the era in which he lives, finds more "heroic" features in Palamedes, the civilizing hero par excellence, than in the very divine Achilles or the treacherous Odysseus.[25]

Odysseus calls Palamedes a sophist in Protesilaos's account (*Her.* 33.25; cf. also Aristophanes *Frogs* 1451 and Plato *Phaedrus* 261d); in his *Palamedes*, Gorgias has the protagonist call himself σοφός and εὐεργέτης, and he could easily be compared to Aeschylus's Prometheus, called a σοφιστής himself (*Palamedes* 16 and 36; cf. Aeschylus *Prometheus Bound* 62 and 944 as well as Lucian *Prometheus* 4–20). A reading of Gorgias's speech reveals Philostratus's source; one by one, the themes of Gorgias's defense are reproduced in the *Heroikos*.

Again, if we look at the other great speech of the sophist of Leontini, the *Encomium of Helen*, which attempts to refute accusations of acts of deceit and at the same time to put an end to ignorance through truth (*Encomium of Helen* 2), we see that Philostratus's debt to the sophistic positions of Gorgias is profound, if implicit, in the *Heroikos*, just as it is (though explicit) in the *Lives of the Sophists*.[26] The words of Gorgias are an indispensable theoreti-

[24] But not by the tragic poets: cf. Aeschylus frgs. 181a, 182 Radt; Sophocles frg. 432 Radt; Euripides frgs. 578, 581, 588 Nauck^2; see *Cypria* frg. 21 Bernabé, as well.

[25] Cf. *Life of Apollonius* 4.13–16, when Apollonius questions Achilles' ghost. The ghost tells him that he should pay homage to Palamedes and briefly summarizes—with the same arguments that Protesilaos uses in the *Heroikos*—the list of good deeds performed by Palamedes and the great injustice the Greeks committed against him because of the lies of Odysseus.

[26] Cf. *Lives of the Sophists* 481–482; on the Gorgian character of the category of the Second Sophistic, which Philostratus defends in the *Lives of the Sophists*, see Francesca Mestre and Pilar Gómez, "Les Sophistes de Philostrate," in *Figures de l'intellectuel en Grèce ancienne* (ed. Nicole Loraux and Carles Miralles; Paris: Belin, 1998), 333–69.

cal reference point for Philostratus, or an example of what he, as a sophist of this new era, aims to establish. The *Heroikos* draws clearly on the first part of Gorgias's *Encomium of Helen*, where the speaker says that the κόσμος of a city is the courage of its men (the heroes, then?), just as the κόσμος of a body is its beauty, that of a soul its wisdom, that of an action its excellence, and that of a speech its truth.[27] Indeed, Philostratus is seeking to define the Greek identity, as if the Greek identity were the city that Gorgias mentions; he is therefore bound to appeal to the heroes and to praise their beauty, wisdom, excellence, whether or not these characteristics are described in the main source, the Homeric poems. He does this via his literary construction in which a fictional character, the vinedresser, inspired by a hero, gives speeches in which he reveals the truth. This truth, needless to say, has nothing to do with history or with fact, but is the truth that is required to meet the objectives that Philostratus has established. For, also following Gorgias,[28] recounting what the hearer already knows creates an atmosphere of trust and familiarity, and persuades, but does not give τέρψις ("pleasure"). The pleasure, then, in the speech of the vinedresser–Protesilaos is to be found above all at the points where it distances itself from Homer: the τέρψις is in the novelty, the surprise, the denial, or the correction of what is already known.

Gorgias is the sophist par excellence, the grand master of sophistic knowledge, a guide without equal for Philostratus. If this is evident in the *Lives of the Sophists*, it is no less so in the *Heroikos:* Philostratus follows the theoretical positions of the *Encomium of Helen* faithfully, and there are compelling reasons for believing that the most important case of refutation of Homer—the one that triggers off practically all the others, that is, the apology of Palamedes as the greatest of the heroes—would not exist at all if it were not for Gorgias's earlier defense. Therefore, though it is true that the refutation of Homer is necessary in the *Heroikos* to adapt and modernize the heroic values to the setting of the second and third centuries C.E., it is no less true that the basis of the refutation and what makes the refutation possible is part of the tradition and not an invention of the Second Sophistic: it is an appropriation of the

[27] *Encomium of Helen* 1: κόσμος πόλει μὲν εὐανδρία, σώματι δὲ κάλλος, ψυχῇ δὲ σοφία, πράγματι δὲ ἀρετή, λόγῳ δὲ ἀλήθεια, "Harmony for a city is courage; for a body, beauty; for a soul, wisdom; for a deed, virtue; for a speech, truth."

[28] *Encomium of Helen* 5: τὸ γὰρ τοῖς εἰδόσιν ἃ ἴσασι λέγειν πίστιν μὲν ἔχει, τέρψιν δὲ οὐ φέρει, "In fact, speaking to those who know what they know shows confidence, but does not give pleasure."

games that the first sophists engaged in to undermine the absolute truths inherited from the Archaic period and thus to modernize the Greeks' worldview. It is an appropriation, it should be said, followed as faithfully as the canons of the tradition itself. The contribution of the Second Sophistic, of which Philostratus is an excellent example, is that following Homer, drawing on his work and his prestige, is not incompatible with following those who surpassed him.

To move on to another point: Homer, during the Roman era, was used as an encyclopedic resource. For the study of people, he was used as a textbook of physiognomy, because according to the sophists, for something to be true one must be able to see it with one's own eyes; for this reason the *ekphrasis* becomes a key genre in the literature of the time.[29] It is practically certain that Philostratus is the author not only of the *Heroikos*, but of one of the series of *Imagines* as well; the similarities between the works cannot, in my view, be a matter of chance. And Philostratus is not the first to reflect on the difference between what is given by poetry and what is given by the image.

Dio Chrysostom's *Olympic Discourse* (*Or.* 12) explains well the frontier between the narrative and the visual, however much the visual takes its inspiration from the narrative. In Dio's speech, Phidias defends his creation, the statue of Zeus in Olympia; he admits that poetry comes before image (*Olympic Discourse* 56–57) and defends himself from the power of representation of his statue in the imagination of the Greeks by saying "I was not the first narrator and master of the truth" (ἐνθυμεῖσθε δὲ ὅτι οὐκ ἐγὼ πρῶτος ὑμῖν ἐγενόμην ἐξηγητὴς καὶ διδάσκαλος τῆς ἀληθείας, *Olympic Discourse* 56). The inference is clear: Homer was the first narrator, the master of truth, and Phidias used his descriptions to make "his" Zeus, which became the Zeus of all the Greeks. However, the features of the finished statue differ from those described in the poetry. The artistic creation does not represent only physically, but morally as well. Phidias's Zeus is calm, gentle, not deceitful, and these qualities now become established once and for all. Homer's Zeus, in contrast,

[29] On the importance of the visual effect in speeches and how this effect is achieved, see Barbara Cassin, "Procédures sophistiques pour construire l'évidence," in *Dire l'évidence (Philosophie et rhétorique antiques): Actes du colloque de Créteil et de Paris (24–25 mars 1995)* (ed. Carlos Lévy and Laurent Pernot; Paris: L'Harmattan, 1997), 15–29; and Ruth Webb, "Mémoire et imagination: Les limites de l'*enargeia* dans la théorie rhétorique grecque," in *Dire l'évidence*, 229–48.

could also be cruel and treacherous. The image, then, can provide a more immutable truth than can poetry.

Philostratus presents the heroes in the *Heroikos* in much the same way as in his *Imagines*, which are close, in terms of their intention and procedure, to Phidias's Zeus in Dio's speech. In the *Heroikos* the plausibility of the qualities of the heroes, in both their physical and moral description, is more the result of the procedure of creating an image than of that of the poetry; precisely for this reason, the poetry that inspires this "gallery of heroes" must be refuted in certain cases. When the Phoenician asks the vinedresser if Protesilaos knows the stories that the poets know (*Heroikos* 7), he implies, even though he is not yet willing to abandon his faith in what Homer says, that there is another way of knowing the facts, that is, the truth. The vinedresser answers that the hero, once dead, can observe everything from his vantage point on high, at first hand, without intermediaries, because he now combines mortal life with divinity. So, when the vinedresser transmits what Protesilaos says, he does so as if he were describing images, a clear example of this direct knowledge: a metahuman knowledge, just as his discourse is metaliterary. Thanks to this, neither Protesilaos when he speaks to the vinedresser, nor the vinedresser when he speaks to the Phoenician, nor Philostratus when he speaks to us, narrates things as Homer would have done; instead, they place it in front of our eyes; they represent it visually. So the *Heroikos*, like the *Imagines*, is like a photograph album, a repository of the history of an individual or in this case of a group. It is thus a place to visit in order to reaffirm our identity and to show to others so that they understand who we are.

There is no doubt that the *Heroikos* refutes, corrects, and rectifies Homer. This is explicitly stated; each episode or detail from the Trojan War, each amendment of the character of the heroes, their qualities and weaknesses or their physical appearance, are adduced either from a particular passage or from the information presented in the Homeric poems as a whole. However, this refutation takes a series of different forms and is motivated by different intentions, as this essay has sought to demonstrate.

Probably the most important aspect is the process of adapting the figures that Philostratus presents as common reference points of identity in terms of contemporary values: the hero of the past must be equated to the πεπαιδευμένος of the present,[30] who must be an

[30] Cf. Anderson, *Philostratus*, 284.

example to imitate in a plausible contemporary situation. This plausibility requires a setting of its own, different from that of the Homeric account.

Second, the visual presentation is better suited both for imitation and for superimposition on the traditional presentation. This is particularly so if we bear in mind that the tradition no longer has an inhibitory effect; it is no longer an edifice that will collapse if a single stone is moved. The tradition is so firmly established, the cultural vitality of the time so intense, that the refutation is legitimized more by the need for correction, in the case of the *Heroïkos*, since it is contemplated from a different perspective, than by the desire to construct something new.

Finally, even though to an extent the decision not to take the Homeric version as the exclusive guide and to draw on other accounts that contradict or challenge Homer and reflect other attitudes and values is a refutation in itself, it is curious that not even this undermines the authority of the Homeric poems as common reference points. It seems that conceiving the tradition as a whole, with its own contradictions, new versions, corrections, modern adaptations, was the only way to respect all the moments and all the contents, and only by incorporating it wholesale as a sign of identity could the Greeks under the empire draw maximum benefit from it, realize its worth, and absorb it in its entirety.

Living in the Past: Allusive Narratives and Elusive Authorities in the World of the *Heroikos*

Jeffrey Rusten

Agamemnon is my long-lost relative, I believe. Sometimes I come by myself during the night and converse with him, as a matter of fact. It's a marvelous feeling . . . of certainty that those things you are around had life once upon a time.

—Archaeologist George Mylonas,
at the site of Mycenae[1]

I

The *Heroikos* is an encounter between a man of action and travel, of the present and commerce, and another man firmly rooted in a simple life of retirement and immersed in the past. In some respects it resembles Dio Chrysostom's *Euboikos* or Herodes Atticus's tales of his meetings with Agathion, the countryside's "Herakles" (Dio Chrysostom *Euboikos;* Philostratus *Lives of the Sophists* 2.552–554); but in the *Heroikos* there is an added twist of its dialogue form. The dominant character is not the Phoenician skeptic whose nationality provokes so much speculation, but the vineyard-keeper, a much more original and dominant creation. In him Philostratus embodies a complex of traits—rusticity, a simple life and occupation, piety and morality, high education and impeccable Attic speech, narrative and physiognomic skill, and finally his unique access to Protesilaos as informant—that makes him the per-

[1] Interviewed by Michael Wood in the BBC documentary "In Search of the Trojan War," episode 2, 1985. The translations below are my own; those from the *Heroikos* were prepared with the aid of an National Endowment for Humanities translation grant for the summer of 1986. All citations from the *Heroikos* are from Ludo de Lannoy, ed., *Flavii Philostrati Heroicus* (Leipzig: Teubner, 1977). I am grateful to the participants at the conference "Philostratus's *Heroikos*, Religion, and Cultural Identity," whose comments improved this paper, and to an anonymous referee.

fect spokesman for the literary, religious, and moral superiority of the world of the Greek heroes.

If we look into the background of the vineyard-keeper's tales and explanations, we often find the trail of evidence hard to follow. A formal barrier to our search is the dialogue's multiple authorities: we think of it as the work of Philostratus, yet every conceivable source he may have adapted is filtered through the mouth of the vineyard-keeper, who has a distinct personality and may not always speak for the author. The vineyard-keeper in turn relies for much of his information on the hero Protesilaos so that, paradoxically, in the world of the *Heroikos* the mythical events have the most immediate authority: an anecdote about Hadrian is oral tradition from one's grandfather (*Her.* 8.1), but for the events at Troy we have "first-hand" evidence.[2] Clearly, to speak of "sources" at all in the *Heroikos* is much less valid than it would be for even another work of this fertile period of reworking of classical texts.[3]

Yet Philostratus is clearly not some *Schwindelautor* like the ficticious Dictys, the presumed author of the *Journal of the Trojan War*, who merely invents and recombines narrative elements in a fantastic context;[4] nor does he declare his independence from his subject while imitating it, like the classical dialogues of Lucian.[5] The *Heroikos* abounds in allusions: to Philostratus's other works, as Friedrich Solmsen showed more than fifty years ago in a groundbreaking article;[6] to his locality and circle of friends, as Simone Follet has shown;[7] to the contemporary world of celebrity athletes

[2] This aspect of the dialogue is also an extension of other works, notably the first-century C.E. account of "Dictys"; see Stefan Merkle, *Die Ephemeris Belli Troiani des Diktys von Kreta* (Studien zur klassischen Philologie 44; New York: Peter Lang, 1989); Peter Grossardt, *Die Trugreden in der Odyssee und ihre Rezeption in der antiken Literatur* (Sapheneia 2; Bern: Peter Lang, 1998).

[3] Despite the title of his work, Grentrup discusses only literary sources for the Trojan War (Henricus Grentrup, "De *Heroici* Philostrati fabularum fontibus" [diss., University of Münster, Westphalia, 1914]).

[4] Simone Follet, "Philostratus's *Heroikos* and the Regions of the Northern Aegean," 221–35 in this volume.

[5] The Phoenician's earlier skepticism is like that expressed by Lucian (*Parliament of the Gods* 12) about six heroes: two oracular ones (Trophônios and Amphilokhos), two athlete-healers (Polydamas and Theagenês), and two Trojan War fighters (Hektor and Protesilaos). Jones plausibly suggests that such an attack contributed to the motives for the *Heroikos* itself. Christopher P. Jones, *Culture and Society in Lucian* (Cambridge, Mass.: Harvard University Press, 1986), 35–37.

[6] Friedrich Solmsen, "Some Works of Philostratus the Elder," *TAPA* 71 (1940): 556–72.

[7] Follet, "Philostratus's *Heroikos* and the Regions of the Northern Aegean."

(Helix and others in *Heroikos* 14–15); possibly even (though more covertly) to the imperial cult and the struggle between Christianity and paganism. Finally, there are especially frequent allusions to Greek literature. Even if we must give up the idea that the *Heroikos* can help us reconstruct lost classical literature (despite his subject he adds almost nothing to the fragments of Euripides or the Epic Cycle), we may recognize that Philostratus has a thorough familiarity, despite his eschewing of pedantic quotations, with Greek literature, which is the foundation of the discourse of Hellenism.

His literary allusions are fascinating and sometimes torturous to trace. One would think that since we possess the complete texts of Homer, identifying allusions to the *Iliad* or the *Odyssey* would be straightforward, but in fact they are often misleading. Note the apparently incorrect Homeric references: at *Her.* 18.2, which mentions "the story in the *Madness*" as if referring to a section of the *Iliad* or a tragedy (neither of which is known to exist); at *Her.* 23.24, which locates Têlephos's healing of Achilles "in Troy" instead of "at Aulis"; at *Her.* 51.7, which mistakes the "Second Weighing of Souls" for "Second Nekyia." Stranger still is *Her.* 51.1, where the vineyard-keeper claims that *Il.* 22.359, which in our texts refers to Achilles' future death at the Skaian gates, is consistent with an ambush at the temple of Thymbraian Apollo. Are these allusions slips by the author (or by the vineyard-keeper), variants, or textual corruptions?[8]

At other times a story is vouched for in a surprising way. The vineyard-keeper gives details from the *Contest of Homer and Hesiod* as secrets from Protesilaos (*Her.* 43.9), but when it comes to a tale that is a mystery to us (*Her.* 56.5), he says, "The story of the golden pitcher which once appeared on the island of Chios has been told by wise men, and why would anyone repeat something told so well?"

The accuracy of site descriptions is sometimes in doubt. Is the description of the ruined shrine of Protesilaos (*Heroikos* 8) based on a place that Philostratus knew well in nearby Elaious, or is it a

[8] Follet notes another slip with "Nemea" for "Tegea" in *Her.* 8.3; she is correct that the former is *lectio difficilior* and should be retained. Follet, "Philostratus's *Heroikos* and the Regions of the Northern Aegean," 225. Some slips elsewhere in Philostratus are noted by Christopher P. Jones, "The Reliability of Philostratus," in *Approaches to the Second Sophistic: Papers Presented at the 105th Annual Meeting of the American Philological Association* (ed. Glen W. Bowersock; University Park, Penn.: American Philological Association, 1974), 15.

reflection of Herodotus *Hist.* 9.116–121?[9] Is Ilion the bustling Roman city adorned by imperial favor,[10] which is now being excavated by a joint United States and German team, or are the heroes' statues and monuments described by the vineyard-keeper, as well as their interventions among mortals (*Heroikos* 19–23), largely imaginary?

Religious cults are similarly slippery. Walter Burkert has drawn attention to the description of the fire ritual in the cult of Hephaistos on Lemnos in *Her.* 53.5–7 as likely to be based on eyewitness testimony (a Lucius Flavius Philostratus was actually a priest of Hephaistos in a third-century C.E. inscription from Hephaistia; *IG* XII 8.27).[11] Yet its description is presented as inside information by the vineyard-keeper, while he takes for granted that the Phoenician will know about the previously unheard-of ritual of the Thessalians at Troy for Achilles (*Her.* 53.8) and even gives a cult hymn to Thetis, apparently invented for this occasion.[12] The eerie description of Achilles' cult on the island of Leukê in the Black Sea, which closes the story, sounds chillingly fantastic, but dedications to Achilles have been found in such a place.[13] Philostratus also tells a story (*Heroikos* 56–57) of the Amazons' attack on the island and a

[9] The archaeological remains are meager: R. Demangel, *Le tumulus dit de Protésilas* (Fouilles du corps d'occupation français de Constantinople 1; Paris: De Boccard, 1926). For the status of Greek mythical/religious localities in this period, see Susan E. Alcock, "Material Witness: An Archaeological Context for the *Heroikos*," in this volume.

[10] Brian Rose, "Ilion in the Early Empire," in *Patris und Imperium: Kulturelle und politische Identität in den Städten der römischen Provinzen Kleinasiens in der frühen Kaiserzeit* (ed. C. Berns, H. von Hesberg, L. Vandeput, and M. Waelkens; Louvain: Peeters, 2002), 32–47.

[11] Walter Burkert, "Jason, Hypsipyle, and New Fire at Lemnos: A Study in Myth and Ritual," 103 in this volume.

[12] The technical correctness of the language of the Thessalians' sacrifice is noted in Albert Henrichs, "Keeping Dead Heroes Alive: The Revival of Hero Cult in the *Heroikos*" (paper presented at the conference "Philostratus's *Heroikos*, Religion, and Cultural Identity," Cambridge, Mass., 4 May 2001), and Christopher Jones pointed out to me that the passage is in many ways a model (although not linguistically) for the long description of a Thessalian sacrifice to Neoptolemos at Delphi, including a hymn to Thetis, in Heliodorus *Aethiopica* 2.34–35 (a work that also alludes to the *Life of Apollonius*), but the skepticism of F. Huhn and E. Bethe ("Philostrats *Heroikos* und Diktys," *Hermes* 52 [1917]: 613–24) still seems warranted.

[13] Christopher P. Jones, *The Roman World of Dio Chrysostom* (Cambridge, Mass.: Harvard University Press, 1978), 62; Guy Hedreen, "The Cult of Achilles in the Euxine," *Hesperia* 60 (1991): 313–30.

defeat that sounds utterly mythical, but then he dates it to 164 B.C.E.![14]

II

Are there, then, literary allusions in *Heroikos* that *are* possible to track down? In the rest of this essay I would like to examine two particularly difficult but instructive challenges to "source criticism" from the beginning of the dialogue, where I think some progress can be made.

The first is at the very outset (*Her.* 1.4–5), when the Phoenician sailor is still skeptical about the farmer's claim to the simple life:

> *Phoenician:* Do you mean, then, that you have no interest in money, even though you live in this vineyard, and doubtless look for men to pick your grapes and pay a drachma for them, or customers for your sweet and fragrant new wine? I suppose you claim to keep it buried underground, like Marôn!
>
> *Vineyard-keeper:* Stranger, if anywhere on earth there live Cyclopes, whom they say the earth feeds with no labor of planting or sowing on their part, then plants would be unguarded—even those of Demeter and Dionysos—and no produce of the earth would be sold; instead, they would grow free for all to share in, just as in a *pigs' marketplace* (ὥσπερ ἐν συῶν ἀγορᾷ). But where it is necessary to sow and plough and plant and toil constantly, attached to the land and in thrall to the seasons, there one must buy and sell.

Most scholars have capitalized "Pigs' Marketplace" and interpreted these words as an allusion to the Roman *Forum Suarium* where Aurelian later sponsored distributions of pork.[15] But given the rural and vegetarian context of this passage, such an allusion seems absurd. Rather, Philostratus has in mind a famous passage from the start of the examination of the ideal city in Plato's *Republic* (372a–d). After Socrates describes an ideal rustic city of simple and unsophisticated pleasures, Adeimantos objects and demands

[14] "I think it was in the year that Leonidas of Rhodes won his first race at the Olympic Games (164 B.C.E.) that Achilles wiped out their warriors on this very island." For Leonidas, see Pausanias *Description of Greece* 6.13.4, and Luigi Moretti, *Olympionikai: I vincitori negli antichi agoni olimpici* (Rome: Accademia Nazionale dei Lincei, 1957), s.v. Leonidas.

[15] R. Muth ("Forum Suarium," *Museum Helveticum* 2 [1945]: 227–36) and many others before him (including reference books on Roman topography).

more civilized foods: "if you were constructing a city of pigs (ὑῶν πόλιν) wouldn't you give them this fodder also?" Once compared, the source of the allusion seems obvious,[16] yet the allusion is not simple or unambiguous; Philostratus's rebuke to the Phoenician's naïveté substitutes "market" for "city" because commercialism is the bone of contention between them. If it were not for the fame of the source and the allusion's similar use—to dismiss one line of discussion at the start of a long conversation—one might wonder whether Philostratus was really thinking of the *Republic* here. The lesson of this allusion is that, even when his source is clear, we can expect it to be varied in ways that exclude unambiguously close verbal reminiscence.

Success with this small problem might encourage us to tackle the much larger complex of allusions that follows, namely, the list of large bone finds at the beginning of the work. Before he can tell of the heroes, the vineyard-keeper must overcome the Phoenician's firm resistance to one initial premise: that the bodies of the heroes were larger than humans of his own day. He confronts the skeptic with a barrage of fourteen instances (*Her.* 8.1–14, see Table 1 below).[17]

Table 1: Bone Finds Attested in the *Heroikos*

	Heroikos	Other attestations
I	I had a grandfather, stranger, who knew as fact many of the stories you don't believe, and he said that the tomb of Ajax was once destroyed by the sea near which it was located, and that in it a skeleton came to light about eleven cubits tall. And he said that the emperor Hadrian went to Troy, laid it out for burial, and built for it the tomb which now exists—he even embraced and kissed some of the bones. (*Her.* 8.1)	Pausanias *Description of Greece* 1.35.4–7 (Mysian informant); Pliny *Natural History* 5.125; Antipater *Epigram* 7 Gow and Page; Strabo *Geography* 13.595

[16] For the background of the concept see Urs Dierauer, *Tier und Mensch im Denken der antike Studien zur Tierpsychologie, Anthropologie und Ethik* (Studien Zur Antiken Philosophie 6; Amsterdam: Grüner, 1977), 180–81n.

[17] A recent book has argued ingeniously and in detail that some of these bone finds were fossils of prehistoric elephants, which are numerous around the Mediterranean and whose skeletal structure (minus the skull, which is fragile and

	Heroikos	Other attestations
II	If I were fond of telling stories I would indeed have told you about Orestes' body, which the Spartans discovered in Nemea—it was seven cubits tall . . . . (*Her.* 8.3)	Herodotus *Hist.* 1.68 (seven-cubit coffin, found in Tegea)
III	. . . or about the body in the Lydian bronze horse, which had been buried in Lydia still before Gyges' time, and miraculously appeared after an earthquake to some shepherds in Lydia, one of whom was Gyges. The horse contained windows on both sides, and in its hollow inside had been stuffed a body, which was greater than a man could imagine. (*Her.* 8.3)	Plato *Republic* 359c–360b
IV	Not long ago an excavation on the banks of the river Orontes brought to light Aryadês—thirty cubits tall—who had been buried in Assyria; some say he was an Ethiopian, others an Indian. (*Her.* 8.3)	Eleven-cubit body on banks of Orontes identified (by Apollo at Klaros) as Orontes of India. Pausanias *Description of Greece* 8.29.3–4
V	And less than fifty years ago, Sigeion over there disclosed on one of its cape's projecting hills the body of a giant, whom Apollo said he himself had killed while defending Troy. I myself sailed to Sigeion, stranger, and witnessed exactly what had happened to the land as well as the giant's size. Many others sailed there also, from the Hellespont, Ionia, and all of the islands and Aeolia, since for two months this huge body lay on the huge cape; until the oracle cleared things up, everyone had offered a different explanation . . . the one on Sigeion measured 22 cubits. He lay in a rocky cave, his head in the inland side, and his feet extended to the end of the cape. There was no sign of a snake on him, and all his skeleton was human. (*Her.* 8.6)	Local observation?

easily lost) would resemble a giant human: Adrienne Mayor, *The First Fossil Hunters: Paleontology in Greek and Roman Times* (Princeton: Princeton University Press, 2000).

	Heroikos	Other attestations
VI	About four years ago, Hymnaios of Peparêthos, a friend of mine, sent one of his sons to have me ask Protesilaos about a similar wonder. For on the island of Ikos (he was its sole owner) he happened to be digging up some vines, when the earth rang under the shovel, as if hollow. When they cleaned it away, there lay exposed a body eleven cubits tall, and in its skull was living a snake. Now the boy came to ask us what should be done with it, and Protesilaos's answer was "let us veil our guest," meaning of course they should bury the corpse and be careful to take nothing from it. He also said it was one of the giants who was laid low. (*Her.* 8.9)	Local observation?
VII	But the largest of all was the one on Lemnos, which Menekratês of Steiria discovered, and I myself sailed over last year from Imbros (I was on the side close to Lemnos) to see it. It wasn't any longer possible to see the bones in their proper position, because the backbone lay in pieces—separated by earthquakes, I imagine—and the ribs had been wrenched from the vertebrae. But as I examined them, both all together and one by one, I received an impression of terrifying size, one I found impossible to describe. The skull alone, when we poured wine into it, was not filled even by two Cretan amphoras. (*Her.* 8.11)	Menekratês of Steiria. Inscription from Myrina; see n. 18
VIII	There is also a cape on Imbros to the southwest called Naulokhos, and in it is nestled a spring that makes eunuchs of all male animals that drink of it, and so intoxicates the females that they fall asleep. Here a broken-off piece of earth has carried with it the body of a huge giant. If you don't believe me, we can sail there; for the body is still stripped and lying there, and it is a short trip to Naulokhos. (*Her.* 8.12)	Local observation?
IX	But you must not believe what I say, stranger, until you sail to the island of Kos, where they say the house of the first earthborn Meropes lie. . . . (*Her.* 8.14)	Giant Meropes. Pindar *Nemean* 4.26; Homer *Il.* 14.255; [Apollodorus] *Library* 2.137; cf. now the poem *Meropis*

	Heroikos	Other attestations
X	. . . and until you see those of Herakles' son Hyllus in Phrygia. . . . (*Her*. 8.14)	False Geryon at upper Lydia = Hyllus the Giant, inspiration for Herakles' son's name (in Lydia with Omphalê). Pausanias *Description of Greece* 1.34
XI	. . . or, by Zeus, even those of the Alôadai in Thessaly—they were actually nine fathoms long, just as the poet says. (*Her*. 8.14)	Homer *Od*. 11.312
XII	And in Italy the Neapolitans have made a wonder of the bones of Alkyoneus; for they say that many of the giants were laid low there, and that Mount Vesuvius smolders over them. (*Her*. 8.15)	?
XIII	Furthermore in Pallênê, which the poets call Phlegra, the earth still contains the bodies of many giants, since that was their camp; thunderstorms and earthquakes have brought many others to the surface. Not even the shepherd takes courage at noonday when the angry spirits of that land clatter about underneath it. (*Her*. 8.16)	?
XIV	. . . disbelief in such things must have been common even in Herakles' day, since after he killed Geryon—the largest being he ever encountered—in Erytheia, he dedicated the bones at Olympia so that his feat would not be dismissed as incredible. (*Her*. 8.17)	?

The sources for the items in the vineyard-keeper's catalog fall into several distinct groups:

1. Four are from well-known works of classical literature, common knowledge to any educated ancient writer. They include the corpse found by Gyges (Plato *Republic* 359c–360b), the bones of Orestes (Herodotus *Hist*. 1.67–68), the Alôadai (Homer *Od*. 11.310–311), and the Meropes of Kos (Pindar *Nemean* 4.26; Homer *Il*. 14.255; [Apollodorus] *Library* 2.137).

2. Four of the winegrower's examples (from Ikos, Lemnos, Cape Naulokhos on Imbros, and Sigeion) are contemporary, having been seen personally by him or his friends. One of the people mentioned, Menekratês of Steiria, has been identified by Simone Follet in an inscription from Lemnos, and there is no reason to doubt the existence either of Hymnaios of Peparêthos or of the finds reported by him and others.[18]

3. Two items are surprising revisions of traditional stories: the body of Alkyoneus the giant is placed in the Phlegraean fields near Naples rather than in northern Greece,[19] and Geryon's bones are claimed to have been dedicated at Olympia by his slayer Herakles rather than buried at his home in Cadiz.[20]

Apart from these groups are three items (Ajax, Orontes, Hyllus) that overlap in a tantalizing way with Pausanias, who catalogs the discoveries of oversize bones on two occasions. In his *Description of Greece* 1.33–35, after discussing the shrine of Amphiaraos at Ôrôpos (for which he cites the shrine of Protesilaos in Elaious as a parallel sanctuary of a human), he turns to Ajax on Salamis, which leads to mention of Ajax's bones, discovered when his supposed burial site split open near Troy.

> A Mysian told me about his size. He said that the sea had flooded the side of the grave facing the beach and removed the difficulty of entering the tomb, and he suggested I estimate the corpse's size in the following way: the bones on his knees, called

[18] Simone Follet, "Inscription inédite de Myrina," *ASAA* NS 36–37 (1974): 309–12. Cape Naulokhos must be identical with modern Cape Pyrgos; on Imbros see C. Fredrich ("Imbros," *Ath. Mitt.* 33 [1908]: 83–84), who reports the coast still shows many sections torn away almost vertically.

[19] Alkyoneus had usually been associated with the Gigantomachy at Pallênê/Phlegra in Chalcidice (Herodotus *Hist.* 7.123); later the volcanic regions between Naples and Cumae became known as Phlegraean fields (Aristotle *Meteorology* 368b30; Timaeus *FGrH* 566 F 89). Philostratus, like Diodorus Siculus (*Library* 5.71) and Claudian (*Rape of Persephone* 3.184–185), assumes there had been Gigantomachies at both sites and places Alkyoneus (called "Phlegraios" in *PMG* frg. 985) there.

[20] Geryon's body at Olympia is an odd story for Philostratus, since it contradicts the placement of his body at Cadiz (where trees dripped blood) not only by Pausanias (*Description of Greece* 1.35.7), but even in Philostratus's own *Life of Apollonius* 5.5. But Geryon's body was also claimed by locals to be at Thebes (Lucian *The Ignorant Book-Collector* 14; Apostolius *Proverbs* 17.23), and Lydia (Pausanias *Description of Greece* 1.35.7, quoted below).

> by doctors knee-pans, were for him as big as the boys' discus in the pentathlon. (Pausanias *Description of Greece* 1.35.4–5)

The oversize corpse of Ajax at Troy is mentioned also as a tale from the vineyard-keeper's grandfather in *Her.* 8.1 (see Table 1, § I). Yet Pausanias is clearly not Philostratus's direct source: the reburial of Ajax seems to have been a historical event[21] with several independent traditions, and both authors cite eyewitness informants and give details not mentioned by the other.

After reporting on Ajax, Pausanias launches into his own catalog of huge bones (*Description of Greece* 1.35.5–6): He says he has viewed alleged Celtic giants (the Celts being proverbially tall; Philostratus *Lives of the Sophists* 2.552) and found them unimpressive, but he counts as credible the huge bones of the athlete Prôtophanês in Magnesia on the river Lêthaios, the bones of a certain Asterios of the island of Ladê near Miletus (ten cubits; cf. Pausanias *Description of Greece* 7.2.5), and finally a personal anecdote (Pausanias *Description of Greece* 1.35.7–8):

> But one thing amazed me: there is a small city of upper Lydia, Temenothyrai. There, when a hill broke off in a storm, some bones were discovered, which had a form that was believably human, though from their large size they would never have seemed so. Immediately most people started saying that it was the corpse of Geryon, the son of Chrysaôr, and that the throne also was his. (There is a man's throne fashioned on a rocky outcrop of the mountain.) And a stream they called the river Okeanos, and said that men while ploughing found the horns of cattle, since the story is that Geryon reared the best cattle. And when I refuted them by explaining that Geryon is at Cadiz, where there is no tomb, but there *is* a tree that assumes different shapes, the Lydian guides explained the real story, that it was the corpse of Hyllus, that Hyllus was a son of Earth, and that the river is named after him; and that Herakles, because he lived with Omphalê, called his son Hyllus after the river.

The story of the bones of "Hyllus" is known only from Pausa-

[21] For the damage to the tomb of Ajax (and the great size of the body it contained), see also Pliny *Natural History* 5.125; Antipater *Epigram* 7 Gow and Page; Strabo *Geography* 13.595; and on its current site see J. M. Cook, *The Troad: An Archaeological and Topographical Study* (Oxford: Clarendon, 1973), 88; for other references to tombs of Ajax, see Ammianus *History* 22.8.4; Strabo *Geography* 13.1.30. For Hadrian's restoration activity at Troy, see Peter Frisch, *Die Inschriften von Ilion* (Bonn: Habelt, 1975), no. 94. For Ajax's original burial without cremation, see *Her.* 35.15; cf. Quintus of Smyrna *Fall of Troy* 5.653.

nias and Philostratus: Pausanias's wording leads naturally to the conclusion that he has seen the bones himself, and that they were a recent discovery.[22] Since Philostratus is the only other author to cite this example, it seems an obvious inference that he read it in Pausanias. But the way Philostratus mentions it in *Her.* 8.14 makes this conclusion difficult to accept: The "Hyllus" whose bones he mentions is in Phrygia, not Lydia, and he is called not a giant after whom Herakles' son was named, but the actual son of Herakles. Doesn't that mean Philostratus has a different source? Not necessarily: "upper Lydia" is virtually the same as Phrygia, and Temenothyrai was placed as often in one as the other;[23] and the "son of Herakles" must be either another careless slip by Philostratus or the vineyard-keeper, or perhaps even an erroneous annotation by a commentator that has crept into the text and should be bracketed: even in *Heroikos*, Hyllus *ought* to have been a giant, as are those named before and after him (Meropes, Alôadai, Alkyoneus) in the vineyard-keeper's catalog.

A significant feature common to Pausanias and Philostratus is the inclusion not only of the bones of heroes but also those of giants (surprising in *Heroikos*, where heroes ought to be strongly distinguished from giants), as well as the use of this evidence to discredit certain artistic Gigantomachies which give the giants snake tails instead of feet.[24] Pausanias makes this point forcefully after describing the Arcadian place claiming to be the site of the Gigantomachy:

> That the giants had serpents for feet is shown to be a ridiculous story in many other ways, as well as the following: the Roman emperor wanted the Syrian river Orontes, which does not flow on a continuously level course to the sea but runs up against a steep cliff-face and is deflected off it, to be navigable from the

[22] The scene is close to the presumed home of Pausanias, Magnesia at Mount Sipylus.

[23] The conflation of Lydia and Phrygia was common at least in the poets according to Strabo *Geography* 14.665; an alternate name of the river Hyllos was Phrygios (Strabo *Geography* 13.626).

[24] Postclassical Gigantomachies (notably the frieze of the great altar at Pergamum) portray giants with two snake-tails for legs, but earlier ones (notably the metopes of the Parthenon) give them human legs (except for Typhôeus, who was snake-legged early). The skeletons, according to Philostratus and Pausanias, refute the anguiped sculptures. See Francis Vian, *La guerre des géants: Le mythe avant l'époque héllenistique* (Paris: Klincksieck, 1952), 14, 147; Hans Christoph Ackermann and Jean-Robert Gisler, eds., *Lexicon Iconographicum Mythologiae Classicae (LIMC)* (8 vols.; Zurich: Artemis, 1981–1997), s.v. Gigantes (F. Vian and M. B. Moore), esp. 253–54.

> sea to the city of Antioch. So with much labor and expense he dug a canal suitable for ships to sail inland, and diverted the river into it. But when the old stream had dried up, there was found in it a clay coffin more than eleven cubits long, and its corpse matched the coffin in size, and was human in all of its body. This corpse the god at Klaros, when the Syrians consulted his oracle there, said was Orontes,[25] and that he was of Indian race. (Pausanias *Description of Greece* 8.29.3–4)

Her. 8.3 (Table 1, §IV) cites a giant on the river Orontes as well, although calling him Aryadês (perhaps another spelling of the same name) and giving him two possible nationalities and different measurements. As for discrediting the concept of snake-feet for giants, *Heroikos* has that as well, but it is applied to a set of bones the vineyard-keeper has seen himself (*Her.* 8.6; Table 1, §V). Pausanias and Philostratus are the only writers known to me who use giants' bones to make such an argument.[26]

Thus we can see that in listing giants' bones Philostratus's vineyard-keeper offers not only a number of literary commonplaces and instances of personal knowledge, but also three examples in common with Pausanias, one of which (Hyllus) is Pausanias's own eyewitness story from near his home and is unknown from other sources. Furthermore, these two writers alone use the bones (although different instances of them) to criticize a particular type of representation of the giants in art. So one can see why Frazer and Gurlitt suggested that Philostratus was directly dependent on Pausanias for at least the bones of Hyllus.[27]

In addition to the frequent variations between the two sources noted above, however, Christian Habicht has recently revived and forcefully endorsed on other grounds—there appear indeed to be no explicit references or direct quotations from Pausanias earlier than Stephanus of Byzantium—the hypothesis that Pausanias's *Description of Greece* was not read at all in the generations following its

[25] Orontes is an Indian giant killed at this site also in Nonnus *Dionysiaca* 17.289.

[26] This conclusion is based on a proximity-search for γιγα- and ὀφ- or δρακ- within five lines in all the current text of the *TLG*. The closest parallels are when Homer's ignorance of anguiped giants is noted by Aristonicus in schol. (PQ) Homer *Od.* 7.59, and snake-footed giants are denied by *Pseudo-Clementine Homilies* 8.15.1, in all cases without any arguments.

[27] J. G. Frazer, trans., *Pausanias' Description of Greece* (London: Macmillian, 1898), on 1.35.7; Wilhelm Gurlitt, *Über Pausanias: Untersuchungen* (Graz: Leuschner & Lubensky, 1890), 11.

composition, and perhaps even entirely lost until the sixth century C.E.[28]

How to sort out these connections? I can imagine three possible ways of accounting for the relationship of *Heroikos* 8 with Pausanias *Description of Greece* 1.35 and 8.29:

1. Philostratus and Pausanias both used a common intermediate source on discoveries of giants' bones. Many other instances of oversize bones are cited by ancient authors,[29] and it might be assumed that there existed some master list of heroes' bones that was the common source of Philostratus and the others. Yet the catalog of bones in *Heroikos* is much more extensive than in any other source, and both Philostratus's vineyard-keeper and Pausanias cite several instances from autopsy. Furthermore, the next-longest catalog, in excerpts from the compiler Phlegon of Tralles, who wrote at the time of Hadrian, does not have a single instance in common with Philostratus or Pausanias.[30] Clearly, reports of discoveries of bones of "heroes" and "giants" were popular enough that Philostratus and Pausanias could assemble a list independently, from a variety of sources, without depending on a single antiquarian catalog.

[28] Christian Habicht, *Pausanias' Guide to Ancient Greece* (Berkeley: University of California Press, 1998), 1, following Otto Regenbogen, "Pausanias," PWSup 8 (1956): 1093, and Aubrey Diller, "The Manuscripts of Pausanias," in *Studies in Greek Manuscript Tradition* (Amsterdam: Hakkert, 1983), 163–82.

[29] Cataloged by Friedrich Pfister, *Der Reliquienkult im Altertum* (2 vols.; Religionsgeschichtliche Versuche und Vorarbeiten 5; Giessen: Töpelmann, 1909–1912), 2:426–27; Eugene Taylor Thompson, "The Relics of the Heroes in Ancient Greece" (Ph.D. diss., University of Washington, 1985). Suetonius (*Divus Augustus* 72) writes that Augustus kept a collection of "so-called giants' bones and heroes' weapons."

[30] *FGrH* 257 F36 11–19 (pp. 1182–83) = Alexander Giannini, *Paradoxographorum Graecorum Reliquiae* (Milan: Istituto Editoriale Italiano, 1966), no. 14, pp. 169–219; William Hansen, trans., *Phlegon of Tralles' Book of Marvels* (Exeter, England: University of Exeter Press, 1996), 43–45, 137–48. It is notable that Philostratus does not cite the most notorious "giant," the one of Crete that was identified as Otos or Orion (Solinus *Collection of Memorable Things* 1.91; Philodemus *On Signs* frg. 4 de Lacy; Pliny *Natural History* 7.16.73). For other giant bones, see Solinus *Collection of Memorable Things* 9.6; Strabo *Geography* 17.829 (on Antaios, cf. Plutarch *Sertorius* 9); Pliny *Natural History* 7.73; on Theseus, see Plutarch *Theseus* 35–36; Plutarch *Cimon* 8.5–6; Diodorus Siculus *Library* 4.62.4; Pausanias *Description of Greece* 1.17.6. For giants elsewhere in Pausanias, see *Description of Greece* 8.29.1; 8.31.5, and cf. Philostratus *Life of Apollonius* 5.16; *Pseudo-Clementine Recognitiones* 1.29.

2. Philostratus read the eyewitness account of Pausanias and reworked part of it here. This would account not only for Hyllus, but also for Orontes and the argument against anguiped giants. Against this view are the many differences of detail (place, Hyllus's father, the giant's size), and especially the prevailing view that Pausanias's work was not known until several centuries later.

3. Philostratus did not read Pausanias nor did he did take "Hyllus" from a common list, but saw or heard independently about the same bones in Lydia as well as those of Orontes, and independently thought of using giants' bones to disprove that they were anguipeds. This would explain the variant in the name of Orontes (if Aryadês is not just a different spelling), the different size given, and the variation Lydia/Phrygia for Hyllus. One might assume that on such a specialized topic some coincidental overlap of topics was inevitable, and here there would be three such overlaps.

The third remains the most likely possibility, given the absence of other testimonia to Pausanias, and explains the variants more naturally than would deliberate alterations or misrememberings by Philostratus. But it is not an easy solution either, and if Pausanias's work could in fact be proved to be circulating, we might long ago have assumed that Philostratus used Pausanias's personal story here, simply making alterations as suited him.[31]

Thus "source criticism" of *Heroikos*, even with the promising material of chapter 8—a passage with a wealth of detail, abundant parallel evidence, and some tantalizingly close correspondences—still ends with mixed results, which establish for certain only the author's desire to keep the real as well as the apparent authorities for the vineyard-keeper's allusions as diverse as possible: classical stories, oral traditions, reports from contemporaries, and the speaker's own autopsy, with some verifications from Protesilaos himself. Such a technique reinforces the timeless world of the dia-

[31] To assume that Pausanias was unread because there exist no references to his work and then to reject possible connections on the grounds that he was unread, seems to me to involve a logical fallacy. If we could allow the possibility that Philostratus read Pausanias, one would certainly want to consider further the relevance of Pausanias *Description of Greece* 7.23.7, where a man from Sidon—a Phoenician—starts an argument with him in a shrine about the parentage of Asclepius, claiming that Phoenicians understand the gods better than the Greeks do.

logue, which rather than idealizing or reconstructing the past, dwells in it, interweaving details from classical literature with appropriate strands of contemporary life, to persuade us of the survival of the classical Greek past into the present of the Troad under Roman rule. Our difficulty of untangling the strands of past and present is a sign of the author's aesthetic success.

Material Witness: An Archaeological Context for the *Heroikos*

Susan E. Alcock

Material context is no bad place to begin when considering the *Heroikos*—indeed, one could even argue that is where Philostratus starts as well. Very early in the text appears a sharp invocation to look down and pay attention, as the vinedresser chides the Phoenician: "Where are you going so proudly and ignoring everything at your feet?" (*Her.* 1.2). This is only the first indication of the dialogue's strong sense of place and of locality. We could also note the tales of bones (e.g., *Her.* 8.1–18), the discovery and personal autopsy of which play no small part in convincing the Phoenician to pay heed, allowing the conversation to proceed in amity.[1] Other episodes of discovery and recovery mark the dialogue; one could expand to include other works of Philostratus and add in Apollonius's restoration of the shrine to Palamedes, complete with excavated cult image (*Life of Apollonius* 4.13). From a modern perspective, even the figure of Protesilaos himself could be seen as a kind of "archaeologist," digging down into layers of tradition, exposing, retrieving, assessing. Places and things, burial and recovery—in other words a material context—are central to interpretations of the *Heroikos*.

This article's title, however—"material witness"—may be a little deceptive. A "material witness," as we all know from television, is one expected to deliver information in time-honored "just the facts, ma'am" style. Until quite recently, such would probably have been the pragmatic role of archaeology in a collection of essays such as this; the archaeologist would be expected to provide the reality check, the physical framework, the "what was really there" to complement and control Philostratus's "fantastic and often childish" treatise (to quote Farnell).[2]

[1] See also Adrienne Mayor, *The First Fossil Hunters: Paleontology in Greek and Roman Times* (Princeton: Princeton University Press, 2000).

[2] Lewis Richard Farnell, *Greek Hero Cults and Ideas of Immortality* (Oxford: Clarendon, 1921), 294.

Such is not the line to be adopted here. My fundamental assertion instead is that the material culture of the period under study (the early centuries of Roman rule in the Greek East) was actively engaged in many of the same processes and anxieties as the *Heroikos* itself. These matters included strategies of authority, competitions over memory, canon building, the creation of cultural identities in a multicultural imperial world, and the redefinition and defense of Hellenism. The material context that can be sketched for the *Heroikos* should not revolve around whether or not "Philostratus stood here," nor will it seek to expose any "fibs" he may have told. The archaeology of his age can be caught fibbing too: under the same pressures and in the same causes.

Out of many possible directions to move, three phenomena can here be traced, phenomena which serve to bring the *Heroikos* in contact and context with archaeologically derived patterns of ritual and commemorative behavior. In good alliterative fashion, I label these phenomena construction, concentration, and convergence. Before I proceed, however, I must establish two introductory points. First, although the *Heroikos* can be dated to within a few decades, the vast majority of the archaeological evidence to be employed here cannot. The patterns discussed, therefore, by and large belong to the early Roman period (the first to third centuries C.E.), not to any specifically Severan manifestation of activity. Such imprecision is simply in the nature of the beast, and analysis must adjust accordingly. Second, as we move through the three categories (from construction, to concentration, to convergence), we shall also be changing the focus and scope of our inquiry: moving from hero cult in the Troad, to a subset of heroes in "Old" (or mainland) Greece, to a more general consideration of commemorative and ritual activity. This leaves us with quite a lot of ground to cover, but it also makes the point of just how far we can trace the cares and concerns expressed in the *Heroikos*.

CONSTRUCTION

We can begin with *construction* and with the proximate setting of the dialogue: the plains of windy Troy. My theme here is the created nature, and mobile character, of memorial traditions. Battles over the identification of tombs, over just who was buried just where, have legendarily raged for centuries. What may be less appreciated are the material interventions that continually remade this particular landscape of memory. To the increasing dismay of early explorers such as Heinrich Schliemann, few of the heroic tumuli of the Trojan plain proved "old enough," being embarassingly exposed as later creations or fabrications. For example, the tumulus now generally agreed to be that hailed in antiquity as the tomb of Achilles—Sivri (or Besik) Tepe, measuring 750 feet wide and nearly 50 feet tall—began life as a prehistoric (Chalcolithic) settlement mound that was then "enhanced" in the Hellenistic period. Kesik Tepe, a nearby, smaller feature probably hailed as the tomb of Patroklos, turned out to be a modified natural hillock.[3]

Today, we are less abashed and more intrigued by such alterings of the earth and by the actors involved. For our purposes, we can focus on practices attested in the early Roman period. The *Heroikos* itself tells us that Hadrian remade the tomb of Ajax when that structure was washed away by the sea, exposing the hero's massive bones (*Her.* 8.1). Archaeological evidence does nothing to dispute this claim.[4] It is to the Severan age, however, that perhaps the most remarkable intervention belongs. Caracalla, of course, paid a well-known visit, presumably to Sivri Tepe, and there (recalling Alexander) honored Achilles with sacrifices and with races in armor around his tomb (Dio Cassius *Roman History* 78.16.7).[5] While there, as Herodian tells us, his favored freedman Festus died, allow-

[3] Sivri (Besik) Tepe: John M. Cook, *The Troad: An Archaeological and Topographical Study* (Oxford: Clarendon, 1973), 173–74, 186; John M. Cook, "The Topography of the Plain of Troy," in *The Trojan War: Its Historicity and Context. Papers of the First Greenbank Colloquium, Liverpool, 1981* (ed. Lin Foxhall and John K. Davies; Bristol, England: Bristol Classical Press, 1984), 170. Kesik Tepe: Cook, *Troad*, 165. The tumulus of Protesilaos at Elaious was similarly (and unhappily) identified as "une tumba—site préhistorique" by Angelika Waiblinger, "La ville grecque d'Éléonte en Chersonèse de Thrace et sa nécropole," CRAI (Nov.–Dec. 1978): 845; see also Robert Demangel, *Le tumulus dit de Protésilas* (Fouilles des corps d'occupation français de Constantinople 1; Paris: De Boccard, 1926).

[4] Usually identified as the site of In Tepe: Cook, *Troad*, 86–89; Cook, "Topography," 163.

[5] On other manifestations of cult to Achilles, especially in the Black Sea region, see Guy Hedreen, "The Cult of Achilles in the Euxine," *Hesperia* 60 (1991): 313–30; James T. Hooker, "The Cults of Achilles," *Rheinisches Museum* 131 (1988): 1–7. For other studies of Roman visitors to Troy, see Cornelius C. Vermeule, "Neon Ilion and Ilium Novum: Kings, Soldiers, Citizens, and Tourists at Classical Troy," in *The Ages of Homer: A Tribute to Emily Townsend Vermeule* (ed. Jane B. Carter and Sarah P. Morris; Austin: University of Texas Press, 1995), 467–82; Michael Siebler, *Troia: Geschichte, Grabungen, Kontroversen* (Mainz, Germany: Zabern, 1994), 16–18.

ing Caracalla a perhaps not unwelcome opportunity to play Achilles to Patroklos (or Alexander to Hephaistiôn; Herodian *History* 4.8.4–5). The resulting tomb of Festus has been identified with Uvecik Tepe—at 75 feet tall and set on high ground, the most outstanding of all tumuli on the Trojan plain. Excavations by Schliemann found late Roman sherds associated with a stone base structure possibly of classical date, suggesting again the later augmentation of an existing feature. The location selected for this monument has been taken to play off and respond to the tomb of Achilles—indeed, J. M. Cook suggested (if without offering exact evidence) that Caracalla "topped up" the height of the Achilles mound at this same time.[6]

The tomb of Festus is a standout in the landscape. Yet this work of "mad extravagance" by a "vain fool . . . who aped the manner of Alexander" (in Schliemann's view) is only scantly regarded in books on the topography of the Trojan hinterland. This is unfortunate, for Uvecik Tepe offers a stunning example of commemorative manipulation, not least in its addition of a novel element to the rituals of Troy. This apparently radical juxtaposition of past and present may strike us as odd today, but it may also be witnessed in the *Heroikos* and indeed as a constant feature in the cultural production of the period.

If some heroes were actively called to mind through the reconstruction of monuments or through the homage of new building, others were not. The obverse side of commemoration, as is everywhere implicit in the *Heroikos*, can be oblivion. Hektor, for one, clearly continues to receive heroic attention in certain contexts. Yet in another tradition, the Phoenician laments, "neither plowman nor goatherd says anything on his behalf, but he is invisible to human beings and simply lies buried" (*Her.* 19.1–2). Lucan, in a passage dripping with anxiety over immortality and remembrance, recounts

[6] On Uvecik Tepe: Heinrich Schliemann, *Ilios: The City and Country of the Trojans* (New York: Harper & Bros., 1881; repr. New York: Arno, 1976), 658–65, plans V–VI; Cook, *Troad*, 172–73, 186; Manfred Korfman, "Troy: Topography and Navigation," in *Troy and the Trojan War: A Symposium Held at Bryn Mawr College, October 1984* (ed. Machteld J. Mellink; Bryn Mawr, Penn.: Bryn Mawr College, 1986), 11 and n. 27. On the possibility of "topping up": Cook, *Troad*, 172; Cook, "Topography," 171 n. 2. For his own account of work at all these various tumuli, see Schliemann, *Ilios;* also Carl Schuchhardt, *Schliemann's Excavations: An Archaeological and Historical Study* (trans. Eugénie Sellers; London: Macmillan, 1891), esp. 83–87. For one map of the relative locations of the tumuli, see Siebler, *Troia*, 25.

how Julius Caesar, striding through tall grass, was brought up short by a local guide who bade him not to step on the body of Hektor (*Civil War* 9.975–977). Piles of stone have, over the past centuries, occasionally been pointed out as this monument (in some instances it would seem, unnervingly, thanks to the grass still growing atop). Yet at least one of the more reliable reconstructors of the Trojan plain, Cook, admits that identifying the tomb of Hektor does remain "a puzzle best left aside."[7]

Of construction, then, two things can be argued in summary. First, the competitions over memory reflected in the *Heroikos* are echoed in material choices taken and manipulations made in this continually redesigned, far from frozen heroic landscape. And second, decisions made about "right memory" in the past (as Philostratus would have warned us) can possess and maintain a robust authority in the present.

CONCENTRATION

Under the rubric of *concentration,* two things can be considered: first, evidence for a spatial concentration in heroic worship, and, related to this, evidence for a social concentration in who wielded authority over such cults. We can tease out these suggested patterns by examining one very specific subset of case studies—shrines to major epic heroes in Greece. Archaeological evidence can shed light on three chief instances: the Agamemnoneion on a Bronze Age causeway near Mycenae in the Argolid; the Pólis Cave, sacred to Odysseus, on Ithaca; and the Menelaion, dedicated to Helen and Menelaus in Laconia.

All three were very long-lived and much-venerated cult places, in each case with activities reaching back into Geometric or Archaic times. Interestingly, each received a boost of attention, often taking the form of new building or renovation, in the Hellenistic period.[8]

[7] Cook, "Topography," 163.

[8] Susan E. Alcock, "The Heroic Past in a Hellenistic Present," in *Hellenistic Constructs: Essays in Culture, History, and Historiography* (ed. Paul Cartledge, Peter Garnsey, and Erich Gruen; Berkeley: University of California Press, 1997), 20–34. Principal publications of the sites include: for the Agamemnoneion, John M. Cook, "The Cult of Agamemnon at Mycenae," in *Geras Antoniou Keramopoullou* (Athens: Typographeion Myrtide, 1953), 112–15; John M. Cook, "Mycenae 1939–52: The Agamemnoneion," *Annual of the British School at Athens* 48 (1953): 30–68; for the Pólis Cave, Sylvia Benton, "Excavations in Ithaca, III: The Cave at Pólis, I," *Annual of the British School at Athens* 35 (1934–1935): 45–

It might be expected—given Homer's ongoing cultural authority, the continuing interest in the Trojan War, and the pervasively backward-looking atmosphere of the Second Sophistic—that these antique shrines would go from strength to strength and that they would be marked out for further construction and renewal. So what happened to them in early Roman times?

Actually, they appear to become defunct at some point around the late first century B.C.E./first century C.E.—the precise time horizon remains unclear. Explanations of their failure have so far tended to the particularistic. The cave of Odysseus, for example, was said to have collapsed through the action of the sea, somewhat reminiscent of the tomb of Ajax in the Troad;[9] the loss of the Agamemnoneion is attributed to the abandonment of Mycenae, its nearest village. But why then did no Hadrian rush in to save the situation on Ithaca, as he did for Ajax? Why did not the neighboring, flourishing city of Argos reach out and adopt the Agamemnoneion, as they did other cults of Mycenae?[10]

One answer may emerge by examining our third case study, the Menelaion. Veneration of Helen by no means came to an end in Roman Sparta. She weaves her way, for example, through Pausanias's account of Spartan topography (e.g., *Description of Greece* 3.12.6–7). More specifically, Paul Cartledge and Antony Spawforth trace how, by Augustan times, her worship moves to join her brothers, the Dioscuri, in a sanctuary below the site of the now abandoned Menelaion. Significantly, they speak of her transfer "to the more accessible sanctuary on the plain below."[11] And there we

---

73; Sylvia Benton, "Excavations in Ithaca, III: The Cave at Pólis, II," *Annual of the British School at Athens* 39 (1938–1939): 1–51; for the Menelaion, Hector W. Catling, "Excavations at the Menelaion, Sparta, 1973–76," *Archaeological Reports* (1976–1977): 24–42; Alan J. B. Wace, Maurice S. Thompson, and John P. Droop, "Laconia I: Excavations at Sparta, 1909. The Menelaion," *Annual of the British School at Athens* 15 (1908–1909): 108–57.

[9] Benton, "Pólis, I," especially 55; for a late-first-century B.C.E. visitor from Italy, see Benton, "Pólis, II," 38.

[10] On the Argive use of Perseus, a hero of Mycenae, see Michael H. Jameson, "Perseus, the Hero of Mykenai," in *Celebrations of Death and Divinity in the Bronze Age Argolid: Proceedings of the Sixth International Symposium at the Swedish Institute at Athens, 11–13 June 1988* (ed. Robin Hägg and Gullög C. Nordquist; Stockholm: Svenska Institutet i Athen, 1990), 213–22. On the Hellenistic settlement at Mycenae, see C. A. Boethius, "Excavations at Mycenae XI: Hellenistic Mycenae," *Annual of the British School at Athens* 25 (1921–1923): 409–28.

[11] Paul Cartledge and Antony Spawforth, *Hellenistic and Roman Sparta: A Tale of Two Cities* (London: Routledge, 1989), 195; Catling, "Excavations," 41–42.

begin to detect a process of concentration. The Menelaion, the Cave of Odysseus, the Agamemnoneion were all in a sense geographical outliers, set in rural locales, perhaps intended originally to define and defend territorial boundaries. Ritual attention to these figures need not necessarily cease, but does arguably shift, becoming concentrated within more central, or more accessible, places.

Why might this development take place? Again, we can look to Helen. The priesthoods of Helen and the Dioscuri became tightly controlled within a group of super-elite Spartan families, at least some of whom claimed personal descent from the Dioscuri.[12] These individuals now actively sought to claim for themselves the epic prestige and charisma the heroes could provide, not least through genealogical connections. Such annexation appears to have involved a desire to have ritual activity under their eye, as well as under their thumb: hence the desire for accessibility, for locating cult in urban or peri-urban locations—a spatial centrality incidentally paralleled in the placement of imperial cult activity at this time.[13] In other words, a concentration of social power over these cults is clearly signaled, a phenomenon to which spatial location is closely linked.

This subset of epic-hero cults is obviously small, and no uniformitarian claims can be made about these consolidating tendencies. On the other hand, this is not an insignificant subset, and it does suggestively point us in certain directions. First, hallowed hero cults were not invulnerable or immovable, but followed and served the needs and exigencies of the present. This should no longer surprise us, nor should the expanding role played by aristocratic families in determining cult location and fate. The *Heroikos*, of course, works inside that aristocratic world, being written by and for such actors. Thinking about this phenomenon of concentration offers a different perspective, however, and a glimpse of matters outside that particular elite domain. The material history of places like the Agamemnoneion and the Menelaion—the passing of landmarks in their local setting—reveals a wider audience affected by these developments, a population arguably more excluded by these centralizing tendencies.

One second century C.E. fibula was, however, found in the fill of the "Great Pit" at the Menelaion.

[12] Cartledge and Spawforth, *Hellenistic*, esp. 162–64.

[13] Susan E. Alcock, *Graecia Capta: The Landscapes of Roman Greece* (Cambridge: Cambridge University Press, 1993), 198–99.

CONVERGENCE

Convergence, our third angle, stands closely related. It is possible, on the basis of archaeological evidence, to make the case for an early imperial convergence of interest on major sanctuaries at the expense of minor cults, for a convergence of interest in dominant memories and myths at the expense of more localized concerns and traditions. In mainland Greece, the Cycladic islands, and Crete, a recurring pattern emerges involving the widespread abandonment of small, relatively "insignificant" rural cult places and monuments, each with its own burden of myths and legends. The pattern is clearest in areas where regional survey work—an investigative technique that can locate otherwise unattested, small-scale rural shrines—has been done. Although such places can be seen to come and go over time, almost none date from the early Roman period.[14] Other examples are more notorious: the reconstruction of the so-called itinerant temples in the Athenian agora (such as the Temple of Ares), whatever else it may indicate, signals the deconstruction of sanctuaries elsewhere in Attica.[15] Some of these now obsolete cult places had once been attached to sites selected for their antique associations, for example, at ancient tombs. Much evidence exists for tomb cult, often associated with hero or ancestor worship, in Greece and the islands: just two instances include Kamilari on Crete, where a shrine nestled by a Minoan tholos tomb, or at Voïdokilia in Messenia, at the so-called tomb of Thrasymêdês outside ancient Pylos.[16] Both produced manifest signs of Hellenistic veneration, but no material traces of

[14] Susan E. Alcock, "Minding the Gap in Hellenistic and Roman Greece," in *Placing the Gods: Sanctuaries and Sacred Space in Ancient Greece* (ed. Susan E. Alcock and Robin Osborne; Oxford: Clarendon, 1994), 247–61.

[15] John M. Camp, *The Athenian Agora: Excavations in the Heart of Classical Athens* (London: Thames and Hudson, 1986), 184–87; Homer A. Thompson and Richard E. Wycherley, *The Agora of Athens: The History, Shape, and Uses of an Ancient City Center* (Athenian Agora 14; Princeton: American School of Classical Studies at Athens, 1972), 160–68.

[16] On Kamilari: Nicola Cucuzza, "Considerazioni su alcuni culti nella Messarà di epoca storica e sui rapporti territoriali fra Festòs e Gortina," *Atti dell'Accademia nazionale dei Lincei. Rendiconti* 9.8 (1997): 72–74; Doro Levi, "La tomba a tholos di Kamilari presso a Festòs," *ASAA* NS 23–24 (1961–1962): 7–148; on Voïdokilia: Carla M. Antonaccio, *An Archaeology of Ancestors: Tomb Cult and Hero Cult in Early Greece* (Lanham, Md.: Rowman and Littlefield, 1995), 80–81; George Korres, "Ê problêmatikê dia tên metagenesteran chrêsin tôn mukênaikôn taphôn Messênias" (in Greek), in *Acts of the Second International Congress of Peloponnesian Studies* (3 vols.; Athens: Hetaira Peloponnêsiako Spoudôn, 1981–1982),

Roman attention or votive dedication (though, interestingly, Pausanias knows the tomb of Thrasymêdês; *Description of Greece* 4.36.2). Finally, of course, we could revert to the epic-hero cults just discussed, which now appear as part of a much wider phenomenon of abandonment. This is not the place for a comprehensive review of the data (which are still being gathered), but this handful of examples points toward an early imperial pattern of the loss of small-scale local cults and monuments. By contrast, on the whole what survives are the large, the mythically significant, the urban, the profoundly antique.

Explaining this abandonment or neglect is a complex matter. Pragmatic factors, such as economic difficulties or realignments in settlement pattern, no doubt played their part. Yet the phenomenon demands to be set within a wider cultural and political context. If, as most would agree, the Hellenic past was at this time being used as a source of social power, as a channel of communication across an imperial, multicultural world, then the need for agreement on where and what was designated "important" becomes increasingly comprehensible. In other words, the pattern observed here is in part the product of a tighter focus on particular mythic tales, on particular dominant cults—a convergence at the expense of other threads of memory.

This pattern can, I think, be related to the emphasis in the *Heroikos*, observed by Maclean and Aitken, on getting the story right. In the dialogue, of course, Homer, along with Homer's particular construction of events, is the specific filter of memory that must be questioned and corrected. My contention would be that Philostratus reflects a *general* concern with such "filters," not least with tensions between overriding panhellenic narratives and resistant local practices and traditions.[17] The *Heroikos* testifies both to the power of the former and the persistence of the latter.

The material record echoes these ongoing contentions, for—side-by-side with the losses we can chart—we can also trace exceptions, observing unpredictable continuities and stubborn survivals. From small rural shrines in the Greek countryside that by

2:394–97; George Korres, "Evidence for a Hellenistic Chthonian Cult in the Prehistoric Cemetery of Voïdokilia in Pylos (Messenia)," *Klio* 70 (1988): 311–28.

[17] Jennifer K. Berenson Maclean and Ellen Bradshaw Aitken, "Introduction," in *Flavius Philostratus: Heroikos* (trans. Jennifer K. Berenson Maclean and Ellen Bradshaw Aitken; SBLWGRW 1; Atlanta: Society of Biblical Literature, 2001), lxxi–lxxvi.

rights should die, to modest cave cults on Crete that by rights should disappear: not all small things were forgotten. Philostratus, with his apparent adherence to northern Aegean traditions and his critique of the Homeric canon, testifies to a similar resistance to convergence.[18] The material record once again places the *Heroikos* within a broader geographical and social context.

The value of material witness to the *Heroikos*, it would seem, does not lie in any chimerical attempt "to tell the truth" about the dialogue. Instead, a focus on processes of construction, concentration, and convergence makes a point vital for our purposes. Far from being a rarefied confection, a nostalgic head trip, or a Homeric snubbing, many of the central themes of the *Heroikos* emerge as both perceived, and acted upon, across a wide cultural domain. Competitions over memory, over authority, and over tradition were not arcane or recondite matters, but instead were materially waged, with material consequences and implications. The archaeology of the *Heroikos*, in the end, provides the dialogue with a surprisingly vigorous context: the vinedresser, inspired as he was, did right to point us downwards.

[18] Maclean and Aitken, "Introduction," l and n. 47.

Philostratus's *Heroikos* and Early Christianity: Heroes, Saints, and Martyrs

Jackson P. Hershbell

Unlike Tacitus and Pliny the Younger, or the later authors Lucian, Galen, and Celsus with whom he was almost contemporary, Flavius Philostratus (ca. 170–249 C.E.) never mentions Christians or the "man who was crucified in Palestine" (Lucian *The Passing of Peregrinus* 11).[1] Whether Philostratus took notice of this superstition in the works attributed to him remains a matter of conjecture. For example, in his *Life of Apollonius* (7.41), Philostratus has Apollonius assure his disciple Damis that after his trial, he will appear to Damis "as I myself believe, alive, but as you will believe, risen from the dead (ἀναβεβιωκότα),"[2] a remark once interpreted as an indirect reference to Christian belief in the resurrection.[3] Yet Apollonius's assurance to Damis is not only vague, but nowhere in the life or elsewhere is Damis associated with Christianity. As Friedrich Solmsen noted in 1941, the view that Philostratus wrote his *Life of Apollonius* to rival the Gospels, thus portraying the wonder-worker from Tyana as a competitor of Jesus, belongs to a past generation of scholars.[4] It also seems quite fanciful to consider mention of the

[1] For a comprehensive study of early non-Christian attitudes to the *superstitio*, see Robert L. Wilken, *The Christians as the Romans Saw Them* (New Haven: Yale University Press, 1984); on Lucian (born ca. 120 C.E.) see pp. 44–45 and 96–98. Wilken makes no mention of Philostratus.

[2] Translations of *The Life of Apollonius* are those of F. C. Conybeare in *Philostratus the Athenian: The Life of Apollonius of Tyana, The Epistles of Apollonius, and the Treatise of Eusebius* (2 vols.; LCL; Cambridge, Mass.: Harvard University Press, 1912; repr. 1960). Hans Dieter Betz ("Hero Worship and Christian Beliefs: Observations from the History of Religion on Philostratus's *Heroikos*," 30 n. 31, in this volume) states that ἀναβιοῦν is a "technical" word for Philostratus, though in LSJ, however, its use by other non-Christian authors is also documented. In early Christian literature it appears only in *2 Clement* 19.4.

[3] See Friedrich Solmsen ("Philostratus," PW 20.1 [1941]: 145), who criticized Richard Reitzenstein's view that Apollonius's remark was intended as a cut or insult against Christian belief in the resurrection.

[4] Solmsen, "Philostratus," 145. To be sure, Apollonius's miracles and power over evil spirits made him a rival to Jesus in the minds of later non-Christians.

people of Antioch who took no interest in Hellenic affairs (*Life of Apollonius* 3.58) as a reference to Christians there. According to Solmsen, any similarities between Philostratus's *Life of Apollonius* and the Gospels are best regarded as arising from a "common atmosphere" in which stories about miracle workers were often believed.

It might be countered, however, that Philostratus's close connections with the imperial court, especially Julia Domna, Caracalla, and possibly with Alexander Severus (222–235 C.E.), early in whose reign the *Heroikos* was probably composed,[5] might have brought Philostratus into contact with Christianity. After all, Philostratus accompanied Caracalla on the emperor's trips and military campaigns and so "traversed most of the earth" (*Life of Apollonius* 7.31). Moreover, if Philostratus had known Alexander Severus well, there is a doubtful report in the *Augustan History* (SHA *Alexander Severus* 29.2) that in the emperor's "private chapel" there were figures of Apollonius, "Christus," Abraham, Orpheus, and other *animae sanctiores*.[6] After the deaths of Caracalla and his mother, however, Philostratus probably took up residence in Athens, and any contact with Alexander Severus remains uncertain.

THE *HEROIKOS* AND EARLY CHRISTIANITY

Since the studies of Samson Eitrem (1929)[7] and Hans Dieter Betz (1996),[8] interest continues to be given to the *Heroikos* and early Christianity, a topic most recently touched on by Jennifer Maclean and Ellen Aitken in their introduction to the first published English

---

Conybeare mentions (*Life of Apollonius* [LCL], 1:xiv) Hieroklês, a provincial governor under Diocletian, who wrote a work to show that Apollonius was as great an exorcist as Jesus.

[5] See Jennifer K. Berenson Maclean and Ellen Bradshaw Aitken, "Introduction," in *Flavius Philostratus: Heroikos* (trans. Jennifer K. Berenson Maclean and Ellen Bradshaw Aitken; SBLWGRW 1; Atlanta: Society of Biblical Literature, 2001), xlix–liii, for Philostratus's connections with the Severan Court and the dating of the *Heroikos*.

[6] See Ronald Syme, *Emperors and Biography: Studies in the "Historia Augusta"* (Oxford: Clarendon, 1971), 27. According to Syme, the report persists "with or without some hint of dubiety." See the later discussion of Ramsey MacMullen, *Paganism in the Roman Empire* (New Haven: Yale University Press, 1981), 92–93.

[7] Samson Eitrem, "Zu Philostrats *Heroikos*," *Symbolae Osloenses* 8 (1929): 1–56.

[8] Betz, "Hero Worship and Christian Beliefs."

translation of the *Heroikos*. All of these scholars have largely avoided "parallelomania"[9] while focusing on comparisons between Philostratus's heroes and early Christian portrayals of Jesus, the saints, and martyrs. Betz, whose study was based partly on that of Eitrem, raises the question of why Christian belief in Jesus as the Messiah did not lead to a hero cult. Like Eitrem, Betz called attention to Jesus' resurrection appearances, which, according to Betz, correspond to the "pattern" of a hero cult. Yet, according to Betz, even though the gospel writers knew about "the possibility of a resurrected Jesus as a hero,"[10] they excluded any "hero-Christology" as "unsuitable" for Christian belief.[11] In *The Quest of the Historical Gospel*, Lawrence Wills considers at length "the hero cult paradigm" in early Christianity and Judaism.[12] His treatment is fuller than that of Betz, and Wills observes that the "missing body" or "empty grave" motif is common to the hero tradition, citing Amphiaraos and Oedipus as examples.[13] Although elements of the hero cult are not explicitly attested in early Christian writings, Wills notes that Justin Martyr (ca. 100–165), a convert to Christianity, made comparisons between the heroes Herakles, Perseus, Asclepius, and Jesus (*First Apology* 54; *Dialogue with Trypho* 69).[14] Moreover, according to Origen's *Against Celsus* (2.56), the non-Christian polemicist Celsus denied in his *True Doctrine* (ca. 178–80) that Jesus' resurrection was unique and cited the "resurrections" of Orpheus, Herakles, Theseus, and Protesilaos. They were all heroes who, according to Celsus, disappeared for a time, and later returned as though risen from the dead.[15]

Before I turn to discussion of Jesus' resurrection and that of Protesilaos, some remarks on the *Heroikos* and its possible connec-

[9] The phrase is that of Samuel Sandmel, "Parallelomania," *JBL* 81 (1962): 1–13. Sandmel does not deny that "literary parallels and literary influence, in the form of source and derivation exist," but he discourages the extravagance of drawing such parallels.

[10] Betz, "Hero Worship and Christian Beliefs," 45.

[11] Betz, "Hero Worship and Christian Beliefs," 46. Betz writes, however, on p. 45 (see also n. 54) about "parallels" between the hero cult and the Gospels, using the term in the broad sense of "similarities." There are, to my knowledge, no clear literary influences of one on the other.

[12] Lawrence M. Wills, *The Quest of the Historical Gospel: Mark, John, and the Origins of the Gospel Genre* (London and New York: Routledge 1997), 23–50.

[13] Wills, *Quest*, 48.

[14] Wills, *Quest*, 33.

[15] See Henry Chadwick, trans. and ed., *Origen: Contra Celsum* (Cambridge and New York: Cambridge University Press, 1980), 110–11, for his translation of the text.

tions with the rise of Christianity are in order. First, although Betz never claimed that Philostratus and early Christian writers knew one another's works, he suggested that Philostratus knew of Christianity. To be sure, this "difficult question" is so difficult that Betz never really answers it in his "Hero Worship and Christian Beliefs."[16]

Second, Philostratus lived at the time of the development of early Christianity, and so a comparison between the *Heroikos* and Christian beliefs about Jesus, the martyrs, and later saints is valuable in showing differences and similarities between two contemporary religious expressions. It also reinforces the hardly novel notion that Christianity did not begin *ex nihilo* as a unique or entirely new religion in the Roman Empire.

JESUS AS HERO

Early in his study, Betz remarks that the "concept" ἥρως is not found in the New Testament, and that the early Christians "consciously" avoided considering Jesus as a hero.[17] As we noted earlier, Wills also suggested that the gospel writers knew about a tradition of Jesus as a risen hero, although "the elements of the hero-cult pattern are not *explicitly* attested in the early Christian texts."[18] Indeed, given the Greco-Roman milieu of early Christianity, both Betz and Wills are probably right, though the absence of the word ἥρως in the New Testament does not prove that its authors or other early Christians "consciously" avoided thinking of Jesus as hero. More germane is that later Christians, especially the patristic writers, gave attention to Jesus and to the non-Christian hero Herakles. To be sure, these theologians' frequent mention of Herakles can be explained by their knowledge of non-Christian literature; yet Jerome's warning (*Letters* 2.13.8) that Christians should not swear by Herakles sug-

[16] Betz, "Hero Worship and Christian Beliefs," 26 n. 8: "The relationship of Philostratus to Christianity involves a difficult question that cannot be discussed here."

[17] Betz, "Hero Worship and Christian Beliefs," 26. More to the point, Eitrem ("Zu Philostrats *Heroikos*," 3–4) noted that "hero" no longer had its former significance, and almost anyone who died could be reverenced as a "hero" by the survivors; he cites here the use of *hêroeion* in *CIG* IV. 9182. The inscription as edited by Ernst Curtius and Adolf Kirchhoff reads †Ηροεῖον Νόννου Μεσσικᾶ (?) ἱματιοπορ(φυρέως) ("the shrine of the hero Nonnus Messika [?] of the purple cloak"). Yet the adjective ἡρωικός, according to Eitrem, still had its old associations with θεῖος. See Eitrem, "Zu Philostrats *Heroikos*," 4 n. 1.

[18] Wills, *Quest*, 50.

gests that this hero and his cult were not far removed from Christian daily life.[19] Moreover, Herakles' decision at the crossroads of virtue and vice was sometimes used to inspire Christians for martyrdom.[20] Patristic writers also made comparisons between Herakles and Jesus, sometimes to combat heresy. For example, in his dispute with Marcion, Tertullian (ca. 160–240 C.E.) argued against the Marcionite insistence that Jesus had a human and a divine father. If this were so, argued Tertullian, Marcion would make Jesus another Herakles (*Against Marcion* 4.10.7).[21] There are many other comparisons between Herakles and Jesus in antiquity which lie beyond the limits of this essay. In a thorough examination of these comparisons, Abraham Malherbe has observed that Christian appropriation of themes to do with Herakles was, in view of the cultural and intellectual background, less a special "Herakleologie" than a set of Christian attempts to express or reinforce hope in a resurrection or overcoming death.[22] The figure of Herakles lent himself to these attempts not least in his triumph over Thanatos ("Death") by returning Alcestis to earth. In one of his contests, moreover, Herakles descended to Hades and brought back the three-headed hound Cerberus; while in Hades he also released Theseus from his imprisonment. In sum, although Jesus may never have been called a "hero" or "consciously" regarded as such, there is evidence in later Christian writers that he and Herakles, perhaps the Greco-Roman hero par excellence, were quite consciously compared.

JESUS, PROTESILAOS, AND THE *HEROIKOS*

The most obvious comparison between Jesus and Protesilaos, the first Achaean warrior to die at Troy, involves their resurrections. A return from the dead or "resurrection" was familiar to the ancient Greeks and Romans and hardly particular to Jewish or Christian belief. As Maclean and Aitken claim, Protesilaos's resurrection was

[19] See Abraham J. Malherbe, "Herakles," *RAC* 14 (1988): 574–75. As Malherbe noted, early Christian remarks about Herakles were polemical (and apologetic); later Christians, e.g., Clement of Alexandria, Justin Martyr, and Gregory of Nazianzus, made positive comparisons.

[20] Malherbe, "Herakles," 574. Malherbe cites Justin's *Second Apology* 11.

[21] Malherbe, "Herakles," 578.

[22] Malherbe, "Herakles," 582–83. See also David E. Aune, "Heracles and Christ: Heracles Imagery in the Christology of Early Christianity," in *Greeks, Romans, and Christians: Essays in Honor of Abraham J. Malherbe* (ed. David L. Balch, Everett Ferguson, Wayne A. Meeks; Minneapolis, Fortress, 1990), 3–19.

so well known in antiquity that Christian writers questioned its possibility in order to "highlight" Jesus' resurrection.[23] Unlike Jesus, however, Protesilaos experiences two resurrections. At *Her.* 2.9–11 the vinedresser and his Phoenician guest discuss Protesilaos's resurrections. According to the vinedresser, Protesilaos died at Troy "because of Helen," but because of his wife Laodameia, he came to life again at Phthia. The Phoenician replies, "And yet he is said to have died after he came to life again and to have persuaded his wife to follow him." The vinedresser's response is veiled in mystery: "How he returned afterwards too, he does not tell me. . . . He is hiding, he says, some secret of the Fates."[24] As Eitrem noted, though Protesilaos's ἀναβίωσις is somewhat like Apollonius of Tyana's apotheosis, it differs in at least one significant feature: already in his lifetime Apollonius was considered a god (Philostratus *Life of Apollonius* 3.50).[25] He is the "divine man" (θεῖος ἀνήρ) who awakens a young woman from death (*Life of Apollonius* 4.45; compare Asclepius and Herakles, who return Alcestis from the dead). Moreover, Apollonius's disappearance at his trial before the emperor Domitian (*Life of Apollonius* 8.9) and his appearance on the afternoon of the same day in Dikaiarchia (*Life of Apollonius* 8.10) suggest that he has joined the gods and is thus removed from time and space. In addition, no grave of Apollonius was to be found (*Life of Apollonius* 8.31).

Given the depiction of Protesilaus in the *Heroikos*, Eitrem formulated what he called Philostratus's "dogmatic of heroification":[26]

1. Heroes have a higher status than souls of the dead because of a special ἀναβίωσις (lit. "a return to life again"), and they enjoy direct association or communion (συνουσία) with the gods, and so heroes have achieved the gift of infallible prophecy.

2. As heroes have attained by their "resurrection" a higher level of existence, so human beings can, because of their "piety" (θεοσέβεια) and the gods' corresponding favor (θεοφιλία), attain communion with the gods.

Eitrem's "dogmatic of heroification" seems generally correct, but in

[23] Maclean and Aitken, *Flavius Philostratus: Heroikos*, liii–liv. They also cite Minucius Felix *Octavius* 11.

[24] See Maclean and Aitken, *Flavius Philostratus: Heroikos*, lxii.

[25] Eitrem, "Zu Philostrats *Heroikos*," 28.

[26] Eitrem, "Zu Philostrats *Heroikos*," 29.

regard to the second point he may have confused the notion of resurrection with that of apotheosis. Elias Bickerman, for example, distinguishes between resurrection of the dead (a reappearance on earth) from an ascension into heaven (or Olympus in the Greco-Roman context).[27] For example, Herakles is transported to Olympus while his shade goes to Hades. In any case, the Greek (Platonic) concept of the soul's immortality and Greek and Roman notions of an apotheosis (deification of a departed hero or emperor) are quite different from Jewish and Christian beliefs in a bodily resurrection. For example, from Paul's First Letter to the Thessalonians, it seems clear that he and other Christians of the first century expected Jesus' return along with a resurrection of those who "sleep in death" (see 1 Thess 4:13–18), and it was difficult for Greeks and Romans to accept the belief in a bodily resurrection.[28]

The myth of Protesilaos's second death and second resurrection may have led Philostratus to make him the main hero of the *Heroikos* and the hero who associates with the vinedresser. There are other significant differences between Protesilaos and Jesus: according to Christian tradition, Jesus died once, and his resurrection was effected by God's power.[29] The agency behind the resurrection of Protesilaos remained unexplained. Moreover, according to the gospels of John, Luke, and Matthew, Jesus did not remain with his disciples after the resurrection, but ascended into heaven, thus changing the location and mode of his existence.[30] These and other accounts of the ascension (the story is explicitly narrated only in Acts 1:9–11) find expression in the simple formulation of later Christian creeds such as the Nicene: "he ascended into heaven."

[27] See Elias Bickerman, "Das leere Grab," *ZNW* 23 (1924): 281–92. Bickerman's view on ascension and that of David Aune ("The Problem of the Genre of the Gospels: A Critique of C. H. Talbert's *What Is a Gospel?*" in *Studies of History and Tradition in the Four Gospels* [ed. R. T. France and David Wenham; Gospel Perspectives 2; Sheffield: JSOT Press, 1981], 9–60) are discussed briefly in Wills, *Quest*, 48.

[28] See, for example, Ramsey MacMullen, *Christianizing the Roman Empire (A.D. 100–400)* (New Haven: Yale University Press, 1984), 12 and 18–19. For more recent and fuller discussion about immortality and resurrection, see Gregory Riley, *Resurrection Reconsidered: Thomas and John in Controversy* (Minneapolis: Fortress, 1995), esp. 23–58, and Alan J. Segal's very interesting sociological interpretation of immortality and resurrection, "Life after Death," in *The Resurrection: An Interdisciplinary Symposium on the Resurrection of Jesus* (ed. Stephen T. Davis, Daniel Kendall, and Gerald O'Collins; Oxford and New York: Oxford University Press, 1997), 90–125.

[29] See, for example, Acts 2:24.

[30] Wills, *Quest*, 48.

There was thus no grave or tomb for Jesus. By contrast, the power or strength of a Greco-Roman hero, especially if a grave existed, was concentrated at the cult center where the hero was buried and revered by those who lived nearby. This phenomenon is not unlike the local veneration of the saints in late antique Christian practice.[31]

In brief, although Jesus was not explicitly called a "hero" by early Christians, later comparison of him with Herakles and some similarities to Protesilaos suggest strongly that Jesus may have been venerated as a hero by some early Christians, especially given variations within the "hero cult paradigm." The extant texts do not rule out such a possibility. Moreover, the canonical Christian texts usually considered in this discussion may not represent the beliefs of many who considered themselves Christians. A thorough examination of apocryphal and noncanonical works may yield further evidence of the use of a "hero cult paradigm" for Jesus.

HEROES, SAINTS, AND MARTYRS

When Philostratus composed his *Heroikos*, there were probably no "saints": formal procedures of sanctification or an official declaration of sainthood did not yet exist.[32] Instead, there was the much less defined notion of the "holy man" since explored by many scholars.[33] Certainly Pythagoras, Apollonius of Tyana, and Jesus were often considered "holy men."[34] Also relevant to the discussion are the similarities between Greco-Roman heroes and the Christian saints. The *Heroikos* provides a focal point for some of these similarities.

[31] See Eitrem, "Zu Philostrats *Heroikos*," 3: "Die lokale Begrenzung war die Stärke des Heros, sein Grab war das sichtbare, unerschütterliche Kultzentrum" ("Locality was the strength of the hero; his grave was the visible, imperturbable center of his cult").

[32] For Paul the term "saints" (ἅγιοι) refers to all Christians, both living and dead. I am indebted to Alexandra Brown for reminding me of this Pauline usage. The terms ἅγιος and *sanctus* came, of course, to be used for those Christians who received cultic veneration. The terms were first applied to martyrs, those who died witnessing to their faith; from the fourth century on it was used often for monastics and bishops. See Theofried Baumeister, "Heiligenverehrung I," *RAC* 14 (1988): 97. My use of "saint" is thus not Pauline, but that of the later church.

[33] For the following discussion, see Averil Cameron, "On Defining the Holy Man," in *The Cult of Saints in Late Antiquity and the Middle Ages: Essays on the Contribution of Peter Brown* (ed. James Howard-Johnston and Paul Antony Hayward; Oxford and New York: Oxford University Press, 1999), 27–43.

[34] The examples are given by A. Cameron in her study mentioned in the previous note.

At *Her.* 10.1 the vinedresser describes Protesilaos as "smelling sweeter than autumn myrtles," and earlier at 3.1 the vineyard itself is described as fragrant.[35] According to Eitrem, there is a Coptic greeting in which the pleasing aroma of a saint is mentioned, and Athenagoras (*Legatio pro Christianis* 13.2) refers to the good odor of God.[36] A second point of similarity is that Protesilaos is a healer (ἰατρός)[37] and cures illness in response to prayer, especially consumption, edema, eye disease, and a form of malaria (*Her.* 16.1). Supernatural healing is also attributed to the saints, and this power is often invoked against illness: for example, Agapitus, martyred ca. 274 C.E., against colic; Cyriacus, martyred ca. 305 C.E., against eye disease; Pantaleon, d. ca. 305 C.E., against consumption. In brief, numerous saints are invoked against physical and mental diseases.[38]

To be sure, there is scholarly dispute about how much the cult of the saints is connected with that of heroes. Yet the influences of the Greco-Roman world on Christianity were great, and in some cases there is a documentable transition from the cult of a hero to that of a saint, or between a *hêrôon* and *martyrium*.[39] Any transformation of a Greco-Roman hero (or deity) into a Christian saint, however, can only be determined if the local legends, the local cult, and feast day somehow coincide with one another; this determination usually requires careful research and treatment of individual cases. With the end of persecutions of Christians, there was an increase in the number of those venerated by the church as saints.

[35] Eitrem, "Zu Philostrats *Heroikos*," 34. According to Eitrem the church accepted the ancient belief that a good odor signifies favor, joy, and grace. See also Gregory Nagy's interesting discussion in "The Sign of the Hero: A Prologue," in Maclean and Aitken, *Flavius Philostratus: Heroikos*, xxvii–xxviii.

[36] See also Irenaeus *Against Heresies* 4.25.3 and 13.2, and 2 Cor. 2:14–16, where Paul refers to Christ's triumphal procession when Christians are to reveal and spread abroad the odor or fragrance (ὀσμή) of the knowledge of himself. Again, my thanks to Alexandra Brown for mentioning this passage.

[37] For a good discussion of Protesilaos as healer, see Teresa Mantero, *Ricerche sull'* Heroikos *di Filostrato* (Genoa, Italy: Instituto di Filologia Classica e Medioevale, 1966), 61–64, where she discusses philosophy, therapy, and initiation.

[38] For brief biographical sketches, see *The Book of Saints: A Dictionary of Servants of God*, by the Benedictine Monks of St. Augustine's Abbey, Ramsgate (6th ed.; Wilton, Conn.: Morehouse, 1989). Sean Kelley and Rosemary Rogers (*Saints Preserve Us!* [New York: Random House, 1993]) provide entertaining descriptions of many saints, their patronage, and reasons for which they are invoked.

[39] See, for example, Baumeister ("Heiligenverehrung I," 104), who notes that parallels between the cult of heroes and that of saints are unmistakable, noting the importance of the grave and regular religious observance for both hero and saint.

Forms of reverence given to the martyrs were now also given to those who had not died because of their Christian belief.[40] It would seem then that from the cult of martyrs developed that of saints, both cults involving an annual day of remembrance, with great attention usually given to the grave site. Thus by the third century the foundations for veneration of the saints were established. In contrast to the prior veneration of apostles and martyrs, the "new" saints were selected from a much larger group of believers, though not every ascetic or bishop was numbered among the saints. How individuals qualified to become saints goes beyond this study, but by the time of Augustine of Hippo, if not before, there was an inclination to apply the concept of hero to Christian martyrs, those who died for the sake of their belief. Thus in *The City of God* (10.21) Augustine writes that he would have used the word "hero" for a martyr if it had not contradicted the language of the church. For Augustine, the heroes live together in the air with daimons, but these Greco-Roman heroes are conquered by the martyrs, who are the true heroes.[41] To be sure, the word "hero" is seldom applied to the saints, although holy persons of the Hebrew scriptures, for example, Samson, Samuel, and even Moses, were called such. Notably, the word is also found in Christian grave inscriptions.[42]

SUMMARY

The *Heroikos* is an important work for giving insights into the concept of the hero in the third century C.E. Its composition occurs at a time when Christianity, despite its persecution, was establishing itself in the Roman Empire. We do not know if Philostratus took much, if any, notice of Christianity. His *Life of Apollonius* and the Christian Gospels, even if they do not have much in common, have all, however, been considered "aretalogies" or accounts of remarkable teachers that have been used for moral instruction.[43] The *Heroikos*, by contrast, seems to be a critique of the Homeric portrayal of some Trojan heroes. At the same time, it gives insights into second- and third-century beliefs about the heroes and their powers. The figure of Jesus is not wholly unlike that of Protesilaos:

[40] Baumeister, "Heiligenverehrung I," 875.

[41] See Speyer, "Heros," 875.

[42] Speyer, "Heros," 875, where he gives several references.

[43] See, for example, Moses Hadas and Morton Smith, *Heroes and Gods: Spiritual Biographies in Antiquity* (New York: Harper & Row, 1965), 3.

both heal illnesses and rise from the dead. It is also possible to say that Protesilaos is a teacher of and companion to the vinedresser, not unlike Jesus' relationship with his disciples, both before and after his death. Jesus, however, is never explicitly called a "hero" in extant Christian writings. He is often compared with Herakles, the Greco-Roman hero par excellence, by early Christian theologians. Some New Testament scholars, furthermore, have argued that Jesus may well fit the paradigm of a cult hero. That the heroes of the *Heroikos* show some similarities to the later martyrs and saints should not be a surprise.

As Eitrem observed, Philostratus's *Heroikos* pursued what might be considered a national or Hellenic purpose.[44] Like other representatives of the Second Sophistic, he fought against all that was anti-Hellenic or was regarded as such by him. In *The Life of Apollonius* (6.20), Thespesian, a *gymnosophist* from Ethiopia,[45] asks Apollonius why the Lacedaemonians do not sacrifice strangers to Artemis as the Scythians formerly did. Apollonius replies, "Because it is not congenial to any of the Hellenes to adopt in their full rigor the manners and customs of barbarians" (ὅτι . . . οὐδενὶ Ἑλλήνων πρὸς τρόπου βάρβαρα ἐξασκεῖν ἤθη). One suspects that if Philostratus had known about Christians, he would have regarded them as "barbarians,"[46] or even "Galileans" as did the emperor Julian.[47]

[44] Eitrem, "Zu Philostrats *Heroikos*," 5.

[45] *Gymnosophists* were Indian ascetics who often lived naked (hence *gymnos*) in forests and were often venerated for their ascetic lives. See J. D. M. Derrett, "Gymnosophisten," *KlPauly* 2:892–93.

[46] Tatian, born in Assyria ca. 120, a convert to Christianity, studied with Justin Martyr, and in his *Oration to the Greeks* was proud of his non-Hellenic origin, and for him the "barbaric" philosophy, that of Christianity, meant far more than Hellenic philosophy. For a good, concise discussion of Tatian's thought, see Etienne Gilson, *History of Christian Philosophy in the Middle Ages* (New York: Random House, 1955), 14–16.

[47] During his brief time as emperor (360–363 C.E.), Julian "the Apostate" wrote a work against Christians whom he always called "Galileans," emphasizing their acceptance of "the creed of fishermen," and perhaps reflecting the statement in John 7:52 that no prophets come from Galilee. *Against the Galileans* was originally in three books, but only the first has survived. For a good introduction and translation, see Wilmar Cave Wright, *The Works of the Emperor Julian* (3 vols.; LCL; Cambridge, Mass.: Harvard University Press, 1923; repr. 1969), 3:313–427.

The *Heroikos* and Popular Christianity in the Third Century C.E.

James C. Skedros

The early Christian *Acts of Peter*, a text which is considered to be part of a larger body of early Christian literature dating from the second and third centuries and commonly referred to as New Testament Apocrypha, was written in the late second century in Greek but survives only in a third-century Latin translation. The *Acts of Peter* opens not with the apostle Peter, but with the apostle Paul conducting evangelical activities in Rome. Quartus, a prison official and newly converted Christian, attempts to convince Paul to leave Rome. In search of God's will, Paul fasts for three days beseeching the Lord (that is, Jesus) for guidance. As one might expect, after three days, guidance comes in the form of a vision in which the Lord himself instructs Paul to travel to Spain. Preparing for his departure, Paul is approached by his Roman Christian brothers and sisters who express their fear that he shall never return. They praise his many accomplishments, most especially his opposition to Jewish customs. As Paul's followers entreat him to return quickly, "there came a sound from heaven and a great voice which said, 'Paul the servant of God is chosen for (this) service for the time of his life; but at the hands of Nero, that godless and wicked man, he shall be perfected before your eyes.' "[1] In a very different yet contemporaneous text, the *Heroikos* shares some significant characteristics with the *Acts of Peter*. Although the rural setting of Protesilaos's shrine at Elaious could not be in greater contrast to the urban Rome of the *Acts of Peter*, the two texts have a common purpose: the defense and propagation of the cult of noted heroes.

The *Acts of Peter* and the *Heroikos* are not only connected by their common desire to support the cults of their respective heroes,

[1] *Acts of Peter* 1.1; for an English translation and notes, see Wilhelm Schneemelcher, ed. and trans., "Acts of Peter," in *New Testament Apocrypha* (ed. Wilhelm Schneemelcher; trans. Robert McL. Wilson; rev. ed. of the collection initiated by Edgar Hennecke; 2 vols.; Louisville: Westminster/John Knox; 1991–1992), 2:288. The *Acts of Peter* were originally composed in Greek, most probably between 180–190 C.E.; see Schneemelcher, "Acts of Peter," 2:283.

but, more importantly, by the religious environment that informs the two texts.[2] Paul's vision and the voice from heaven are certainly not unusual or unbelievable experiences within the first three centuries of Christianity. Such heavenly epiphanies and divine appearances are found throughout the New Testament, the Apocryphal Acts of the Apostles, and other early Christian literature.[3] Nor are they unusual within the religious milieu of the Mediterranean world of the third century. In Philostratus's *Heroikos*, the steward of the shrine of Protesilaos offers several examples of the appearance of the heroes in order to convince his Phoenician visitor of the continued existence of these heroes. Although separated by theological, ritualistic, and mythic differences, the *Acts of Peter* and the *Heroikos* share some rather significant features in the area of popular religiosity. Using the *Heroikos* as a springboard, this essay explores some of the popular religious expressions found within Christianity of the third century C.E.

At the outset, a couple of methodological observations are in order. First, popular Christianity, as broadly conceived, encompasses a variety of practices and beliefs, including baptism and eucharist.[4] Because of the almost universal importance of baptism and eucharist within earliest Christian praxis, these two rituals are excluded from the present discussion of popular Christianity in the third century. I employ, moreover, as a working definition of "popular religion" in this period that it "was not so much superstition or magic as the set of beliefs and practices that arose outside the context of the temple cults, which had a normative effect on how men approached the resident deities."[5] Second, just as myth and cult varied considerably from one place to another in pagan religion of

[2] It should be noted, however, that the two texts reflect different genres: the *Heroikos* is a literary piece influenced by Plato's famous dialogue *Phaedrus* and exhibits "characteristic sophistic exercises" (Jennifer K. Berenson Maclean and Ellen Bradshaw Aitken, "Introduction," in *Flavius Philostratus: Heroikos* [trans. Jennifer K. Berenson Maclean and Ellen Bradshaw Aitken; SBLWGRW 1; Atlanta: Society of Biblical Literature, 2001], xlv–xlvi) while the Apocryphal Acts of the Apostles are written on a more popular level and are often influenced by the Hellenistic and Roman romance novel. I thank François Bovon for pointing out this distinction.

[3] See, for example, Acts 9:4–6; 2 Cor 12:2–4; *Acts of John* 18 and 87; *Acts of Thomas* 1.11–12; *Martyrdom of Polycarp* 9.1.

[4] Arthur Darby Nock, *Early Gentile Christianity and its Hellenistic Background* (New York: Harper & Row, 1964), 59–84.

[5] Frank R. Trombley, *Hellenic Religion and Christianization, c. 370–529* (2 vols.; Leiden and New York: Brill, 1993), 1:36. See also H. J. Carpenter, "Pop-

the Greco-Roman world, such was also the case with the myth and cult of Christian religion in the third century.[6] My observations are not limited to one geographical area or to one Christian orthodoxy and therefore cannot avoid "the inaccuracies and contradictions inherent in [such a] synoptic approach."[7]

As Ellen Aitken and Jennifer Berenson Maclean have pointed out, one of the primary goals of the *Heroikos* is the "correction of Homer," a task that focuses on "Homeric doctrine" or "Homeric myth."[8] Philostratus's reworking of Homer's account of events and actions surrounding certain Trojan and Greek heroes is told within the framework of the early-third-century hero cult and provides the reader with several examples of the rituals, practices, and beliefs associated with this cult. Two such popular religious practices found in the *Heroikos* are also found in the opening pages of the *Acts of Peter:* these are epiphanies and visionary experiences.

EPIPHANIES AND VISIONARY EXPERIENCES

Found in the *Heroikos* are several examples of popular religious practices associated with the cult of the Homeric heroes. One such example parallels the opening of the *Acts of Peter*. In an attempt to convince the Phoenician that the heroes continue to live centuries after their death, the vinedresser relates a story of an appearance of Ajax on the plain of Troy. Two strangers, states the vinedresser, were playing with some gaming stones in front of the tomb of Ajax. Suddenly, Ajax emerges and admonishes them to quit playing the game since it reminds him of his close companion, Palamedes (*Her.* 20.2). Although the appearance is relatively undramatic, it does reflect Philostratus's attempt to confirm belief in the reality of the Trojan War heroes and their continued efficacy in the third century.

When we turn to Christian praxis, we notice that the power of revelation within Christian life is highlighted in a very brief, yet revealing, ordinance found in *The Apostolic Tradition* attributed to Hippolytus of Rome and usually dated to the first half of the third century. Within the context of a series of ordinances governing the

---

ular Christianity in the Theologians in the Early Centuries," *JTS* 14 (1963): 294–310.

[6] Jon D. Mikalson, *Athenian Popular Religion* (Chapel Hill: University of North Carolina Press, 1983), 4.

[7] Mikalson, *Athenian Popular Religion*, 5.

[8] Maclean and Aitken, *Flavius Philostratus: Heroikos,* xlix.

imposition of hands upon various individuals, the order states, "If any one among the laity appear to have received a gift of healing by a revelation, hands shall not be laid on him, because the matter is manifest."[9] The placing of hands upon the infirm is well attested in early Christianity.[10] What is of note here is that the Christian believer has received restoration to health through a revelation. Just what kind of revelation is not specified. It is clear, however, that direct revelation, that is, direct communication with the source of healing, whether in this case God or an intermediary, is part of acceptable Christian praxis of the third century.[11]

Like the hero Protesilaos, the Christian martyr was capable of appearing to individuals at moments of need. The third-century martyrdom account of the two martyrs Potamiaina and Basileidês provides such an example. Eusebius, who preserves the story for us, places their martyrdom during the reign of Septimius Severus.[12] In this extremely brief martyrdom account, a young Alexandrian maiden, Potamiaina, is condemned to die for her Christian faith. After being tortured, she is led to the site of her impending execution by a certain Basileidês, who is described in the text as being a member of the military. As the crowd hurls abuses at Potamiaina, Basileidês, feeling pity toward her, does what he can to prevent them from insulting her. To show her appreciation, Potamiaina assures Basileidês that when she meets her Lord she will repay his kindness. After these words she received the martyr's crown by having boiling pitch poured over her entire body.

So far, there is nothing out of the ordinary, in comparison to other accounts of martyrdom. The story now shifts to Basileidês, who, in the presence of his fellow soldiers, is asked to swear an oath. He refuses, since, as he confesses, he is a Christian. When he is placed in prison, fellow Christians come to visit him and inquire

[9] Hippolytus, *The Apostolic Tradition* 15; translation from Gregory Dix, ed., *Apostolikê Paradosis: The Treatise on the Apostolic Tradition of St. Hippolytus of Rome, Bishop and Martyr* (London: SPCK, 1937), 22. For a more complete discussion of this ordinance see Paul F. Bradshaw, Maxwell E. Johnson, and L. Edward Phillips, *The Apostolic Tradition: A Commentary* (Hermeneia; Minneapolis: Fortress, 2002), 80, who date *The Apostolic Tradition* from as early as the mid–second century to the mid–fourth century (pp. 14–15).

[10] For New Testament examples see Mark 5:23; 6:5; and Acts 28:8. Post–New Testament examples include *Acts of Peter* 20 and *Pseudo-Clementine Homilies* 8.24; 9.23.

[11] It is interesting that Protesilaos, the protagonist of the *Heroikos*, is noted for his healing capabilities; see *Her.* 16.1–3.

[12] Eusebius *Ecclesiastical History* 6.5.

how it is that he has become a Christian. He replies that three days after the martyrdom of Potamiaina, the martyr appeared to him at night and placed a crown upon his head informing him that she had beseeched the Lord to allow Basileidês to join the ranks of the martyrs. The Lord answered her prayer, for the very next day Basileidês was crowned with the victory of martyrdom. The story ends by noting that many other pagans joined the ranks of the Christians through nocturnal appearances of Potamiaina.

This martyrdom story has an interesting parallel with the *Heroikos*—the postmortem appearances of the Christian hero to individuals. These appearances are intended to convince unbelievers of the truth of the Christian faith and the power of the Christian message. This they certainly do. Yet they are also evidence of the martyr's existence after death, her power of intercession, and her ability to aid those in need. Such postmortem appearances serve a similar function to those of the appearances of the Trojan and Achaean heroes in Philostratus's *Heroikos*. The vinedresser goes to great lengths to convince the Phoenician of the existence of the heroes by relating several examples of the appearances of these heroes to particular individuals in various places and times.[13] It is the appearance of the heroes, both Christian and pagan, which confirms their existence and justifies the continuation of their cults.

MATERIALITY IN THE PRACTICE OF EARLY CHRISTIANITY

Another significant expression of popular religious practice found in the *Heroikos* is the physicality or materiality of the religious environment associated with the cult of the heroes and, more specifically, with Protesilaos. The opening part of the *Heroikos* contains several examples of the physical and material character of the worship surrounding the Greek heroes. For example, the physical remains of the heroes figure prominently in the vinedresser's attempt to convince his guest of the historical existence of the heroes (*Her*. 8.1). Protesilaos can be seen by the physical eyes as he appears several times a month to the vinedresser (*Her*. 11.3). Recent footprints of the hero can be found on the grounds around the shrine (*Her*. 13.2–3). Statues of the heroes are common, and close examination of them reveals much about these great men for those who have the eyes to see (*Her*. 9.5–10.5; 19.3; 26.13). Perhaps most dramatic is

[13] *Her*. 2.11; 3.6; 13.3–4; 18.1–23.1.

the vinedresser's statement that on occasion he greets Protesilaos with an embrace and a kiss (*Her.* 11.2).

Christian religious practices of the third century were equally sensual in nature. In a fascinating treatise on marriage and remarriage addressed to his wife, Tertullian exhorts her not to remarry after his death, fearing that she might marry a pagan. In defense of his position he notes how difficult it would be for her, or any Christian woman, to marry a non-Christian man. By marrying a pagan, a Christian woman would give up the "pearls . . . (and) distinctive religious practices of (her) daily life." How could she possibly fulfill the obligations and expressions of Christian practice? "For," contends Tertullian,

> If a station [= feast day] is to be kept, her husband will make an early appointment with her to go to the baths; if a fast is to be observed, her husband will, that very day, prepare a feast; if it be necessary to go out on an errand of Christian charity, never are duties at home more urgent. Who, indeed, would permit his wife . . . to spend the whole night away from the house during the Paschal solemnities? Who will suffer her to slip into prison to kiss the fetters of a martyr? Or, for that matter, to salute any one of the brethren with a kiss? Who would allow her to wash the feet of the saints? . . . The more you attempt to conceal them [these distinctive religious observances], the more suspect they become and the more they arouse a pagan's curiosity. Do you think to escape notice when you make the sign of the cross on your bed or on your body? Or when you blow away, with a puff of your breath, some unclean thing? Or when you get up, as you do even at night, to say your prayers? In all this will it not seem that you observe some magic ritual? (Tertullian *To His Wife* 2.4–5)[14]

This litany of Christian practices is of interest for its emphasis on religious activities with particularly physical characteristics that take place outside of the context of baptism and eucharist. I would like to examine a few of these examples of popular Christianity in more detail.

Christian practices of fasting and making the sign of the cross were widespread. Fasting as a ritual exercise surfaces in the Greek

[14] Translation from *Tertullian: Treatises on Marriage and Remarriage* (trans. William P. Le Saint; ACW 13; Westminster, Md.: Newman, 1952), 29–30.

world through the introduction of the mystery cults. Privately, fasting was "deliberately practiced at cults and oracles to elicit significant dreams and receive the gods' inspiration."[15] For Christians, fasting had been prescribed from the first century and seems to have been introduced into nascent Christianity through its Jewish roots.[16] By the third century, fasting is not only a well-established practice among Christians but becomes associated with a particular ascetic strain in early Christianity. The second- and third-century Apocryphal Acts of the Apostles are flooded with references to fasting, abstinence, and similar practices. This emphasis is often interpreted as evidence for the more ascetic nature of this literature. A third-century Syrian church order, the *Didascalia Apostolorum*, speaks of several fasting periods: Wednesdays and Fridays, a paschal fast of six days prior to Easter Sunday, and fasting imposed for penance.[17]

The sign of the cross, tracing a cross on one's forehead or chest, is a Christian practice attested as early as the second century in the *Acts of Peter*.[18] It is Tertullian, however, who gives us the best description of this practice. "At every forward step and movement," the North African Christian writes, "at every going in and out, when we put on our clothes and shoes, when we bathe, when we sit at table, when we light the lamps, on couch, on seat, in all the ordinary actions of daily life, we trace upon the forehead the sign."[19] References could be multiplied, demonstrating the relatively common use of the sign of the cross in Christian praxis.[20]

ANGELS AND DAIMONS

In addition to the talismanic use of the sign of the cross, Tertullian makes reference to what appears to be an almost magical action of

[15] Robin Lane Fox, *Pagans and Christians* (New York: Knopf, 1987), 396.

[16] See *Didache* 8.1 where the reference to fasting "presupposes the customary fasting of pious Jews," Kurt Niederwimmer, *The Didache: A Commentary* (trans. Linda M. Maloney; ed. Harold Attridge; Hermeneia; Minneapolis: Fortress, 1998), 131.

[17] *Didascalia Apostolorum* 2.16 and 5.10–20. For the text and translation, see *Didascalia Apostolorum: The Syriac Version Translated and Accompanied by the Verona Latin Fragments* (trans. R. Hugh Connolly; Oxford: Clarendon, 1929), 52, 178–92.

[18] *Acts of Peter* 2.5.

[19] Tertullian *The Crown* 3.4 (*ANF* 3:94–95).

[20] These include Tertullian *The Resurrection of the Flesh* 8; Hippolytus *The Apostolic Tradition* 37; *Acts of Thomas* 50.

exhalation to extricate the presence of something unclean. A pagan, says Tertullian, will notice that you are a Christian "when you blow away, with a puff of your breath, some unclean thing" (*To His Wife* 2.5). Tertullian seems to be referring to the practice of insufflation, a popular form of exorcism in the early church. His reference to "some unclean thing" (*aliquid immundum*) is not entirely clear.[21] It is probable, however, that he is referring to the world of daimons, those beings or spirits which are intermediaries between God and mortal humanity.[22] Within the diversity of religious beliefs, popular religious practices, and official cults that characterized the third-century Greco-Roman world, there was a shared belief among pagans, Jews, and Christians of the existence of intermediate beings whose ontological existence was somewhere between that of a god and a human being. There was nothing inherently evil or bad about these intermediary beings. For the Greeks, they were called daimons, for the Jews, angels.[23] The religious context of the *Heroikos* is imbued with this common popular belief. In the *Heroikos*, the vinedresser, responding to the inquiry of the Phoenician about the death of Protesilaos, notes that the hero's death at Troy was the result of an "unjust" and "malicious" daimon who was against Protesilaos (*Her.* 12.1).[24]

Earliest Christianity adopted the popular notion of the existence of daimons, and much of Jesus' active ministry as recorded in the Gospels is dedicated to the exorcising of such daimons (Mark 5:1–13; Luke 11:14; Acts 19:11–16). Other examples of Christian practices which reflect the common belief in daimons abound in the first three centuries C.E.[25] *The Apostolic Tradition* of Hippolytus speaks of daily exorcisms prior to baptism for those who have been chosen for this initiation ritual.[26] In one of the few surviving "statistics" of the church prior to Constantine, we are told that in the

[21] Tertullian *To His Wife* 2.5 (PL 1:1296a); see Le Saint, *Tertullian*, 129 n. 117.

[22] E. R. Dodds, *Pagan and Christian in an Age of Anxiety: Some Aspects of Religious Experience from Marcus Aurelius to Constantine* (Cambridge: Cambridge University Press, 1965), 37–38.

[23] John Ferguson, *The Religions of the Roman Empire* (London: Thames & Hudson, 1970), 224.

[24] Protesilaos, as a hero, is considered to be a daimon (*Her.* 43.3).

[25] Justin Martyr (*Dialogue with Trypho* 76) claims that Christians can drive out demons simply by mentioning the name of Jesus. In *Acts of Thomas* 42–49 a woman previously possessed by a demon seeks baptism from Thomas to ensure that the demon will not return.

[26] Hippolytus *The Apostolic Tradition* 20.

year 251 the church of Rome had fifty-two exorcists enrolled among its clergy.[27] At the same time in North Africa, Cyprian tells us that exorcists were used to expel demons, combat female heretics, and heal those with mental disorders.[28] The prominent position given to the act of exorcism in relation to the initiation ritual of baptism and the existence of the office of the exorcist indicate the widespread belief in invisible evil forces permeating the world of third-century Christians.

THE CULT OF THE CHRISTIAN MARTYRS

One further aspect of popular Christianity has its religious counterpart in the *Heroikos*. The affinities and similarities between the cult of the Christian martyrs and the cult of the Greek heroes have been aptly noted by historians of religion since the late nineteenth century.[29] It is not my intention to enter here into a lengthy discussion. Rather, I would simply offer a few observations regarding the *Heroikos* and the cult of the martyrs in third-century Christianity.

As heroes of the faith, Christian martyrs were venerated and respected for their courage and fortitude in the face of impending death. These Christian heroes were objects of veneration not only after receiving their crown of victory, that is, death, but prior to it as well, while they were still alive. Third-century Christians in Syria were encouraged to visit martyrs who had been condemned to death and to rejoice with the martyrs as if they were sharing in their suffering.[30] Tertullian, in the passage quoted above, acknowledges

[27] Eusebius *Ecclesiatical History* 6.43.11.

[28] Cyprian *Letters* 69.15 and 75.10; references taken from W. H. C. Frend, *The Rise of Christianity* (Philadelphia: Fortress, 1984), 406.

[29] Hermann Usener, "Gottliche Synonyme," *Rheinisches Museum für Philologie* 53 (1898): 329–79; Ernst Lucius, *Die Anfänge des Heiligenkults in der christlichen Kirche* (Tübingen: Mohr, 1904); Hippolyte Delehaye, *Les origines du culte des martyrs* (Brussels: Bureaux de la Société des Bollandistes, 1912); Arthur Darby Nock, "The Cult of Heroes," *HTR* 37 (1944): 141–74; repr. in *Essays on Religion and the Ancient World* (ed. Zeph Stewart; 2 vols.; Oxford: Clarendon, 1972), 2:575–602. More recently see Paul-Albert Février, "Le culte des morts dans les communautés chrétiennes durant le IIIe siècle," *Atti del IX congresso internazionale di archeologia cristiana, Roma, 21–27 settembre 1975* (2 vols.; Rome: Pontificio Instituto di archeologia cristiana, 1978), 1:211–74; and Speros Vryonis, "The Panegyris of the Byzantine Saint," in *The Byzantine Saint: University of Birmingham Fourteenth Spring Symposium of Byzantine Studies* (ed. Sergei Hackel; London: Fellowship of St. Alban and St. Sergius, 1981), 196–228. For a contrary view see Fox, *Pagans and Christians*, 446–50.

[30] *Didascalia Apostolorum* 19.1.

the Christian practice of visiting martyrs in prison and expressing devotion to the martyrs by kissing the chains that bind them. Some fifty years later, Christians in North Africa sought out martyrs on death row in hopes of receiving from them spiritual healing and absolution of sins.[31]

Yet it was the postmortem commemoration of the Christian martyr that had the greatest and most lasting impact upon the development of popular religion in Christianity and which has close affinities with the Greek hero cult. Like the Greek hero cult, the Christian commemoration of its own heroes had two fundamental elements: the heroic story of the life and death of the martyr—the martyrdom account—and a physical location for the cultic commemoration of the martyr—the place of burial of the martyr. In Philostratus's *Heroikos*, both characteristics are present. The primary purpose of the *Heroikos* is to retell several of the stories of Greek and Trojan heroes. It is within the retelling of these stories that the cult sites of these heroes and the cultic practices associated with them are highlighted (*Her.* 26.13–20; 37.5). In particular, the cult site of Protesilaos, as the setting for the *Heroikos*, figures prominently in the text.

What then do these two fundamental aspects of the veneration of martyrs and the Greek hero cult suggest about popular Christianity in the third century and its relationship to the religious world of that time? First, Christians of the third century had a concept of sacred space. The vinedresser of the *Heroikos*, responding to the comments of his Phoenician guest concerning the beauty of the property surrounding the shrine of Protesilaos, states "the walkways are sacred, stranger, for the hero exercises on them" (*Her.* 3.6). The ground is sacred because of the presence of the hero. In the *Acts of Thomas*, a text dating to the mid–third century C.E., one of the sons of King Misdaeus of India is possessed by a daimon. Misdaeus visits the place where the apostle Thomas was buried and, unable to find the bones of the apostle since they had been taken away, the king procures some dirt "from the place where the bones of the apostle had lain" and attaches it to his son, who is shortly thereafter healed.[32] For the author and audience of the *Acts of Thomas*, the ground is sacred because it once housed the hallowed bones of the apostle Thomas.

The story of King Misdaeus's son reveals a second aspect of

[31] Cyprian *Letters* 15 and 33.
[32] *Acts of Thomas* 170.

popular Christianity, namely, that physical objects are capable of transmitting divine or supernatural power. For the cult of the martyrs this popular religious belief is exemplified through the nascent cult of relics or physical remains of the martyrs. Sufficient evidence exists to suggest that this belief was well established by the third century. The martyrdom account of Fructuosus and his companions who were burned alive in January 259 C.E., records that after the death of the martyrs, faithful Christians gathered up their ashes in order to keep them for themselves.[33] In an interesting parallel, the vinedresser tells us that the emperor Hadrian himself showed respect for the physical remains of the heroes, when upon his arrival at Troy he "embraced and kissed" some of the bones of the hero Ajax which had become unintentionally exposed. After venerating the bones, Hadrian had them properly restored in Ajax's tomb (*Her*. 8.1).

A third and final characteristic of the third-century cult of the martyrs is the didactic nature of this popular religious phenomenon. The opening lines of the rather lengthy martyrdom account of Pionius, a presbyter martyred at Smyrna during the Decian persecution, express this aspect of the cult of the martyrs:

> The Apostle urges us to share in the remembrances of the saints, fully aware that to call to mind those who have passed their lives in the faith wisely with all their heart gives strength to those who are striving to imitate the better things. . . . Indeed, the martyr Pionius has left us this writing for our instruction that we might have it even to this day as a memorial of his teaching.[34]

Prologues from other early Christian martyrdom accounts emphasize as well the moralistic value of the stories of their Christian heroes. In the *Heroikos*, explicit references to the moralistic value of the stories of the heroes told by the vinedresser are lacking. Rather, what is emphasized is the fact that the Phoenician's doubts regarding the existence and, therefore, power of the heroes are overcome as the stories of these great men unfold.

[33] Herbert Musurillo, trans. and ed., *Acts of the Christian Martyrs* (Oxford: Clarendon, 1972), 183. One hundred years earlier, the often-referenced martyrdom account of Polycarp of Smyrna describes the martyr's relics as "more valuable than precious stones," stating that they were collected and honored with a memorial service for the saint at the place where they were laid (*Martyrdom of Polycarp* 18).

[34] Musurillo, *Acts of the Christian Martyrs*, 137.

CONCLUSION

An ancient reader of the *Heroikos* may have been struck by the discrepancy between what Philostratus had to say about the ancient Greek and Trojan heroes and the actual practice of the hero cult in the third century C.E. Yet what was most likely not strange for the pagan reader of the *Heroikos* was the religious environment and presuppositions which inform the text. The more common characteristics of this third-century religiosity included epiphanies, visions, dreams, daimons, hero worship, relics, heroic deeds, and sacred space. Add to these fasting, making the sign of the cross, exhalation, and you have a list of popular religious activities practiced by third-century Christians. Yet even these latter practices have parallels among non-Christian groups. Special dietary practices and fasting were observed by others,[35] and the making of the sign of the cross, though Christian, as an apotropaic gesture certainly has parallels elsewhere.[36]

What is the significance of these observations? Taken together, they suggest that the popular religious culture of third-century Christianity and that reflected in the *Heroikos* were not so far removed from one another. This is not a novel idea; the work of Robin Lane Fox, Ramsey MacMullen, and others has already demonstrated this point.[37] Removed from doctrine (that is, myth or theology) and official cult (that is, ritual), the popular religious practices and beliefs of pagans and Christians in the third century share many commonalities. The importance of this observation is that it forces historians of Christianity to reconsider whether the monumental sociopolitical events of the fourth century, following the accession of Constantine, were the precipitating factor in the "steady absorption or soaking up of pagan concepts . . . [and] customs" by Christianity.[38] Rather, as the religious world of the *Heroikos* and third-century Christianity reveals, the evidence of commonalities between pagan popular religion and Christian popular religious practices and beliefs dates much earlier. Constantine's conversion can no longer be seen as the watershed event of early

[35] See esp. *Her.* 33.14–15.

[36] I thank the editors for this observation.

[37] Robin Lane Fox, *Pagans and Christains* (New York: Knopf, 1987); Ramsey MacMullen, *Christianizing the Roman Empire* (New Haven: Yale University Press, 1984).

[38] Vivian H. H. Green, *A New History of Christianity* (New York: Continuum, 1996), 26.

Christianity that unleashed the "steady absorption of pagan . . . customs" into Christianity. These practices were present among Christian communities at least a century earlier. Even the history of religions' view of pagan influences upon Christianity needs to be reassessed. Perhaps a more useful paradigm is the one reflected in the sources themselves: that the religious world of the early third century, for both pagans and Christians, is a world where both groups express their distinctive religious beliefs in common popular practices.

Jesus as Cult Hero in the Fourth Gospel

Jennifer K. Berenson Maclean

The relevance of the *Heroikos* for the study of hero cult is obvious, and many of the essays in this volume explore its details, including how heroes and hero cult could be invoked for a variety of cultural agendas. Some essays in this volume have tried in various ways to address a less obvious issue: the relevance of the *Heroikos* for the study of early Christianity.[1] These essays represent the beginnings of research into how the *Heroikos* might illumine early Christian experience; in particular, the formation of a canon, the phenomena of prophecy and mysticism, and the development of Christian worship and Christology could all be fruitfully investigated in conversation with the *Heroikos*. In this essay I address one small part of this broad investigation: the question of the heroic status of Jesus. To put it more precisely, I wish to investigate whether any of Jesus' earliest followers understood him through the cultural lens of the Greek hero and related to him through a cult modeled on that of a hero. It should be clear at this point that I am not engaging in normative theological construction nor am I naively attempting an objective solution to the identity of Jesus. I am, however, interested in whether early Christians, in their pressing need to comprehend and speak about their experience of Jesus, drew upon this one particular and ancient mode of talking about and relating to extraordinary humans.

JESUS AS HERO: A VIEW OF THE LAST THIRTY YEARS

A consensus that the Greek heroes provided a pattern for early Christian writers and storytellers in their presentation of Jesus has

[1] See the essay by Hans Dieter Betz (focusing on gospel literature), and those by Jackson Hershbell and James Skedros (looking primarily at the religiosity associated with the veneration of martyrs and saints). See also Ellen Bradshaw Aitken, "The Cult of Achilles in Philostratus's *Heroikos*: A Study in the Relation of Canon and Ritual," in *Between Magic and Religion: Interdisciplinary Studies in Ancient Mediterranean Religion and Society* (ed. Sulochana R. Asirvatham, Corinne Ondine Pache, and John Watrous; New York: Rowman & Littlefield, 2001), 127–35.

been slowly emerging. This question was reopened nearly thirty years ago by folklorist Alan Dundes in his essay "The Hero Pattern and the Life of Jesus."[2] Dundes analyzes the heroic patterns, that is, the collection of discrete narrative elements proposed by his predecessors, especially Otto Rank and Lord Raglan, and interprets Jesus' heroic status through the lens of Freudian Oedipal desire.[3] Not surprisingly, biblical scholars were hesitant to embrace Dundes' conclusions, although their criticisms had little to do with the application of the Greek hero to the study of Jesus and more to do with the perceived artificiality of the so-called heroic pattern, its lack of specificity to ancient Greek culture, and its refusal to engage redactional-critical issues in the Gospels.[4] Some years earlier, Moses Hadas and Morton Smith investigated the aretalogies of divine men and their relevance for the depiction of Jesus, among other figures.[5] The following decades witnessed numerous writings on the divine man (θεῖος ἀνήρ),[6] but the hero as the object of cult and whose powers

[2] Alan Dundes, "The Hero Pattern and the Life of Jesus," in *Protocol of the Twenty-fifth Colloquy, The Center for Hermeneutical Studies in Hellenistic and Modern Culture, Berkeley, California, 12 December 1976* (ed. W. Wuellner; Berkeley, Calif.: The Center for Hermeneutical Studies in Hellenistic and Modern Culture, 1977), 1-32; repr. in *In Quest of the Hero* (ed. Robert A. Segal; Princeton: Princeton University Press, 1990), 179–223.

[3] Dundes, "The Hero Pattern," 188–203.

[4] See the responses to Dundes' paper by Samuel Sandmel, Morton Smith, Charles H. Talbert, and Herman C. Waetjen printed in the *Protocol* cited above at pp. 61, 62–63, 64–65, and 66–67.

[5] Moses Hadas and Morton Smith, *Heroes and Gods: Spiritual Biographies in Antiquity* (New York: Harper and Row, 1965). For a brief evaluation of their work, see Lawrence M. Wills, *The Quest for the Historical Gospel: Mark, John, and the Origins of the Gospel Genre* (London and New York: Routledge, 1997), 35. Approaching the question from a different angle, Martin Hengel (*The Atonement: The Origins of the Doctrine in the New Testament* [Philadelphia: Fortress, 1981], esp. 4–32) argues that the interpretation of Jesus' death as "for us" would have been intelligible to a Greek audience, which was well aware of the heroic idea of vicarious suffering.

[6] The bibliography on the θεῖος ἀνήρ is vast. See, e.g., Carl Holladay, *Theios Aner in Hellenistic Judaism* (SBLDS 40; Missoula, Mont.: Scholars Press, 1977); Aage Pilgaard, "The Hellenistic *Theios Aner*—A Model for Early Christian Christology?" in *The New Testament and Hellenistic Judaism* (ed. Peder Borgen and Søren Giversen; Århus: Århus Univeristy Press, 1995), 101–22; Nikolaus Walter, "Der Mose-Roman des Artapanos und die Frage nach einer Theios-Anër Vorstellung im hellenistischen Judentum sowie nach 'paganen' Einflüssen auf die neutestamentliche Christologie," in *Jüdische Schriften in ihrem antik-jüdischen und urchristlichen Kontext* (ed. Hermann Lichtenberger and Gerbern S. Oegema; Gütersloh, Germany: Gütersloher Verlagshaus, 2002), 284–303; Dieter Zeller, "The θεῖα φύσις of Hippocrates and of Other Divine Men," in *Early Christianity*

transcended the grave was lost amidst the arguments swirling around the divine man. The 1990s saw a fruitful revival of interest in heroes by biblical scholars, all of whom to varying degrees do justice to the particularly Greek conception of heroes and respect the diversity of portrayals of Jesus in early Christian literature. David E. Aune attributes previously noted similarities between Herakles and Christ "to the more general tendency of traditions about great personalities to conform to the morphology of Greco-Roman heroes through the folkloristic process of communal re-creation of tradition";[7] he does, however, argue that there are striking similarities between Herakles and the portrayal of Christ in the Epistle to the Hebrews.[8] In his 1997 article Hans Dieter Betz identifies numerous parallels between the *Heroikos* and a wide variety of early Christian literature,[9] and concludes that "the violent, premature death of Jesus brought about by an unjust legal verdict, as well as the appearances after his death, correspond to the basic pattern of a hero cult."[10] Thus Betz ultimately agrees with Samson Eitrem that narratives of the post-Easter appearances of Jesus were initially based on a heroic model.[11]

---

and Classical Culture: Comparative Studies in Honor of Abraham J. Malherbe (ed. J. T. Fitzgerald, T. H. Olbricht, and L. M. White; NovTSup 110; Leiden: Brill, 2003), 49–69.

[7] David E. Aune, "Heracles and Christ: Heracles Imagery in the Christology of Early Christianity," in *Greeks, Romans, and Christians: Essays in Honor of Abraham J. Malherbe* (ed. David L. Balch, Everett Ferguson, and Wayne A. Meeks; Minneapolis: Fortress, 1990), 19.

[8] Aune, "Heracles and Christ," 13–19. On Herakles in Hebrews, see also Harold W. Attridge, "Liberating Death's Captives: Reconsideration of an Early Christian Myth," in *Gnosticism and the Early Christian World: In Honor of James M. Robinson* (ed. James E. Goehring et al.; Sonoma, Calif.: Polebridge, 1990), 103–15. The hero Odysseus has also been suggested as the heroic model for Jesus in Hebrews. Ellen Bradshaw Aitken, "The Hero in the Epistle to the Hebrews: Jesus as an Ascetic Model," in *Early Christian Voices: In Texts, Traditions, and Symbols. Essays in Honor of François Bovon* (ed. David H. Warren, Ann Graham Brock, and David W. Pao; Leiden and Boston: Brill, 2003), 179–88.

[9] Hans Dieter Betz, "Hero Worship and Christian Beliefs: Observations from the History of Religions on Philostratus's *Heroikos*," in this volume. He notes, for example, the similar use of πίστις and ἀπιστία for defining correct and incorrect responses to the hero; the common emphasis on the πάθος of Protesilaos's and Jesus' death; the eroticization of the hero in his epiphany; the cultic meal; the presence of wounds on the hero's body; the emphasis on shared sufferings as a part of community ethos; the motif of a recognition scene; and the motif of secrecy/mystery in reference to resurrection. Betz, "Hero Worship and Christian Beliefs," 29–30, 33–35, 37–38, 44.

[10] Betz, "Hero Worship and Christian Beliefs," 45.

[11] Betz, "Hero Worship and Christian Beliefs," 45.

Much broader claims for the influence of a hero pattern have emerged as well. Drawing on a wide variety of Christian sources, Gregory J. Riley argues that the earliest stories of Jesus were based on the culturally powerful pattern of the Greek hero, which for Riley can be summed up as follows: the hero experienced antagonistic relationships with both a god and with human rulers; in these conflicts the character of the hero was tested, and the character of those who encountered him was simultaneously put to the test; the hero usually suffered an agonizing death at a young age, but gained the prize of immortality and the role of protector of and example to the living.[12]

Two other scholars have recently argued much more specific theses concerning the role of heroic traditions—specifically of the poet-hero—in the formation of Christian literature. Building upon an earlier article in which she suggests that the ending of the Gospel of Mark (Mark 16:1–8) was modeled upon ancient translation stories,[13] Adela Yarbro Collins notes that the biographical traditions of Aesop, Hesiod, Archilochus, and Homer portray the poet-hero simultaneously as both outcast and benefactor.[14] This narrative pattern, she contends, "served to structure the narrative as a whole and thus to provide the dominant framework of meaning" for the Gospel of Mark.[15] The *Life of Aesop* was independently taken up by Lawrence M. Wills in his investigation of the origin of the gospel genre.[16] Wills describes the life of the poet-hero similarly to Collins: the poet reproaches his city, the city responds antagonistically and violently, its violence renders it impure, and its impurity is expiated through cult that immortalizes the poet-hero; simultaneous with this course of events, the poet also experiences an antagonistic relationship with the deity, which is likewise remedied through cult.[17] This same novelistic pattern, Wills argues, can be

[12] Gregory J. Riley, *One Jesus, Many Christs: How Jesus Inspired Not One True Christiantiy, But Many* (San Francisco: HarperSanFrancisco, 1997), chs. 3–4. While many of these heroic characteristics are well chosen and illuminating, others are more debatably standard heroic features and still others are not given adequate emphasis. See my review of Riley's book in *JBL* 119 (2000): 131–33.

[13] Adela Yarbro Collins, "The Empty Tomb and Resurrection according to Mark," in *The Beginning of the Gospel: Probings of Mark in Context* (Minneapolis: Fortress, 1992), 147.

[14] Adela Yarbro Collins, "Finding Meaning in the Death of Jesus," *JR* 78 (1998): 191.

[15] Collins, "Finding Meaning," 196.

[16] Wills, *The Quest*.

[17] Wills, *The Quest*, esp. 23–28. Both Wills and Collins are indebted to Gregory Nagy's (*The Best of the Achaeans: Concepts of the Hero in Archaic Greek*

fruitfully compared with the basic structure of both Mark and John.[18] More so than any of his predecessors, Wills is attentive to the fact that heroes are not heroes without cult, although he concludes that like the *Iliad*, the *Odyssey*, and the *Life of Aesop*, which are largely silent on matters of cult, the Gospels rarely comment on cult, although they served as its "charter myth."[19]

FOCUSING ON THE CULT IN HERO CULT

Scholarship since Dundes has sought greater and greater precision in defining a hero pattern within the cultural world of the Greeks and in focusing investigation on the heroic themes in individual Christian texts or trajectories. Attention to a narrative pattern is, of course, important, but the narrative motifs ascribed to heroes' lives transcend the particular designation of "hero."[20] The institution of *cult* is the decisive indication of heroic status. Exclusive attention to narrative patterns has thus resulted in the exclusion of an essential aspect of Greek heroes, namely the *mechanics* of cult (prayer, sacrifice, libation, oracular inquiry, etc.) and the *worshiper's relationship with the hero* through cult. No examination of the heroes' relevance to early Christianity can be complete without attention to the question of cult. I propose to use the *Heroikos* as an entrée into investigating whether a particular early Christian text—the Gospel of John—bears evidence of hero-cult worship of Jesus.

This goal may appear problematic from the start since while elements of early Christian traditions and even whole units of literature (e.g., Mark and John) have been linked to a heroic pattern, Christian cult (i.e., the worship of Jesus) is generally held to be distinct from hero cult. The crucial issue has been understood as whether cultic worship took place at the tomb of Jesus during the first century,[21] a practice that would be a clear marker of early

Poetry [Baltimore: Johns Hopkins University Press, 1979], esp. 301–8) work on the poet-hero.

[18] Wills, *The Quest*, 23–50.

[19] Wills, *The Quest*, 45, 50, 179. But see Wills's comments on the "cult of remembrance" (pp. 46–48).

[20] Christopher Jones, "Apollonius of Tyana, Hero and Holy Man," in this volume.

[21] For those who have supported this view, see the references in Pheme Perkins, *Resurrection: New Testament Witness and Contemporary Reflection* (Garden City, N.Y.: Doubleday, 1984), 109–10 n. 73, 143 n. 36. During Constantine's rule, Jesus' tomb was "discovered" and the Church of the Holy Sepulchre was erected

Christian understanding of Jesus as a hero. Pheme Perkins points to a lack of evidence for such a cult and to the lack of homogeneity in the tomb traditions.[22] Betz, whose work was discussed above, asserts that the early heroic Christology was later purposefully rejected through the narratives of ascension and empty tomb, which he deems incompatible with hero cult.[23] Erwin Rohde seems to support this contention when he states "belief in Heroes required a *grave* at which the continued existence and potency of the 'Hero' was localized,"[24] but according to Rohde a cenotaph could also bind the hero to that locality so that "his psyche, his invisible counterpart and double, hovers in the neighbourhood of the body and grave."[25] Wills rightly recognizes that a body is not essential for hero cult to be performed and be effective. The missing body, he eloquently puts, "indicates not a lack of tangible evidence of divinization, but an indeterminacy of status for the hero that is meant to be provocative and suggestive."[26] The *translation* of Jesus' body does not preclude heroic status either: Gregory Nagy demonstrates that the immortalization of the hero in cult is fully compatible (from the perspective of the ancients) with the immortalization of the hero via transportation to Elysium or other idyllic locations, such as Leukê.[27] These observations reopen the theoretical possibility that early followers of Jesus might have seen hero cult as a viable option for expressing their reverence for him and their conviction that he

---

on the site. Eusebius tells us that the site had been "consigned to the darkness of oblivion" prior to the imperial-sponsored excavations (*Life of Constantine* 3.25). Socrates Scholasticus's contention that the earliest Christians venerated the tomb of Jesus does not appear to be based on any historical source (*Ecclesiastical History* 1.17).

[22] Perkins, *Resurrection*, 93–94.

[23] Betz, "Hero Worship and Christian Beliefs," 46–47. See also Helmut Koester, "On Heroes, Tombs, and Early Christianity: An Epilogue," in *Flavius Philostratus: Heroikos* (trans. Jennifer K. Berenson Maclean and Ellen Bradshaw Aitken; SBLWGRW 1; Atlanta: Society of Biblical Literature, 2001), 257–64, esp. 259–60. On the incompatibility of hero cult and an empty tomb, see also Peter G. Bolt, "Mark 16:1–8: The Empty Tomb of a Hero?" *Tyndale Bulletin* 47 (1996): 27–37.

[24] Erwin Rohde, *Psyche: The Cult of Souls and Belief in Immortality among the Greeks* (London: Routledge & Kegan Paul, 1925), 98.

[25] Rohde, *Psyche*, 122; see also p. 134. For a critique of Rohde on the local power of the hero, see Nagy, *Best of the Achaeans*, 116–17.

[26] Wills, *The Quest*, 49. For a review of Jewish reverence for the dead, including those heroized, i.e., whose graves remain effective after death, see Wills, *The Quest*, 37–43.

[27] Nagy, *Best of the Achaeans*, 189–210. (See also p. 175, which deals with their compatibility in the *Aithiopis*, in contrast to the *Iliad* and *Odyssey*.)

had achieved a superhuman status. While I will make no attempt to argue definitively for tomb-side cult in the case of Jesus, we must acknowledge that such a cult would not have been de facto incompatible with Jesus' resurrection or ascension.[28] In addition, hero cult encompassed more than just sacrifices at a particular locale; the appearance of the hero, his oracular functions, his intimacy with worshipers, and his inculcation of a defining ethos all must be included under the rubric of hero cult. Thus when looking for a hero-cult pattern in early Christianity, we must attend to more than just the tomb (i.e., locale) and its contents.

A second potential obstacle to the search for traces of hero cult in the Fourth Gospel stems from the fact that this gospel is notoriously difficult in respect to cultic practice. Baptism and eucharist are the two widely recognized foundational cultic acts of early Christian communities, but the Fourth Gospel narrates neither Jesus' baptism nor the institution of a meal in his honor. Debate has swirled around the significance of the sacramental "hints" in John (e.g., John 3:5; 6:48–58; 13:8–10; 19:34; 21:13), but these most likely are a redactor's additions and many scholars hold John to be anti-sacramental.[29] However, if we understand cult[30] as the actions of a community by which it incorporates new members or reconstitutes its identity, then we must acknowledge that the Johannine Christians did value cultic actions, different though they may have been from those practiced by the communities of Mark, Matthew, Luke, or Paul. Right worship is of great importance to the Johannine Jesus, as a brief look at John 4 demonstrates. Jesus' conversation with the Samaritan woman culminates in a discussion of right versus wrong worship (John 4:20–24). The key terms used throughout this passage are προσκυνέω and its cognate noun προσκυνητής,

[28] Collins ("The Empty Tomb," 141) correctly suggests that "even if there were no cultic observances at the site of the tomb, it would still be important as a *literary* motif in characterizing Jesus as herolike."

[29] See the helpful summary of this issue in Robert Kysar, "John, Gospel of," *ABD* 3.929–30.

[30] I prefer the terms "cult" and "ritual" to the more theologically loaded "sacrament," as the former facilitate comparison with other Greco-Roman religious practices. Margaret Y. Macdonald, "Ritual in the Pauline Churches," in *Social-Scientific Approaches to New Testament Interpretation* (ed. David G. Horrell; Edinburgh: T&T Clark, 1999), 236. Wayne A. Meeks, *The First Urban Christians: The Social World of the Apostle Paul* (New Haven: Yale University Press, 1983), 140–63. Bruce J. Malina, *Christian Origins and Cultural Anthropology: Practical Models for Biblical Interpretation* (Atlanta: John Knox, 1986), 140–43.

which when used in reference to God refer to cultic action and not simply an internal attitude of reverence.[31] That cultic action is also *central* to John's ecclesiology is clear as well: the mission of Jesus will create these true worshipers, and the Father himself is seeking those who will continually worship him in this way.[32] The Johannine community no doubt organized its communal gatherings to reflect this "true worship"; discovering its various aspects may only require a new hermeneutical lens.

I will argue that the cultic practices of the Johannine community—as revealed by the Farewell Discourse in John 13:31–17:26—display important similarities to the type of hero cult presented in the *Heroikos*. If I am correct, early christological reflection may be more indebted to hero cult than previously recognized; rather than only a literary model used to shape the gospel story, hero cult may also have been for some early Christians the paradigm according to which they organized their worship and community life.

THE CULT OF THE HERO

In addition to solemn and sometimes elaborate offerings, hero cult also offered the worshiper an intimate experience of the hero and access to his wisdom and beneficent powers.[33] In the *Heroikos* the vinedresser is the active worshiper of the hero, while the Phoenician undergoes a process of transformation into a devotee.[34] The vinedresser lives and works among the tomb of the hero and its gardens, cultivating the plants and presenting offerings and libations to the hero (*Her.* 2.1–5.6; 9.1–13.4). This way of life grants him a special relationship with the hero, an intimate association (*ξυνουσία*; *Her.* 4.11; 7.1) that is expressed in the language of *eros* (*Her.* 11.2–3; cf. 21.4–6).[35] This *ξυνουσία* encompasses the appearances of the hero

[31] BDAG, s.v. προσκυνέω (b); Heinrich Greeven, "προσκυνέω, προσκυνητής," *TDNT* 6.758–66; also John 12:20; Acts 8:27; 24:11; Rev 4:10; 5:14; 7:11; 11:16; 19:4. See also Karen H. Jobes, "Distinguishing the Meaning of Greek Verbs in the Semantic Domain for Worship," *Filologia Neotestamentaria* 4 (1991): 186–87.

[32] John 4:23. Note the invocation of "the hour" and the use of the present participle. Cf. John 9:38. All biblical translations are from the NRSV.

[33] This brief description of hero cult is not meant to be exhaustive. Readers may consult the other essays in the first section of this volume for more detailed analysis of hero cult.

[34] On this transformation, see my article "The *αἶνοι* of the *Heroikos* and the Unfolding Transformation of the Phoenician Merchant" in this volume.

[35] On this emotion bond, see Corinne Ondine Pache, "Singing Heroes—The Poetics of Hero Cult in the *Heroikos*," 7–9 in this volume; Casey Dué and Gregory

(*Her.* 2.7–11; 4.2–5.6; 10.1–13.4) and the communication of "divine and pure wisdom" (*Her.* 4.10–11; 6.1; on Palamedes' wisdom, see *Her.* 21.9; 23.23; 33.1, 11, 14, 19; 34.7). In the *Heroikos,* Protesilaos is the quintessential interpreter of Homer and all the epic tradition (*Her.* 7.4; 11.4; 25.1 and passim);[36] his insights allow human beings to understand the truth about what it means to be Greek and the ethical standards appropriate to that reformulated identity.[37] Protesilaos's insights are passed on to the vinedresser through their ξυνουσία, and the vinedresser is the medium for Protesilaos's oracular advice: he begins his two extended monologues (*Her.* 23.3–30; 25.18–42.4) with ritual offerings (*Her.* 23.3) and invocations of the hero's inspiration (*Her.* 25.18), and proceeds to report all that Protesilaos "says" (note the consistent use of the present tense; *Her.* 23.12, 18, 20, 24, 28 and passim), even immediately relaying Protesilaos's response to the Phoenician's request for stories of Hades (*Her.* 58.3) Thus during ritual, Protesilaos inspires the vinedresser, and their identities become melded: he is the oracular presence of the hero.[38]

The role of the gods in the *Heroikos* is admittedly minor, although one passage gives a brief framework for their relationship to the heroes. The heroes, as "attendants" (ὀπαδοί) of the gods, have "visible association" (ξυνουσίας φανεράς) with them; this exalted position grants the heroes their superhuman insight concerning the world of humans, which can be communicated through oracles (*Her.* 7.3). The relationship that the hero has with the gods (ξυνουσία leading to insight) is identical to that between humans and the hero himself. Inquiring of the hero is the key to revealing these insights (*Her.* 6.1; 7.3; 14.1–16.6; cf. 33.15), although he must be approached with devotion and the proper ethical commitments or his response will be silence (*Her.* 4.7) or worse (*Her.* 16.3–4).

Nagy, "Illuminating the Classics with the Heroes of Philostratus," 61–63 in this volume.

[36] See Francesca Mestre, "Refuting Homer in the *Heroikos* of Philostratus," in this volume. See also Jennifer K. Berenson Maclean and Ellen Bradshaw Aitken, *Flavius Philostratus: Heroikos* (SBLWGRW 1; Atlanta: Society of Biblical Literature, 2001), lx–lxxvi.

[37] Maclean and Aitken, *Flavius Philostratus: Heroikos,* lxxvi–lxxxvii.

[38] On the superhuman consciousness of the hero and his possession of the poet in cult, see Dué and Nagy, "Illuminating the Classics," 57–60; and Gregory Nagy, *Poetry as Performance: Homer and Beyond* (Cambridge: Cambridge University Press, 1996). On oracular consultation of heroes, see Dué and Nagy, "Illuminating the Classics," 63–64 and Rohde, *Psyche,* 132–33.

The *Heroikos* thus portrays hero cult as stemming from the appearance of the hero through the ritual acts of consultation; this epiphany allows for the communication of wisdom, the establishment of a deep union with the worshiper, and the inculcation of a particular ethical perspective. In brief, hero cult makes one wise (σοφός), intimate with the hero (φίλος), and ethically noble (ἀγαθός).[39] My aim in this essay is to investigate whether this pattern of worship is evident in the Gospel of John. The *Heroikos* was obviously composed long after the Gospel of John, but this pattern, while not emphasized in epic, has a long history in cult practice.[40]

THE HERO'S EPIPHANY, RITUAL CONSULTATION, AND WISDOM

The Johannine paradigm of "true worship" is not tied to a place, but is intimately connected with accurate knowledge gained through insight granted by the spirit ("we worship what we know . . . true worshipers will worship the Father in spirit and truth"; John 4:22–23). The revelation of truth by Jesus is a Johannine theme established from the very first chapter (1:14, 17; see also, e.g., 8:32, 40–46; 18:37–38), and this theme is once again closely associated with the Spirit in the final discourse in John. It is in these chapters, also known as the Farewell Discourse (John 13:31–17:26),[41] that we discover the first element of hero cult,

[39] I borrow this triad from Gregory Nagy (*Pindar's Homer: The Lyric Possession of an Epic Past* [Baltimore and London: Johns Hopkins University Press, 1990], 146–98, 314–38), who utilizes it to understand the use of marked (ambiguous) speech to create and maintain community. Aitken ("The Cult of Achilles") offers a similar analysis of the cult of Achilles in the *Heroikos*.

[40] Dué and Nagy, "Illuminating the Classics," 65–73; Pache, "Singing Heroes," 11–23.

[41] On the inclusion of 13:31–38 in the Farewell Discourse, see Fernando F. Segovia, "The Structure, *Tendenz*, and *Sitz im Leben* of John 13:31–14:31," *JBL* 104 (1985): 476. The coherence of the Farewell Discourse is problematic at best, since it returns again and again to a few basic points, each elaborated with a slightly different emphasis. I will not address the questions of the composition or the overall coherence of the Farewell Discourse, although the "contradictions" within the discourse in my judgment stem from (*a*) the continual process of reinterpreting Jesus' sayings and (*b*) the discourse's reflection of both the narrative setting of Jesus' final evening and the "now" of the gospel's author. My reading of the Farewell Discourse here is synchronic, without denying the validity of diachronic analysis. On theories of composition and coherence, see Rudolf Bultmann, *The Gospel of John: A Commentary* (Philadelphia: Westminster Press, 1971), 680; trans. of *Das Evangelium des Johannes* (Göttingen: Vandenhoeck & Ruprecht, 1964), 457–61; Raymond E. Brown, *The Gospel according to John* (2 vols.; AB 29–29A; Garden

namely, the hero's epiphany and the attainment of wisdom through his ritual consultation.

This key passage, set in the night of Jesus' betrayal and composed in the form of a farewell speech,[42] offers the reader clues to the post-Easter cult practices of the Johannine community.[43] The discourse is replete with future-tense verbs, imperatives, and purpose clauses: the focus is clearly on the future experience of the community, that is, the present of the author and his community. One of the most significant themes in this extended discourse is that of memory and remembrance. Jesus commands the disciples, "*Remember* the word that I said to you" (μνημονεύετε τοῦ λόγου οὗ ἐγὼ εἶπον ὑμῖν, John 15:20), and indicates that the reason he has mentioned certain things now is so that later they "may *remember* that I told you about them" (ἵνα . . . μνημονεύητε αὐτῶν ὅτι ἐγὼ εἶπον ὑμῖν, John 16:4). Jesus' words were not only forward-looking, but prior to his death; they were also perplexing, parables or riddles,[44] whose meaning would only become clear later: "I have said these things to you in figures of speech (ἐν παροιμίαις). The hour is coming when I will no longer speak to you in figures, but will tell you plainly of the Father" (John 16:25). The Johannine disciples are expected to recall Jesus' words, and aided by the Holy Spirit, who engages in a complementary act of calling to mind Jesus' words and interpreting them (ὑμᾶς διδάξει πάντα καὶ ὑπομνήσει ὑμᾶς πάντα ἃ εἶπον ὑμῖν [ἐγώ], "[the Spirit] will teach you everything, and *remind* you of all that I

City, N.Y.: Doubleday, 1966–1970), 2:583–97; Wayne Brouwer, *The Literary Development of John 13–17: A Chiastic Reading* (SBLDS; Atlanta: Society of Biblical Literature, 2000), esp. 11–20; Fernando F. Segovia, *The Farewell of the Word: The Johannine Call to Abide* (Minneapolis: Fortress, 1991), 24–47, 299–308.

[42] Brown, *John*, 2:598–601. Segovia, *The Farewell of the Word*, 5–20.

[43] This assertion differs from that of Edwyn C. Hoskyns (*The Fourth Gospel* [2d ed.; London: Faber and Faber, 1947], 495), who suggests that the *structure* of the Farewell Discourse corresponds to the *structure* of Johannine worship.

[44] Riddles demand special knowledge and thus draw community boundaries. Tom Thatcher, "The Riddles of Jesus in the Johannine Dialogues," in *Jesus in Johannine Tradition* (ed. Robert T. Fortna and Tom Thatcher; Louisville: Westminster John Knox, 2001), 263–77; see also Tom Thatcher, *The Riddles of Jesus in John: A Study in Tradition and Folklore* (SBLMS 53; Atlanta: Society of Biblical Literature, 2000). Nagy's understanding of αἶνος as a mode of speech that similarly requires the interpreter to be φίλος, σοφός, and ἀγαθός is also applicable here (see above). The disciples' declaration that Jesus is no longer speaking in "figures" (John 16:29) must be understood as the post-Easter affirmation that Jesus' words have become clear, since Jesus in John 16:31–32 questions their belief.

have said to you"; John 14:26), the disciples will learn their true meaning. The Spirit

> becomes the agent of memory, the spur generating the community's meaningful recollection of Jesus. The presence of [the Spirit] justifies new and different understandings of Jesus as the community puts together the words and deeds of Jesus in juxtaposition with the sacred writings.[45]

The Spirit is the key to knowledge of the truth (see, e.g., John 14:17; 15:26; 16:7, 13; 17:17–19), which can only be ascertained through the proper interpretation of the words of Jesus. Such knowledge is not possible in the pre-Easter world (John 2:17, 22; 12:16; 13:7), but will become the possession of the disciples through their Spirit-guided recollection of Jesus' words.

Remembrance, however, is neither a fleeting noetic exercise nor an individual activity. In the biblical tradition, to *remember* means "to recall something or to think about it in such a way that it is expressed in speech or is formative for attitude and action."[46] Remembrance is also a communal practice that redefines the community's understanding of itself: it is a cultic activity. This is seen in the use of the Hebrew *zakār* ("to remember") to refer to cultic commemoration of God's great deeds, and the designation of the eucharist in some communities as an act of remembrance (ἀνάμνησις; 1 Cor 11:24–25; Luke 22:19).[47] Another aspect of communal remembrance was the citation, memorization, and interpretation of the sacred traditions, a diction that is common in rabbinic sources in reference to the scriptures.[48] In the New Testament one likewise *remembers* (i.e., cites and interprets) scripture (John 2:17, 22; 12:16; 2 Pet 3:2) and, as we have seen in the Johannine Farewell Discourse, the sayings of Jesus (see also Matt. 26:75; 27:63 [ironically]; Mark 11:21; 14:72; Luke 22:61; 24:6–8; John 2:22; Acts 11:16; 20:35; 2 Pet 3:2). Thus if the Fourth Gospel contains any counterpart to the Lord's Supper, initiated according to Paul and Luke in Jesus' own

[45] Arthur J. Dewey, "The Eyewitness of History: Visionary Consciousness in the Fourth Gospel," in *Jesus in Johannine Tradition* (ed. Robert T. Fortna and Tom Thatcher; Louisville: Westminster John Knox, 2001), 67.

[46] Nils Alstrup Dahl, "Anamnesis: Memory and Commemoration in Early Christianity," in *Jesus in the Memory of the Early Church* (Minneapolis: Augsburg, 1976), 13.

[47] Dahl, "Anamnesis," 14, 21–23.

[48] See the sources cited in Dahl, "Anamnesis," 15 n. 22.

command[49] to "do this in remembrance of me" (τοῦτο ποιεῖτε εἰς τὴν ἐμὴν ἀνάμνησιν; Luke 22:19; 1 Cor 11:24–25), it must be this expectation that the disciples will *remember* his words. This community gathers not around a table to commemorate Jesus' death, but their foundational cultic act is to engage in the communal recollection of Jesus' words, encompassing no doubt their recital, memorization, interpretation, and application.

If the disciples' remembrance of Jesus' words is a cultic practice, we must inquire what specific cultic acts were involved. Let us begin with the oft-repeated assertion of Jesus in the Farewell Discourse that after going away (i.e., dying) he will come to his disciples (ἔρχομαι, John 14:3, 18, 23, 28; 16:16), he will manifest himself (ἐμφανίζω, 14:21–22), and the disciples will "see" him (θεωρέω, 14:19; ὁράω, 16:16–19).[50] The Johannine disciples believed that after his death they experienced Jesus through the Holy Spirit,[51] entitled in this gospel "Paraclete" (John 14:16, 26; 15:26; 16:7), whose coming is described in similar language (John 15:26; 16:7–8, 13). Most interpreters of this enigmatic title[52] have translated it as "advocate," "counselor," "comforter," or "intercessor." The last two are simply not appropriate for the Johannine usages,[53] and since Kenneth Grayston has convincingly refuted a specifically forensic meaning of the term in non-Christian literature,[54] a reinvestigation seems in order.

As a verbal adjective ending in -τος and accented on the antepenult, παράκλητος should have the meaning of the perfect-passive participle of παρακαλέω,[55] a verb whose range of meanings includes "to send for," "to summon," "to invite," and "to appeal to."[56] In his

[49] Ellen Bradshaw Aitken, "τὰ δρώμενα καὶ τὰ λεγόμενα: The Eucharistic Memory of Jesus' Words in First Corinthians," *HTR* 90 (1997): 366–70.

[50] "The whole dialogue, indeed, is dominated by the ideas of going and coming." C. H. Dodd, *The Interpretation of the Fourth Gospel* (Cambridge: Cambridge University Press, 1968), 403.

[51] Bultmann, *John*, 567. Brown, *John*, 2:710.

[52] See the helpful summary of interpretative issues by John Ashton in "Paraclete," *ABD* 5:152–54.

[53] Bultmann, *John*, 569–70. Brown, *John*, 2:1136–37.

[54] Kenneth Grayston, "The Meaning of PARAKLĒTOS," *JSNT* 13 (1981): 67–82. Both Dodd (*Interpretation*, 414–15) and Brown (*John*, 2:1137) had previously noted the difficulty of sustaining a forensic meaning in all the Johannine uses of παράκλητος. "[N]o one translation . . . captures the complexity of the functions . . . this figure has." Brown, *John*, 2:1137.

[55] Smyth 425c n. See also Ashton, *ABD* 5:152. Johannes Behm, "παράκλητος," *TDNT* 5:800.

[56] LSJ, s.v. παρακαλέω II.

thorough study of the uses of παράκλητος, Grayston variously translates it as "supporter," "sponsor," or "patron." The key idea in each case is that the παράκλητος has been summoned by another for some specific purpose: one may be called in to act as a witness in court on another's behalf (Demosthenes *False Embassy* [*Or.* 19] 1; Dionysius of Halicarnassus *Roman Antiquities* 11.37.1), to aid a friend in need (Philo *Against Flaccus* 22, 151, 181; *P. Lit. Lond.* 97; Diogenes Laertius *Lives of the Eminent Philosophers* 4.50; Eusebius *Ecclesiastical History* 5.1.10), to pay a deposit for another (BGU II.601.12), or even to instigate gang chaos (Dio Cassius *Roman History* 46.20.1; *Didache* 5.2; *Barnabas* 20.2). In religious contexts a deity or suprahuman power is the object of the summons for help.[57] For example, according to a Stoic allegory, Hermes accompanied Priam as his παράκλητος to help convince Achilles to release the body of Hektor (Heraclitus *Allegoriae* 59). According to Philo, Jews may invoke three παράκλητοι, the first two of which are the "merciful, and gentle, and compassionate nature" of God and the founders of Jewish nation, whose souls are now able to pray effectively on behalf of others (Philo *On Rewards and Punishments* 166–167 Yonge). God himself, however, has no παράκλητος; that is, there is no one he can or need invoke (Philo *On the Creation of the World* 23).[58] Christians, however, can expect no divine aid (i.e., no παράκλητος) without obedience (*2 Clem.* 6.9). Given the Johannine understanding of the παράκλητος as the reappearance of the otherworldly Jesus, the term might then best be translated as "the one summoned" or "the one invoked."

In our search for the cultic life of the Johannine community, this title—"the one summoned" or "the one invoked"—has important implications. If *remembering* is a cultic act of the community in which the Paraclete plays an essential role, then this title may well refer to a cultic invocation. In their quest to realize the presence of Jesus and understand his cryptic words, Johannine Christians evidently invoked his presence[59] and gave this name to the Spirit they

[57] This meaning is also attested in the active use of παρακαλέω. BDAG, s.v. παρακαλέω (c). LSJ, s.v. παρακαλέω II.1. In Christian literature, see, e.g., Matt 26:53; 2 Cor 12:8.

[58] All these references are cited and discussed in Grayston, "The Meaning of PARAKLĒTOS," 72–78. Other references not included in Grayston's study include the Letter of Besas (*P. Harr.* 1.107.6, τῷ παρακλήτῳ πνεύματι) and *P. Oxy.* 34.2725.10.

[59] One thinks of the invocation "Come, Lord Jesus!" (ἔρχου κύριε Ἰησοῦ, Rev 22:20; μαράνα θά, 1 Cor 16:22; *Didache* 10:6). While the usage in Revelation and

believed came among them. A further linguistic clue confirms that the Paraclete was understood as the invoked presence of Jesus the hero: Five times the Paraclete is referred to as ἐκεῖνος (14:26; 15:26; 16:8; 16:13–14), which conforms to the standard diction of referring to the hero in his epiphany.[60] The Paraclete is the presence of the hero. The distinction between this proposed meaning of παράκλητος and the general "one who is called to help" is thus one of emphasis, albeit a key emphasis in our investigation. The Paraclete in John certainly refers to one who helps, but the title emphasizes its presence through invocation or summoning and not its "helping" function. Although the Christian interpretive tradition may have understood this title in other ways,[61] I suggest that it originated in the cultic life of the community as it *remembered* the words of Jesus and designated the Spirit the community experienced after their ritual invocation/summoning of Jesus, who had promised his presence among them.[62]

An additional clue to the community's cultic practices is found in the repeated promise that after his departure, Jesus or the Father will do whatever believers ask in Jesus' name (καὶ ὅ τι ἂν αἰτήσητε ἐν τῷ ὀνόματί μου τοῦτο ποιήσω, John 14:13; see also 14:14; 15:7, 16; 16:23, 24, 26). The Q version of this saying (11:9–10), linked to the Lord's Prayer and the difficulties of itinerant existence, refers no

1 Corinthians must be understood in a future eschatological sense, the invocation in the *Didache* belongs to the ritual of the eucharist (cf. 1 Cor 11:26?). Kurt Niederwimmer, *The Didache* (Hermeneia; Minneapolis: Fortress, 1998), 161–64. Joseph A. Fitzmyer, "New Testament *Kyrios* and *Maranatha* and Their Aramaic Background," in *To Advance the Gospel* (New York: Crossroad, 1981), 223–29.

[60] Dué and Nagy, "Illuminating the Classics," 62 n. 29.

[61] On this see Behm, *TDNT* 5:805–6.

[62] Most commentators assume that the *Sitz im Leben* of this title was the community's conflict with the synagogue and the Spirit's role in witnessing or convincing/convicting the world (John 15:26; 16:7); I suggest that this forensic application of the title is a secondary outgrowth of the initial context of communal remembrance. The meaning of παράκλητος proposed here may solve the persistent problem of the first παράκλητος implied by ἄλλον παράκλητον in John 14:16. The Messiah's "coming" (mentioned in John 4:25; 7:27, 31; see also 7:40–42; 10:24; 12:34) may have been invoked by something akin to the fourteenth and fifteenth benedictions (Babylonian recension) or the various Talmudic variations (R. Ulla: "Let him [the Messiah] come, but let me not see him"; R. Rabbah: "Let him come, but let me not see him"; R. Joseph: " Let him come and may I be worthy of sitting in the shadow of his ass's saddle"; *b. Sanh.* 98*b* Epstein). Perhaps in John, Jesus as Messiah is the first παράκλητος sent in response to cultic invocation; Jesus as the Spirit of Truth is the second.

doubt to the provision of daily needs.[63] The Johannine version, located in a different context, demands a distinct interpretation.[64] Brown asserts that the "ordinary needs of life" are not in view, but rather "whatever will deepen eternal life and make fruitful the work of the Paraclete."[65] I suggest that the type of inquiry to be made by the disciples can be sharpened even further.

The key lies both in the continuity of these future requests with the questions posed by the disciples in the Farewell Discourse and in their fundamental difference. The questions addressed to Jesus in these chapters all pertain to the meaning of his cryptic sayings:[66]

> Simon Peter said to him, "Lord, where are you going?" (John 13:36a, referring back to Jesus' assertion in 13:33);
>
> Thomas said to him, "Lord, we do not know where you are going. How can we know the way?" (John 14:5, referring back to 14:4);
>
> Judas (not Iscariot) said to him, "Lord, how is it that you will reveal yourself to us, and not to the world?" (John 14:22, referring to 14:21).

The connection between the post-Easter practice of "asking for something in Jesus' name" and the interpretation of his words is made clear in 16:17–26, where we are privy to a bit of Johannine *remembrance* as the disciples ponder the precise meaning of μικρόν in Jesus' statement "A little while (μικρόν), and you will no longer see me, and again a little while (μικρόν), and you will see me" (John 16:17–18). Knowing that they wish to inquire about the meaning of μικρόν, Jesus raises the question himself and responds (16:19–22). Immediately following this interpretive interchange the disciples are told that although they will no longer be able to pose questions to Jesus directly after he has departed, they will be able to ask the Father for anything (16:23–24). The next two verses repeat this pat-

[63] Dale C. Allison, Jr., *The Jesus Tradition in Q* (Harrisburg, Pa.: Trinity Press International, 1997), 11–15. The saying in Matt 7:7–8 and Luke 11:9–10 retains this material/economic context.

[64] Dodd, *Interpretation*, 392. Bultmann (*John*, 584; see also pp. 540 and 546) does not narrow down the scope of this prayer, but simply states that it represents "faith's highest possibility."

[65] Brown, *John*, 2:734; see also p. 636.

[66] Not only is the Farewell Discourse structured around the disciples' questions about Jesus' teachings, but the entirety of this gospel is filled with similar such questions (e.g., John 3:4–9; 4:10–15; 6:27–29, 52–59; 7:19–24, 32–36; 8:21–24, 31–59; 12:30–36; 13:21–26).

tern: Jesus returns to the disciples' present inability to understand his words (v. 25) and then reiterates their future ability to "ask in my name" (v. 26). The double juxtaposition of the problem of interpreting Jesus' words and the efficacy of "asking in Jesus' name" indicates the proper context in which to understand the inquiry itself: The disciples can expect the Father to respond when they inquire about the meaning of Jesus' words. This connection is also clear in John 14:13–17. The initial "asking in Jesus' name" saying (14:13–14) is immediately followed by the first reference to the παράκλητος (14:6). Thus once again, efficacious prayer is linked to the presence of the Spirit, who reveals the truth (14:17). There is, of course, also a fundamental difference between the questioning of Jesus during the Farewell Discourse and the questioning of the post-Easter community. Jesus' words in the Farewell Discourse are cryptic and difficult to decipher (ἐν παροιμίαις, 16:25a). In contrast, his post-Easter responses will be characterized by openness and clarity (παρρησίᾳ, 16:25b). It seems clear then that the promise of fulfilled prayer in John must be understood as a kind of oracular inquiry: through ritual invocation of the presence of Jesus,[67] the disciples inquire into the meaning of his words and receive a clear interpretation from the hero himself.

Like the hero Protesilaos, the Johannine Jesus responds to rituals of invocation, appears to his followers (as Paraclete), and makes them wise (σοφός) through consultation concerning the sacred traditions. A clear difference between the two cults lies in the object of consultation: Protesilaos's wisdom is based on his ability to properly interpret and critique Homer and the poetic tradition, while the Spirit's wisdom consists in the proper interpretation of Jesus' own words. These two types of wisdom, though, are similar in that both are only possible after the death of the hero.[68]

THE ξυνουσία OF THE HERO

We have already seen that the Paraclete is the presence of Jesus among the disciples in cult and that the Paraclete, by bringing to

[67] Bultmann interprets the key phrase "in my name" (ἐν τῷ ὀνόματί μου) as "by invocation of Jesus" (*John*, 585).

[68] Protesilaos's insight is only gained after becoming "free of the body and its diseases" (*Her.* 7.3). The Paraclete's insight is not based on a dualistic anthropology, but rather on its mediation of the Father's and Jesus' wisdom (see, e.g., John 16:13–14). On the necessity of Jesus' death for the Spirit's presence, see, e.g., John 16:7.

mind Jesus' words and their correct interpretation, makes the disciples wise (σοφοί). The second aspect of hero cult in the *Heroikos* is the intimacy of the hero with his devotee (they are φίλοι). As the vinedresser enjoys an intimate relationship (ξυνουσία)[69] with the hero Protesilaos, so also do the disciples with Jesus. This immediate experience of Jesus is expressed in the Farewell Discourse as their mutual indwelling, abiding, and love.[70]

This intimacy is first hinted at in John 14:20, where Jesus declares that his reappearance will bring the disciples into a new relationship with the Father and with himself. The inclusion of the Father will be discussed below; for now what concerns us is the new relationship between Jesus and his disciples: "you in me, and I in you" (ὑμεῖς ἐν ἐμοι κἀγὼ ἐν ὑμῖν, 14:20). Whatever this saying actually might mean,[71] one can hardly dispute that it is a statement of the most intimate of associations, with a surprising emphasis on its mutuality. In John 15 vegetal imagery is employed to describe this relationship: Jesus is the true vine; the disciples are the branches (15:1, 4).[72] Such imagery is particularly appropriate in a heroic context, since heroes are connected with the seasonality of nature, and their bodies—when properly honored in cult—bring fertility to the surrounding land (see, e.g., *Her.* 4.10; cf. 18.2–4; note that both Protesilaos and Palamedes are depicted as gardeners; *Her.* 11.3–6; 21:8). As "the true vine" Jesus is the source of true life—life that comes from the Father.[73] But this passage goes beyond naming Jesus as a life-giving figure: it also emphasizes his relationship with the disciples as vine to branch. The disciples are not simply the beneficiaries of Jesus' bounty, but by their connection to him are part of the entire plant; they are members of a new community, the new Israel.[74] The disciples are repeatedly commanded to abide in Jesus the vine (15:4–7, 9–10). Although it is very difficult to define pre-

[69] Throughout this discussion I retain the Ionic spelling of ξυνουσία, which is used in the *Heroikos*.

[70] I will not discuss here the use of the verb πιστεύω in the Fourth Gospel to designate the proper response to Jesus. The similar use of this terminology in the *Heroikos*, noted by Betz ("Hero Worship and Christian Beliefs," 29 n. 25), merits further inquiry.

[71] This theme is usually referred to as the "indwelling" motif. Brown (*John*, 2:646) speaks of "the profound insight that the real gift of the post-resurrectional period was a union with Jesus that was not permanently dependent on bodily presence." Dodd, *Interpretation*, 187–200.

[72] On the background of this imagery, see Brown, *John*, 2:669–72.

[73] Brown, *John*, 2:674. Bultmann, *John*, 530.

[74] Brown, *John*, 2:670.

cisely the meaning of "abide" in this context, Bultmann is probably correct when he asserts this is a demand for loyalty.[75] Note, however, that loyalty, like the indwelling motif above, is reciprocal: "abide in me as I abide in you" (μείνατε ἐν ἐμοί, κἀγὼ ἐν ὑμῖν, 15:4). The same fidelity that Jesus pledges to the believer, the believer can expect from Jesus himself. The worshiper's relationship to the hero is also eroticized: The disciples are to "abide in [Jesus'] love" for them (μείνατε ἐν τῇ ἀγάπῃ, 15:9; cf. 14:21)—a love that the disciples are expected to return (14:15, 23; 16:27).[76] The community of those who live in such intimate association, demonstrating mutual loyalty and love, Jesus names his "friends" (φίλοι, John 15:14), the nearest and most valued of associates.[77] The Farewell Discourse thus shows that the Johannine Christians understood their relationship with Jesus through the Paraclete as one of utmost intimacy (ξυνουσία), and as in the heroic pattern, that intimacy is often described in the language of *eros*.

Before turning to the ethical component of the community as created through cult, I briefly sketch some differences between the Johannine conception of ξυνουσία and that described in the *Heroikos*. These differences are founded upon the fundamental Johannine theme of the incarnation of Wisdom. Unlike Protesilaos, who upon death becomes the attendant of the gods (*Her.* 7.3), Jesus is presented as the visible manifestation of the Father (see, e.g., John 14:8–11; cf. 1:1–18; 8:58). Jesus is the mediator between the Father and humans (see, e.g., John 14:6), whereas while Protesilaos benefits from his association (ξυνουσία) with the gods, he does not bring the gods closer to his worshiper. Intimacy with Jesus moreover not only brings the worshiper into contact with the Father, but the worshiper is exalted to a union with Jesus of astounding depth, implying a fluidity of identity and power. The hatred of the world for Jesus will likewise be experienced by his disciples (John 15:20; 15:18–16:4). The power of Jesus to do mighty works will also be transferred to his followers (John 14:12). Even Jesus' intimacy with the Father will now be their prized possession (John 16:26–27). This final theme is most explicitly described in 17:21–23:

[75] Bultmann, *John*, 535–36.

[76] Betz ("Hero Cult and Christian Beliefs," 34 n. 37) notes the eroticization of Jesus in his resurrection appearances.

[77] The use of φιλέω and its cognates should not be misinterpreted as connoting a love inferior to that of ἀγαπάω, as their connection in this passage makes clear. See also Ann Graham Brock, "The Significance of φιλέω and φίλος in the Tradition of Jesus Sayings in the Early Church," *HTR* 90 (1997): 405–8.

> As you, Father, are in me and I am in you, may they also be in us, so that the world may believe that you have sent me. The glory that you have given me I have given them, so that they may be one, as we are one, I in them and you in me, that they may become completely one, so that the world may know that you have sent me and have loved them even as you have loved me.

Johannine Christians understand themselves as lifted up to an immediate relationship with the Father, just as Jesus himself enjoys. This contrasts significantly with the chain of relationships implied by the *Heroikos*, where Protesilaos's relationship to the gods is only a paradigm for the human worshiper's relationship to the hero (not the gods). These distinctive elements of Johannine ξυνουσία do not, however, invalidate the presence of the basic heroic paradigm. Johannine Christians drew upon many cultural lenses to interpret Jesus, and the interaction between these lenses within the Fourth Gospel provides a unique portrait of Jesus. He is portrayed as a hero, but he is not simply a hero.

THE HERO AND THE ETHICAL LIFE

The last aspect of hero cult—the inculcation of a particular lifestyle leading to ethical nobility (ἀγαθοί)—is also a focal point of the Farewell Discourse. Admittedly, there is less detail in the Farewell Discourse than inquisitive believers have desired, but a new ethic is clearly promulgated by Jesus nonetheless: "I give you a new commandment, that you love one another" (John 13:34a). The love that Jesus requires is modeled on the ethic of Jesus himself: "Just as I have loved you, you also should love one another" (John 13:34b; cf. 15:12). This is later explained as Jesus' willingness to die for others: "No one has greater love than this, to lay down one's life for one's friends" (John 15:13). This love is clearly tied to the intimacy with Jesus created through cult: It both is the natural outgrowth of that intimacy ("If you love me, you will keep my commandments"; John 14:15; cf. 14:21, 23–24) and deepens it ("If you keep my commandments, you will abide in my love"; John 15:10; cf. 15:14). This complete commitment to the well-being of other members is believed to be the distinctive mark of membership in the community: "By this everyone will know that you are my disciples, if you have love for one another" (John 13:35).

There is not nearly the same emphasis on relations among the devotees of the hero in the *Heroikos*, although through tales of the heroes, the vinedresser and Protesilaos certainly advocate a particular way of life for those who take seriously the heroes as models for imitation.[78] Ethical ideals such as courage and composure in battle (*Her.* 23.16–19), ambition (*Her.* 26.7–10), eloquence (*Her.* 26.1), endurance (*Her.* 27.10), modesty (*Her.* 27.11), and simplicity of life (*Her.* 27.11; 33.41–45) are praised, whereas vices such as flattery, quickness to anger, unwillingness to be rebuked, and predilections for luxury (*Her.* 26.1; 27.9; 40.4–6) are held up as blameworthy. Friendship is also a primary heroic virtue.[79] The heroes, especially Achilles and Ajax, are depicted as the most loyal of friends. Achilles was devoted to his friends (avenging the deaths of Patroklos and Antilokhos; withdrawing from the battle on account of the murder of Palamedes), understanding that friendship requires dangerous risks to oneself (*Her.* 48.20), but also that these risks are undertaken with great pleasure (*Her.* 48.21). Indeed, Achilles claimed that his friends were no less dear to him than his own body (*Her.* 48.21–22); the same kind of loyalty in the face of extreme danger—pain of death—was displayed by Ajax when he buried Palamedes (*Her.* 33.32–33). It seems to me that the Fourth Gospel's emphasis on love as the community ethic does not differ greatly from the *Heroikos*'s ideal of friendship.

The presence of a new commandment that regulates the interpersonal life of the community leads to an issue of great importance. Cultic action implies the existence of a *cult legend.* If, as I have argued, the Farewell Discourse contains clues to the community's cultic practices, we must inquire what cult legend lay behind the ritual invocation of Jesus' presence and the spiritually aided interpretation of his words. A number of scholars argue that the Farewell Discourse bears important similarities to Moses' discourses in Deuteronomy: the unique status of Moses and Jesus as mediators, the function of "signs and wonders," the intimacy of God with his people, the promulgation of a central commandment that includes faith, love, and obedience, the promised rewards to the faithful, and the command to read/remember these words in the

[78] On the heroes as models for imitation, see Mestre, "Refuting Homer," 135, 140–41.

[79] On friendship in ancient literature, see John T. Fitzgerald, ed., *Greco-Roman Perspectives on Friendship* (Atlanta: Scholars Press, 1997); John T. Fitzgerald, ed., *Friendship, Flattery, and Frankness of Speech: Studies on Friendship in the New Testament World* (NovTSup 82; Leiden: Brill, 1996).

future in order to promote obedience.[80] This construction of the Farewell Discourse implies that the evangelist wished his readers to understand Jesus as the originator of a new covenant[81] and thus as the creator of a new community. The invocation of the Spirit, as practiced by the Johannine community, is therefore a reenactment of the giving of the new covenant, as the Lord's Supper was for other communities.[82] Just as Moses commanded the sabbatical rereading of the Law (Deut 31:9–13, 24–28), so Jesus commanded the remembrance of his words. However, Jesus' words, as remembered in the community, differ fundamentally from those of Moses. Moses' words are set down in written form and are read aloud; Jesus' teaching is not fundamentally a written tradition, and the meaning of his words are not thought to be evident from the mere process of reading. These words are to be *remembered* and in that process continually reinterpreted through the aid of the Spirit. They are thus more fruitfully compared to the practice of reading and interpretation of the Law described in Neh 8:1–8. When the Johannine community obeys Jesus' command to *remember* (understood here as invocation of his presence, inquiring about the meaning of his sayings, as well as gaining intimacy and adopting the community ethic of love), it reaffirms the covenant and its identity as the covenant community.

CONCLUSION: LAMENTATION AND GLORY AND THE JOHANNINE CHRIST

A fundamental aspect of hero cult has to this point been neglected: ritual lamentation for the dead hero.[83] While this cult action does not receive the repeated attention to which many of the other themes in the Farewell Discourse are subjected, it is here nonethe-

[80] Aelred Lacomara, "Deuteronomy and the Farewell Discourse (Jn 13:31–16:33)," *CBQ* 36 (1974): 65–84. See also Yves Simoens, *La gloire d'aimer: Structures stylistiques et interprétatives dans le Discours de la Cène (Jn 13–17)* (AnBib 90; Rome: Biblical Institute, 1981), 202–3, cited in and followed by Brouwer, *Literary Development*, 101, 104, 160. Brown, *John*, 2:600.

[81] Lacomara, "Deuteronomy," 83. So also Simoens, *La gloire d'aimer*, 204, cited in Brouwer, *Literary Development*, 160.

[82] Aitken, "τὰ δρώμενα καὶ τὰ λεγόμενα," 366–70. Ellen Bradshaw Aitken, *Jesus' Death in Early Christian Memory: The Poetics of the Passion* (Novum Testamentum et Orbis Antiquus; Göttingen: Vandenhoeck & Ruprecht, 2004).

[83] Nagy, *Best of the Achaeans*, 94–117. See also Pache, "Singing Heroes," 10–11, 22–23. On ritual lamentation of Jesus in Revelation, see Leonard L. Thompson, "Lamentation for Christ as Hero: Revelation 1:7," *JBL* 119 (2000): 683–703.

less. Jesus' going away (a euphemism for his death) will cause the disciples to weep (κλαύσετε) and lament (θρηνήσετε) and experience pain (λυπηθήσεσθε, John 16:20). All this might be expected upon the death of any loved one. But the context of this assertion implies that their weeping and lamentation are ongoing. The preceding verses, to which this saying of Jesus responds, concern the meaning of the "little while" (μικρόν) during which the disciples will not see Jesus. Rather than answering this question with a time frame (the *length* of μικρόν), Jesus' response describes the *quality* of this time: their tears, mourning, and pain will be turned to joy. This is the experience of "a little while, and you will no longer see me, and again a little while, and you will see me" (John 16:16). Lamentation and joy correspond to not seeing and seeing. The connection of this twofold experience to the community's ritual is made in the following verses through the metaphor of a woman giving birth: "When a woman is in labor, she has pain, because her hour has come. But when her child is born, she no longer remembers the anguish because of the joy of having brought a human being into the world" (John 16:21).[84] Labor brings pain, but what is remembered is not pain but joy; likewise, the pain of Jesus' death and absence is alleviated in cult through the process of *remembering*—they rejoice when they encounter him as Paraclete (John 16:22). Joy is also found in the proper perspective of Jesus' death/departure: His death is necessary, beneficial, and, most of all, it is the path for Jesus to attain glory (δόξα; see, e.g., 17:1–5).[85]

The cultic experience of Jesus by Johannine Christians was indeed very much like that of a hero. Heroes like Protesilaos bring grief to their worshipers in cult, but this grief is alleviated by the appearance of the hero, who transmits divine wisdom, shares an intimacy with the worshiper, and promotes an ethical lifestyle. The hero makes his worshipers φίλοι, σοφοί, and ἀγαθοί. The same heroic pattern is at work in the Fourth Gospel: The community's ritual, though born out of lamentation and grief, ultimately brings joy as the hero Jesus appears as Paraclete; by answering their inquiries, he becomes the authoritative interpreter of the sacred tradition (i.e., of Jesus' words), pursues an intimate, life-giving relationship with his followers, and requires of them a rigorous ethical stance. This for-

[84] Labor is a traditional image for the Day of the Lord. Brown, *John*, 2:731.

[85] The Fourth Gospel may thus be likened to epic, which emphasizes the heroes' glory (κλέος), whereas the cult of the community encompasses both lamentation of a hero's death and joy in his continued presence and power.

mation of a distinct community is succinctly summed up in John 15:14–15: Jesus' disciples are his friends (φίλοι), a relationship that is predicated upon their new knowledge (they have become σοφοί) and upon their ethical behavior (they must be ἀγαθοί). Jesus' heroic status is therefore not confined to the narrative elements of the Fourth Gospel, but the pattern of hero *cult* appears to have been the very basis upon which the community's identity and ritual practices were founded.

To be sure, the Christology of the Fourth Gospel is complex, and my investigation here is not intended to deny the importance of many other lenses employed by the evangelist to portray Jesus.[86] I have demonstrated above that the hero-cult paradigm has at times been modified to accommodate nonheroic aspects of the gospel's Christology, for example, the incarnation and Christ's role as mediator. The early Christians readily drew upon various cultural resources at their disposal—Jewish and Greek—to help them speak about Jesus and to organize their communal lives around him. That no single paradigm was sufficient testifies not to scholarly inability to "nail down" John's Christology, but rather to the enduring and multifaceted impact of this undoubtedly most enigmatic of figures, who was, at least for the Johannine Christians, a hero.

[86] E.g., Wayne Meeks, *The Prophet King: Moses Traditions and the Johannine Christology* (NovTSup 14; Leiden: Brill, 1967). Wayne A. Meeks, "The Man From Heaven in Johannine Sectarianism," in *The Interpretation of John* (ed. John Ashton; Philadelphia: Fortress, 1986), 169–205; repr. from *JBL* 91 (1972): 44–72. Michael E. Willett, *Wisdom Christology in the Fourth Gospel* (San Francisco: Mellen, 1992). Jennifer K. Berenson Maclean, "The Divine Trickster in John: A Tale of Two Weddings," in *A Feminist Companion to John* (ed. Amy-Jill Levine; 2 vols.; Sheffield: Sheffield Academic Press, 2003), 1:48–77.

Part III

The Phoenician: Hellenes and Foreigners

Philostratus's *Heroikos* and the Regions of the Northern Aegean

Simone Follet

Setting his dialogue in a rural estate near Elaious, in the Thracian Chersonesus, with the Troad within sight, Philostratus gave the *Heroikos* a very precise frame. This does not imply that all the *realia* that he happens to mention belong to this area. However, if we gather all the toponyms included in this text and compare them with those of a standard mythology handbook, the *Library* and *Epitome* of Apollodorus, for instance, we realize that he is especially concerned with regions he knows well, those of the northern Aegean Sea. After a brief recapitulation of the places where there is evidence for the author, his family, and his friends, I shall try to gather and check all the details he gives about landscapes or modes of life; if they appear reliable, we shall perhaps have to trust him when he describes heroic sanctuaries or archaic rituals of these countries, even if he is a *testis unus*, a sole witness.

EVIDENCE ABOUT PHILOSTRATUS'S FAMILY AND FRIENDS

Since there are good recent studies of Philostratus's life,[1] I shall only recall the main places where he, his relatives, or his friends are known from inscriptions, coins, or literary evidence.

Athens: L. Flavius Philostratus of Steiria (such was his full name) appears in three *prytany* lists[2] as a hoplite general (στρατηγός) under the archon M. Munatius Themison of Azenia, between

[1] For instance, Friedrich Solmsen, "Some Works of Philostratus the Elder," *TAPA* 71 (1940): 556–72; repr. in *Kleine Schriften* (3 vols.; Hildesheim, Germany: Olms, 1968), 1:74–90; Graham Anderson, *Philostratus: Biography and* Belles Lettres *in the Third Century A.D.* (London: Croom Helm, 1986), 291–96; Simon Swain, *Hellenism and Empire: Language, Classicism, and Power in the Greek World, A.D. 50–250* (Oxford: Clarendon, 1996), 380–400; Ludo de Lannoy, "Le problème des Philostrate (État de la question)," *ANRW* 34.3:2362–2449; Alain Billault, *L'univers de Philostrate* (Collection Latomus 252; Brussels: Latomus, 2000), 5–31.

[2] Benjamin D. Meritt and John S. Traill, *Inscriptions: The Athenian Councillors* (The Athenian Agora xv; Princeton: American School of Classical Studies at Athens, 1975), 313–15 nos. 447–49.

202/203 and 208/209 C.E.; he was then at least thirty. He was also a *prytanis* of his tribe, the Pandionis, in the first quarter of the third century;[3] his name is written in large letters immediately after that of the benefactor who is called "eponymous." A younger member of the family, called νεώτερος,[4] was probably στρατηγός between 220 and 235;[5] he may be the younger relative called Lemnian by the author of the *Life of Apollonius* and the *Lives of Sophists*. Two generations later, another person of the same name was eponymous archon in 254/255.[6] Several contemporary sophists, known from the *Lives of Sophists*, are also present in Attic epigraphy.[7]

Olympia: "Fl. Philostratus, the Athenian sophist," was honored in Olympia "by his glorious mother-city";[8] we can still see the high pillar that supported his statue near the entrance to the Altis. Olympia is also the place where the Lemnian Philostratus, then twenty-two years old, lectured in the presence of his teacher Hippodromus in 213[9] and where the wrestler and pancratiast Helix[10] was twice crowned, but missed a third victory; the mention of the victories of this athlete in Olympia (*Her.* 15.8–10) offers a *terminus post quem* for the date of both *Heroikos* and *On Gymnastics*.

[3] John S. Traill, "Prytany and Ephebic Inscriptions from the Athenian Agora," *Hesperia* 51 (1982): 231–33 no. 34, pl. 66.

[4] The additional adjective means that he must not be confused with a living person of the same name.

[5] James H. Oliver, "Greek Inscriptions," *Hesperia* 4 (1935): 50–52 no. 13; Meritt and Traill, *Agora* XV, 335 no. 485.

[6] Or 255/256, year of the 35th (new) Panathenaic celebration (*IG* II^2 2245). Since he has the same *praenomen* and *nomen* as the most famous sophist, he probably is the grandson of a brother rather than of a sister of this Philostratus. He may be the author of the second set of *Imagines*, but we have no proof; it is merely possible from the chronological point of view.

[7] For example, Valerius Apsinês, of Gadara (*IG* II^2 4007, completed by James H. Oliver, "Greek and Latin Inscriptions," *Hesperia* 10 [1941]: 260–61 no. 65); Junius Nikagoras, sacred herald at Eleusis (*IG* II^2 3814).

[8] *I. Olympia* 476; *Sylloge*^{3} 878.

[9] *Lives of Sophists* 2.27.3. For a different, less probable chronology, see Ivars Avotins, "The Year of Birth of the Lemnian Philostratus," *L'Antiquité classique* 47 (1978): 538–39.

[10] The most complete study of this athlete is that of Christopher P. Jones, "The Pancratiasts Helix and Alexander on an Ostian Mosaic," *JRA* 11 (1998): 293–98. Since the emphasis in Dio Cassius *Roman History* 79.10.2–3 is on his Olympic victory under the reign of Elagabalus, his half-success in Olympia may be dated in 221 and the later victory in the Roman Capitolia in 222, so that the *Heroikos* must belong to the first years of Alexander Severus and the *On Gymnastics* must be a little later, as Julius Jüthner saw ("Der Verfasser des Gymnastikos," in *Festschrift Theodor Gomperz* [ed. Moritz von Schwind; Vienna: Hölder, 1902; repr. Aalen, Germany: Scientia, 1979], 225–32).

Lemnos: The Romans left Lemnos and Imbros to Athens. The Philostrati lived in Lemnos, but were Athenian citizens; so all the members of the family may be called either Athenian or Lemnian.[11] One of them, a priest of Hephaistos, has set up at Hephaistia an honorific inscription for his nephew, P. Aelius Ergokharês of Prospalta, who had then already assumed several ἀρχαί and λειτουργίαι in Athens.[12] Another inscription, which I published in 1975,[13] mentions a Menekratês of Steiria, a deme companion of Philostratus, who is surely identical to the person bearing this name quoted in the *Heroikos* (*Her.* 8.11). The Menekratês who, in the dialogue entitled *Nero*, speaks with Musonius Rufus (probably in Gyaros, where the latter was exiled), is thought to belong to the same family, since he also is a Lemnian.[14]

Imbros: In his *Letter* 70, Philostratus states that, being a Lemnian, he considers Imbros also as his homeland. The name of the Imbrian Cleophôn, to whom *Letter* 70 is addressed, is present at least twice in Imbrian inscriptions.[15]

Ionia: At Erythrai (modern Ritri), Philostratus probably owned an estate, from where he could send a gift of ten pomegranates (*Letter* 45). He is mentioned with his wife Aurelia Melitinê, of senatorial rank, and one of their sons, in an inscription found in this city.[16] This son will appear as a στρατηγός on the city coinage between 244 and 249 C.E.[17] At Ephesus, Philostratus paid several

[11] This fact has not always been clearly understood, but the Attic demotics are sufficient proofs.

[12] *IG* XII 8.27. For Ergokharês' father, Mêtrophanês, see Meritt and Traill, *Agora* XV, 443; and perhaps *IG* V 1.563.

[13] Simone Follet, "Inscription inédite de Myrina," *ASAA* NS 36–37 (1974–1975): 309–12, with photograph in fig. 1.

[14] About this Menekratês, see, for instance, de Lannoy, "Le problème des Philostrate," 2383–84 n. 144; Timothy Whitmarsh, "Greek and Roman in Dialogue: The Pseudo-Lucianic *Nero*," *JHS* 119 (1999): 142–60.

[15] *IG* XII 8.113, 114. See Simone Follet, "Dédicataire et destinataires des *Lettres* des Philostrates," in *Titres et articulations du texte dans les oeuvres antiques: Actes du Colloque international de Chantilly, 13–15 décembre 1994* (ed. Jean-Claude Fredouille et al.; Paris: Institut d'études augustiniennes, 1997), 139–41.

[16] Helmut Engelmann and Reinhold Merkelbach, *Die Inschriften von Erythrai und Klazomenai* (Inschriften griechischer Städte aus Kleinasien 1–2; 2 vols.; Bonn: Habelt, 1972), 1:158–61 no. 63. The initial of the *praenomen* was present in the *editio princeps*, *BCH* 4 (1880): 153–55 no. 1, but omitted in *Sylloge*[3] 879 and *IGR* IV 1544.

[17] See Friedrich Imhoof-Blumer, *Monnaies grecques* (Amsterdam: Müller, 1883), 288 no. 63b; Rudolf Münsterberg, *Numismatische Zeitschrift* 45 (1912): 28; 48 (1915): 121. See further Christopher P. Jones, "*Trophimos* in an Inscription of Erythrai," *Glotta* 67 (1989): 195 n. 2.

visits to an elder sophist, Damianos, a member of a family whose inscriptions and monuments were discovered in the ruins of Ephesus.[18]

Syria: The author of the *Lives of Sophists* had spent some time in Syria: he reminds Antonius Gordianus, the future emperor Gordian I,[19] in his dedicatory letter, of their former talks in Daphne, near Antioch on the Orontes (this river is mentioned in the *Heroikos* [8.5]). He probably stayed also in some other Syrian cities, such as Tyre, with the empress Julia Domna and her son Caracalla.

These were not the only regions he knew: we learn from the *Life of Apollonius* (5.3) that he had seen the Atlantic Ocean and its tides and, from the prologue to the *Imagines*, that he probably stayed some time in a Campanian villa. Writing the *Heroikos*, however, he had in mind readers living in the eastern part of the Roman Empire, for whom he had to be precise, for instance, that Naples (*Her.* 8.15) and Mount Vesuvius (*Her.* 8.16) were in Italy. He focused attention on northern Aegean regions: the only places that are carefully described belong to this area and were known to him by autopsy. This appears especially true when he gives a detailed account of some landscapes and modes of life.

LANDSCAPES AND MODES OF LIFE

A preliminary observation may be useful. Philostratus mentions some places that perhaps he does not know, but either he discards them as literary (especially Homeric) fictions (such are the lands of the Kikones, Laestrygonians, Cyclopes, Circe, and others) or borrows traditional lists—for instance, a list of drowned cities or islands (Boura and Helikê[20] on the Corinthian Gulf, Atalantê in

[18] Ekrem Akurgal, *Civilisations et sites antiques de Turquie* (Istanbul: Haset Kitabevi, 1986), 190 and pl. 52.

[19] I agree with Ivars Avotins, "The Date and the Recipient of the *Vitae Sophistarum* of Philostratus," *Hermes* 106 (1978): 242–47.

[20] On these cities, ruined by an earthquake in 373/372 B.C.E., and modern archaeological research, cf. Dôra Katsônopoulou, "Archaia Elis: Istoria kai synchronê ereuna" (in Greek), in *Archaia Achaia kai Eleia* (ed. Athanase D. Rizakis: Athens: Kentron Hellênikês kai Rômaïkês Archaiotêtos, 1991), 227–34; Dôra Katsônopoulou, "Helikê" (in Greek), *Archaiologia* 54 (March 1995): 35–40; Nestor E. Courakis, "A Contribution to the Search for Ancient Helike," in *TIMAI Iôannou Triantaphyllopoulou* (Athens and Komotiní, Greece: Sakkoulas, 2000), 23–38. All the sources are quoted in Athanase D. Rizakis, ed., *Achaïe I: Sources textuelles et histoire régionale* (Athens: Kentron Hellênikês kai Rômaïkês Archaiotêtos, 1995), see indices s.v. Boura, 424, and Helikê, 437.

East Locris; *Her.* 53.21) or lists of places where giants' bones were found (*Her.* 8.3–17).[21] Alternatively, he draws heavily upon classical sources, without adding anything personal: Isocrates[22] for Messene (*Her.* 26.3); Plato[23] for the story of Gyges (*Her.* 8.3); Herodotus[24] for Orestes' bones (with a slip, Nemea for Tegea; *Her.* 8.3); Thucydides[25] for alluvial islands, the Ekhinades, in the mouth of the Akhelôos river in Acarnania (*Her.* 54.5)—the source here supports the reading "under the sun" (de Lannoy) against "under Ilion" (Kayser). He may also exclude the heroes who have no appeal to him, along with their countries: Ethiopia and Egypt with Memnôn (*Her.* 26.16), Crete with Idomeneus (*Her.* 30.1), Cyprus with Teukros (*Her.* 36.1); for Teukros, his lack of interest is patent, especially when we consider the bulk of testimonies collected in the *Testimonia Salaminia*[26] about this hero.

In contrast, he relates with greater detail what can be seen on the islands or continental shores between Athens and Lemnos. In addition to a brief mention of the Cyclades (Andros, Tênos; *Her.* 31.5), Chalcis (*Her.* 43.7), and the "hollows of Euboea" (*Her.* 33.47), he offers interesting information (*Her.* 8.9) about two of the Sporades, Peparêthos (modern Skopelos) and Ikos[27] (modern Alonnisos). First, he notes that the Peparethian Hymnaios (we must write Hym[e]naios with the authors of the *Lexicon of Greek Per-*

[21] See Jeffrey Rusten, "Living in the Past: Allusive Narratives and Elusive Authorities in the World of the *Heroikos*," 143–58 in this volume; and, on Hyllos, Peter Weiss, "Eumeneia und das Panhellenion," *Chiron* 30 (2000): 630–34; on Orontes, Christopher P. Jones, "The Emperor and the Giant," *CP* 95 (2000): 476–81.

[22] Isocrates *Archidamus* 19 (*Or.* 6).

[23] Plato *Republic* 2.359c–e.

[24] Herodotus *Hist.* 1.67–68; cf. also Pausanias *Description of Greece* 3.3.5–7; Barbara McCauley, "Heroes and Power: The Politics of Bone Transferal," in *Ancient Greek Hero Cult: Proceedings of the Fifth International Seminar on Ancient Greek Cult, Organized by the Department of Classical Archaeology and Ancient History, Göteborg University, 21–23 April 1995* (ed. Robin Hägg; Stockholm: Svenska Institutet i Athen, 1999), 85–98.

[25] Thucydides *Peloponnesian War* 2.102.2–6. For the countryside, see Klaus Freitag, "Oiniadai als Hafenstadt—Einige historisch-topographische Überlegungen," *Klio* 76 (1994): 212–38; Eric Fouache, *L'alluvionnement historique en Grèce occidentale et au Péloponnèse: Géomorphologie, archéologie, histoire* (BCH suppl. 35; Athens and Paris: École française d'Athènes, 1999), 55–73.

[26] Marie-José Chavane and Marguerite Yon, *Testimonia Salaminia* (Salamine de Chypre 10; Paris: De Boccard, 1978), 31–91.

[27] Of course we adopt the emendation of Kos to Ikos, as does Ludo de Lannoy, following Ulrich von Wilamowitz-Moellendorff, "Lesefrüchte CXLIII," *Hermes* 44 (1909): 475.

sonal Names, volume 2) possessed the whole of Ikos (sixty-two square kilometers) and grew vineyards there—wine was in fact the main production of these islands from classical to imperial times, as a ship full of wine amphoras sunk in the fifth century B.C.E.,[28] literary allusions,[29] and the Peparethian coinage bearing the effigy and abbreviated name of the god Dionysos[30] all testify. Commercial links between Peparêthos and the Troad are also well documented,[31] so that every detail here sounds true.

Relating Theseus's death in a very different way from Aristotle's bare statement,[32] Philostratus allows us to recognize the situation of modern Skyros,[33] on the eastern coast of this island: it is a city that is "high in the air, established on a rocky hill" (*Her.* 46.2). We may notice that his grandson, the author of the second set of *Imagines*, also had a personal knowledge of Skyros and could describe other pleasant landscapes there.[34]

About Lemnos, Philostratus cites toponyms that are not attested elsewhere (such as Akesa, supposed to be the place where Philoktêtês was cured; *Her.* 28.6); he describes the rocky shore where the hero was left and also the red earth from Mount Mosykhlos, so praised by physicians (Galen landed twice on the island to get this precious earth);[35] all these places are not far from the large city of Hephaistia,[36] the Philostrati's fatherland, presented here as the place where Hephaistos fell. For Imbros, Philostratus cites a

[28] Cf. Elpida Hadjidaki, "Underwater Excavations of a Late Fifth-Century Merchant Ship at Alonnesos, Greece: The 1991–1993 Seasons," *BCH* 120/2 (1996): 559–93.

[29] These are collected by Argyroula Doulgéri-Intzessiloglou and Yvon Garlan, "Vin et amphores de Péparéthos et d'Ikos," *BCH* 114 (1990): 361–64.

[30] See Doulgeri-Intzessiloglou and Garlan, "Vin et amphores," 366 n. 10, for a bibliography about this coinage.

[31] Cf. Argyroula Intzessiloglou, "Chronika," *Archaiologikon Deltion* 39 (1984): 146–47; 43 (1998): 250–52; and Doulgeri-Intzessiloglou and Garlan, "Vin et amphores," 361–89.

[32] Aristotle *Athenian Constitution* frg. 6 ("he was pushed down the rocks").

[33] In the Middle Ages the hill was crowned with a Venetian *kastro*.

[34] Philostratus the Younger *Imagines* 1.1.2.

[35] For an account of Galen's two trips to Lemnos, see Paul Moraux, *Galien de Pergame: Souvenirs d'un médecin* (Paris: Société d'éditions "Les Belles Lettres," 1985), 74–78.

[36] For a planimetry of Hephaistia, see *ASAA* NS 54–55 (1992–1993): text plate 9. For a list of the publications concerning the Italian excavations, see Luigi Beschi, "Cabirio di Lemno: Testimonianze letterarie ed epigrafiche," *ASAA* NS 58–59 (1996–1997): 7–146 and plates 1–46, with planimetry of the Cabeirion at the end of the volume.

toponym that is not mentioned elsewhere, but sounds authentic, Naulokhos (*Her.* 8.12),[37] probably on the southern part of the island (the name is more suitable for a harbor than for a promontory). He also describes collapsing cliffs, which Carl Fredrich could still observe in 1908 in the southern part of this island.[38]

The author of the *Heroikos* knows equally well the continental route from Athens to Lemnos. He mentions Boeotia, especially the harbor of Aulis; Locris, with Atalantê (*Her.* 53.21); and, as we shall see, Naryka. He has much to say about Thessaly, its mountains (Ossa, Pelion; *Her.* 32.1; 45.2–3; 53.9), river (Sperkheios; *Her.* 53.9), cities (Phthia [*Her.* 2.9; 11.7; 16.5; 46.5; 53.16], Phulakê [*Her.* 16.5; 33.22]). He tells how Achilles was educated on Mount Pelion by the centaur Kheirôn, how they hunted together and how the centaur cut him a spear made from the wood of an ash tree (*Her.* 45.4). He mentions Thessalian illustrious horses (*Her.* 50.2; 53.16; he perhaps heard about them from one of his teachers, Hippodromus from Larissa, the son of a horse breeder).[39] Combining the data of the *Life of Apollonius* (4.12, 16) and of the *Heroikos*, we get a vivid picture of what happened to Thessalians who had violated the imperial purple regulations: families ruined, houses sold or mortgaged, slaves who have run away, and even the ancestors' tombs which have been sold (*Her.* 53.22–23). Archaeology and inscriptions confirm the economic importance of purple fabrication and commerce for several Thessalian cities and the creation of an imperial monopoly on purple under Alexander Severus.[40]

Thrace is also well known to Philostratus, with its large rivers (Axios, Haimos), important cities such as Abdera and Maroneia, evoked through their eponymous heroes (*Her.* 48.14; 23.13; 26.4;

[37] A harbor, Pyrgos, is present on the maps of Heinrich Kiepert and Eugen Oberhummer, in Eugen Oberhummer, "Imbros," *Beiträge zur alten Geschichte und Geographie: Festschrift für Heinrich Kiepert* (Berlin: Reimer, 1898), 281. It is mentioned, with the name Pyrgos, by Alexander Conze, *Reise auf den Inseln des thrakischen Meeres* (Hannover: Rümpler, 1860), 102, 104; Charles Picard and Adolphe-Joseph Reinach, "Voyage dans la Chersonèse et aux îles de la mer de Thrace," *BCH* 36 (1912): 325–26; Oberhummer, "Imbros," 285 and 303.

[38] Carl Fredrich, "Imbros," *Ath. Mitt.* 33 (1908): 83–84.

[39] *Lives of Sophists* 2.27.1.

[40] Cf. *ILS* 1575, 2952; SHA *Alexander Severus* 39. W. Adolph Schmidt, *Die griechischen Papyrusurkunden der königlichen Bibliothek zu Berlin* (part 1 of *Forschungen auf dem Gebiete des Alterthums*; Berlin: Fincke, 1842), 96–212; Meyer Reinhold, *History of Purple as a Status Symbol in Antiquity* (Collection Latomus 116; Brussels: Latomus, 1970), 58; Peter Herrmann, "Milesisches Purpur," *Ist. Mitt.* 25 (1975): 141–47.

45.6; 1.4; 17.2), and special methods of dressing vines (*Her.* 17.2; κυκλοῦν, with its scholion λακκίζειν, probably means digging hollows around each vine to keep it wet as long as possible).[41] Rhêsos's homeland, Mount Rhodopê, is notably a place for horsemen and hunters, but the author also gives notice of the large population and the many villages, attesting to the prosperity of the country (*Her.* 17.3–6), a fact which is confirmed from several other sources, especially for those settlements along the *Via Egnatia*.

Starting, now, from the southeast, we may sail with the Phoenician merchant from Syria to Elaious. One important piece of information is given at the very beginning of the dialogue: Phoenicia is now completely hellenized, and Ionian refinement has conquered the whole country (*Her.* 1.1). We receive only brief mention of some places that are still far away from the Troad: the river Orontes in Syria (*Her.* 8.5); the oracle of Amphilokhos at Mallos in Cilicia (*Her.* 17.1); the former inhabitants of Kos, called Meropes (*Her.* 8.14); a κάλπις ("pitcher") which mysteriously appeared on the island of Chios (*Her.* 56.5); and the Baths of Agamemnon,[42] not far from Smyrna—a well-identified site for which Philostratus provides us a precise description (*Her.* 23.30).

There are more particulars and colors in the pictures of the regions that are nearer his homeland. He describes, for instance, the Troad and Mysia, the country around Pergamum, with pastures coming down to the seaside (*Her.* 23.6). He states that the river Scamander is rather unimpressive, so that Homeric descriptions may be labeled ὑπερβολαί ("hyperboles"; *Her.* 48.11–12). He knows the changing winds and how sailors use them to sail away at dawn.[43] There are wolves in the mountains (*Her.* 33.14) and groups of cranes flying south in their usual order (*Her.* 33.11). He also mentions the visitors coming to the Troad to see the *tumuli* of ancient heroes on Cape Sigeion or Cape Rhoiteion (*Her.* 8.6).[44]

He also knows the regions of the Hellespont as the place where

[41] On this practice, see Raymond Billiard, *La vigne dans l'antiquité* (Lyon: Lardanchet, 1914), 326–28.

[42] Cf. Cecil John Cadoux, *Ancient Smyrna: A History of the City from the Earliest Times to 324 A.D.* (Oxford: Blackwell, 1938), 17 n. 1 and plate facing p. 359; M. B. Sakellariou, *La migration grecque en Ionie* (Collection de l'Institut français d'Athènes 17; Athens: n.p., 1958), 116–18. These hot springs were between Smyrna and Clazomenai, about six miles from Smyrna.

[43] He mentions them, for instance, in reference to the funeral ship of the Locrian Ajax (*Her.* 31.9); see also *Life of Apollonius* 4.13.

[44] See Susan E. Alcock, "Material Witness: An Archaeological Context for the *Heroikos*," 160–63 in this volume.

travelers and sailors tell more-or-less fantastic stories about the Amazons, upper Colchis (*Her.* 57.2–17), and Achilles' island (*Her.* 54.7–11). The traffic is so intense in these straits that the sea is like a river (*Her.* 22.4).

Coming to the Chersonesian peninsula, Philostratus gives a pleasant picture of the suburban estate where the vinedresser is living—there is a variety of agricultural products, such as vineyards with Thasian plants for the best production, and everywhere irrigation channels, olive trees, fruit trees, beehives, and cattle (*Her.* 3.1–6; 4.10–11). It contains a charming κῆπος ("garden"; *Her.* 9.3; 58.5), similar to that of Longus, with soft grass, clear water, flowers, tunnels, and nice fragrances of flowers and trees. Agricultural implements did not change in the course of centuries, so that the author is still able to mention the traditional hoe and the plain tunic of the farmer (*Her.* 4.10). Residing on his estate and producing everything he needs, according to the old ideal of self-sufficiency, the vinedresser is free and happy, even after having been deprived of most of his former lands by a mighty neighbor (*Her.* 4.2; such encroachments are well known under the Roman Empire, through repressive legislation, literary allusions, and inscriptions).[45] This place has much of the character of a *locus amoenus* created by poets or painters, or of a philosophical Thebais,[46] but it also calls to mind the suburban villas which are better known from archaeology and inscriptions, as well as the ideals of the urban societies of the Hellenistic and imperial periods.

Describing areas that he does know thus, with realistic or typical details, Philostratus sets his dialogue in a landscape that looks real; it is a part of his literary creation, just as such sceneries were for Plato in the *Phaedrus* or Plutarch in the *Eroticus*. So he is for us an eyewitness of landscapes and modes of life modeled through many centuries by human activity, and this witness may be trusted. We shall have to decide whether the same is true or not when he describes heroic sanctuaries or archaic rituals.

[45] For example, *IG* II^2 1035; André Piganiol, *Les documents cadastraux de la colonie romaine d'Orange* (Gallia suppl. 16; Paris: Centre national de la recherche scientifique, 1962), 81; Dio Chrysostom *Euboikos* 27; Lucian *The Ship, or The Wishes* 38.

[46] See Rüdiger Vischer, *Das einfache Leben: Wort- und motivgeschichtliche Untersuchungen zu einem Wertbegriff der antiken Literatur* (Göttingen: Vandenhoeck & Ruprecht, 1965); Philostratus's *Heroikos* might have been included in this study.

HEROIC SANCTUARIES AND RITUALS

This dialogue, having heroes as its main argument, provides us with much information about hero cults in general and individual *hêrôa* and rituals, either past or contemporary, in particular.

Most of the specific features of hero cults have been recently gathered by Robin Hägg.[47] From what Philostratus tells us, these cults are usually related to an altar or a statue. Devotees pour libations and offer prayers; the statue may even be defaced by votive tablets (*Her.* 9.6). Usually the hero is benevolent: Palamedes knows how to protect vineyards against hail, hanging in them the skin of an animal, perhaps a seal[48] (*Her.* 21.8); Protesilaos cures diseases such as phthisis, dropsy, hemorrhages (*Her.* 16.1–2), and Têlephos is capable of healing wounds (*Her.* 23.24). They may also be angry, as Protesilaos is with Xeinis the Chersonesian (*Her.* 4.2), or as Achilles is with the Thessalians who had neglected the sacrifices due to him (*Her.* 53.17–23). Some heroes also have *manteia*, or oracles: Protesilaos in Elaious (*Her.* 14.4–15.10), Orpheus in Antissa (on Lesbos; *Her.* 28.7–9),[49] or Amphilokhos in Mallos (in Cilicia; *Her.* 17.1). Some *hêrôa* are adorned with trophies: Mysian helmets thus surround the Baths of Agamemnon near Smyrna (*Her.* 23.30). *Hêrôa* may also be the seat of miracles: Philostratus tells us, following Herodotus,[50] how in Elaious the salted fish came back to life against the Mede Artayktes (*Her.* 9.5). Τελεταί, or secret ceremonies, may be included in the cult: thus it is in Lemnos (*Her.* 51.5–7; Philostratus alludes to the Cabeirion),[51] in Corinth (*Her.*

[47] Robin Hägg, ed., *Ancient Greek Hero Cult: Proceedings of the Fifth International Seminar on Ancient Greek Cult, Organized by the Department of Classical Archaeology and Ancient History, Göteborg University, 21–23 April 1995* (Stockholm: Svenska Institutet i Athen, 1999).

[48] See *Geoponica* 1.14, and its source Anatolius of Berytus, in *Paris. gr.* 2313, f. 49v.

[49] Cf. *Life of Apollonius* 4.14; Salomon Reinach, "La mort d'Orphée," *RAr* 2 (1902): 242–79; repr. in *Cultes, mythes et religions* (3d ed.; 3 vols.; Paris: Leroux, 1928), 2:45–122; Waldemar Deonna, "Orphée et l'oracle de la tête coupée," *REG* 38 (1925): 44–69.

[50] Herodotus *Hist.* 9.116, 120; cf. also 7.33; Pausanias *Description of Greece* 3.4.6.

[51] Cf. Silvio Accame, "Iscrizioni del Cabirio di Lemno," *ASAA* NS 3–5 (1941–1943): 75–105; Doro Levi, "Il Cabirio di Lemno," in *Charisterion eis Anastasion K. Orlandon* (Bibliothêkê tês en Athênais Archaiologikês Hetaireias 54; 4 vols.; Athens, 1965–1968), 3:110–32 and plates 30–44. Cf. note 36 above.

52.4; with rites of propitiation for Medea's children),[52] and in Isthmia (*Her.* 52.4; sacrificial pits for Palaimôn-Melikertês have been found there, confirming and clarifying Philostratus's allusions).[53]

Some places are described more precisely. About the sanctuary of Protesilaos at Phulakê, we know little, but we learn that the statue there was thought to be efficacious (*Her.* 16.5). The famous statue in the Metropolitan Museum is supposed to be a copy of it.[54]

Philostratus also describes the statue of the hero exactly as it was standing in Elaious, on the prow of a ship (*Her.* 9.6);[55] we know it from the contemporary coinage of the city. The miracle of the trees losing a part of their foliage early (*Her.* 9.1–3) is mentioned by several writers from the first to the third century C.E.[56]

In Ilion, it is Hektor's statue that requires atttention (*Her.* 37.5). The emperor Julian[57] could still see it in 354 C.E., shining with unguents; its special hair-dressing was the origin of a proverbial expression.[58] Competitions, too, are well attested, but we must read ἀγωνοθετοῦσιν at *Her.* 19.4 (ἀγῶνα θύουσιν in the manuscripts

[52] Cf. Nikolaos D. Papachatzis, "To Hêraio tês Korinthou kai hê latreia tôn 'paidiôn tês Mêdeias'" (in Greek), in *Philia epê eis Geôrgion E. Mylônan* (Bibliothêkê tês en Athênais Archaiologikês Hetaireias 103; Athens: Hê en Athênais Archaiologikê Hetaireia, 1986–1987), 2:396–404; Pierre Bonnechère, *Le sacrifice humain en Grèce ancienne* (Kernos suppl. 3; Athens and Liège, Belgium: Centre international d'étude de la religion grecque antique, 1994), 70–74; Christine Harrauer, "Der korinthische Kindermord—Eumelos und die Folgen," *Wiener Studien* 112 (1999): 5–28.

[53] Cf. David W. Rupp, "The Lost Classical Palaimonion Found?" *Hesperia* 48 (1979): 64–72 and pl. 18; Marcel Piérart, "Panthéon et hellénisation dans la colonie romaine de Corinthe: La 'redécouverte' du culte de Palaimon à l'Isthme," *Kernos* 11 (1998): 85–109; Elizabeth R. Gebhard and Matthew W. Dickie, "Melikertes-Palaimon, Hero of the Isthmian Games," in Hägg, *Ancient Greek Hero Cult*, 159–65. The *enagistêrion* is explicitly mentioned in an inscription: cf. Daniel J. Geagan, "The Isthmian Dossier of P. Licinius Priscus Juventianus," *Hesperia* 58 (1989): 349–60 and pl. 56.

[54] Cf. José Dörig, "Deinoménès," *Antike Kunst* 37 (1994): 67–80.

[55] Cf. Barclay V. Head, *Historia Numorum: A Manual of Greek Numismatics* (2d ed.; Oxford: Clarendon, 1906), 259–60.

[56] *Anthologia palatina* 7.141 (Antiphilus), 385 (Philip); Pliny *Natural History* 16.88; Pomponius Mela *De chorographia* 2.2.30; Quintus of Smyrna *Fall of Troy* 7.408–411.

[57] Julian *Letter* 79 Bidez; Alfred R. Bellinger, *Troy: The Coins* (Princeton: Princeton University Press, 1961), 48–78; Ruth Lindner, *Mythos und Identität: Studien zur Selbstdarstellung kleinasiatischer Städte in der römischen Kaiserzeit* (Stuttgart: Steiner, 1994), 25–102; Dennis D. Hughes, "Hero Cult, Heroic Honors, Heroic Dead: Some Developments in the Hellenistic and Roman Periods," in Hägg, *Ancient Greek Hero Cult*, 167–75.

[58] See R. G. Austin, "Hector's Hair-Style," *CQ* NS 22 (1972): 199.

means nothing, despite the scholiast's efforts; I received Louis Robert's approval for this slight paleographical emendation).

In contrast with these cult places, which were well known and attracted tourists, Palamedes' *hêrôon*, as it is presented in the *Heroikos* (21.2) and the *Life of Apollonius* (4.13), was already ruined in the first century C.E. The statue bore a plain dedication, "to the divine Palamedes." It was set up on the continent, not far from Assos, in front of Methymna and Mount Lepetumnos, not, as many people think, on the island of Lesbos.[59]

If we usually have several testimonies about the sanctuaries of the Greek and Trojan heroes, we face a somewhat different situation when we consider the rituals mentioned in the course of the *Heroikos*.[60] Philostratus is frequently the only witness for the information he provides.

Even with respect to Attic festivals, Philostratus sometimes gives original information. Adhering firmly to the Attic version of the Aiakids' legend,[61] he presents the Telamonian Ajax as an Athenian child and then provides more information than any other writer concerning the second day of the Anthestêria, the Choes (*Her.* 35.6–9); archaeology, especially vase-painting and small jugs found in children's graves, confirms these indications.[62] We may

[59] Cf. Emily Ledyard Shields, *The Cults of Lesbos* (Menasha, Wis.: Banta, 1917), 82–83; and Simone Follet, "Remarques sur deux valeurs de κατά dans l'*Héroïque* de Philostrate," in *Cas et prépositions en grec ancien: Contraintes syntaxiques et interprétations sémantiques. Actes du colloque international de Saint-Étienne (3–5 juin 1993)* (ed. Bernard Jacquinod; Saint-Étienne: Université de Saint-Étienne, 1994), 113–16.

[60] Albert Henrichs ("Keeping Dead Heroes Alive: The Revival of Hero Cult in the *Heroikos*" [paper presented at the conference "Philostratus's *Heroikos*, Religion, and Cultural Identity," Cambridge, Mass., 4 May 2001]) addressed the precise vocabulary used by Philostratus to describe heroic rituals; cf. Gunnel Ekroth, "Pausanias and the Sacrificial Rituals of Greek Hero-Cults," in Hägg, *Ancient Greek Hero Cult*, 145–58.

[61] On this set of legends, cf. Alwine Zunker, *Untersuchungen zur Aiakidensage auf Aigina* (St. Ottilien, Germany: EOS Verlag, 1988); Louise-Marie L'Homme-Wéry, "Les héros de Salamine en Attique: Cultes, mythes et intégration politique," in *Héros et héroïnes dans les mythes et les cultes grecs: Actes du colloque organisé à l'Université de Valladolid du 26 au 29 mai 1999* (ed. Vinciane Pirenne-Delforge and Emilio Suárez de la Torre; Kernos suppl. 10; Liège, Belgium: Centre international d'étude de la religion grecque antique, 2000), 333–49.

[62] Cf. Gerard Van Hoorn, *Choes and Anthesteria* (Leiden: Brill, 1951); Henri Metzger, *Recherches sur l'imagerie athénienne* (Paris: De Boccard, 1965), 55–76; H. W. Parke, *Festivals of the Athenians* (Ithaca, N.Y.: Cornell University Press, 1977), 107–20.

also see an example of "Athenian myth-making" in the *aition* he gives to what should be the name of the Amazon *Peisianassa* ("the one who persuades the queen"; *Her.* 57.10); the name Peisianassa, for an Amazon, is attested early.[63]

In regard to Achilles' cult in the Euxine (*Her.* 54.3, 11), what could be considered pure fancy is now increasingly confirmed by archaeology and inscriptions. Around Olbia, the cult of the hero Achilles is well documented at least from the sixth century B.C.E. The double aspect of this cult, half-human and half-divine, is now confirmed by literature, epigraphy, and archaeology.[64] Even if the Thessalian ritual is not known from other sources, it bears a number of archaic features: two groups of seven θεωροί or ambassadors (this reminds us of the story of Theseus), the importance of the number nine (a festival every ninth year, the extinction of the fire for nine days),[65] water from the river Sperkheios, and amarantine ("unfading") crowns (*Her.* 53.9). Even the reduction of offerings over the course of centuries (*Her.* 53.14, 17; lambs instead of bulls, etc.) may be paralleled: for example, the Pythaïs, a brilliant Athenian procession to Delphi in the second century B.C.E., with more than a hundred people representing all the categories of the city and many beautiful victims, became, under Augustus, a small *dôdekaïs*, with few priests and victims, as the inscriptions engraved on the Athenian Treasury at Delphi record.[66]

Archaic and authentic, too, is the information given about the renewal of the sacred fire on Lemnos every nine years (*Her.* 53.5–7; Adolf Wilhelm[67] understood that this was the right reading). After

[63] Pierre Devambez and Aliki Kauffmann Samaras, "Amazones," *LIMC* 1.1 (1982): no. 724, pp. 631 and 653 (index of Amazons' names).

[64] H. Koehler, "Mémoire sur les îles et la course consacrée à Achille dans le Pont-Euxin," *Mémoires de l'Académie impériale des sciences de Saint-Pétersbourg* 10 (1824): 531–819; Hildebrecht Hommel, *Der Gott Achilleus* (Heidelberg: Winter, 1980); Zunker, *Untersuchungen zur Aiakidensage auf Aigina*, 167–91, esp. 187–91; Guy Hedreen, "The Cult of Achilles in the Euxine," *Hesperia* 60 (1991): 313–30; Laurent Dubois, "Oiseaux de *Nostoi*," in *Poésie et lyrique antiques* (ed. Laurent Dubois; Villeneuve d'Ascq, France: Presses universitaires du Septentrion, 1996), 149–60; Laurent Dubois, *Inscriptions grecques dialectales d'Olbia du Pont* (Geneva: Droz, 1996), 95–107.

[65] See, e.g., Wilhelm Heinrich Roscher, *Die Sieben- und Neunzahl im Kultus und Mythus der Griechen* (Leipzig: Teubner, 1904).

[66] Gaston Colin, *Inscriptions du Trésor des Athéniens* (Fouilles de Delphes 3.2; Paris: Fontemoing, 1909–1913).

[67] Adolf Wilhelm, "Die Pyrphorie der Lemnier," *Anzeiger der (K.) Akademie der Wissenschaften in Wien. Philosophisch-historische Klasse* 76 (1939): 41–46; repr.

nine days without fire, Lemnians could get new fire from the Pythion on Delos, as René Vallois[68] suggested, and it was later given to ordinary people for the needs of everyday life, but also to ironworkers—this corporation was always important in Hephaistos's city, which, as we know, was the Philostrati's homeland.

About the Locrian Ajax, Philostratus follows a favorable tradition, with original details. He mentions a tame serpent that followed the hero everywhere (*Her.* 31.3); this has sometimes been thought as a fanciful invention, but this serpent was already present on ceramics of the classical age;[69] we must thus conclude that here the author could be following an authentic tradition. Two Locrian inscriptions allow us to understand how these traditions could survive: the first one, the famous inscription about the tribute of Locrian maidens,[70] mentions a group called "Aianteioi," which was probably an association in charge of the cult and legend of the hero in Naryka. The second, still unpublished,[71] is a letter of Hadrian who in 138 C.E. recalls the reasons why Naryka could be admitted into the Panhellenion, including the particular fact that she had borne heroes who were famous through Greek and Roman poets (the main such hero was certainly Ajax, the son of Oileus).

---

in *Akademieschriften zur griechischen Inschriftenkunde [1895–1951]* (part 8 of *Opuscula*; 3 vols.; Leipzig: Zentralantiquariat der Deutschen Demokratischen Republik, 1974), 1/3:43–48. See also Follet, "Remarques," 116–19. My emendation is accepted by Bernadette Leclercq-Neveu in her re-edition of Georges Dumézil, *Le crime des Lemniennes: Rites et légendes du monde égéen* (Paris: Macula, 1998), 125–26.

[68] René Vallois, *L'architecture hellénique et hellénistique à Délos: I. Les monuments* (Paris: De Boccard, 1944), 35 and n. 1. This was not admitted by Philippe Bruneau, *Recherches sur les cultes de Délos à l'époque hellénistique et à l'époque impériale* (Paris: De Boccard, 1970), 115, 120–21.

[69] Cf. Juliette Davreux, *La légende de la prophétesse Cassandre d'après les textes et les monuments* (Paris: Droz, 1942), figs. 39, 41, 62 and pp. 144, 146, 169–70; Barclay V. Head, *British Museum: Catalogue of Greek Coins, I. Central Greece* (London: The Trustees of the British Museum, 1884), nos. 7–17; S. W. Grose, *Fitzwilliam Museum: Catalogue of the McClean Collection of Greek Coins* (Cambridge: Cambridge University Press, 1926), nos. 5425 and 5436.

[70] *IG* IX 1^2 3.706; Hatto H. Schmitt, *Die Verträge der griechisch-römischen Welt von 338 bis 200 v. Chr.* (vol. 3 of *Die Staatsverträge des Altertums*; 3 vols.; Munich: Beck, 1969), 118–26 no. 472; for a full bibliography, see Giuseppe Ragone, "Il millennio delle vergini locresi," in *Studi ellenistici* (Studi ellenistici 8; Biblioteca di studi antichi 78; ed. Biagio Virgilio; Pisa and Rome: Istituti editoriali e poligrafici internazionali, 1996), 7–95.

[71] It will be published by Dominique Jaillard; see already his paper "À propos du fragment 35 de Callimaque," *ZPE* 132 (2000): 143–44.

I quote, with more hesitation, a tantalizing passage about the city of Lyrnêssos, "in a fortified site and not missing fortifications,"[72] which is usually thought to be on the continent,[73] but appears, in our text, as a city on the island of Lesbos (*Her.* 33.28). It was the place where Orpheus's lyre had landed, carried there by the waves after his death. Since, according to some authors, the lyre and the head of the poet had sailed from Thrace together, the city might be in the neighborhood of Antissa, but it is difficult to find the exact place, especially since the archaeological exploration of Lesbos is far from complete. I wish only to stress that the precise description given in our dialogue has not yet been seriously taken into account.

In conclusion, I would draw attention to the fact that, for the regions of the northern Aegean, Philostratus is an eyewitness and can usually be trusted. Much attention has been spent in recent years on the *realia* of the Greek novel, especially such features as landscapes, institutions, cities, harbors, porticoes, and sanctuaries. If, like Plato in his *Phaedrus* or Plutarch in his *Eroticus*, Philostratus chose a real setting for his dialogue, if he knows well the places he describes because he lived there for at least some time, if he is really interested in hero cults and sanctuaries, then his text may be scrutinized just as those of other antiquarians such as Strabo or Pausanias are. The presentation of Hellenic landscapes, shrines, rituals is an interesting part of his "Hellenism."[74]

[72] On this expression, see Minos M. Kokolakis, "Apo to thematologio tôn sophistôn: Hê ateichistos Spartê" (in Greek), *Lakônikai Spoudai* 10 (1990): 1–24. The meaning may be literal or metaphorical.

[73] See Walter Leaf, ed., *Strabo on the Troad: Book XIII, Cap. 1* (Cambridge: Cambridge University Press, 1923), 308–10; Walter Leaf, "Notes on the Text of Strabo XIII. 1," *JHS* 37 (1917): 24–25; Josef Stauber, *Die Bucht von Adramytteion: I. Topographie (Lokalisierung antiker Orte/Fundstellen von Altertümer)* (Inschriften griechischer Städte aus Kleinasien 50; Bonn: Habelt, 1996), 66–71.

[74] On other aspects of his Hellenism, see Simone Follet, "Divers aspects de l'hellénisme chez Philostrate," in *ΕΛΛΗΝΙΣΜΟΣ: Quelques jalons pour une histoire de l'identité grecque: Actes du colloque de Strasbourg, 25–27 octobre 1989* (ed. Suzanne Saïd; Leiden: Brill, 1991), 205–15. On the *realia* in the *Heroikos*, see also Christopher P. Jones, "Philostratus' *Heroikos* and its Setting in Reality," *JHS* 121 (2001), 141–49 and pl. 1, which I read only after delivering my paper at the conference "Philostratus's *Heroikos*, Religion, and Cultural Identity," May 2001 in Cambridge, Massachusetts.

The Harvest of Wisdom: Landscape, Description, and Identity in the *Heroikos*

Tim Whitmarsh

The *Heroikos*, this wonderfully rich, plural text now rightly sited at the heart of imperial Greek culture, has many aspects to it. Homeric criticism, Platonic dialogue, eschatological rumination, novelistic encounter, even miniature lyric: all these generic strands are deftly woven into its elegant tapestry. Rather than attempt to offer an exhaustive reading of the text (a feat presuming the superhuman knowledge and insight of an undead hero), my scope in this essay is narrower: to focus upon the *Heroikos* within the genre of imperial travel writing.[1] Why is there so much emphasis upon siting

[1] For ancient travel-writing in general see Jean-Marie André and Marie-Françoise Baslez, *Voyager dans l'antiquité* (Paris: Fayard, 1993); also James S. Romm, *The Edges of the Earth in Ancient Thought: Geography, Exploration, and Fiction* (Princeton: Princeton University Press, 1991); Jaś Elsner and Joan-Pau Rubiès, "Introduction," in *Voyages and Visions: Towards a Cultural History of Travel* (ed. Jaś Elsner and Joan-Pau Rubiès; London: Reaktion, 1999), 8–15. For Pausanias within the genre of ancient travel-writing, see especially Christian Habicht, *Pausanias' Guide to Ancient Greece* (Berkeley: University of California Press, 1985), 19–27; Jaś Elsner, "Pausanias: A Greek Pilgrim in the Roman World," *Past and Present* 135 (1992): 3–29, repr. with modifications in *Art and the Roman Viewer: The Transformation of Art from the Pagan World to Christianity* (Cambridge and New York: Cambridge University Press, 1995); Karim Arafat, *Pausanias' Greece: Ancient Artists and Roman Rulers* (Cambridge and New York: Cambridge University Press, 1996), 8–12; also the various contributions in Susan E. Alcock, John F. Cherry, and Jaś Elsner, eds., *Pausanias: Travel and Memory in Roman Greece* (Oxford and New York: Oxford University Press, 2001). For Philostratus's interest in travel-writing elsewhere, see Jaś Elsner, "Hagiographic Geography: Travel and Allegory in the *Life of Apollonius of Tyana*," *JHS* 117 (1997): 22–37. For an argument that Philostratus uses Pausanias (or a common source) in the *Heroikos*, see Jeffrey Rusten's contribution to this volume. This essay is a shorter version of my "Performing Heroics: Language, Landscape, and Identity in Philostratus' *Heroicus*," in *Philostratus* (ed. Ewen Bowie and Jaś Elsner; Cambridge: Cambridge University Press, forthcoming). I am grateful to audiences in the universities of Harvard, Oxford, and Cambridge for their comments on versions of this chapter. All translations are taken from *Flavius Philostratus: Heroikos* (trans. Jennifer K. Berenson Maclean and Ellen Bradshaw Aitken; SBLWGRW 1; Atlanta: Society of Biblical Literature, 2001), sometimes with modifications.

the text in the Chersonesus?[2] Why is the cult site described in such detail? What literary "voice" is adopted in these descriptions, and why? And in particular—this will be my focus—how are Philostratus's Greek readers encouraged to explore their own cultural self-positioning through this dialogue?

Within the vast expanse of the Roman Empire, geography is always a marked discourse, whether appropriating alien territory and rendering it amenable to imperializing knowledge,[3] or idealizing an impossibly primitive countryside as a counterpart to the ambiguous sophistication of modern urban life.[4] The *Heroikos* intersects with a tradition of texts that strategically relocate the centers of Hellenism away from the traditional, grand cult sites of Athens and Olympia to rural backwaters.[5] Dio's seventh oration, the *Euboikos*, is a case in point. This text (discussed in Philostratus's *Lives of the Sophists*, and important for the *Heroikos*, as we shall see) begins by siting the tale "in practically the middle of Greece" (ἐν μέσῃ σχεδόν τι τῇ Ἑλλάδι, Dio Chrysostom *Euboikos* 7.1), a marker of cultural centrality that underscores the normative, moralizing narrative.[6] These hunters of Euboea are "true" Greeks,

[2] See especially Christopher P. Jones, "Philostratus' *Heroikos* and Its Setting in Reality," *JHS* 121 (2001): 144–46, on the geographical location of the scene, particularly its location in "real" space. On the *Heroikos*'s "rooted connection to the ground of history," see now also Richard P. Martin, "A Good Place to Talk: Discourse and Topos in Achilles Tatius and Philostratus," in *Space in the Ancient Novel* (Ancient Narrative suppl. 1; ed. Michael Paschalis and Stavros A. Frangoulidis; Groningen, Netherlands: Barkhuis, 2002), 156–58 (quotation from p. 158). This article appeared too late to integrate fully into this chapter.

[3] Arnaldo Momigliano, *Alien Wisdom: The Limits of Hellenization* (Cambridge and New York: Cambridge University Press, 1975), 65–66; and especially Claude Nicolet, *Space, Geography, and Politics in the Early Roman Empire* (Ann Arbor: University of Michigan Press, 1991).

[4] Tim Whitmarsh, *Greek Literature and the Roman Empire: The Politics of Imitation* (Oxford and New York: Oxford University Press, 2001), 100–108, with further references.

[5] Teresa Mantero, *Ricerche sull'* Heroikos *di Filostrato* (Genoa, Italy: University of Genoa, Instituo di Filologia Classica e Medioevale, 1966), 45–47, on "motivi nazionalistici"; Froma I. Zeitlin, "Visions and Revisions of Homer," in *Being Greek under Rome: Cultural Identity, the Second Sophistic, and the Development of Empire* (ed. Simon Goldhill; Cambridge and New York: Cambridge University Press, 1990), 430–36.

[6] For this point, see Michael B. Trapp, "Sense of Place in the Orations of Dio Chrysostom," in *Ethics and Rhetoric: Classical Essays for Donald Russell on His Seventy-fifth Birthday* (ed. Doreen Innes, Harry Hine, and Christopher Pelling; Oxford: Clarendon, 1995), 164–65; also John Moles, "Dio Chrysostom, Greece, and Rome," in Innes, *Ethics and Rhetoric*, 177–80.

preserving their traditions through innocence of city traditions: the "center" has been provocatively shifted away from the usual claimants (Athens, Olympia, Delphi) to rural Euboea. In another passage with important implications for the *Heroikos*, Philostratus himself in the *Lives of the Sophists* discusses at one point a certain Agathion, who decries the corrupted, "barbaric" speech to be found in the center of Athens, whereas "the interior of Attica is pure of barbarians, and hence its language remains uncorrupted and its dialect sounds the purest strain of Atthis" (ἡ μεσογεία δὲ ἄμικτος βαρβάροις οὖσα ὑγιαίνει αὐτοῖς ἡ φωνὴ καὶ ἡ γλῶττα τὴν ἄκραν Ἀτθίδα ἀποψάλλει, *Lives of the Sophists* 553).[7] Once again, the relocation from mainstream urban center to a rustic context (which in this account becomes a new "center") is constructed as a search for Hellenic purity.

In the *Heroikos*, the cult site of Protesilaos is strategically marked as a hyperhellenic space. In literary terms, it is constructed from a series of pastoral features that are drawn from the central texts of the Hellenic heritage: in particular the locus both *amoenus* and *classicus*, Plato's *Phaedrus*, bulks large in the text's intertextual self-substantiation. There are, however, more pronounced indices of the emblematic Hellenism of the landscape. Even the nightingales, the vinegrower reports, "Atticize" here (ἐναττικίζουσιν, *Her.* 5.4). The nightingale, however, is an elegiac bird: the Phoenician responds that from what he has heard, they do not "lament" (θρηνεῖν), they merely sing here—this hint of tragedy, albeit tragedy supplanted by pleasure, may allude subtly to the narrative of the Athenian Procne, who suffered violent rape at the hands of the Thracian tyrant Têreus (most famously in Sophocles' play of that name). The theme of violent intrusion of Thracians is also prominent in an earlier episode in the *Heroikos*, in which the vinegrower reports the attempts by one of the local potentates (οἱ δυνατοί), the suggestively named Xeinis ("Foreigner"), to acquire the cult site forcibly, whereupon Protesilaos forcibly blinded him (*Her.* 4.2). Although an apparently Greek Chersonesian, Xeinis occupies the negative role in a series of overlapping polarities: urban-rural, wealthy-peasant, outsider-insider. The cult site of Protesilaos is constructed as a space protected from incursion by quasi-tyrannical quasi-Thracians.

On the other hand, the Chersonesus is positioned on the ful-

[7] A more complex story, however, than is often assumed: I attempt to unpack it at Whitmarsh, *Greek Literature*, 105–8.

crum between East and West, the meeting point for both a Greek vinegrower and a Phoenician sailor. Protesilaos, the in-between figure par excellence, embodies the geographical liminality of his shrine. Homer refers to the "half-built house" (δόμος ἡμιτελής, *Il.* 2.701; compare Catullus 68.74–75) he began with his wife. Philostratus underlines his junctural status, in terms of religion (he is semidivine: *Her.* 7.3; 16.4) and age (he is an ephebe: *Her.* 10.2). He died *just as* he alighted on the shore, *just when* he had married, and he has his cult site at the exact point where the Hellenic meets the nonhellenic. This cultural difference between the two is thematized in the dialogue, as the Phoenician protests that the vinegrower is favoring the Greeks (*Her.* 19.1–2; 19.8), and the latter teases the former for his partiality toward the Trojans (*Her.* 20.1). If this landscape is—or can be constructed as—hyperhellenic, it is also a boundary, a site of negotiation and problematization.

The setting, moreover, alludes to Herodotus's narrative of the Persian Wars, the paradigmatic exploration of relations between Greek and barbarian. At one point, the vinegrower points to the temple "in which the Mede committed sacrilege in our forefathers' time. It was because of this, they say, that even the preserved fish came back to life" (ἐφ' ᾧ καὶ τὸ τάριχος ἀναβιῶναί φασι, *Her.* 9.5). The allusion (signaled by "they say," which serves as the marker of a kind of "Alexandrian footnote")[8] is to the end of Herodotus's text, where Xerxes' governor Artayktes deviously gains permission to ransack Protesilaos's temple by describing the latter to his master simply as "a Greek who attacked your territory and rightly died for it" (ἀνδρὸς Ἕλληνος . . . ὃς ἐπὶ γῆν τὴν σὴν στρατευσάμενος δίκης κυρήσας ἀπέθανε, Herodotus *Hist.* 9.116; cf. 7.33). The horrible irony is that Artayktes employs this pretext to effect a transgressive incursion himself, into the sacred space of the temple—and is subjected to divine vengeance, including the preserved fish (τάριχος) coming to life (a prognostication of the reanimation of the "corpse" [τάριχος] of Protesilaos) as a result. Geographical boundaries in Herodotus are protected by supernatural powers.[9] Philostratus's

[8] That is, an appeal to the reader's specific knowledge of an intertext masquerading as a reference to a generalized tradition; see Stephen Hinds, *Allusion and Intertext: Dynamics of Appropriation in Roman Poetry* (Cambridge and New York: Cambridge University Press, 1998), 2.

[9] James Romm, *Herodotus* (New Haven: Yale University Press, 1998), 77–93; also Deborah Boedeker, "Protesilaos and the End of Herodotus' *Histories*," *Classical Antiquity* 7/1 (1988): 42, and esp. 45: "As a hero buried at the entrance to the Hellespont, and one not fated to survive a hostile crossing between the continents,

knowing echo of Herodotean narrative, the paradigmatic exploration of the cultural-political-sacral-cosmic ramifications of military invasion, serves once again to reinforce the construction of Protesilaos as the protector of this enclosed, Hellenic space (this in turn also lends a retrospective depth to the account of Protesilaos's blinding of the appropriative Xeinis at *Her.* 4.2). It also reminds us, however, that identity is most insistently defined where it is most at risk; that is to say, boundaries can only be imagined at the moment of their transgression.

The liminality of the siting invokes the interpretative crisis that Daniel L. Selden has named "syllepsis":[10] like the Chersonesus, the text is equipoised between East and West and can be approached from either side. Indeed, to a degree, it *must* be approached as an outsider. The protected space of the cult site and the protected knowledge of Protesilean revelations inevitably construct the reader as an interloper, an invader into this privileged space. Despite the welter of more-or-less familiar literary reference points, the central "revelations" of the text are, by definition, anticanonical, predicated as they are on an idiosyncratic, exclusive, and wholly "private" modality of knowledge gathering: the ξυνουσία, or direct, epiphanic encounter with a deity.[11] The reader's status as outsider is also enforced by the dialogic form. The familiar world of Philostratus's readers lies (by presumption) west of the Chersonesus, but their point of access into the protected spaces of this text is focalized through the Phoenician easterner. Although the *Heroikos* parades the culturally iconic status of pastoral landscape, then, the reader's status—insider or outsider? resident or invader?—is put on the line.

If the *Heroikos* is a dialogic or sylleptic text at the level of cultural identity, it also exposes the reader to a cunning performativity in relation to social identity. As is now well understood, the distinction between elite and nonelite is conventionally articulated in the literature of the period through the polarity of "the educated"

Protesilaos colors Herodotus' logos about the Persian invasion of Europe. His vengeance against Artayktes suggests a broader justice directed against the entire armada."

[10] Daniel L. Selden, "Genre of Genre," in *The Search for the Ancient Novel* (ed. James Tatum; Baltimore: Johns Hopkins University Press, 1994), 39–64.

[11] See Mantero, *Ricerche*, 64–68, interpreting the focus on ξυνουσία "straight," that is, as evidence of the text's religious dimension.

(πεπαιδευμένοι) and the "rustic" (ἄγροικοι).[12] I wish to turn now to consider how this quasi-pastoral text implicates and interrogates the reader's implied self-construction as an urban sophisticate in its dialogic exploration of identity.

The first sections of the text (*Heroikos* 1–5) establish the rural setting, and this is at first blush constructed as an idealized golden age offset against the decadence of the *polis* (a strong theme in the literature of the age: Dio Chrysostom's *Euboikos* is only the most prominent example).[13] The Phoenicians represent, paradigmatically, the vices of the city. The vinegrower is quick to note the sailor's extravagant dress, commenting that "Ionian Sybaris has captivated all Phoenicia at once; and there, I think, one would be prosecuted for *not* living luxuriously" (Σύβαρις Ἰωνικὴ τὴν Φοινίκην κατέσχεν ὁμοῦ πᾶσαν, καὶ γραφὴν ἐκεῖ ἄν τις, οἶμαι, φύγοι μὴ τρυφῶν, *Her.* 1.1). He proceeds to observe that Phoenicians "have earned a negative reputation" (διαβέβλησθε) for being "money-lovers and nibblers" (φιλοχρήματοί τε καὶ τρῶκται, *Her.* 1.3). This allusion to the Phoenicians' "reputation" constitutes another "Alexandrian footnote": Homer uses the rare word "nibblers" (τρῶκται) of the Phoenicians in the *Odyssey* (15.416; cf. 14.289), while Plato refers to the "money-loving" (φιλοχρήματον) aspect of the Phoenicians in the *Republic* (436a).

Commerce and its absence become the central focus of the ethical polarization of Phoenician and vinegrower. The former, apparently piqued by the charge laid against his people, asks whether the vinegrower is not himself affected by any commercial pressures, or whether instead he buries his wine in the ground like Maron (another Odyssean reference: see *Od.* 9.196–211, although Homer has no mention of burying the wine). The vinegrower counters with an equally Homeric riposte: Cyclopes, he says, have no need for money, but farmers do, in order to make a livelihood and in order to hire labor (*Her.* 1.5–7). Even so, he himself does not deal with merchants, nor "do I even know what the drachma is" (οὐδὲ τὴν δραχμὴν ὅ τι ἐστὶ γινώσκω, *Her.* 1.7), an assertion which clearly has more to it than meets the eye (and to which I shall return

[12] See in general Simon Swain, *Hellenism and Empire: Language, Classicism, and Power in the Greek World A.D. 50–250* (Oxford: Clarendon, 1996), 113–14; Whitmarsh, *Greek Literature*, 100–101. This polarity is of course central to Longus *Daphnis and Chloe*: on the self-conscious play between naïveté and knowingness in *Daphnis and Chloe*, see especially R. L. Hunter, *A Study of Daphnis and Chloe* (Cambridge and New York: Cambridge University Press, 1983), 45 and 59.

[13] Hunter, *Study*, 119 n. 29.

presently). The attack on mercantilism reinforces the paradigmatic status of the two interlocutors, the Phoenician embodying urban commerce and the rural vinegrower the uncomplicated generosity of the land. The Phoenician's response styles the vinegrower's barter economy as a golden age: "That is a golden marketplace that you are talking of" (χρυσῆν ἀγορὰν λέγεις, *Her.* 2.1).

The countryside is thus constructed as a place of freedom from mercantile values; indeed, it is even metaphysically defended against commercial appropriation, as Xeinis the now-blind Chersonesian has discovered (*Her.* 4.2). It is, moreover, consistently presented in positive terms as a place of divinity and eroticized beauty. When the two speakers relocate to another spot to exchange stories (an obvious reworking of Plato *Phaedrus* 227a–230e),[14] the Phoenician comments that the fragrance from the flowers is "pleasant" (ἡδύ, *Her.* 3.3), a word with strongly metapoetical pastoral connotations.[15] The vinegrower replies "What do you mean? Pleasant? It's divine!" (τί λέγεις ἡδύ; θεῖον, *Her.* 3.4). This countryside is constructed as hyperpastoral, an especially privileged space. Hence the superlative-heavy description: the cult site is, according to the Phoenician, "the most pleasant and divine . . . portion of the land" (τὸ μέρος τοῦ ἀγροῦ . . . ἥδιστον τε . . . καὶ θεῖον, *Her.* 5.2; cf. ἥδιστα, ἀλυπότατα, ὑπερμήκη, *Her.* 5.2–3). The language of divinity is used to describe a site that transcends "normal" description, or, better, it marks the failure of received language, including (self-reflexively) that of the pastoral literary tradition, to generate an adequate simulacrum of a space that is (only just) beyond the reader's imagination. Philostratus's (non-)descriptive strategy abuts the discourse of the sublime, as articulated by Pseudo-Longinus and—according to a scintillating article by James I. Porter—as practised by Pausanias in his topographic descriptions. "Sublimity in its most startling form," writes Porter, "is to be found in the won-

[14] Michael B. Trapp, "Plato's *Phaedrus* in the Second Century," in *Antonine Literature* (ed. D. A. Russell; Oxford: Clarendon, 1990), 171, with copious contemporary parallels.

[15] Thanks primarily to its programmatic placement at the start of Theocritus *Idyll* 1: see Richard Hunter, *Theocritus: A Selection* (Cambridge and New York: Cambridge University Press, 1999), 70, on Theocritus; and Hunter, *Study*, 92–97, on later theorizations of ἡδονή and its close ally, γλυκύτης. A significant parallel to Philostratus's usage comes at Achilles Tatius *The Adventures of Leucippe and Cleitophon* 1.2.3 (another reworking of the *Phaedrus*; see Trapp, "Plato's *Phaedrus*," 171): "a place like this is altogether sweet and appropriate for erotic stories" (πάντως δὲ ὁ τοιοῦτος τόπος ἡδὺς καὶ μύθων ἄξιος ἐρωτικῶν). See further Martin, "A Good Place to Talk."

drous and the miraculous, and above all in what lies beyond reach in the present."[16] This ancient cult site, suffused with ancient, indescribable divinity, is awesomely sublime, a decayed relic of a formerly great past and a location reanimated by a living presence:

> καταλείπεται δὲ αὐτοῦ ὁρᾷς ὡς ὀλίγα. τότε δέ, οἶμαι, χαρίεν τε ἦν καὶ οὐ μικρόν, ὡς ἔστι τοῖς θεμελίοις ξυμβαλέσθαι. τὸ δὲ ἄγαλμα τοῦτο βέβηκε μὲν ἐπὶ νεώς, τὸ γὰρ τῆς βάσεως σχῆμα πρῷρα, ἵδρυται δὲ ναύαρχος. περιτρίψας δὲ αὐτὸ ὁ χρόνος καὶ νὴ Δί' οἱ ἀλείφοντές τε καὶ ἐπισφραγιζόμενοι τὰς εὐχὰς ἐξηλλάχασι τοῦ εἴδους. ἐμοὶ δὲ οὐδὲν τοῦτο· αὐτῷ γὰρ ξύνειμι καὶ αὐτὸν βλέπω καὶ οὐδὲν ἄν μοι γένοιτο ἄγαλμα ἐκείνου ἥδιον.
>
> You see how little of the sanctuary is left. But back then it was lovely and not small, as can be made out from its foundations. This cult statue stood upon a ship, since its base has the shape of a prow, and the ship's captain dedicated it. Time has worn it away and, by Zeus, those who anoint it and seal their vows here have changed its shape. But this means nothing to me, for I spend time with him and see him, and no statue could be more pleasant than he. (*Her.* 9.5–7)

Furthermore, following a characteristically Philostratean metatextualism, the beauty of topography is intimately connected with the beauty of language and knowledge. The vinegrower's rural labor is explicitly cast as a form of philosophy (*Her.* 2.5–6), contrasting with the ruinous urban philosophy which he undertook earlier in his life (*Her.* 4.6). Literary culture and viticulture are metaphorically interlinked: *il faut cultiver son jardin.* Conversely, the land embodies intellectual values. The fertility of the soil ("there is no stinting," φθόνος οὐδείς, *Her.* 2.3; "everything on the land teems for me," βρύει μοι τὰ ἐν τῷ ἀγρῷ πάντα, *Her.* 4.10) is matched by the abundance of Protesilaos's wisdom ("he has wisdom to spare," περίεστι . . . καὶ σοφίας αὐτῷ, *Her.* 4.10). On hearing of the intellectual fertility of this space, the Phoenician responds with a praise of this site, on the grounds that "you do not only cultivate olives and grapes in it, but you also harvest divine and

[16] James I. Porter, "Ideals and Ruins: Pausanias, Longinus, and the Second Sophistic," in *Pausanias: Travel and Memory in Roman Greece* (ed. Susan E. Alcock, John F. Cherry, and Jaś Elsner; Oxford and New York: Oxford University Press, 2001), 71–72. The similarities between the literary effects of Protesilean narrative and the Longinian sublime are already adverted to by Mantero, *Ricerche*, 153–57. Philostratus may have used Pausanias as a source elsewhere in the *Heroikos*: see Rusten's contribution in this volume.

pure wisdom" (μὴ μόνον ἐλάας καὶ βότρυς ἐν αὐτῷ τρυγᾶς, ἀλλὰ καὶ σοφίαν δρέπῃ θείαν τε καὶ ἀκήρατον, *Her.* 4.11). The transferability of metaphors from Protesilaos's landscape to his knowledge signals that the latter partakes of the same fructose qualities. Moreover, the land itself seems to assume the mythical, storied aspect of Protesilaos himself. This is imaged in a later, ekphrastic description of Protesilaos himself that employs markedly vegetal imagery: "he teems with soft down, and his fragrance is sweeter than autumn myrtles" (ἁβρῷ ἰούλῳ βρύει καὶ ἀπόζει αὐτοῦ ἥδιον ἢ τὸ μετόπωρον τῶν μύρτων, *Her.* 10.2).[17] The verb βρύειν ("to teem") has already been used of the vegetal abundance of the cult site (*Her.* 4.10, quoted above), and "sweet" (ἡδύς) is, as we have seen, a key marker of pastoral landscape. In this divine, hyperpastoral space, the hero's presence and the erotic tenor of his myths inhabit the very soil of the land.

One of the many messages of the *Heroikos* is that the landscape is even now—despite the passing of time, and our hypermodern skepticism and sophistication—inhabited by traditional, heroic energies.[18] Homeric Greece maintains a physical reality in the present. The mythical heroes of the past are not simply the stuff of tales told to children by their nurses, as the Phoenician puts it in his early, skeptical phase (*Her.* 7.10; 8.2); heroes inhabit, and share potency with, the landscape of their cult sites. The Achaeans, for example, embraced Achilles' tomb "and believed that they were embracing Achilles" (τὸν Ἀχιλλέα ᾤοντο περιβάλλειν, *Her.* 51.13). Enormous footprints (ἴχνη), traces of Protesilaos's presence, are left in the soil of the cult site (*Her.* 13.2–3). These marks have a semiotic, almost graphematic quality, like the "spoors" (στίβη) of her brother that Electra tracks (compare ἰχνοσκοποῦσα) in Aeschylus's *Libation-Bearers*.[19] The past is legible in the text of the rural landscape. But it is deeply significant that Protesilaos's footsteps are said to be not always visible: when the hero runs too fast to leave a trace, the ground is ἄσημος, literally "without a sign/signifier" (*Her.*

[17] This is not so much evidence that Protesilaos was "originally" a vegetal god (so Mantero, *Ricerche*, 113–19; compare Boedeker, "Protesilaos," 37–38), as a marker of the intense interrelationship between hero and landscape in Philostratus's artfully contrived discourse.

[18] Samson Eitrem, "Zu Philostrats *Heroikos*," *Symbolae Osloenses* 8 (1929): 38–42.

[19] Aeschylus *Libation-Bearers* 228: see especially Simon Goldhill, *Language, Sexuality, and Narrative: The Oresteia* (Cambridge and New York: Cambridge University Press, 1984), 128–29.

13.3). If we are right about the self-reflexivity of this text, then this episode can be read as a meditation upon the process of reading as reinscribing, *reincorporating*, the plenitude of the past, even as it evanesces.

Reading is an act of traversal of the boundaries that separate past from present. When the Phoenician asks, prompted by a passing remark of the vinegrower's, when the heroes "were seen" (ὤφθησαν) on the plain of Troy, the vinegrower replies by correcting his interlocutor's tense:

> ὁρῶνται, ἔφην, ὁρῶνται ἔτι βουκόλοις τε τοῖς ἐν τῷ πεδίῳ καὶ νομεῦσι μεγάλοι καὶ θεῖοι, καὶ θεῶνται ἔστιν ὅτε ἐπὶ κακῷ τῆς γῆς.
>
> They *are* seen, I said, they *are still* seen great and divine to herdsmen and shepherds on the plain, and they are seen whenever there is evil upon the land. (*Her.* 18.2)

The word "still" (ἔτι), repeated twice, marks the crucial juncture between traditional narrative and actuality. Philostratus's vinegrower adopts the voice of Herodotean archaeology, as mediated through Hellenistic aetiology, recording the visible traces of the past.[20] In Philostratus's account, exceptionally, a mystical power grants the heroes of the past a capacity to transcend the etiolating effects of time, to retain across the ages an existential plenitude. And yet there is a palpable tension here: the present is inhabited by the past, but *only just*, and with a certain strain or surprise ("still" carries a concessive force: *even so, nevertheless*).

There is, however, a knowingly fictitious undercurrent to this idealized construction of a primitivist, hyperhellenic countryside. Let us return to the vinegrower's odd assertion that he does not know what a drachma is (*Her.* 3.2), an assertion the force of which seems to depend upon the very knowledge it denies. Pastoral innocence conventionally precludes such self-consciousness, or at least self-consciousness marks the puncturing of the hermetic pastoral space. When Virgil's Corydon tells himself "you are a rustic, Cory-

[20] The persistence of Greek tradition is signaled in Herodotus by such expressions as "still in my day" (ἔτι ἐς ἐμέ, *Hist.* 1.52). On this Herodotean device, see Wolfgang Rösler, "Die 'Selbsthistorisierung' des Autors: Zur Stellung Herodots zwischen Mündlichkeit und Schriftlichkeit," *Philologus* 135 (1991): 215–20, arguing that they demonstrate a new awareness of the fixity of the written text. The exact phrase is paralleled at *Hist.* 7.178 (cf. the slightly different use at 8.22); see also Pausanias *Description of Greece* 1.8.1; 1.10.5; 1.39.4; 3.16.8; 8.15.5; 8.23.7; 9.37.4; 10.12.4.

don" ("rusticus es, Corydon," *Eclogues* 2.56), this is not only a Theocritean resignation to failure in his pursuit of the urban Alexis;[21] it also represents the encroachment of civic consciousness onto the rural, the point of evanescence of the very premises that make pastoral possible.

One crucial marker of the self-conscious fictionalizing of the presentation of the countryside is the use of language and literary culture, an eminently Philostratean concern. The vinegrower speaks in perfect Attic, brandishing optatives and deictic iotas with a flourish. At one level, this is part of the standard texture of the Roman Greek countryside: the peasants in Dio Chrysostom's *Euboikos*, for example, puncture the surface of Lysianic naïveté with such showy words as ἁμηγέπη ("somehow or other").[22] Philostratus's vinegrower is, however, on any terms an extreme case: not only is his Greek faultlessly Attic, but also, as we have seen, right from the start he trades more-or-less recondite allusions (particularly Homeric) with the Phoenician sailor. Yet the paradoxical tradition of eloquent peasants is given a self-conscious spin. In what I take as a knowing play upon this topos, he makes the Phoenician sailor ask the eminently reasonable question, "How were you trained in speaking? You do not seem to me to be among the uneducated" (τὴν . . . φωνὴν . . . πῶς ἐπαιδεύθης; οὐ γάρ μοι τῶν ἀπαιδεύτων φαίνῃ, *Her.* 4.5). Herodes Atticus asks an almost identical question of Agathion, the autochthon from Marathon, in the *Lives of the Sophists* 553.[23] But whereas Agathion responds that the countryside is the best source of education, the vinegrower of the *Heroikos* turns out to be an impersonator of a rustic: he spent the first part of his life "in the city" (ἐν ἄστει), "being educated and philosophizing" (διδασκάλοις χρώμενοι καὶ φιλοσοφοῦντες, *Her.* 4.6); eventually,

[21] Modeled primarily, of course, on Polyphemus's famous (and famously problematic) self-conscious address to himself at Theocritus *Idylls* 11.72 (ὦ Κύκλωψ Κύκλωψ, πᾷ τὰς φρένας ἐκπεπότασαι, "Cyclops, Cyclops, where has your mind wandered?"). See further Ian DuQuesnay, "From Polyphemus to Corydon: Virgil, *Eclogues* 2, and the *Idylls* of Theocritus," in *Creative Imitation in Latin Literature* (ed. David West and Tony Woodman; Cambridge and New York: Cambridge University Press, 1979), 56–58, noting Virgil's introduction of the motif of *rustic* self-identification (which may, however, allude to Eunica's rejection of her rustic lover at Theocritus *Idylls* 20.3–4).

[22] D. A. Russell, ed., *Dio Chrysostom,* Orations *VII, XII, XXXVI* (Cambridge and New York: Cambridge University Press, 1990), 116, on this term as "a conspicuous Atticism."

[23] Whitmarsh, *Greek Literature*, 106.

his fortunes sank so low that he consulted Protesilaos in desperation, who advised him "change your clothes" (μεταμφίασαι, *Her.* 4.9). The vinegrower presently understood that this was a suggestion to change his mode of life (τὸ τοῦ βίου σχῆμα, *Her.* 4.10). So the vinegrower is not a "real" peasant, but a transvestite. Appearances can be deceptive—a lesson both for the Phoenician and for the reader, who may have been misled into believing that this is a conventionally "unrealistic" account of Atticizing peasants.

The *Heroikos* is centrally about the saturation of the present with the rich limpidity of the Greek heritage: "the ghosts of the past . . . return in material form and hover about the scenes of their former heroic existence."[24] But they are ghosts nonetheless, absent presences, easy for the casual (or skeptical) eye to miss. The *Heroikos* offers its readers a privileged insight into the art of reading the rich texture of landscape. The informed reader comes to know that the horizontal plane of geographical space is intersected by vertical shafts of historical experience. The education of the Phoenician becomes paradigmatic of this intense understanding of space: where formerly he thought of the Chersonesus as a stopping-off point, a place of transition between destination and arrival, he now comes to appreciate its value on its own terms. (Analogously, on the narrative axis he comes to understand digressions as a form of "profit" [ἐπικέρδειαν]—to use his own mercantile idiom—on their own terms [*Her.* 53.3].) There are strong continuities between Philostratus's construction of geographical space as the repository of identity and that of Pausanias: the subject of the latter's narrative accumulation, famously encapsulated at one point by the phrase "everything Greek" (πάντα . . . τὰ Ἑλληνικά, *Description of Greece* 1.26.4), is later glossed as "the most memorable phenomena in both stories and sights" (γνωριμώτατα . . . ἔν τε λόγοις καὶ θεωρήμασιν, *Description of Greece* 1.39.3). The "sights" are the objects of the traveler's perception, but it is the intellectual and imaginative pleasure that accrues from the "stories" which accords the sights their value. There is seeing, and then there is *understanding*. As Lucian writes, "There is not the same law about looking at sights for ordinary people and for educated people" (οὐχ ὁ αὐτὸς περὶ τὰ θεάματα νόμος ἰδιωταῖς τε καὶ πεπαιδευμένοις, *The Hall* 2). The visual differential that operates in the *Heroikos* is in terms not so much of class and education (in the received sense), or even of religious initiation

[24] Zeitlin, "Visions and Revisions," 214; see further pp. 213–17, 255–62.

(in any formal guise), as of *sympathy*: it is a willingness to suspend the brutal skepticism of a prosaic age that qualifies the insightful viewer to understand this landscape.

At the same time, the *Heroikos* parades an ongoing self-consciousness about its own intractable textuality; after all, rewriting the "true story" of the Trojan War is by now a deeply established element in the sophistic repertoire.[25] Is this text a pious homage,[26] or a sophistic joke?[27] An unanswerable question, but this unanswerability is meaningful: the text teasingly strains its readers' credibility with the marvelous proposition of a metaphysical dynamism still permeating the landscape of Greece. The Phoenician's conversion from skepticism to belief provides one model for the reader, but it is an extreme model which also serves as a kind of challenge. Can we—*could* we—share in his swift metamorphosis from sophisticated hypercritic to drooling mythomaniac? A question that readers will have to decide for themselves, but the implications are profound for one's sense of self, or of how "Greek" one is; or (perhaps better), of *how one is Greek*.

[25] Graham Anderson, *The Second Sophistic: A Cultural Phenomenon in the Roman Empire* (London: Routledge, 1993), 174–76; Stefan Merkle, "Telling the True Story of the Trojan War: The Eyewitness Account of Dictys of Crete," in *The Search for the Ancient Novel* (ed. James Tatum; Baltimore: Johns Hopkins University Press, 1994), 183–96; Zeitlin, "Visions and Revisions."

[26] Eitrem, "Zu Philostrats *Heroikos*," 1–5; Mantero, *Ricerche*, 13–14.

[27] Ulrich von Wilamowitz-Moellendorff, *Der Glaube der Hellenen* (2 vols.; Berlin: Weidmann, 1931–1932; repr., Basel: Schwabe, 1956), 2:514; Graham Anderson, *Philostratus: Biography and* Belles Lettres *in the Third Century A.D.* (London: Croom Helm, 1986), 241–57.

The αἶνοι of the *Heroikos* and the Unfolding Transformation of the Phoenician Merchant

Jennifer K. Berenson Maclean

Characters in classical literature, whether epic, novel, or biography, have sometimes been construed as single-dimensional, static, and "flat,"[1] the idea that character might change over time deemed largely the product of Christianity's concern with the inner life.[2] Set up in stark contrast to Achilles, Odysseus, and their ilk were biblical characters, who rather than being fixed were "in the process of becoming."[3] This portrayal of biblical characters may hold some truth,[4] but the sweeping judgment on classical figures can no longer stand. Despite his tenacious demand to receive rightful honor, Achilles is ultimately not a flat character. His confrontation with Priam in Book 24 of the *Iliad* ends with his transformation into a more humane figure, who is able to see and respond to the pain of another—even of an enemy.[5] Likewise, a gradual shift in studies of biography is taking place, seeing the possibility of more complex

[1] Robert Scholes and Robert Kellogg, *The Nature of Narrative* (Oxford and New York: Oxford University Press, 1966), 161–64. Scholes and Kellogg utilize E. M. Forster's distinction between "flat" and "round" characters. E. M. Forster, *Aspects of the Novel* (New York: Harcourt, Brace, and Co., 1927), 103–18. On biography, note the oft-repeated dictum that ancient biographers showed no interest in a character's development; instead, character was linked to an individual's essence, and the episodes of a βίος were intended to display that constant essence. See, e.g., Charles H. Talbert, *What Is a Gospel? The Genre of the Canonical Gospels* (Philadelphia: Fortress, 1977), 3 and 16.

[2] Scholes and Kellogg, *The Nature of Narrative*, 165.

[3] Scholes and Kellogg, *The Nature of Narrative*, 123.

[4] See, e.g., Robert Alter, *The Art of Biblical Narrative* (New York: Basic Books, 1981), 114–30.

[5] Gregory Nagy, *The Best of the Achaeans: Concepts of the Hero in Archaic Greek Poetry* (Baltimore: Johns Hopkins University Press, 1979), 110 and the citations in the note. See also Graham Zanker, *The Heart of Achilles: Characterization and Personal Ethics in the "Iliad"* (Ann Arbor: University of Michigan Press, 1994), esp. 127–30.

characterization in later Greco-Roman biographies, while still acknowledging the heavy use of stereotyping.[6]

Forster's alternative to the "flat" character is the "round" character, who is complex, undergoes change, displays various motivations, and is "capable of surprising" the reader.[7] This polarized approach to characterization is clearly too simplistic, whereas Baruch Hochman's more complex taxonomy, which understands characters on a continuum between flat and round according to eight criteria, allows for greater precision and distinction in character analysis.[8] Hochman's work provides freedom to eschew labeling a character like the Phoenician as "flat" without having to defend his thoroughgoing complexity or believability.

Flat, round, or anywhere in the continuum between, characterizations of literary figures are in the end creations from particular perspectives.[9] The characterization of the Phoenician offered in this essay is the product of one cognizant of hero cult, the epic tradition, and many of the layered allusions in the text. A different reader—one with fewer sympathies toward the heroes and less knowledge about them—would no doubt come to a different reading of the Phoenician, seeing him as less coherent, dynamic, or complex. As it turns out, perspective—understood as the possession (or lack) of knowledge to interpret coded speech correctly—plays a significant role in the development of the Phoenician's character. Thus Philostratus recognized that texts (and characters) can be the object of multiple interpretations, although in contrast to the common postmodern refusal to privilege any one interpretation, Philostratus clearly prioritizes one reading of the Phoenician over others.

[6] Richard A. Burridge, *What Are the Gospels? A Comparison with Graeco-Roman Biography* (SNTSMS 70; Cambridge: Cambridge University Press, 1992), 124–25, 148–49, 182–84. See also Stephen Halliwell, "Traditional Greek Conceptions of Character," in *Characterization and Individuality in Greek Literature* (ed. Christopher Pelling; Oxford: Clarendon, 1990), 32–59. On the development of Pericles in Plutarch's biography, see Christopher Pelling, "Childhood and Personality in Greek Biography," in *Characterization and Individuality in Greek Literature* (ed. Christopher Pelling; Oxford: Clarendon, 1990), 232–33.

[7] Forster, *Aspects of the Novel*, 103–18. The quotation is from p. 118.

[8] Baruch Hochman, *Character in Literature* (Ithaca, N.Y., and London: Cornell University Press, 1985), 86–140. For a different critique of the applicability of Forster's terminology to ancient literature, see Margaret Anne Doody, *The True Story of the Novel* (New Brunswick, N.J.: Rutgers University Press, 1996), 126–31.

[9] Hochman, *Character in Literature*, 31–34, 38–39. This characterization is no doubt also highly influenced by modern, rather than ancient, conceptions of what constitutes a realistic and whole person. Hochman, *Character in Literature*, 55–57.

The Phoenician may well be the most interesting character of the *Heroikos* simply because he undergoes change and because the reader is given a window into the dynamics of his metamorphosis. Protesilaos's transformation occurred at death when his soul was freed from his body (*Her.* 7.3); the vinedresser's, when the hero ordered him to change his way of life (*Her.* 4.7–10). The latter is narrated briefly, the former a forbidden topic (*Her.* 2.9; 58.2). The Phoenician's transformation, however, spans the entirety of the dialogue and probably functioned as a model for the ancient reader. Hans Dieter Betz has suggested that the Phoenician's transformation entails the movement from skepticism to belief;[10] Tim Whitmarsh has termed it a "swift metamorphosis from sophisticated hypercritic to drooling mythomaniac."[11] I wish to suggest that the Phoenician's movement is more subtle than either of these options implies and that it is effected through a series of αἶνοι—coded speech—at first misunderstood, but eventually grasped.

Ellen Aitken and I have argued that the construction of foreignness is central to the purposes of the *Heroikos*.[12] This foray into characterization must therefore be guided by the observation that Philostratus is reconstituting the ancient topos of the foreigner. On the level of myth, a Phoenician might well represent the archetypical foreigner, but within the cultural realities of the third century C.E., such an identification is too simplistic. So the real question is not whether the Phoenician is a foreigner, but rather how Philostratus defined foreignness (and its opposite, Greekness) through the Phoenician's characterization.

We first meet the Phoenician through the eyes of the vinedresser, whom the Phoenician encounters at the very beginning of the dialogue. Although Phoenicia had been part of the Roman province of Syria since 64 B.C.E. and Greek cities and cultural institutions had flourished there since at least the reign of Antiochus IV Epiphanes, this region of the empire nevertheless retained the aura of cultural foreignness, perhaps due to the resilience of distinctive Syrian practices.[13] Thus the vinedresser's surprise that a Phoenician

[10] Betz, "Hero Worship and Christian Beliefs: Observations from the History of Religion on Philostratus's *Heroikos*," 29–31 in this volume.

[11] Tim Whitmarsh, "The Harvest of Wisdom: Landscape, Description, and Identity in the *Heroikos*," 249 in this volume.

[12] See the introduction to this volume (pp. xxiii–xxv).

[13] Fergus Millar, "The Problem of Hellenistic Syria," in *Hellenism in the East: Interaction of Greek and Non-Greek Civilizations from Syria to Central Asia after*

might wear Greek clothing (*Her.* 1.1) does not represent the historical reality of a distinctive Phoenician dress, but rather is a rhetorical strategy used to indicate the type of Greek culture that has molded this Phoenician. Ionian Sybaris—perhaps a reference to Miletus in particular—is labeled the culprit. The Ionians had long been considered as dedicated to luxury as were the Sybarites (Diodorus Siculus *Library* 8.18.2; *Suda*, s.v. Sybaritikais; see also Herodotus *Hist.* 6.21; Athenaeus *Deipnosophists* 12.518; Diodorus Siculus *Library* 8.20; Juvenal *Satires* 6.296), and the Phoenician openly tells the vinedresser that indulgence in luxury was the expected way of life (*Her.* 1.1). A few lines later the vinedresser pulls out the old slander of the Phoenicians as "money-loving and greedy rascals" (*Her.* 1.3; cf. Homer *Od.* 14.288–289), and once again the Phoenician makes no attempt to refute this reputation; his only response is to hint that the vinedresser is motivated by the same desires as he is (*Her.* 1.4), although the reader soon learns that the vinedresser lives in the world of the heroes, whose values are antithetical to those of commerce and self-indulgence. The text thus from the start plays upon the established contrast of city-dweller vs. rustic, in which authentic Greek values are to be found in the countryside rather than in the rarified and decadent world of the city.[14] While the Phoenician accepts the vinedresser's portraiture without any regret or embarrassment, Philostratus's audience is no doubt expected to categorize this self-indulgence as a trait of non-Greek—Persian, if one has Herodotus in mind—rather than of authentic Greek culture. The Phoenician, in both name and primary cultural commitments, is a foreigner.

In contrast to the vinedresser's casting of him as non-Greek, the Phoenician presents himself as no stranger to Greek literature, religious practices, or philosophy. By his own account, he was raised on the tales of the poets (*Her.* 7.10), and from the very beginning of the dialogue he demonstrates his knowledge of the poets by his ability to recognize poetic allusions and to create his own, seemingly without effort. For example, after the vinedresser describes at length his rejection of money and the marketplace, the Phoenician immediately recognizes the allusion to Hesiod's golden age (*Her.*

Alexander (ed. Amélie Kuhrt and Susan M. Sherwin-White; Berkeley: University of California Press, 1987), 110–33; John D. Grainger, *The Cities of Seleukid Syria* (Oxford and New York: Oxford University Press, 1990).

[14] Whitmarsh, "The Harvest of Wisdom," 238–39.

2.1; cf. Hesiod *Works and Days* 109–126). It is at this point that the heroes, the inhabitants of the golden age, are first mentioned in the text—by the Phoenician, surprisingly not by the vinedresser. What else does the Phoenician know from the poets? Concerning Protesilaos, he knows that this hero hailed from Thessaly (*Her.* 2.7; cf. Homer *Il.* 2.695–710), that he died before engaging the enemy at Troy (*Her.* 7.2; cf. Homer *Il.* 2.701–702), and that he returned from the dead because of his devotion to Laodameia, a story not narrated in Homer, but widely elaborated on in later literature (*Her.* 2.10; cf. Apollodorus *Epitmore* 3.30; Hyginus *Fabulae* 103–104; Catullus 68; Ovid *Heroides* 13.153–157). Naturally, he knows of Achilles' "ruinous" anger (*Her.* 54.1; cf. Homer *Il.* 1.2) and that Achilles now dwells on an island in the Pontus (*Her.* 54.1; cf. Pindar *Nemean* 4.49; Euripides *Iphigeneia in Tauris* 436–438; *Aithiopis*). As for the *Odyssey*, he knows of Odysseus's encounter with the Sirens (*Her.* 8.13; cf. Homer *Od.* 12.154–200), with the dead in Hades (*Her.* 11.2; cf. Homer *Od.* 11.204–222, 390–394), and with the Lotus-Eaters (*Her.* 43.1; cf. Homer *Od.* 9.82–104). He also recognizes that there was no established story of a contest over a shield associated with the Achaean's battle against the Mysians (*Her.* 14.1). He is especially well acquainted with Hektor's exploits (*Her.* 19.1–2), and even the mention of Paris is enough to vex him (*Her.* 40.1). When it comes to literary *paideia*, the Phoenician displays more than adequate training to engage in conversation with the eloquent and educated vinedresser.

Nor can the Phoenician be accused of ignorance or skepticism of common Greek religious practices. He wanders into the sanctuary of Protesilaos while seeking an omen (*Her.* 1.2), he understands himself to be led in some sense by the gods (*Her.* 6.1), and by the vinedresser's account he is adept at dream interpretation (*Her.* 6.2–7). The Phoenician even proves himself to be attuned to the numinous presence in the sanctuary of Protesilaos (*Her.* 5.2–3). Nevertheless, the dialogue is filled with statements of his unbelief and, then later, his belief. What then does the Phoenician doubt? In contrast to his respectable knowledge about the heroes, whose existence in the past he does not seem to doubt, the Phoenician does not believe that they still appear to humans and have the power to affect their lives, for good or for ill (*Her.* 2.11–3.1; 7.9–10; 19.1); put another way, the Phoenician has not understood that the heroes are not limited by death, that their consciousness has been elevated by their association with the gods, and that the heroes can thus medi-ate truth to humans through oracular pronouncements (*Her.* 7.2–3). He is, nevertheless, an eager learner: he regrets his skepticism about the power of the heroes and presents himself as willing to go to excessive lengths to be persuaded by the vinedresser (*Her.* 3.1–2). It is difficult to evaluate the truthfulness of his regret, but his claim to perseverance will initially be proved false (see below). In any case, his religious practices are not distinctively Syrian, but rather are fully at home in the Greek world.

The Phoenician constructs the grounds of his disbelief in the language of observation and evidence: he "observes things according to nature, for which contemporary humans provide the measure" (*Her.* 7.9).[15] This statement positions him as part of the Greek philosophical tradition that asserted the trustworthiness of sense perception.[16] Thus the tales that entertained[17] him in his youth should not be accepted without detailed examination and questioning (οὐκ ἀβασανίστως, *Her.* 7.10). He rigorously demands that the vinedresser speak from his own experience and refrain from simply passing on the stories of others (*Her.* 8.2). This philosophical approach marks the Phoenician once again as a highly educated Greek.

What are we to make of the tension between the vinedresser's portrayal of the Phoenician as foreign (i.e., sybaritic) and the Phoenician's self-presentation as a highly educated, even religious, Greek? Herein lies the heart of Philostratus's construction of foreignness. The foreigners that concern him are not so much those who dwell beyond the borders of the empire, but those who live within, who despite their education, sophistication, and piety fail to embody the values and lifestyle of the Hellenic tradition. Philostra-

[15] The similarity of the final clause to Protagoras's famous dictum ("man is the measure of all things"; DK 80b1) is only superficial; the Phoenician's philosophical stance is in fact in direct contrast to that of Protagoras. See the discussion of Protagoras's teachings in Plato *Theaetetus* 151e–164d.

[16] Both Aristotelians and Epicureans held this position. On Aristotle's meaning of θεωρία, see W. K. C. Guthrie, *A History of Greek Philosophy* (6 vols.; Cambridge: Cambridge University Press, 1962–1981), 6:396–97. On Epicureanism, see, e.g., Norman W. DeWitt, *Epicurus and His Philosophy* (Cleveland and New York: Word, 1967), esp. ch. 11. I am indebted to Hans Zorn for his insight on this point.

[17] As the Phoenician becomes enamored once again with the stories of the heroes, he regains the pleasure of the stories (*Her.* 24.1; 25.18; cf. 7.10), but this time with an educative value more in accord with Plato's demand for the virtues of self-control (*Republic* Book 3).

tus utilized the topos of the foreigner to frame a discourse of internal rather than external critique.[18]

When the vinedresser complies with his demands for firsthand evidence (*Her.* 8.4–17), the Phoenician responds with his first statement of belief (*Her.* 8.18); subsequent stories about Protesilaos (*Her.* 9.1–16.5), again based for the most part on the vinedresser's personal knowledge, are greeted with similar statements of belief: "Finally I am on your side, vinedresser, and no one hereafter will disbelieve such stories" (*Her.* 18.1; cf. 16.6). The transformation of the Phoenician, however, extends considerably beyond the movement from skepticism to affirmation of belief.[19]

More revealing are the series of αἶνοι utilized both by the vinedresser to describe the Phoenician and by the Phoenician in acts of self-definition.[20] As Gregory Nagy has argued, in Pindar's diction αἶνος refers to the medium of praise poetry, and "[t]he **ainos** is an affirmation, a marked speech-act, made by and for a marked social group."[21] This social group consists of those who are skilled (σοφός) in interpreting the coded message, ethically noble (ἀγαθός), and part of this elite community (φίλος). This audience proves itself by

[18] Jennifer K. Berenson Maclean and Ellen Bradshaw Aitken, trans. *Flavius Philostratus: Heroikos* (SBLWGRW 1; Atlanta: Society of Biblical Literature, 2001), lxxxiii. Gregory Nagy, *Pindar's Homer: The Lyric Possession of an Epic Past* (Baltimore and London: Johns Hopkins University Press, 1990), 308. I do not deny the political impetus for the writing of the *Heroikos*. In fact, as the Phoenician moves from cultural foreigner to model Hellene, Philostratus offers a series of new "others" to take his place (*Her.* 4.2; 19.5–9; 20.2; 56.1–57.17). It is not possible here to enter into a detailed examination of these other "others." Let it suffice to say that their utter destruction is the persistent theme, with the last destruction—that of the Amazons—being the most complete and vengeful of them all. On Philostratus's concern with foreigners external to the empire, see the articles by Ellen Aitken and Rahim Shayegan in this volume.

[19] One of the difficulties with this formulation is that "belief" does not explicitly encompass the totality of the transformation, which includes commitment to the hero and to a particular ethical lifestyle. The Pauline use of πίστις and πιστεύω is enlightening in this regard. Dieter Georgi, "Who Is the True Prophet?" in *Paul and Empire: Religion and Power in Roman Imperial Society* (ed. Richard A. Horsley; Harrisburg, Penn.: Trinity Press International, 1997), 148–57, esp. 149; repr. from *HTR* 79 (1986): 100–126.

[20] These αἶνοι function similarly to Christopher Gill's concept of "character-markers," which include "character-indicating speeches and actions by the relevant figures and significant statements about them by the narrator or other figures." Christopher Gill, "The Character-Personality Distinction," in *Characterization and Individuality in Greek Literature* (ed. Christopher Pelling; Oxford: Clarendon, 1990), 7.

[21] Nagy, *Pindar's Homer*, 147–48.

being able to interpret rightly the poet's message; outsiders, however, will take away the wrong meaning.[22] As a "mode of discourse," αἶνοι appear in various poetic forms, and narratives (e.g., history, fable) can utilize αἶνοι as well, with the same social functions.[23] Careful attention to the αἶνοι in the *Heroikos* will allow us to chart the Phoenician's transformation from foreigner to friend (φίλος), from ignorant to wise (σοφός), from indulgent to noble (ἀγαθός). These αἶνοι constitute a shifting set of comparisons of the Phoenician with other heroic characters, primarily Odysseus.[24] The meaning of each αἶνος is gradually revealed from one αἶνος to the next, but the meaning of the last αἶνος is never fully resolved.

The first αἶνος occurs at the very beginning of the dialogue where the vinedresser queries the Phoenician: "Where are you going so proudly and ignoring everything at your feet?" (*Her.* 1.2). This coded reference to the philosopher Thales, who fell into a pit when he failed to pay attention to what was in front of his feet (see Plato *Theaetetus* 174a), is completely opaque to the Phoenician. By this association the vinedresser hints that the Phoenician may end up like Thales if he too pays more attention to the sky rather than what lies before his eyes (i.e., the sanctuary of Protesilaos and the world of the heroes). The right answer to the vinedresser's question would be "headed for danger because of an inappropriate focus" (as was the case with Thales); the Phoenician misses this hidden meaning entirely and proceeds to answer the question plainly, "I need a sign and an omen for good sailing" (*Her.* 1.2),[25] indicating his commitment to participating in the culture of luxury. The Phoenician fails to grasp the αἶνος and thus remains outside the circle of φίλοι, σοφοί, and ἀγαθοί. A further irony should not be lost. The Phoenician, who claims to be dedicated to close observation (*Her.* 7.9), turns out to have been as nonobservant as the ill-fated Thales (*Her.* 1.2); Protesilaos, however, is the quintessential examiner of

[22] Nagy, *Pindar's Homer*, 148.

[23] Nagy, *Pindar's Homer*, 149–50, 324, 329.

[24] According to Hochman (*Character in Literature*, 66), characters are often drawn through their interactions through parallel characters or situations. "These patterns provide not only the scaffolding on which we construct an understanding of his character but also the configuration of issues on which the novel's whole thematic structure finally rests." Hochman, *Character in Literature*, 71.

[25] The conflict between Odysseus and Palamedes that eventually leads to Palamedes' death (*Her.* 33.4–9) concerns exactly this issue: heavenly observation versus a chthonic source of authority and knowledge. On this point, see Maclean and Aitken, *Flavius Philostratus: Heroikos*, lxxxi–lxxxii.

Homer's poems (*Her.* 7.4) and the authoritative source of a truly reflective life.[26]

In the next αἶνος the vinedresser recalls an episode from Odysseus's wanderings: just as Odysseus encountered Hermes and learned from him about the *moly*, the magical antidote to Circe's enchantments, so the Phoenician will become wise through conversation with Protesilaos (*Her.* 6.1; cf. Homer *Od.* 10.274–306). The Phoenician believes the vinedresser has likened him to Odysseus, a comparison he accepts, quibbling only with the adjective "perplexed" (*Her.* 6.2). He later promotes his association with Odysseus in *Her.* 8.13, where he declares himself "bound to my ship" (an allusion to Odysseus's machinations to hear the Sirens; Homer *Od.* 12.154–200) and implies that he will only allow the vinedresser's storytelling to entertain him until he is able to continue his voyage. His purported willingness to follow the vinedresser "even beyond the interior of Thrace" (*Her.* 3.2) or "beyond Okeanos" (*Her.* 8.13) apparently was no more than bravado. The Phoenician also takes from the αἶνος the importance that Protesilaos will play in his future: he interprets the αἶνος in the context of his dream and concludes that just as the *moly* facilitated Odysseus's homecoming, so only talking about the heroes ("cataloguing them on the ship") will bring favorable winds, allowing him to embark (*Her.* 6.3–6).

Yet the Phoenician has not fully grasped the αἶνος, as reading further in the text proves. First, likening the merchant to Odysseus is no compliment at all, since Odysseus is revealed to be the most disgraceful of all heroes for his fatal rivalry with Palamedes, whose knowledge he did not acknowledge and whose advice he did not heed (see especially *Her.* 33.1–34.7). Second, the allusion to Odysseus's encounter with Hermes implies more than just a superficial similarity between two figures who happen to learn something from a divine being; rather—and this is the core of the αἶνος—the allusion hints at the *kind* of knowledge needed by the Phoenician and the *kind* of predicament he faces. Circe's magic had turned Odysseus's companions into swine (Homer *Odyssey* 10); their only chance for a homecoming was their retransformation into human beings through the *moly*. Conversation with the vinedresser thus offers the Phoenician a similarly transformative antidote: Protesi-

[26] The Phoenician is also described as "going so proudly" (βαδίζεις . . . μετέωρος, *Her.* 1.2). μετέωρος is used twice in the dialogue to describe the heroes (of Protesilaos and of Ajax; *Her.* 13.3; 35.2). Perhaps the vinedresser is also implying that the Phoenician is improperly mimicking a stance only appropriate for a hero.

laos's knowledge has the power to transform the Phoenician from beast (i.e., foreignlike self-indulgent money-lover) to human being (i.e., Greek). The city vs. rustic dichotomy has now been superseded by the more charged animal vs. human dichotomy. The Phoenician, of course, has yet to learn the truth about Odysseus, and he is blind to the hidden implications of the vinedresser's words, but his ability to decode at least a portion of this αἶνος has provided a response to the first. Where is the Phoenician going (*Her.* 1.2)? To hear the stories of the heroes.

The next two αἶνοι continue the process of the Phoenician's transformation from outsider to insider (i.e., φίλος, σοφός, and ἀγαθός). The Phoenician demonstrates his grasp of the vinedresser's second αἶνος through a third, partially unconscious αἶνος that comes soon after his declaration of belief in the reality and power of the heroes. No longer is the point of reference the disgraceful Odysseus.[27]

> Not even the wild beasts listened as intently to Orpheus when he sang as I, listening to you, prick up my ears, rouse my mind, and gather every detail into my memory. I even consider myself to be one of those encamped at Troy, so much have I been possessed by the demigods about whom we are speaking. (*Her.* 23.2)

The Phoenician aptly likens himself to a wild beast being tamed by listening to the stories of the heroes. Whereas in the previous αἶνος, he assumed that he was the parallel to Odysseus, he now acknowledges himself to be the beast, like the companions of Odysseus. The taming of the wild beasts through Orpheus's singing is a common theme in literature and art and implies the same transformation (from beast to human) as the first Odyssean allusion.[28] The stories, received with the attitude of belief, have begun the transformation of the Phoenician, and the *moly* is taking effect. This αἶνος not only looks back to the previous one, but it also remains partly unresolved, hiding a warning not fully grasped by the

[27] Perhaps the Phoenician has taken to heart the fate of Odysseus related in *Her.* 21.1–8.

[28] W. K. C. Guthrie, *Orpheus and Greek Religion: A Study of the Orphic Movement* (London: Methuen, 1952; repr. Princeton: Princeton University Press, 1993), 21–23, 40–41. Note the association of foreigner and beast in this description of Orpheus: "by his playing and singing won over the Greeks, changed the hearts of barbarians and tamed wild beasts" (Pseudo-Callisthenes *Alexander Romance* 1.42.6.7; cited in Guthrie, *Orpheus and Greek Religion*, 40).

Phoenician. The beasts that listen to Orpheus are potentially dangerous. They are "possessed" by supernatural forces, not unlike the ecstatic women who dismembered him (*Her.* 28.9–13).[29] Moreover, Orpheus is a riddler himself, and interpreting his words incorrectly can have disastrous consequences, as Cyrus learned (*Her.* 28.11–12). The αἶνος thus leaves the attentive reader uncertain whether the transformation of the Phoenician will result in madness or a sound mind and whether he will ultimately be able to grasp the heroes' message.

As the catalog of the heroes (*Her.* 25.18–42.4) draws to a close, the Phoenician offers another αἶνος that again recalls the wanderings of Odysseus. The Phoenician likens himself to those from Odysseus's crew who, having tasted the lotus, were unwilling to return home (*Her.* 43.1; cf. *Od.* 9.82–104). To the outsider, this allusion would bring negative connotations—the lack of a homecoming. But from the Phoenician's perspective the motif of the return has been subverted: the Phoenician no longer wishes to gain a homecoming (i.e., a return to the life of a merchant), and now stands in marked contrast to Odysseus. The Phoenician has tasted the lotus—the prophetic powers of the heroes—and he is addicted. To sever him from the fount of heroic wisdom would require force (another interesting play on his earlier statement that he was "bound" to his ship) and would be a cause of great lamentation. In stark contrast to his earlier refusal to delay his business venture (*Her.* 8.13), the Phoenician now demonstrates that his devotion to the heroes supersedes his earlier devotion to the acquisition of wealth: "Farewell then to the ship and all that is on board! The soul's cargo is sweeter to me and more profitable" (*Her.* 53.3). He is now φίλος, σοφός, and ἀγαθός, and the vinedresser can declare that his transformation from beast to human—from barbarian to Greek—from decadent Greek to authentic Greek—is complete: "You are of sound mind [ὑγιαίνεις], my guest, thinking in this way" (*Her.* 53.4). His possession by the heroic daimons has not led to madness and destruction, but to wholeness and perception.

This recognition of the Phoenician's transformation is immediately followed by the stories of heroic initiation (*Her.* 53.4–23). Since the Phoenician accepts the superhuman consciousness of

[29] Philostratus seems to play with the double meaning of κατέχω (in *Her.* 23.2, "to be possessed"). In *Her.* 28.9, the head of Orpheus "resides" (κατασχοῦσα) in Lesbos, and in *Her.* 28.11, Cyrus thinks he will "occupy" (καθέξων) certain territories. Both figures experience a similar fate of dismemberment by frenzied women.

Protesilaos (*Her*. 43.3), is obedient to hero's requirement of silence (*Her*. 44.5; 55.1; cf. 58.2), rejects luxury, and is capable of interpreting αἶνοι, he is now ready to hear the stories of initiation.[30]

The dialogue concludes with a final αἶνος. At first the ending seems painfully anticlimactic: the Phoenician is utterly devoted to Protesilaos and recognizes the special status of the vinedresser (*Her*. 58.1); nevertheless, he wants to return the following day to hear stories connected to rivers (the Kôkytos, Pyriphlegethôn, and Akherousias) and the judgments of Hades (*Her*. 58.3). Precisely what relevance do such stories have to the previous stories of the heroes? How is this a fitting completion of the heroic stories? The rivers mentioned in *Her*. 58.3 were all located in the ancient imagination in Epirus, near the entrance to Hades (see, e.g., Homer *Od*. 10.513–514; Aeschylus *Agamemnon* 1160; Plato *Phaedo* 113a–114c), and thus the Phoenician's αἶνος evokes Odysseus's trip to the Underworld (*Odyssey* 11). This perilous journey was necessary for Odysseus to achieve his homecoming. But recall that the Phoenician has refused the Odyssean homecoming; for the Phoenician the borders of Hades instead represent his final destination.

Gregory Nagy has argued that the river Styx is the elixir of life, holding the possibilities of immortality when it is approached in the right way, at the right time.[31] That the mention of these rivers hints at immortality is supported by the preceding sentence, in which Protesilaos's immortality—his returning to life—is raised a final time and the requirement of silence honored by the Phoenician. Plato's *Phaedo* supports this direction of interpretation: After describing the geography of Hades (*Phaedo* 112a–113c), including all the rivers mentioned here, Socrates turns to the fates of various types of characters (*Phaedo* 113d–115a). Of interest here is his description of the final group:

> But those who are found to have excelled in holy living are freed from these regions within the earth and are released as from prisons; they mount upward into their pure abode and dwell upon the earth. And of these, all who have duly purified themselves by philosophy live henceforth altogether without bodies, and pass to still more beautiful abodes which it is not easy to describe. (*Phaedo* 114b–c Fowler [LCL])

[30] On the importance of initiation in hero cult, see Casey Dué and Gregory Nagy, "Illuminating the Classics with the Heroes of Philostratus," esp. 60–65 in this volume.

[31] Nagy, *Best of the Achaeans*, 189.

Although the Underworld holds nothing promising from a Homeric viewpoint (as the memorable words of Achilles prove; Homer *Od.* 11.488–491), the *Heroikos* shares certain philosophical perspectives with the *Phaedo*—death as freedom from the prison of the body, pleasure as an impediment to human fulfillment (*Her.* 7.3; see also Plato *Phaedo* 80e–84b; 114e–115a)—that open the possibility of a radically different view of death. Corinne Pache rightly notes the Phoenician's persistence in wanting to hear these stories and that the etymological connotations of these rivers point toward the lamentation of the hero: Kôkytos ("wailing" or "shrieking"), Pyriphlegethôn ("blazing fire"), and Akherousias ("woe").[32] This αἶνος thus hints that a trip to the Underworld would be the ultimate fulfillment of association with the hero: the attainment of immortalization. In the end this αἶνος remains enigmatic in its details. Death, lamentation for the hero, and immortalization are all evoked, but the hope held out by the Phoenician is something that must be experienced rather than narrated. Philostratus artfully refuses to tell such a story, mimicking in narrative the silence required by cult.[33]

Through a chain of interconnected αἶνοι, each individual riddle partially interpreting the previous, the Phoenician is continually redefined. The first αἶνος (Thales) hints that he is lacking in true wisdom, a judgment his inability to decode the αἶνος confirms. The second αἶνος (Odysseus and the *moly*), which the Phoenician in part grasps, hints at the path along which the Phoenician is traveling. In the third (Orpheus and the beasts), the Phoenician realizes his beastlike nature—revising his previous self-identification with Odysseus—and his need to be tamed, although through his words Philostratus unconsciously hints that possession by the heroes may hold dangers. In the fourth αἶνος (the Lotus-Eaters), the Phoenician proves himself to be not only dedicated to the heroes, but of sound mind, eschewing the vices of luxury and self-indulgence. The final αἶνος picks up the per-

[32] Corinne Pache, "Singing Heroes—The Poetics of Hero Cult in the *Heroikos*," 23–24 in this volume.

[33] A similar rhetorical device may be at work in the original ending of the Gospel of Mark. After Jesus' tomb has been discovered to be empty, an angelic figure announces the resurrection, but the women flee, "for terror and amazement had seized them; and they said nothing to anyone, for they were afraid" (Mark 16:8). See John Paul Heil, *The Gospel of Mark as a Model for Action: A Reader-Response Commentary* (New York: Paulist, 1992), 350; Joan L. Mitchell, "Silence, Secrets, and Speech," in *Beyond Fear and Silence: A Feminist-Literary Reading of Mark* (New York: Continuum, 2001), 76–82.

sistent Odyssean theme of homecoming and hints that it is to be found in the nexus of death, lamentation for the hero, and immortality through the virtuous life. By the end of the dialogue the Phoenician has become a true companion of the hero since he has deciphered the αἶνοι and modified his life in accordance with them.

Whitmarsh claims that the Phoenician's transformation is extreme and hints that few would choose to emulate it.[34] I suggest that understanding the transformation in terms of a series of αἶνοι has two benefits. First, it allows us to see that his transformation, while occurring all within the space of a single afternoon, actually takes place over the entire course of the dialogue and in small, discrete steps. Second, the use of αἶνοι forces us to reconsider exactly how the Phoenician might have a mimetic function. Let us return briefly to αἶνος and its relationship to κλέος. According to Nagy, the key difference between αἶνος (praise poetry) and κλέος (epic) is the occasionality of praise poetry. Epic praises the deeds of heroes from the past, whereas αἶνος speaks to contemporaries and has a specific moral agenda (i.e., reinforcing the cultural values of the elite).[35] The *Heroikos*, filled with stories of κλέος, forges the connection between κλέος and αἶνος: The κλέος of the heroes, mediated through αἶνοι, becomes the possession of the Phoenician. I therefore suggest that the audience of the *Heroikos* is invited to imitate the Phoenician, but only in a highly specific way. Recall that the riddling aspect of αἶνος ensures that only the worthy will understand correctly; misunderstanding and further confusion await all others. The Phoenician struggles through the αἶνοι and eventually gains wisdom and knowledge. Individual readers will respond to the αἶνοι and the text as a whole as their own abilities and dispositions (whether they are φίλοι, σοφοί, and ἀγαθοί) allow. Certain readers will observe the Phoenician's struggle and engage in their own parallel struggles to decode the text—carefully reading and rereading—and modify their lives. In this reading of the text the Phoenician is neither a background character nor a *ficelle*,[36] but rather the protagonist, the character who "evokes our beliefs, sympathies, revulsions."[37]

[34] Whitmarsh, "The Harvest of Wisdom," 249.

[35] Nagy, *Pindar's Homer*, 149–51.

[36] Background characters are "merely useful cogs in the mechanism of the plot"; a *ficelle* is an intermediate character, "who while more fully delineated and individualized than any background character, exists in the novel primarily to serve some function." W. J. Harvey, *Character and the Novel* (Ithaca, N.Y.: Cornell University Press, 1965), 56 and 58.

[37] Harvey, *Character and the Novel*, 56.

The text itself then, and not just individual scenes, functions as an extended αἶνος. The text attracts, creating not just readers, but rereaders struggling to grasp all its complex allusions[38] and purposes, or it alienates. A similar thesis about the Gospel of John was advanced by Wayne Meeks in his article "The Man From Heaven in Johannine Sectarianism." Both the Fourth Gospel itself and the Johannine Jesus are fundamentally enigmatic, evoking one of two responses: the disdain of one who finds the text and its protagonist more maddening than attractive or the devotion of a committed disciple who engages in a process of rereading and interpretation to grasp the message of Jesus.[39] I do not address here the question of a Johannine parallel to Protesilaos,[40] but only suggest that the two texts—the Fourth Gospel and the *Heroikos*—may well have functioned in the same way. Such a text has the potential to create the most devoted of readers, and I suggest that it is this process of reading and interpretation, with its attendant transformations, that ultimately succeeds in locating one within the dynamic legacy of Homer.[41]

[38] See Jeffrey Rusten, "Living in the Past: Allusive Narratives and Elusive Authorities in the World of the *Heroikos*," in this volume.

[39] Wayne A. Meeks, "The Man from Heaven in Johannine Sectarianism," in *The Interpretation of John* (ed. John Ashton; Philadelphia: Fortress, 1986), esp. 162; repr. from *JBL* 91 (1972): 44–72.

[40] On this issue, see my essay "Jesus as Cult Hero in the Fourth Gospel," in this volume.

[41] See the insightful conclusion to Francesca Mestre's article in this volume.

Why a Phoenician? A Proposal for the Historical Occasion for the *Heroikos*

Ellen Bradshaw Aitken

Cicero, speaking in defense of Scaurus, averred, "All the monuments of the ancients and all histories have handed down to us the tradition that the nation of the Phoenicians is the most treacherous of all nations."[1] With this broad stroke, Cicero draws upon a tradition of ethnic prejudice not infrequently articulated in Greek and Roman literature. He does so in his oration *In Defense of Scaurus* so as to dismiss the testimony of the Sardinian witnesses in the case against Scaurus in 54 B.C.E. According to Cicero, the problem with the Sardinians is that they are Punic by descent, and thus untrustworthy, not least in the forensic arena. Indeed this perceived treachery of the Phoenicians had been demonstrated in more recent Roman memory by the Punic Wars, in which the Carthaginians were thought to have exhibited the same perfidious characteristics by which their Phoenician ancestors were distinguished.[2] I begin with this example from republican Rome in order to highlight the way in which a tradition of ethnic caricature, particularly about the Phoenicians, can become active in relation to the here and now of political discourse.

In the study of early Christian narratives, investigations into the strategies for marking the boundaries between one group and another begin with the observation of the place-names and other geographical markers found in the text.[3] The point in doing so is not, in the first place, to engage in naive historical reconstruction, but rather to analyze the rhetoric of the text and the world that it

[1] Cicero *In Defense of Scaurus* 42; the translation is that of N. H. Watts, *Cicero* (LCL; Cambridge, Mass.: Harvard University Press; London: Heinemann, 1979), 297.

[2] Cicero *In Defense of Scaurus* 38–45.

[3] See, for example, Robert T. Fortna, "Theological Use of Locale in the Fourth Gospel," *Anglican Theological Review Supplement Series* 3 (1974): 58–95; Richard A. Horsley, *Galilee: History, Politics, People* (Valley Forge, Pa.: Trinity Press International, 1995).

constructs. It entails asking such questions as the following: How do the geographical markers contribute to the narrative and rhetorical world of the text? What is the valence of the particular places and regions named, and how does this valence contribute to the persuasive goals of the text? Assessing such rhetorical valence needs, moreover, to take into account the contributions both of historical events and of the earlier stories and traditions associated with these places, as well as examining the ways in which these places function within the narrative. From this basis, it may then be possible to reconstruct a plausible historical occasion for the composition of the text and to understand its persuasive aims in relation to a larger socio-political and religious world. That is, it may become possible to identify the circles of discourse and signification in which these strategies of community definition are effective.[4] Thus, for example, in the study of the Gospel of John, we may ask about the distinctions drawn between Galileans, Judeans, and Samaritans, noting how differences in responses to Jesus are grouped by ethnic markers, inquiring into the situation of each group at the end of the first century C.E., and then formulating such hypotheses as the role of this gospel in addressing the incorporation of Samaritans into a predominantly Galilean group.[5] The story of the baptism of the Ethiopian eunuch in Acts 8 provides another brief example. Here understanding the valence of Ethiopia both in terms of the ancient geographical traditions, on the one hand,[6] and in relation to the references to Ethiopia in the scriptures of Israel, on the other,[7] suggests how this story contributes to Acts' overall narrative of the eschatological gathering of the ends of the earth into God's reign.[8]

A sense of place is similarly indispensable to the *Heroikos*. In other words, when we consider the rhetorical strategies of this dia-

[4] Elisabeth Schüssler Fiorenza, *Rhetoric and Ethic: The Politics of Biblical Studies* (Minneapolis: Fortress, 1999), 105–48.

[5] Thus, Raymond E. Brown, *The Community of the Beloved Disciple* (New York: Paulist Press, 1979), 34–39; Wayne Meeks, *The Prophet King: Moses Traditions and the Johannine Christology* (NovTSup 14; Leiden: Brill, 1967), 318–19; Elisabeth Schüssler Fiorenza, *In Memory of Her: A Feminist Reconstruction of Christian Origins* (New York: Crossroad, 1983), 327–28.

[6] For example, Homer *Od.* 1.23–25; Herodotus *Hist.* 3.17–20; Strabo *Geography* 17.2.1–3.

[7] For example, Psalm 68:31; "Let bronze be brought from Egypt; let Ethiopia hasten to stretch out its hands to God" (LXX; NRSV).

[8] Thus, Robert C. Tannehill, *The Acts of the Apostles* (vol. 2 of *The Narrative Unity of Luke–Acts, a Literary Interpretation*; Minneapolis: Fortress, 1994), 107–12.

logue, we need to begin by recognizing that this is a highly *locative* text. It is thus a rich text to which we may address questions concerning the rhetorical function of geography and locale. The dialogue is replete with references to places,[9] locating, for example, appearances of heroes in specific sites, connecting ritual practices to locales, and drawing attention to the places where evidence for the "truth" of myth (e.g., the bones of the giants) is to be found.[10] Indeed to read the *Heroikos* successfully requires a geographical knowledge almost equal to that of a sea captain or merchant who sails the eastern Mediterranean. Above all, however, the locative quality of the text is determined by the emphasis on the very presence (the *here* and now) of the cult sanctuary of Protesilaos on the Thracian Chersonesus (*Her*. 5.1–2). *Here*, at this site, from this tumulus that you see *right there*, comes the hero (*Her*. 9.1); here the vinedresser has intimate conversation with him (*Her*. 5.1). It is here, moreover, on the left-hand side of the Hellespont, overlooking Sigeion where Achilles and Patroklos are buried, that Protesilaos lives as the guardian hero of all Hellas. The frequency of deictic suffixes on pronouns to do with location emphasizes the intensity of interest in space.[11] Clearly the identity and the authority of the vinedresser is tied to his region, to the sanctuary he cultivates and the locale where he consorts with Protesilaos.[12]

The other participant in the dialogue is a figure who is marked primarily by a geographical reference. He is "the Phoenician stranger" (ξένε Φοῖνιξ, *Her*. 1.5), described at the outset in terms of land of origin,

> *Vinedresser:* Stranger, are you an Ionian, or where are you from?
>
> *Phoenician:* I am a Phoenician (Φοῖνιξ), vinedresser, one of those who live near Sidon and Tyre.

[9] See Simone Follet, "Philostratus's *Heroikos* and the Regions of the Northern Aegean," 221–35 in this volume.

[10] See Jeffrey Rusten, "Living in the Past: Allusive Narratives and Elusive Authorities in the World of *Heroikos*," 143–58 in this volume.

[11] For example, κολωνὸς δὲ αὐτὸν ἐπέχει μέγας οὑτοσὶ δήπου ὁ ἐν ἀριστερᾷ ("this large mound here on the left no doubt contains him," *Her*. 5.1); see also the use of deictic suffixes at *Her*. 8.6 and 1.2. I am grateful to Christopher P. Jones for this observation.

[12] The vinedresser, upon his return to the Chersonesus from the city and following the advice of Protesilaos, "devotes himself to the land" (τῇ γῇ προσκείμενος, *Her*. 4.11), by which he becomes "wiser" (σοφώτερος) as a result of such locative association with the hero.

> *Vinedresser:* But what about the Ionic fashion of your dress?
>
> *Phoenician:* It is now the local dress also for those of us from Phoenicia. (*Her.* 1.1)

Why a Phoenician? In other words, what is the rhetorical valence of identifying the interlocutor in the dialogue as a Phoenician from the region of Sidon and Tyre? I would suggest that there are two separate but converging tracks toward answering this question: the profile of the Phoenicians developed by the literary texts and heroic traditions upon which Philostratus draws, on the one hand, and, on the other, the role of "Phoenicians" in the religio-political world in which and for which the *Heroikos* was composed. I contend, moreover, that these two aspects of what it means to be a "Phoenician" work together to convey an important statement about the political, social, and religious values at the heart of the *Heroikos*. Correlated with information from Roman historians, it permits the identification of a likely historical occasion for the composition and reception of the *Heroikos*.

Aside from the attempts to situate the *Heroikos* in connection with Caracalla's visit to the Troad in 214–215 C.E.[13] and Julia Domna's patronage of Philostratus,[14] discussions of the aims of the *Heroikos* have tended to speak little of the text's historical and political aspects, in favor of religious and literary questions.[15] Given that the religious and the political were inseparably intertwined in the early third century C.E. and that many sophists held religious and political offices, it is appropriate to inquire into the political dimen-

[13] For example, Samson Eitrem, "Zu Philostrats Heroikos," *Symbolae Osloenses* 8 (1929): 1; Friedrich Solmsen, "Some Works of Philostratus the Elder," *TAPA* 71 (1940): 558–59; and Graham Anderson, *Philostratus: Biography and* Belles Lettres *in the Third Century A.D.* (London: Croom Helm, 1986), 241. I would defer from this association on the grounds that the *Heroikos* should be dated after 222 C.E., most likely to the early years of Alexander Severus's reign. See the discussion in Jennifer K. Berenson Maclean and Ellen Bradshaw Aitken, *Flavius Philostratus: Heroikos* (SBLWGRW 1; Atlanta: Society of Biblical Literature, 2001), xlii–xlv, lxxvii.

[14] See Glen W. Bowersock, *Greek Sophists in the Roman Empire* (Oxford: Clarendon, 1969), ch. 8.

[15] An exception is Georges Radet ("Notes sur l'histoire d'Alexandre: II. Les théores Thessaliens au tombeau d'Achille," *Revue des études anciennes* 27 [1925]: 81–96), who discusses the *Heroikos* in relation to Severan economic policies. See now, however, M. Rahim Shayegan, "Philostratus's *Heroikos* and the Ideation of Late Severan Policy toward Arsacid and Sasanian Iran," 285–315 in this volume.

sion.[16] I turn first, however, to the literary and cultural heritage of the *Heroikos*, and in particular to the role of "Phoenician" character and identity within this heritage.

It might be supposed that the seafaring merchant in the *Heroikos* is identified as a Phoenician simply because Phoenicians were the archetypal sailors and merchants of the Greek world.[17] That is, attribution of Phoenician origin makes for a realistic portrayal of a merchant who sails the eastern Mediterranean and might set ashore along the banks of the Hellespont. The references to Phoenicians in Homer, however, indicate a more complex characterization. The high degree to which the *Heroikos* engages the *Iliad* and *Odyssey*, moreover, suggests that the Homeric conceptualization of Phoenicians is crucial, even though there are only a few instances when Phoenicians are mentioned. When they do appear, they are enmeshed in a world of deceit and trickery. Central are the so-called Cretan lies of Odysseus, in which the disguised Odysseus tells a false story about his supposedly Cretan identity and adventures in order to test the mettle of his audience.[18] In the first Cretan lie in *Odyssey* 13, Odysseus tells how he, having killed the son of Idomeneus, was rescued by the Phoenicians, but then blown off course with them—"it was not as if they wished to deceive me," he says in his own deceit (*Od.* 13.277). In the second Cretan lie, Odysseus relates being taken from Egypt to Phoenicia by a Phoenician man, "well skilled in beguilements" (*Od.* 14.288), who would have, but for a shipwreck, sold him into slavery. The swineherd Eumaios in *Odyssey* 15, moreover, relates to Odysseus his own lengthy tale of how he was abducted by Phoenicians, through the deceit of a

[16] A similar direction is indicated in a recent paper by T. J. G. Whitmarsh, "Performing Heroics: Language, Landscape, and Identity in Philostratus' Heroicus," in *Philostratus* (ed. E. Bowie and J. Elsner; Cambridge: Cambridge University Press, forthcoming), in which he discusses the text in terms of the cultural politics of its time.

[17] Donald B. Harden, *The Phoenicians* (New York: Praeger, 1962), esp. 170–77. See also Franz Cumont, "The Frontier Provinces in the East," in *Cambridge Ancient History* (1st ed.; 11 vols.; Cambridge: Cambridge University Press, 1936), 11:633; and John D. Grainger, *Hellenistic Phoenicia* (Oxford: Clarendon, 1991), 189.

[18] On the Cretan lies in general, see Gregory Nagy, *Greek Mythology and Poetics* (Myth and Poetics; Ithaca, N.Y., and London: Cornell University Press, 1990), 44–45; Adele J. Haft, "Odysseus, Idomeneus, and Meriones: The Cretan Lies of *Odyssey* 13–19," *CJ* 79 (1983–1984): 289–306; Hugh Parry, "The *Apologos* of Odysseus: Lies, All Lies?" *Phoenix* 48 (1994): 1–20; Steve Reece, "The Cretan Odyssey: A Lie Truer Than Truth," *AJP* 115 (1994): 157–73; and P. Walcot, "Odysseus and the Art of Lying," *AncSoc* 8 (1977): 1–19.

Phoenician woman in his father's house. The overall characterization here is clearly that Phoenicians are treacherous deceivers, foreigners who are not to be trusted.

The alliance between the Phoenicians and the Persians in the Persian Wars is taken for granted in the Greek world. The way in which Herodotus portrays this association, however, is particularly illuminating for the significance of the Phoenician in the *Heroikos*, not least because the rhetorical strategies of the *Heroikos* draw upon the end of Herodotus's *Histories*. In the strategic final episode of the *Histories* (9.116–120), Protesilaos the *revenant* appears, a frightening ghost who brings vengeance and terror, but who does so in order to defend Greek territory against the outrages of the Persian governor, Artayktes. The crimes of the Persian governor include his personal offenses against Protesilaos, namely, the looting of the sanctuary and conducting improper sexual relations within its boundaries. In addition, however, Protesilaos takes revenge upon him as a representative of Xerxes, the Asian invader, for all the Persian offenses against the Greeks.[19] The image of the *revenant* is manifested by the resurrection of dried fish, which leap from the fiery grill as a sign of Protesilaos's resurrection and coming vengeance.[20] The vinedresser alludes to this story in *Her.* 9.5.

Herodotus's concluding narrative is matched, however, by the opening of the *Histories*, which provides a genealogy for the conflict between the Persians and the Hellenes. "The Persian learned men say that the *Phoenicians* were the cause of the feud," (*Hist.* 1.1; my emphasis)[21] because the Phoenicians abducted Io, the daughter of the Argive king. This genealogy of reciprocal stealing of women continues in what Herodotus identifies as the "next generation" with Alexander's abduction of Helen (*Hist.* 1.3); thus, the Phoenicians are blamed not only for the Persian Wars but also the Trojan

[19] On the importance of this passage for understanding Herodotus's aims, see the excellent discussion by Gregory Nagy, "The Sign of Protesilaos," *ΜΗΤΙΣ: Revue d'anthropologie du monde grec ancien* 2/2 (1987): 207–13; elaborated in Gregory Nagy, *Pindar's Homer: The Lyric Possession of an Epic Past* (Baltimore: Johns Hopkins University Press, 1990), 268–73. See also Deborah Boedeker, "Protesilaos and the End of Herodotus' *Histories*," *Classical Antiquity* 7/1 (1988): 30–48.

[20] See the note on *Her.* 9.5 in Maclean and Aitken, *Flavius Philostratus: Heroikos*; as well as Nagy, "The Sign of Protesilaos," 207–13; and Boedeker, "Protesilaos," 41.

[21] Translations of Herodotus are from Herodotus, *Histories* (trans. A. D. Godley; LCL; 4 vols.; Cambridge, Mass., and London: Harvard University Press, 1997).

War.[22] Throughout the *Histories* the Phoenicians are allied with the Persians, providing them with the ships they need and aiding them in the invasion of Ionia. According to Herodotus, moreover, it is the Phoenicians who are responsible for taking the Thracian Chersonesus and burning its towns. After the fall of Miletus to the Phoenicians,

> Then the [Phoenician] fleet departed from Ionia and took all that lay on the left hand of the entrance of the Hellespont; for what was to the right had been subdued by the Persians themselves from the side of the land. These are the regions of Europe that belong to the Hellespont,—the Chersonese, wherein are many towns. . . . The Phoenicians, having burnt these places aforesaid, turned against the Proconnesus and Artace, and having given these also to the flames sailed back to the Chersonese to make an end of the remnant of the towns, as many as they had not destroyed at their first landing. (*Hist.* 6.33)

Although Protesilaos is not named in this passage, the alert reader would recognize that this territory now captured by Phoenicians includes the hero's sanctuary on the western bank of the Hellespont.

Inasmuch as the *Heroikos* adopts and reactivates the Herodotean perspective that sees Protesilaos as the defender of Hellas, the arrival of a Phoenician on the left-hand side of the Hellespont, on the Chersonesus, would immediately signal danger at the outset of the dialogue. Philostratus thus raises the possibility that this is a Phoenician, who, like his ancestors, allied with the Persians, may subdue, burn, and desecrate the Chersonesus and the home of Protesilaos. The *Heroikos*'s emphasis on the Phoenician qua Phoenician, however, functions within a larger discussion of foreigners and their behavior. This discussion is necessary in order to understand the potential danger that the Phoenician poses.

Throughout the *Heroikos*, a parallelism is drawn between Achilles and Protesilaos, and both appear at times as avenging *revenants*. Protesilaos's tomb guards Hellenic territory and culture and is matched on the other side of the Hellespont by the tomb of Achilles. A wrathful Protesilaos regained his sanctuary from the possession of a man named Xeinis ("foreigner"; *Her.* 4.2). The dia-

[22] See the discussion in François Hartog, *Memories of Odysseus: Frontier Tales from Ancient Greece* (trans. Janet Lloyd; Chicago: University of Chicago Press, 2001), 79–85.

logue ends with two stories of Achilles' brutal wrath: in the first case upon a young girl, one of the last of Priam's descendants (*Her.* 56.6–10); in the second upon the Amazons who invade Achilles' island in the Black Sea (*Her.* 56.11–57.17). These stories appear, at first reading, to be an abrupt shift from the relatively peaceful descriptions of Protesilaos's and Achilles' current lifestyles, but their position as the climax of the dialogue suggests their importance for its overall purpose.[23] There is, as Graham Anderson points out, a certain "similarity between the vengeance of Achilles at the end of the *Heroicus* and that of Protesilaos at the end of Herodotus's *Histories*: both have the last blood."[24]

It is important to notice not only the wrath of the heroes but also at whom it is directed—in each case at those who are quintessentially foreign or "other" from the Hellenic perspective: Xeinis, the Trojan girl, and the Amazons. Hektor, to cite another instance, returns as *revenant* to avenge the insults hurled at him by the offending *Assyrian* youth (*Her.* 19.5–9). In this regard, it is also notable that Achilles' victims are women; the particular juxtaposition of gender and alterity bears further examination in the context of the politics of empire in Philostratus's time.

The Phoenician merchant is, of course, also a foreigner, from the region of Tyre and Sidon (*Her.* 1.1), but one who is realistically depicted as a "hellenized" Phoenician: he wears an Ionic style of dress, knows all about Homer, and speaks Greek.[25] At the beginning of the dialogue, because of the valence of being a Phoenician in the *Heroikos*'s literary and cultural heritage, he is also marked as a liminal character: potentially deceitful and treacherous, potentially destructive, and potentially subject to destruction at the hands of Protesilaos. He is, moreover, skeptical about the heroes of old, and from the outset of the dialogue he is associated with the values of luxury and love of money (*Her.* 1.1–7), values which are typically understood as non-Greek, but which can also be employed to critique Hellenic behavior.[26] Throughout he is called ξένος ("stranger, foreigner, guest"), and it is possible to read his passage from foreign

[23] See Maclean and Aitken, *Flavius Philostratus: Heroikos*, lvi–lx.

[24] Anderson, *Philostratus*, 247.

[25] See Jennifer K. Berenson Maclean, "The αἶνοι of the *Heroikos* and the Unfolding Transformation of the Phoenician Merchant," 253–56 in this volume.

[26] Thus, Nagy argues that in Herodotus the story of Artayktes is directed at the Athenians and "signals the threat of *hubris* from within, not from without" (*Pindar's Homer*, 308).

stranger to guest, within the hospitality of the vinedresser and Protesilaos, as taking place in tandem with his growing acceptance of the matters to do with the heroes.[27] This foreigner, moreover, ends up being a listener devoted to Protesilaos, prepared to abide by the hero's reluctance to speak of certain matters, and ready to pour a libation to Protesilaos (*Her.* 58.1–6). It is perhaps not going too far to say that this foreigner, unlike Artayktes and Xeinis, becomes subject to Protesilaos, and that this Phoenician, unlike his ancestors, is welcome on the Chersonesus.

I turn now to the other strand of the investigation, namely, the valence of being a Phoenician within the socio-political-religious world in which and for which the *Heroikos* was composed. I adopt here the dating of the *Heroikos* to the reign of Alexander Severus (222–235 C.E.).[28] The composition of the *Heroikos* in the early third century C.E., during the later Severan period, situates it in a time when the government of the Roman Empire was strongly influenced by such imperial women as Julia Domna, Julia Maesa, Julia Mamaea, and Julia Soemias, all from the Syrian religious aristocracy. Religious practices were redefined, not only by a new wave of what might be called syncretism, but also by Elagabalus's introduction into Rome of the Syrian sun god (Herodian *History* 5.5.6–10) and his installation of the Black Rock of Emesa on the Palatine (SHA *Elagabalus* 3.4). One result was a heightened awareness of the relationship between foreignness and what was perceived as authentically "Hellenic" or Greek.

We may note first of all that the Phoenician merchant in the *Heroikos* would be considered an inhabitant of the Roman province of Syria, and thus a Syrian. He is from the vicinity of Sidon and Tyre (*Her.* 1.1); following Septimius Severus's division of Syria into two provinces in 194 C.E., this merchant would come from the province of Syria Phoenice, which was governed from Tyre.[29] The

[27] See the note on *Her.* 6.1 in Maclean and Aitken, *Flavius Philostratus: Heroikos*; the shift is also marked through the customs of hospitality.

[28] Maclean and Aitken, *Flavius Philostratus: Heroikos,* xlii–xlv, lxxvii. Simone Follet also argues that the *Heroikos* was composed in the first years of the reign of Alexander Severus; see the abstract of her unpublished dissertation, "Édition critique, avec introduction, notes et traduction, de l'*Héroïque* de Philostrate," *Annuaire de l'école practique des hautes études: Section des sciences historiques et philologiques* (1969/1970): 747–48. Radet ("Notes sur l'histoire d'Alexander," 92) refers more generally to the reign of Alexander Severus.

[29] Fergus Millar, *The Roman Near East, 31 BC–AD 337* (Cambridge, Mass., and London: Harvard University Press, 1993), 121–22. Septimius Severus divided

city of Emesa, the home of Julia Domna, Julia Maesa, Julia Mamaea, and Julia Soemias, was located in eastern Syria Phoenice.[30] It is thus striking that this dialogue, written by an author who at least early in his career was closely associated with the Severan court, features an interlocutor from the same geographical province as the empresses themselves. Herodian refers to Julia Maesa as a "Phoenician" (Φοίνισσα, *History* 5.3.2), and in his description of the religious practices of Elagabalus he emphasizes their Phoenician character (*History* 5.5.3–4).[31] We may be accustomed to refer to the Severan emperors as Syrian, but they may be equally considered "Phoenician."

Even in the case of the first Severan emperor, Septimius Severus, we find a Phoenician connection. Septimius Severus came from the North African city of Lepcis Magna, not from Syria. Lepcis, along with Carthage and other North African cities, was founded by Phoenicians from Tyre;[32] Lepcis, moreover, claimed Tyre as its mother-city.[33] Warwick Ball emphasizes the persistent Phoenician character of the city, apparent in the number of bilingual (Punic and Latin) inscriptions and prominence of the Phoenician gods Melqart and Shadrapa.[34] The admittedly problematic *Historia Augusta* suggests the epithets "Punic Sulla" and "Punic Marius" for Septimius Severus.[35] Thus, there is considerable evidence that

---

Syria into Syria Phoenice (governed from Tyre) and Syria Coele (governed from Antioch, then from Laodicea). Tyre, in contrast to Antioch, enjoyed imperial favor for its support of Septimius Severus against Pescennius Niger; Tyre became a *colonia* in 201 and was given the *ius Italicum*, whereas Antioch was stripped of civic status and deprived of its games (see Anthony Birley, *Septimius Severus: The African Emperor* [London: Eyre & Spottiswood, 1971], 180). Indicating that the Phoenician merchant comes from the vicinity of Tyre may be a way of showing his allegiance to the Severans.

[30] Millar, *The Roman Near East*, 122.

[31] See the discussion in Millar, *The Roman Near East*, 305–6; Millar also cites the self-identification of the author of the *Aithiopica* as "a Phoenician man, an *Emisênos*, by race belonging to those from the Sun, Heliodorus the son of Theodosios" (p. 306). See also Grainger, *Hellenistic Phoenicia*, 115 n. 41.

[32] Pliny *Natural History* 5.12; Millar, *The Roman Near East*, 265–66.

[33] Warwick Ball, *Rome in the East: The Transformation of an Empire* (London and New York: Routledge, 2000), 404. Lepcis Magna became a Roman *colonia* in 112 C.E.

[34] Ball, *Rome in the East*, 421; see also Birley, *Septimius Severus*, 62. Birley (p. 124) also cites the report that Septimius Severus and his sister spoke Punic (SHA *Septimius Severus* 15.7; 19.10).

[35] SHA *Pescennius Niger* 6.4; see the discussion in Birley, *Septimius Severus*, 280; and Ball, *Rome in the East*, 404. Both Birley (p. 124) and Ball (pp. 17, 404)

the Severan emperors and their wives were perceived at least in some circles as Phoenician.

Herodian's account of the emperor Elagabalus's religious practices also highlights their Phoenician (and possibly Persian) customs.

> Setting out from Syria, Antoninus [= Elagabalus] reached Nicomedia, where he was forced by the season of the year to spend the winter. Straight away he began to practice his ecstatic rites and go through the ridiculous motions of the priestly office belonging to his local god in which he had been trained. He wore the most expensive types of clothes, woven of purple and gold, and adorned himself with necklaces and bangles. On his head he wore a crown in the shape of a tiara glittering with gold and precious stones. The effect was something between the sacred garb of the Phoenicians and the luxurious apparel of the Medes. Any Roman or Greek dress he loathed because, he claimed, it was made out of wool, which is a cheap material. Only seric silk was good enough for him. He appeared in public accompanied by flutes and drums, no doubt because he was honoring his god with special rites. (Herodian *History* 5.5.3–4)

Herodian emphasizes their problematic character when he speaks of Julia Maesa's concerns about how such non-Roman activities would be perceived in Rome and of her futile attempts to dissuade her grandson from them (*History* 5.5.5).[36] In particular, he remarks on Julia Maesa's wish that Elagabalus wear Roman clothing; this resonates with the opening of the *Heroikos*, in which the non-Phoenician, but rather "Ionic" appearance of the merchant's attire is accentuated.

In Herodian's account, Elagabalus's extreme foreignness serves as a foil to Alexander Severus's "self-control." Although both

propose the recognition of shared "Phoenician" identity as an element of the bond between Septimius Severus and Julia Domna. Millar (*The Roman Near East*, 266) suggests that Septimius Severus's choice of "Phoenice" as the name of the new province of Syria Phoenice derived from both the Phoenician heritage of Lepcis Magna and the home of his wife.

[36] Dio Cassius (*Roman History* 80.11) includes Julia Soemias and Julia Maesa in Elagabalus's religious activities, thus painting a much less positive view of the Syrian women than Herodian does. In Dio's account, these rites are similarly aligned with effeminate behavior, including cross-dressing, and sexual immorality (*Roman History* 80.13)

young men appear to have been "dedicated to" the Emesene god (*History* 5.3.4),[37] Alexander's *Romanitas* is stressed:

> After Alexander's appointment as Caesar, Antoninus wanted him to be trained in his own pursuits of leaping and dancing, and to share in his priesthood by wearing the same dress and following the same practices. But his mother, Mamaea, removed him from contact with such activities which were shameful and unbecoming for emperors. In private she summoned teachers of all the arts, and trained him in the exercise of self-control, introducing him to the wrestling schools and manly exercises, and gave him both a Latin and a Greek education. (Herodian *History* 5.7.4–5)

This description of Alexander Severus's upbringing mirrors the depiction of the education of Achilles in the *Heroikos* (45.5–8). In particular, the role of *paideia* in inculcating non-foreign behavior and self-control as "manly" characteristics is important and in contrast to what both Herodian and Philostratus construe as "feminine" customs.[38] Herodian indicates that he regards Elagabalus's behavior and dress as "more appropriate for women than men" (*History* 5.5.5); Philostratus dismisses the story that Achilles was hidden among the women on Skyros as inconsistent with Achilles' love of honor (*Her.* 45.8).

To be perceived as "Phoenician" was in the Roman world to have an ambiguous status. On the one hand, the alliances of the Phoenicians with the Persians in the Persian Wars combined with the memory of the Phoenician-Punic threat in the Roman wars with Carthage to produce the caricature of Phoenicians as deceitful and treacherous: the ultimate anti-Romans. On the other hand, Philostratus writes in a world where Phoenicians are emperors and

[37] Millar (*The Roman Near East*, 145) regards both Elagabalus and Alexander Severus as priests of the god Elagabal. There remains, however, uncertainty about Alexander Severus's participation in the priesthood, not least given his mother's attempts to separate him from his cousin's excesses (Herodian *History* 5.7.4–5). In Herodian's account (*History* 5.3.3 and 5.3.6) the matter depends in part on how one accentuates the text, namely, whether one reads ἱέρωντο or ἱερῶντο at 5.3.3 and similarly ἱερώμενος or ἱερωμένος at 5.3.6; see the discussion in C. R. Whittaker's notes in his translation of Herodian *History* (LCL; Cambridge, Mass.: Harvard University Press; London: Heinemann, 1970), 18–20.

[38] This contrast is stressed in R. V. Nind Hopkins, *The Life of Alexander Severus* (Cambridge Historical Essays 14; Cambridge: Cambridge University Press, 1907), 38–40.

Phoenician women exercise considerable power both as cultural patrons and political agents. This ambiguity is also inscribed in gendered terms: the capacity of Phoenicians to be "foreign" (non-Roman, non-Hellenic), as in the case of Elagabalus, is aligned with being effeminate, extreme, and a lover of luxury, whereas the capacity to be Roman (in the model of the Greek heroes) is marked as properly masculine. It is perhaps not coincidental that, in the *Heroikos,* Achilles' wrath is directed toward women (the Trojan girl and the Amazons) who broke the taboos of the hero's sanctuary (*Her.* 56.6–57.17). What Philostratus does in these stories is an example of using women as instruments with which to think about cultural difference and the violation of cultural values.[39]

As we have seen, the *Heroikos* develops a contrast between two opposing stances toward the heroes of Hellenic culture, that is, between proper honor, as exemplified by the attitude of the Phoenician (Syrian) merchant by the end of the dialogue, and the extremes of dishonor exemplified by the quintessential foreigners—the Amazons, the Trojan girl, Xeinis, and the Assyrian youth. Such a contrast, therefore, may well serve to highlight attempts by the Phoenician women of the Severan dynasty to present themselves as authentically "Greek" by engaging in the practices proper to the cult and culture of the Hellenic heroes. The *Heroikos* may thus serve to advertise and promote the Hellenic piety of the emperor Alexander Severus and his highly influential mother, Julia Mamaea.[40] The degree to which Philostratus is also concerned with the gender of the Phoenician empresses in relation to the political power they wielded is difficult to evaluate. The dialogue displays a very high regard for the Mysian queen, Hiera (*Her.* 23.26–30); this creates a striking contrast between the women who violate Achilles'

[39] For a discussion of the role of gender and foreignness in the construction of the other, see Sandra Joshel, "The Body Female and the Body Politic: Livy's Lucretia and Verginia," in *Pornography and Representation in Greece and Rome* (ed. Amy Richlin; New York: Oxford University Press, 1992); and Sandra Joshel and Sheila Murnaghan, *Women and Slaves in Greco-Roman Culture: Differential Equations* (London: Routledge, 1998).

[40] The references to the imperially established "Market of the Swine" and the identification of Achilles' wrath with the punishment for Thessaly's violation of the imperial purple monopoly suggest a complimentary, rather than critical, attitude toward imperial policies. See Robert Muth, "Forum suarium," *Museum Helveticum* 2 (1945): 227–36. For an alternative interpretation of this expression, see Jeffrey Rusten's article in this volume, 147–48.

sanctuary and those (foreign) royal women who exhibit both martial courage and extreme beauty.[41]

Dating the dialogue to the reign of Alexander Severus, moreover, suggests a political context in which the themes of the *Heroikos* would have had specific resonance, namely, renewed threats and campaigns from the East against the Romans. In the 220s, after the accession of Alexander Severus as emperor in 222, the Parthian empire was overthrown by the Sasanian ruler, Ardašīr I.[42] This new Sasanian empire not only ruled formerly Parthian territory but also, during the attack on the Mesopotamian city of Hatra, declared an intent to reclaim the full extent of the Persian empire under the Achaemenids, namely, to the Aegean Sea.[43] Alexander Severus launched a campaign against the Sasanians in the early 230s, in response to their invasion of Roman

[41] According to Philostratus, Mysian women "fought from horses alongside the men, just as the Amazons do, and the leader of the cavalry was Hiera, wife of Têlephos" (*Her.* 23.26); Hiera also surpassed Helen in beauty (*Her.* 23.28). The comparison with the Amazons is notable given the Amazons' fate at the end of the *Heroikos*. It is also important that Hiera is Mysian, an ally of the Trojans, and is engaged in battle against the Achaean forces. Both Julia Domna and Julia Mamaea were accorded the title "Mater Castrorum" ("mother of the [army] camps"). On Julia Domna, see the discussion in Birley, *Septimius Severus*, 183 n. 1; and H. U. Instinsky, "Studien zur Geschichte des Septimius Severus," *Klio* 35 (1942): 200–211. For a list of such inscriptions for Julia Mamaea, see Hopkins, *Alexander Severus*, 275. The title certainly indicates their association with the Roman army and may honor their accompanying of the army on campaign.

[42] When he became emperor, Alexander Severus (b. Gessius Alexianus Bassianus) adopted the name M. Aurelius Severus Alexander, which combined elements from the Antonine and Severan dynasty and the name Alexander. Millar points out (*The Roman Near East*, 149) that this is the sole use of the name Alexander by a Roman emperor, suggesting that he was drawing upon the memory of Alexander the Great as the "liberator" of Greece from the Persians and presenting himself as the deliverer of the Roman Empire from the renewed Persian threat. An inscription from Palmyra names him as "the deified Alexander Caesar" (*CIS* II, no. 3932, cited in Millar, *The Roman Near East*, 149). See also Dio Cassius *History* 80.17–18. Ball emphasizes the confrontation between the rulers: "Thus the two emperors faced each other, a new Artaxerxes facing a new Alexander, both of them natives of the East, both descendants of priests" (*Rome in the East*, 22); he suggests that this comparison was available in the Roman imagination (Aurelius Victor, for example, calls Ardašīr "Xerxes"; see Ball, *Rome in the East*, 455 n. 80). See also Shayegan, "Philostratus's *Heroikos* and the Ideation of Late Severan Policy."

[43] Millar, *The Roman Near East*, 146–47; G. W. Bowersock, *Roman Arabia* (Cambridge, Mass.: Harvard University Press, 1983), 126–28. Birley (*Septimius Severus*, 278) dates the accession of Ardašīr to 226 C.E., his invasion of Roman Mesopotamia to 230, and Alexander Severus's campaign to 231–232.

Mesopotamia. In describing the Sasanian threat at the very end of his *Roman History*, Dio Cassius writes of Ardašīr I,

> He accordingly became a source of fear to us; for he was encamped with a large army so as to threaten not only Mesopotamia but also Syria, and he boasted that he would win back everything that the ancient Persians had once held, as far as the Grecian sea, claiming that all this was his rightful inheritance from his forefathers. The danger lies not in the fact that he seems to be of any particular consequence in himself, but rather in the fact that our armies are in such a state that some of the troops are actually joining him and others are refusing to defend themselves. They indulge in such wantonness, licence, and lack of discipline, that those in Mesopotamia even dared to kill their commander, Flavius Heracleo. . . . (Dio Cassius *Roman History* 80.4.1–2)[44]

In order to understand the particular valence Protesilaos may have had in this political situation, it is instructive to recall Herodotus's use of Protesilaos as the protector of Greece against the Persians. The *Heroikos* invokes Protesilaos, together with devotion to his hero and his lifestyle, at a point when Rome needs him. That is, Rome, however Phoenician it may be, needs not only the heroic protection and vengeance of Protesilaos, but also to be recalled to the values and behaviors associated with his cult. I suggest, therefore, that the *Heroikos* may have been written around the time of Alexander Severus's Sasanian campaign in order to promote Greek (and hence Roman) identity and piety, by recalling not only the memory of the preeminent heroes of the Trojan War but most notably that of Protesilaos.[45]

The episode of the Amazons' attack on the abode of Achilles on the island of Leukê can also be understood within this political framework. In the fifth century B.C.E., at the time of the Persian

[44] The translation is that of Earnest Cary, *Dio's Roman History* (LCL; 9 vols.; Cambridge, Mass.: Harvard University Press; London: Heinemann, 1982), 9:483–85. The mention of "wantonness, licence, and lack of discipline" in this context coincides with the *Heroikos*'s criticism of such behavior on the part of warriors (e.g., Paris, *Her*. 25.11; and Euphorbos, *Her*. 42.1). See also Herodian *History* 6.2.1–2.

[45] In recalling the heroes' protection of Greece, Philostratus offers a more hopeful view of a Roman victory against Sasanians than does Dio Cassius in concluding his history on what Millar (*The Roman Near East*, 147) terms a "deeply pessimistic" note.

Wars, the story of the Amazons' invasion of Attica and their defeat by Theseus was added to earlier stories about the Amazons and was used as pro-Athenian propaganda against the Persian invasion.[46] Thus Philostratus in the *Heroikos* may employ the literary topos of the Amazons in order to represent a contemporary foreign threat to Greek identity.[47] Achilles' destruction of the Amazons, like their defeat by Theseus, would then communicate the certainty of Roman success against the Sasanians, so long as the heroes receive due honor. Given this interpretation, the *Heroikos* exhibits a strong anti-Persian perspective, which coheres well with Alexander Severus's campaign against the Sasanians. Moreover, since being a Phoenician in the literary and cultural heritage of *Heroikos* signals the possibility of a treacherous alliance with the Persians, the "acceptance" of things Hellenic by the Phoenician merchant in the *Heroikos* signals a different outcome. I would venture to say that through the Phoenician merchant the Phoenician/Syrian imperial family becomes a presence in the dialogue. The unrealized potential of the merchant to "go bad" provides a narrative space for negotiating the cultural dangers perceived in the Phoenician rulers of Rome; in the hands of Philostratus, it provides a narrative space for demonstrating the "Hellenic" character and behavior of Alexander Severus and thus also the anti-Persian stance of this Phoenician.

I would stress, moreover, that the enigmatic message of the *Heroikos* is aimed also at a Roman audience, at insiders, not only at Phoenicians and other foreigners. Gregory Nagy has argued that the end of Herodotus's *Histories* should be read as directed at Herodotus's Athenian audience and that it "signals the threat of *hubris* from within, not from without."[48] Similarly, the way of life

[46] See Josine H. Blok, *The Early Amazons: Modern and Ancient Perspectives on a Persistent Myth* (Religions in the Greco-Roman World 120; Leiden: Brill, 1995), 182, 441; John Boardman, "Herakles, Theseus, and the Amazons," in *The Eye of Greece: Studies in the Art of Athens* (ed. D. C. Kurtz and B. Sparkes; Cambridge: Cambridge University Press, 1982), 1–28. According to Herodotus (*Hist.* 9.27), before the Battle of Plataea the Athenians referred to the Amazons' invasion. The story also appears in Aeschylus's *Eumenides* (657–66), first performed ca. 460–458 B.C.E., during the Persian Wars; see Blok, *The Early Amazons*, 182. On Greek iconography for Amazons as Scythians and its implications for Athenian attitudes toward Persians, see H. A. Shapiro, "Amazons, Thracians, and Scythians," *GRBS* 24 (1983): 105–14.

[47] If Whitmarsh is correct in his argument ("Performing Heroics") that Leukê represents a place of ideal "Greekness," then the Amazons' invasion replays the invasion of Attica in the Theseus stories and the invasion of Greece by the Persians.

[48] Nagy, *Pindar's Homer*, 308.

espoused by the *Heroikos* is not only that adopted by Alexander Severus and Julia Mamaea, but is also promoted for Roman society. I would suggest a few points of connection between the lifestyle upheld by the *Heroikos* and the aspects perceived as problematic in the behavior of the Severan emperors. Both Dio Cassius in his account of Alexander Severus and Lampridius in the *Historia Augusta* speak of Alexander's moral cleansing of the imperial palace after the excesses of Elagabalus[49] and his insistence on a "pure" way of life following the rule of the Eleusinian mysteries.[50] His own daily regime, according to Lampridius (admittedly a problematic and later source), of study, exercise, a vegetarian meal, and hospitality[51] matches well the description of Protesilaos's favorite fellow hero, Palamedes. Similarly, Alexander's austere lifestyle, drawn from the life of the army camps, is much like that of Palamedes (the sophist). In contrast, Protesilaos's censure of luxury, flattery, bribery, sexual immorality, and general laxity[52] matches Lampridius's portrayal of the lifestyle of Alexander's predecessor and cousin Elagabalus.[53] Thus, particularly in Protesilaos's praise for Palamedes and his way of life, but also in the values espoused throughout the dialogue, we find not so much a xenophobic message, but more a warning against *hubris* directed at the insiders, an audience well situated within the Roman world.

Moreover, if the legions under Alexander Severus's command in the Sasanian campaign were largely or even in part drawn from among the inhabitants of Syria,[54] then issues of Syrian loyalty to Rome and conformity to Romano-Hellenic values may have been perceived as an area of greater vulnerability. Were these Roman legions, like the Phoenicians in Roman memory, potentially treacherous and treasonous? This potential is emphasized in the conclusion to Dio Cassius's account of the campaign, quoted above, in which he identifies the danger as lying not so much with

[49] For references, see Hopkins, *Alexander Severus*, 38–39.

[50] Hopkins, *Alexander Severus*, 70–71.

[51] Hopkins, *Alexander Severus*, 80–81.

[52] See, for example, Protesilaos's attitude toward Paris, whom he mocks for his luxury, "self-love" (τὸ φίλαυτον), and vanity (*Her*. 40.1–6). Odysseus is similarly the object of the hero's criticism for his use of bribery and flattery (see, e.g., *Her*. 34.1–7; 43.13–14).

[53] Another possible connection might be the *Heroikos*'s concern for burial even of those denied burial according to customary law, in light of the despoiling of Elagabalus's body after his murder.

[54] See the discussion of this issue in Nigel Pollard, *Soldiers, Cities, and Civilians in Roman Syria* (Ann Arbor: University of Michigan Press, 2000), 111–67.

Artaxerxes' might, as in the laxity and treachery of the legions themselves (*Roman History* 80.4.1–2). As with the ending of Herodotus's *Histories*, in the *Heroikos* the hero Protesilaos has a message for these insiders—a message about an appropriately austere lifestyle, avoidance of *hubris*, and a devotion to the cults of the heroes of old.

In conclusion, then, the question of the valence of the Phoenician merchant, qua Phoenician, indicates a historical occasion for the *Heroikos* in the context of Alexander Severus's campaigns against the Sasanian incursion into Mesopotamia and Syria. Signaling Alexander Severus as a trustworthy Phoenician who loves and honors Protesilaos, and who is certainly not allied with the Persians or Sasanians, the dialogue aims at promoting a way of life according to a Hellenic, Palamedean ethic as a means of establishing a "healthy" society that can resist this new Persian threat. In addition, however, the dialogue opens up narrative space for exploring the potential dangers within Roman society. By relating Protesilaos's vengeance upon the Persian governor Artaykes and Achilles' violent destruction of the invading Amazons to the Phoenician merchant, the vinedresser allows this Phoenician to situate himself either as a threatening foreigner or as a lover of the heroes and a loyal "Hellene."

Philostratus's *Heroikos* and the Ideation of Late Severan Policy toward Arsacid and Sasanian Iran*

M. Rahim Shayegan

In 224 C.E., the Persian magnate Ardašīr I (Ardaxšahr), having overpowered his Arsacid suzerain Ardawān IV, founded the Sasanian Empire, named after his eponymous forefather Sāsān, and launched an aggressive expansionist foreign policy in Asia Minor. Alexander Severus, the last of the Syrian *augusti*, was temporarily able to defend the *limes* and to reestablish the *status quo ante*, without being lured into a most perilous war of conquest against the Sasanian Empire. The emperor's resolution to refrain from an offensive campaign, possibly reached in light of the redoubtable Sasanian war machinery, was at odds with one of the main tenets of late Severan political ideology: the *imitatio Alexandri* and its call for eastern conquest.

Thus, the aim of this essay is manifold: (1) it seeks to demonstrate how two concomitant, but at times conflicting, currents of thought shaped the late Severan political ideology, namely, the *imitatio Alexandri* and the Second Sophistic's reception of the Hellenic past; furthermore, (2) it shall illustrate how instrumental Philostratus's *Heroikos* was in reconciling the urge to eastern conquest inherent in the *imitatio* with the exigencies of a defensive warfare by portraying the archetypal hero-conquerors Achilles and Protesilaos as guardians of Hellenic territories, whose actions were worthy of emulation by a *novus Alexander;* and finally, (3) it will argue that the resurgence, under the Severans, of the Achaemenids either as intrinsic part of the *imitatio* (as the vanquished enemies of Alexander), or consequent upon the celebration of Hellas's past triumphs (as aggressors who were warded off), as well as their equation with the Sasanians, led to the incorporation of the *idea* of an Achaemenid heritage in the Sasanian political ideology: henceforth, the Sasanians would refer to their ancestral rights as the

* I wish to extend my thanks to the Society of Fellows, Harvard University, for affording me, during my tenure, the leisure to put pen to paper for this study.

rationale to claim back formerly Achaemenid territories from the Roman Empire.

First, however, I shall review succinctly the Roman perception of the Arsacids in the Augustan Age, in order to expose the historical background indispensable for our understanding of the Severan policy vis-à-vis Sasanian Persia.[1]

THE REPRESENTATION OF THE PARTHIANS IN THE AUGUSTAN AGE

We can distinguish two stages in the Roman perception of the Parthians: before *and* after the Augustan Parthian policy. Before Augustus's official renunciation of a war of conquest against the Arsacids and the ensuing ideological consequences, Rome's perception of the Parthians was initially led by the idea of a rich and lucrative "Oriental" realm beyond the Euphrates, where abundant spoils could be gained, but where Roman uncertainty about the people and the land also imperiled the success of military offensives.[2] Of interest to the present discussion, however, are the changes that occurred in the Roman perception of the Parthians after the Augustan policy shift in 20 B.C.E. The increasing importance of the Arsacid realm in Roman foreign policy, especially after the defeat of Crassus at Carrhae, seems to have produced a variegated, but stereotyped, literature on the Arsacids that compensated for Rome's lack of genuine knowledge of the Parthians by associating them with the Achaemenids as known to the Romans from the

[1] The following chapter relies to a considerable extent on the works of Holger Sonnabend, *Fremdenbild und Politik: Vorstellungen der Römer von Ägypten und dem Partherreich in der späten Republik und frühen Kaiserzeit* (Europäische Hochschulschriften[3]: Geschichte und ihre Hilfswissenschaften 286; Frankfurt am Main: Lang, 1986); Antony Spawforth, "Symbol of Unity? The Persian-Wars Tradition in the Roman Empire," in *Greek Historiography* (ed. Simon Hornblower; Oxford: Clarendon, 1994), 233–69; Rolf Michael Schneider, *Bunte Barbaren: Orientalstatuen aus farbigem Marmor in der römischen Repräsentationskunst* (Worms, Germany: Wernersche Verlagsgesellschaft, 1986); Rolf Michael Schneider, "The Barbarian in Roman Art: A Countermodel of Roman Identity," in *The Roman Period (in the Provinces and the Barbaric World)* (ed. Bruno Luiselli and Patrizio Pensabene; XIII International Congress of Prehistoric and Protohistoric Sciences, Fórli, Italy, 8–14 September 1996; Fórli, Italy: A.B.A.C.O. edizioni, 1996), 19–30; and Rolf Michael Schneider "Die Faszination des Feindes: Bilder der Parther und des Orients in Rom," in *Das Partherreich und seine Zeugnisse* (ed. Josef Wiesehöfer; Beiträge des internationalen Colloquiums, Eutin, 27–30 June 1996; Stuttgart: Steiner, 1998), 95–127, pl. 19.

[2] Sonnabend, *Fremdenbild und Politik*, 162, 167–68.

Greek tradition, as well as with images of an Orient plagued by luxury and decadence.[3] Augustus's adoption of a policy of coexistence with the Arsacid Empire paved the way for the elaboration of a new political ideology that could account for Rome's relinquishment of the idea of world dominion without suffering any loss of prestige and without any fundamental changes to the prevailing image of the Parthians in Rome.[4] Augustus's ingenuity, according to Holger Sonnabend, did not consist in his mere acquiescence in the balance of power (*Machtdualismus*) between Rome and Parthia, that is, the reality of the *divisio orbis* between the two empires,[5] but in his decision officially to recognize the division by rendering it the bedrock of his political ideology.[6] Thus, Augustus created the concept of another world (*alter orbis/alius orbis*), a decadent and uncivilized (Parthian) world, against which the Roman world (*orbis Romanus*) was determined to protect itself.[7] This (Oriental) world was characterized in the Augustan propaganda by decadence (*degeneratio*)—despotism, luxury, and polygamy among other commendable virtues—the causes of which were readily ascribed, through the Roman reception of Greek thought, to the ancient Persians, the Achaemenids. Indeed, since they regarded the Arsacids as the new occupants of the geographic expanse once held by the ancient Persians,[8] the same inventory of (often pejorative) attributes the Greeks used in order to characterize their former adversaries, the Achaemenids, was also applied to the Arsacids. The Arsacid military might, however, which, after its repeated victories over the Romans, did not fit the picture of the "degenerate Oriental," was explained as a remnant of the Arsacids' Scythian descent, but even this feature was deemed to have been exposed to the process of degeneration once the Arsacids became the hegemones of the Orient and heirs to the ancient Persians.[9]

Thus, Sonnabend's exhaustive study demonstrates that after Augustus's policy shift towards the Arsacid Empire, the Arsacids, who were deemed to be invincible in their own realm, were cast out from the "civilized world" (= *orbis Romanus*), where Rome ruled supreme, into another "parallel world," the *alter orbis*, where

[3] Sonnabend, *Fremdenbild und Politik*, 198–199.
[4] Sonnabend, *Fremdenbild und Politik*, 200.
[5] Sonnabend, *Fremdenbild und Politik*, 202–3.
[6] Sonnabend, *Fremdenbild und Politik*, 209–10.
[7] Sonnabend, *Fremdenbild und Politik*, 211–21.
[8] Sonnabend, *Fremdenbild und Politik*, 264–72.
[9] Sonnabend, *Fremdenbild und Politik*, 273–88, especially pp. 277–81.

Roman dominion was considered to be neither possible nor desired, for it ran the danger of succumbing to the degeneration plaguing the East.[10] Encouraged by Rome's reception of Greek thought and her lacunary knowledge of the Parthians, the *literati* sought the causes of Arsacid degeneration in the Arsacid past, in the Achaemenid Empire, with which Parthia, from this time on, became increasingly associated. It is, therefore, not surprising that poets of the Augustan Age referred to Parthians as *Persae* or *Medi*, and occasionally as *Achaemenii*.[11] In a striking passage in one of Horace's *Odes*, the throne of the Arsacid king Frahād IV (ca. 40 B.C.E. to 3/4 C.E.)—which he defended successfully against Tiridatês, the pretender backed by Rome—is described as that of Cyrus (*Cyri solium*), so as to establish unmistakably the link between the Parthians and the Achaemenids:[12]

> redditum *Cyri solio* Phraaten
> dissidens plebi numero beatorum
> eximit *virtus* populumque falsis
> dedocet uti ocibus

> [A]lthough Phraates has been restored to the *throne of Cyrus*, yet *virtus*, at variance with the populace, will bar (him) from the number of the happy, and teaches the people to employ false words. (Horace *Odes* 2.2.17–21)

Moreover, having indicated his dissatisfaction with the recovery of the Arsacid throne by Frahād, Horace, in an ode to his patron

[10] The substrate of the Augustan propaganda against Antonius, whom Augustus accused of "degeneration" and "orientalization," was similar to the essence of his foreign policy vis-à-vis the Arsacid realm, which was also based upon the notion that the opposition between East and West ought to be preserved, as suggested by Dietmar Kienast, "Augustus und Alexander," *Gymnasium* (Heidelberg) 76 (1969): 446.

[11] Some passages illustrating this phenomenon are Horace *Odes* 1.2.21–24; 1.2.49–52; 1.21.13–16; 2.16.5–8; 3.5.1–9; Ovid *Art of Love* 1.223–226. See also Sonnabend, *Fremdenbild und Politik*, 244–46, 255–58, 268–74, 280–88, 304; Schneider, "Die Faszination des Feindes," 106, 110–11; see also p. 111 n. 121 for a very useful and succinct list of passages—pertinent to the works of Virgil, Properce, Horace, and Ovid—in which Parthians are referred to as Medes, Persians, and Achaemenids (the reference to Virgil's "populi Parthorum aut Medes Hydaspes" should be emended to Virgil *Georgica* 4.211, instead of 5.211; and that to Horace's "Achaemenium" to *Odes* 3.1.44, instead of 2.12.21). For references to Achaemenid Persia in Horace and Ovid, see also Michael Wisseman, *Die Parther in der augusteischen Dichtung* (Frankfurt am Main: Lang, 1982), 71, 122–23.

[12] See Sonnabend, *Fremdenbild und Politik*, 255; also Wisseman, *Die Parther*, 68–69; and Schneider, "Die Faszination des Feindes," 111.

Maecenas, expresses his anxiety about the consequences of Frahād's superiority for Parthian–Roman relations; in this ode, the Parthian dominion is described as *regnata Cyro Bactra* "Bactra (once) ruled by Cyrus":[13]

> tu civitatem quis deceat status
> curas et urbi sollicitus times
> quid Seres et *regnata Cyro*
> *Bactra* parent Tanaisque discors.
>
> [Y]ou look to what condition is proper for the state, and, troubled for the city, you fear what the Sereans (= Chinese) and *Bactra (once) ruled by Cyrus* will comply with, as well as the rebellious (people) on the Tanais. (Horace *Odes* 3.29.25–28)

The consequence of this Roman equation between Arsacids and Achaemenids was that, to the extent the Parthians became heirs to the Persians in the Augustan propaganda, the Romans themselves were eventually identified with the ancient Greeks. The most remarkable manifestation of this identification consisted in the staged reenactment of episodes from the Persian Wars.[14] Significantly, the Roman emulation of past battles, or other events from the Persian Wars, was first introduced under Augustus with the reenactment of the Salaminian naumachia in 2 B.C.E., which took place in an arena by the Tiber excavated for that purpose.[15] The occasion for the staged sea battle of Salamis, in which the Athenians were triumphant, was the inauguration of the temple of Mars Ultor at the *Forum Augustum*,[16] where captured Roman standards were deposited after the peace treaty of 20 B.C.E. between Rome and Parthia. It is probable, as mentioned by Ovid (*Art of Love* 1.171–172), that the naumachia was prompted by the imminent departure of Augustus's grand- and adoptive son Gaius Caesar for an eastern campaign aiming at reimposing Roman suzerainty over Armenia,[17]

[13] Wisseman, *Die Parther*, 69.

[14] See Spawforth, "Symbol of Unity?" 237–43; Schneider, *Bunte Barbaren*, 63–67, and his "Die Faszination des Feindes," 112–13.

[15] Spawforth, "Symbol of Unity?" 238.

[16] On the temple of Mars Ultor, see Franz Alto Bauer, *Stadt, Platz und Denkmal in der Spätantike: Untersuchungen zur Ausstattung des öffentlichen Raumes in den spätantiken Städten Rom, Kontantinopel und Ephesos* (Mainz, Germany: Zabern, 1996), 86–89; also Joachim Ganzert, *Der Mars-Ultor-Tempel auf dem Augustusforum in Rom* (Deutsches Archäologisches Institut Rom 11; Mainz, Germany: Zabern, 1996).

[17] See Spawforth, "Symbol of Unity?" 238; Schneider, "Die Faszination des Feindes," 113.

where the Arsacids—in violation of the treaty of 20 B.C.E. that had placed Armenia under the protectorate of Rome[18]—had interfered, in order to facilitate the accession of their own candidates, Tigranês II's children Tigranês III and his sister Eratô.[19]

The reenactments of the Persian Wars initiated by Augustus with the Salaminian naumachia of 2 B.C.E. and continued by later emperors have been exhaustively surveyed by Antony Spawforth and Rolf Michael Schneider; in the following I shall be referring to their works.

Augustus's motives for having recourse to the symbolism of the Persian Wars on the eve of an eastern campaign are intriguing. Indeed, one would expect that Augustus, faced with an eastern foe who was increasingly associated with the ancient Persians, would make use of the same symbolism that the triumvirs of the Republic—Pompeius, Caesar, and Antonius—had utilized,[20] namely, the Alexander myth. But, despite his well-attested reverence for Alexander,[21] Augustus exploited the Persian Wars parallelisms. There are several reasons why Augustus adopted the Persian Wars motif in his ideological discourse: (1) the presence of Alexander in the Arsacid political ideology may have diminished the appeal of Alexander as the champion of the "West" against the "Eastern" Arsacids; but, more important, (2) the referral to Alexander would have forcibly evoked the notions of world conquest and world monarchy, both of which were irreconcilable with the princeps's political solution of the year 20 B.C.E.: the *divisio orbis*.[22] The notion

[18] On the treaty of 20 B.C.E. and its implications for Rome and the Arsacid Empire, see Karl-Heinz Ziegler, *Die Beziehungen zwischen Rom und dem Partherreich* (Wiesbaden: Steiner, 1964), 45–52; on the establishment of the *status quo ante* in an encounter between Gaius Caesar and Frahād V on the banks of the Euphrates, see pp. 53–57.

[19] On the Armenian problem, see Marie-Louise Chaumont, "L'Arménie entre Rome et l'Iran: De l'avènement d'Auguste à l'avènement de Dioclétien," *ANRW* 9.1:76–82.

[20] On the Alexander imitation of Pompeius, Caesar, and Antonius, see Dorothea Michel, *Alexander als Vorbild für Pompeius, Caesar und Marcus Antonius: Archäologische Untersuchungen* (Latomus 94; Brussels: Latomus, 1967), 35–135.

[21] On Augustus's *imitatio Alexandri*, see Kienast, "Augustus und Alexander," 430–56, especially 446–48. See similarly P. Ceauşescu, "La double image d'Alexandre le Grand à Rome," *Studi Clasice* (Bucharest) 16 (1974): 167–68.

[22] According to Kienast, the notion of Alexander as a source of emulation lost its appeal for Augustus after the treaty of 20 B.C.E., that is, following the realization of the concept of the *divisio orbis;* see Kienast, "Augustus und Alexander," 453; see also Ceauşescu, "La double image d'Alexandre," 167, who says: "[l]a politique *nationale* inaugurée par Auguste et *l'imitation* d'Alexandre étaient donc

of *degeneratio*, of which the Parthians were accused, not only made their conquest undesirable, but also rendered the idea of Roman world dominion through fusion of the two empires inconceivable. While the symbolism of the Alexander imitation was fraught with consequences, the Persian Wars motif implied neither the indispensable conquest of the East nor any fusion with it, *but rather the successful defense of the West against Eastern aggression.*[23]

Now we must recall that the Armenian succession, which had progressed contrary to Rome's interests with the unsanctioned accession of Tigranês III and his sister Eratô after Tigranês II's death (ca. 6 B.C.E.),[24] was probably conceived by Rome as the direct result of tacit Arsacid support for the Armenian pro-Parthian faction.[25] The naumachia of the year 2 B.C.E. could therefore have been Augustus's response to covert Parthian assistance to the accession of Tigranês III and his sister, although incontestable evidence for Arsacid intervention in the Armenian succession emerged only after the enthronement of the new Arsacid king Frahād V (ca. 3–2 B.C.E.),[26] who at that time began openly to support Tigranês III and his sister against Augustus's attempt to instate his own candidate Artavasdes with an escort of Roman troops (ca. 1 B.C.E.).[27] Therefore, Arsacid backing for the pro-Parthian faction in Armenia could have been perceived as a violation of Roman suzerainty and could consequently be paralleled with the Persian (= Achaemenid) attempt to subdue Athenian sovereignty by war.

The battle of Salamis, in which the Athenians had triumphed (Dio Cassius *Roman History* 55.10.7–8), provided not only a historical precedent with which to compare the present aggression of the Arsacids against Roman sovereignty, but, more important, was also envisioned as a response to the Arsacid aggression: a moderate and limited military intervention aimed only at reestablishing the *status*

irréconciliables" ("the *national* policy instated by Augustus and the Alexander *imitation* were thus irreconcilable").

[23] See Spawforth, "Symbol of Unity?" 240.

[24] Chaumont, "L'Arménie entre Rome et l'Iran," 76–77; also Klaus Schippmann, *Grundzüge der parthischen Geschichte* (Darmstadt, Germany: Wissenschaftliche Buchgesellschaft, 1980), 48.

[25] See Edward Dąbrowa, *La politique de l'état parthe à l'égard de Rome* (Krakow: Jagiellonian University Press, 1983), 43.

[26] On the chronology of Frahād V's accession, see Georges Le Rider, *Suse sous les Séleucides et les Parthes* (Paris: Guethner, 1965), 418–19.

[27] On this episode, see David Magie, *Roman Rule in Asia Minor* (2 vols.; Princeton: Princeton University Press, 1950), 1:481–85.

quo ante in Armenia, without the inconvenience of a war of conquest required by the *imitatio*.

To sum up:

1. Following the treaty of 20 B.C.E. between Rome and the Arsacid Empire, which led to the recognition of the Euphrates as the border between the two realms and the acknowledgment of Roman suzerainty over Armenia, Augustus initiated a new eastern policy by renouncing the aggressive stance of its predecessors;

2. The ideological foundation for this renouncement rested on the new definition of the Arsacid realm as an *alter orbis*, a degenerate world, whose conquest was undesirable for Rome;

3. The equation of the Parthians with the ancient Persians, an equation deemed to be the source of Arsacid degeneration, prepared the way for the identification of Romans with the former champions of the West: ancient Hellas and/or Alexander;

4. The Salaminian naumachia of 2 B.C.E. illustrates that the symbolism of an *Alexander redivivus*—notwithstanding Augustus's continued veneration for the Macedonian—was substituted for, or at least supplemented by, another one more in line with the exigencies of Augustus's eastern *Realpolitik*. The *imitatio Alexandri* with its inevitable call for eastern conquest was fundamentally at odds with the Augustan conception of a *divisio orbis*. In anticipation of an impending eastern campaign, Rome, through the symbolism of the Persian Wars, as illustrated by the staged battle of Salamis, not only acquiesced to the reality of an eastern power capable of endangering Roman interest, but, more important, also set the limit for the military riposte when faced with Arsacid aggression; under Augustus, Rome's military campaigns would aim at preserving Roman suzerainty to the extent stipulated by the treaty of 20 B.C.E., and, whenever infringed, it would reestablish the *status quo ante*, like the Athenians who preserved their sovereignty against the Persians in the sea battle at Salamis.

In conclusion, we can say that the equation of the Arsacids with the Achaemenids, which was prompted by Roman political exigencies and possibly inspired by the simultaneous Achaemenid reminiscences within the Arsacid Empire, led to the identification of the Romans with the ancient Greeks. The equation of *the Arsacids with the Achaemenids* can be observed in literary and artistic productions of the Augustan era, whereas, the equation of *Romans with the ancient Greeks* was first illustrated in the Salaminian naumachia of 2 B.C.E.

IMITATIO ALEXANDRI AND THE SASANIAN "ACHAEMENID REVIVAL"

What did the Sasanians know about the Achaemenids? Can we assume that the equations of the Augustan era lasted until the advent of the Sasanians, who then replaced the Arsacids as the successors of the Achaemenids in the Roman *imaginaire*? In order to answer this question, I shall first address the striking revival in Rome of the Alexander symbolism at the end of the second century, in the decades immediately preceding the advent of the Sasanians.

What we can see during these decades, when, as eloquently worded by Alfred Heuss, "Alexander von einer erregenden Gegenwärtigkeit [war]" ("Alexander [remained] ever present"),[28] is not so much that Arsacids and Achaemenids, Romans and Greeks of old, were equated—although there were occasional allusions to the Persian Wars under Caracalla (214) and Gordian III (235)[29]—as an increasing urgency to imitate Alexander.

The advent of the Severans gave rise to a renewed interest in Alexander in Rome. Despite Septimius Severus's considerable expansion of the *limes* beyond the Euphrates,[30] following the short-

[28] Alfred Heuss, "Alexander der Große und die politische Ideologie des Altertums," *Antike und Abendland* 4 (1954): 98.

[29] See Spawforth, "Symbol of Unity?" 239–40.

[30] On the eastern campaigns of Septimius Severus (195 and 197 C.E.) and the creation of the provinces of Osrhoênê and Mesopotamia, see Magie, *Roman Rule in Asia Minor,* 1:672–75 and 2:1543–45 n. 26; also Maria Gabriella Angeli Bertinelli, "I Romani oltre l'Eufrate nel II secolo d. C. (le province di Assiria, di Mesopotamia e di Osroene)," in *ANRW* 9.1:34–41; Schippmann, *Grundzüge der parthischen Geschichte,* 68–69; Edward Dąbrowa, "Le programme de la politique en Occident des derniers Arsacides," *Iranica Antiqua* 19 (1984): 155–57; Anthony R. Birley, *Septimius Severus: The African Emperor* (rev. and enl. ed.; New Haven: Yale University Press, 1989), 129–31; and Marcelo Tilman Schmidt, *Die römische Außenpolitik des 2. Jarhunderts n. Chr.: Friedenssicherung oder Expansion?* (Stuttgart: Steiner, 1997), 69–72; see also Ziegler, *Die Beziehungen zwischen Rom und dem Partherreich*, 129–32.

lived success of Trajan and the reaffirmation of the Augustan policy by Hadrian and his successors,[31] the Alexander myth was undoubtedly *not* the cause of Severus's eastern campaign,[32] in spite of his veneration for the Macedonian.[33] The same, however, cannot safely be assumed with respect to the eastern campaigns of his successors Caracalla and Alexander Severus.

Caracalla's *imitatio*, which has been reported by Dio Cassius[34] and Herodian,[35] and which manifested itself variously,[36] could have

[31] On Hadrian's eastern policy, see Magie, *Roman Rule in Asia Minor*, 1:611–29; Ziegler, *Die Beziehungen zwischen Rom und dem Partherreich*, 105–10; M. K. Thornton, "Hadrian and his Reign," *ANRW* 2:435–37; Schmidt, *Die römische Außenpolitik*, 63–64. On Lucius Verus's successful Parthian campaign, which led to minor territorial gains and the military penetration of the Osrhoênê and possibly also of the Adiabene, although the Euphrates continued to constitute the boundary between the two realms, see Magie, *Roman Rule in Asia Minor*, 1:660–62; Angeli Bertinelli, "I Romani oltre l'Eufrate nel II secolo d. C.," 30–31; Schippmann, *Grundzüge der parthischen Geschichte*, 67; Dąbrowa, "Le programme de la politique en Occident," 153–54; and Schmidt, *Die römische Außenpolitik*, 65–68; a different opinion in Ziegler, *Die Beziehungen zwischen Rom und dem Partherreich*, 114.

[32] Septimius Severus's first Parthian campaign in 195 was essentially motivated by the desire to reestablish Roman authority in Osrhoênê and possibly to extend it onto the Parthian vassal state of Adiabene; Roman authority was conceivably shaken after the Parthian provocation during Severus's power struggle with Pescennius Niger. The second Parthian campaign of Severus in 197 followed upon an Arsacid counteroffensive that led to the conquest of Adiabene and the thwarted siege of Nisibis, which was abandoned as the Roman forces approached; see Ziegler, *Die Beziehungen zwischen Rom und dem Partherreich*, 130–31; Schippmann, *Grundzüge der parthischen Geschichte*, 68–69; Józef Wolski, *L'empire des Arsacides* (Acta Iranica 32; Louvain: Peeters, 1993), 188–90.

[33] On Severus's Alexander imitation, see still Adrien Bruhl, "Le souvenir d'Alexandre le Grand et les Romains," *Mélanges d'Archéologie et d'Histoire* 47 (1930): 214; Heuss, "Alexander der Große und die politische Ideologie des Altertums," 98–99; and Birley, *Septimius Severus*, 135–36.

[34] Dio Cassius *Roman History* 78.7.1–78.8.3; 78.22.1–2; 79.1.1–2; on Dio's judgment of Caracalla, see Rosemarie Bering-Staschewski, *Römische Zeitgeschichte bei Cassius Dio* (Bochum, Germany: Brockmeyer, 1981), 77–92, especially pp. 83–84. For a comparative summarized table of classical reports on Caracalla's alleged Alexander imitation, see Urbano Espinosa, "La Alejandrofilia de Caracala en la antigua historiografia," in *Neronia IV: Alejandro Magno, modelo de los emperadores romanos. Actes du IVe colloque de la SIEN* (ed. Jean-Michel Croisille; Latomus 209; Brussels: Latomus, 1990), 40–41.

[35] Herodian *History* 4.8.1–2; 4.8.6–7, 9; 4.9.3–5; 4.10.1–5.

[36] On Caracalla's *imitatio Alexandri*, see Bruhl, "Le souvenir d'Alexandre le Grand et les Romains," 214–18; Heuss, "Alexander der Große und die politische Ideologie des Altertums," 99–100; on Caracalla's "Alexandrophilia," on the other hand, see Espinosa, "La Alejandrofilia de Caracala," 37–51; also Michel Christol, *L'empire romain du IIIe siècle: Histoire politique (de 192, mort de Commode, à 325,*

constituted the stimulus for his Parthian campaign, since the Arsacids had provided no *casus belli*. Already in an article published in 1974, P. Ceauşescu put forth the thesis that the sum of Caracalla's political measures—such as the bestowal of Roman citizenship on the entire population of the empire, as reflected in the *constitutio Antoniniana* and in Dio Cassius's account, as well as Caracalla's reported offer to marry King Artabanus's daughter—could suggest that the *imitatio Alexandri* was a decisive force that strongly determined the emperor's course of political actions.[37] These actions could have been animated by the illusive hope of a world monarchy through fusion of the two realms, for which the *constitutio Antoniniana* and the marriage proposal to the Arsacid king Artabanus constituted the prelude.[38] Although there may have been numerous other motivations for introducing the *constitutio Antoniniana*[39] and, although Caracalla's marriage proposal could be viewed as a mere pretext to wage a war of conquest with the Arsacid realm (Dio Cassius *Roman History* 79.1.1) or even an invention,[40] the fact remains

concile de Nicée) (Paris: Éditions Errance, 1997), 40–41. On other manifestations of Caracalla's Alexander imitation, notably the herd of elephants that reportedly accompanied him on his itinerary (Dio Cassius *Roman History* 78.7.4), see Julien Guey, "Les éléphants de Caracalla (216 après J.-C.)," *REA* 49/3–4 (1947): 248–73, especially pp. 268–73, and Julien Guey, "Les animaux célestes du nouvel édit de Caracalla," CRAI (Jan.–Apr. 1948): 128–30.

[37] Ceauşescu, "La double image d'Alexandre," 166–67; see also Fergus Millar, *The Roman Near East: 31 B.C.–A.D. 337* (Cambridge, Mass.: Harvard University Press, 1993), 142, who states: "Abundant contemporary evidence makes perfectly clear that Caracalla's imitation of Alexander was no superficial whim, but the determinating factor in his actions as Emperor. It is surely relevant also to his historic proclamation that the entire population of the Empire should become Roman citizens." See also Joseph Vogt, "Zu Pausanias und Caracalla," *Historia* 18 (1969): 306–7.

[38] Herodian *History* 4.2–4; see Ceauşescu, "La double image d'Alexandre," 166; also Ziegler, *Die Beziehungen zwischen Rom und dem Partherreich*, 133; On the marriage proposal, see also Joseph Vogt, "Die Tochter des Großkönigs und Pausanias, Alexander, Caracalla," in *Gesetz und Handlungsfreiheit in der Geschichte* (Lebendiges Wissen 8; Stuttgart: Kohlhammer, 1955), 72–80; and Vogt, "Zu Pausanias und Caracalla," 303–8.

[39] For a recent and succinct review of various interpretations of the *constitutio*, see Christol, *L'empire romain du IIIe siècle*, 38–39; for a survey of past scholarship up to 1972, see Gerold Walser and Thomas Pekáry, *Die Krise des römischen Reiches: Bericht über die Forschungen zur Geschichte des 3. Jahrhunderts (193–284 n. Chr.) von 1939 bis 1959* (Berlin: de Gruyter, 1962), 11–12; and Gerold Walser, "Die Severer in der Forschung 1960–1972," *ANRW* 2:627–28.

[40] See Dieter Timpe, "Ein Heiratsplan Kaiser Caracallas," *Hermes* 95 (1967): 470–95, especially the author's concluding remark on p. 494. Cf. also the convincing criticism of Timpe's thesis by Vogt, "Zu Pausanias und Caracalla," 303–6.

that Caracalla's policy toward the Arsacids, his willingness to provoke an unjustified war of *conquest*, or *fusion*, was governed by the exploits of Alexander the Great.[41]

The *imitatio* of Alexander Severus (Bassianus Alexianus), the main source for whose life remains the *Historia Augusta*, is absent from the account of Herodian and is more ambiguous than the one documented for Caracalla. The fact that Herodian does not mention any instance of *imitatio* for Alexander Severus, and, more important, the fact that the composition of the *Historia Augusta* in general and that of the *vita Alexandri Severi* in particular are commonly ascribed to the late fourth century C.E.[42]—when, due to the revival of the Alexander myth,[43] the *vita* evolved into a treatise of good government, rather than a historical biography[44]—do not support the veracity of the Alexander imitation that the *vita* attributes to Alexander Severus. Indeed, aside from the account of the *Historia Augusta*, there is little evidence to validate Severus's *imitatio*; in contrast to Caracalla, there are no allusions in Severus's inscriptions and on his coins to Alexander the Great,[45] and intriguingly, against the testimony of *Historia Augusta*,[46] Severus seems to have neither

[41] See Vogt, "Zu Pausanias und Caracalla," 306–7. On the chronology of Caracalla's campaign of 216–217 against Parthia, see André Maricq, "La chronologie des dernières années de Caracalla," in *Classica et Orientalia: Extrait de Syria 1955–1962, revu et corrigé, augmenté d'un article inédit et d'un index* (Institut Français d'Archéologie de Beyrouth 11; Paris: Geuthner, 1965), 27–32; on the campaign itself, see Chaumont, "L'Arménie entre Rome et l'Iran," 152–56; Schippmann, *Grundzüge der parthischen Geschichte*, 71–72; Dąbrowa, "Le programme de la politique en Occident," 158–59; and Wolski, *L'empire des Arsacides*, 192.

[42] See Cécile Bertrand-Dagenbach, *Alexandre Sévère et l'Histoire Auguste* (Latomus 208; Brussels: Latomus, 1990), 76–80.

[43] See L. Cracco-Ruggini, "Sulla cristianizzazione della cultura pagana: Il mito greco e latino di Alessandro dall'età Antonina al medioevo," *Athenaeum* (Pavia) 43/1–2 (1965): 4–56; and L. Cracco-Ruggini, "Un riflesso del mito di Alessandro nella 'Historia Augusta,'" in *Bonner Historia-Augusta-Colloquium, 1968–1969* (Antiquitas 4; Beiträge zur Historia-Augusta-Forschung 7; ed. Johannes Straub; Bonn: Habelt, 1970), 79–89.

[44] See Bertrand-Dagenbach, *Alexandre Sévère*, 120; also José Maria Blázquez, "Alejandro Magno: Modelo de Alejandro Severo," in *Neronia IV: Alejandro Magno, modelo de los emperadores romanos: Actes du IVe colloque de la SIEN* (ed. Jean-Michel Croisille; Latomus 209; Brussels: Latomus, 1990), 35.

[45] See Blázquez, "Alejandro Magno," 35, who states: "La no alusión a Alejandro Magno en las inscripciones y en las monedas y en Herodiano, nos parece fundamental *para negar esta imitación* [italics mine]" ("The lack of any reference to Alexander the Great in inscriptions and on coinage, as well as in Herodian's work, seems essential to us, *in order to refute this imitation*").

[46] SHA *Alexander Severus* 11.2; 56.9.

carried the title of *magnus*,[47] nor the victory title(s) *Parthicus/Persicus (maximus)*,[48] which, according to Peter Panitschek, "im gegebenen Rahmen der Kaiseridee am ehesten das Bindeglied zum realpolitischen Alexandermythos hätten darstellen können" ("would have been most likely to represent, within the prevailing framework of the imperial ideology, the link to the realpolitical Alexander myth").[49] Despite the lack of direct evidence for Severus's *imitatio*, there is still sufficient indication that the emperor consciously embraced the Alexander myth either on his own initiative or encouraged by his entourage. The fact that Severus (Bassianus Alexianus) was named "Alexander" when adopted by his predecessor, Elagabalus,[50] and later was proclaimed Caracalla's son,[51] means that Severus was consciously associated with Alexander the Great, probably in order to strengthen in the public eye his affinity with Caracalla, whose infatuation with the Macedonian was well known.

[47] For a discussion of the historicity of the title *magnus* for Alexander Severus, see Jacques Gascou, "Une énigme épigraphique: Sévère Alexandre et la titulature de Giufi," *Antiquités Africaines* 17 (1981): 231–40; and Gianna Dareggi, "Severo Alessandro: *Romanus Alexander*," *Latomus* (Brussels) 53/3 (1994): 848–58, especially p. 855; also Dietmar Kienast, *Römische Kaisertabelle: Grundzüge einer römischen Kaiserchronologie* (Darmstadt: Wissenschaftliche Buchgesellschaft, 1990), 177.

[48] See Peter Kneissl, *Die Siegestitulatur der römischen Kaiser: Untersuchungen zu den Siegerbeinamen des ersten und zweiten Jahrhunderts* (Hypomnemata 23; Göttingen: Vandenhoeck & Ruprecht, 1969), 167–68; also Peter Panitschek, "Zur Darstellung der Alexander- und Achaemenidennachfolge als politische Programme in kaiserzeitlichen Quellen," *Klio* 72 (1990): 465; also Kienast, *Römische Kaisertabelle*, 178; a different opinion in Christol, *L'empire romain du IIIe siècle*, 76. For a more nuanced view, see Engelbert Winter, *Die sasanidisch-römischen Friedensverträge des 3. Jahrhunderts n. Chr.: Ein Beitrag zum Verständnis der außenpolitischen Beziehungen zwischen den beiden Großmächten* (New York: Lang, 1988), 60–62.

[49] Panitschek, "Zur Darstellung der Alexander– und Achaemenidennachfolge," 464.

[50] See Auguste Jardé, *Études critiques sur la vie et le règne de Sévère Alexandre* (Paris: De Boccard, 1925), 1–3; Bruhl, "Le souvenir d'Alexandre le Grand et les Romains," 218–19.

[51] Initially Alexander Severus was adopted by Elagabalus, who himself was proclaimed Caracalla's son (see Erich Kettenhoffen, *Die syrischen Augustae in der historischen Überlieferung: Ein Beitrag zum Problem der Orientalisierung* [Antiquitas 3; Abhandlungen zur Vor- und Frühgeschichte, zur klassischen und provinzial-römischen Archäologie und zur Geschichte des Altertums 24; Bonn: Habelt, 1979], 25–28, 36–37), but after his own ascension, Alexander Severus eliminated all reference to Elagabalus, becoming himself directly Caracalla's son (see Kettenhoffen, *Die syrischen Augustae*, 36–37; also Kienast, *Römische Kaisertabelle*, 177–78; and Christol, *L'empire romain du IIIe siècle*, 49, 51–52, 67 nn. 10–11).

The episode of Severus's adoption by Elagabalus under the name of "Alexander" is reported by Dio Cassius, who associates this event with the account of the short-lived insurrection of a pseudo-Alexander.[52] Dio mentions that the adoption and naming of Severus by Elagabalus came about by some divine arrangement (ἐκ θείας τινὸς παρασκευῆς, Dio Cassius *Roman History* 80.17.3), for which he (Dio) provides two foregoing omens: the first of these was, as Dio reports, a statement made to Elagabalus that an Alexander should come from Emesa to succeed him (Ἀλέξανδρος ἐξ Ἐμέσης ἐλθὼν αὐτὸν διαδέξεται, Dio Cassius *Roman History* 80.17.3), and the second, which occurred before the adoption of Severus by Elagabalus, was the successful crusade of a pseudo-Alexander—literally a δαίμων ("soul") claiming to be Alexander of Macedonia—who throughout his itinerary via Moesia and Thrace as far as Byzantium did not encounter any resistance either from the officials or from the populace. What is more, the communal officials in Thrace, far from opposing the δαίμων, provided for him at public expense (Dio Cassius *Roman History* 80.18.1–2). This pseudo-Alexander, according to Dio, finally vanished after having performed sacred rites by night in Chalcedon (Dio Cassius *Roman History* 80.18.3). It follows from Dio's passage that the conferral of the name "Alexander" on Severus (Bassianus Alexianus) bore out the general belief that Severus was identical with the awaited Alexander from Emesa[53] and possibly, as Dio's report or our understanding of it seems to suggest, was the resurrection/continuation of the very δαίμων that had so mysteriously vanished. An inscription found in Moesia at the end of the nineteenth century and convincingly interpreted by Edmund Groag in 1909[54] seems to confirm the historicity of Dio's account. It is dedicated to a group of divinities by a certain Epi-

[52] Dio Cassius *Roman History* 80.17.1–18.3. On this episode see the important contribution of Jean Gagé, "L'horoscope de Doura et le culte d'Alexandre sous les Sévères," *Bulletin de la Faculté de Lettres de Strasbourg* 33 (1954–1955): 151–68, especially 164–66.

[53] The family of the Syrian *augusti* Elagabalus and Severus Alexander had its roots in the Syrian city of Emesa, where the cult of the Elagabal divinity, as whose high priest Emperor Elagabalus was groomed, was exercised; on the Elagabal cult of Emesa, see Martin Frey, *Untersuchungen zur Religion und zur Religionspolitik des Kaisers Elagabal* (Historia Einzelschriften 62; Stuttgart: Steiner, 1989), 45–71, especially pp. 45–49.

[54] See Edmund Groag, "Alexander in einer Inschrift des 3. Jahrhunderts n. Chr.," in *Wiener Eranos: Zur fünfzigsten Versammlung deutscher Philologen und Schulmänner in Graz 1909* (Wien: Hölder, 1909), 252–55, whose interpretation I have followed. See also Gagé, "L'horoscope de Doura," 166.

tynchanus, slave of Furius Octavianus, a well-known senator under the Severan emperors Caracalla, Elagabalus, and Alexander Severus, who had estates in Moesia ("Epitynchanus servus Furi Octavi clarissimi viri").[55] The divinities comprise Jupiter (Jove) and Juno, but also a male and a female serpent, as well as an Alexander ("Jovi et Junoni et dracconi et draccenae et *Alexandro* . . . posuit"). Groag interpreted the *dracco* and *draccena* of the inscription as elements of the Moesian popular cult,[56] but he identified *Alexander* with the same δαίμων who, operating in Moesia and Thrace, claimed to be the resurrected Alexander of Macedonia shortly before Severus's adoption by Elagabalus. Thus, Epitynchanus, who made his dedication possibly stimulated by the deeds of the δαίμων, ensured also the benevolence of the δαίμων by including him with Roman and Moesian divinities in his dedication.[57]

That the Alexander symbolism held a vigorous sway over people's imagination under the Severans is illustrated by yet another circumstance. Among the Greek graffiti discovered during the excavations of Dura-Europus and estimated to date back to the years 230–235 C.E., the horoscope of a certain Alexander Macedon (Ἀλέξανδρος Μακεδών), born 11 December 218 C.E., is of special interest.[58] While the name "Macedon" was commonly used as a personal name during the empire, as other examples bear witness,[59] its occurrence in association with another Greek name, "Alexander," led the editors of the horoscope to believe that "Macedon" was in reality an ethnic designation.[60] Jean Gagé, however,

[55] Groag, "Alexander in einer Inschrift," 251–53.

[56] Groag, "Alexander in einer Inschrift," 255.

[57] Groag, "Alexander in einer Inschrift," 255.

[58] On the graffiti in general see C. B. Welles, "Graffiti," in *The Excavations at Dura-Europos: Preliminary Report of Fourth Season of Work, October 1930–March 1931* (ed. P. V. C. Baur, Michael I. Rostovtzeff, and Alfred R. Bellinger; New Haven: Yale University Press, 1933), 79–177; on the horoscope in particular see item 232, pp. 105–10; see also Gagé, "L'horoscope de Doura," 151–68, to whose views I subscribe. The complete text and translation of the horoscope (Welles, "Graffiti," 107) are as follows: ἔτους λφʹ, μηνὸς Αὐδνέου θʹ κατὰ σελήνην εʹ, ἡμέρᾳ Κρόνου, περὶ γʹ ὥρ(ας) ἡμερινῆς, ἐγενήθη Ἀλέξαν(δρος) Μακεδὼν Ἀπολλωνίκου· ἐν Ἰχθυδίῳ ὡρ(οσκόπος) Ὑδροχοῦς ("In the year 530, on the ninth of the month Audnaeus and on the fifth day of the moon, Saturday, about the third hour of the day, was born Alexander Macedonius son of Apollonicus; in the constellation of Pisces; Aquarius was rising on the horizon").

[59] Welles, "Graffiti," 110.

[60] Welles, "Graffiti," 110: ". . . Μακεδών was common under the empire as a personal name . . . [t]he double name, however, Alexandros Macedon, offers difficulties. Double names are common where the first is non-Greek, especially with

whose views have been embraced here, proposed some time ago that Μακεδών should be regarded as a personal name; according to him, "Alexander Macedon" could well be the personal name of an inhabitant of Dura-Europus named after the Great Macedonian, because the stellar constellation of his birth recalled that of Alexander. What is more, the reason for bestowing so illustrious a name on a private citizen in December 218 C.E.—that is, shortly after the rise of Elagabalus and more than two years before the occurrence of a pseudo-Alexander in Moesia—resided, according to Gagé, in the growing importance of the Alexander legend among the empire's Oriental population.[61] One other aspect of the horoscope needs to be discussed. While there is a plausible reason for naming a private citizen "Alexander Macedon" in 218 C.E., the appearance of *his* horoscope as graffiti in the years 230–235 C.E. requires an explanation. The recurrence of the horoscope over a decade following its genesis can only be attributed to the emerging danger to which the rise of the Sasanians and the aggressive campaigns of King Ardašīr in the years 230–233 C.E.[62] had exposed the eastern boundaries of the Roman Empire, notably Dura-Europus. In such circumstances, Gagé argues, it was not surprising that the expectations for the appearance of a *novus Alexander*, which had been stirred up by the deliberate association of Severus with Alexander the Great already at his adoption by Elagabalus, who could preempt the Sasanian menace, grew stronger as the emperor committed himself to a Persian campaign in 232.[63] Thus, while the horoscope was originally made to celebrate the birth of a certain Alexander Macedon of Dura, whose claim to fame was the similarity the stellar constellation of his birth displayed with the one ascribed to Alexander the Great, when it recurred on a wall a decade later it was meant to celebrate both the Macedonian hero, whom the horoscope recalled, and his incarnation Alexander Severus.[64]

Roman citizens . . . [b]ut double Greek names ran counter to the principles of ancient nomenclature, and it is probably better here to take Macedon as an ethnic. It is not impossible that at Dura as generally in Mesopotamia there was a social class which called its members Μακεδόνες. . . ."

[61] Gagé, "L'horoscope de Doura," 156.

[62] On Ardašīr's Roman campaign in general, see Josef Wiesehöfer, "Ardašīr I (?–242 A.D.): The Founder of the Sasanian Empire," *Encyclopaedia Iranica* 2.371–76; on Ardašīr's first confrontation with the Roman Empire in the years 230–233 C.E., see Winter, *Die sasanidisch-römischen Friedensverträge*, 45–68.

[63] Gagé, "L'horoscope de Doura," 166–67.

[64] Gagé, "L'horoscope de Doura," 168.

A final source for Alexander Severus's *imitatio* is provided by Jacques Gascou's relatively recent interpretation of two inscriptions from the North African town of Giufi.[65] According to these inscriptions, the city of Giufi became a free town (*municipium*) sometime between December 228 and March 235 C.E.,[66] with the impressive title of *municipium Aurellium Alexandrianum Augustum Magnum Giufitanum*[67] after Alexander Severus's imperial appellation *Imperator Caesar Marcus Aurel(l)ius Severus Alexander Augustus*.[68] Gascou demonstrated beyond doubt that the adjective *magnum*, although not otherwise attested for Alexander Severus on epigraphic and numismatic material,[69] referred in this context to him.[70] The inclusion of the title *magnus* in the inscriptions of Giufi was interpreted by Gascou as a deliberate attempt, possibly by the municipal authorities, to flatter the emperor by associating him with Alexander of Macedonia, either before or during Severus's Persian campaign or upon his return or even during the celebration of his triumph in Rome. Whether or not the emperor knew about or approved of the honor bestowed upon him by Giufi's authorities is of no consequence; important is solely the fact that they (the town's authorities) used the *epithet of Alexander the Great* in order to flatter him.[71]

However, an important point distinguishes the *imitatio* of Alexander Severus from that of Caracalla: Severus's eastern campaign was a direct response to Sasanian aggression in Mesopotamia, and it is unclear whether it ever intended, beyond the recovery of wrested Roman territory, to penetrate deep into the Sasanian realm in an effort to subdue eastern lands.[72] The Persian campaign of Alexander Severus, despite being depicted by Herodian as an ill-fated expedition,[73] seems nonetheless to have resulted in a temporary

[65] See Gascou, "Une énigme épigraphique," 231–40.

[66] See Gascou, "Une énigme épigraphique," 232; see also R. Duncan-Jones, "Patronage and City Privileges: The Case of Giufi," *Epigraphische Studien* 9 (1971): 12–16.

[67] Gascou, "Une énigme épigraphique," 233.

[68] Gascou, "Une énigme épigraphique," 233; and Kienast, *Römische Kaisertabelle*, 177.

[69] Gascou, "Une énigme épigraphique," 239.

[70] Gascou, "Une énigme épigraphique," 233–34.

[71] Gascou, "Une énigme épigraphique," 230.

[72] For a succinct description of Alexander Severus's eastern expedition, see Magie, *Roman Rule in Asia Minor*, 1:695–96; 2:1560–61; also Christol, *L'empire romain du IIIe siècle*, 75–76.

[73] See Herodian *History* 6.5.1–6.6.3.

cessation of hostilities with the Sasanians and in the reestablishment of the territorial *status quo ante*.[74] The very fact that Alexander Severus did not exhibit any particular predisposition for an offensive warfare during his military venture in Germany as well and was, according to Herodian, who accuses him of being a coward (ἄνανδρος),[75] far more disposed to conclude peace with the Germans[76] (and to fortify his defensive positions against Persians)[77] than to cross the Rhine, could indicate that Alexander was as a matter of policy inclined toward defensive warfare, rather than a campaign of expansion, which could have been expected from a *novus Alexander*. Here lies the ambiguity of Alexander Severus's ideological foundation and *Realpolitik*: On one hand, he clearly sought to emulate the great Macedonian, for all the aforementioned reasons; on the other hand, however, his policy is a measured military response in the best Augustan tradition, a policy that follows the paradigm of the Salaminian naumachia, that is, a policy inspired by the fifth-century Athenians who defended their territories against invading Persian armies.

These tensions within Alexander Severus's political ideology and policy are unmistakably reflected in Flavius Philostratus's *Heroikos*, which, in my opinion, simultaneously captures and resolves the dichotomy of Severus's ideological representation(s) and foreign policy. We shall therefore briefly discuss the *Heroikos* in view of Severus's policy vis-à-vis the Persian empire of the Sasanians.

[74] See Herodian *History* 6.6.4–6.7.1. Compare also SHA *Alexander Severus* 15.1–17.

[75] Herodian accuses Alexander Severus in several passages of cowardice: during his campaign against the Persians (*History* 6.5.9); again while depicting the despair of the Illyrian soldiers at the announcement of the German raid into Illyria, they (the soldiers) are reported to have ascribed their misfortunes in the war against the Persians, as well as the devastation of their homes, to Alexander's cowardice (*History* 6.7.3); and finally, in his description of Maximinus's plot against Alexander, Herodian contrasts the *soldatesque*'s admiration for the courage of the former with its despite for the cowardice of the latter (*History* 6.8.3); see also *History* 6.9.5. In contrast, the *Historia Augusta* (SHA *Alexander Severus* 19.5) reports that the mutiny against Alexander was triggered by his excessive severity.

[76] See Herodian *History* 6.7.9.

[77] See Herodian *History* 6.7.5.

PHILOSTRATUS'S *HEROIKOS*

The *Heroikos*, which has been the subject of intense study in recent years,[78] is a dialogue between a local Greek vineyard worker in charge of the gardens and the vineyard surrounding the tomb of the hero Protesilaos and a Phoenician merchant waiting for more favorable winds to set forth on his journey. The setting is Elaious, a southern city on the Thracian Chersonesus on the European side of the Hellespont. The vineyard worker is an intimate of Protesilaos, the first Achaean to fall in Troy, and relates to the Phoenician merchant the hero's account of the Trojan War and his discussion of Homer's poems; Ellen Aitken and Jennifer Maclean have eloquently described Protesilaos's retrospective musings in the introduction to their new *Heroikos* edition:

> . . . the dialogue is dedicated to a discussion of the heroes, but not simply as a retelling of Homer. Protesilaos is, after all, a more trustworthy witness not only of the events prior to landing at Troy (when he died), but also of those that occurred afterward, since he is "free from the body and diseases" and thus can "observe the affairs of mortals" (*Her.* 7.3). From this privileged vantage point, Protesilaos the hero is both reader and critic of Homer.[79]

Two aspects of the *Heroikos* make it invaluable for the purposes of the present study: On the one hand, Philostratus belonged to the Second Sophistic (with its reception and exaltation of the Hellenic past),[80] was included in Julia Domna's Circle (κύκλος), and was

[78] See Valeria Rossi, ed. and trans., *Filostrato: Eroico* (Venice: Marsilio, 1997); Andreas Beschorner, *Helden und Heroen, Homer und Caracalla: Übersetzung, Kommentar und Interpretationen zum* Heroikos *des Flavios Philostratos* (Pinakes 5; Bari, Italy: Levanti, 1999); and Jennifer K. Berenson Maclean and Ellen Bradshaw Aitken, trans., *Flavius Philostratus: Heroikos* (SBLWGRW 1; Atlanta: Society of Biblical Literature, 2001).

[79] Maclean and Aitken, *Flavius Philostratus: Heroikos*, xxxviii.

[80] On the Second Sophistic, its ethos, affected archaism, and yearning for the Hellenic past, see Graham Anderson, *The Second Sophistic: A Cultural Phenomenon in the Roman Empire* (London: Routledge, 1993), 1–12, 86–100, 101–43, 234–46; Ewen L. Bowie, "Greeks and Their Past in the Second Sophistic," *Past and Present* 46 (1970): 3–41; also Lukas de Blois, "The Third-Century Crisis and the Greek Elite in the Roman Empire," *Historia* 33 (1984): 358–77, and "Emperor and Empire in the Works of Greek-Speaking Authors of the Third Century AD," *ANRW* 34.4:3391–3404.

closely associated with the Severan court,[81] at least until Julia Domna's demise in 217[82]—all reasons that suggest the *Heroikos* could reflect, if not the official Severan political ideology under Alexander Severus, at least some of the tensions that characterized the late Severan imperial policy vis-à-vis Sasanian Iran. On the other hand, the *Heroikos*'s chief heroes, Protesilaos and Achilles, these "watchful defenders of all that is Greek from all that is not"[83] in afterlife, reflect the defensive (but ideologically dilemmatic) character of Alexander Severus's campaign against Sasanian expansionism: while both heroes are depicted in the *Heroikos* as "protective guardians" of Hellas, Achilles' more aggressive disposition differs markedly from Protesilaos's more defensive nature. Thus, their juxtaposition in the *Heroikos* closely mirrors the tensions and contradictions in Severus's policy between the *ideological* imperative to emulate Alexander's act of conquest and that of the *Realpolitik* to lead a more contained eastern campaign.

Let us first turn our attention to the second point. Aitken and Maclean, in their introduction of the *Heroikos*,[84] and Aitken separately,[85] have placed the composition of the *Heroikos* in the early years of Alexander Severus. Indeed, considering the Trojan War motif and the preeminence of Protesilaos in the *Heroikos*, the hero, with whose revenge upon the Persian governor of Chersonesus the final *logos* of the Herodotean cycle on the *Persian Wars* concludes,[86]

[81] For a more detailed description of Philostratus's life, see Graham Anderson, *Philostratus: Biography and* Belles Lettres *in the Third Century A.D.* (London: Croom Helm, 1986), 1–22; also Jaap-Jan Flinterman, *Power,* Paideia *and Pythagoreanism: Greek Identity, Conceptions of the Relationship between Philosophers and Monarchs, and Political Ideas in Philostratus'* Life of Apollonius (Dutch Monographs on Ancient History and Archaeology 13; Amsterdam: Gieben, 1995), 15–28. On Julia Domna's Circle, see in particular Glen W. Bowersock, *Greek Sophists in the Roman Empire* (Oxford: Clarendon, 1969), 101–9.

[82] We do not know much about Philostratus's association with the Severan court after the death of Julia Domna in 217, but it is not unlikely that he might have been involved indirectly with Elagabalus and Alexander Severus, see Anderson, *Philostratus*, 7; Flinterman, *Power,* Paideia *and Pythagoreanism*, 26–27; and Maclean and Aitken, *Flavius Philostratus: Heroikos*, lxxxvii.

[83] Maclean and Aitken, *Flavius Philostratus: Heroikos*, lviii.

[84] Maclean and Aitken, *Flavius Philostratus: Heroikos*, xliv–xlv, lxxxv–lxxxvi.

[85] Ellen Bradshaw Aitken, "Why a Phoenician? A Proposal for the Historical Occasion of the *Heroikos*," 275 in this volume.

[86] Maclean and Aitken, *Flavius Philostratus: Heroikos*, lxxxv: "In order to understand the particular valence Protesilaos may have had in this political situation, it is instructive to recall Herodotus's use of Protesilaos as the protector of Greece against the Persians."

we see that everything in the *Heroikos* seems to hint at the reign of Alexander Severus, when the Roman Empire was faced with the reality of invading Persian armies and ideologically in need of recalling heroes and events of the past whose projection into the present presaged a successful outcome for Rome's defense. It is thus possible that the *Heroikos* was written "around the time of Alexander Severus's Persian campaign in order to promote Greek (and hence Roman) identity and piety, by recalling not only the memory of the preeminent heroes of the Trojan War but most notably that of Protesilaos."[87]

Let us once more recall the last *logos* of Herodotus's *Histories*, which is indispensable for understanding the strategies of the *Heroikos*:[88] here, Protesilaos, the first of the Achaeans to fall during the Trojan War, is vindicated for the past outrage of Artayktes, the Persian administrator of the Chersonesus. Artayktes, who ruled this region in the manner of a tyrant (ἐτυράννευε δὲ τούτου τοῦ νομοῦ Ξέρξεω ὕπαρχος Ἀρταΰκτης), is accused of having deceived King Xerxes with the intent to seize the riches (χρήματα) attached to Protesilaos's precinct (οἶκος). Accordingly, he requested from Xerxes the ownership of Protesilaos's precinct by presenting it as the "house" (οἶκος)[89] of a Greek man who had made war against the king's land and has died deservedly:[90]

> ὃς καὶ βασιλέα ἐλαύνοντα ἐπ Ἀθήνας ἐξηπάτησε, τὰ Πρωτεσίλεω τοῦ Ἰφίκλου χρήματα ἐξ Ἐλαιοῦντος ὑπελόμενος. ἐν γὰρ Ἐλαιοῦντι τῆς Χερσονήσου ἐστὶ Πρωτεσίλεω τάφος τε καὶ τέμενος περὶ αὐτόν, ἔνθα ἦν χρήματα . . . τὰ Ἀρταΰκτης ἐσύλησε βασιλέος δόντος. λέγων δὲ τοιάδε Ξέρξην διεβάλετο. δέσποτα, ἔστι οἶκος ἀνδρὸς Ἕλληνος ἐνθαῦτα, ὃς ἐπὶ γῆν σὴν στρατευσάμενος δίκης κυρήσας ἀπέθανε· τούτου μοι δὸς τὸν

[87] Maclean and Aitken, *Flavius Philostratus: Heroikos*, lxxxv–lxxxvi.

[88] See also Deborah Boedeker, "Protesilaos and the End of Herodotus' *Histories*," *Classical Antiquity* 7/1 (1988): 30–48.

[89] On this entire passage and the double meaning of οἶκος in Herodotus's *logos*, see Gregory Nagy, *Pindar's Homer: The Lyric Possession of an Epic Past* (Baltimore: Johns Hopkins University Press, 1990), 268–69, where the author states: "At least Xerxes was led to believe that Artayktes was to occupy the house of 'a Greek man.' The story is actually being told by Herodotus in a mode analogous to that of an **ainos**, in that double meanings abound. To begin with, the 'house' of the 'Greek man' is really the sacred precinct of the hero Protesilaos, a cult center filled with riches supplied by the hero's worshipers (9.116.2)."

[90] Artayktes' denunciation of Protesilaos obviously refers to him being the first Achaean who died attacking Troy (Homer *Il.* 2.700–702); see also *Her.* 12.3–4.

> οἶκον, ἵνα καί τις μάθῃ ἐπὶ γῆν τὴν σὴν μὴ σταρτεύεσθαι. ταῦτα λέγων εὐπετέως ἔμελλε ἀναπείσειν Ξέρξην δοῦναι ἀνδρὸς οἶκον, οὐδὲν ὑποτοπηθέντα τῶν ἐκεῖνος ἐφρόνεε. ἐπὶ γῆν δὲ τὴν βασιλέος στρατεύεσθαι Πρωτεσίλεων ἔλεγε νοέων τοιάδε· τὴν Ἀσίαν πᾶσαν νομίζουσι ἑωυτῶν εἶναι Πέρσαι καὶ τοῦ αἰεὶ βασιλεύοντος.
>
> [H]e deceived the king marching toward Athens, he stole away the riches from Protesilaos, son of Iphiklos. There is in Elaious in the Chersonesus the tomb of Protesilaos and a precinct about it, where the riches were . . . that Artayktes carried away by the king's gift. He misled Xerxes in the following way: "*Master, there is a house belonging to a Greek man who had made war against your land. Getting his just deserts, he had died. Give me this man's house, so that everyone may learn not to make war against your land.*"[91] It was to be thought that this plea would easily persuade Xerxes to give him the man's house, having no suspicion of what Artayktes had in mind, whose reason for saying that Protesilaos had invaded the king's territory was that *the Persians believe all Asia to belong to themselves and whosoever is their king.* (Herodotus *Hist.* 9.116)

After looting Protesilaos's precinct, Artayktes continued violating Protesilaos's cult by having intercourse with women in the hero's sanctuary (αὐτός τε ὅκως ἀπίκοιτο ἐς Ἐλαιοῦντα ἐν τῷ ἀδύτῳ γυναιξὶ ἐμίσγετο, Herodotus *Hist.* 9.116).

In the aftermath of the successful Athenian offensive in the Chersonesus and the siege of Sestos, Artayktes was then captured and executed by the Athenian forces for the wrongs he had perpetrated against Protesilaos and the responsibility that he, the official representative of the Persian authority in Chersonesus, was symbolically bearing for the bridging of the Hellespont by King Xerxes (Herodotus *Hist.* 9.116–120). Before the execution of Artayktes, however, Protesilaos came back to life through the agency of dried fish (τάριχος)—which, being miraculously restored to life, leapt off the fire while being roasted by an Athenian—to announce his vengeance and exact retribution from Artayktes, who addressed his frightened Athenian captor as follows:

[91] The translation of the passage from δέσποτα to σταρτεύεσθαι is taken from Nagy, *Pindar's Homer*, 269.

> ξεῖνε Ἀθηναῖε, μηδὲν φοβέο τὸ τέρας τοῦτο· οὐ γὰρ σοὶ πέφηνε, ἀλλ' ἐμοὶ σημαίνει ὁ ἐν Ἐλαιοῦντι Πρωτεσίλεως ὅτι καὶ τεθνεὼς καὶ τάριχος ἐὼν δύναμιν πρὸς θεῶν ἔχει τὸν ἀδικέοντα τίνεσθαι.
>
> Athenian Stranger, do not be frightened of this portent [τέρας]. For it was manifested not for you. Rather, Protesilaos—the one who abides in Elaious—is making a sign [σημαίνει] to me that, even though he is dead—and a τάριχος—*he has the power* [δύναμις] *from the gods to exact retribution from the one who commits wrongdoing.*" (Herodotus *Hist.* 9.120)[92]

Nagy describes this episode as follows:

> In the narrative of Herodotus, the dead hero Protesilaos "gives a sign" (σημαίνει) to the living. . . . Through a "power" (δύναμις) given to Protesilaos by the gods, the hero can uphold justice by punishing the unjust—just as surely as he can give a mystical sign, as narrated immediately beforehand: an Athenian is roasting τάριχοι ("preserved fish"), and the dead fish suddenly come back to life. . . . So also Protesilaos is now being called a τάριχος: even though he is dead, and thus a τάριχος, he still has the power to intervene in the world of the living. . . . By implication, Protesilaos has mystically come back to life, just like the preserved fish.[93]

The importance of this passage[94] resides in the fact that Protesilaos, the first Achaean to die in the Trojan War, the hero who could not prove himself in the world of the living, is offered a *comeback as revenant* in the final *logos* of Herodotus's *Histories* on the origins of the antagonism between Asia and Europe, in order to inflict punishment upon Artayktes, not only because of the wrongs he committed against the hero, but also because of those his master, King Xerxes, inflicted upon Hellas by bridging the Hellespont.[95] There is perfect symmetry in this *logos* between the actions and

[92] The translation of this passage is taken from Nagy, "A Sign of the Hero: A Prologue," in Maclean and Aitken, *Flavius Philostratus: Heroikos*, xvii.

[93] Nagy, "A Sign of the Hero," xvi–xvii, and *Pindar's Homer*, 269–70.

[94] See also discussion by Boedeker, "Protesilaos and the End of Herodotus' *Histories*," 41.

[95] See Maclean and Aitken, *Flavius Philostratus: Heroikos*, liv–lv: "Not only has the Persian governor offended Protesilaos personally by looting his sanctuary and having sex within its boundaries, but Protesilaos also takes revenge upon him as a representative of Xerxes, the Asian invader, for all the Persian offenses against the Persians."

reactions of Artayktes and Protesilaos, Asians and Hellenes: Protesilaos's precinct fell prey to looting only because he was presented as a Hellene who dared attack Asia; Artayktes was executed on the very spot where Xerxes had crossed over to Europe because the king dared attack Hellas. Thus, already in the Herodotean *logos*, Protesilaos as *revenant* appears as the champion of the Hellenic cause against the Persian invader, fulfilling the promise that the living hero had failed to meet at Troy.[96]

Now let us return to the *Heroikos*. Reactivating the Herodotean perspective, Philostratus depicts the *revenant* Protesilaos as the guardian of Hellas in tandem with Achilles. In analogy to Herodotus, who had recourse to the Trojan War motif in his depiction of the Persian Wars,[97] Philostratus, confronted with the prospect of a looming conflict between Rome and Persia, actualizes both themes and projects the tenor of these hereditary conflicts upon the reality of his own age.

In the *Heroikos*, Achilles, the vanquisher of Troy par excellence, is juxtaposed to Protesilaos the *revenant*—a Herodotean reinvention of the hero, whereupon Philostratus seems to have constructed his own narrative[98]—and presented as Hellas's defender against all for-

[96] Contrast the following passage of the *Heroikos*, where the vineyard worker renders Protesilaos's own judgment of his deeds in Troy (*Her*. 12.4): ἑαυτὸν δὲ ὀλοφύρεται μηδὲν ἐν Τροίᾳ ἐργασάμενον, ἀλλὰ πεσόντα ἐν γῇ ἧς οὐδὲ ἐπέβη ("[h]e grieves that he accomplished nothing at Troy, and how he fell in a land that he had not even assaulted"; all translations of the *Heroikos* are taken from the edition of Maclean and Aitken).

[97] See Boedeker, "Protesilaos and the End of Herodotus' *Histories*," 42: "Within the framework of division and hostility between the two continents, the Protesilaos-Artayktes story develops a special connection between the Trojan and the Persian Wars—with an ancient hero linking past and present, as often in Herodotus"; and pp. 47–48: "More than just providing a structural framework for the *Histories*, rounding off the work with references to the division between Asia and Europe, the Protesilaos *logos* bridges the temporal boundaries between the two greatest transcontinental invasions. At the same time it proposes, by setting forward suggestive parallels for a perceptive audience, that just as the Trojans were long ago punished by the gods for great injustices, so too perhaps were the Persians within recent memory. With subtle but insistent metonymy, Herodotus sets the vengeance of Protesilaos—or better, his restoration of balance—against the background of the whole invasion of Xerxes."

[98] See Anderson, *Philostratus*, 249: "As Pan at Marathon repels the first Persian invasion, so Protesilaos takes the final vengeance of Greek over Persian by bringing about the crucifixion of the Persian desecrator Artayktes. Much of Philostratus's *mise-en-scène* could have been deduced, developed or reconstructed from this passage." Contrast also the following passage of the *Heroikos* (9.5), which refers in a striking manner to the Herodotean *logos:* τὸ δέ γε ἱερόν, ἐν ᾧ κατὰ τοὺς

eign (Persian/Asian) foes. In spite of the fact that, unlike Protesilaos, whose *heure de gloire* was consequent upon his manifestation as *revenant*, Achilles' exploits are extensively celebrated in the *Iliad*, in the *Heroikos* he, too, experiences a second career as *revenant*; as such, Achilles like Protesilaos is depicted guarding Hellas against foreign (eastern) invaders, as the story of Achilles' annihilation of the Amazons illustrates (*Her*. 56.1–57.1). By depicting the lives and exploits of Achilles and Protesilaos in the afterlife, that is, through the artifice of resurrecting them as *revenants*, Philostratus is able not only to invest these heroes with attributes more fitted to reflect the urgencies of his own time, but also to make them more alike: whatever Protesilaos lacks in exploits in the *Iliad*, he acquires as *revenant* by being the avenger of Hellas against the Persians, and Achilles from the wrathful destroyer of Troy, the aggressor of Asia, becomes the—still irate—defender of Hellas against foreign (Asian) invaders. The overwhelming similarities between the two heroes,[99] despite the differences they exhibit, seem to symbolize those prevailing between another "couple," that is, Alexander Severus and the object of his emulation, Alexander of Macedonia.

Here, we must recall that the two ideological tenets, upon which Alexander Severus's legitimacy and imperial policy were grounded, were incompatible, even antinomic, and called for harmonization. On the one hand, Severus's legitimacy was based upon his filiation from Caracalla, whose imitation of Alexander of Macedonia is well attested, hence the imperative for Severus and his entourage to maintain and promote the cult of Alexander (despite its perilous implications for foreign policy). On the other hand, as the Persian campaign had barely reestablished the *status quo ante*, without any territorial gain for Rome, possibly as a consequence of the emperor's defensive posture, but most importantly as a result of the limitations imposed upon Roman legions by the formidable Sasanian war machinery, the image of a vanquishing *novus Alexander* was hard to maintain.

πατέρας ὁ Μῆδος ὕβριζεν, ἐφ' ᾧ καὶ τὸ τάριχος ἀναβιῶναί φασι. τοῦτο ἡγοῦ, ὦ ξένε· καταλείπεται δὲ αὐτοῦ ὁρᾷς ὡς ὀλίγα ("[c]onsider this sanctuary, my guest, where the Mede committed a sacrilege in our forefathers' time. It was because of this they say even the preserved fish came back to life. You see how much of the sanctuary is left").

[99] For a discussion of the heroes' similarities, see Boedeker, "Protesilaos and the End of Herodotus' *Histories*," 36–37; and Maclean and Aitken, *Flavius Philostratus: Heroikos*, lvi–lx.

It is difficult to gauge to what extent Severus's defensive posture in the face of Sasanian expansionism was cognizant of, or tributary to, the Augustan political doctrine of the *divisio orbis*, which owed its existence to circumstances comparable to those affecting Severus. The policy of the *divisio orbis* emerged out of the realization that the eastern foe was invincible in its own realm, hence the imperative to deal with its occasional aggression by a moderate and limited military response. This is precisely why Rome, on the eve of Gaius Caesar's eastern expedition, felt compelled to resort to the Persian Wars symbolism—in order to justify its campaign against the perceived Arsacid aggression in Armenian affairs—for it best illustrated Rome's defensive posture.

Equally difficult to assess is the part of the Second Sophistic in inspiring the emperor's actions vis-à-vis the Sasanians, or, in the absence of such inspiration, to appraise the share of the Second Sophistic in adorning Severus's pragmatic foreign policy with referrals to Hellas's "heroic" exploits of the past. Suffice to say that whatever the motivations of Severus's measured foreign policy may have been, they were at odds with the emperor's Alexander emulation.

Philostratus seems to have countered this predicament by altering and rendering less forceful the drive to conquest inherent in the Alexander symbolism itself, by turning the archetypal hero/conqueror Achilles from the aggressor of Troy into the guardian of Greeks against foreigners (as *revenant*). Consequently, in the same fashion as the impetus of conquest was counterpoised in the *Heroikos*, by casting Achilles' aggressive force into a protective bellicosity, the defensive posture of Severus's policy was sanctioned through the protective characterization of yet another reinvented *revenant*. In this function, Protesilaos, although vengeful and formidable, very much symbolized the defensive character of Roman policy: a measured military action in the defense of the territories, rather than a war of conquest.

Thus, the resurrection of Protesilaos and Achilles as *revenants* served several purposes: (1) as guardians of Hellas against "foreigners," they came to represent Rome's defensive stance against the Sasanian Empire; (2) to the extent that the two heroes were equated to each other in the *Heroikos*—albeit, Protesilaos displayed a more pronounced affinity with Alexander Severus, as did Achilles with Alexander of Macedonia—they helped bridge (and cloud) in fiction the divide between their respective historical counterparts, that is, Severus and his source of emulation Alexander of Macedonia; finally, (3) the projection of the harmonized image of Protesilaos and Achilles upon the relationship of Severus and Alexander enabled the former (or those in charge of his memory) to reconcile the two antinomic principles of his rule: the simultaneous emulation of the Macedonian and the urge to eastern conquest inherent to the *imitatio*, on the one hand, with his own policy of defensive posture toward the Sasanian East, on the other.

Let me illustrate in greater detail some of the parallels between *Heroikos*'s heroes Achilles/Protesilaos and the rulers Alexander/Severus:

1. Both Achilles and Alexander were the vanquishers of Asia: Troy would not have fallen without Achilles, the Persian Empire not without Alexander. Both Protesilaos and Alexander Severus perished, their promises unfulfilled, during or following their attack upon/campaign against Asia, unlike Achilles and Alexander, who completed the cycle of conquest, paying with their lives for their victory.
2. Although both Protesilaos and Achilles are depicted as the *guardians* of all that is Greek, there is a particularly bellicose quality to Achilles, best captured in the episode of Achilles' active pursuit of the last descendant of King Priam, whom he dismembers alive (*Her.* 56.6–10). Through the agency of the merchant charged with bringing the Trojan maiden to Leukê, Achilles *actively* and without provocation attacks Ilion anew and, thereby, Asia, and by dint of the maiden's gruesome killing, reenacts the destruction of Troy/Asia. This offensive attitude toward Asia cannot avoid recalling the drive to conquest and desire for revenge in Alexander of Macedonia, who laid waste Persepolis to exact retribution for the burning of Athens at Persian hands. In contrast, Protesilaos's deeds are always in *reaction* to offenses or insults to which he has been subjected. He is resurrected in order to punish Artayktes (*Her.* 9.5); he wreaks vengeance upon Xeinis, the former owner of his precinct (*Her.* 4.2); and he chastises with a dog-bite the adulterer(s) in his sanctuary (*Her.* 16.3–4; reminiscent of Artayktes' sacrileges). In this respect he provides a perfect heroic model for Severus's defensive campaign in *response* to Persian aggression.

3. Moreover, the location of the heroes' tombs may allude to the two historical rulers. Achilles' tomb on the Asian shore of the Hellespont is not only a reminder of his true identity as the vanquisher of Troy who found death in Asia, but also seems to hint at Alexander, the conqueror of Asia, who died in Babylon. By contrast, Protesilaos's tomb is located on the European shore of the Hellespont, "a memorial at the extreme edge of Europe to a Greek hero who never gained a foothold across the strait,"[100] but, also an implicit reference to Severus's decision not to (or failure to?) gain new territories in the East.

We return now to the first point raised above: Is the *Heroikos* an official representation of the Severan political ideology under Alexander Severus or does it reflect Philostratus's independent attempt at capturing (and interpreting?) the tensions that characterized the late Severan imperial policy vis-à-vis the Sasanian Empire? The question can obviously not be answered in full, but were the association of Alexander Severus with Protesilaos to prove correct, then one might surmise that the *Heroikos* was written *after* Alexander Severus's demise as a posthumous justification (*Rechtfertigungszeugnis*) of the emperor's cautious and defensive policy, as it seems unlikely that the identification of the emperor with Protesilaos, the hero with the house half-built (δόμος ἡμιτελής, Homer *Il.* 2.701), could have occurred during his lifetime. Intriguingly, we encounter, in the Indian episode of Philostratus's *Life of Apollonius*—the "romanticised biography of Apollonius, a first-century Pythagorean philosopher and miracle-worker who was born in Cappadocian Tyana"[101]—written at the behest of Julia Domna, some of the themes that also occur in the *Heroikos* as justification of Severus Alexander's defensive policy.

In his journey beyond the Indus River, Apollonius is received by Phraôtês, the philosopher-king of India, who exalts the virtues of a (foreign) policy that seeks to turn foes into friends by paying them off (ὑποποιοῦμαι τουτοισὶ τοῖς χρήμασι, "I subject them [the barbarians] to myself with money"; Philostratus *Life of Apollonius* 2.26). It is, indeed, difficult not to see in this policy an implicit allusion to Alexander Severus's intended disbursements to the Germans in exchange for peace (πάντα τε ὑπισχνεῖτο παρέξειν ὅσων δέονται, καὶ χρημάτων ἀφειδῶς ἔχειν, "he promised to grant all they [the Ger-

[100] See Boedeker, "Protesilaos and the End of Herodotus' *Histories*," 37.
[101] Flinterman, *Power,* Paideia *and Pythagoreanism*, 1.

mans] required and to have ample of money"; Herodian *History* 6.7.9). What is more, Philostratus reports the encounter between Apollonius and the leader of the Indian Sages, Iarchas, who, during their conversation, compares the legendary Indian king Ganges with Achilles (see Philostratus *Life of Apollonius* 3.20). In contrast to Achilles, whose motives in the Trojan War Iarchas questions, and whose deeds, which led to the destruction of numerous cities, he denounces (αὐτὸν δώδεκα μὲν πόλεις ἐκ θαλάττης ᾑρηκέναι, πεζῇ δὲ ἕνδεκα, "he [Achilles] took twelve cities by sea and eleven on land"; Philostratus *Life of Apollonius* 3.20), the sage praises the Indian hero-king Ganges for having founded new cities (πόλεων μὲν τοίνυν ἑξήκοντα οἰκιστὴς ἐγένετο, "he [Ganges] accordingly became the founder of many cities"; Philostratus *Life of Apollonius* 3.20). More important, Philostratus, by the intermediary of the Indian sage Iarchas, seems to sanction Ganges' defensive posture in face of invading foreign (Scythian) enemies, in contrast to Achilles' capture of Troy that led to the city's subjugation (τὸ δὲ ἐλευθεροῦντα τὴν ἑαυτοῦ γῆν ἄνδρα ἀγαθὸν φαίνεσθαι πολλῷ βέλτιον τοῦ δουλείαν ἐπάγειν πόλει, "it is by far more fitting to become a good man by setting free your country than to bring slavery to a city"; Philostratus *Life of Apollonius* 3.20).[102] Ganges' much-admired protective policy against invading Scythians is undeniably reminiscent of the Athenian stance against invading Achaemenid armies—especially as Scythians were often equated with Persians—as the destructive and belligerent depiction of Achilles is evocative of Alexander of Macedonia. On another level, Ganges' policies call to mind Severus's prudent guiding principle toward the Sasanians, who could equally be referred to as the "Scythian" enemies; in contrast, Achilles' deeds may well have alluded to Caracalla's ill-fated policy of expansion,[103] from which Severus's course of action departed. Another

[102] Already Elena M. Schtajerman, *Die Krise der Sklavenhalteordnung in Westen des römischen Reiches* (trans. W. Seyfarth; Berlin: Akademie, 1964), 250–66, 278–81, based her interpretation on this passage (and a Marxist interpretation of the *Life of Apollonius*) to demonstrate that Philostratus's advocacy of a defensive foreign policy (as reflected in this passage) was part of a wider program aimed at rallying the municipal aristocracy—with whom Julia Domna's circle was associated. In his critique of Schtajerman, Flinterman, *Power,* Paideia *and Pythagoreanism*, 223, not only questions the alleged political and programmatic nature of Philostratus's *Life of Apollonius,* but also draws attention to the topicality of the aforementioned passage.

[103] On Caracalla's honoring Achilles with sacrifices and races about his tomb, following the crossing of the Hellespont, see Dio Cassius *Roman History* 78.17.7; similarly also Herodian *History* 4.8.4–5.

similarity between the hero-king Ganges and Severus is their respective ends at their subjects' hands, which set off a time of broad decay (Ganges) and political turmoil (Severus) leading in both cases to the violent demise of the murderers and the reestablishment of the troubled order. In the case of Ganges, the sacrifice of the king's murderers ended the cycle of unnatural calamities that had befallen the lands, and in that of Severus, the establishment of Gordian III closed the chapter of anomaly that the advent of Maximinus appears to have represented.[104]

Thus, both the *Heroikos* and the *Life of Apollonius* seem to allude to Alexander Severus's reign, and, although one might be in agreement with Jaap-Jan Flinterman in assuming that Philostratus did not have a consistent set of political beliefs,[105] it is nonetheless probable that his writings did not merely capture the political beliefs of the late Severan court, but also expressed his adherence to a broadly defined defensive foreign policy, best epitomized by Alexander Severus.

The purpose of the preceding discussion is not only to illustrate the extent of Severan infatuation with Alexander, but also to underscore the ubiquity of two concomitant, at times contrasting, currents of thought in the late second and early third centuries C.E.: the *imitatio Alexandri* and the Sophistic glorification of things Greek. It was in a climate filled with "Alexandromania" and pervaded by the Second Sophistic's reception and veneration of the Hellenic past that the Sasanians rose to power and Ardašīr set out for his campaigns of expansion against Rome.[106] Confronted with

[104] On the rise of Maximinus, his murder, and the advent of Gordian III, see Christol, *L'empire romain du IIIe siècle*, 79–91; on Herodian's severe judgment of Maximinus, see *History* 7.1.1–4.

[105] See Flinterman, *Power,* Paideia *and Pythagoreanism*, 227: ". . . the positive evaluation of the allusion to the buying off of barbarian invasions no doubt indicates that Philostratus was aware to a certain extent of the problems connected with the defence of the borders; after all, he had followed Caracalla's operations on the Rhine and Danube border from the imperial headquarters. As Schtajerman suggested, he perhaps had a certain preference for a low-profile military policy, but it would be going too far to credit the author of the *VA* with a *consistent set of views on the financial and military aspects of imperial government* [italics mine] on the basis of a policy ascribed to an Indian philosopher king. . . . There simply is no evidence to support the assumption that he was genuinely interested in such matters."

[106] See also Wiesehöfer, "Ardashir I," 373: "It is noteworthy that the Sasanian evocation of the traditional view of Alexander as the great wrecker of Iran was matched by a contemporary Roman emphasis on the idea of *imitatio Alexandri*";

an aggression that evoked Xerxes' assault on Hellas, Severus succeeded in preserving the eastern *limes*, but was unwilling or unable to wrest new territories from the Sasanians. His conscious or imposed defensive posture, although in the best Augustan tradition, was, however, at odds with his *imitatio*, the very principle of his legitimacy. The author of the *Heroikos* seems to have attempted to solve this discrepancy within the imperial ideology by superimposing upon the Trojan War narrative the Herodotean *logos* on the Persian Wars, by turning the two fallen heroes-aggressors of Troy into the two *revenants*-guardians of Hellas, following in whose footsteps Severus was to become a *novus Alexander*, not by an act of conquest, but by safeguarding the empire against a new Xerxes.

---

and Josef Wiesehöfer, "Zum Nachleben von Achaimeniden und Alexander in Iran," in *Continuity and Change: Proceedings of the Last Achaemenid History Workshop, April 6–8, 1990, Ann Arbor, Michigan* (ed. Heleen Sancisi-Weerdenburg, Amelie Kuhrt, and Margaret Cool Root; Achaemenid History 8; Leiden: Nederlands Instituut voor het Nabije Oosten, 1994), 392.

Beyond the Euphrates in Severan Times: Mani, Bar Daysan, and the Struggle for Allegiance on the Syrian Frontier

Sidney H. Griffith

I

During the years when the Severans ruled in Rome, to the east of Antioch in Syria, Edessa, the ancient Urhay and modern Sanli Urfa, became the center for a revived Aramean culture. The language that in due course was to carry the literature of this revival to the very ends of the East was a dialect of ancient Aramaic that modern, Western scholars call "Syriac."[1] For the Persians, that is, the Parthians, Edessa was the capital of the province of Osrhoênê; in the 160s of the Common Era it came under Roman domination.[2] As Steven K. Ross has recently written, "By the end of the century between Trajan (97–117 C.E.) and Septimius Severus (193–211 C.E.), the king of Edessa was squarely within Roman *clientela*, and the groundwork was laid for the even firmer incorporation of his realm into the empire."[3] King Abgar VIII, "the Great" (178/9–212 C.E.), was the king at the time. It was during his reign, as a client king of Rome, that "pre-Christian Edessan culture reached its zenith."[4] Edward Gibbon gave this still-apt description of Osrhoênê as it was just prior to the Severan period:

[1] On the development of classical Syriac, see Lucas Van Rompay, "Some Preliminary Remarks on the Origins of Classical Syriac as a Standard Language: The Syriac Version of Eusebius of Caesarea's Ecclesiastical History," in *Semitic and Cushitic Studies* (ed. Gideon Goldenberg and Shlomo Raz; Wiesbaden, Germany: Harrossowitz, 1994), 70–89.

[2] See Fergus Millar, *The Roman Near East: 31 B.C.–A.D. 337* (Cambridge, Mass.: Harvard University Press, 1993), 472–81; Warwick Ball, *Rome in the East: The Transformation of an Empire* (London and New York: Routledge, 2000), 87–94.

[3] Steven K. Ross, *Roman Edessa: Politics and Culture on the Eastern Fringes of the Roman Empire, 114–242 CE* (London and New York: Routledge, 2001), 29.

[4] Ross, *Roman Edessa*, 57.

> That little state occupied the northern and most fertile part of Mesopotamia, between the Euphrates and the Tigris. Edessa, its capital, was situated about twenty miles beyond the former of those rivers; and the inhabitants, since the time of Alexander, were a mixed race of Greeks, Arabs, Syrians, and Armenians. The feeble sovereigns of Osrhoene, placed on the dangerous verge of two contending empires, were attached from inclination to the Parthian cause; but the superior power of Rome exacted from them a reluctant homage.[5]

Gibbon here put his finger on a salient fact about life in Edessa and the Syriac-speaking milieu generally. It was life on the frontier. Wars between the Romans and the Persians were an ever-present factor in this territory, in which the borders between the two empires were constantly shifting, depending on unpredictable military sallies and excursions from one side or the other. Moreover, another constant feature of life in this milieu was the often forced transfer of whole populations from one jurisdiction to the other, depending on the fortunes of the wars.[6] Intellectual life was deeply imbued with both Roman and Persian features; Hellenism and the indigenous, Semitic modes of thought and expression often clashed in both religious and more broadly cultural discourse.[7]

In these cross-frontier circumstances, some measure of local identity was preserved in the burgeoning success of the Syriac language; it was spoken and understood on both sides of the indefinite, great divide between Rome and Persia, thereby creating a cross-frontier community. The language carried with it a family relationship to the Jewish world in which Christianity first appeared in the synagogue communities of Mesopotamia and Syria/Palestine. It was this language that eventually carried the Christian faith across the trade routes of Central Asia, eastward into China and southward

[5] Edward Gibbon, *The History of the Decline and Fall of the Roman Empire* (ed. David Womersley; 3 vols.; London: Penguin, 1994), 1:224; repr. of *The History of the Decline and Fall of the Roman Empire* (6 vols.; London: Straham, 1774–1788).

[6] See Samuel N. C. Lieu, "Captives, Refugees, and Exiles: A Study of Cross-Frontier Civilian Movements and Contacts between Rome and Persia from Valerian to Jovian," in *The Defence of the Roman and Byzantine East* (ed. Philip Freeman and David Kennedy; 2 vols.; British Institute of Archaeology at Ankara 8; Oxford: B.A.R., 1986), 2:475–508.

[7] See Glen W. Bowersock, *Hellenism in Late Antiquity* (Ann Arbor: University of Michigan Press, 1990), esp. 29–40.

into India,[8] for it was Christianity that provided the cultural élan that made Syriac much more than just the Aramaic dialect of Edessa. From the third century onward it became the lingua franca of a sizeable, mostly mercantile population group in Mesopotamia, who, until well into Islamic times, carried their cultural identity in their own distinctive idiom far and wide.

II

One no longer knows for sure when or exactly how Christianity first came to the Syriac-speaking communities. Modern scholars are divided between supporters of the view that it first appeared in the kingdom of Adiabene, to the north and east of Osrhoênê, among Jews who had close ties to Palestine, and those who think that Christianity came first to Edessa from Antioch. What is clear is that by the time of Septimius Severus there was a large enough community to support a church building in the city. The *Chronicle of Edessa* records the fact that in the year 201 C.E. the church of the Christians was destroyed by a flood. The same sixth-century chronicle dates the "apostasy" of Marcion to the year 138 C.E. It also records the date of Bar Daysan's birth in Edessa in the year 154 C.E.[9] Both Marcion and Bar Daysan will figure prominently in the discussion to follow. The earliest, independent historical document concerning this community, dating from around the year 192 C.E., is the epitaph of Abercius Marcellus, bishop of Hierapolis in Phrygia, which mentions the presence of Christians in the environs of Edessa from the second half of the second century onward. Finally, Sextus Julius Africanus (ca. 160–240), who in 195 C.E. came with Septimius Severus's expedition to Osrhoênê, mentions in his *Kestoi* or *Embroideries*, that he had met Bar Daysan in Edessa and had admired his skill in archery.[10]

Tatian the Syrian (ca. 160 C.E.), who says of himself that he was

[8] See Ian Gillman and Hans-Joachim Klimkeit, *Christians in Asia before 1500* (Ann Arbor: University of Michigan Press, 1999).

[9] See Ignatius Guidi, *Chronica Minora* (CSCO 1–2; Louvain: Secretariat du CSCO, 1903–1907). Composed ca. 540 C.E., the *Chronicle of Edessa* presents many problems for the historian. See Witold Witakowski, "Chronicles of Edessa," *Orientalia Suecana* 33–34 (1984–1986): 486–98.

[10] Cf. Sextus Julius Africanus *Kestoi* (PG 10:45c). See Jean-René Vieillefond, *Les "Cestes" de Julius Africanus: Étude sur l'ensemble des fragments* (Florence: Sansoni Antiquariata; Paris: Didier, 1970).

from Assyria,[11] by which he presumably meant northern Mesopotamia, is perhaps the earliest Christian whom we know by name to have come from the Syriac-speaking milieu. He had gone to Rome to study philosophy and there he converted to Christianity under the influence of Justin Martyr (ca. 100–ca. 165). Sometime after Justin's death, perhaps around the year 172, Tatian returned to his native land. Therefore, Tatian himself may well have played a significant role in the dissemination of Christianity beyond the Euphrates. In the works of early Christian heresiographers he is often accused of the heresy of the "Encratites," a somewhat vague doctrine involving excessive ascetical practice.[12] He is also remembered for two works that have survived: his *Oration to the Greeks*, written in Greek, and the *Diatessaron*, a presentation of the four Gospels in a continuous narrative, which Tatian put together while he was still in Rome. While the original language of the latter is uncertain, it nevertheless had a wide circulation in Syriac, at least until the time of Bishop Rabbula of Edessa (d. 435), when it was officially banned.[13]

The translation of the Bible into Syriac was an important part of the introduction of Christianity into the Syriac-speaking milieu. It appears that all the translators of the Old Testament into the Syriac version that would come to be called the Peshitta or "Simple" version by the ninth century C.E., worked primarily from a Hebrew original. Many of them seem also sporadically to have consulted the Greek Bible, and there are parallels with the Targums that suggest dependence on a common oral tradition. As for the translators themselves, the current scholarly consensus is that "they constituted a single school, a non-rabbinic Jewish community, which eventually accepted Christianity. The evidence suggests that the work spanned perhaps one or two generations, toward the end of the second century C.E., and that the likeliest location is Edessa."[14] The evidence is compatible

[11] See Molly Whittaker, ed. and trans., *Tatian,* Oratio ad Graecos *and Fragments* (Oxford: Clarendon, 1982), 76–77, sec. 42.

[12] See Robert M. Grant, "The Heresy of Tatian," *JTS* 5 (1954): 62–68; Leslie W. Barnard, "The Heresy of Tatian—Once Again," *JEH* 19 (1968): 1–10.

[13] See William L. Peterson, *Tatian's Diatessaron: Its Creation, Dissemination, Significance, and History in Scholarship* (Suppl. to *VC* 25; Leiden: Brill, 1994). See also Nicholas Perrin, *Thomas and Tatian: The Relationship between the* Gospel of Thomas *and the* Diatessaron (Atlanta: Society of Biblical Literature, 2002).

[14] Michael P. Weitzman, *The Syriac Version of the Old Testament: An Introduction* (University of Cambridge Oriental Publications 56; Cambridge: Cambridge University Press, 1999), 13.

with a date circa 150 for the translation of the earlier books of the Hebrew Bible.[15]

A number of other Christian works in Syriac from the early period suggest vigorous literary activity by the Severan period. In this connection one might mention the *Odes of Solomon*, the *Acts of Thomas* (including the *Hymn of the Pearl*), and the *Gospel of Thomas*.[16] But these works are all problematic in terms of our knowledge of their origins; most of what we think we know about them is the product of modern scholarly surmise. The earliest Syriac writer whose name and work we actually know is Bar Daysan (154–222 C.E.), of whom we will speak at greater length below. For now what is important to emphasize is the fact that all of the earliest Christian texts in Syriac supply ample evidence of a wide acquaintance with the rest of the world. Indeed, on the face of it, the Syriac-speaking milieu in the Severan period, along with its entire heritage from the East and with its continuing fascination with Persia and Persians, was nevertheless busy absorbing Christian ideas from the wider Roman world into which Septimius Severus and his successors were bringing the East. To this phenomenon Abercius, Tatian, Julius Africanus, and the others also testify. By the time Eusebius of Caesarea (ca. 260–340) was writing his *Ecclesiastical History* (before 300?), Edessa and Osrhoênê were seen to be playing a role in what was by now an empire-wide Christian movement; he reports events in the church there on the basis of documents in the city's archives, including the rudiments of what would become the legend of its apostolic origins.[17] Eusebius also reports more-ordinary events in the city's ecclesiastical life, such as its participation in early doctrinal and liturgical controversies. This fact has led Steven K. Ross to make the following observation:

> Eusebius, however, reports (*Hist. Eccl.* 5.23.4) that the churches of Osrhoene were consulted when a controversy arose in the church over the date of Easter, around 197. If this report is genuine, it offers confirmation for the establishment of at least a small Catholic community in

[15] Weitzman, *The Syriac Version*, 258.

[16] See Robert Murray, *Symbols of Church and Kingdom: A Study in Early Syriac Tradition* (Cambridge: Cambridge University Press, 1975), esp. 24–38.

[17] See Sebastian Brock, "Eusebius and Syriac Christianity," in *Eusebius, Christianity, and Judaism* (ed. Harold W. Attridge and Gohei Hata; Detroit: Wayne State University Press, 1992), 212–34.

Osrhoene, and probably in its capital of Edessa, around 190–200.[18]

III

From the later heresiographical literature in Syriac, notably the works of Ephraem the Syrian (306–373 C.E.), one learns that already in the second century the ideas of Marcion of Sinope (d. ca. 154), who had become a Christian in Rome circa 140, exerted a major influence in Syriac-speaking Edessa and its environs.[19] Given the wide range of his ideas in the Christian world generally, it would be surprising if this had not been the case; at the time Edessa seems to have been absorbing Christianity in its entirety, including the ideas of that other daring thinker from Rome, Valentinus (d. ca. 165), along with the ever more popular Roman, political suzerainty. Although he was never a resident there, Marcion in particular became such an important figure in Osrhoênê that the *Chronicle of Edessa* mentions it as a notable fact in the city's official memory that "in the year 449 [of the Seleucid era, i.e., 137/138 C.E.] Marcion left the Catholic church."[20]

Marcion's ideas had a powerful effect on Edessa's native intellectual, Bar Daysan (154–222), whom Julius Africanus met in Abgar VIII's court in the days of Septimius Severus. As we learn from Eusebius, Bar Daysan composed polemical works against the teaching of Marcion. This "Aramean Philosopher," as Ephraem later called Bar Daysan,[21] was himself the author of a formidable system of thought, putting together elements from his own world beyond the Euphrates and from the philosophy of the Greeks, as we shall discuss below.

Radiating from Edessa, Bar Daysan's teaching had a wide dissemination in the Aramaic-speaking world. In the next generation it was to have a profound effect on a teacher from southern Mesopotamia named Mani (216–276), who had been brought up in the Aramaic-speaking, Jewish-Christian milieu of the Elkasaites. Mani was to become the founder of a major world religion, with the Per-

[18] Ross, *Roman Edessa*, 127–28.

[19] See Han J. W. Drijvers, "Marcionism in Syria: Principles, Problems, Polemics," *SecCent* 6 (1987–1988): 153–72.

[20] Quoted from Drijvers, "Marcionism in Syria," 153. See Guidi, *Chronica Minora*, 3.

[21] Charles W. Mitchell, *S. Ephraim's Prose Refutations of Mani, Marcion, and Bardaisan* (2 vols.; London and Oxford: Williams and Norgate, 1912–1921), 2:225.

sian court as the focal point of his activity. But this fact should not blind us to his Edessan connections. Not only was he indebted in important ways to Bar Daysan, Edessa's own "Aramean philosopher,"[22] but Mani himself addressed one of his epistles to a community of his followers in Edessa,[23] where by Ephraem's day, in the judgment of Han J. W. Drijvers, Manichaeism had gained a commanding presence.[24]

From the vantage point of Edessa, Bar Daysan and Mani can be seen to represent two responses from the Aramaic-speaking world beyond the Euphrates to the intellectual challenges presented by the irruption of the influences of Roman arms and ideas into the frontier region of Syria in Severan times. In personal terms, these influences came with Tatian, Julius Africanus, and others who brought ideas from the imperial city to the eastern shores of the Mediterranean, including the ideas of their contemporaries, Marcion and Valentinus. But they were not the only ones to come, nor were they the only Christians in evidence in Edessa and its environs. There was, presumably, the presence of a larger community to welcome them. Later Christian legend, recorded in the famous *Doctrina Addai*, a work of the first half of the fifth century,[25] would put forward other names from the Severan period as the ancestors of those who would come to profess the "orthodox" faith of the

[22] See O. G. von Wessendonk, "Bardesanes und Mani," *AcOr* 10 (1932): 336–63; Han J. W. Drijvers, "Mani und Bardaisan: Ein Beitrag zur Vorgeschichte des Manichäismus," in *Mélanges d'histoire des religions offerts à Henri-Charles Puech* (Paris: Presses universitaires de France, 1974), 459–69; Barbara Aland, "Mani und Bardesanes—zur Entstehung des manichäischen Systems," in *Synkretismus im syrisch-persischen Kulturgebiet* (ed. Albert Dietrich; Göttingen: Vandenhoeck & Ruprecht, 1975), 123–43.

[23] See Ron Cameron and Arthur J. Dewey, eds., *The Cologne Mani Codex (P. Colon. Inv. Nr. 4780): Concerning the Origin of His Body* (SBLTT 15; Early Christian Literature Series 3; Missoula, Mont.: Scholars Press, 1979), 50–51.

[24] Drijvers made this point in a number of publications, most succinctly in Han J. W. Drijvers, "Addai und Mani, Christentum und Manichäismus im dritten Jahrhundert in Syrien," in *III Symposium Syriacum 1980* (ed. René Lavenant; OrChrAn 221; Rome: Pontificium Institutum Studiorum Orientalium, 1983), 171–85.

[25] In this connection see the important remarks of Han J. W. Drijvers, "The Image of Edessa in the Syriac Tradition," in *The Holy Face and the Paradox of Representation: Papers from a Colloquium Held at the Bibliotheca Hertziana, Rome, and the Villa Spelman, Florence, 1996* (ed. Herbert L. Kessler and Gerhard Wolf; Villa Spelman Colloquia 6; Bologna: Nuova Alfa, 1998), 13–31. See also Sidney H. Griffith, "The *Doctrina Addai* as a Paradigm of Christian Thought in Edessa in the Fifth Century," *Hugoye* 6 (2003). Available online at http:/syrcom.cua.edu/Hugoye/Vol6No2/HV6N2Griffith.html.

Roman Empire. The most important of these was Bishop Palut (ca. 200), who was said to have been consecrated bishop by Serapion of Antioch (ca. 190–209), who in turn was consecrated by Zephyrinus of Rome (d. 217).[26] It was their lineage that was claimed by Bishop Qune (reigned ca. 289–313), who according to Walter Bauer "organized orthodoxy in Edessa in an ecclesiastical manner and gave to it significant impetus."[27]

Looking back from the second half of the fourth century, Ephraem the Syrian, who was then the major voice in support of Roman ecclesiastical orthodoxy in the Syriac-speaking world, considered Bishop Palut to have been the man in Severan times who represented orthodoxy's best interest. Nevertheless, Ephraem renounced the name "Palutians" for the orthodox Christians, maintaining that the true followers of Christ are known simply as "Christians."[28] Furthermore, Ephraem considered Marcion, Bar Daysan, and Mani to have been the principal "outsider" adversaries to Christian faith in Edessa and its environs in the early years of the Roman imperial hegemony. Here is what he said about them in his *Hymns against Heresies*:

> Let them be interrogated about their times,
> about who is older than his associate.
> Would Mani seize primogeniture?
> Bar Daysan is prior to him.
> Would Bar Daysan claim to be older?
> His age is younger than the earlier ones.
> Marcion was the first thorn,
> the first-born of the thicket of sin,
> the tare that was the first to spring up.

[26] See George Howard, trans., *The Teaching of Addai* (SBLTT 16; Early Christian Literature Series 4; Chico, Calif.: Scholars Press, 1981), 52 (Syriac), 105 (English).

[27] Walter Bauer, *Orthodoxy and Heresy in Earliest Christianity* (ed. Robert A. Kraft and Gerhard Krodel; Philadelphia: Fortress, 1971), 33; trans. of *Rechtgläubigkeit und Ketzerei im ältesten Christentum* (2d ed.; Tübingen: Mohr, 1964).

[28] See Sidney H. Griffith, "Setting Right the Church of Syria: Saint Ephraem's *Hymns against Heresies*," in *The Limits of Ancient Christianity: Essays on Late Antique Thought and Culture in Honor of R. A. Markus* (ed. William E. Klingshirn and Mark Vessey; Ann Arbor: University of Michigan Press, 1999), 97–114; Sidney H. Griffith, "The Marks of the 'True Church' according to Ephraem's *Hymns against Heresies*," in *After Bardaisan: Studies on Continuity and Change in Syriac Christianity in Honor of Professor Han J. W. Drijvers* (ed. G. J. Reinink and Alexander C. Klugkist; OLA 89; Louvain: Peeters, 1999), 125–40.

May the Just One trample his growth.[29] (*Hymns against*
Heresies 22.17 Beck)

Ephraem viewed the famous teachers of Severan times, both those from abroad, such as Marcion and Valentinus, and those local to the Syriac-speaking world, such as Quq,[30] Bar Daysan, and Mani, to have been anxious to corral disciples from the Christian church of Edessa for their own doctrines.

Valentinus stole a flock
from the church and called it by his own name;
the 'Potter' (i.e., Quq) made a denomination in his own
name.
The crafty Bar Daysan stole some sheep
and they acted like the flock universal.
Marcion deserted his sheep;
Mani fell upon them to capture them from him.
The one mad man was biting the other one!
They called the flock by their own names.
Blessed is the One who has thrown them out of his
house. (*Hymns against Heresies* 22.3 Beck)

In his polemical zeal, Ephraem even liked to make fun of the names of the great teachers whose doctrines he loathed.

Whoever gave the name of the Daysan[31]
to Bar Daysan,
has caused more to die in Bar Daysan
than [ever died in] the Daysan.
His volume swelled up to bring forth
thistles and tares.
Marcion (*Mrqyon*) he rubbed (*mraq*) so much
as to make him rusty.
He scoured him to the point of blunting
his mind with blasphemy.
Mani (*Mani*) became a garment (*mana*)

[29] Occasionally, Ephraem would add the names of other "outsider" adversaries. For example, in one stanza he wrote of Valentinus and Quq, in addition to the more frequently mentioned troika of Marcion, Bar Daysan, and Mani. See, e.g., Ephraem *Hymns against Heresies* 22.3, quoted below.

[30] Quq was a native of Edessa, who also lived in Severan times, but whose teachings, so objectionable to Ephraem, are now largely unknown. See Han J. W. Drijvers, "Quq and the Quqites: An Unknown Sect in Edessa in the Second Century A.D.," *Numen* 14 (1967): 104–29.

[31] In ancient times, Daysan was the name of the river that flows by Edessa.

> apt to wear out its wearers (*Hymns against Heresies* 2.1 Beck).

This polemical zeal on the part of Ephraem and the writers against heresies who came after him convinced Walter Bauer that they were inventing the history of Christianity in Edessa in the third century in order to support the cause of Roman imperial, ecclesiastical orthodoxy in the fourth century. He thought that heresy came first in Edessa and only later what could be called "orthodoxy," and then only as a small, embattled group. More specifically, Bauer thought that in Edessa "Christianity was first established in the form of Marcionism, probably imported from the West and certainly not much later than the year 150."[32] Here is not the place to argue about the Bauer hypothesis. True or false, it does nevertheless call attention to the tremendous intellectual vitality in Edessa and the Syriac-speaking world in the Severan period. Two thinkers in particular, Bar Daysan and Mani, were to have major roles in the struggle for Christian allegiance in Syria in the third century and later. To them, and to the nature of that struggle, we now turn our attention.

IV

Bar Daysan (154–222 C.E.) and Mani (216–276 C.E.) were frontier figures; they were native sons of the Aramaic-speaking world of the frontier between Rome and Persia in the days of the Severan emperors in Rome. Their doctrines were made up of elements from both East and West, displaying a syncretism that one might think of as characteristic of a frontier culture.[33] In this milieu their teachings dominated the intellectual and religious life of the third century.[34]

[32] Bauer, *Orthodoxy and Heresy*, 29.

[33] See Geo Widengren, "'Synkretismus' in der syrischen Christenheit," in *Synkretismus im syrisch-persischen Kulturgebiet* (ed. Albert Kietrich; Göttingen: Vandenhoeck & Ruprecht, 1975), 38–64.

[34] For Bar Daysan, see Han J. W. Drijvers, *Bardaisan of Edessa* (SSN 6; Assen, Netherlands: Van Gorcum, 1966); Edmund Beck, "Bardaisan und seine Schule bei Ephraem," *Le Museon* 91 (1978): 324–33; Javier Teixidor, *Bardesane d'Edesse: La primiere philosophie syriaque* (Paris: Cerf, 1992); Alberto Camplani, "Note Bardesanitiche," *Miscellanea Marciana* 12 (1997): 11–43; Alberto Camplani, "Rivisitando Bardesane: Note sulle fonti siriache del bardesanismo e sulla sua collocazione storico-religiosa," *Cristianesimo nella Storia* 19 (1998): 519–96. For Mani, see Edmund Beck, *Ephraems Polemik gegen Mani und die Manichaeer: Im Rahmen der zeitgenoessischen griechischen Polemik und der des Augustinus* (CSCO 391; Louvain: Secretariat du CSCO, 1978); Samuel N. C. Lieu, *Manichaeism in the*

In the fourth century, Ephraem the Syrian (ca. 306–373) emerged as the strongest voice in Syrian Christianity. He espoused Nicene orthodoxy and Roman political allegiance in a flawless Syriac idiom that set the standard for literary excellence in that language ever afterward.[35] Bar Daysan and Mani, the dominant voices of the previous century, were his principal intellectual adversaries. Due to his popular success in refuting their teachings and the zeal with which later Christians destroyed or neglected their writings, in later centuries Ephraem's works became important sources for the reconstruction of their teachings. But in the third century, when Philostratus traveled in the entourage of the wife of Septimius Severus, Julia Domna (193–217 C.E.), who was originally from Emesa in Syria, the voice of Bar Daysan was the dominant one in the native intellectual circles beyond the Euphrates in the Aramaic-speaking world, followed by that of Mani in the next generation. The one took his inspiration from Rome and the West; the other hearkened to the wisdom of the East. Julia Domna, and not to forget the Phoenician in the *Heroikos*, coming as they did from the environs of Antioch, Tyre, Emesa, and Palmyra, may well have heard echoes of the fame of Bar Daysan, if not of Mani, whose career was just getting under way in the last years of Alexander Severus (222–235 C.E.).

Bar Daysan looked west. Epiphanius of Salamis (ca. 315–403 C.E.), the heresiographer, wrote in his *Panarion* that Bar Daysan was "a learned man in both Greek and Syriac" (*Panarion* 56). Although he was well schooled in the astral sciences of the Babylonians and the cosmogonical myths of the Persians and was much concerned with planetary influences over human affairs, he was also occupied with the science and philosophy of the Greeks. In fact, following the perception of Ephraem, who called him "the

Later Roman Empire and Medieval China: A Historical Survey (Manchester, England: Manchester University Press, 1985); Samuel N. C. Lieu, *Manichaeism in Mesopotamia and the Roman East* (Religions in the Graeco-Roman World 118; Leiden: Brill, 1994); Jason David BeDuhn, *The Manichaean Body: In Discipline and Ritual* (Baltimore: Johns Hopkins University Press, 2000). See also Sidney H. Griffith, "'The Thorn among the Tares': Mani and Manichaeism in the Works of St. Ephraem the Syrian," in *Ascetica, Gnostica, Liturgica, Orientalia* (vol. 2 of *Studia Patristica: Papers Presented at the Thirteenth International Conference on Patristic Studies Held in Oxford, 1999*; ed. Maurice F. Wiles and Edward J. Yarnold; StPatr 35; Louvain: Peeters, 2001), 403–35.

[35] See Sidney H. Griffith, "Setting Right the Church of Syria," 97–114.

Aramean philosopher,"[36] modern commentators have been inclined to consider Bar Daysan to have been more of a philosopher than a religious teacher.[37] They find in his ideas about the origins of the world and human destiny reminiscences of the teachings of the Stoics and the Platonists.[38] Perhaps in this connection, recalling Pierre Hadot's reminders about the pursuit of philosophy as a spiritual exercise in antiquity, one should think of him as a philosopher with a definite program for the spiritual life to commend to his followers.[39] But from a cultural point of view, what is more interesting is that while the notes of his students portray him as almost a Socratic teacher,[40] Ephraem presents Bar Daysan as a particularly successful composer of Syriac *madrāshê* (sg., *madrāshâ*). The *madrāshâ* is a poetic "teaching song" in Syriac,[41] which in Ephraem's later hands was to become the literary and musical medium of choice for winning the allegiance of the Syriac-speaking population in Osrhoênê to the twin loyalties of the Roman Empire and Nicene orthodoxy. Indeed, as we shall see, according to Ephraem, Bar Daysan was the first one to set the traditional *madrāshâ*, hitherto more of a recitative, to music.[42] Ephraem, moreover, claims

[36] Mitchell, *Prose Refutations*, 2:225.

[37] See Teixidor, *Bardesane d'Edesse*, esp. 105–14.

[38] See, e.g., Han J. W. Drijvers, "Bardaisan von Edessa als Repräsentant des syrischen Synkretismus im 2. Jahrhundert n. Chr.," in *Synkretismus im syrisch-persischen Kulturgebiet* (ed. Albert Dietrich; Göttingen: Vandenhoeck & Ruprecht, 1975), 109–22.

[39] See Pierre Hadot, *Philosophy as a Way of Life* (trans. Arnold I. Davidson; Oxford: Blackwell, 1995); Pierre Hadot, *What Is Ancient Philosophy?* (trans. Michael Chase; Cambridge, Mass.: Harvard University Press, 2002).

[40] The only sustained record of Bar Daysan's teaching still extant is contained in a work put together by one of his interlocutors, Awida by name. The text usually carries the title *The Book of the Laws of Countries*; sometimes it is called *De Fato* or *On Fate*. See François Nau, *Bardesanes: Liber Legum Regionum* (Patrologia Syriaca 1; Paris: Firmin-Didot, 1907), cols. 536–611; Han J. W. Drijvers, ed. and trans., *The Book of the Laws of Countries: Dialogue on Fate of Bardaisan of Edessa* (Semitic Texts with Translations 3; Assen, Netherlands: Van Gorcum, 1965).

[41] Usually called simply a "hymn" in English translation, Andrew Palmer has proposed the alternative translation "teaching song," a rendering that certainly comes closer to the original sense of the term. See A. Palmer, "The Merchant of Nisibis: Saint Ephrem and His Faithful Quest for Union in Numbers," in *Early Christian Poetry: A Collection of Essays* (ed. J. den Boeft and A. Hilhorst; Suppl. to *VC* 22; Leiden: Brill, 1993), 167–233. On the inappropriateness of calling the *madrāshâ* a "hymn," see Michael Lattke, "Sind Ephraems *Madrāshê* Hymnen?" *OrChr* 73 (1989): 38–43.

[42] See Kathleen E. McVey, "Were the Earliest *Madrāshê* Songs or Recitations?" in *After Bardaisan: Studies on Change and Continuity in Syriac Christianity*

that Bar Daysan made these compositions the effective vehicles of his ideas in the larger Aramaic-speaking milieu. He complains of this in his own *Hymns against Heresies*:

> In the lairs of Bar Daysan
> are melodies and chants.
> Since he saw the youth
> longing for sweets,
> with the harmony of his songs
> he excited the youngsters. (Ephraem *Hymns against Heresies* 1.17 Beck)

For Ephraem the seduction of Bar Daysan's Syriac melodies was virtually sexual:

> Bar Daysan's speech
> outwardly displays chastity.
> Inwardly it is perverted
> into the very symbol of blasphemy.
> It is a stealthy woman;
> she commits adultery in the inner room. (Ephraem *Hymns against Heresies* 1.11 Beck)

The real issue here is that Bar Daysan, according to Ephraem, excelled in the composition of the rhythmically metrical teaching songs that were the masterpieces of Aramaic didactic poetry. He goes on to say:

> For he composed *madrāshê*
> and put them to music.
> He wrote songs,
> and introduced metres.
> According to the quantities and measures
> he distributed the words.
> To the innocent he proffered
> the bitter in the sweet,
> the sick, who do not choose
> healthy food. (Ephraem *Hymns against Heresies* 53.6 Beck)

Ephraem said that Bar Daysan emulated the biblical King David, in that he composed 150 such teaching songs, on the model of David's 150 Psalms. But from Ephraem's own point of view they

---

in Honor of Professor Han J. W. Drijvers (ed. G. J. Reinink and Alexander C. Klugkist; OLA 89; Louvain: Peeters, 1999), 185–99.

were "the music of the infidels, whose lyre is falsehood" (*Hymns against Heresies* 53.6 Beck). The reason was that these teaching songs, as embellished by Bar Daysan, became the effective means of transmitting what Ephraem regarded as "the Aramean philosopher's" erroneous religious teaching. In this manner, too, according to Ephraem, Bar Daysan was responsible for an even graver mischief; he provided the entrée for Mani and his doctrines into the minds and hearts of the Arameans.

Mani looked east. He was born near Seleucia-Ctesiphon, the capital of the Persian Empire; Ephraem said he was from Babylon (Ephraem *Hymns against Heresies* 14.8). While Mani was religiously nurtured in the Aramaic-speaking milieu of the Elkasaites, a Judeo-Christian group in lower Mesopotamia, the backbone of his mature teaching was the dualism that Ephraem always claimed Mani received from the Persians, whom Ephraem polemically refers to in this connection as "Hindus."[43] For a while Mani enjoyed the protection of the Persian royal court, in the person of the Shah Shapur I (241–272 C.E.), and his teachings spread far and wide, both westward into the Roman Empire and eastward, across Central Asia into China. They exercised a major appeal in the Syriac-speaking environs of Edessa. According to Ephraem, Mani, like Bar Daysan, and perhaps in imitation of his practice, disseminated his teachings in Nisibis and Edessa in *madrāshê* (Ephraem *Hymns against Heresies* 1.16). It is possible that Ephraem had in mind what modern scholars know as Mani's book of *Psalms and Prayers*, composed originally in Aramaic, perhaps even in Syriac, that was one of the seven works in the official canon of Manichaean scriptures.[44] But other Manichaean works were also available, and, as John Reeves has shown, Ephraem himself not infrequently quotes from them and alludes to them in his polemical writings.[45] Nevertheless, it appears that Ephraem regarded what he called Mani's *madrāshê* to be the most formidable expressions of Manichaean

[43] See Ephraem *Hymns against Heresies* 3.7. Citing other passages, Beck shows that by the term "Hindus," Ephraem actually means Persians rather than Indians. See Edmund Beck, *Des heiligen Ephraem des Syrers Hymnen contra Haereses* (CSCO 169–170; Louvain: Secretariat du CSCO, 1957), 2.13 n. 8, and Beck, *Ephraem's Polemik*, 25.

[44] See Lieu, *Manichaeism in the Later Roman Empire*, 6.

[45] See John C. Reeves, "Manichaean Citations from the *Prose Refutations* of Ephrem," in *Emerging from Darkness: Studies in the Recovery of Manichaean Sources* (ed. Paul Mirecki and Jason BeDuhn; Nag Hammadi and Manichaean Studies 43; Leiden: Brill, 1997), 217–88.

teachings; they are the only Manichaean scriptures he actually names. According to Ephraem, then, it was in his so-called *madrāshé* that Mani made his strongest appeal for the allegiance of the Syriac-speaking peoples on the Aramean frontier of the Roman and Persian Empires.

V

While in Severan times, just across the Euphrates from Roman Syria, Bar Daysan and Mani came successively to excite the minds of the Syriac-speaking communities on the frontier and to solicit their allegiance, Philostratus in Rome was celebrating the glories of Hellenism in the context of Roman political allegiance. Sextus Julius Africanus (ca. 180–ca. 250), a Palestinian who found his way into imperial circles already in the time of Septimius Severus, is the one person whose name we know who frequented the courts of both Rome and Edessa at that time, and who, as we noted above, had actually met Bar Daysan. It is not so far-fetched then to think that he must also have known Philostratus. If the latter was actually writing the *Heroikos* in the days of Alexander Severus,[46] and the former brought out his *Kestoi* in 221 and dedicated the work to that same Alexander Severus, while reportedly organizing the library of the Pantheon at the emperor's request,[47] one may well imagine that the two literati had met in the circle of Julia Domna[48] and elsewhere in the imperial entourage of those days.

Philostratus (d. ca. 244–249 C.E.) and Bar Daysan (d. 222 C.E.)

[46] See Jennifer K. Berenson Maclean and Ellen Bradshaw Aitken, trans., *Flavius Philostratus: Heroikos* (SBLWGRW 1; Atlanta: Society of Biblical Literature, 2001), lxxxv.

[47] For more information and further bibliography on Sextus Julius Africanus, who is usually remembered as the earliest Christian chronographer, see the entries *sub nomine* in Angelo Di Berardino, ed., *Encyclopedia of the Early Church* (trans. A. Walford, 2 vols.; New York: Oxford University Press, 1992); Everett Ferguson, Michael P. McHugh, and Frederick W. Norris, eds., *Encyclopedia of Early Christianity* (2d ed.; 2 vols.; New York: Garland, 1997); Elizabeth A. Livingstone and Frank L. Cross, eds., *The Oxford Dictionary of the Christian Church* (3d ed.; Oxford: Oxford University Press, 1997); Siegmar Döpp and Wilhelm Geerlings, eds., *Dictionary of Early Christian Literature* (trans. Matthew O'Connell; New York: Crossroad, 2000).

[48] See Glen W. Bowersock, *Greek Sophists in the Roman Empire* (Oxford: Clarendon, 1969), 101–9. Bowersock does not mention Bar Daysan as a member of Julia Domna's circle, but the description he gives of it provides a fetching description of the circumstances in which both men lived at court.

were roughly contemporaries, the latter being the elder by at least a generation, depending on when one dates the birth of the former.[49] In Rome, Philostratus, with his works such as the *Heroikos*, the *Lives of the Sophists*, and the *Life of Apollonius* in particular, championed Hellenism in its pre-Christian expression, perhaps consciously acting in response to the growing Christian claim to allegiance. In Edessa, Bar Daysan, "the Aramean philosopher," imbued as he was with a deep love of Greek learning and a familiar in the court of the Edessan king, gave his allegiance to Christianity, coming to what Javier Teixidor calls the rather banal conclusion that "the Christian religion would transcend nationalism in imposing a new order in the known world."[50]

Mani, who was much indebted to the teachings of Bar Daysan, also looked further to the east from his Aramean, frontier homeland for his inspiration. He was just a youngster in late Severan times, when Alexander Severus pursued his Persian expedition. But Mani was destined to found a religion, which in spite of its origins across the frontier in Aramaic-speaking Mesopotamia, was to become a major rival to mainline Christianity well within the borders of the Roman Empire in the following century. In the West, the young Augustine of Hippo (354–430 C.E.) in North Africa was to become for a time one of Mani's better-known devotees and subsequently a major polemicist against Manichaeism.[51] In the days of Julia Domna, Philostratus, Julius Africanus, Bar Daysan, and the rest, it would probably have been unthinkable that a man from the Aramaic-speaking world beyond the Euphrates should so soon after their lifetimes have brought such a major challenge to both the ancient Hellenism and the then burgeoning Christianity right into the heart of the empire of the Romans.

[49] See Maclean and Aitken, *Flavius Philostratus: Heroikos*, xlv–xlvi.

[50] Teixidor, *Bardesane d'Edesse*, 113–14.

[51] See Lieu, *Manichaeism in the Late Roman Empire*, 117–53.

Bibliography

EDITIONS AND TRANSLATIONS OF THE *HEROIKOS*

Maclean, Jennifer K. Berenson, and Ellen Bradshaw Aitken, trans. *Flavius Philostratus: On Heroes*. SBLWGRW 3. Atlanta: Society of Biblical Literature, 2003.

———, trans. *Flavius Philostratus: Heroikos*. SBLWGRW 1. Atlanta: Society of Biblical Literature, 2001.

Beschorner, Andreas. *Helden und Heroen, Homer und Caracalla: Übersetzung, Kommentar und Interpretationen zum Heroikos des Flavios Philostratos*. Pinakes 5. Bari, Italy: Levante, 1999.

Rossi, Valeria, ed. and trans. *Filostrato: Eroico*. Venice: Marsilio, 1997.

Mestre, Francesca, ed. and trans. *Heroico; Gimnastico; Descripciones de cuadros; Filostrato. Descripciones; Calistrato*. Biblioteca clasica Gredos 217. Madrid: Gredo, 1996.

Mandilaras, Vassilios, ed. Ἡρωικός—Νέρων. Archaia Hellênikê Grammateia (Hoi Hellênes) 311. Athens: Kaktos, 1995.

de Lannoy, Ludo, ed. *Flavii Philostrati Heroicus*. Leipzig: Teubner, 1977.

Kayser, Carl Ludwig. *Flavii Philostrati opera auctiora edidit C. L. Kayser; accedunt Apollonii Epistolae, Eusebius Adversus Hieroclem, Philostrati junioris Imagines, Callistrati Descriptiones*. 2 vols. Leipzig: Teubner, 1870–1871. Repr., Hildesheim, Germany: Olms, 1964.

Westermann, Anton. *Philostratorum et Callistrati opera recognovit Antonius Westermann. Eunapii Vitae Sophistarum, iterum edidit Jo. Fr. Boissonade. Himerii Sophistae Declamationes, accurate excusso codice optimo et unico XXII declamationum emendavit Fr. Dübner*. Scriptorum Graecorum bibliotheca. Paris: Didot, 1849.

Kayser, Carl Ludwig. *Flavii Philostrati quae supersunt: Philostrati junioris Imagines, Callistrati Descriptiones edidit C. L. Kayser*. Zurich: Meyer & Zeller, 1844.

Jacobs, Friedrich, trans. *Flavius Philostratus Werke*. Edited by G. L. F. Tafel, C. N. Osiander, and G. Schwab. Griechische Prosaiker in neuen Übersetzungen 25. Stuttgart: Metzler, 1828.

Boissonade, Jean François, ed. *Philostrati Heroica ad fidem codicum manuscriptorum IX recensuit, scholia graeca adnotationesque suas addidit J. Fr. Boissonade*. Paris: n.p., 1806.

Olearius, Gottfried. *Philostratorum quae supersunt omnia: Vita Apollonii libris VIII. Vitae Sophistarum libris II. Heroica. Imagines priores atque posteriores et Epistolae. Accessere Apollonii Tyanensis Epistolae, Eusebii liber adversus Hieroclem, Callistrati descript. statuarum. Omnia ex mss. codd. recensuit notis perpetuis illustravit versionem totam fere novam fecit Gottfridus Olearius*. Leipzig: Thomam Fritsch, 1709.

Morel, Federic. *Philostrati Lemnii Opera quae exstant: Philostrati Iunioris Imagines et Callistrati Ecphrases. Item Eusebii Caesariensis episcopi liber contra Hieroclem, qui ex Philostrati historia aequipararat Apollonium Tyaneum saluatori nostro Iesu Christo. Graeca Latinis e regione posita; Fed. Morellus professor et interpres regius cum mnss. contulit, recensuit et hactenus nondum Latinitate donata, vertit.*

Ad virum amplissimum D. Nic. Brulartum, summum Galliarum Procancellarium. Paris: Claudii Morelli, 1608.

Que hoc volvmine continentur. Luciani opera. Icones Philostrati. Eiusdem Heroica. Eiusdem uitae Sophistarum. Icones Iunioris Philostrati. Descriptiones Callistrati. Loukianou eis ten eautou biblon. Venice: Aldi, 1503.

OTHER PRIMARY LITERATURE: EDITIONS AND TRANSLATIONS

Adler, Ada, ed. *Suidae Lexicon.* 5 vols. Leipzig: Teubner, 1928–1938.

Austin, Colin, ed. *Nova fragmenta Euripidea.* Berlin: de Gruyter, 1968.

Bekker, Immanuel, ed. *Anecdota Graeca.* 3 vols. Berlin: Nauckium, 1814–1821.

Bernabé Pajares, Alberto, trans. *Fragmentos de épica griega archaia.* Madrid: Gregos, 1979.

Bidez, Joseph. *L'Empereur Julian: Oeuvres complètes.* 2 vols. Paris: Société d'édition "Les Belles Lettres," 1932–1964.

Blundell, Mary Whitlock, trans. *Sophocles' Oedipus at Colonus.* Newburyport, Mass.: Focus Information Group, 1990.

Bond, G. W., ed. *Euripides: Hypsipyle.* London: Oxford University Press, 1963. Repr. with corrections, Oxford: Clarendon, 1969.

Butler, Samuel, trans. *The Odyssey.* London: Longmans, Green & Co., 1900.

Cameron, Ron, and Arthur J. Dewey, eds. *The Cologne Mani Codex (P. Colon. Inv. Nr. 4780): Concerning the Origin of His Body.* SBLTT 15. Early Christian Literature Series 3. Missoula, Mont.: Scholars Press, 1979.

Cary, Earnest, trans. *Dio's Roman History.* 9 vols. LCL. Cambridge, Mass.: Harvard University Press; London: Heinemann, 1982.

Cervantes Saavedra, Miguel de. *The Ingenious Hidalgo Don Quixote de la Mancha.* Translated by John Rutherford. New York: Penguin, 2001.

Chadwick, Henry, trans. and ed. *Origen: Contra Celsum.* Cambridge and New York: Cambridge University Press, 1953. Repr., 1980.

Connolly, R. Hugh, trans. *Didascalia Apostolorum: The Syriac Version Translated and Accompanied by the Verona Latin Fragments.* Oxford: Clarendon, 1929.

Conybeare, F. C., trans. *Philostratus the Athenian: The Life of Apollonius of Tyana, The Epistles of Apollonius, and the Treatise of Eusebius.* 2 vols. LCL. Cambridge, Mass.: Harvard University Press, 1912. Repr., 1960.

Diels, Hermann, and Walter Kranz, eds. *Die Fragmente der Vorsokratiker.* 6th ed. 3 vols. Zurich: Weidmann, 1985.

Dindorf, Wilhlem, ed. *Aelius Aristides: Works.* Hildesheim, Germany: Olms, 1964.

Dittenberger, Wilhelm, ed. *Sylloge inscriptionum Graecarum.* 3d ed. Hildesheim, Germany: Olms, 1982.

Dix, Gregory, ed. *Apostolikê Paradosis: The Treatise on the Apostolic Tradition of St. Hippolytus of Rome, Bishop and Martyr.* London: SPCK, 1937.

Dodds, E. R., ed. *Euripides: Bacchae.* 2d ed. Oxford: Clarendon, 1960.

Drachmann, Anders Björn, ed. *Scholia vetera in Pindar Carmina.* 3 vols. Leipzig: Teubner, 1903–1927. Repr., Amsterdam: Hakkert, 1966–1967.

Drijvers, Han J. W., ed. and trans. *The Book of the Laws of Countries: Dialogue on Fate of Bardaisan of Edessa.* Semitic Texts with Translations 3. Assen, Netherlands: Van Gorcum, 1965.

Epstein, Isidore, ed. *The Babylonian Talmud.* 18 vols. London: Soncino, 1961.

Erbse, Hartmut. *Untersuchungen zu den attizistischen Lexika.* Abhandlungen der

Deutschen Akademie der Wissenschaften zu Berlin: Philosophisch-historische Klasse 1949 no. 2. Berlin: Akademie, 1950.

Foerster, Richard, ed. *Libanii Opera.* 12 vols. Leipzig: Teubner, 1903–1927. Repr., Hildesheim, Germany: Olms, 1963.

Frazer, J. G., trans. *Pausanias' Description of Greece.* London: Macmillian, 1898.

Gaertringen, F. Hiller von. *Inscriptiones Epidauri. IG* 4.1. Berlin: de Gruyter, 1929.

Giannini, Alexander, ed. *Paradoxographorum Graecorum reliquiae.* Milan: Istituto Editoriale Italiano, 1966.

Godley, A. D., trans. *Herodotus: Histories.* 4 vols. LCL. Cambridge, Mass., and London: Harvard University Press, 1997.

Gow, Andrew S. F., and Denys L. Page, eds. *The Greek Anthology: Hellenistic Epigrams.* 2 vols. Cambridge: Cambridge University Press, 1965.

Guidi, Ignatius, ed. and trans. *Chronica Minora.* CSCO 1–2. Louvain: Secretariat du CSCO, 1903–1907.

Hansen, William, trans. *Phlegon of Tralles' Book of Marvels.* Exeter, England: University of Exeter Press, 1996.

Howard, George, trans. *The Teaching of Addai.* SBLTT 16. Early Christian Literature Series 4. Chico, Calif.: Scholars Press, 1981.

Hunter, Richard, ed. *Theocritus: A Selection.* Cambridge and New York: Cambridge University Press, 1999.

Jacoby, Felix, ed. *Die Fragmente der griechischen Historiker (FGrHist).* Berlin: Weidmann, 1923–1958.

Jebb, Richard C., trans. *Sophocles: The Philoctetes.* Vol. 4 of *Sophocles: Works.* 7 vols. Cambridge: Cambridge University Press, 1890–1924.

Jones, William H. S., ed. *Pausanias: Description of Greece.* 5 vols. LCL. Cambridge, Mass.: Harvard University Press, 1935–1955.

Kassel, Rudolf, and Colin Austin, eds. *Poetae Comici Graeci (PCG).* 8 vols. Berlin: de Gruyter, 1983–1995.

Keil, Bruno, ed. *Aelius Aristides: Works.* Berlin: Weidemann, 1958. Repr., Hildesheim, Germany: Weidmann, 2000.

Kühn, Karl Gottlob, ed. *Galen: Opera Omnia.* 20 vols. Leipzig: Cnobloch, 1821–1833.

Lacy, Phillip Howard de, and Estelle Allen de Lacy, eds. and trans. *Philodemus* On Methods of Inference: *A Study in Ancient Empiricism.* Philadelphia: American Philological Association, 1941.

Le Saint, William P., trans. *Tertullian: Treatises on Marriage and Remarriage.* ACW 13. Westminster, Md.: Newman, 1952.

Lentz, August, ed. *Herodiani technici reliquiae.* 2 vols. Hildesheim, Germany: Olms, 1965.

Lloyd-Jones, Hugh, ed. *Sophocles: Works.* 3 vols. LCL. Cambridge, Mass.: Harvard University Press, 1994–1996.

Lobel, Edgar, and Denys Page, eds. *Poetarum Lesbiorum fragmenta.* Oxford: Clarendon, 1955.

Maehler, Herwig, ed. *Pindari carmina cum fragmentis.* 8th ed. 2 vols. Leipzig: Teubner, 1987–1989.

Mazon, Paul, trans. *Philoctète: Oedipe à Colone.* Vol. 3 of *Sophocle.* Edited by Alphonse Dain and Paul Mazon. Paris: Société d'édition "Les Belles Lettres," 1955–1960.

Merkelbach, R., and M. L. West, eds. *Fragmenta Hesiodea.* Oxford: Clarendon, 1967.

Mette, Hans Joachim, ed. *Die Fragmenta der Tragödien des Aischylos*. Berlin: Akademie, 1959.
Miller, Emmanuel, ed. *Mélanges de littérature grecque*. Paris: Imprimerie impériale, 1868.
Musurillo, Herbert, trans. and ed. *Acts of the Christian Martyrs*. Oxford: Clarendon, 1972.
Nauck, August, ed. *Tragicorum Graecorum fragmenta*. 2d ed. Hildesheim, Germany: Olms, 1964.
Page, Denys L., ed. *Poetae Melici Graeci*. Oxford: Clarendon, 1962.
Pfeiffer, Rudolf. *Callimachus*. 2 vols. Oxford: Clarendon, 1949–1953. Repr., Salem, N.H.: Ayer, 1988.
Pintaudi, Rosario, ed. *Miscellanea papyrologica*. Florence: Gonnelli, 1980.
Rabe, Hugo, ed. *Scholia in Lucianum*. Leipzig: Teubner, 1906. Repr., Stuttgart: Teubner, 1971.
Radt, S. L., ed. *Tragicorum Graecorum fragmenta*. 4 vols. Edited by Bruno Snell. Göttingen: Vandenhoeck & Ruprecht, 1971–1997.
Ribbeck, Otto, ed. *Comicorum Romanorum praeter Plautum et Terentium fragmenta*. Vol. 2 of *Scaenicae Romanorum poesis fragmenta*. Leipzig: Teubner, 1873.
———, ed. *Tragicorum Romanorum fragmenta*. Leipzig: Teubner, 1897.
Roberts, Alexander, and James Donaldson, eds. *The Ante-Nicene Fathers*. 1885–1887. 10 vols. Repr., Peabody, Mass.: Hendrickson, 1994.
Russell, D. A., ed. *Dio Chrysostom: Orations VII, XII, XXXVI*. Cambridge and New York: Cambridge University Press, 1990.
Scheer, Eduard, ed. *Lycophron: Alexandra*. 2 vols. Berlin: Weidmann, 1881–1908. Repr., 1958.
Schneemelcher, Wilhelm, ed. *Neutestamentliche Apokryphen*. 5th ed. Tübingen: Mohr Siebeck, 1987.
———, ed. *New Testament Apocrypha*. Translated by Robert McL. Wilson. Rev. ed. of the collection initiated by Edgar Hennecke. 2 vols. Louisville: Westminster/John Knox, 1991–1992.
Smith, Charles Forster, trans. *Thucydides: History of the Peloponnesian War*. 4 vols. LCL. Cambridge, Mass: Harvard University Press, 1965–1969.
Spiro, Friedrich, ed. *Pausanias: Description of Greece*. Leipzig: Teubner, 1903. Repr., Stuttgart: Teubner, 1959.
Watts, N. H., trans. *Cicero: Orations*. Vol. 14 of 28. LCL. Cambridge, Mass.: Harvard University Press; London: Heinemann, 1979.
Whittaker, Molly, ed. and trans. *Tatian:* Oratio ad Graecos *and Fragments*. Oxford: Clarendon, 1982.
Wilamowitz-Moellendorff, Ulrich von, ed. *Euripides: Herakles*. 3 vols. Berlin: Weidmann, 1889.
———, trans. *Griechische Tragoedien*. 7th ed. Berlin, 1926.
Wright, Wilmar Cave. *The Works of the Emperor Julian*. 3 vols. LCL. Cambridge, Mass.: Harvard University Press, 1923. Repr., 1969.
Wyss, Bernhard, ed. *Antimachus of Colophon: Works*. Berlin: Weidmann, 1936.
Yonge, C. D., trans. *Philo: Works*. 4 vols. London: Bohn, 1854–1855. Rev. ed., Peabody, Mass.: Hendrickson, 1993.

SECONDARY LITERATURE

Accame, Silvio. "Iscrizioni del Cabirio di Lemno." *ASAA* NS 3–5 (1941–1943): 75–105.

Ackermann, Hans Christoph, and Jean-Robert Gisler, eds. *Lexicon Iconographicum Mythologiae Classicae (LIMC)*. 8 vols. Zurich: Artemis, 1981–1997.
Aitken, Ellen Bradshaw. "The Cult of Achilles in Philostratus' *Heroikos*: A Study in the Relation of Canon and Ritual." Pages 127–35 in *Between Magic and Religion: Interdisciplinary Studies in Ancient Mediterranean Religion and Society*. Edited by Sulochana R. Asirvatham, Corinne Ondine Pache, and John Watrous. Lanham, Md.: Rowman & Littlefield, 2001.
———. "The Hero in the Epistle to the Hebrews: Jesus as an Ascetic Model." Pages 179–88 in *Early Christian Voices: In Texts, Traditions, and Symbols. Essays in Honor of François Bovon*. Edited by David H. Warren, Ann Graham Brock, and David W. Pao. Leiden and Boston: Brill, 2003.
———. *Jesus' Death in Early Christian Memory: The Poetics of the Passion*. Novum Testamentum et Orbis Antiquus. Göttingen: Vandenhoeck & Ruprecht, 2004.
———. "τὰ δρώμενα καὶ τὰ λεγόμενα: The Eucharistic Memory of Jesus' Words in First Corinthians." *HTR* 90 (1997): 359–70.
Akurgal, Ekrem. *Civilisations et sites antiques de Turquie*. Istanbul: Haset Kitabevi, 1986.
Aland, Barbara. "Mani und Bardesanes—zur Entstehung des manichäischen Systems." Pages 123–43 in *Synkretismus im syrisch-persischen Kulturgebiet*. Edited by Albert Dietrich. Göttingen: Vandenhoeck & Ruprecht, 1975.
Alcock, Susan E. *Graecia Capta: The Landscapes of Roman Greece*. Cambridge: Cambridge University Press, 1993.
———. "The Heroic Past in a Hellenistic Present." Pages 20–34 in *Hellenistic Constructs: Essays in Culture, History, and Historiography*. Edited by Paul Cartledge, Peter Garnsey, and Erich Gruen. Berkeley: University of California Press, 1997.
———. "Minding the Gap in Hellenistic and Roman Greece." Pages 247–61 in *Placing the Gods: Sanctuaries and Sacred Space in Ancient Greece*. Edited by Susan E. Alcock and Robin Osborne. Oxford: Clarendon, 1994.
Alcock, Susan E., John F. Cherry, and Jaś Elsner, eds. *Pausanias: Travel and Memory in Roman Greece*. Oxford and New York: Oxford University Press, 2001.
Alexiou, Margaret. *The Ritual Lament in Greek Tradition*. Cambridge: Cambridge University Press, 1974. 2d ed., Lanham, Md.: Rowman & Littlefield, 2002.
Allen, Thomas W. *Homer: The Origins and the Transmission*. Oxford: Clarendon, 1924.
Allison, Dale C., Jr. *The Jesus Tradition in Q*. Harrisburg, Pa.: Trinity Press International, 1997.
Alter, Robert. *The Art of Biblical Narrative*. New York: Basic Books, 1981.
Anderson, Carl, Klaus Bartels, and Ludwig Huber, eds. *Lexikon der Alten Welt*. Zurich: Artemis, 1965.
Anderson, Graham. *Philostratus: Biography and* Belles Lettres *in the Third Century A.D.* London: Croom Helm, 1986.
———. *The Second Sophistic: A Cultural Phenomenon in the Roman Empire*. London: Routledge, 1993.
André, Jean-Marie, and Marie-Françoise Baslez. *Voyager dans l'antiquité*. Paris: Fayard, 1993.
Angeli Bertinelli, Maria Gabriella. "I Romani oltre l'Eufrate nel II secolo d. C. (le province di Assiria, di Mesopotamia e di Osroene)." *ANRW* 9.1:3–45. Part 2, *Principat*, 9.1. Edited by H. Temporini and W. Haase. New York: de Gruyter, 1979.
Antonaccio, Carla M. *An Archaeology of Ancestors: Tomb Cult and Hero Cult in Early Greece*. Lanham, Md.: Rowman and Littlefield, 1995.

Arafat, Karim. *Pausanias' Greece: Ancient Artists and Roman Rulers*. Cambridge and New York: Cambridge University Press, 1996.

Asheri, D. "Studio sulla storia della colonizzazione di Anfipoli sino alla conquista macedone." *Rivista di filologia e d'istruzione classica* 95 (1967): 5–30.

Ashton, John. "Paraclete." *ABD* 5:152–54.

Attridge, Harold W. "Liberating Death's Captives: Reconsideration of an Early Christian Myth." Pages 103–15 in *Gnosticism and the Early Christian World: In Honor of James M. Robinson*. Edited by James E. Goehring et al. Sonoma, Calif.: Polebridge, 1990.

Aubriot-Sévin, D. *Prière et conceptions religieuses en Grèce ancienne jusqu'à la fin du Ve siècle av. J.-C.* Lyon: Maison de l'Orient méditerranéen, 1992.

Aune, David E. "Heracles and Christ: Heracles Imagery in the Christology of Early Christianity." Pages 3–19 in *Greeks, Romans, and Christians: Essays in Honor of Abraham J. Malherbe*. Edited by David L. Balch, Everett Ferguson, and Wayne A. Meeks. Minneapolis, Fortress, 1990.

———. "The Problem of the Genre of the Gospels: A Critique of C. H. Talbert's *What Is a Gospel?*" Pages 9–60 in *Studies of History and Tradition in the Four Gospels*. Edited by R. T. France and David Wenham. Gospel Perspectives 2. Sheffield: JSOT Press, 1981.

Austin, R. G. "Hector's Hair-Style." *CQ* NS 22 (1972): 199.

Avotins, Ivars. "The Date and the Recipient of the *Vitae Sophistarum* of Philostratus." *Hermes* 106 (1978): 242–47.

———. "The Year of Birth of the Lemnian Philostratus." *L'Antiquité classique* 47 (1978): 538–39.

Babelon, Jean. "Protésilas à Scioné." *Revue Numismatique* 5th ser. 3 (1951): 1–11.

Bachofen, Johann J. *Das Mutterrecht*. Stuttgart: Krais & Hoffman, 1861. Repr. in *Gesammelte Werke*. 7 vols. Edited by Karl Meuli. Basel: Schwabe, 1943.

———. *Gesammelte Werke*. 7 vols. Edited by Karl Meuli. Basel: Schwabe, 1943.

Balch, David, Everett Ferguson, and Wayne A. Meeks, eds. *Greeks, Romans, and Christians: Essays in Honor of Abraham J. Malherbe*. Minneapolis: Fortress, 1990.

Ball, Warwick. *Rome in the East: The Transformation of an Empire*. London and New York: Routledge, 2000.

Barnard, L. W. "The Heresy of Tatian—Once Again." *JEH* 19 (1968): 1–10.

Basanoff, V. *Evocatio: Étude d'un rituel militaire romain*. Paris: Presses universitaires de France, 1947.

Bauer, Franz Alto. *Stadt, Platz und Denkmal in der Spätantike: Untersuchungen zur Ausstattung des öffentlichen Raumes in den spätantiken Städten Rom, Kontantinopel und Ephesos*. Mainz, Germany: Zabern, 1996.

Bauer, Walter. *Das Leben Jesu im Zeitalter der neutestamentlichen Apokryphen*. Tübingen: Mohr Siebeck, 1909.

———. *Orthodoxy and Heresy in Earliest Christianity*. Edited by Robert A. Kraft and Gerhard Krodel. Philadelphia: Fortress, 1971. Trans. of *Rechtgläubigkeit und Ketzerei im ältesten Christentum*. 2d ed. Tübingen: Mohr, 1964.

Bauer, Walter, Frederick W. Danker, W. F. Arndt, and F. W. Gingerich, eds. *A Greek-English Lexicon of the New Testament and Other Early Christian Literature*. 3d ed. Chicago: University of Chicago Press, 2000.

Baumeister, Theofried "Heiligenverehrung I." *RAC* 14 (1988): 96–150.

Beard, Mary, John North, and Simon Price. *Religions of Rome*. 2 vols. Cambridge: Cambridge University Press, 1998.

Beazley, John D. *Attic Red-Figure Vase-Painters*. 2d ed. Oxford: Clarendon, 1963.

Beck, Edmund. "Bardaisan und seine Schule bei Ephraem." *Le Museon* 91 (1978): 324–33.
———. *Ephräms Polemik gegen Mani und die Manichäer: Im Rahmen der zeitgenössischen griechischen Polemik und der des Augustinus.* CSCO 391. Louvain: Secrétariat du CSCO, 1978.
———. *Des heiligen Ephraem des Syrers Hymnen contra Haereses.* CSCO 169–170. Louvain: Secretariat du CSCO, 1957.
BeDuhn, Jason David. *The Manichaean Body: In Discipline and Ritual.* Baltimore: Johns Hopkins University Press, 2000.
Behm, Johannes. "παράκλητος." *TDNT* 5:800–814.
Bellinger, Alfred R. *Troy: The Coins.* Princeton: Princeton University Press, 1961.
Benton, Sylvia. "Excavations in Ithaca, III: The Cave at Pólis, I." *Annual of the British School at Athens* 35 (1934–1935): 45–73.
———. "Excavations in Ithaca, III: The Cave at Pólis, II." *Annual of the British School at Athens* 39 (1938–1939): 1–51.
Bérard, C. "Récupérer la mort du prince: Héroïsation et formation de la cité." Pages 89–105 in *La mort: Les morts dans les sociétés anciennes.* Edited by Gherardo Gnoli and Jean-Pierre Vernant. Cambridge: Cambridge University Press, 1982.
Berger, Dietrich, and Johannes Nollé. *Tyana: Archäologisch-historische Untersuchungen zum südwestlichen Kappadokien.* Inschriften griechischer Städte aus Kleinasien 57. Bonn: Habelt, 2000.
Bering-Staschewski, Rosemarie. *Römische Zeitgeschichte bei Cassius Dio.* Bochum, Germany: Brockmeyer, 1981.
Bernabò-Brea, L. "Lemno." Pages 4:542–45 in *Enciclopedia dell'arte antica, classica e orientale.* 7 vols. Rome: Istituto della Enciclopedia italiana, 1958–1966.
Bertram, Georg. "Erhöhung." *RAC* 6 (1966): 22–43.
Bertrand-Dagenbach, Cécile. *Alexandre Sévère et l'Histoire Auguste.* Latomus 208. Brussels: Latomus, 1990.
Beschi, Liugi. "Cabirio di Lemno: Testimonianze letterarie ed epigrafiche." *ASAA* NS 58–59 (1996–1997): 7–146.
Betz, Hans Dieter. *Gesammelte Aufsätze.* 4 vols. Tübingen: Mohr Siebeck, 1990–1998.
———. "Lukian von Samosata und das Christentum." Pages 10–21 in *Hellenismus und Urchristentum.* Vol. 1 of *Gesammelte Aufsätze.* Tübingen: Mohr Siebeck, 1990.
———. *Lukian von Samosata und das Neue Testament: Religionsgeschichtliche und paränetische Parallelen.* TU 76. Berlin: Akademie-Verlag, 1961.
———. "Das Problem der Auferstehung Jesu im Lichte der griechischen magischen Papyri." Pages 230–61 in *Hellenismus und Urchristentum.* Vol. 1 of *Gesammelte Aufsätze.* Tübingen: Mohr Siebeck, 1990.
Bickerman, Elias. "Das leere Grab." *ZNW* 23 (1924): 281–92.
Billault, Alain. *L'univers de Philostrate.* Collection Latomus 252. Brussels: Latomus, 2000.
Billiard, Raymond. *La vigne dans l'antiquité.* Lyon: Lardanchet, 1914.
Birley, Anthony R. *Septimius Severus: The African Emperor.* London: Eyre & Spottiswood, 1971. Rev. and enlarged ed., New Haven: Yale University Press, 1989.
Blackburn, Stuart H., Peter J. Claus, Joyce B. Flueckiger, and Susan S. Wadley, eds. *Oral Epics in India.* Berkeley: University of California Press, 1989.
Blázquez, José Maria. "Alejandro Magno: Modelo de Alejandro Severo." Pages

25–36 in *Neronia IV: Alejandro Magno, modelo de los emperadores romanos. Actes du IVe Colloque de la SIEN*. Edited by Jean-Michel Croisille. Latomus 209. Brussels: Latomus, 1990.

Bleeker, Claas J. *Egyptian Festivals: Enactment of Religious Renewal*. Leiden: Brill, 1967.

Blois, Lukas de. "Emperor and Empire in the Works of Greek-Speaking Authors of the Third Century AD." *ANRW* 34.4:3391–3443. Part 2, *Principat*, 34.4. Edited by H. Temporini and W. Haase. New York: de Gruyter, 1998.

———. "The Third-Century Crisis and the Greek Elite in the Roman Empire." *Historia* 33 (1984): 358–77.

Blok, Josine H. *The Early Amazons: Modern and Ancient Perspectives on a Persistent Myth*. Religions in the Greco-Roman World 120. Leiden: Brill, 1995.

Blomart, Alain. "Devotio." *RGG* 2:775–76.

———. "Evocatio." *RGG* 2:1749.

———. "Die *evocatio* und der Transfer 'fremder' Götter von der Peripherie nach Rom." Pages 99–111 in *Römische Reichsreligion und Provinzialreligion*. Edited by Hubert Cancik and Jörg Rüpke. Tübingen: Mohr Siebeck, 1997.

———. "Les manières grecques de déplacer les héros: Modalités religieuses et motivations politiques." Pages 351–64 in *Héros et héroïnes dans les mythes et les cultes grecs: Actes du colloque organisé à l'Université de Valladolid, 26–29 May 1999*. Edited by Vinciane Pirenne-Delforge and Emilio Suárez de la Torre. Kernos suppl. 10. Liège, Belgium: Centre international d'étude de la religion grecque antique, 2000.

Boardman, John. "Herakles, Theseus, and the Amazons." Pages 1–28 in *The Eye of Greece: Studies in the Art of Athens*. Edited by D. C. Kurtz and B. Sparkes. Cambridge: Cambridge University Press, 1982.

Boedeker, Deborah. "Hero Cult and Politics in Herodotus: The Bones of Orestes." Pages 164–77 in *Cultural Poetics in Archaic Greece*. Edited by Carol Dougherty and Leslie Kurke. Cambridge: Cambridge University Press, 1993.

———. "Protesilaos and the End of Herodotus' *Histories*." *Classical Antiquity* 7/1 (1988): 30–48.

Boethius, C. A. "Excavations at Mycenae XI: Hellenistic Mycenae." *Annual of the British School at Athens* 25 (1921–1923): 409–28.

Bolt, Peter G. "Mark 16:1–8: The Empty Tomb of a Hero?" *Tyndale Bulletin* 47 (1996): 27–37.

Bonnechère, Pierre. *Le sacrifice humain en Grèce ancienne*. Kernos suppl. 3. Athens and Liège, Belgium: Centre international d'étude de la religion grecque antique, 1994.

Borgeaud, Philippe. "Rhésos et Arganthoné." Pages 51–59 in *Orphisme et Orphée: En l'honneur de Jean Rudhardt*. Edited by Philippe Borgeaud. Geneva: Droz, 1991.

Bowersock, Glen W. *Fiction as History: Nero to Julian*. Berkeley: University of California Press, 1994.

———. "Greek Intellectuals and the Imperial Cult in the Second Century A.D." Pages 293–326 in *Studies on the Eastern Roman Empire: Social, Economic, and Administrative History, Religion, Historiography*. Goldbach, Germany: Keip, 1994. Repr. from *Le culte des souverains*. Edited by Willem den Boer. Entretiens sur l'Antiquité Classique 19. Geneva: Hardt, 1973.

———. *Greek Sophists in the Roman Empire*. Oxford: Clarendon, 1969.

———. *Hellenism in Late Antiquity*. Ann Arbor: University of Michigan Press, 1990.

———. *Roman Arabia*. Cambridge, Mass.: Harvard University Press, 1983.

Bowie, Ewen L. "Greeks and Their Past in the Second Sophistic." *Past and Present* 46 (1970): 3–41. Rev. in *Studies in Ancient Society*. Edited by M. I. Finley. London: Routledge, 1974.

———. "Philostratus: Writer of Fiction." Pages 181–99 in *Greek Fiction: The Greek Novel in Context*. Edited by J. R. Morgan and Richard Stoneman. New York: Routledge, 1994.

Bradshaw, Paul F., Maxwell E. Johnson, and L. Edward Phillips. *The Apostolic Tradition: A Commentary*. Hermeneia. Minneapolis: Fortress, 2002.

Brelich, Angelo. *Gli eroi greci: Un problema storico-religioso*. Rome: Edizioni dell'Ateneo, 1958.

Brock, Ann Graham. "The Significance of φιλέω and φίλος in the Tradition of Jesus Sayings in the Early Church." *HTR* 90 (1997): 393–409.

Brock, Sebastian. "Eusebius and Syriac Christianity." Pages 212–34 in *Eusebius, Christianity, and Judaism*. Edited by Harold W. Attridge and Gohei Hata. Detroit: Wayne State University Press, 1992.

Broneer, Oscar. *Isthmia I: Temple of Poseidon*. Princeton: American School of Classical Studies at Athens, 1977.

———. *Isthmia III: Terracotta Lamps*. Princeton: American School of Classical Studies at Athens, 1977.

Brouwer, Wayne. *The Literary Development of John 13–17: A Chiastic Reading*. SBLDS. Atlanta: Society of Biblical Literature, 2000.

Brown, Raymond E. *The Community of the Beloved Disciple*. New York: Paulist, 1979.

———. *The Gospel according to John*. 2 vols. AB 29–29A. Garden City, N.Y.: Doubleday, 1966–1970.

Bruhl, Adrien. "Le souvenir d'Alexandre le Grand et les Romains." *Mélanges d'Archéologie et d'Histoire* 47 (1930): 202–21.

Bruneau, Philippe. *Recherches sur les cultes de Délos à l'époque hellénistique et à l'époque impériale*. Paris: De Boccard, 1970.

Budde, L., and R. V. Nicholls. *A Catalogue of the Greek and Roman Sculpture in the Fitzwilliam Museum Cambridge*. Cambridge: Cambridge University Press, 1964.

Buffière, Félix. *Allégories d'Homère*. Paris: Société d'édition "Les Belles Lettres," 1962.

Bultmann, Rudolf. *The Gospel of John: A Commentary*. Philadelphia: Westminster Press, 1971. Translation of *Das Evangelium des Johannes*. Göttingen: Vandenhoeck & Ruprecht, 1964.

Burg, M. N. H. van den. "ΑΠΟΡΡΗΤΑ ΔΡΩΜΕΝΑ ΟΡΓΙΑ." Diss., Amsterdam, 1939.

Burgess, Jonathan S. "The Non-Homeric *Cypria*." *TAPA* 126 (1996): 77–99.

———. *The Tradition of the Trojan War in Homer and the Epic Cycle*. Baltimore: Johns Hopkins University Press, 2001.

Burkert, Walter. *Ancient Mystery Cults*. Cambridge, Mass.: Harvard University Press, 1987.

———. *Greek Religion*. Cambridge, Mass.: Harvard University Press, 1985. Translation of *Griechische Religion der archaischen und klassischen Epoche*. Stuttgart: Kohlhammer, 1977.

———. "Greek Tragedy and Sacrificial Ritual." *GRBS* 7 (1966): 102–21.

———. *Homo Necans: The Anthropology of Ancient Greek Sacrifical Ritual and Myth*. Berkeley: University of California Press, 1983. Translation of *Homo Necans: Interpretationen griechischen Opferriten und Mythen*. Religionsgeschichtliche Versuche und Vorarbeiten 32. Berlin: de Gruyter, 1972.

———. "Kekropidensage und Arrhephoria: Vom Initiationsritus zum Panathenenfest." *Hermes* 94 (1966): 1–25.

Burnet, John. *Early Greek Philosophy*. 4th ed. London: Black, 1958.

Burridge, Richard A. *What Are the Gospels? A Comparison with Graeco-Roman Biography*. SNTSMS 70. Cambridge: Cambridge University Press, 1992.

Cadoux, Cecil John. *Ancient Smyrna: A History of the City from the Earliest Times to 324 A.D.* Oxford: Blackwell, 1938.

Calame, Claude. "Mort héroïque et culte à mystère dans l'*Oedipe à Colone* de Sophocle: Aspects rituels au service de la création mythique." Pages 326–56 in *Ansichten griechischer Rituale: Geburtstags-Symposium für Walter Burkert, Castelen bei Basel, 15. bis 18. Marz 1996*. Edited by Fritz Graf. Stuttgart: Teubner, 1998.

———. *Thésée et l'imaginaire athénien: Légende et culte en Grèce antique*. Lausanne: Editions Payot, 1990.

Cameron, Averil. "On Defining the Holy Man." Pages 27–43 in *The Cult of Saints in Late Antiquity and the Middle Ages: Essays on the Contribution of Peter Brown*. Edited by James Howard-Johnston and Paul Antony Hayward. Oxford and New York: Oxford University Press, 1999.

Camp, John M. *The Athenian Agora: Excavations in the Heart of Classical Athens*. London: Thames and Hudson, 1986.

Camplani, Alberto. "Note Bardesanitiche." *Miscellanea Marciana* 12 (1997): 11–43.

———. "Rivisitando Bardesane: Note sulle fonti siriache del bardesanismo e sulla sua collocazione storico-religiosa." *Cristianesimo nella Storia* 19 (1998): 519–96.

Carpenter, H. J. "Popular Christianity in the Theologians in the Early Centuries." *JTS* 14 (1963): 294–310.

Cartledge, Paul, and Antony Spawforth. *Hellenistic and Roman Sparta: A Tale of Two Cities*. London: Routledge, 1989.

Cassin, Barbara. "Procédures sophistiques pour construire l'évidence." Pages 15–29 in *Dire l'évidence (philosophie et rhétorique antiques): Actes du colloque de Créteil et de Paris (24–25 mars 1995)*. Edited by Carlos Lévy and Laurent Pernot. Paris: L'Harmattan, 1997.

Cassola, F. "La leggenda di Anio e la preistoria Delia." *PP* 60 (1954): 345–67.

Catling. Hector W. "Excavations at the Menelaion, Sparta, 1973–76." *Archaeological Reports* (1976–1977): 24–42.

Ceauşescu, P. "La double image d'Alexandre le Grand à Rome." *Studii Clasice* (Bucharest) 16 (1974): 153–68.

Chaumont, Marie-Louise. "L'Arménie entre Rome et l'Iran: De l'avènement d'Auguste a l'avènement de Dioclétien." *ANRW* 9.1:71–194. Part 2, *Principat*, 9.1. Edited by H. Temporini and W. Haase. New York: de Gruyter, 1979.

Chavane, Marie-José, and Marguerite Yo. *Testimonia Salaminia*. Salamine de Chypre 10. Paris: De Boccard, 1978.

Christol, Michel. *L'empire romain du IIIe siècle: Histoire politique (de 192, mort de Commode, à 325, concile de Nicée)*. Paris: Éditions Errance, 1997.

Claus, Peter J. "Behind the Text: Performance and Ideology in a Tulu Oral Tradition." Pages 55–74 in *Oral Epics in India*. Edited by Stuart H. Blackburn, Peter J. Claus, Joyce B. Flueckiger, and Susan S. Wadley. Berkeley: University of California Press, 1989.

Clay, Diskin. "The Cults of Epicurus." *Cronache Ercolanesi* 16 (1986): 11–28.

Colin, Gaston. *Inscriptions du Trésor des Athéniens*. Fouilles de Delphes 3.2. Paris: Fontemoing, 1909–1913.

Collins, Adela Yarbro. "The Empty Tomb and Resurrection according to Mark." Pages 119–48 in *The Beginning of the Gospel: Probings of Mark in Context*. Minneapolis: Fortress, 1992. Rev. as "Apotheosis and Resurrection." Pages 88–100 in *The New Testament and Hellenistic Judaism*. Edited by Peder Borgen and Søren Giversen. Århus: Århus University Press, 1995.

———. "Finding Meaning in the Death of Jesus." *JR* 78 (1998): 175–96.

———. "From Noble Death to Crucified Messiah." *NTS* 40 (1994): 481–503.

———. "The Genre of the Passion Narrative." *ST* 47 (1993): 3–28.

Conze, Alexander. *Reise auf den Inseln des thrakischen Meeres*. Hannover: Rümpler, 1860.

Cook, Arthur B. *Zeus: A Study in Ancient Religion*. 3 vols. Cambridge: Cambridge University Press, 1914–1940.

Cook, John M. "The Cult of Agamemnon at Mycenae." Pages 112–15 in *Geras Antoniou Keramopoullou*. Athens: Typographeion Myrtide, 1953.

———. "Mycenae 1939–52: The Agamemnoneion." *Annual of the British School at Athens* 48 (1953): 30–68.

———. "The Topography of the Plain of Troy." Pages 163–72 in *The Trojan War: Its Historicity and Context: Papers of the First Greenbank Colloquium, Liverpool, 1981*. Edited by Lin Foxhall and John K. Davies. Bristol, England: Bristol Classical Press, 1984.

———. *The Troad: An Archaeological and Topographical Study*. Oxford: Clarendon, 1973.

Courakis, Nestor E. "A Contribution to the Search for Ancient Helike." Pages 23–38 in *TIMAI Iôannou Triantaphyllopoulou*. Athens and Komotiní, Greece: Sakkoulas, 2000.

Cracco-Ruggini, L. "Un riflesso del mito di Alessandro nella 'Historia Augusta.'" Pages 79–89 in *Bonner Historia-Augusta-Colloquium, 1968–1969*. Antiquitas 4. Beiträge zur Historia-Augusta-Forschung 7. Edited by Johannes Straub. Bonn: Habelt, 1970.

———. "Sulla cristianizzazione della cultura pagana: Il mito greco e latino di Alessandro dall'età Antonina al medioevo." *Athenaeum* (Pavia) 43/1–2 (1965): 4–56.

Crittenden, J. "Armenian Hero Laid to Rest after Journey from Watertown." *Boston Herald*, 29 May 2000.

Croisille, Jean-Michel, ed. *Neronia IV: Alejandro Magno, modelo de los emperadores romanos. Actes du IVe colloque de la SIEN*. Latomus 209. Brussels: Latomus, 1990.

Cucuzza, Nicola. "Considerazioni su alcuni culti nella Messarà di epoca storica e sui rapporti territoriali fra Festòs e Gortina." *Atti dell'Accademia nazionale dei Lincei. Rendiconti* 9.8 (1997): 72–74.

Cumont, Franz. "The Frontier Provinces in the East." CAH 11:606–48.

Dąbrowa, Edward. *La politique de l'état parthe à l'égard de Rome*. Krakow: Jagiellonian University Press, 1983.

———. "Le programme de la politique en Occident des derniers Arsacides." *Iranica Antiqua* 19 (1984): 149–65.

Dahl, Nils Alstrup. "Anamnesis: Memory and Commemoration in Early Christianity." Pages 11–29 in *Jesus in the Memory of the Early Church*. Minneapolis: Augsburg, 1976.

Dareggi, Gianna. "Severo Alessandro: *Romanus Alexander*, e il complesso santuariale di Thugga." *Latomus* (Brussels) 53/3 (1994): 848–58.

Daux, Georges. "La grande démarchie: Un nouveau calendrier sacrificiel d'Attique (Erchia)." *BCH* 87 (1963): 603–34.

Davies, Malcolm. *The Epic Cycle*. Bristol, England: Bristol Classical Press, 1989.

Davreux, Juliette. *La légende de la prophétesse Cassandre d'après les textes et les monuments*. Paris: Droz, 1942.

de Lannoy, Ludo. "Le problème des Philostrate (État de la question)." *ANRW* 34.3:2362–2449. Part 2, *Principat*, 34.3. Edited by H. Temporini and W. Haase. New York: de Gruyter, 1997.

Delcourt, Marie. *Héphaistos ou la légende du magicien*. Paris: Société d'édition "Les Belles Lettres," 1957.

———. *Légendes et cultes de héros en Grèce*. Paris: Presses universitaires de France 1942.

Delehaye, Hippolyte. *Les origines du culte des martyrs*. Brussels: Bureaux de la Société des Bollandistes, 1912.

Della Seta, A. "Arte Tirrenica di Lemno." *Archaeologike Ephemeris* (1937): 629–54.

Demangel, Robert. *Le tumulus dit de Protésilas*. Fouilles des corps d'occupation français de Constantinople 1. Paris: De Boccard, 1926.

Deonna, Waldemar. "Orphée et l'oracle de la tête coupée." *REG* 38 (1925): 44–69.

Deubner, Ludwig. *Attische Feste*. Berlin: Keller, 1932.

Dewey, Arthur J. "The Eyewitness of History: Visionary Consciousness in the Fourth Gospel." Pages 59–70 in *Jesus in Johannine Tradition*. Edited by Robert T. Fortna and Tom Thatcher. Louisville: Westminster John Knox, 2001.

DeWitt, Norman W. *Epicurus and His Philosophy*. Cleveland and New York: Word, 1967.

Di Berardino, Angelo, ed. *Encyclopedia of the Early Church*. Translated by A. Walford. 2 vols. New York: Oxford University Press, 1992.

Dierauer, Urs. *Tier und Mensch im Denken der antike Studien zur Tierpsychologie, Anthropologie und Ethik*. Studien Zur Antiken Philosophie 6. Amsterdam: Grüner, 1977.

Dihle, Albrecht. *Greek and Latin Literature of the Roman Empire: From Augustus to Justinian*. London and New York: Routledge, 1994. Translation of *Die griechische und lateinische Literatur der Kaiserzeit*. Munich: Beck, 1989.

Diller, Aubrey. "The Manuscripts of Pausanias." Pages 163–82 in *Studies in Greek Manuscript Tradition*. Amsterdam: Hakkert, 1983.

Dodd, C. H. *The Interpretation of the Fourth Gospel*. Cambridge: Cambridge University Press, 1968.

Dodds, E. R. *Pagan and Christian in an Age of Anxiety: Some Aspects of Religious Experience from Marcus Aurelius to Constantine*. Cambridge: Cambridge University Press, 1965.

Doody, Margaret Anne. *The True Story of the Novel*. New Brunswick, N.J.: Rutgers University Press, 1996.

Döpp, Siegmar, and Wilhelm Geerlings, eds. *Dictionary of Early Christian Literature*. Translated by Matthew O'Connell. New York: Crossroad, 2000.

Dörig, José. "Deinoménès." *Antike Kunst* 37 (1994): 67–80.

Doulgeri-Intzessiloglou, Argyroula, and Yvon Garlan. "Vin et amphores de Péparéthos et d'Ikos." *BCH* 114 (1990): 361–89.

Dow, Sterling. "The Greater Demarkhia of Erchia." *BCH* 89 (1965): 180–213.

Drijvers, Han J. W. "Addai und Mani, Christentum und Manichäismus im dritten

Jahrhundert in Syrien." Pages 171–85 in *III Symposium Syriacum 1980*. Edited by René Lavenant. OrChrAn 221. Rome: Pontificium Institutum Studiorum Orientalium, 1983.

———. *Bardaisan of Edessa*. SSN 6. Assen, Netherlands: Van Gorcum, 1966.

———. "Bardaisan von Edessa als Repräsentant des syrischen Synkretismus im 2. Jahrhundert n. Chr." Pages 109–22 in *Synkretismus im syrisch-persischen Kulturgebiet*. Edited by Albert Dietrich. Göttingen: Vandenhoeck & Ruprecht, 1975.

———. "The Image of Edessa in the Syriac Tradition." Pages 13–31 in *The Holy Face and the Paradox of Representation: Papers from a Colloquium Held at the Bibliotheca Hertziana, Rome, and the Villa Spelman, Florence, 1996*. Edited by Herbert L. Kessler and Gerhard Wolf. Villa Spelman Colloquia 6. Bologna, Italy: Nuova Alfa, 1998.

———. "Mani und Bardaisan: Ein Beitrag zur Vorgeschichte des Manichäismus." Pages 459–69 in *Mélanges d'histoire des religions offerts à Henri-Charles Puech*. Paris: Presses universitaires de France, 1974.

———. "Marcionism in Syria: Principles, Problems, Polemics." *SecCent* 6 (1987–1988): 153–72.

———. "Quq and the Quqites: An Unknown Sect in Edessa in the Second Century A.D." *Numen* 14 (1967): 104–29.

Dubois, Laurent. *Inscriptions grecques dialectales d'Olbia du Pont*. Geneva: Droz, 1996.

———. "Oiseaux de *Nostoi*." Pages 149–60 in *Poésie et lyrique antiques*. Edited by Laurent Dubois. Villeneuve d'Ascq, France: Presses universitaires du Septentrion, 1996.

Dué, Casey. "Achilles' Golden Amphora and the Afterlife of Oral Tradition in Aeschines' *Against Timarchus*." *CP* 96 (2001): 33–47.

———. *Homeric Variations on a Lament by Briseis*. Lanham, Md.: Rowman & Littlefield, 2002.

Dué, Casey, and Gregory Nagy. "Preliminaries to Philostratus's *On Heroes*." Pages xv–xli in *Flavius Philostratus: On Heroes*. Translated by Jennifer K. Berenson Maclean and Ellen Bradshaw Aitken. SBLWGRW 3. Atlanta: Society of Biblical Literature, 2003.

Dulière, W. L. "Protection permanente contre des animaux nuisibles assurée par Apollonius de Tyane dans Byzance et Antioche: Evolution de son mythe." *ByzZ* 63 (1970): 247–77.

Dumézil, Georges. *Le crime des Lemniennes: Rites et légenedes du monde égéen*. Paris: Geuthner, 1924. Repr., Paris: Macula, 1998.

Duncan-Jones, R. P. "Patronage and City Privileges: The Case of Giufi." *Epigraphische Studien* 9 (1971): 12–16.

Dundes, Alan. "The Hero Pattern and the Life of Jesus." Pages 1–32 in *Protocol of the Twenty-fifth Colloquy, the Center for Hermeneutical Studies in Hellenistic and Modern Culture, Berkeley, California, 12 December 1976*. Edited by W. Wuellner. Berkeley, Calif.: The Center for Hermeneutical Studies in Hellenistic and Modern Culture, 1977. Repr. pages 179–223 in *In Quest of the Hero*. Edited by Robert A. Segal. Princeton: Princeton University Press, 1990.

Du Quesnay, Ian M. Le M. "From Polyphemus to Corydon: Virgil, *Eclogues* 2, and the *Idylls* of Theocritus." Pages 35–69 in *Creative Imitation in Latin Literature*. Edited by David West and Tony Woodman. Cambridge and New York: Cambridge University Press, 1979.

Dzielska, Maria. *Apollonius of Tyana in Legend and History*. Rome: Bretschneider, 1986.

Edmunds, Lowell. "The Cults and the Legend of Oedipus." *HSCP* 85 (1981): 221–38.

———. *Theatrical Space and Historical Place in Sophocles'* Oedipus at Colonus. Lanham, Md.: Rowman & Littlefield, 1996.

Eitrem, Samson. "Heros." PW 8.1 (1913): 1111–45.

———. "Philostratea: Ad textum dialogi Heroici adnotationes." *Symbolae Osloenses* 9 (1930): 51–61.

———. "Zu Philostrats *Heroikos*." *Symbolae Osloenses* 8 (1929): 1–56.

Ekroth, Gunnel. "Pausanias and the Sacrificial Rituals of Greek Hero-Cults." Pages 145–58 in *Ancient Greek Hero Cult: Proceedings of the Fifth International Seminar on Ancient Greek Cult, Organized by the Department of Classical Archaeology and Ancient History, Göteborg University, 21–23 April 1995*. Edited by Robin Hägg. Stockholm: Svenska Institutet i Athen, 1999.

Eliade, Mircea. "Schöpfungsmythos und Heilsgeschichte." *Antaios* 9 (1968): 329–45.

Elsner, Jaś. "Hagiographic Geography: Travel and Allegory in the *Life of Apollonius of Tyana*." *JHS* 117 (1997): 22–37.

———. "Pausanias: A Greek Pilgrim in the Roman World." *Past and Present* 135 (1992): 3–29. Repr. with modifications in *Art and the Roman Viewer: The Transformation of Art from the Pagan World to Christianity*. Cambridge and New York: Cambridge University Press, 1995.

Elsner, Jaś, and Joan-Pau Rubiès. "Introduction." Pages 8–15 in *Voyages and Visions: Towards a Cultural History of Travel*. Edited by Jaś Elsner and Joan-Pau Rubiès. London: Reaktion, 1999.

Engelmann, Helmut, and Reinhold Merkelbach. *Die Inschriften von Erythrai und Klazomenai*. Inschriften griechischer Städte aus Kleinasien 1–2. 2 vols. Bonn: Habelt, 1972.

Engels, Friedrich. *Der Ursprung der Familie, des Privateigentums und des Staats*. Hottingen-Zürich: Schweizerische Genossenschaftsbuchdruckerei, 1884.

Ernout, Alfred, and A. Meillet. *Dictionnaire étymologique de la langue latine*. 4th ed. Paris: Klincksieck, 1959.

Espinosa, Urbano. "La Alejandrofilia de Caracala en la antigua historiografia." Pages 37–51 in *Neronia IV: Alejandro Magno, modelo de los emperadores romanos. Actes du IVe colloque de la SIEN*. Edited by Jean-Michel Croisille. Latomus 209. Brussels: Latomus, 1990.

Faraone, Christopher A. *Talismans and Trojan Horses: Guardian Statues in Ancient Greek Myth and Ritual*. New York: Oxford University Press, 1992.

Farnell, Lewis R. *Cults of the Greek States*. 5 vols. Oxford: Clarendon, 1896–1909.

———. *Greek Hero Cults and Ideas of Immortality*. Oxford: Clarendon, 1921.

Ferguson, Everett, Michael P. McHugh, and Frederick W. Norris, eds. *Encyclopedia of Early Christianity*. 2d ed. 2 vols. New York: Garland, 1997.

Ferguson, John. *The Religions of the Roman Empire*. London: Thames & Hudson, 1970.

Festugière, A.-J. "Tragédie et tombes sacrées." Pages 47–68 in *Études d'histoire et de philologie*. Paris: Vrin, 1975.

Février, P.-A. "Le culte des morts dans les communautés chrétiennes durant le IIIe siècle." Pages 1:211–74 in *Atti del IX congresso internazionale di archeologia cristiana, Roma, 21–27 settembre 1975*. 2 vols. Rome: Pontificio Instituto di archeologia cristiana, 1978.

Figueira, Thomas J. *Athens and Aigina in the Age of Imperial Colonization*. Baltimore: Johns Hopkins University Press, 1991.

———. "The Chronology of the Conflict between Athens and Aegina in Herodotus Bk. 6." *Quaderni urbinati di cultura classica* 28 (1988): 49–89.

Fitzgerald, John T., ed. *Friendship, Flattery, and Frankness of Speech: Studies on Friendship in the New Testament World*. NovTSup 82. Leiden: Brill, 1996.

———, ed. *Greco-Roman Perspectives on Friendship*. Atlanta: Scholars Press, 1997.

Fitzmyer, Joseph A. "New Testament *Kyrios* and *Maranatha* and Their Aramaic Background." Pages 218–35 in *To Advance the Gospel*. New York: Crossroad, 1981.

Flinterman, Jaap-Jan. *Power,* Paideia, *and Pythagoreanism: Greek Identity, Conceptions of the Relationship between Philosophers and Monarchs, and Political Ideas in Philostratus'* Life of Apollonius. Dutch Monographs on Ancient History and Archaeology 13. Amsterdam: Gieben, 1995.

Follet, Simone. *Athènes au IIe et au IIIe siècle: Études chronographiques et prosopographiques*. Paris: Les Belles Lettres, 1976.

———. "Dédicataire et destinataires des *Lettres* des Philostrates." Pages 139–41 in *Titres et articulations du texte dans les oeuvres antiques: Actes du colloque international de Chantilly, 13–15 décembre 1994*. Edited by Jean-Claude Fredouille et al. Paris: Institut d'études augustiniennes, 1997.

———. "Divers aspects de l'hellénisme chez Philostrate." Pages 205–15 in *ΈΛΛΗΝΙΣΜΟΣ: Quelques jalons pour une histoire de l'identité grecque. Actes du colloque de Strasbourg, 25–27 octobre 1989*. Edited by Suzanne Saïd. Leiden: Brill, 1991.

———. "Édition critique, avec introduction, notes et traduction, de l'*Héroïque* de Philostrate." *Annuaire de l'école practique des hautes études. Section des sciences historiques et philologiques* (1969–1970): 747–48.

———. "Inscription inédite de Myrina." *ASAA* NS 36–37 (1974): 309–12.

———. "Remarques sur deux valeurs de κατά dans l'*Héroïque* de Philostrate." Pages 113–19 in *Cas et prépositions en grec ancien: Constraintes syntaxiques et interprétations sémantique. Actes du colloque international de Saint-Étienne (3–5 juin 1993)*. Edited by Bernard Jacquinod. Saint-Étienne, France: Université de Saint-Étienne, 1994.

Fontenrose, Joseph. *Python*. Berkeley: University of California Press, 1959.

———. *The Ritual Theory of Myth*. Berkeley: University of California Press, 1966.

Forrest, W. G. "Oracles in Herodotus." *Classical Review* NS 8 (1958): 122–24.

Forster, E. M. *Aspects of the Novel*. New York: Harcourt, Brace, 1927.

Fortna, Robert T. "Theological Use of Locale in the Fourth Gospel." *AThR* Suppl. Ser. 3 (1974): 58–95.

Fouache, Eric. *L'alluvionnement historique en Grèce occidentale et au Péloponnèse: Géomorphologie, archéologie, histoire*. BCH suppl. 35. Athens and Paris: École française d'Athènes, 1999.

Fox, Robin Lane. *Pagans and Christians*. New York: Knopf, 1987.

Frazer, J. G. *The Golden Bough*. 3d ed. 12 vols. London: Macmillan, 1911.

Fredrich, Carl. "Imbros." *Ath. Mitt.* 33 (1908): 81–112.

———. "Lemnos." *Ath. Mitt.* 31 (1906): 60–86.

Freedman, David Noel, ed. *The Anchor Bible Dictionary*. 6 vols. New York: Doubleday, 1992.

Freitag, Klaus. "Oiniadai als Hafenstadt—Einige historisch-topographische Überlegungen." *Klio* 76 (1994): 212–38.

Frend, W. H. C. *The Rise of Christianity*. Philadelphia: Fortress, 1984.

Frey, Martin. *Untersuchungen zur Religion und zur Religionspolitik des Kaisers Elagabal*. Historia Einzelschriften 62. Stuttgart: Steiner, 1989.

Frisch, Peter. *Die Inschriften von Ilion*. Bonn: Habelt, 1975.

Gagé, Jean. "L'horoscope de Doura et le culte d'Alexandre sous les Sévères." *Bulletin de la Faculté de Lettres de Strasbourg* 33 (1954–1955): 151–68.

———. *Matronalia*. Brussels: Latomus, 1963.

Gantz, Timothy. *Early Greek Myth: A Guide to Literary and Artistic Sources*. Baltimore: Johns Hopkins University Press, 1993.

Ganzert, Joachim. *Der Mars-Ultor-Tempel auf dem Augustusforum in Rom*. Deutsches Archäologisches Institut Rom 11. Mainz, Germany: Zabern, 1996.

Gascou, Jacques. "Une énigme épigraphique: Sévère Alexandre et la titulature de Giufi." *Antiquités Africaines* 17 (1981): 231–40.

Gaster, Theodor H. *Thespis: Ritual, Myth, and Drama in the Ancient Near East*. 2d ed. Garden City, N.Y.: Doubleday, 1961.

Geagan, Daniel J. "The Isthmian Dossier of P. Licinius Priscus Juventianus." *Hesperia* 58 (1989): 349–60.

Gebhard, Elizabeth. "The Beginnings of Panhellenic Games at the Isthmus." Pages 221–37 in *Akten des Internationalen Symposions Olympia, 1875–2000*. Edited by Helmut Kyrieleis. Mainz am Rhein, Germany: Zabern, 2002.

———. "Child in the Fire, Child in the Pot: The Making of a Hero." Paper presented at the Seventh International Seminar on Ancient Greek Cult, Göteborg University, Sweden, 16–18 April 1999.

Gebhard, Elizabeth R., and Matthew W. Dickie. "Melikertes-Palaimon, Hero of the Isthmian Games." Pages 159–65 in *Ancient Greek Hero Cult: Proceedings of the Fifth International Seminar on Ancient Greek Cult, Organized by the Department of Classical Archaeology and Ancient History, Göteborg University, 21–23 April 1995*. Edited by Robin Hägg. Stockholm: Svenska Institutet i Athen, 1999.

Georgi, Dieter. "Who Is the True Prophet?" Pages 148–57 in *Paul and Empire: Religion and Power in Roman Imperial Society*. Edited by Richard A. Horsley. Harrisburg, Pa.: Trinity Press International, 1997. Repr. from *HTR* 79 (1986): 100–126.

Ghedini, Francesca. *Giulia Domna tra Oriente e Occidente: Le fonti archaeologiche*. Rome: "L'Erma" di Bretschneider, 1984.

Gibbon, Edward. *The History of the Decline and Fall of the Roman Empire*. Edited by David Womersley. 3 vols. London: Penguin, 1994. Repr. of *The History of the Decline and Fall of the Roman Empire*. 6 vols. London: Straham, 1774–1788.

Gill, Christopher. "The Character-Personality Distinction." Pages 1–31 in *Characterization and Individuality in Greek Literature*. Edited by Christopher Pelling. Oxford: Clarendon, 1990.

Gillman, Ian, and Hans-Joachim Klimkeit. *Christians in Asia before 1500*. Ann Arbor: University of Michigan Press, 1999.

Gilson, Etienne. *History of Christian Philosophy in the Middle Ages*. New York: Random House, 1955.

Gjerstad, E. "Das Attische Fest Der Skira." *AR* 27 (1929–1930): 189–240.

Goldhill, Simon. *Language, Sexuality, and Narrative: The Oresteia*. Cambridge and New York: Cambridge University Press, 1984.

Gómez, Pilar, and Francesca Mestre. "Lo religioso y lo político: Personajes del mito y hombres de la historia." Pages 365–78 in *Estudios sobre Plutarco: Misti-*

cismo y religiones mistéricas en la obra de Plutarco. Edited by A. Pérez Jiménez and F. Casadesús Bordoy. Actas del VII Simposio Español sobre Plutarco, Palma de Mallorca, 2–4 noviembre 2000. Madrid and Málaga, Spain: Ediciones Clásicas & Charta Antiqua, 2001.

Gorman, P. "The 'Apollonius' of the Neoplatonic Biographies of Pythagoras." *Mnemosyne* 38 (1985): 130–44.

Graf, Fritz. Introduction to Samson Eitrem's "Dreams and Divination in Magical Ritual." Pages 175–76 in *Magika Hiera: Ancient Greek Magic and Religion*. Edited by Christopher A. Faraone and Dirk Obbink. Oxford and New York: Oxford University Press, 1991.

Grainger, John D. *The Cities of Seleukid Syria*. Oxford and New York: Oxford University Press, 1990.

———. *Hellenistic Phoenicia*. Oxford: Clarendon, 1991.

Grant, Robert M. "The Heresy of Tatian." *JTS* 5 (1954): 62–68.

Grayston, Kenneth. "The Meaning of PARAKLĒTOS." *JSNT* 13 (1981): 67–82.

Green, Vivian H. H. *A New History of Christianity*. New York: Continuum, 1996.

Greene, Thomas M. "The Natural Tears of Epic." Pages 189–202 in *Epic Traditions in the Contemporary World: The Poetics of Community*. Edited by Margaret Beissinger, Jane Tylus, and Susanne Wofford. Berkeley: University of California Press, 1999.

Greeven, Heinrich. "προσκυνέω, προσκυνητής." *TDNT* 6:758–66.

Grentrup, Henricus. "De *Heroici* Philostrati fabularum fontibus." Diss., University of Münster, Westphalia, 1914.

Griffin, J. "The Epic Cycle and the Uniqueness of Homer." *JHS* 97 (1977): 39–53.

Griffin, Nathaniel Edward. *Dares and Dictys: An Introduction to the Study of Medieval Versions of the Story of Troy*. Baltimore: J. H. Furst, 1907.

Griffith, Sidney H. "The *Doctrina Addai* as a Paradigm of Christian Thought in Edessa in the Fifth Century." *Hugoye* 6 (2003). Available online at http://syrcom.cua.edu/Hugoye/Vol6No2/HV6N2Griffith.html.

———. "The Marks of the 'True Church' according to Ephraem's *Hymns against Heresies*." Pages 125–40 in *After Bardaisan: Studies on Continuity and Change in Syriac Christianity in Honor of Professor Han J. W. Drijvers*. Edited by G. J. Reinink and Alexander C. Klugkist. OLA 89. Louvain: Peeters, 1999.

———. "Setting Right the Church of Syria: Saint Ephraem's *Hymns against Heresies*." Pages 97–114 in *The Limits of Ancient Christianity: Essays on Late Antique Thought and Culture in Honor of R. A. Markus*. Edited by William E. Klingshirn and Mark Vessey. Washington, D.C.: Catholic University of America Press, 1999.

———. "'The Thorn among the Tares': Mani and Manichaeism in the Works of St. Ephraem the Syrian." Pages 403–35 in *Ascetica, Gnostica, Liturgica, Orientalia*. Vol. 2 of *Studia Patristica: Papers Presented at the Thirteenth International Conference on Patristic Studies Held in Oxford, 1999*. Edited by Maurice F. Wiles and Edward J. Yarnold. StPatr 35. Louvain: Peeters, 2001.

Groag, Edmund. "Alexander in einer Inschrift des 3. Jahrhunderts n. Chr." Pages 252–55 in *Wiener Eranos: Zur fünfzigsten Versammlung deutscher Philologen und Schulmänner in Graz 1909*. Vienna: Hölder, 1909.

Grose, S. W. *Fitzwilliam Museum: Catalogue of the McClean Collection of Greek Coins*. Cambridge: Cambridge University Press, 1926.

Grossardt, Peter. *Die Trugreden in der Odyssee und ihre Rezeption in der antiken Literatur*. Sapheneia 2. Bern: Peter Lang, 1998.

Guey, Julien. "Les animaux célestes du nouvel édit de Caracalla." CRAI (Jan.–Apr. 1948): 128–30.

———. "Les éléphants de Caracalla (216 après J.–C.)." *REA* 49/3–4 (1947): 248–73.

Gurlitt, Wilhelm. *Über Pausanias: Untersuchungen*. Graz, Austria: Leuschner & Lubensky, 1890.

Guthrie, W. K. C. *A History of Greek Philosophy*. 6 vols. Cambridge: Cambridge University Press, 1962–1981.

———. *Orpheus and Greek Religion: A Study of the Orphic Movement*. London: Methuen, 1952. Repr., Princeton: Princeton University Press, 1993.

Habicht, Christian. *Die Inschriften des Asklepieions*. Altertümer von Pergamon 8.3. Berlin: de Gruyter, 1969.

———. *Pausanias' Guide to Ancient Greece*. Berkeley: University of California Press, 1985. Repr., 1998.

Hadas, Moses, and Morton Smith. *Heroes and Gods: Spiritual Biographies in Antiquity*. New York: Harper & Row, 1965.

Hadjidaki, Elpida. "Underwater Excavations of a Late Fifth-Century Merchant Ship at Alonnesos, Greece: The 1991–1993 Seasons." *BCH* 120/2 (1996): 559–93.

Hadot, Pierre. *Philosophy as a Way of Life*. Translated by Arnold I. Davidson. Oxford: Blackwell, 1995.

———. *What Is Ancient Philosophy*? Translated by Michael Chase. Cambridge, Mass.: Harvard University Press, 2002.

Haft, Adele J. "Odysseus, Idomeneus, and Meriones: The Cretan Lies of *Odyssey* 13–19." *CJ* 79 (1983–1984): 289–306.

Hägg, Robin, ed. *Ancient Greek Hero Cult: Proceedings of the Fifth International Seminar on Ancient Greek Cult, Organized by the Department of Classical Archaeology and Ancient History, Göteborg University, 21–23 April 1995*. Stockholm: Svenska Institutet i Athen, 1999.

Hainsworth, Bryan. *The Iliad: A Commentary. Books 9–12*. Vol. 3 of *The Iliad: A Commentary*. Edited by G. S. Kirk. Cambridge and New York: Cambridge University Press, 1993.

Halfmann, Helmut. *Itinera principum: Geschichte und Typologie der Kaiserreisen im Römischen Reich*. Stuttgart: Steiner, 1986.

Hall, A. "New Light on the Capture of Isaura Vetus by P. Servilius Vatia." Pages 568–71 in *Akten des VI Internationalen Kongresses für Griechische und Lateinische Epigraphik, München 1972*. Munich: Beck, 1973.

Halliwell, Stephen. "Traditional Greek Conceptions of Character." Pages 32–59 in *Characterization and Individuality in Greek Literature*. Edited by Christopher Pelling. Oxford: Clarendon, 1990.

Hammond, N. G. L. "The War between Athens and Aegina circa 505–481." *Historia* 4 (1955): 406–11.

Harden, Donald B. *The Phoenicians*. New York: Praeger, 1962.

Harrauer, Christine. "Der korinthische Kindermord—Eumelos und die Folgen." *Wiener Studien* 112 (1999): 5–28.

Harrison, Jane E. *Mythology and Monuments of Ancient Athens*. London: Macmillan, 1890.

———. *Themis: A Study of the Social Origins of Greek Religion*. 2d ed. Cambridge: Cambridge University Press, 1927.

Hartog, François. *Memories of Odysseus: Frontier Tales from Ancient Greece*. Translated by Janet Lloyd. Chicago: University of Chicago Press, 2001.

Harvey, W. J. *Character and the Novel*. Ithaca, N.Y.: Cornell University Press, 1965.
Hasluck, F. W. "Terra Lemnia." *Annual of the British School at Athens* 16 (1909–1910): 220–31.
Head, Barclay V. *British Museum: Catalogue of Greek Coins, I. Central Greece*. London: The Trustees of the British Museum, 1884.
———. *Historia Numorum: A Manual of Greek Numismatics*. 2d ed. Oxford: Clarendon, 1911.
Hedreen, Guy. "The Cult of Achilles in the Euxine." *Hesperia* 60/3 (1991): 313–30.
Hemberg, Bengt. *Die Kabiren*. Uppsala, Sweden: Almqvist & Wilksells, 1950.
Hengel, Martin. *The Atonement: The Origins of the Doctrine in the New Testament*. Philadelphia: Fortress, 1981.
Hengel, Martin, and Anna Maria Schwemer. *Königsherrschaft Gottes und himmlischer Kult im Judentum, Urchristentum und in der hellenistischen Welt*. WUANT 55. Tübingen: Mohr Siebeck, 1991.
Hennig, R. "Altgriechische Sagengestalten als Personifikation von Erdfeuern." *JDAI* 54 (1939): 230–46.
Henrichs, Albert. "Keeping Dead Heroes Alive: The Revival of Hero Cult in the *Heroikos*." Paper presented at the conference "Philostratus's *Heroikos*, Religion, and Cultural Identity," Cambridge, Mass., 4 May 2001.
———. "The Tomb of Aias and the Prospect of Hero Cult in Sophokles." *Classical Antiquity* 12 (1993): 165–80.
Herkenrath, Emil. "Mykenische Kultszenen." *AJA* NS 41 (1937): 411–23.
Herrmann, Peter. "Milesisches Purpur." *Ist. Mitt.* 25 (1975): 141–47.
———. *Tituli Lydiae: Regio septentrionalis ad Orientem vergens*. Vol. 5.2 of *Tituli Asiae Minoris*. Vienna: Verlag der Österreichischen Akademie der Wissenschaften, 1989.
Herrmann, Peter, and Kemal Ziya Polatkan. *Das Testament der Epikrates und andere neue Inschriften aus dem Museum von Mainsa*. SÖAW 265.1. Vienna: Böhlau, 1969.
Heuss, Alfred. "Alexander der Große und die politische Ideologie des Altertums." *Antike und Abendland* 4 (1954): 65–104.
Hinds, Stephen. *Allusion and Intertext: Dynamics of Appropriation in Roman Poetry*. Cambridge and New York: Cambridge University Press, 1998.
Hochman, Baruch. *Character* in *Literature*. Ithaca, N.Y., and London: Cornell University Press, 1985.
Holl, Karl. *Epiphanius (Ancoratus und Panarion)*. GCS 25, 31, 37. Leipzig: Hinrichs, 1915–1933.
Holladay, Carl. *Theios Aner in Hellenistic Judaism*. SBLDS 40. Missoula, Mont.: Scholars Press, 1977.
Hommel, Hildebrecht. *Der Gott Achilleus*. Heidelberg: Winter, 1980.
Hooke, Samuel H., ed. *Myth and Ritual*. London: Oxford University Press, 1933.
———. *Myth, Ritual, and Kingship*. Oxford: Clarendon, 1958.
Hooker, James T. "The Cults of Achilles." *Rheinisches Museum* 131 (1988): 1–7.
Hopkins, R. V. Nind. *The Life of Alexander Severus*. Cambridge Historical Essays 14. Cambridge: Cambridge University Press, 1907.
Horsley, Richard A. *Galilee: History, Politics, People*. Valley Forge, Pa.: Trinity Press International, 1995.
———, ed. *Paul and Empire: Religion and Power in Roman Imperial Society*. Harrisburg, Pa.: Trinity Press International, 1997.

Hoskyns, Edwyn C. *The Fourth Gospel*. 2d ed. London: Faber and Faber, 1947.
Hughes, Dennis D. "Hero Cult, Heroic Honors, Heroic Dead: Some Developments in the Hellenistic and Roman Periods." Pages 167–75 in *Ancient Greek Hero Cult: Proceedings of the Fifth International Seminar on Ancient Greek Cult, Organized by the Department of Classical Archaeology and Ancient History, Göteborg University, 21–23 April 1995*. Edited by Robin Hägg. Stockholm: Svenska Institutet i Athen, 1999.
Huhn, F., and E. Bethe. "Philostrats *Heroikos* und Diktys." *Hermes* 52 (1917): 613–24.
Hunter, R. L. *A Study of Daphnis and Chloe*. Cambridge and New York: Cambridge University Press, 1983.
Hüttenbach, Fritz Lochner von. *Die Pelasger*. Vienna: Gerold, 1960.
Huxley, George L. *Crete and the Luwians*. Oxford: n.p., 1961.
Imhoof-Blumer, Friedrich. *Monnaies grecques*. Amsterdam: Müller, 1883.
Innes, Doreen, Harry Hine, and Christopher Pelling, eds. *Ethics and Rhetoric: Classical Essays for Donald Russell on His Seventy-fifth Birthday*. Oxford: Clarendon, 1995.
Instinsky, H. U. "Studien zur Geschichte des Septimius Severus." *Klio* 35 (1942): 200–211.
Intzessiloglou, A. "Chronika." *Archaiologikon Deltion* 39 (1984): 146–47.
———. "Chronika." *Archaiologikon Deltion* 43 (1998): 250–52.
Jaillard, Dominique. "À propos du fragment 35 de Callimaque." *ZPE* 132 (2000): 143–44.
Jameson, Michael H. "Perseus, the Hero of Mykenai." Pages 213–22 in *Celebrations of Death and Divinity in the Bronze Age Argolid: Proceedings of the Sixth International Symposium at the Swedish Institute at Athens, 11–13 June 1988*. Edited by Robin Hägg and Gullög C. Nordquist. Stockholm: Svenska Institutet i Athen, 1990.
———. "Theoxenia." Pages 35–57 in *Ancient Greek Cult Practice from the Epigraphic Evidence: Proceedings of the Second International Seminar on Ancient Greek Cult, Organized by the Swedish Institute at Athens, 22–24 November 1991*. Svenska Institutet i Athen 8/13. Edited by Robin Hägg. Stockholm: Åströms, 1994.
Jardé, Auguste. *Études critiques sur la vie et le règne de Sévère Alexandre*. Paris: De Boccard, 1925.
Jobes, Karen H. "Distinguishing the Meaning of Greek Verbs in the Semantic Domain for Worship." *Filologia Neotestamentaria* 4 (1991): 183–91.
Johansen, Knud Friis. *The Iliad in Early Greek Art*. Copenhagen: Muksgaard, 1967.
Jones, Christopher P. *Culture and Society in Lucian*. Cambridge, Mass.: Harvard University Press, 1986.
———. "The Emperor and the Giant." *CP* 95 (2000): 476–81.
———. "Neryllinus." *CP* 80 (1985): 40–45.
———. "The Pancratiasts Helix and Alexander on an Ostian Mosaic." *JRA* 11 (1998): 293–98.
———. "Philostratus' *Heroikos* and Its Setting in Reality." *JHS* 121 (2001): 141–49.
———. "The Reliability of Philostratus." Pages 11–16 in *Approaches to the Second Sophistic: Papers Presented at the 105th Annual Meeting of the American Philological Association*. Edited by Glen W. Bowersock. University Park, Pa.: American Philological Association, 1974.

———. *The Roman World of Dio Chrysostom*. Cambridge, Mass.: Harvard University Press, 1978.

———. "Time and Place in Philostratus' *Heroikos*." *JHS* 121 (2001): 141–48.

———. "*Trophimos* in an Inscription of Erythrai." *Glotta* 67 (1989): 194–97.

Joshel, Sandra. "The Body Female and the Body Politic: Livy's Lucretia and Verginia." Pages 112–30 in *Pornography and Representation in Greece and Rome*. Edited by Amy Richlin. New York: Oxford University Press, 1992.

Joshel, Sandra, and Sheila Murnagha. *Women and Slaves in Greco-Roman Culture: Differential Equations*. London: Routledge, 1998.

Jost, Madeleine. *Sanctuaires et cultes d'Arcadie*. Paris: Vrin, 1985.

Jouan, François. "Héros d'Euripide et dieux des cités." *Kernos* 11 (1998): 63–72.

Jouanna, Jacques. "Espaces sacrés, rites et oracles dans *l'Oedipe à Colone* de Sophocle." *REG* 108 (1995): 38–58.

Jüthner, Julius. "Der Verfasser des Gymnastikos." Pages 225–32 in *Festschrift Theodor Gomperz*. Edited by Moritz von Schwind. Vienna: Hölder, 1902. Repr., Aalen, Germany: Scientia, 1979.

Katsônopoulou, Dôra. "Archaia Elis. Istoria kai synchroni ereuna" (in Greek). Pages 227–34 in *Archaia Achaia kai Eleia*. Edited by Athanase D. Rizakis. Athens: Kentron Hellênikes kai Rômaïkês Archaiotêtos, 1991.

———. "Helikê" (in Greek). *Archaiologia* 54 (March 1995): 35–40.

Kearns, E. *Heroes of Attica*. London: University of London, 1989.

Kelley, Sean, and Rosemary Rogers. *Saints Preserve Us!* New York: Random House, 1993.

Kerényi, Karl. *Die Eröffnung des Zugangs zum Mythos*. Darmstadt: Wissenschaftliche Buchgesellschaft, 1967.

———. *Umgang mit Göttlichem*. Göttingen: Vandenhoeck & Ruprecht, 1955.

Kern, O. "Kabeiros und Kabeiroi: Samothrake." PW 10 (1913): 1423–50.

Kettenhoffen, Erich. *Die syrischen Augustae in der historischen Überlieferung: Ein Beitrag zum Problem der Orientalisierung*. Antiquitas 3. Abhandlungen zur Vor- und Frühgeschichte, zur klassischen und provinzial-römischen Archäologie und zur Geschichte des Altertums 24. Bonn: Habelt, 1979.

Kienast, Dietmar. "Augustus und Alexander." *Gymnasium* (Heidelberg) 76 (1969): 130–456.

———. *Römische Kaisertabelle: Grundzüge einer römischen Kaiserchronologie*. Darmstadt: Wissenschaftliche Buchgesellschaft, 1990.

Kinsella, Thomas. *The Táin: From the Irish Epic Táin Bó Cuailnge*. Oxford: Oxford University Press, 1969.

Kittel, G., and G. Friedrich, eds. *Theological Dictionary of the New Testament*. Translated by G. W. Bromiley. 10 vols. Grand Rapids: Eerdmans, 1964–1976.

Kluckhohn, Clyde. "Myths and Rituals: A General Theory." *HTR* 35 (1942): 45–79.

Kneissl, Peter. *Die Siegestitulatur der römischen Kaiser: Untersuchungen zu den Siegerbeinamen des ersten und zweiten Jahrhunderts*. Hypomnemata 23. Göttingen: Vandenhoeck & Ruprecht, 1969.

Knight, William F. Jackson. *Cumaean Gates*. Oxford: Blackwell, 1936.

Koehler, H. "Mémoire sur les îles et la course consacrée à Achille dans le Pont-Euxin." *Mémoiresde l'Académie impériale des sciences de Saint-Pétersbourg* 10 (1824): 531–819.

Koester, Helmut. "Melikertes at Isthmia: A Roman Mystery Cult." Pages 355–66 in *Greeks, Romans, and Christians: Essays in Honor of Abraham J. Malherbe*.

Edited by David Balch, Everett Ferguson, and Wayne A. Meeks. Minneapolis: Fortress, 1990.

———. "On Heroes, Tombs, and Early Christianity: An Epilogue." Pages 257–64 in *Flavius Philostratus: Heroikos*. Translated by Jennifer K. Berenson Maclean and Ellen Bradshaw Aitken. SBLWGRW 1. Atlanta: Society of Biblical Literature, 2001.

Kokolakis, Minos M. "Apo to thematologio tôn sophistôn: hê ateichistos Spartê" (in Greek). *Lakônikai Spoudai* 10 (1990): 1–24.

Kondoleon, Christine. *Antioch: The Lost Ancient City*. Princeton: Princeton University Press, 2000.

Korfman, Manfred. "Troy: Topography and Navigation." Pages 1–16 in *Troy and the Trojan War: A Symposium Held at Bryn Mawr College, October 1984*. Edited by Machteld J. Mellink. Bryn Mawr, Pa.: Bryn Mawr College, 1986.

Korres, George. "Ê problêmatikê dia tên metagenesteran chrêsin tôn mukênaikôn taphôn Messênias" (in Greek). Pages 2:394–450 in *Acts of the Second International Congress of Peloponnesian Studies*. 3 vols. Athens: Hetaira Peloponnêsiako Spoudôn, 1981–1982.

———. "Evidence for a Hellenistic Chthonian Cult in the Prehistoric Cemetery of Voïdokilia in Pylos (Messenia)." *Klio* 70 (1988): 311–28.

Koskenniemi, Erkki. *Apollonios von Tyana in der neutestamentlichen Exegese: Forschungsbericht und Weiterführung der Diskussion*. WUNT 2/61. Tübingen: Mohr Siebeck, 1994.

Kysar, Robert. "John, Gospel of." *ABD* 3.912–31.

Lacomara, Aelred. "Deuteronomy and the Farewell Discourse (Jn 13:31–16:33)." *CBQ* 36 (1974): 65–84.

Lacroix, Léon. "Quelques aspects du 'culte des reliques' dans les traditions de la Grèce ancienne." *Bulletin de la classe des Lettres et des sciences morales et politiques de l'Académie Royale de Belgique* 75 (1989): 58–99.

Latte, Kurt. *Römische Religionsgeschichte*. Munich: Beck, 1960.

Lattke, Michael. "Sind Ephraems *Madrāshê* Hymnen?" *OrChr* 73 (1989): 38–43.

"Lavori della Scuola Italiana a Lemnos nel 1939." *ASAA* NS 1–2 (1939–1940): 221–24.

Le Gall, J. "Evocatio." Pages 1:519–24 in *Italie préromaine et la Rome républicaine*. Edited by Jacques Heurgon. 2 vols. Rome: École française de Rome, 1976.

Le Rider, Georges. *Suse sous les Séleucides et les Parthes*. Paris: Guethner, 1965.

Leach, Edmund R. "Critical Introduction." Pages 1–20 in Mikhail I. Steblin-Kamenskij. *Myth*. Translated by Mary P. Coote. Ann Arbor, Mich.: Karoma, 1982.

Leaf, Walter. "Notes on the Text of Strabo XIII.1." *JHS* 37 (1917): 19–30.

———, ed. *Strabo on the Troad: Book XIII, Cap. 1*. Cambridge: Cambridge University Press, 1923.

Leahy, D. M. "The Bones of Tisamenus." *Historia* 4 (1955): 26–38.

Leschhorn, Wolfgang. *Gründer der Stadt: Studien zu einem politisch-religiösen Phänomen der griechischen Geschichte*. Stuttgart: Steiner, 1984.

Levi, Doro. "Il Cabirio di Lemno." Pages 3:110–32 in *Charistêrion eis Anastasion K. Orlandon*. 4 vols. Bibliothêkê tês en Athênais Archaiologikês Hetaireias 54. Athens, 1965–1968.

———."La tomba a tholos di Kamilari presso a Festòs." *ASAA* NS 23–24 (1961–1962): 7–148.

Lévi-Strauss, Claude. *Le totémisme aujourd'hui*. Paris: Presses universitaires de France, 1962.

Lévy, Carlos, and Laurent Pernot. *Dire l'évidence (Philosophie et rhétorique antiques): Actes du colloque de Créteil et de Paris (24–25 mars 1995)*. Paris: L'Harmattan, 1997.

L'Homme-Wéry, Louise-Marie. "Les héros de Salamine en Attique: Cultes, mythes et intégration politique." Pages 333–49 in *Héros et héroïnes dans les mythes et les cultes grecs: Actes du colloque organisé à l'Université de Valladolid, 26–29 May 1999*. Edited by Vinciane Pirenne-Delforge and Emilio Suárez de la Torre. Kernos suppl. 10. Liège, Belgium: Centre international d'étude de la religion grecque antique, 2000.

———. *La perspective éleusinienne dans la politique de Solon*. Geneva: Droz, 1996.

Liddell, H. G., R. Scott, and H. S. Jones, *A Greek-English Lexicon*. 9th ed. with revised supplement. Oxford: Clarendon, 1996.

Lieu, Samuel N. C. "Captives, Refugees, and Exiles: A Study of Cross-Frontier Civilian Movements and Contacts between Rome and Persia from Valerian to Jovian." Pages 2:475–508 in *The Defence of the Roman and Byzantine East*. Edited by Philip Freeman and David Kennedy. 2 vols. British Institute of Archaeology at Ankara 8. Oxford: B.A.R., 1986.

———. *Manichaeism in Mesopotamia and the Roman East*. Religions in the Graeco-Roman World 118. Leiden: Brill, 1994.

———. *Manichaeism in the Later Roman Empire and Medieval China: A Historical Survey*. Manchester, England: Manchester University Press, 1985.

Lindner, Ruth. *Mythos und Identität: Studien zur Selbstdarstellung kleinasiatischen Städte in der römischen Kaiserzeit*. Stuttgart: Steiner, 1994.

Livingstone, Elizabeth A., and Frank L. Cross, eds. *The Oxford Dictionary of the Christian Church*. 3d ed. Oxford: Oxford University Press, 1997.

Loeff, A. Rutgers van der. "De Athena Scirade." *Mnemosyne* NS 44 (1916): 7–112.

Lonis, Raoul. *Guerre et religion en Grèce à l'époque classique: Recherches sur les rites, les dieux, l'idéologie de la victoire*. Paris: Belles Lettres, 1979.

Loraux, Nicole. *Mothers in Mourning*. Ithaca, N.Y.: Cornell University Press, 1998.

Lorber, Catharine C. *Amphipolis: The Civic Coinage in Silver and Gold*. Los Angeles: Numismatic Fine Arts International, 1990.

Lorenz, Konrad. *On Aggression*. London: Methuen, 1966.

Lucius, Ernst. *Die Anfänge des Heiligenkults in der christlichen Kirche*. Tübingen: Mohr, 1904.

Lüdemann, Gerd. *Die Auferstehung Jesu: Historie, Erfahrung, Theologie*. Göttingen: Vandenhoeck & Ruprecht, 1994.

Macdonald, Margaret Y. "Ritual in the Pauline Churches." Pages 233–47 in *Social-Scientific Approaches to New Testament Interpretation*. Edited by David G. Horrell. Edinburgh: T&T Clark, 1999.

Maclean, Jennifer K. Berenson. "The Divine Trickster in John: A Tale of Two Weddings." Pages 1:48–77 in *A Feminist Companion to John*. Edited by Amy-Jill Levine. 2 vols. Sheffield: Sheffield Academic Press, 2003.

MacMullen, Ramsey. *Christianizing the Roman Empire (A.D. 100–400)*. New Haven: Yale University Press, 1984.

———. *Paganism in the Roman Empire*. New Haven: Yale University Press, 1981.

Magie, David. *Roman Rule in Asia Minor*. 2 vols. Princeton: Princeton University Press, 1950.

Malherbe, Abraham J. "Herakles." *RAC* 14 (1988): 559–83.

Malina, Bruce J. *Christian Origins and Cultural Anthropology: Practical Models for Biblical Interpretation*. Atlanta: John Knox, 1986.

Malinowski, Bronislaw. *Cults, Myths, Oracles, and Politics in Ancient Greece*. Lund, Sweden: Gleerup, 1951.

———. *Myth in Primitive Psychology*. London: Paul, Trench, Trubner, 1926.

Malkin, Irad. "Land Ownership, Territorial Possession, Hero Cults, and Scholarly Theory." Pages 225–34 in *Nomodeiktes: Greek Studies in Honor of Martin Ostwald*. Edited by Ralph Mark Rosen and Joseph Farrell. Ann Arbor: University of Michigan Press, 1993.

———. *Religion and Colonization in Ancient Greece*. Leiden: Brill, 1987.

Malten, L. "Hephaistos." *JDAI* 27 (1912): 232–64.

———. "Hephaistos" PW 8 (1913): 311–66.

Manfredini, Mario, and Luigi Piccirilli. *La vita di Solone*. Milan: Mondadori, 1977.

Mannhardt, Wilhelm. *Wald- und Feldkulte*. 2 vols. Berlin: Gebrüder Borntraeger, 1875–1877.

Mantero, Teresa. *Ricerche sull'* Heroikos *di Filostrato*. Genoa, Italy: University of Genoa, Istituto di Filologia Classica e Medioevale, 1966.

Maricq, André. "La chronologie des dernières années de Caracalla." Pages 27–32 in *Classica et Orientalia: Extrait de Syria 1955–1962, revu et corrigé, augmenté d'un article inédit et d'un index*. Institut Français d'Archéologie de Beyrouth 11. Paris: Geuthner, 1965.

Marinatos, S. *Proceedings of the Cambridge Colloquium on Mycenaean Studies*. Edited by L. R. Palmer and John Chadwick. Cambridge: Cambridge University Press, 1966.

Marlow, A. N. "Myth and Ritual in Early Greece." *BJRL* 43 (1960–1961): 373–402.

Martin, Richard P. "A Good Place to Talk: Discourse and Topos in Achilles Tatius and Philostratus." Page 143–60 in *Space in the Ancient Novel*. Edited by Michael Paschalis and Stavros A. Frangoulidis. Ancient Narrative suppl. 1. Groningen, Netherlands: Barkhuis, 2002.

———. *The Language of Heroes: Speech and Performance in the Iliad*. Myth and Poetics. Ithaca, N.Y.: Cornell University Press, 1989.

Marx, Karl, and Friedrich Engels. *Werke*. 39 vols. Berlin: Dietz, 1961–1974.

Mastrocinque, Attilio. "Gli dei prottettori della città." Pages 3–21 in *Religione e politica nel mondo antico*. Edited by Marta Sordi. Milan: Vita e pensiero, 1981.

Mayor, Adrienne. *The First Fossil Hunters: Paleontology in Greek and Roman Times*. Princeton: Princeton University Press, 2000.

McCauley, Barbara. "Heroes and Power: The Politics of Bone Transferal." Pages 85–98 in *Ancient Greek Hero Cult: Proceedings of the Fifth International Seminar on Ancient Greek Cult, Organized by the Department of Classical Archaeology and Ancient History, Göteborg University, 21–23 April 1995*. Edited by Robin Hägg. Stockholm: Svenska Institutet i Athen, 1999.

McClure, Laura. *Spoken Like a Woman: Speech and Gender in Athenian Drama*. Princeton: Princeton University Press, 1999.

McVey, Kathleen E. "Were the Earliest *Madrāshê* Songs or Recitations?" Pages 185–99 in *After Bardaisan: Studies on Change and Continuity in Syriac Christianity in Honor of Professor Han J. W. Drijvers*. Edited by G. J. Reinink and Alexander C. Klugkist. OLA 89. Louvain: Peeters, 1999.

Meeks, Wayne A. *The First Urban Christians: The Social World of the Apostle Paul*. New Haven: Yale University Press, 1983.

———. "The Man from Heaven in Johannine Sectarianism." Pages 141–73 in *The Interpretation of John*. Edited by John Ashton. Philadelphia: Fortress, 1986. Repr. from *JBL* 91 (1972): 44–72.

———. *The Prophet King: Moses Traditions and the Johannine Christology*. NovTSup 14. Leiden: Brill, 1967.

Meritt, Benjamin D., and John S. Traill. *Inscriptions: The Athenian Councillors*. The Athenian Agora xv. Princeton: American School of Classical Studies at Athens, 1975.

Merkle, Stefan. *Die Ephemeris Belli Troiani des Diktys von Kreta*. Studien Zur Klassischen Philologie 44. New York: Peter Lang, 1989.

———. "Telling the True Story of the Trojan War: The Eyewitness Account of Dictys of Crete." Pages 183–96 in *The Search for the Ancient Novel*. Edited by James Tatum. Baltimore: Johns Hopkins University Press, 1994.

Mestre, Francesca. "Por qué miente Homero (Una visión histórica sobre los poemas homéricos en época imperial)." Pages 1:533–40 in *Actas del X congreso español de estudios clásicos: 21–25 de septiembre de 1999*. Edited by Emilio Crespo and Maria José Barrios Castro. 3 vols. Madrid: Ediciones Clásicas, 2000.

———. "Urbanidad y autosuficiencia: La moneda no es *physis*." Pages 239–45 in *Actas del XIII simposio nacional de estudios clásicos*. La Plata, Argentina: Universidad Nacional de La Plata, 1997.

Mestre, Francesca, and Pilar Gómez. "Les Sophistes de Philostrate." Pages 333–69 in *Figures de l'intellectuel en Grèce ancienne*. Edited by Nicole Loraux and Carles Miralles. Paris: Belin, 1998.

Metzger, Henri. *Recherches sur l'imagerie athénienne*. Paris: De Boccard, 1965.

Meuli, K. "Bettelumzüge im Totenkult, Opferritual und Volksbrauch." *Schweizer Archiv für Volkskunde* 28 (1927–1928): 1–38.

Michel, Dorothea. *Alexander als Vorbild für Pompeius, Caesar und Marcus Antonius: Archäologische Untersuchungen*. Latomus 94. Brussels: Latomus, 1967.

Mikalson, Jon D. *Athenian Popular Religion*. Chapel Hill: University of North Carolina Press, 1983.

———. *Honor Thy Gods: Popular Religion in Greek Tragedy*. Chapel Hill: University of North Carolina Press, 1991.

Millar, Fergus. "The Problem of Hellenistic Syria." Pages 110–33 in *Hellenism in the East: Interaction of Greek and Non-Greek Civilizations from Syria to Central Asia after Alexander*. Edited by Amélie Kuhrt and Susan M. Sherwin-White. Berkeley: University of California Press, 1987.

———. *The Roman Near East: 31 B.C.–A.D. 337*. Cambridge, Mass.: Harvard University Press, 1993.

Mitchell, Charles W. *S. Ephraim's Prose Refutations of Mani, Marcion, and Bardaisan*. 2 vols. London and Oxford: Williams and Norgate, 1912–1921.

Moles, John. "Dio Chrysostom, Greece, and Rome." Pages 177–92 in *Ethics and Rhetoric: Classical Essays for Donald Russell on His Seventy-fifth Birthday*. Edited by Doreen Innes, Harry Hine, and Christopher Pelling. Oxford: Clarendon, 1995.

Momigliano, Arnaldo. *Alien Wisdom: The Limits of Hellenization*. Cambridge and New York: Cambridge University Press, 1975.

Moraux, Paul. *Galien de Pergame: Souvenirs d'un médecin*. Paris: Société d'éditions "Les Belles Lettres," 1985.

Moreau, A. "Le retour des cendres: Oreste et Thésée, deux cadavres au service de la propagande politique." Pages 209–18 in *Mythe et politique: Acts du colloque de Liège, 14–16 septembre 1989*. Edited by François Jouan and André Motte. Paris: Société d'édition "Les Belles Lettres," 1990.

Moretti, Luigi. *Olympionikai: I vincitori nelgi antichi agoni olimpici*. Rome: Accademia Nazionale dei Lincei, 1957.
Morgan, J. "De ignis eliciendi modis." *HSCP* 1 (1890): 50–64.
Muellner, Leonard. *The Meaning of Homeric εὔχομαι through Its Formulas*. Innsbrucker Beiträge zur Sprachwissenschaft 13. Innsbruck: Institut für Sprachwissenschaft der Universität Innsbruck, 1976.
Münscher, Karl. "Die Philostrate." *Philologus* suppl. 10/4 (1907): 469–558.
Münsterberg, Rudolf. "Die Beamtennamen auf den griechischen Münzen." *Numismatische Zeitschrift* 45 (1912): 1–111.
———. "Die Münzen der Sophisten." *Numismatische Zeitschrift* 48 (1915): 119–24.
Murray, Robert. *Symbols of Church and Kingdom: A Study in Early Syriac Tradition*. Cambridge: Cambridge University Press, 1975.
Mustilli, Domenico. "Efestia." Pages 3:230–31. *Enciclopedia dell'arte antica, classica e orientale*. 7 vols. Rome: Istituto della Enciclopedia italiana, 1958–1966.
———. "La necropoli tirrenica di Efestia." *ASAA* NS 15–16 (1932–1933): 1–278.
Muth, R. "Forum Suarium." *Museum Helveticum* 2 (1945): 227–36.
Nagy, Gregory. "As the World Runs Out of Breath: Metaphorical Perspectives on the Heavens and the Atmosphere in the Ancient World." Pages 37–50 in *Earth, Air, Fire, Water: Humanistic Studies of the Environment*. Edited by Jill K. Conway, Kenneth Keniston, and Leo Marx. Amherst: University of Massachusetts Press, 1999.
———. *The Best of the Achaeans: Concepts of the Hero in Archaic Greek Poetry*. 2d rev. ed. Baltimore: Johns Hopkins University Press, 1999.
———. *Greek Mythology and Poetics*. Ithaca, N.Y.: Cornell University Press, 1990.
———. "Homer and Plato at the Panathenaia: Synchronic and Diachronic Perspectives." Pages 123–50 in *Contextualizing Classics: Ideology, Performance, Dialogue. Essays in Honor of John J. Peradotto*. Edited by Thomas M. Falkner, Nancy Felson, and David Konstan. Lanham, Md.: Rowman & Littlefield, 1999.
———. *Homeric Questions*. Austin: University of Texas Press, 1996.
———. "The Library of Pergamon as a Classical Model." Pages 185–232 in *Pergamon: Citadel of the Gods*. Edited by Helmut Koester. HTS 46. Harrisburg, Pa.: Trinity Press International, 1998.
———. "Phaethon, Sappho's Phaon, and the White Rock of Leukas: 'Reading' the Symbols of Greek Lyric." Pages 223–62 in *Greek Mythology and Poetics*. Ithaca, N.Y.: Cornell University Press, 1990.
———. *Pindar's Homer: The Lyric Possession of an Epic Past*. Baltimore and London: Johns Hopkins University Press, 1990.
———. *Poetry as Performance: Homer and Beyond*. Cambridge: Cambridge University Press, 1996.
———. "The Sign of Protesilaos." *ΜΗΤΙΣ: Revue d'anthropologie du monde grec ancien* 2/2 (1987): 207–13.
———. "The Sign of the Hero: A Prologue." Pages xv–xxxv in *Flavius Philostratus: Heroikos*. Translated by Jennifer K. Berenson Maclean and Ellen Bradshaw Aitken. SBLWGRW 1. Atlanta: Society of Biblical Literature, 2001.
Nagy, Joseph F. "Orality in Medieval Irish Narrative." *Oral Tradition* 1 (1986): 272–301.
Nau, F. *Bardesanes: Liber Legum Regionum*. Patrologia Syriaca 1. Paris: Firmin-Didot, 1907.

Neumann, Karl, and Josef Partsch. *Physikalische Geographie von Griechenland.* Wroclaw, Poland: Koebner, 1885.

Nicolet, Claude. *Space, Geography, and Politics in the Early Roman Empire.* Ann Arbor: University of Michigan Press, 1991.

Niederwimmer, Kurt. *The Didache: A Commentary.* Translated by Linda M. Maloney. Edited by Harold Attridge. Hermeneia. Minneapolis: Fortress, 1998.

Nilsson, Martin P. *Geschichte der griechischen Religion.* 2 vols. Munich: Beck, 1941–1950. 2d ed. Munich: Beck, 1961. 3d ed., Munich: Beck, 1967–1974.

———. *Griechische Feste von religioser Bedeutung.* Leipzig: Teubner, 1906.

Nock, Arthur Darby. "The Cult of Heroes." Pages 2:575–602 in *Essays on Religion and the Ancient World.* Edited by Zeph Stewart. 2 vols. Oxford: Clarendon, 1972. [Repr., Oxford and New York: Oxford University Press, 1986.] Repr. from *HTR* 37 (1944): 141–74.

———. *Early Gentile Christianity and Its Hellenistic Background.* New York: Harper & Row, 1964.

———. "Hellenistic Mysteries and Christian Sacraments." Pages 2:791–820 in *Essays on Religion and the Ancient World.* Edited by Zeph Stewart. 2 vols. Oxford: Clarendon, 1972. [Repr., Oxford and New York: Oxford University Press, 1986.] Repr. from *Mnemosyne* Fourth Series 5 (1952): 177–213.

———. "Notes on Ruler-Cult." Pages 1:134–57 in *Essays on Religion and the Ancient World.* Edited by Zeph Stewart. 2 vols. Oxford: Clarendon, 1972. [Repr., Oxford and New York: Oxford University Press, 1986.] Repr. from *JHS* 48 (1928): 21–43.

Oberhummer, Eugen. "Imbros." *Beiträge zur alten Geschichte und Geographie: Festschrift für Heinrich Kiepert.* Berlin: Reimer, 1898.

Oliver, James H. "Greek and Latin Inscriptions." *Hesperia* 10 (1941): 237–61.

———. "Greek Inscriptions." *Hesperia* 4 (1935): 50–70.

Otto, Eberhard. *Das Verhältnis von Rite und Mythus im Ägyptischen.* Heidelberg: Winter, 1958.

Otto, W. F. *Dionysos: Mythos und Kultus.* Frankfurt am Main: Klostermann, 1934.

Pache, Corinne Ondine. *Baby and Child Heroes in Ancient Greece.* Urbana: University of Illinois Press, 2004.

Palmer, A. "The Merchant of Nisibis: Saint Ephrem and His Faithful Quest for Union in Numbers." Pages 167–233 in *Early Christian Poetry: A Collection of Essays.* Edited by J. den Boeft and A. Hilhorst. Suppl. to *VC* 22. Leiden: Brill, 1993.

Panitschek, Peter. "Zur Darstellung der Alexander– und Achaemenidennachfolge als politische Programme in kaiserzeitlichen Quellen." *Klio* 72 (1990): 457–72.

Papachatzis, Nikolaos D. "To Hêraio tês Korinthou kai hê latreia tôn 'paidiôn tês Mêdeias' " (in Greek). Pages 2:396–404 in *Philia epê eis Geôrgion E. Mylônan.* Bibliothêkê tês en Athênais Archaiologikês Hetaireias 103. Athens: Hê en Athênais Archaiologikê Hetaireia, 1986–1987.

Pariente, A. "Le monument argien des 'Sept contre Thèbes.' " Pages 195–230 in *Polydipsion Argos: Argos de la fin des palais mycéniens à la constitution de l'Etat classique. Freibourg, Suisse, 7–9 May 1987.* Edited by Marcel Piérar. BCH suppl. 22. Paris: De Boccard, 1992.

Parke, H. W. *Festivals of the Athenians.* Ithaca, N.Y.: Cornell University Press, 1977.

Parker, Robert. *Athenian Religion: A History.* Oxford: Clarendon, 1996.

Parry, Hugh. "The Apologos of Odysseus: Lies, All Lies." *Phoenix* 48 (1994): 1–20.

Pauly, A. F. *Paulys Realencyclopädie der classischen Altertumswissenschaft*. Edited by G. Wissowa. New ed. 49 vols. Munich: Druckenmüller, 1980.

Pechuel-Loesche, Eduard. *Volkskunde von Loango*. Vol. 3.2 of *Die Loango-Expedition ausgesandt von der deutschen Gesellschaft zur Erforschung Aequatorial-Africas, 1873–1876*. Stuttgart: Strecker & Schröder, 1907.

Pelekidis, C. "Les Grecs en Thrace: Les premiers rapports entre les Grecs et les Thraces." Pages 98–114 in *La Thrace*. Edited by V. Papoulia et al. Athens: n.p., 1994.

Pelling, Christopher. "Childhood and Personality in Greek Biography." Pages 213–44 in *Characterization and Individuality in Greek Literature*. Edited by Christopher Pelling. Oxford: Clarendon, 1990.

Pembroke, S. "Last of the Matriarchs." *Journal of the Economic and Social History of the Orient* 8 (1965): 217–47.

Perkins, Pheme. *Resurrection: New Testament Witness and Contemporary Reflection*. Garden City, N.Y.: Doubleday, 1984.

Perrin, Nicholas. *Thomas and Tatian: The Relationship between the* Gospel of Thomas *and the* Diatessaron. Atlanta: Society of Biblical Literature, 2002.

Peterson, William L. *Tatian's* Diatessaron*: Its Creation, Dissemination, Significance, and History in Scholarship*. Suppl. to *VC* 25. Leiden: Brill, 1994.

Petzke, Gerd. *Die Traditionen über Apollonios von Tyana und das Neue Testament*. Studia ad corpus hellenisticum Novi Testamenti 1. Leiden: Brill, 1970.

Pfister, Friedrich. *Der Reliquienkult im Altertum*. 2 vols. Religionsgeschichtliche Versuche und Vorarbeiten 5. Giessen, Germany: Töpelmann, 1909–1912.

Picard, Charles. "Une peinture de vase lemnienne, archaïque, d'après l'Hymne de Démodocos: Odyss., VIII, 256 sqq." *Revue Archéologique* 20 (1942–1943): 97–124.

Picard, Charles, and Adolphe-Joseph Reinach. "Voyage dans la Chersonèse et aux îles de la mer de Thrace." *BCH* 36 (1912): 275–352.

Piccirilli, Luigi. "Solone e la guerra per Salamina." *Annali della Scuola Normale Superiore di Pisa, Cl. di Lettere e Filosofia* 8.1 (1978): 1–13.

Piérart, Marcel. "Panthéon et hellénisation dans la colonie romaine de Corinthe: La 'redécouverte' du culte de Palaimon à l'Isthme." *Kernos* 11 (1998): 85–109.

Piganiol, André. *Les documents cadastraux de la colonie romaine d'Orange*. Supplément à "Gallia" 16. Paris: Centre national de la recherche scientifique, 1962.

Pilgaard, Aage. "The Hellenistic *Theios Aner*—A Model for Early Christian Christology?" Pages 101–22 in *The New Testament and Hellenistic Judaism*. Edited by Peder Borgen and Søren Giversen. Århus: Århus Univeristy Press, 1995.

Pirenne-Delforge, Vinciane, and Emilio Suárez de la Torre, eds. *Héros et héroïnes dans les mythes et les cultes grecs: Actes du colloque organisé à l'Université de Valladolid, 26–29 May 1999*. Liège, Belgium: Centre international d'étude de la religion grecque antique, 2000.

Podlecki, A. J. "Cimon, Skyros, and 'Theseus' Bones.'" *JHS* 91 (1971): 141–43.

Pollard, Nigel. *Soldiers, Cities, and Civilians in Roman Syria*. Ann Arbor: University of Michigan Press, 2000.

Porter, James I. "Ideals and Ruins: Pausanias, Longinus, and the Second Sophistic." Pages 63–92 in *Pausanias: Travel and Memory in Roman Greece*. Edited by Susan E. Alcock, John F. Cherry, and Jaś Elsner. Oxford and New York: Oxford University Press, 2001.

Preller, Ludwig, and Carl Robert. *Griechische Mythologie*. 4th ed. 2 vols. Berlin: Weidmann, 1894–1926.

Price, Simon R. F. "Religious Pluralism in the Roman World: Pagans, Jews, and

Christians." Paper presented at the Annual Meeting of the Society of Biblical Literature, Nashville, Tennessee, November 2000.

Pritchett, W. Kendrick. *The Greek State at War*. 5 vols. Berkeley: University of California Press, 1979.

Radet, Georges. "Notes sur l'histoire d'Alexandre: II. Les théores Thessaliens au tombeau d'Achille." *REA* 27 (1925): 81–96.

Radke, Gerhard. *Die Götter Altitaliens*. Munich: Aschendorff, 1965.

———. "Protesilaos." PW 43. half vol. (1957): 932–39.

Ragone, Giuseppe. "Il millennio delle vergini locresi." Pages 7–95 in *Studi ellenistici*. Edited by Biagio Virgilio. Studi ellenistici 8. Biblioteca di studi antichi 78. Pisa and Rome: Istituti editoriali e poligrafici internazionali, 1996.

Ratinaud-Lachkar, Isabelle. "Héros homériques et sanctuaires d'époque géométrique." Pages 247–62 in *Héros et héroïnes dans les mythes et les cultes grecs: Actes du colloque organisé à l'Université de Valladolid, 26–29 May 1999*. Edited by Vinciane Pirenne-Delforge and Emilio Suárez de la Torre. Kernos suppl. 10. Liège, Belgium: Centre international d'étude de la religion grecque antique, 2000.

Raynor, D. H. "Moeragenes and Philostratus: Two Views of Apollonius of Tyana." *CQ* 34 (1984): 222–26.

Reece, Steve. "The Cretan Odyssey: A Lie Truer Than Truth." *AJP* 115 (1994): 157–73.

Reeves, John C. "Manichaean Citations from the *Prose Refutations* of Ephrem." Pages 217–88 in *Emerging from Darkness: Studies in the Recovery of Manichaean Sources*. Edited by Paul Mirecki and Jason BeDuhn. Nag Hammadi and Manichaean Studies 43. Leiden: Brill, 1997.

Regenbogen, Otto. "Pausanias." PWSup 8 (1956): 1008–97.

Rehm, Albert. *Die Inschriften*. Vol. 2 of *Didyma*. Edited by Theodor Wiegand. Berlin: Mann, 1958.

Reinach, Salomon. "La mort d'Orphée." *RAr* 2 (1902): 242–79. Repr. pages 2:45–122 in *Cultes, mythes et religions*. 3d ed. 3 vols. Paris: Leroux, 1928.

Reinhold, Meyer. *History of Purple as a Status Symbol in Antiquity*. Collection Latomus 116. Brussels: Latomus, 1970.

Reynolds, Dwight Fletcher. *Heroic Poets, Poetic Heroes: The Ethnography of Performance in an Arabic Oral Tradition*. Ithaca, N.Y.: Cornell University Press, 1995.

Richter, Gisela M. A. *The Furniture of the Greeks, Etruscans, and Romans*. London: Phaidon, 1966.

———. "A Statue of Protesilaos in the Metropolitan Museum." *Metropolitan Museum Studies* 1 (1928–1929): 187–200.

Ricl, Marijana. *The Inscriptions of Alexandreia Troas*. Inschriften griechischer Städte aus Kleinasien 53. Bonn: Habelt, 1997.

Riley, Gregory J. *One Jesus, Many Christs: How Jesus Inspired Not One True Christiantiy, but Many*. San Francisco: HarperSanFrancisco, 1997.

———. *Resurrection Reconsidered: Thomas and John in Controversy*. Minneapolis: Fortress, 1995.

Rizakis, Athanase D., ed. *Achaïe I: Sources textuelles et histoire régionale*. Athens: Kentron Hellênikes kai Rômaïkês Archaiotêtos, 1995.

Robert, Jeanne, and Louis Robert. "Bulletin épigraphique." *REG* 83 (1970): 362–488.

Robert, Louis. "Addenda aux Tomes I–X." *Hell* 11/12 (1960): 542–95.

———. *Études anatoliennes: Recherches sur les inscriptions grecques de l'Asie Mineure*. Paris: De Boccard, 1937.
———. *Études de numismatique Grecque*. Paris: Collège de France, 1951.
Rohde, Erwin. *Psyche: The Cult of Souls and Belief in Immortality among the Greeks*. London: Routledge & Kegan Paul, 1925.
Romm, James S. *The Edges of the Earth in Ancient Thought: Geography, Exploration, and Fiction*. Princeton: Princeton University Press, 1991.
———. *Herodotus*. New Haven: Yale University Press, 1998.
Roscher, Wilhelm Heinrich. *Ausführliches Lexikon der griechischen und römischen Mythologie*. 7 vols. Leipzig: Teubner, 1884–1937. Repr., 7 vols. Hildesheim, Germany: Olms, 1965–1978.
———. *Die Sieben- und Neunzahl im Kultus und Mythus der Griechen*. Leipzig: Teubner, 1904.
Rose, Brian. "Ilion in the Early Empire." Pages 32–47 in *Patris und Imperium: Kulturelle und politische Identität in den Städten der römischen Provinzen Kleinasiens in der frühen Kaiserzeit*. Edited by C. Berns, H. von Hesberg, L. Vandeput, and M. Waelkens. Louvain: Peeters, 2002.
Rose, H. J. "Myth and Ritual in Classical Civilisation." *Mnemosyne* 4th ser. 3 (1950): 281–87.
Rösler, Wolfgang. "Die 'Selbsthistorisierung' des Autors: Zur Stellung Herodots zwischen Mündlichkeit und Schriftlichkeit." *Philologus* 135 (1991): 215–20.
Ross, Steven K. *Roman Edessa: Politics and Culture on the Eastern Fringes of the Roman Empire, 114–242 CE*. London and New York: Routledge, 2001.
Rougé, J. "Ὁ ΘΕΙΟΤΑΤΟΣ ἈΥΓΟΥΣΤΟΣ." *RevPhil* 43 (1969): 83–92.
Rupp, David W. "The Lost Classical Palaimonion Found?" *Hesperia* 48 (1979): 64–72.
St. Augustine's Abbey (Ramsgate, England). *The Book of Saints: A Dictionary of Servants of God*. 6th ed. Wilton, Conn.: Morehouse, 1989.
Sakellariou, M. B. *La migration grecque en Ionie*. Collection de l'Institut français d'Athènes 17. Athens: n.p., 1958.
Sallet, Alfred von, and Julius Friedlaender. *Beschreibung der antiken Münzen*. Königliche Museen zu Berlin. Berlin: Spemann, 1888–1894.
Sandmel, Samuel. "Parallelomania." *JBL* 81 (1962): 1–13.
Sartori, Paul. *Sitte und Brauch*. 3 vols. Leipzig: Heims, 1910–1914.
Scaife, Ross. "The *Kypria* and Its Early Reception." *Classical Antiquity* 14 (1995): 164–92.
Schachter, A. "Policy, Cult, and the Placing of Greek Sanctuaries." Pages 1–57 in *Le sanctuaire grec*. Geneva: Fondation Hardt, 1992.
Schippmann, Klaus. *Grundzüge der parthischen Geschichte*. Darmstadt: Wissenschaftliche Buchgesellschaft, 1980.
Schliemann, Heinrich. *Ilios: The City and Country of the Trojans*. New York: Harper & Bros., 1881. Repr., New York: Arno, 1976.
Schmid, Wilhelm. *Der Attizismus in seinem Hauptvertretern von Dionysius von Halikarnass bis auf den zweiten Philostratus*. 5 vols. Stuttgart: Kohlhammer, 1887–1897.
Schmid, Wilhelm, and Otto Stählin. *Geschichte der griechischen Literatur*. 2 vols. Handbuch der Altertumswissenschaft. Munich: Beck, 1924.
Schmidt, Ernst A. *Kultübertragungen*. Giessen, Germany: Töpelmann, 1909.
Schmidt, Marcelo Tilman. *Die römische Außenpolitik des 2. Jarhunderts n. Chr.: Friedenssicherung oder Expansion?* Stuttgart: Steiner, 1997.
Schmidt, W. Adolph. *Die grieschischen Papyrusurkunden der königlichen Bibliothek*

zu Berlin. Part 1 of *Forschungen auf dem Gebiete des Alterthums.* Berlin: Fincke, 1842.
Schmitt, Hatto H. *Die Verträge der griechisch-römischen Welt von 338 bis 200 v. Chr.* Vol. 3 of *Die Staatsverträge des Altertums.* 3 vols. Munich: Beck, 1969.
Schmitt, J.-Cl. "Translation d'image et transfert de pouvoir: Le crucifix de pierre de Waltham (Angleterre, XIe–XIIIe siècle)." *Bulletin de l'institut historique belge de Rome* 69 (1999): 245–64.
Schneider, Rolf Michael. "The Barbarian in Roman Art: A Countermodel of Roman Identity." Pages 19–30 in *The Roman Period (in the Provinces and the Barbaric World).* Edited by Bruno Luiselli and Patrizio Pensabene. XIII International Congress of Prehistoric and Protohistoric Sciences, Fórli, Italy, 8–14 September 1996. Fórli, Italy: A.B.A.C.O. edizioni, 1996.
———. *Bunte Barbaren: Orientalstatuen aus farbigem Marmor in der römischen Repräsentationskunst.* Worms, Germany: Wernersche Verlagsgesellschaft, 1986.
———. "Die Faszination des Feindes: Bilder der Parther und des Orients in Rom." Pages 95–146 in *Das Partherreich und seine Zeugnisse.* Edited by Josef Wiesehöfer. Beiträge des internationalen Colloquiums, Eutin, June 1996. Stuttgart: Steiner, 1998.
Scholes, Robert, and Robert Kellogg. *The Nature of Narrative.* Oxford and New York: Oxford University Press, 1966.
Schtajerman, Elena M. *Die Krise der Sklavenhalteordnung in Westen des römischen Reiches.* Translated by W. Seyfarth. Berlin: Akademie, 1964.
Schuchhardt, Carl. *Schliemann's Excavations: An Archaeological and Historical Study.* Translated by Eugénie Sellers. London: Macmillan, 1891.
Schüssler Fiorenza, Elisabeth. *In Memory of Her: A Feminist Reconstruction of Christian Origins.* New York: Crossroad, 1983.
———. *Rhetoric and Ethic: The Politics of Biblical Studies.* Minneapolis: Fortress, 1999.
Scullion, Scott. "Olympian and Chthonian." *Classical Antiquity* 13 (1994): 75–119.
Sealey, F. L. W. "Lemnos." *Annual of the British School at Athens* 22 (1918–1919): 148–72.
Segal, Alan J. "Life after Death." Pages 90–125 in *The Resurrection: An Interdisciplinary Symposium on the Resurrection of Jesus.* Edited by Stephen T. Davis, Daniel Kendall, and Gerald O'Collins. Oxford and New York: Oxford University Press, 1997.
Segal, Charles P. *Euripides and the Poetics of Sorrow.* Durham, N.C.: Duke University Press, 1993.
———. *Tragedy and Civilization: An Interpretation of Sophocles.* Cambridge, Mass.: Harvard University Press, 1981. Repr., Norman: University of Oklahoma Press, 1999.
Segovia, Fernando F. *The Farewell of the Word: The Johannine Call to Abide.* Minneapolis: Fortress, 1991.
———. "The Structure, *Tendenz*, and *Sitz im Leben* of John 13:31–14:31." *JBL* 104 (1985): 471–93.
Selden, Daniel L. "Genre of Genre." Pages 39–64 in *The Search for the Ancient Novel.* Edited by James Tatum. Baltimore: Johns Hopkins University Press, 1994.
Severyns, Albert. *Le cycle épique dans l'école d'Aristarque.* Liège, Belgium: Champion, 1928.
Shapiro, H. A. "Amazons, Thracians, and Scythians." *GRBS* 24 (1983): 105–14.
Shields, Emily Ledyard. *The Cults of Lesbos.* Menasha, Wis.: Banta, 1917.

Siebler, Michael. *Troia: Geschichte, Grabungen, Kontroversen.* Mainz, Germany: Zabern, 1994.
Simoens, Yves. *La gloire d'aimer: Structures stylistiques et interprétatives dans le Discours de la Cène (Jn 13–17).* AnBib 90. Rome: Biblical Institute, 1981.
Sissa, Giulia, and Marcel Detienne. *La vie quotidienne des dieux grecs.* Paris: Hachette, 1989.
Smith, R. R. R. "Late Roman Philosopher Portraits from Aphrodisias." *JRS* 80 (1990): 127–55.
Smith, W. Robertson. *Lectures on the Religion of the Semites.* Edinburgh: Black, 1889. 3d ed., London: Black, 1927.
Smyth, Herbert Weir. *Greek Grammar.* Revised by Gordon M. Messing. Cambridge, Mass.: Harvard University Press, 1984.
Snodgrass, Anthony M. *An Archaeology of Greece: The Present State and Future Scope of a Discipline.* Berkeley: University of California Press, 1987.
———. "Les origines du culte des héros dans la Grèce antique." Pages 107–19 in *La mort: Les morts dans les sociétés anciennes.* Edited by Gherardo Gnoli and Jean-Pierre Vernant. Cambridge: Cambridge University Press, 1982.
Solmsen, Friedrich. "Philostratus." PW 20.1 (1941): 124–77.
———. "Some Works of Philostratus the Elder." *TAPA* 71 (1940): 556–72. Repr. pages 1:74–90 in *Kleine Schriften.* 3 vols. Hildesheim, Germany: Olms, 1968.
Sonnabend, Holger. *Fremdenbild und Politik: Vorstellungen der Römer von Ägypten und dem Partherreich in der späten Republik und frühen Kaiserzeit.* Europäische Hochschulschriften[3]: Geschichte und ihre Hilfswissenschaften 286. Frankfurt am Main: Lang, 1986.
Spawforth, Antony S. "Families at Roman Sparta and Epidauros: Some Prosopographical Notes." *Annual of the British School at Athens* 80 (1985): 191–258.
———. "Symbol of Unity? The Persian-Wars Tradition in the Roman Empire." Pages 233–69 in *Greek Historiography.* Edited by Simon Hornblower. Oxford: Clarendon, 1994.
Speyer, Wolfgang. "Gigant." *RAC* 10 (1978): 1247–76.
———. "Heros." *RAC* 14 (1988): 861–77.
———. "Zum Bild des Apollonius von Tyana bei Heiden und Christen." Pages 176–92 in *Frühes Christentum im antiken Strahlungsfeld: Augewählte Aufsätze.* WUNT 50. Tübingen: Mohr Siebeck, 1989. Repr. from JAC 17 (1974): 47–63.
Stauber, Josef. *Die Bucht von Adramytteion: I. Topographie (Lokalisierung antiker Orte/Fundstellen von Altertümer).* Inschriften griechischer Städte aus Kleinasien 50. Bonn: Habelt, 1996.
Stewart, Andrew. "Stesichoros and the François Vase." Pages 53–74 in *Ancient Greek Art and Iconography.* Edited by Warren G. Moon. Madison: University of Wisconsin Press, 1983.
Stubbings, Frank H. "The Rise of Mycenaean Civilization." CAH 2.1:635–38.
Suksi, Aara. "The Poet at Colonus: Nightingales in Sophocles." *Mnemosyne* 54 (2001): 646–58.
Susini, Giancarol. "Note di epigrafia lemnia." *ASAA* NS 14–16 (1952–1954): 317–40.
Swain, Simon. *Hellenism and Empire: Language, Classicism, and Power in the Greek World, A.D. 50–250.* Oxford: Clarendon, 1996.
Syme, Ronald. *Emperors and Biography: Studies in the "Historia Augusta."* Oxford: Clarendon, 1971.

Talbert, Charles H. *What Is a Gospel? The Genre of the Canonical Gospels.* Philadelphia: Fortress, 1977.

Tannehill, Robert C. *The Acts of the Apostles.* Vol. 2 of *The Narrative Unity of Luke–Acts, a Literary Interpretation.* Minneapolis: Fortress, 1994.

Tatum, James. *The Search for the Ancient Novel.* Baltimore: Johns Hopkins University Press, 1994.

Teixidor, Javier. *Bardesane d'Edesse: La primiere philosophie syriaque.* Paris: Cerf, 1992.

Thatcher, Tom. *The Riddles of Jesus in John: A Study in Tradition and Folklore.* SBLMS 53. Atlanta: Society of Biblical Literature, 2000.

———. "The Riddles of Jesus in the Johannine Dialogues." Pages 263–77 in *Jesus in Johannine Tradition.* Edited by Robert T. Fortna and Tom Thatcher. Louisville: Westminster John Knox, 2001.

Thompson, Eugene Taylor. "The Relics of the Heroes in Ancient Greece." Ph.D. diss., University of Washington, 1985.

Thompson, Homer A., and Richard E. Wycherley. *The Agora of Athens: The History, Shape, and Uses of an Ancient City Center.* Athenian Agora 14. Princeton: The American School of Classical Studies at Athens, 1972.

Thompson, Leonard L. "Lamentation for Christ as Hero: Revelation 1:7." *JBL* 119 (2000): 683–703.

Thomson, George D. *Aeschylus and Athens: A Study in the Social Origins of Drama.* London: Lawrence & Wishart, 1941. 2d. ed., 1966.

———. *Studies in Ancient Greek Society.* London: Lawrence & Wishart, 1949.

Thornton, M. K. "Hadrian and His Reign." *ANRW* 2:432–76. Part 2, *Principat*, 2. Edited by H. Temporini and W. Haase. New York: de Gruyter, 1975.

Timpe, Dieter. "Ein Heiratsplan Kaiser Caracallas." *Hermes* 95 (1967): 470–95.

Tobler, Ludwig. "Die Mordnächte und ihre Gedenktage." Pages 79–105 in *Kleine Schriften zur Volks- und Sprachkunde.* Frauenfeld, Switzerland: Huber, 1897.

Toepffer, Johannes. *Attische Genealogie.* Berlin: Weidmann, 1889.

Toit, David. S du. *Theios Anthropos: Zur Verwendung von "theios anthrôpos" und sinnverwandten Ausdrücken in der Literatur der Kaiserzeit.* Tübingen: Mohr Siebeck, 1997.

Traill, John S. "Prytany and Ephebic Inscriptions from the Athenian Agora." *Hesperia* 51 (1982): 197–235.

Trapp, Michael B. "Plato's *Phaedrus* in the Second Century." Pages 141–73 in *Antonine Literature.* Edited by D. A. Russell. Oxford: Clarendon, 1990.

———. "Sense of Place in the Orations of Dio Chrysostom." Pages 163–75 in *Ethics and Rhetoric: Classical Essays for Donald Russell on His Seventy-fifth Birthday.* Edited by Doreen Innes, Harry Hine, and Christopher Pelling. Oxford: Clarendon, 1995.

Trombley, Frank R. *Hellenic Religion and Christianization, c. 370–529.* 2 vols. Leiden and New York: Brill, 1993.

Usener, Hermann. "Gottliche Synonyme." *Rheinisches Museum für Philologie* 53 (1898): 329–79.

Vallois, René. *L'architecture hellénique et hellénistique à Délos: I. Les monuments.* Paris: De Boccard, 1944.

Van Hoorn, Gerard. *Choes and Anthesteria.* Leiden: Brill, 1951.

Van Rompay, Lucas. "Some Preliminary Remarks on the Origins of Classical Syriac as a Standard Language: The Syriac Version of Eusebius of Caesarea's Ecclesiastical History." Pages 70–89 in *Semitic and Cushitic Studies.* Edited by Gideon Goldenberg and Shlomo Raz. Wiesbaden, Germany: Harrossowitz, 1994.

Vermeule, Cornelius C. "Neon Ilion and Ilium Novum: Kings, Soldiers, Citizens, and Tourists at Classical Troy." Pages 467–82 in *The Ages of Homer: A Tribute to Emily Townsend Vermeule*. Edited by Jane B. Carter and Sarah P. Morris. Austin: University of Texas Press, 1995.

———. "Protesilaos: First to Fall at Troy and Hero in Northern Greece and Beyond." Pages 341–46 in *Florilegium Numismaticum: Studia in Honorem U. Westermark*. Numismatiska Meddelanden 38. Stockholm: Svenska Numismatiska Föreningen, 1992.

Vian, Francis. *La guerre des géants: Le mythe avant l'époque héllenistique*. Paris: Klincksieck, 1952.

Vidal-Naquet, Pierre. "Oedipe entre deux cités: Essai sur Oedipe à Colone." Pages 2:175–211 in *Mythe et tragédie en Grèce ancienne*. Edited by Jean-Pierre Vernant and Pierre Vidal-Naquet. 2 vols. Paris: Éditions la découverte, 1986.

Vieillefond, Jean-René. *Les "Cestes" de Julius Africanus: Étude sur l'ensemble des fragments*. Florence: Sansoni Antiquariata; Paris: Didier, 1970.

Vischer, Rüdiger. *Das einfache Leben: Wort- und motivgeschichtliche Untersuchungen zu einem Wertbegriff der antiken Literatur*. Göttingen: Vandenhoeck & Ruprecht, 1965.

Vogt, Joseph. "Die Tochter des Großkönigs und Pausanias, Alexander, Caracalla." Pages 72–80 in *Gesetz und Handlungsfreiheit in der Geschichte*. Lebendiges Wissen 8. Stuttgart: Kohlhammer, 1955.

———. "Zu Pausanias und Caracalla." *Historia* 18 (1969): 299–308.

Von Ungern-Sternberg, J. "Das Grab des Theseus und andere Gräber." Pages 321–29 in *Antike in der Moderne*. Edited by Wolfgang Schuller. Xenia 15. Constance, Germany: Universitätsverlag Konstanz, 1986.

Vries, Jan de. *Forschungsgeschichte der Mythologie*. Freiburg, Germany: Alber, 1961.

Vryonis, S. "The Panegyris of the Byzantine Saint." Pages 196–228 in *The Byzantine Saint: University of Birmingham Fourteenth Spring Symposium of Byzantine Studies*. Edited by Sergei Hackel. London: Fellowship of St. Alban and St. Sergius, 1981.

Wace, Alan J. B., Maurice S. Thompson, and John P. Droop. "Laconia I. Excavations at Sparta, 1909: The Menelaion." *Annual of the British School at Athens* 15 (1908–1909): 108–57.

Waiblinger, Angelika. "La ville grecque d'Éléonte en Chersonèse de Thrace et sa nécropole." CRAI (Nov.–Dec. 1978): 843–57.

Walcot, Peter. *Hesiod and the Near East*. Cardiff: Wales University Press, 1966.

———. "Odysseus and the Art of Lying." *AncSoc* 8 (1977): 1–19.

Walker, Henry J. *Theseus and Athens*. Oxford and New York: Oxford, 1995.

Walser, Gerold. "Die Severer in der Forschung 1960–1972." *ANRW* 2:614–56. Part 2, *Principat*, 2. Edited by H. Temporini and W. Haase. New York: de Gruyter, 1975.

Walser, Gerold, and Thomas Pekáry. *Die Krise des römischen Reiches: Bericht über die Forschungen zur Geschichte des 3. Jahrhunderts (193–284 n. Chr.) von 1939 bis 1959*. Berlin: de Gruyter, 1962.

Walter, Nikolaus. "Der Mose-Roman des Artapanos und die Frage nach einer Theios-Anër Vorstellung im hellenistischen Judentum sowie nach 'paganen' Einflüssen auf die neutestamentliche Christologie." Pages 284–303 in *Jüdische Schriften in ihrem antik-jüdischen und urchristlichen Kontext*. Edited by Hermann Lichtenberger and Gerbern S. Oegema. Gütersloh, Germany: Gütersloher Verlagshaus, 2002.

Webb, Ruth. "Mémoire et imagination: Les limites de l'*enargeia* dans la théorie rhétorique grecque." Pages 229–48 in *Dire l'évidence (Philosophie et rhétorique antiques): Actes du colloque de Créteil et de Paris (24–25 mars 1995)*. Edited by Carlos Lévy and Laurent Pernot. Paris: L'Harmattan, 1997.

Weiss, Peter. "Eumeneia and the Panhellenion." *Chiron* 30 (2000): 630–34.

Weitzman, Michael P. *The Syriac Version of the Old Testament: An Introduction*. University of Cambridge Oriental Publications 56. Cambridge: Cambridge University Press, 1999.

Welcker, Friedrich G. *Die aeschylische Trilogie: Prometheus und die Kabirenweihe zu Lemnos*. Darmstadt: Leske, 1824.

Welles, C. B. "Graffiti." Pages 79–177 in *The Excavations at Dura-Europos: Preliminary Report of Fourth Season of Work, October 1930–March 1931*. Edited by P. V. C. Baur, Michael I. Rostovtzeff, and Alfred R. Bellinger. New Haven: Yale University Press, 1933.

Wessendonk, O. G. von. "Bardesanes und Mani." *AcOr* 10 (1932): 336–63.

Whitmarsh, Tim. "Greek and Roman in Dialogue: The Pseudo-Lucianic *Nero*." *JHS* 119 (1999): 142–60.

———. *Greek Literature and the Roman Empire: The Politics of Imitation*. Oxford and New York: Oxford University Press, 2001.

———. "Performing Heroics: Language, Landscape, and Identity in Philostratus' *Heroicus*." In *Philostratus*. Edited by Ewen Bowie and Jaś Elsner. Cambridge: Cambridge University Press, forthcoming.

Widengren, Geo. "'Synkretismus' in der syrischen Christenheit." Pages 38–64 in *Synkretismus im syrisch-persischen Kulturgebiet*. Edited by Albert Kietrich. Göttingen: Vandenhoeck & Ruprecht, 1975.

Wiesehöfer, Josef. "Ardašir I (?–242 A.D.): The Founder of the Sasanian Empire." Pages 371–76 in *Encyclopaedia Iranica*. Edited by Ehsan Yar-Shater. 11 vols. London: Routledge & Kegan Paul, 1982–.

———. "Zum Nachleben von Achaimeniden und Alexander in Iran." Pages 389–97 in *Continuity and Change: Proceedings of the Last Achaemenid History Workshop, April 6–8, 1990, Ann Arbor, Michigan*. Edited by Heleen Sancisi-Weerdenburg, Amelie Kuhrt, and Margaret Cool Root. Achaemenid History 8. Leiden: Nederlands Instituut voor het Nabije Oosten, 1994.

Wilamowitz-Moellendorff, Ulrich von. *Der Glaube der Hellenen*. 2 vols. Berlin: Weidmann, 1931–1932. Repr., Basel: Schwabe, 1956. Repr., 3d ed. Darmstadt: Wissenschaftliche Buchgesellschaft, 1959.

———. *Hellenistische Dichtung in der Zeit des Kallimachos*. 2 vols. Berlin: Weidmann, 1924.

———. "Hephaistos." *Nachrichten von der Königliche Gesellschaft der Wissenschaften zu Göttingen: Historisch-philologische Klasse* 3 (1895): 217–45. Repr. 2:5–35 in *Kleine Schriften*. 5 vols. Berlin: Academie, 1962–1971.

———. "Lesefrüchte CXLIII." *Hermes* 44 (1909): 474–75.

———. "Pausanias-Scholien." *Hermes* 29 (1894): 240–48.

Wilhelm, Adolf. "Die Pyrphorie der Lemnier." *Anzeiger der (K.) Akademie der Wissenschaften in Wien: Philosophische-historische Klasse* 76 (1939): 41–46. Repr. 1/3:43–48 in *Akademieschriften zur griechischen Inschriftenkunde [1895–1951]*. Part 8 of *Opuscula*. 3 vols. Leipzig: Zentralantiquariat der Deutschen Demokratischen Republik, 1974.

Wilken, Robert L. The *Christians as the Romans Saw Them*. New Haven: Yale University Press, 1984.

Will, Edouard. *Le monde grec et l'Orient*. Vol. 1 of *Le Vè siècle (510–403)*. Paris: Presses universitaires de France, 1972.

Willett, Michael E. *Wisdom Christology in the Fourth Gospel.* San Francisco: Mellen, 1992.

Wills, Lawrence M. *The Quest for the Historical Gospel: Mark, John, and the Origins of the Gospel Genre.* London and New York: Routledge, 1997.

Winter, Engelbert. *Die sasanidisch-römischen Friedensverträge des 3. Jahrhunderts n. Chr.: Ein Beitrag zum Verständnis der außenpolitischen Beziehungen zwischen den beiden Großmächten.* New York: Lang, 1988.

Wisseman, Michael. *Die Parther in der augusteischen Dichtung.* Frankfurt am Main: Lang, 1982.

Wissowa, Georg. *Religion und Kultus der Römer.* 2d ed. Munich: Beck, 1912.

Witakowski, Witold. "Chronicles of Edessa." *Orientalia Suecana* 33–34 (1984–1986): 486–98.

Wolski, Józef. *L'empire des Arsacides.* Acta Iranica 32. Louvain: Peeters, 1993.

Zanker, Graham. *The Heart of Achilles: Characterization and Personal Ethics in the* Iliad. Ann Arbor: University of Michigan Press, 1994.

Zeitlin, Froma I. "Viewing the Heroes: Philostratus's *Heroikos* and the Culture of Visuality in the Second Sophistic." Paper presented at "Philostratus's *Heroikos*: Religion and Cultural Identity," Harvard Divinity School, Cambridge, Mass., 4–6 May 2001.

———. "Visions and Revisions of Homer." Pages 430–36 in *Being Greek under Rome: Cultural Identity, the Second Sophistic, and the Development of Empire.* Edited by Simon Goldhill. Cambridge and New York: Cambridge University Press, 1990.

Zeller, Dieter. "The θεῖα φύσις of Hippocrates and of Other Divine Men." Pages 49–69 in *Early Christianity and Classical Culture: Comparative Studies in Honor of Abraham J. Malherbe.* Edited by J. T. Fitzgerald, T. H. Olbricht, and L. M. White. NovTSup 110. Leiden: Brill, 2003.

Ziegler, Karl-Heinz. *Die Beziehungen zwischen Rom und dem Partherreich.* Wiesbaden, Germany: Steiner, 1964.

Ziegler, Konrad, and Walther Sontheimer, eds. *Der kleine Pauly: Lexicon der Antike.* Munich: Taschenbuch, 1979.

Zimmer, Heinrich. "Keltische Studien." *Zeitschrift für vergleichende Sprachforschung* 28 (1887): 417–689.

Zunker, Alwine. *Untersuchungen zur Aiakidensage auf Aigina.* St. Ottilien, Germany: EOS Verlag, 1988.

Index of Ancient Writings

Subject Index